THE ENTREPRENEURSHIP OF GF SECURITIES IN CHINA'S CAPITAL MARKETS

The Entrepreneurship of GF Securities in China's Capital Markets

Advised by Chen Yunxian
Edited by Ma Qingquan

Bridge21 | Alhambra, CA

The Entrepreneurship of GF Securities in China's Capital Markets
Advised by Chen Yunxian
Edited by Ma Qingquan

Published by Bridge21 Publications, LLC

Distributed by Casemate Group
Casemate Academic: USA and North America
Oxbow Books: UK, Europe, and the Rest of the World

This edition is an authorized translation from the Chinese language edition.
Published by arrangement with Foreign Language Teaching and Research Publishing Co., Ltd.
Translated by Tong Xiaohua and Shao Yanan

Published in the United States of America

ISBN 978-1-62643-081-5 Hardcover
ISBN 978-1-62643-082-2 ePub | ebook pdf | Kindle

Figure 1

In 1992, Dr. Chen Yunxian was presented with this calligraphy work by Mr. Chen Jingshu, chairman of the Guangdong Calligraphers Association. The ancient motto—"The way ahead is long; I see no ending, yet high and low I'll search with my will unbending"—has also become a reflection of Dr. Chen's state of mind in the securities industry during years of "exploring theories, practicing in the market, and uniting knowledge and practice."

Figure 2

Dr. Chen Yunxian, chairman of GF Securities, and Dr. Ma Qingquan, president of GF Securities, on a hike in 1997. As the leading figures of GF Securities during its founding period, Dr. Chen Yunxian and Dr. Ma Qingquan went south in the early 1990s, focusing on both theoretical research and practical exploration, leading GF Securities to grow into a unique "PhD Legion" in the securities industry.

Figure 3

Photograph of the first leadership team of GF Securities taken in January 1997 (Chairman Dr. Chen Yunxian, President Dr. Ma Qingquan, Executive Vice President Dr. Fang Jiachun, Vice Presidents Wang Hongmao, Ye Junying, Li Shuzhi, and Dong Zhengqing). Among the seven members of the team, there were three PhDs (Chen Yunxian, Ma Qingquan, and Fang Jiachun) and three masters (Wang Hongmao, Ye Junying, and Dong Zhengqing). Before joining GF Securities, Chen Yunxian, Ma Qingquan, Fang Jiachun, and Dong Zhengqing had all taught in higher education institutions. Dr. Ma Qingquan was a professor at the Central Party School in Beijing.

Figure 4

In March 2000, the postdoctoral R&D base of GF Securities was founded as the first postdoctoral R&D base of a financial company in China. Dr. Chen Yunxian (front left) and Lu Zhonghe (front right), former vice governor of Guangdong Province, inaugurated the postdoctoral R&D base of GF Securities.

Figure 5

On February 12, 2010, GF Securities was listed on the Shenzhen Stock Exchange and had a new start. Dr. Chen Yunxian (sixth from right), mayor of Foshan, attends the listing ceremony. Chairman Wang Zhiwei (sixth from left) rings the listing bell.

Figure 6

On April 10, 2015, GF Securities was successfully listed on the main board of the Hong Kong Stock Exchange and enters a new era in its internationalization process. Dr. Chen Yunxian (seventh from left), vice governor of Guangdong Province, attends the listing ceremony. Chairman Sun Shuming (seventh from right) rings the listing bell.

Figure 7

The senior management of E Fund in 2007. Front row from left: Ye Junying and Liang Tang. Back row from left: Zhang Nan, Liu Xiaoyan, Zhang Youzao, and Jiang Zuoliang.

Figure 8

In August 2003, GF Fund staff members marked its establishment.

Figure 9

In May 2006, GF Celüe Youxuan, the sixth fund managed by GF, was launched with an initial offering of 18.4 billion yuan, making it the fund with the largest initial offering, the shortest initial subscription period, and the largest number of valid initial subscriptions in China's fund industry at that time. The seventh person from left in the front row in the photo is General Manager Lin Chuanhui of GF Fund.

Figure 10

In 2013, GF Futures officially signed an agreement to acquire a UK subsidiary.

Contents

Preface

It is September again, and when the thick manuscript of *The Entrepreneurship of GF Securities in China's Capital Markets* is laid out in front of me, my heart is filled with emotions.

The year 2020 marks the thirtieth anniversary of the establishment of China's capital markets, and many knowledgeable people are now reviewing and writing this history of vicissitudes. Among their writings, there are both vertical analyses of the industry and reviews of outstanding figures. The publication of *The Entrepreneurship of GF Securities in China's Capital Markets* is timely and will provide a new perspective on the study of China's capital markets, namely the perspective of the securities operating institutions.

Mr. Liang Qichao, a great scholar of Chinese culture, said, "The most ancient history is actually local history." *The Entrepreneurship of GF Securities in China's Capital Markets* is just like a "local history" of China's capital markets, detailing the history of GF Securities from its establishment to its rise. It vividly reflects the brilliant history of China's capital markets of which GF Securities is part.

As one of the first securities companies in China, GF Securities possesses many commonalities of the industry and era as well as distinctive and even unique individualities. As early as 1996, GF Securities was reported by authoritative media such as Xinhua News Agency and Nanfang Daily for its individualities, and has since been called the "PhD Legion" in the capital markets for many years.

Because of this far-reaching significance, it has become the common wish of many old colleagues and friends to use a book to record the people and events of the PhD Legion. Dr. Ma Qingquan, who volunteered to write this book, was my confidant on the way to academic studies in 1985, and also my closest partner during the years in GF Securities. As the first president of GF Securities, he has presented the difficulties, struggles, and thoughts of a securities company in this book to the greatest possible extent. Reading the manuscript of this book, I once again feel that I share with Dr. Ma "an essential identification and a heartfelt echo, which are beyond words." Zhao Guiping and Wang Liangzhong also responded positively and served as the associate editors of this book, including in the book everyone's memories of the passionate years.

While appreciating the profound writing capacity of Dr. Ma and other editors, I was also able to re-examine my own experience and decision making in GF Securities and have a deeper feeling in reading their book. In the torrent of China's capital markets, GF Securities is "a small but all-inclusive company." Some inspirations on the development of entrepreneurship may be useful for those who come after us and for those in the same industry.

On September 8, 1991, the Securities Department of Guangdong Development Bank was established; in December 1993, it was restructured into Guangdong GF Securities Company; in December 1996, it was restructured into GF Securities; in June 1998, it increased its capital and expanded its shares; and in June 2001, it was restructured into GF Securities. Since then, the company went public, became a conglomerate, and developed its international business. "The expansion of the company and the development opportunities of the employees are linked together," which became one of the motives for the development of GF Securities.

In 1993, the employees of GF Securities started to raise the issue of material compensation; in 1996, the call for improving material benefit was even louder; in 1998, the issue of benefit distribution was put on the agenda of the board of directors; along with the reform of the national property rights system and the implementation of the stock option system, as well as the improvement of relevant welfare measures of the company, "benefit guarantee" became one of the motives for the development of GF Securities.

GF Securities had been implementing a series of systems such as "competition for jobs," "merit-based recruitment," "employment system for talents," and "contract system for employees." This, combined with the "strengthening and improvement of the moral and political work, pressure of competition and elimination," and employees' identification and sense of belonging to the company's culture, formed a management mechanism, which became one of the driving forces for the development of GF Securities.

However, when the company has developed to a certain scale, when economic reforms in China have been deepened so that the property rights system and material compensation have become more reasonable, and when the moral and cultural system and management mechanism of the company have been gradually improved, does it mean that GF Securities lacks vitality?

In fact, through the early development of GF Securities, we can see that behind the "scale motive force," "interest motive force," and "mechanism motive force," there lies the core factor of the development of GF Securities: the "knowledge motive force," "unity and synergy motive force," and "courage to shoulder social missions and responsibilities" driven and formed by a group of high-quality employees. It is these "forces" that play a fundamental role in the gradual improvement of the "organization scale," "benefit distribution," and "management mechanism" of GF Securities.

The "scale motive force," "benefit motive force," and "mechanism motive force" are the extrinsic motive forces of GF Securities' development; the "knowledge motive force," "synergy motive force," and "mission motive force" are the intrinsic motive forces of GF Securities' development. The "extrinsic motive force" has a certain limit, which will "diminish in marginal utility" with the development of the company and the deepening of China's economic reforms; the "intrinsic motivation" is infinite, which is the real power of the company's existence and development. It is the real power of the company's existence and development. The knowledge and quality of each employee, the unity and cooperation among employees, and the sense of mission and responsibility for the pursuit of one's career, the survival and development of the company, and the rise and fall of the country and society undertaken by each employee are the eternal power and source of the development of GF Securities.

Therefore, the development path of GF Securities is not only the path to constantly tap the "scale motive force," "benefit motive force," and "mechanism motive force," but also, more importantly, the path to encourage our employees to develop on the strength of knowledge, unity, and the courage to shoulder the mission of history and develop a sense of responsibility. "Knowledge," "synergy," and "mission" have been the inherent and fundamental eternal motive forces of the development of GF Securities for many years.

Inspired by the motive forces of development, and reviewing the word "entrepreneurship" with the values of GF Securities, we can further realize that the criterion of successful entrepreneurship should not be personal financial freedom, nor should it be limited to the company's profit and market value, but should be the contribution to the country and society. Establishing a stable management structure, exploring the cutting-edge capital markets theories, and leaving a relatively unique growth experience in the industry are the only successful entrepreneurship that can stand the test of history. In the face of the changes of a kind unseen for a century that have been brought about by technological revolution and the international landscape, we believe that GF Securities employees can uphold this value, make more achievements in future development, and deliver satisfactory answers to history.

After 30 years, the capital markets have reached an unprecedented height in China's economy, and many securities companies have formed their own characteristics in their development, which are worthy of respect and learning by GF Securities. In addition, under the effect of various factors, outsiders still have some cognitive limitations on the securities industry, and foreign institutions still have some prejudices on the Chinese capital markets. Then, the publication of the Chinese version and the subsequent English version of *The Entrepreneur of GF Securities in China's Capital Markets* will be a good opportunity for more securities companies to tell their own history and present a confident, open, and prosperous image of China's capital markets. This will be a form of "letting a hundred flowers bloom" that we want to see. Perhaps, this is the charm of history.

Chen Yunxian
September 2020, Guangzhou

Introduction: Majesty and Brilliance

In the early morning of March 19, 2019, with the dawn in the east and the clouds in the sky, Guangzhou, a millennia-old city, woke up from its sleep once again. If you take a bird's eye view of the city's rich and prosperous central axis, you will find that Guangzhou is different this day.

On the east side of Zhujiang New Town, Guangzhou, a new skyscraper, was officially opened by lighting up in the morning sun. The diamond-shaped main tower is covered with crystal-clear glass curtain walls, and the four-beam and eight-pillar structure is complemented by the linear rhythm of waterfalls, thus marking a new height of 308 meters in the eastern part of Zhujiang New Town. This new landmark is geographically located amidst Zhujiang New Town, Guangzhou International Financial City, and the Pazhou Convention and Exhibition Area. Like the finishing touch with the flow of light, the move-in ceremony attracted more attention to the land on both sides of the Pearl River with great development potential.

Rising by the central axis, soaring to the skyline, as a super 5A intelligent business and financial building, the skyscraper announces to the world its dignity and energy. It also draws people's attention to the skyline and the striking name hanging high on the building—GF Securities.

A tree in south China

To move into a landmark building named after itself is a big event with milestone significance for any company.

GF Securities Tower was dressed up on this day, with the red color favored by the securities industry reflecting every corner of the moving ceremony site. Every employee who came to work was the protagonist of the ceremony. They walked through the red carpet stretching from the main road to the main entrance of the building, surrounded by the red lion dancers in Lingnan flavor, and received the joyful red envelopes from the executives of GF Securities.

At 8:30 a.m., company leaders had already handed out more than 2,000 red envelopes to the headquarters employees moving into the new building. On the same day, employees from 264 brokerage branches in 31 provinces, autonomous regions, and municipalities directly under the central government, employees in foreign offices engaged in investment banking, institutional services and investment management, and employees of subsidiaries in Hong Kong, Vancouver, and London shared the joy of the move. They comprised more than 10,000 people.

This hub of 10,000 people has since been located at 26 Machang Road, Tianhe District, Guangzhou.

The morning breeze comes from the Pearl River Park adjacent to GF Securities Tower, a 28-hectare urban ecological park with thousands of trees, creating a rich ecological landscape. GF Securities has also planted a huge "banyan tree" next to its building: when you stand in the lobby of the first floor of the main tower, you can see through the 10.2-meter-high glass curtain wall that the building's second tower is shaped as a banyan tree. The tower has five stories, with a canopy-like roof facing the sea of traffic and people.

The banyan tree, a common tree in the warm South, is also the most sentimental tree in many people's eyes. It is a strong, sturdy tree with a strong trunk that defies the cold and the heat and thrives in all four seasons. The most amazing thing is that the branches of the banyan tree are able to grow "air roots" downward, which become "pillar roots" when they hit the ground, and over time, the pillar roots are connected, the pillar branches are supported by each other, and the branches and leaves expand to form a "single tree into a forest." The famous story "Bird's Paradise" by the writer Ba Jin depicts the scene of a single tree forming a forest and ten thousand birds flying on Banyan Island in Xinhui, Guangdong. The largest projection of a great banyan tree in the tropical rainforest is said to cover an area of up to 10,000 square meters and the tree is said to be able to accommodate an army of thousands of men under it.

In the ecology of China's securities market, GF Securities is like a banyan tree born in the South, which takes root in the ground, with a canopy that is strong and self-improving. At the end of 2019, the total assets of GF Securities reached 394.391 billion yuan, the owner's equity attributable to shareholders of listed companies was 91.234 billion yuan, the operating income was 22.81 billion yuan, and the net profit attributable to shareholders of listed companies was 7.539

billion yuan. This makes the capital strength and profitability of GF Securities outstanding in Guangzhou and even in south China. GF Securities has also remained at the top of domestic listed securities companies for many years in a row and has created the "GF phenomenon" in the capital markets.

As a reputation, what does the "GF phenomenon" mean specifically? How does one define its connotation and extension? There does not seem to be a definite answer.

If you ask a financial practitioner, he may say that the "GF phenomenon" refers to a group of companies constructed by equity relations. GF Securities has formed a clear financial conglomerate structure: it holds the controlling share in a number of subsidiaries, including GF Futures, GF Fund Management, GF Holdings (Hong Kong), GF Xinde Investment, GF Qianhe Investment, GF Asset Management, GF Leasing, and GF Hexin. It has also invested in E Fund as the joint largest shareholder.

Unlike some company groups that are keen on "collecting" financial licenses, GF Securities' holding (participation) companies not only have a full range of business licenses in the securities industry, but also have subsidiaries that are among the top in each sector of the securities industry, and most of them have reached an industry status matching that of their parent companies. In the field of public funds, the participating company E Fund and the holding subsidiary GF Fund ranked first and fourth, respectively, in the average monthly size of non-monetary public funds in 2019.[1]

In the field of brokerage fund management, GF Asset Management, a wholly-owned subsidiary, is the first brokerage asset management company in south China and ranked fifth in the industry in terms of average monthly scale of asset management of securities companies in 2019.

In the field of private equity fund management, GF Xinde, a wholly-owned subsidiary, and the funds it manages had completed about 250 equity projects as of the end of 2019, and had been awarded the "Golden Bull Brokerage Equity Investment Annual Winning Institution" for many years in a row.

In the field of internationalization, GF Holdings (Hong Kong), a wholly-owned subsidiary, has become one of the comprehensive brokerage firms with a full range of business lines and licenses in Hong Kong, providing a full range of cross-border securities financial services such as cross-border financing and institutional services.

In the futures industry, GF Futures, a wholly-owned subsidiary, as a senior futures company in China, not only has a relatively complete operating network in key cities, but also has actively set up overseas operations, and is one of the few futures companies in China that can provide comprehensive, 24-hour, bilingual services for domestic and foreign institutional clients in major international commodity markets such as London and Hong Kong for global bulk commodity

1 Source: Asset Management Association of China, same below.

trading.

If you ask a veteran stockholder, he or she will probably report that the "GF phenomenon" is a series of "bull stocks" in the market, such as 000776.SZ and 1776.HK, as well as the brokerage shares—the three GF related stocks (Liaoning Cheng Da, Jilin Aodong, and Zhongshan Utilities) which have been outstanding in every bull market. What impresses young new stockholders more is that the "GF phenomenon" is the technology finance tools that can help them capture bull stocks, such as the industry's first financial engineering theory and big data technology-based smart investment advisor Betanew, "GF Yitaojin E-commerce," a comprehensive advisory investment and financial service APP, as well as "Real-time Investment Advisor" "GF Trader," which are powerful and convenient to operate.

GF Securities has long attached importance to fintech. Its online account opening and 24/7 online services have enabled it to take the lead in the bull market and become the object of imitation in the industry. In the new round of development planning, fintech becomes an important sub-strategy that GF Securities spares no effort to support their development. By 2019, GF Securities has launched its self-developed cloud services, micro services, robotic investment advisors and other technology finance platforms, and cooperated in the development of the industry's first big data-based full-chain quantitative investment research cloud platform and comprehensive smart service platform (GF-SMART), laying a solid foundation for the subsequent development of technology finance. By the end of 2019, the number of GF Securities mobile securities users exceeded 27.2 million, the number of followers of its WeChat platform exceeded three million, and the sales and transfer of financial products on the Yitaojin E-commerce platform reached 366.2 billion; the total number of clients served by the smart investment advisor "Betanew" exceeded 800,000, and the sales of financial products were achieved while the sales of financial products reached 22.8 billion yuan.

If you ask a reporter of financial media, he or she may think that the "GF phenomenon" refers to the many ranking data, project cases, and research opinions that converge into the GF brand. GF Securities has been ranked among the top brokerages in China in the Hurun Brand List for many years. The brand value reached 5.5 billion yuan in 2019, and many mainstream media and lists have praised the brand influence of GF Securities. Behind the data of these lists, there are star projects in the primary market and explosive products in the secondary market. In 2019, the corporate bonds project of China National Aviation Holding Corporation Limited and the asset-backed special plan of Zhengjia Company Group Co., Ltd. continued to show the strength of GF Securities in the capital markets where star projects shine, and GF Fund set a record of one manager being responsible for three products and taking the top three positions in active equity fund performance.

In today's world where research is increasingly regarded as a core brand by leading securities firms, GF Securities is popular for its research strength in the industry. Without aggressive experts and views popular in the market, GF Securities' research team has won the appreciation of knowledgeable people for its professional and pragmatic character. GF Securities' equity research covers 28 industries and nearly 700 A-share listed companies, as well as nearly 110 Hong Kong-listed companies. In 2017 and 2019, the team won first place for "Best Local Research Team" in New Fortune, and was awarded the "Golden Bull Research Team" for six consecutive years, and second place for "Best Analyst Team" in the "Institutional Investor: Caixin Capital Markets Analyst Achievement Award" in 2019.

There are many alternative answers to what the "GF phenomenon" is.

But on March 19, 2019, if you walk past the tall "banyan tree" in the secondary tower of GF Securities Tower to the housewarming ceremony being held on the square with this question in mind, you will get a very concise answer the "GF phenomenon" originates from a group of outstanding GF Securities employees.

This group of employees is looking up at the building on the square, as if it is an ivory tower carrying dreams.

This group of employees, like the pillar roots of the giant banyan, has created a world.

This group of employees has some with grey hair after having passed on the flame.

This group of employees glimmers like starlight.

The glory of Hong Kong

In his masterpiece *Sternstunden der Menschheit* (*The Tide of Fortune*), the Western biographer Stefan Zweig spared no effort to promote "the moment when the stars shine":

> In history, once such starry moments occur, they will determine the course of the coming decades and centuries. Just as the tip of a lightning rod concentrates the currents of the entire atmosphere, so too do the countless events that tend to crowd together in the shortest of times. Those events that normally occur in a slow and leisurely sequence and are compressed into a unique moment that will determine everything and change everything: a simple yes or no, a decision that comes too early or too late, will make the lives of hundreds of generations irreversible, and determine the life or death of a person, the survival of a nation, or even the fate of the entire human race.
>
> Such moments may be concentrated in a single day, a single moment, or often even in a single minute, but their decisive impact transcends time. I call them moments when the stars of humanity shine, because in this dark night of

time, which is beyond human reach and immortal, they are like stars that pierce the darkness and radiate eternal light.

In Zweig's passionate book, the Ottoman Turkish Empire's conquest of Constantinople and Roald Amundsen and Robert Falcon Scott's race to be the first man to reach the South Pole are all "starry moments" in his eyes. Zweig's point of view applies to human history at the macro level, and it also seems to apply to the history of companies at the micro level. Tracing the reflection of history, GF Securities also has its own "stars" and its own "starry moments."

To this day, many employees of GF Securities still remember a memorable day five years ago.

It was on the early morning of April 10, 2015, when the company's leaders announced a series of important messages to all employees in an email message:

In a few hours, GF Securities will be listed on the Hong Kong Stock Exchange.

The H-share listing of GF Securities was the largest IPO of a brokerage firm in the world up to that time, and was also the largest IPO in Asia and the second largest in the world up to that time that year.[2]

The H-share listing project took only 141 days exactly to the day from the adoption of a resolution on it by the board of directors of GF Securities to the successful listing.

Due to the strict confidentiality of the project, the majority of GF Securities employees were not aware of the progress of their company's IPO, so you can imagine their excitement when reading this email message. As a securities firm, helping clients to achieve IPO is a "specialty," which makes GF Securities employees understand how difficult it is to "make it happen exactly to the day within 141 days of the project schedule," as stated in the email message.

In China's mainland IPO projects, it is not impossible to achieve the goal of "making a stock start trading exactly to the day," and there have been such cases in GF's own investment banking business. However, H-share IPO projects and China's mainland investment banking projects are obviously very different as the former need to coordinate many intermediaries, consider overseas roadshows, put a lot of energy into the issuance process, and face many institutional investors in the highly market-oriented Hong Kong market. All this means a huge workload and work intensity. Many other mainland financial institutions such as banks and securities companies tried to get listed in Hong Kong too, but they did not always have a smooth sailing. Some institutions started the listing process twice, some institutions went back and forth for as long as three years, and there was more than one case where the delay was too long and the listing plan eventually failed.

The project team in charge of the GF Securities' H-share listing had researched several financial institutions with experience in listing in Hong Kong, and had a psychological expectation of the risks involved. In the decision of the audit

2 Source: the co-sponsor Goldman Sachs & Co.

benchmark date for the listing, the company leaders finally chose the difficult part by pushing back the original plan of December 31, 2014 as the audit benchmark date, advancing the audit benchmark date to September 30, 2014, and scheduling the listing date at April 10, 2015. This stretched the project team of over 100 employees in more than 20 departments to a spring near its limits. The peak of the production of audit materials was followed by the peak of the roadshows, an experience that is difficult for others to share: during the roadshows, more than 400 meetings were held worldwide, more than 100 domestic investors and more than 200 foreign investors were met, and more than 700 institutional orders were placed for international placement. The "Future Glory" project, code-named after the GF Securities anthem, created a miracle of execution in 141 days, at a pace that many people thought was impossible.

The glory was finally created here at 19 Des Voeux Road Central, Hong Kong, on the morning of April 10.

At 9:25 a.m., the hands of Sun Shuming, chairman of GF Securities, and Charles Li Xiaojia, CEO of the Hong Kong Stock Exchange, were clasped together. Near 9:30 a.m., the crowded Exchange Hall began to count down together in exuberance, "10, 9, 8..." red silk fluttered, a gong sounded, and 1776.HK was born. The electronic screen in the lobby was flooded with flashing lights, the trading data flashed in high frequency as the time progressed, and the scene resounded with exclaims from time to time.

The brief but solemn listing ceremony also became a stage for several generations of GF employees to gather together. Dr. Chen Yunxian, vice governor of Guangdong Province and founder of GF Securities, was present to congratulate the event and witnessed the historical moment surrounded by GF Securities employees.

The global offering of GF Securities H-shares amounted to 1.48 billion shares at an issue price of HK$18.85 per share, rising to a high of HK$26.80 per share, or 42.18 percent, during the day. After the full exercise of the over-allotment option on April 13, the number of shares offered reached 1.702 billion, raising total proceeds of HK$32.079 billion (US$4.13 billion).

Since then, GF Securities has become the third mainland securities company to successfully achieve A+H listing, and the fourth mainland securities firm to be listed on the Hong Kong Stock Exchange.

Many mainstream financial media in China paid high attention to GF Securities' H-share listing, while China's Hong Kong media such as *Hong Kong Economic Times*, *Sing Tao Daily*, and *The New Paper* also followed the company's roadshows and listing, and perceptive stock commentators in the Hong Kong stock market published reports such as "GF Securities opens for trading today and may become the king of IPO fund raising."

This achievement is a testament to GF Securities and, to some extent, a reflection of how hot the capital markets had been in 2015. From November 5,

2014 to April 10, 2015, GF Securities had a high-intensity march, while the Hang Seng Index soared from 24836 points to 27272 points during the same period. Along with the ideal market, the GF Securities H-share listing project achieved "riding the bull" by virtue of its gaming and timing ability.

This achievement also encouraged the project's co-sponsors, global coordinators, and many other institutions. At the IPO celebration dinner on April 10, Matthew Westerman, head of investment banking for Asia Pacific at Goldman Sachs, congratulated the company on the completion of the world's largest IPO of a securities company from China that day. He also humorously poked fun at his own firm, saying that the record was previously held by a "small" US firm, Goldman Sachs.

Asiamoney, Asia's leading financial magazine with a reputation for professionalism, also awarded GF Securities the "IPO of the Year" for its H-share IPO in the subsequent Global Capital Asia Awards, describing it to the magazine's main audience of Asia-Pacific investment bankers as follows:

> There couldn't have been a better time. Chinese brokers were seeing their biggest rally in years as the A-share market exploded. But of all the FIG deals on the table, GF was the first to take the plunge, setting the bar high.
>
> By coming first GF Securities became the standard bearer and the trade everyone looked to as the yardstick for their own success. GF Securities deserves the title of Best IPO of 2015.

On the evening of April 10, the project team, codenamed "Future Glory," appeared at the IPO Gala Dinner surrounded by congratulatory baskets from dozens of international financial institutions. The occasion of congratulating each other was also a time to vent out the pressure, as the project team members who had been "grinding" together for more than a hundred days gathered together to vent out the pressure after a hard battle, as well as the pressure of GF Securities' thirst for capital replenishment and integration into the securities industry.

The H-share listing project was a deep coordination between GF Securities and the international capital markets. During the roadshows, GF Securities had to go global to tell international investors about itself, cooperate and play with international top-ranking investment banks, and face various rules of overseas regulation that are very different. After these deep collisions, the prejudices of many international investors about "Chinese securities industry's license protection, single business and live at the mercy of the market" have been changed to a certain extent, allowing GF Securities to make a deep mark in the dramatic capital markets in 2015, with a rich harvest that goes far beyond its industry status as the "third A+H listed company."

In this sense, it is an indelible highlight: on April 10, 2015, the flashing lights at the Hong Kong Stock Exchange listing ceremony to welcome the birth of 1776.

HK recorded a "starry moment" for GF Securities.

Before the birth of 1776.HK, GF Securities had a similar memory.

A decade of lushness

It was February 2010, when the new century entered its second decade. The newspapers and magazines on the street were full of reports on "ten-year stocktaking" and "new year's outlook," with the eagerness for more success by building on past experiences. The newly emerged microblogging platform continued comments on hot topics, and people who frequently swipe their phones had yet to fully anticipate the huge changes that mobile information technology would bring. The Chinese New Year coincided with the Western "Valentine's Day." In the midst of the warm winter, Guangzhou citizens were either wandering around the bustling Spring Festival flower market, discussing with their friends about seeing an IMAX version of *Avatar*, or looking forward to the 16th Guangzhou Asian Games to be held in the same year. In the office building at 183 Tianhe North Road, Guangzhou, GF Securities was working day and night to change its destiny in one fell swoop.

On February 12, the last trading day before the Chinese New Year, stockholders in front of the trading screen were full of good expectations on this day when the year of the ox and the year of the tiger intersected, hoping to seize the robust "tail of the ox" and usher in the "tiger's power." And institutional investors and old stock investors had long been concerned about the Shenzhen Stock Exchange news, where a "tiger's roar" was about to come.

This was an "ox tail" far better than a limit up; this was a hundred billion yuan "tiger's roar"; this was the "blue chip securities company"; this was 000776.SZ.

At 9:24 a.m., Song Hai, vice governor of Guangdong Province, and Wang Zhiwei, chairman of GF Securities, rang the trading bell of the Shenzhen Stock Exchange together, and GF Securities officially landed on the mainland securities market through a shell. The LED screen of the exchange answered the predictions of various institutions on the share price in big, bold red letters.

It was indeed the "No. 1 high-priced brokerage stock in the Chinese capital markets." Opening price 54 yuan! Up 411.8 percent! This figure reached the upper limit of many institutions' predictions.

After four hours of trading time, the market value of GF Securities reached 125.478 billion yuan at the closing price, ranking among the top Chinese securities companies and becoming a "heavyweight stock" of the Shenzhen Stock Exchange.

After four hours of trading time, the sound of the trading bell still seems to be ringing in the ears of many people. For the company's leaders at the scene of the ceremony represented by the vast number of employees of GF Securities, for tens of thousands of the original "Yanbian Highway" shareholders who followed the road to the listing of the shell for three years, the sound of the bell made them intoxicated.

The listing was a highlight of the company's development. The listing was also an excellent answer sheet for the company's entrepreneurship. Dr. Chen Yunxian, the then mayor of Foshan, as the core figure of the "PhD Legion" entrepreneurial team, made a short speech at the ceremony, reviewing what the company had paid for and gained from the listing, with plain language and heartfelt sentences. Off stage, the leadership team and staff representatives of GF Securities could not repress their deep feelings and their eyes were moistened.

Vice Governor Song Hai, who was in charge of financial work in Guangdong Province, understood this sentiment. He has witnessed GF Securities from being the first in the industry to launch a listing based on the shell, to a three-year delay, and finally seeking progress in the midst of crisis and successfully fulfilling the dream of listing on that day. In his speech on the spot, Song Hai encouraged GF Securities: "The process of listing was tortuous, during which many parties gave support and assistance, and the company itself was also motivated to make good efforts to finally succeed in listing. I believe GF will add glory to the securities market with its unique style and good performance in the future."

The phrase "make good efforts" is true. When Dr. Li Jianyong, then president of GF Securities, received the commemorative gift of a heavy bronze statue "Pioneering Bull," he felt the weight of these two words even more vividly. During the three-year suspension period, the A-share market surged from 1792.25 points to 6124.04 points, then fell to 1664.93 points, and then rose to 2985.5 points on the trading day before the listing. The ebb and flow of the securities market had enabled GF Securities to develop more stable operation and stronger belief.

During these three years, GF Securities continued to rank among the top ten in the industry in terms of major business indicators and top five in the industry in terms of profitability, and its robust market image and good business performance won the trust and support of regulators and investors.

Li Jianyong was one of the commanders of the battle for the listing of the shell. This battle also left a record in the history of Chinese securities: from the restart of the project to the successful resumption of trading, it took only 48 days; from the approval of the China Securities Regulatory Commission (CSRC) to the resumption of trading, it took only 12 days; from the issuance of the approval document to the resumption of trading, it took only 6 days.

It was December 25, 2009. It was a Friday afternoon after the market closed when the company leaders received a notice on the phone that they had been waiting for three years: GF Securities could restart its bid for the listing of the shell of Yanbian Highway.

The listing project team immediately entered a "wartime state." That night, the project team got together to study directed repurchase of Yanbian Highway shares and the exchange of shares for the merger of GF Securities, analyzing the problems and difficulties in the implementation of the project after three years in the case of significant changes in the subject of the transaction and regulatory rules.

The next day, the CSRC convened a meeting of Guangdong and Jilin provincial governments, Guangdong and Jilin securities regulatory bureaus, GF Securities, Yanbian Highway, as well as Liaoning Cheng Da, Jilin Aodong, and Zhongshan Utilities, to conduct a special study and coordination on Yanbian Highway's share swap and absorption to merge GF Securities and to determine the basic principles of the listing of the shell.

In the following 48 days, members of the project team were divided into multiple routes. In Yanbian Prefecture, Jilin Province, where it was more than 20 degrees Celsius below zero, the project team members, with their skillful business knowledge and infectious enthusiasm, worked with Yanbian Highway personnel until late at night to complete the tax clearance and industrial and commercial changes in a short period of time. In the bright Guangzhou Metropolitan Plaza, the financial staff cooperated with the accounting firm to complete the "9–30" audit report by January 6, 2010 in accordance with the data accuracy requirements, and also finished the year-end accounts. The confirmation of the transfer of debts and liabilities was one of the most mobilized tasks, which involved all accounting units under GF Securities, creditors, and debtors from all over the country, in addition to newspaper notification and confirmation letters. However, under the "system mobilization," 152 debtor acknowledgement letters of about 40 million were completed in just one day. During these 48 days, GF Securities was always in a tense atmosphere, like a countdown to a rocket launch.

The listing bell stirred people's hearts, and "Blue Chip GF" stood on a new starting point. This securities company, which had completed its main underwriting business 159 times from its establishment to listing, and had been awarded "Best Small and Medium-Sized Enterprise Board Sponsor" by the Shenzhen Stock Exchange three times, finally rang its own listing bell and entered the fast development road of modern investment banking.

After 18 years of pursuit, GF Securities' dream of going public finally came true. The listing ceremony is the best rite of passage, and GF Securities started to transform into a public company from February 12, 2010, at the "starry moment" to become a listed company with a market capitalization of 100 billion yuan. It shouldered the development mission of value creation, showing its lush growth.

The tree is big because of its deep roots

It takes about 30 minutes for the Pearl River to flow from Haizhu Square to the south bank of Zhujiang New Town. It took nearly 30 years for GF Securities employees to move all the way from the counter in Haizhu Square to GF

Securities Tower in Zhujiang New Town. The long-established "PhD Legion" in China's capital markets finally got its own central premise on March 19, 2019.

Employees gathered in the square, leaning on the banyan tree-shaped secondary tower, looking up from time to time at the 308-meter-high "ivory tower" of their own company. The streamlined glass curtain wall seemed to pull the time, allowing every shining milestone moment in the company's history to flow down, looking back to April 10, 2015, to February 12, 2010, and more.

In the many eyes that trace back to the source, there was a pair of hale and hearty eyes connecting all the "starry moments" in the history of GF Securities.

Those were the eyes of Dr. Chen Yunxian, the founder of GF Securities and the leader of the "PhD Legion." He and his entrepreneurial team, as the first generation of veterans in China's capital markets, opened up the entrepreneurial pattern of GF Securities. Even during the years when he turned to politics until his promotion to vice governor of Guangdong Province, Dr. Chen Yunxian has witnessed all the major moments such as the company's IPO.

At the relocation ceremony, he used a magnetic voice with a slight southern Fujian accent to guide everyone's thoughts to retrace the steps of GF Securities:

> In 1991, our headquarters was in Haizhu Square; immediately after that, we moved to Huanshizhong Road; in the third step, we moved to the guest house of Guangdong Province Materials Building; in the fourth step, we moved to Huashan Hotel; in the fifth step, we moved to Huatai Hotel; in the sixth step, we returned from Huatai Hotel to the fourth floor of Guangdong Development Bank Building; in the seventh step, we moved to Metropolitan Plaza. Today is our big move to GF Securities Tower.

GF Securities moved seven times to eight sites. The company once did not have a permanent site, whereas now it has this enviable landmark building. Climbing the tower and looking at the cloudy mountains and the Pearl River would become the exclusive benefit for the employees of GF Securities working in this building in the future after their intense work.

When you eat fruit, you think of the tree that bears the fruit, and when you drink water, you think of its source. High in GF Securities Tower, in an elegant and gorgeous exhibition hall, a photo titled "Entrepreneurship in the South" is hung. The decorative wall of the exhibition hall depicts an abstract K-line diagram, which starts from this photo and continues to the present. This photo comes from the temporal and spatial origin of GF Securities: on September 8, 1991, the day the Securities Department of Guangdong Development Bank was established, Dr. Chen Yunxian posed with his staff in front of the counter labeled "Securities Trading." On that day, there were only six "GF Securities employees" and the capital was only 10 million yuan.

Dr. Chen Yunxian himself was also thinking of his roots. In his speech at the housewarming ceremony, he recalled the great support he received from the leaders of Guangdong Development Bank at the beginning of his business:

> GF Securities' housewarming ceremony is based on the foundation of carrying on the past and opening up the future. With the support and encouragement of Mr. Wu Chixin, former chairman of Guangdong Development Bank, GF Securities allowed the young people to open up a new world, just like rivers returning to the sea and an eagle in the clouds spreading its wings and flying to a new height.

Many things seem to be unknown in GF Securities' nearly 30 years. And what has been repeatedly asked by outsiders in recent years, is:

What did GF Securities rely on to grow into a leading securities company with a small start-up, through decades of turbulent waves in China's capital markets?

What did GF Securities, as a non-state company, rely on to be unique among first-tier securities firms and to have never been placed under trusteeship, merged or received policy assistance in its history?

As a public company, GF Securities has repeatedly disclosed its core competencies in its own IPO prospectus and annual reports: a market-oriented mechanism, a balanced and diversified shareholding structure and sound corporate governance, an excellent corporate culture and a stable management team, and sound business philosophy.

But these seem to be too general, and those who are interested often hope to get "genetic" and "pixel" answers, and thus continue to ask one more question: why GF Securities?

At this moment, in the square of GF Securities Tower, the lion dance and fireworks were in full swing, and the housewarming ceremony had reached its climax. People who witnessed the opening of GF Securities Tower got up together and used their cell phone cameras to record another "starry moment."

GF Securities did not invite outside guests to attend the moving ceremony, and the honor of the building's inaugurators was reserved for a series of familiar and affectionate names. In a boisterous cheer, company leaders rose to eagerly invite Chen Yunxian, Wu Chixin, Lu Jinchang, Wang Zhiwei, Ma Qingquan, Fang Jiachun, Wang Hongmao, and Ye Junying. This list of names, connected with more names, are the key to the question: "Why GF Securities?"

The red silk floated up, the sunlight sprinkled down, and the ivory-colored words "GF Securities Tower" reflected a warm glow. The tree in south China is with big deep roots, a grand narrative throughout the nearly 30 years of GF Securities is still continuing.

Chapter I: He Comes from Peking University

Learning is the sweet fruit of the root of bitterness.

—David Ricardo

1. Origins: the mission of intellectuals of the times

It has been 30 years since the official inception of China's capital markets in 1990. As a new economic model in the history of the socialist economy, the birth and development of China's capital markets was not only a major innovation in reform, but also a major breakthrough in the exploration of socialist economic theory. Today, as China's capital markets enter their thirtieth year, people admire the wisdom of reform policymakers, appreciate the courage of market leaders, and equally miss the significant contributions of many economists to economic reforms and capital markets development.

As the torrent of history moves forward like a towering wave, economists are like the watchmen in the lighthouse, continuing the light of reason with their exhaustive thinking. As a group with a special status, generations of economists have devoted themselves to reform and opening up and national rejuvenation, which extends far beyond the 30-year time span.

A long line of scholarship

In September 1982, Deng Xiaoping clearly put forward the proposition of "building socialism with Chinese characteristics" at the twelfth National Congress of the Communist Party of China (CPC), which became the symbol of the formation of the theory of building socialism with Chinese characteristics. Sun Yefang, a famous economist and a proletarian revolutionary of the older generation, attended this congress despite an illness and was elected as a member of the CPC Central Advisory Commission.

Born in 1908, Sun Yefang was a rigorous scholar and adherent to the truth throughout his life. He put forward many creative ideas in the light of China's economic reality and became a leader in theoretical exploration of economic reforms, but also suffered from this. In the 1960s, he was vilified as "the biggest revisionist in Chinese economics" and was imprisoned for seven years. As the twelfth CPC Congress opened a new chapter of the era, this "model soldier and scholar"[1] was already in his twilight years. Also in 1982, his old friends Xue Muqiao and Xu Xuehan made a proposal to him, while his deathbed, to establish a prize for economic science in his name.

In February 1983, Sun Yefang passed away in Beijing. Four months later, the Sun Yefang Economic Science Award Committee was established to commemorate the significant contributions of this outstanding economist and to recognize and reward collectives and individuals who had made outstanding contributions to economic science. The Sun Yefang Economic Science Award is recognized as the highest award in Chinese economics.

The theory of economic reforms was passed on. The first Sun Yefang Economic Science Award was awarded in the time frame of 1977 (after the Cultural Revolution ended) to 1984 for works and papers which focused on hot topics of reform such as "working to expand decision-making power of state-owned enterprises (SOEs)" and "the opening up of the commodity economy." The list of winners included a number of names that shine in Chinese economics: Xiao Zhuoji, author of "Some Ideas on Economic Management Reforms," Dong Fureng, author of "Economic Interest, Economic Leverage and Economic Organization," and Wei Xinghua, author of "Marx's Theory of Productive Labor."[2]

Mr. Xiao Zhuoji had since been widely known as "Xiao the Stock Market," and in the early 1980s, he was one of the earliest experts in China to study and advocate the commodity economy and market economy, and was active in the forefront of economic theory. The award of the first Sun Yefang Economic Science Award was a recognition of Xiao Zhuoji as the first Chinese scholar to create and systematically demonstrate the theory of "separation of ownership and use (management) rights of SOEs." Earlier, in 1981, Xiao's bold ideas were even criticized by the authoritative economist Sun Yefang himself in an article.

Xiao Zhuoji recalled:

---

1 Zhang Jinfu. Sun Yefang: A Model Soldier and Scholar [N]. *People's Daily*, February 24, 1984.
2 The first Sun Yefang Economic Science Award essay award was in order of date of publication.

> In September 1981, at the inaugural meeting of the China Federation of Economic Organizations in Dalian, some people complained for me, saying that the great economist should not criticize me, an "unknown person," by name because it would put me under great pressure. When Professor Sun Yefang heard such comments, he also felt uneasy. During the meeting, he met me and said, "So you are so young. I thought you were a senior scholar." He asked me very kindly whether I would be under pressure for his critique of my article. I told Professor Sun clearly: "I am not under any pressure at Peking University because this is an academic issue. It is normal to express different opinions on academic issues, and Peking University, with its scientific and democratic spirit, will not put pressure on those who express creative ideas." Professor Sun was very happy to hear this and said with a sense of relief, "That's very good; that's very good."[3]

In fact, Mr. Song Tao, Xiao Zhuoji's mentor and the first head of the Department of Economics of Renmin University of China, was also a long-time friend and staunch supporter of Mr. Sun Yefang. When Sun was under political attack in the early 1960s, Mr. Song Tao believed that many of his views were correct and invited him to come to Renmin University of China to teach his students.[4]

Before receiving the first Sun Yefang Economic Science Award, the life of Xiao Zhuoji and other economists was also a reflection of that era. In 1959, the young Xiao Zhuoji was assigned to the Economics Department of Peking University after graduating from Renmin University of China with a master's degree. Inspired by the moral character of Professor Chen Daisun, head of the Department of Economics at Peking University, he aspired to teach for the rest of his life. However, he stayed with the title of assistant professor for 20 years. During this period, China's higher education was paralyzed, and a large number of intellectuals with a passion to serve their country lacked the social status and job opportunities they deserved. Like most professors, Xiao Zhuoji did not escape the decade of turmoil, and he was imprisoned for more than ten months and put on trial for four months. But Xiao still seized every opportunity to study Marxist works and Western economic classics. It was not until 1978, when the National Conference on Science and the National Conference on Education were held, at which Deng Xiaoping blazed out the assertions that "science and technology are the primary productive forces" and "intellectuals are part of the working class," that millions of intellectuals got rid of the stigma of "stinking Number Nine," and the culture of respecting knowledge and teachers became stronger and stronger.

In 1979, Xiao Zhuoji was promoted to lecturer, in 1980 to associate professor, in 1985 to professor, and in 1986 he was approved by the Academic Degrees

---

3 Xiao Zhuoji. Lifelong Love for Teaching [EB/OL]. http://pkunews.pku.edu.cn, May 7, 2012.

4 Jiang Lihua. Mr. Song Tao and His Admiration of Talented Students [N]. *Journal of Renmin University of China*, May 18, 2015.

Committee of the State Council as a doctoral supervisor. In addition to winning the first Sun Yefang Economic Science Award, many of Xiao Zhuoji's theses had had a significant impact on academia and economic practice, such as "The Theory of Price Elasticity," "The Theory of Compatibility between Public Ownership and the Market Economy," "The Theory of the Commodity Economy as the Market Economy," and "The Theory of Adaptation of Securities Market to Socialism." During this period, Professor Xiao Zhuoji presided over the national social science key research project of China's Seventh Five-Year Plan period, "Research on Shareholding Economy," and began to take the securities market as an object of research, becoming one of the earliest experts to study the shareholding economy and securities market.

Jingji, the ancient Chinese for "economics," means to save the world and govern the nation and represents one of the responsibilities of intellectuals; modern economists spend their lives exploring economic theories and are concerned about the livelihood of the country. China's economic reforms, which began after the Third Plenary Session of the 11th CPC Central Committee, led more and more intellectuals to explore economic theories, and economics became more and more of a "prominent science" in the 1980s.

In addition, as a profound science, economics requires a rigorous attitude and an open mind to learning. The exchange, cooperation, and even debate among economists in the academic field is mutually beneficial. Professor Xiao Zhuoji participated in the launching of the large economic theory journal *Economist*. Together with Professors Liu Shibai and Wang Yongxi of Southwest University of Finance and Economics, he built a platform for the exchange of theoretical research results in the economics community.

At the end of the 1980s, during the debate on whether what China was doing was capitalist or socialist, Professor Xiao Zhuoji published an article entitled "A New Understanding of Socialism," in which he clearly proposed that socialism and capitalism are both different and related, and that socialism should draw upon the beneficial experience of capitalism. Because of the academic controversy, Professor Xiao was misunderstood by some people. The economist Mr. Dong Fureng wrote a handwritten banner, "A debate between right and wrong is admirable; chasing fame and profit is despicable." Xiao replied: "A debate between right and wrong is admirable: upholding truth and theoretical innovation; chasing fame and profit is despicable: staying uninterested in fame and fortune, and loving my students, friends, and relatives."

The "loving my students" in this case reflects the rigor and open-mindedness of Professor Xiao Zhuoji. On the one hand, Professor Xiao was very strict in choosing his students. Even in the School of Economics of Peking University, which has a strong academic style, he was known for his strict teaching; on the other hand, he boldly encouraged his students to be innovative in their theories and asked them to dare to outdo their teachers. As the saying goes, "A famous teacher makes good students." Xiao said the reverse: "A good student makes famous teachers." He often joked that he did not have a doctorate, but he had a team of PhD candidates. He often praised the theoretical innovations of his early doctoral students, such as Dr. Liu Wei's "The Theory of the Incompatibility between State-Owned Economy Monopoly and the Market Economy," Dr. Du Hui's "Theory of Economic Cycle Fluctuation," Dr. Mo Fumin's "The Theory of Compatibility between Socialism and the Market Economy," and Dr. Sun Qixiang's "A Hypothesis for the Optimal Macro Control of Risk Constraints."

One of "Xiao, the Stock Market's" most popular disciples is Chen Yunxian, a doctoral student who began to study under his supervision in 1988 and one of the first in China to start studying the theory of securities markets. In one of his articles, Professor Xiao Zhuoji said:

> Among my students, there are many who are of high quality and have outstanding achievements.... Dr. Chen Yunxian, who graduated in 1991, was the first Chinese economist to propose the law governing correlation between risk and return of securities investment. He not only studies investment banking theory, but also engages in investment banking. In just a few years, the securities company he managed grew at a high speed with remarkable benefits.

Times change, and scholars' self-regeneration is ceaseless as generations of them have gone on to break through the barriers of thinking. The economic theory of the People's Republic of China had been passed down to 1988 when China was about to achieve a theoretical breakthrough in capital markets under the catalyst of the times.

From working in the countryside to studying at Peking University

In the summer of 1988, Chen Yunxian was a lecturer at the School of Finance and Economics of Fuzhou University at the age of 33.

Like most people born in the 1950s, Chen Yunxian was personally involved in the movement to go to work in the countryside after graduating from secondary school. His experience in the rural areas of his hometown in Shanghang, Fujian Province, improved his physique and broadened his knowledge. The hardships of peasants and the various aspects of grassroots society were unforgettable to Chen Yunxian, a Hakka about 18 years old.

During the period of his countryside experience, Chen Yunxian was working as a peasant in a rural production team in a poor mountainous area on the provincial border, and at a young age he was already serving as a production leader. In that small mountain village, the rice flour factory was the only industry, and what Chen Yunxian had to do was to balance the relationship between the urban intellectuals and local peasants earning work points and the benefits of the rice flour factory. At this time, Chen Yunxian had already shown his unusual management talent. Due to his good performance, Chen Yunxian was recommended to study in Fujian Construction Engineering School, and from this time on, his thirst for knowledge sprang up deep inside him.

With the official resumption of the college entrance examination, the tradition of education in Fujian Hakka areas was rapidly restored, and large numbers of students sat the examination. Chen Yunxian had already been working in society for several years, but he turned to study and enrolled in Fujian Normal University majoring in economics, where he met the first person who greatly influenced his study career, namely his master's degree advisor, Mr. Chen Zheng, a famous economist and president of Fujian Normal University.

Mr. Chen Zheng began to teach and research on *Capital* and political economy in 1949, and began to publish his masterpiece *Explanation of "Capital"* (vol. 1–5) in 1978. This is the first comprehensive and systematic monograph on *Capital* in China. In the early days of reform and opening up, with the restoration of the college entrance examination system and rapid economic and social development, domestic education and academic circles were in urgent need of the study of classical works such as *Capital*. Mr. Chen Zheng's *Explanation of "Capital"* was widely used as a textbook throughout the country, influencing several generations of students.

It was Mr. Chen Zheng who founded the economics major at Fujian Normal University. Chen Yunxian, a master's student, studied depreciation compensation of financial fixed assets under the personal guidance of Mr. Chen Zheng. Mr. Chen Zheng not only guided Chen Yunxian's academic research, but also deeply influenced his research vision and attitude toward study. Also studying for his master's degree under Mr. Chen Zheng was Fang Jiachun, a student from Fujian.

In order to help Chen Yunxian better develop his academic horizons, Mr. Chen Zheng fully supported his participation in academic exchanges. In 1985, Chen Yunxian went to Beijing to attend an academic exchange program at Renmin University of China. At this event, he got to know many famous economists and met Ma Qingquan, who was studying for his PhD under Professor Wei Xinghua at Renmin University of China. Ma Qingquan was a few years older than Chen Yunxian and had an unassuming personality. Their common pursuit of economics made them instantly acquainted and they started a deep friendship that lasted for most of their lives.

After receiving his master's degree in economics, Chen Yunxian was assigned to the School of Finance and Economics of Fuzhou University as a lecturer. Teaching and educating others was Chen Yunxian's favorite career, but in his prime, he also wanted to have deeper attainments in economics research. While teaching at the university, he continued his research and published more than 10 academic research reports including "On the Intangible Loss of Commodities," "On the Effect of Intangible Loss of Commodities on the Economic Efficiency of

Commercial Companies," and "Controlling the Scale of Investment from Meso Economics," "On the Establishment and Development of the Scientific System of the Open Economy." In addition, Chen Yunxian launched himself to the pinnacle of education, hoping to obtain a doctorate in economics.

At that time, there were only a handful of PhD supervisors in economics in China, and Chen Yunxian's goal was to learn the most cutting-edge theoretical knowledge of economics, which meant that the competition for the doctoral exam was very fierce. At the beginning, Chen Yunxian's goal was to get a PhD from the famous economist Liu Shibai at Southwest University of Finance and Economics, but unfortunately, he was not successful. In the process, he met Li Jianyong, the first doctoral student of Southwest University of Finance and Economics, who was the "great disciple" of Professor Liu Shibai. Like Ma Qingquan and Fang Jiachun whom he met before, Chen Yunxian and Li Jianyong also formed a deep friendship on the way to study.

Throughout the 1980s, when all industries were yet to be developed, the fresh social atmosphere was blowing to the heart of every intellectual youth. As master's and doctoral students, they were the ones standing at the top of the "pyramid." They were full of ideals and passion, eager to innovate and change, not willing to be left behind, good at accepting new things, and eager to realize their value with knowledge in the era of reform.

In 1988, the hardworking Chen Yunxian knocked on the door to change his destiny and finally entered Peking University, the highest school in China, where students dream of being enrolled, and began his doctoral studies under the prestigious Professor Xiao Zhuoji.

The year 1988 marked the thirtieth year of Professor Xiao Zhuoji's tenure at Peking University, a year in which he admitted only two doctoral students. Professor Xiao's teaching style was also unique. He often instructed students at home while teaching, drinking tea, and discussing, which was laughingly called a "private school" by students. Chen Yunxian, then 33 years old and a little younger than the other students, attracted Professor Xiao's special attention as soon as he joined Xiao's team.

Thanks to his master's degree, Chen had a good understanding of Marxist economic theory such as Capital. The study of Marxist economic theory had also been a lifelong commitment of Professor Xiao Zhuoji, who, as early as his youth, set two ambitions: first, to read the works of Marx and Engels, and second, to write his own biographies of them. In addition, Professor Xiao Zhuoji boldly applied his study of Capital to practice, and his keen ideas and insights were known as "reform economics" and "news economics" at that time. During his teaching, Professor Xiao led Chen Yunxian and other students to study Soviet and Eastern European socialist political economy, make comparative studies of Western economics, and put forward new ideas in the light of the actual situation of China's reform and opening up.[5]

In the late 1980s, the sudden debate on whether what China was doing was capitalist or socialist did not change Professor Xiao's belief in the direction of academic research, and he clearly emphasized the importance of the market economy, encouraging his students to do more research along this direction. During this period, Chen Yunxian, under the guidance of Professor Xiao, published important theoretical discoveries such as "The Policy of Inflation Control and the Choice of Policy Tools," "The Changes, Development and Implementation Conditions of the Socialist Theory of Distribution According to Labor," "Emphasizing and Strengthening the Research of Portfolio Investment Theory," "The Characteristics, Kernel and Defects of Bruce's Economic Model," "The Virtual Characteristics of Stocks and the Analysis of Investor Behavior," and "Stock Investors Should Grasp Stock Prices at the Right Time to Make Investments."

In 1990, Professor Xiao Zhuoji began to lead the research project "Research on the Securities Market," a key national social science research topic during China's Eighth Five-Year Plan period, while his student Chen Yunxian was actively preparing his doctoral dissertation, the research direction of which was determined to be a frontier topic in economic theory: comparing the financial systems of the United States, the United Kingdom, Germany and Japan, and exploring the development model of China's multilevel capital markets.

Riding a bicycle, Chen Yunxian moved between Professor Xiao's "private school," the library of Peking University, and his student dormitory, immersing himself in his research for a long time. As winter turned to spring, the picturesque Peking University did not attract him to stop and appreciate it. Because Chen Yunxian found that there was basically no reference material available for theoretical research related to China's capital markets, his doctoral dissertation was quite difficult from the very beginning. As his research progressed, the pressure on Chen Yunxian increased day by day, which made him unhappy. In addition to the lack of materials, he also encountered a huge theoretical bottleneck.

In the history of natural science, the three laws of classical mechanics had long been dominant, and the research on quantum mechanics started in its background was destined to be difficult and incomprehensible to common people. Similarly, according to the domestic political economy theory in 1980s, the factors of production only included the so-called "three factors" of labor, tools of labor, and objects of labor, so Chen Yunxian had to face the theoretical bottleneck when he studied the capital markets on this basis: can capital be incorporated into the factors of production? Can "finance" become the blood of the economy?

Moreover, after some social events, the debate on whether the capital markets are socialist or capitalist was still going on in the theoretical circles at that time. As

5 Dr. Chen Yunxian's article in memory of Professor Xiao Zhuoji in 2017.

a current student, he chose such a topic for his dissertation at the risk of not being able to graduate. Chen Yunxian, a doctoral student, thoroughly understood that it was never easy to make breakthroughs and innovations in theory.

Professor Xiao Zhuoji, who "removed a hundred obstacles with one smile," helped his student with his own open-mindedness and teaching style at this time.

Under the tolerant and liberal academic style of Peking University, Professor Xiao encouraged his student to cross the threshold to ask other economists for advice, "to learn from all and form his own ideas." During his three years at Peking University, Chen Yunxian received guidance from a number of economics professors, including Chen Zhenhan, Hu Daiguang, Fan Jiaxiang, Zhang Youren, Li Yining, and Liu Fangyu. Facing the bottleneck in his doctoral dissertation, Chen Yunxian was most helped by the economics master Chen Daisun.

Born in 1900, Mr. Chen Daisun made great achievements in his research in finance, statistics, international finance, and history of economic theory. After graduating from Tsinghua University in 1920, Chen Daisun was qualified to study in the US at the public expense of the Gengzi Compensatory Education Fund, and studied at the University of Wisconsin and Harvard University. After receiving his PhD degree with his dissertation "A Statistical Analysis of Local Fiscal Expenditures in Massachusetts,"[6] he went to England, France, and Italy for short research trips. In 1927, Mr. Chen Daisun returned to China to teach, and taught at Tsinghua University, National Southwest Associated University, and Peking University for dozens of years, teaching undergraduates until he was over 80 years of age and doctoral students in his nineties. His academic status and moral character are respected by the teachers and students of Peking University and Tsinghua University.

With his extraordinary life history and academic vision, Mr. Chen became one of the few famous scholars in China who had systematically studied Western financial models. What made Chen Yunxian feel fortunate was that Mr. Chen Daisun, who was respectfully called "Respected Chen Dai" by his classmates, was his fellow townsman from Fujian. As a result, Chen Yunxian frequently stayed with the 90-year-old "Respected Chen Dai," respectfully asking for advice on his doubts and opening up the ideas of his dissertation step by step.

Under the analysis and encouragement of Mr. Chen Daisun and Professor Xiao Zhuoji, Chen Yunxian boldly incorporated capital into the factors of production. After removing this bottleneck, Chen Yunxian's theoretical musings were further extended.

According to the original economic theory, there are two major categories of assets. One is money and the other is commodities, and the theory focused on studying how to coordinate the two effectively. After the emergence of capital markets, besides the effective coordination of commodities and money, should

6 Wu Lin. Chen Daisun's Peach and Plum Spring Breeze [N]. *Beijing Evening News*, January 24, 2019.

securities be included as a third party in the coordination problem?

Under the view that capital is a factor of production, people, property, and goods are hard factors, money is a soft factor, and stocks and bonds are also soft factors. How will they play a positive role in promoting economic development?

Finally, in his doctoral dissertation, Chen Yunxian developed three major hypotheses of securities investment: the expected return theory, the risk premium theory, and the holding period preference theory. He revealed three laws of the capital markets: the law of expected return guidance, the law of equal increase of return and risk, and the law of resonance of securities and money.

From the content, direction, and results of his research, Chen Yunxian not only studied the model of Chinese capital markets, but also studied a series of financial market systems such as bonds, funds, and futures within this model. Some of the theories not only filled the theoretical gap in China, but even went beyond the regulatory practice in the United States which did not use the investment ratio of the securities market as one of the tools of monetary regulation until the 1990s to directly regulate the market from the perspective of the Federal Reserve. The theoretical research direction revealed by Chen Yunxian's proposal to "incorporate the elements of capital into the factors of production" was clearly ahead of its time.

As a doctoral supervisor who constantly led theoretical innovation, Professor Xiao Zhuoji gave high praise to this research result of Chen Yunxian, saying that the dissertation "explores a major theoretical and practical issue in the current international economic activities and domestic economic reforms, with a novel and pioneering topic, and is the first doctoral dissertation on the theory of securities investment in China.... It proposes a novel theoretical framework and basic ideas for the establishment of a theory of portfolio investment with Chinese characteristics, which should be recognized."

In 1991, Chen Yunxian successfully defended his doctoral dissertation "A Comparative Study of Chinese and Foreign Portfolio Investment," and at Peking University he became China's first PhD in research on the theory of securities market. Chen Yunxian has been called "Dr. Chen" since then.

The first job chosen following graduation as the first PhD of securities investment theory

At the end of 1990, at the age of 35, the general manager of the Shanghai Stock Exchange, Mr. Wei Wenyuan, rang the gong at the Pujiang Hotel, and a stock exchange trader on the floor took the lead and completed a purchase and sale of the stock Vacuum Electronics. The first step was taken in the Chinese securities market to "cross the river by feeling the stones."

Dr. Chen Yunxian was the same age as Wei Wenyuan, and at the time when the latter started the Chinese securities market, he was writing his graduation thesis to fill the theoretical gap of the securities market. He could not remember how many times he rode his bicycle to and from his teachers, and how many times he discussed with his grey-haired teachers until late at night. It was not until he was close to graduation that Dr. Chen began to think seriously about his career direction.

In the context of economic reforms in China at that time, most of the PhDs in economics from famous universities went to work in the Central Policy Research Office and relevant ministries and commissions of the State Council after graduation. Dr. Chen Yunxian's initial idea after graduation was to "stay in Beijing" and continue his theoretical research there, or to "go back to Fujian" and work in his hometown where he was familiar with the local culture and people. Until the beginning of the last semester, Chen Yunxian did not have the idea of "going to work in a securities company."

This is because although the Chinese securities market had already started in 1990, securities companies, as market operating entities, were still distant from the theoretical circles of universities in terms of talent employment.

In 1987, Shenzhen Special Economic Zone Securities Company was established as the first professional securities company after the introduction of the reform and opening up reform. In 1988, in order to adapt to the nationwide promotion of treasury bond transfer, the People's Bank of China allocated funds to set up 33 securities companies in various provinces. In addition, a number of securities companies were also established in the financial system. These securities companies, established before the 1990s, all had a common characteristic: they were created for the circulation of treasury bonds. Several of the early securities companies in Shanghai made their first lots of money quickly by trading treasury bonds off-site, but this idea came from the initiative of stockholders such as "Millionaire Yang" (Yang Huaiding). The brainy Yang Huaiding was able to achieve this "practical breakthrough" because, according to his own account, "the Shanghai newspapers published the news that Shanghai was going to open up the trading of government bonds. I had read *Midnight*[7] and knew that there would definitely be benefits in it."

Before and after the official establishment of the Shanghai Stock Exchange, most of these securities companies and banks' securities departments did not understand the business structure and management model of modern securities companies. They did whatever the government told them to do; they concentrated their efforts on what was profitable. Their long-term development ideas were vague, and they seldom took the initiative to think about the role of securities companies at the macroeconomic level.

Generally speaking, in 1990, the securities companies, which were aggressive but not rational, had neither subjective awareness nor realistic motivation to "seek help from the theoretical circles of universities."

It is remarkable that in Guangdong Province, the forefront of reform and opening up, a few knowledgeable people knew the reputation of Dr. Chen from

7 A novel written by Mao Dun about Chinese capitalists in the 1930s.

Peking University. What is even more remarkable is that they believed in the value of academic theories to the practice of securities market and that a fledgling PhD could create a career in the securities market at its nascent stage.

When Dr. Chen Yunxian entered Peking University in September 1988, the same people established China's tenth bank.

As the frontline of reform and opening up, Guangdong Province has long led the way. The year 1984 saw Deng Xiaoping's visit to Guangdong, which greatly freed people's minds and further developed reform and opening up, and as a result, Guangdong's economy flourished. According to incomplete statistics, the demand for loans around 1985 exceeded 10 billion yuan in Guangdong Province. After research at home and abroad, the Guangdong Provincial Government submitted a request to the State Council on January 7, 1988 on deepening reform, expanding opening up and accelerating economic development in Guangdong Province. The State Council officially approved on February 10 of that year that "Guangdong Province, as an experimental zone for comprehensive reform, will continue to be a step ahead in reform and opening up" and "approved the establishment of Guangdong Development Bank."[8]

Lin Ruo, then secretary of the CPC Guangdong Provincial Committee, attached great importance to the establishment of "Guangdong's own bank" and named Yang Deyuan, executive vice governor, to be responsible for the preparation of Guangdong Development Bank. After several considerations, Yang Deyuan instructed Wu Chixin, then deputy director of the Guangdong Provincial Government Economic Research Center, and Qiu Zhenlan, chief of the Finance and Banking Section of the Guangdong Provincial Finance and Trade Office, to prepare the relevant matters.

Wu Chixin later recalled the situation when he was "appointed." He thought that "I was just a deputy director who did research," and even though he personally participated in writing the request to the State Council on deepening reform, expanding opening up and accelerating economic development in Guangdong Province, he had not expected that he would come to Guangdong Development Bank and become its first president, legal representative, chairman, and CPC secretary. At the bank, he went through a bumpy and glorious period.

On September 8, 1988, Guangdong Development Bank was officially opened, a pilot bank for China's financial reforms, one of the earliest joint-stock commercial banks established in China, and the tenth bank in Chinese history since the Westernization Movement. The first employees posed for a group photo in front of the headquarters at 1 Qiyi Road, Haizhu District, Guangzhou. Among these employees, there were officials transferred from the provincial Party committee, the provincial government and the People's Bank of China, talents from the four state-owned commercial banks, and young employees under 20

8 " '30 Years, 30 People' of Guangdong Development Bank: The Pioneers Who Dare to Be the First," September 8, 2018.

years old who had just graduated from school.

Among the preparers of Guangdong Development Bank was Ding Lisong, who studied in the Sociology Department of Tsinghua University in 1947 and served as the secretary of Tao Zhu, former vice premier of the State Council, for eight years. In Guangdong Province, Ding Lisong served as deputy secretary general of the provincial government and director of the Provincial Office of Special Economic Zones, and participated in the drafting of the Regulations of Economic Special Zones. In 1988, he became an important member of Guangdong Development Bank. During one of his financial projects, Ding Lisong met Fu Ge, a graduate of Fujian Normal University, who happened to be Chen Yunxian's master's degree classmate. Through Fu Ge's introduction, Ding Lisong learned about Dr. Chen Yunxian and his research on China's capital markets. By coincidence, on the eve of his graduation, Chen Yunxian got in touch with Ding Lisong and agreed to have a face-to-face meeting at Guangdong Mansion in Beijing. One evening, Dr. Chen rode his bicycle along the West Third Ring Road to Guangdong Building on time for the appointment, and Ding Lisong was already waiting for Chen Yunxian in his suite on the top floor of the building.

The atmosphere at the first meeting was very calm. Ding Lisong, a literary man, was very subtle and did not use a long speech to persuade Dr. Chen Yunxian, but said something that impressed Dr. Chen to this day: "The north is short of vitality, so I hope you can come to Guangdong, which is at the forefront of reform and opening up." Ding is a senior who had rich experience in revolutionary work and reform and opening up, and Chen is a PhD graduate who was in his prime and full of ambition. The two seemed to have reached some kind of consensus.

Before the meeting, Dr. Chen Yunxian had a preliminary understanding of Guangdong Development Bank and had rethought his career path, and had an additional choice besides "staying in Beijing" and "going back to Fujian." What impressed Dr. Chen the most about Guangdong Development Bank in Guangzhou was that it could be the best "testing ground" to put his theories into practice. Many of Chen's schoolmates who had studied under Professor Xiao Zhuoji, had established good careers in the theoretical field in universities and government departments. With the pioneering spirit of the Hakka people in Fujian, Dr. Chen, who had just achieved a breakthrough in the academic field, developed a new vision: to go south to Guangzhou and put his theories into practice in the emerging Chinese securities market.

On the recommendation of Ding Lisong, Chen Yunxian went to Guangdong to meet with Wu Chixin, president of Guangdong Development Bank, before graduating from his doctoral program. Dr. Chen briefed Wu on his views on the securities market and made it very clear to Wu that he would join Guangdong Development Bank to develop the securities business. President Wu Chixin had heard about Dr. Chen from Peking University and expressed a very welcoming attitude, and formally invited Dr. Chen to come to his bank to prepare for the establishment of the Securities Department. Dr. Chen was the first PhD in Guangdong Development Bank.

So Dr. Chen started to establish the Securities Department of Guangdong Development Bank, the predecessor of GF Securities, and started his journey in the securities market in 1991.

In 1991, Ren Zhongyi, a member of the Central Advisory Commission and former first secretary of the CPC Guangdong Provincial Committee, wrote an inscription for Guangdong Development Bank, "Be a pioneer of exploration bravely," in a strong and powerful script. From the perspective of talent introduction and career development, employing young Dr. Chen Yunxian to establish the Securities Department of Guangdong Development Bank is a footnote of the spirit of "being a pioneer of exploration bravely."

In the history of the world securities industry, Marcus Goldman, the founder of Goldman Sachs, came to New York from Germany in the wave of immigrants. He was a tailor struggling to make ends meet before engaging in the commercial paper business. John Pierpont Morgan, the founder of J.P. Morgan Consortium, came from a family of merchants during the American Civil War. Tokichi Nomura, the founder of Nomura Securities in Japan, came from a famous family during the Meiji Restoration period. All these investment banking giants had their own entrepreneurial legends and belonged to their respective historical trends.

In China, a series of securities firms born around 1990 also have their own legends and collectively belong to the grand historical context of China's reform and opening up. Among them, the case of Dr. Chen Yunxian and the GF Securities group is unique in that a fledgling PhD led the securities business in the absence of many conditions, and then attracted a group of university intellectuals to start a business together, eventually exerting considerable influence on the market.

This "history of entrepreneurship intellectuals from colleges and universities" is extremely rare even in the global securities history; it was a phenomenon under the specific historical background of China's reform and opening up. In a sense, from the first generation of economists after the founding of the People's Republic of China, to Professor Xiao Zhuoji, Wu Chixin, and Ding Lisong of Guangdong Development Bank, and to every entrepreneurial employee who would join GF Securities, all were contributors to this historical case.

2. The "three theories," GF Securities' priori advantages in the securities market

On Securities Investment in China

At the end of June 1991, after defending his doctoral dissertation, Chen

Yunxian left Beijing and set off on the train to the South. His luggage was simple, but in the deepest part of his suitcase was the manuscript of his thesis, "A Comparative Study of Chinese and Foreign Portfolio Investment." After discussing with the editors of Peking University Press, this doctoral thesis, one of the earliest studies on the theory of securities investment in China, would be officially published under the title of "On Securities Investment" after editing and finishing touches.

When he arrived in Guangzhou, Dr. Chen reported directly to the Head Office of Guangdong Development Bank. At that time, Ms. Li Shuzhi, who was in charge of employee deployment in the Personnel Department, had a deep impression of the first time she met Dr. Chen.

At that time in Guangzhou, doctoral talents were very rare, and Li Shushi was curious about the PhD from Peking University she was about to meet, and had imagined the image of a PhD in a suit in her mind. On the day of check-in, Dr. Chen Yunxian wore a sports suit with the words "Peking University" printed on it and a pair of white washed sneakers. It was a surprise to Li Shuzhi that Dr. Chen, who was the first PhD of Guangdong Development Bank, was so simple. A few simple words of communication during the process of joining the bank made Li Shuzhi feel that the gentleman in front of her was knowledgeable, modest, and simple, with a strong sense of scholarship between his words, yet exuding the vigor of youth, giving her a spring-like feeling.

After joining the bank at the end of June, Dr. Chen Yunxian worked in the Trust and Investment Department to prepare and develop the bank's securities business. At that time, all the non-banking businesses of Guangdong Development Bank were placed in the Trust and Investment Department, including securities business, investment business, technology business, and guarantee business. There were more than ten colleagues in the department, including Wang Zhiwei, Huang Xiaoxuan, Wang Hongmao, Hu Yousheng, and Li Weixiong.

After a short period of adaptation, Dr. Chen Yunxian formally reported to President Wu Chixin his ideas on the development of the securities business.

President Wu had several titles among his colleagues. The first was "Boss Wu," rich in southern characteristics, which also reflected Wu Chixin as he had the final say as the first president and chairman of the board. He was known for his decisiveness and temper to middle-level officials. The second was "Uncle Wu," which is full of affinity and human touch. The title of "Uncle Wu" and the other vice president, Lu Jinchang, who was called "Uncle Lu," coincide with the capitalized numbers for 5 (伍) and 6 (陆) commonly used in the banking industry. They were also well supported by the grassroots staff.

After the interview with "Boss Wu," Dr. Chen Yunxian did not have an easy time. Although he had already created an academic theory, when he came to Guangzhou and joined Guangdong Development Bank, the first thing he had to consider was how the securities business could hold ground and survive.

At the beginning of the establishment of Guangdong Development Bank, Wu Chixin foresaw a great potential for the development of the securities market. However, due to various conditions, during the first three years of bank's development, its securities business was basically limited to the distribution and purchase of treasury bonds, and generally did not take off, and could not even be called a specialized business. During this period, a number of securities institutions had emerged in Guangzhou alone. How did these peers operate in the vicinity? What were the inspirations for Guangdong Development Bank? No answers could be found in the Trust Investment Department.

Dr. Chen quickly got to work. The bicycle he rode at Peking University was shipped from Beijing to Guangzhou, where it continued to be his mode of transportation for many years. Dr. Chen went out to research during the day and came back to write reports at night, and with the energy of an academic researcher, he analyzed the strengths and weaknesses of the securities institutions in Guangzhou.

After his research, he was surprised to find that the soon-to-be-established Securities Department of Guangdong Development Bank was not only not a "local leader," but also had fallen to about tenth place in the securities industry in Guangzhou.

On August 18, 1991, Dr. Chen Yunxian put his three research reports on "Guangdong Development Bank's Securities Business Vision" on Wu Chixin's desk. The reports analyzed the business scope and development of nearly 10 securities institutions in Guangzhou up to that time. In general, they could be divided into three categories.

> The first category: securities institutions whose business have a good development trend and have the potential to form securities trading centers in Guangzhou, such as Guangdong Securities Company, Guangzhou Securities Company, and Guangzhou Financial Market. Their common characteristics are: more sound organization, sufficient manpower, clearer securities business objectives, better business area and location conditions, longer experience in securities business, and direct support from the People's Bank of China Guangdong Branch or Guangzhou Branch.
>
> The second category: securities institutions with greater autonomy and vitality and better prospects for securities business, such as the Securities Department of Bank of Communications and the Securities Finance Department of Guangdong International Trust and Investment Corporation.
>
> The third category: securities institutions with average business development, such as the Securities Department of Bank of China Guangzhou Branch, the Securities Department of China Construction Bank Guangdong Branch, and the Securities Department of Guangdong Yuecai Trust and Investment Company. None of these institutions have implemented independent

> accounting and self-financing, and the size of securities business and the level of profitability are not linked to the personal interests of business personnel.
>
> In terms of the types of securities business, the standard of the three types of securities institutions is generally comparable: first, the business varieties are limited to treasury bonds and a small amount of corporate bonds, while stocks and international securities business have not yet been launched; second, the business scope is basically limited to Guangzhou, and there is no vertical and horizontal securities business beyond Guangzhou; third, the business level is basically limited to securities issuance, and there are gaps in securities trading; fourth, there is a general lack of collection of national securities information and exploration of theories of securities operation. They do what they want to do. Although they are pioneering, but there is blindness.

In the reports, Dr. Chen Yunxian concluded that the securities business of Guangdong Development Bank should seize the time to effectively overcome and avoid the four defects mentioned above and develop toward a first-class securities institution in Guangzhou in the spirit of "being practical and pragmatic." He also put forward the business development policy of the Securities Department of "laying a good foundation, exploring horizontally and vertically, and leaning outward" to continuously improve the profit level and explore the way for financial reforms.

Wu Chixin, who had been the deputy director of the Guangdong Provincial Government's Economic Research Center, was extremely critical of wording and cared a lot about every word and even punctuation of work reports submitted to him for approval. He often gave annotations in them, and even once tore up the reports directly in front of those who had prepared them. However, he approved Dr. Chen's report without changing a single word.

Soon after, Dr. Chen Yunxian integrated the essence of the three reports and formed another report, "Vision for the Development of Guangdong Securities Market," from the perspective of the overall development of Guangdong's securities industry. In Dr. Chen's view, Guangdong's securities market should deal with both equity and debt, both primary and secondary markets, and both domestic and international markets, synchronize securities circulation and securities management, and establish a core Guangdong securities market network.

If you describe that Dr. Chen was in control of GF Securities' future in his reports, just as Zhuge Liang was in control of Liu Bei's future when he first joined him, you may be overrating Dr. Chen. However, the top-level planning of GF Securities before its birth, as well as the source of its rapid emergence at a later stage, can be seen in these reports. In 1991 when China's securities market had not yet taken shape, the regulatory system had just started, and securities companies made selling treasury bonds their main business, Dr. Chen Yunxian's ideas of dealing with both equity and debt, both primary and secondary markets, and even both domestic and international markets were very much ahead of their time.

The correctness of these development ideas has been proved in the "three decades" of GF Securities and the "three decades" of China's securities market.

Several years later, Dr. Ma Qingquan, Dr. Chen Yunxian's entrepreneurial partner, said in his analysis of the development of GF Securities: "China's capital markets crossed the river by feeling the stones, but Dr. Chen led GF Securities not by feeling the stones; he had a clear idea of what a securities company should be and what GF Securities should be at the very beginning."

There is no prophet in the world, and the "priori advantage" of GF Securities at the beginning originated from the manuscript that Dr. Chen brought with him when he went south to Guangzhou in June 1991. This book, *On Securities Investment*, based on his doctoral dissertation, is divided into three parts, namely, the first part "The Law of Securities Investment," the second part "Comparison of Securities Investment between China and Foreign Countries," and the third part "The Practice of Securities Investment in China." In addition to achieving the theoretical breakthrough of "incorporating capital into the factors of production," he also developed the three hypotheses of securities investment and the three laws of the capital markets, and applied the empirical analytical method to conduct a detailed comparative study of the securities market models of the United Kingdom, Germany, the United States, and Japan. The study was a pioneer in the comparative study of securities investment in China and abroad. For the United States securities market, which had the most significance, the development process and specific forms of securities investment were examined in detail, and a "multi-element, multilevel, multi-stage" securities investment operation model was proposed, taking into account China's national conditions. This book, which followed Dr. Chen's journey south, combined with his "research on the bicycle" in Guangzhou, became the basis for him to quickly figure out how to develop the Securities Department of Guangdong Development Bank.

At the beginning of 1992, *On Securities Investment* was officially published by Peking University Press, with a simple blue cover covering several years of Dr. Chen Yunxian's research. As a book to fill the theoretical gap, it was highly sought after by economics theorists and university teachers and students, and has been reprinted several times since its publication, becoming a must-read for the whole industry to study the theory of securities investment for a longer period of time. It was not until several years later that when Dr. Ma Qingquan was communicating with a scholar at Renmin University of China, the scholar suddenly exclaimed, "Oh, you are talking about the same Dr. Chen, author of *On Securities Investment*!"

On September 8, 1991, the Securities Department of Guangdong Development Bank was officially established with Dr. Chen Yunxian as general manager. On that day, Guangdong Development Bank celebrated its third anniversary, and the Guangdong Trade Center Building in Haizhu Square was filled with a joyful atmosphere. Dr. Chen Yunxian came to the business counter marked "securities trading" and posed for a group photo with Hu Yousheng, Liu Lin, Li Weixiong, Zhang Hairong, and others with a youthful atmosphere. This was the place where the dream of GF Securities began.

On Investment Banking which clarifies the essence

Securities business was the business entrusted to Dr. Chen Yunxian by President Wu and other leaders; securities theory was Dr. Chen Yunxian's own spiritual kingdom.

At the beginning of his work, Dr. Chen Yunxian often appeared at the counters of the brokerage branches, and when the counter staff was too busy, he sold bonds and counted cash together with his colleagues. This behavior of his puzzled many people, and Huang Xiaoxuan, deputy general manager of the Trust Investment Department, asked Dr. Chen in a serious manner, "Do you think it is appropriate for you, a graduate of Peking University and a PhD of China's highest academic institution, to come here to sell bonds and count money as well?" However, what Dr. Chen was thinking was that as a pioneer in the securities business, he must not be far from the grassroots, and selling bonds over the counter was a process to grasp the real situation of the market. In the face of others' confusion, Dr. Chen still enjoyed what he was doing.

In addition to the complicated business and management affairs, Dr. Chen Yunxian did not stop thinking about and innovating his theory, and he kept deepening his research content. After the establishment of the Securities Department, Dr. Chen published research articles such as "Ways to Revitalize SOEs," "The Management and Effectiveness of Bond Investment in the US," "The Similarities and Differences of Securities Market Systems in Hong Kong and China's Mainland and Their Implications," "A Survey of China's Securities Investment and Its Development Trend," and "China's Securities Investment Target Model and Its Realization Conditions."

At the beginning of 1992, Deng Xiaoping inspected the South and delivered important talks, which laid the theoretical foundation for developing the socialist market economy with Chinese characteristics. The young securities market ushered in another development opportunity, and the trend of the industry developing from secondary market to primary market, from a single business to all-around businesses, and from domestic business to international business became more and more obvious.

In accordance with the advance layout of President Wu and Dr. Chen, as soon as the Securities Department was established, Guangdong Development Bank prepared to apply to the People's Bank of China for the establishment of a wholly-owned subsidiary securities company. The plan was supported by the Guangdong Branch of the People's Bank of China, but after nearly three months of review, the Head Office of the People's Bank of China replied that "a joint-stock securities company should be established." Guangdong Development Bank then adjusted the plan to form a joint-stock securities company with 11 shareholders and submitted it to the Head Office of the People's Bank of China. This time it took longer for the Head Office to review and reply. Finally, the Head Office decided that the securities company formed by a bank should still be a wholly-owned subsidiary.

The main reason for such a long and tangled approval process was that policymakers were considering a major change in the financial industry to separate banking and securities operations.

As a pioneer in the comparative study of Chinese and foreign securities investment, Dr. Chen was familiar with the origins of the separation of banking and securities. After the US experienced the world economic crisis from 1929 to 1933, it was found that one of the main causes of the crisis was the use of short-term funds as long-term investments in the securities market. This led to a crisis in the securities industry and the banking industry, and the crisis extended to industrial and commercial companies and various other fields. In view of this profound historical lesson, the US passed the Glass-Steagall Act in 1933 and the Securities Exchange Act of 1934, which prohibited affiliated companies of commercial banks from engaging mainly in securities issuance, listing, and underwriting, marking the formal entry of the US financial industry into the era of separate banking and securities operation and regulation.

After the initiative to rectify the economic order and improve the economic environment in the early 1990s, the separation of banking and securities was also tried out in China. In October 1992, three national securities companies—Huaxia Securities, Southern Securities, and Guotai Securities—were established, relying on the Industrial and Commercial Bank of China, the Agricultural Bank of China, and the China Construction Bank. These three national joint-stock securities companies were established so that the People's Bank of China could try out separate banking and securities operation and regulation through them. As envisaged by the People's Bank of China, the establishment of the three major joint-stock securities companies would enable separate banking and securities operation and regulation.

In order to achieve this goal, the three national securities companies had strong capital strength. In 1992, the registered capital of Huaxia Securities and Southern Securities was one billion yuan when they were established. The registered capital of Guotai Securities was 918 million yuan, and was subsequently increased. In contrast, the Securities Department of Guangdong Development Bank, which was established a year before, had a registered capital of only 10 million yuan, of which only two million yuan was in cash and the remaining eight million yuan was treasury bonds allocated by Guangdong Development Bank.

However, the development of the industry pattern was not as good as the People's Bank of China had hoped it would be. The three major securities companies had business outlets all over the country, and the original commercial bank securities department continued to exist and operate as usual. The number of securities companies increased sharply, and most of the trust and investment companies also engaged in securities business.

By the beginning of 1993, there were nearly 7,000 securities trading institutions and agents nationwide, including more than 70 securities companies, more than 1,000 brokerage branches, and more than 5,000 securities trading points, basically forming a nationwide securities trading network in cities and villages.[9]

In 1993, the stock market trading volume had risen, with the annual turnover of Shanghai and Shenzhen reaching 377.2 billion yuan, 5.53 times that of the previous year. At this time, the Securities Department of Guangdong Development Bank not only could hardly compete with the industry giants, but also faced more hidden dangers for its very survival: in addition to facing local protectionism, it also had to deal with the business crossover among banks, securities, and trust institutions. Most importantly, the entire securities industry was facing the problem of lack of clarity in business scope and boundaries, and unclear concepts of the industry.

How do we view separate banking and securities operation? How do we scientifically define the business substance of securities companies? Dr. Chen Yunxian started to think again.

On June 1, 1993, as planned by the Securities Association of China, Dr. Chen Yunxian went to the United States to attend the one-month business training program "Foreign Seminar of National Senior Securities Managers." This was the first high-profile training session organized by the Securities Association of China, and it came at the right time for Dr. Chen, who was thinking about the direction of the industry and the company.

The training was mainly conducted at Merrill Lynch and was attended by executives from various domestic securities firms, including officials from the People's Bank of China system and a few highly educated professionals. Most of the participants were drowsy, probably due to jet lag or English unproficiency. Given the size and volume of Guangdong Development Bank's Securities Department, it was fortunate for its representative to have the opportunity to attend such an industry-wide training session abroad. Dr. Chen Yunxian braced himself to drink a few more cups of coffee rather than miss a single moment.

During the study in the United States, Dr. Chen had no distractions. The close observation and study of Merrill Lynch further deepened his understanding of international investment banking. When he heard something he could learn from, it would stir and swirl in his mind for a long time, and he was excited. He

9 *Economist*, 1993.

concentrated on writing about the content on what he heard and thought, creating a large amount of material.

Gradually, he approached the crux of the problem he had been thinking about for some time: the separation of the securities and banking industries in China first required a clear concept—investment banking. On this basis, he further clarified investment banks and commercial banks.

In the 1980s and 1990s, the international concept of "investment banking" was introduced into China and increasingly discussed, but there was no domestic institution corresponding to international investment banking at first. When people mentioned investment banks, they generally thought of the banks under the State Development Bank that carried out infrastructure investment, not securities companies. In addition, many people simply equated foreign "investment banking" with investment through mergers and acquisitions.

After deep thinking, Dr. Chen Yunxian proposed for the first time in China that the concept of "investment banking" should be in both a broad and a narrow sense.

In his view, the essence of commercial banks in the narrow sense is the deposit and loan business, while the essence of investment banking in the narrow sense is the securities dealer. After the 1933 Glass-Steagall Act and the 1934 Securities Exchange Act, investment banks in the United States engaged in securities brokerage business separated from banks. Although retaining their names as banks, they, in essence, were securities companies, such as the United States' Merrill Lynch and Morgan Stanley, and Japan's Nomura Securities. Investment banks were only a theoretical designation.

However, with the new characteristics of diversification, specialization, internationalization, and conglomeration of investment banking, the business scope of investment banks was no longer limited to traditional business, but expanded to a broader scope, so the concept of investment banking also needed to be broadened.

Investment banking in a narrow sense mainly includes securities underwriting and securities brokerage, but investment banking in a broad sense should also include project financing, corporate finance, fund management, securities investment consulting, venture capital, and leasing. The expansion of investment banking from the narrow scope to the broad scope was the trend of the development of investment banks in the world, and also the future development trend of domestic securities companies.

Dr. Chen's theoretical exploration became clear, and good news came from the application for the establishment of a securities company.

In June 1993, Wang Qishan became vice president of the People's Bank of China, with the main task of cooperating with the central government to deal with the runaway inflation, and one of the measures to be taken was to cultivate and support securities institutions. After several rounds of screening and inspection,

Wang Qishan did not award his first approval to financial institutions in Shenzhen and Shanghai, but to Guangdong GF Securities Company. President Wu Chixin made a promise to Wang Qishan face to face that the formation of GF Securities Co., Ltd. in Guangdong would certainly enable the operation and regulation of securities business to reach a high level of standardization.

In December 1993, Guangdong GF Securities Company was established on the basis of the former Securities Department with a registered capital of 150 million yuan, with Chen Yunxian as the legal representative and general manager and Wu Chixin as the chairman of the supervisory board, as approved by the People's Bank of China in the document Yinfu [1993] No. 432.

GF Securities moved to Huatai Hotel in Guangzhou. In January 1994, at the 1993 annual work summary meeting held in Huatai Hotel, Dr. Chen Yunxian formally stated that Guangdong GF Securities Company should operate as an investment bank.

By investment bank, Dr. Chen was referring to an investment bank in a broad sense. He emphasized that securities companies should clarify their business nature and their business model should be different from that of commercial banks, and conform to the trend to separate banking and securities operations. This is because Dr. Chen, after clarifying the essence of investment banking and securities business, concluded that commercial banks and investment banks are different in three areas: business essence, profit sources, and management styles, and therefore need to implement separate business operation and regulation.

In this way, Dr. Chen Yunxian successfully solved the two most troubling problems in the securities industry in its early stage in China in 1993 after careful research, using the "theory + practice" approach.

During this period, Dr. Chen's favorite example was the J.P. Morgan Consortium in the United States. In accordance with the Glass-Steagall Act and the Securities Exchange Act, the J.P. Morgan Consortium was separated into two banks—J.P. Morgan and Morgan Stanley—in 1934. Among them, J.P. Morgan was mainly a commercial bank, while Morgan Stanley was mainly an investment bank, and the two Morgan banks worked in different business areas. Since its independence, Morgan Stanley has gradually surpassed J.P. Morgan in terms of its international influence and development prospects. Even though J.P. Morgan returned to the mixed business path in 1989 with the concession of the US government, the popularity of the two Morgans is no longer the same.

The long-term flourishing of Morgan Stanley and other international investment banks made Dr. Chen Yunxian realize with great excitement that it was not impossible for an investment bank to emerge in China with reasonable forward-looking planning and standardized management.

On March 28, 1994, the founding celebration of Guangdong GF Securities Company was held at Oriental Hotel in Guangzhou. Ren Zhongyi, who congratulated the establishment of Guangdong Development Bank six years previous, was pleased to inscribe "Rising Sun" for Guangdong GF Securities Company. Dr. Chen Yunxian wore a corsage and delivered a speech with great enthusiasm. On this day, GF Securities officially entered the securities market as an independent legal entity.

In the second half of the year, Dr. Chen Yunxian, who was also the assistant to the governor of Guangdong Development Bank, was sent to the Guangdong Provincial Party School for half a year as a training target of the CPC. During his study at the Party School, Dr. Chen Yunxian applied to the Party School to live in a room by himself to conduct research. He solemnly indicated to the Party School that he had some theoretical thinking of his own and was eager to compile and form research results. The leadership of the Party School readily supported his request, and Dr. Chen finally settled down and put his thoughts on investment banking into writing systematically.

In 1995, Dr. Chen Yunxian's second theoretical monograph *On Investment Banking* was successfully published, which is a work based on four years of securities market operation, and thus more practical, relevant, and operational. In the book, Dr. Chen firstly analyzes the nature and functions of commercial banks, then discusses the characteristics of investment banks, and defines and compares the business of commercial banks and investment banks on the basis of foreign experience, and argues the necessity and specific model of the separation of the securities industry and banking industry in China.

For the Chinese securities industry, *On Investment Banking* and Dr. Chen's previous series of discussions clarified the essence of the business and introduced the term "investment banking" to the industry. The book is realistic and targeted, and provides the industry with many insightful operational guidelines. For example, in "The Business of Investment Banks in a Broad Sense," the book makes specific comments on financing forms, financial management methods, and fund management, among which, "shell listing" and "comparison of listing procedures, requirements and costs for Chinese companies in the United States, the United Kingdom, and Hong Kong, China," have become the basis for policy formulation and practical guidelines for the industry. Further, *On Investment Banking* also provides theoretical reference for financial regulatory practice. On May 10, 1995, the Law on Commercial Banks of the People's Republic of China was passed, which legally established the financial model of separating the banking, trust, and securities industries.

The Guangdong Provincial Party School, which facilitated Dr. Chen's writing, also attached great importance to this achievement, and Dr. Chen Yunxian was invited to the Party School several times to give lectures on *On Investment Banking*.

For GF Securities, it was even more beneficial. At the beginning of 1993, GF Securities formally put forward the goal of "developing investment banking" and broadened its business thinking before others did in the industry, as Dr. Chen Yunxian said in his book:

> The competition of business, the pressure of market, and the drive of interests have made investment banks abandon the narrow business frame confined to securities underwriting and securities brokerage, and join in the diversification, specialization, concentration, and internationalization of financial business, and strive to develop various comprehensive businesses, presenting the distinctive characteristics of modern investment banking.

After the publication of *On Investment Banking,* GF Securities held several training courses and system-wide theoretical seminars. When GF Securities first started its business as an independent legal person, *On Investment Banking* laid the foundation for the company's medium and long-term strategy, and the a priori advantages from the theory further guided the company's business practice.

The unique leading-edge book on Risk-Return Correspondence

Dr. Chen Yunxian once asked Mr. Chen Jingshu, chairman of the Guangdong Calligraphers Association, for a piece of calligraphy, and displayed it in his office for a long time. The calligraphy work in ancient and strong clerical script—"The way ahead is long; I see no ending, yet high and low I'll search with my will unbending"—is a famous statement of the cultural sage Qu Yuan. It reflected Dr. Chen's state of mind. He was very clear about his purpose of joining the capital markets, and had changed his identity from a university intellectual to the helm of a securities company for many years, but along the way, his original intention remained unchanged. (See Figure 1)

Business development, back-office management, and theoretical research inevitably produced conflicts in time and energy. Dr. Chen's spare time was very limited, and when he had a spark of theoretical ideas, he often wrote until late at night when he came home from work. With a weak wife and a young child, the longstanding night writing further compressed the normal sleep of mother and child, which made Dr. Chen feel very guilty all the time.

In a speech at the company's meeting, Dr. Chen suddenly said he wanted to confide in his colleagues, saying, "I am very tired of working here, and recently the thought has often occurred to me: if possible, I can return to studying at the university, so that my life can be calmer and more stable. With more power comes more risk. Funds are under my management, and I have to make decisions. I have to be careful with auditing and precautionary measures; otherwise, it is easy to make mistakes, so I feel very tired. This tiredness is physical, but also psychological. But things have developed to the point where there seems to be no choice."

During this period of forming the company, Dr. Chen Yunxian began to feel his body changing. Yet, apart from the obvious visible fatness, it was not clear what was wrong. Once his condition was more serious, Dr. Chen was admitted to Zhuangjiang Hospital directly because of his heart difficulty. In fact, Dr. Chen had been hospitalized and examined more than once because of work strain, but the cause could not be detected. At that time, there was no such thing as "sub-health" in medicine, but on that occasion, a doctor in the Neurology Department of Zhujiang Hospital told him seriously that although he was not yet 40 years old and did not seem to have any physical problems, he was already in a physical state like an old man in his 60s, with many symptoms only found in the elderly.

Indeed, as Dr. Chen said in his speech, "With more power comes more risk." The first thing that Dr. Chen, the decision maker of Guangdong GF Securities Company, which was successfully established with great efforts, felt was not the promotion of power, but the fear of risk.

Around 1995, when the Chinese securities market was in the doldrums, the regulator took a number of measures to activate the market, including the introduction of some new trading varieties, such as funds and treasury bond futures. It once adopted the T+0 trading and clearing method, which was rare even in developed countries. Due to the relative lag in supervision and management, speculation in the securities market became prevalent, leading to the 327 Bond Futures Incident in February 1995, which led to the collapse of China's largest securities firm, Wanguo Securities, and the imprisonment of its founder.

Outside of the stock market, some securities firms "took a different route" into industrial investment and capital lending. For example, during the real estate bubble, Wanguo Securities poured hundreds of millions of yuan into Hainan Island, but many of the real estate projects invested were left unfinished. During the Hainan real estate peak, Southern Securities was said to have bought nearly half of the real estate property in a county in Hainan. In addition to investing in real estate, highways, restaurants, and pawn shops, Huaxia Securities also spent hundreds of millions of yuan to buy the Ukrainian aircraft carrier "Varyag."

With a rational understanding of the laws of the industry, Dr. Chen Yunxian curbed the impulse to use the company's capital for "diversified investment." GF Securities maintained a sound business in the primary and secondary markets, and became one of the top ten brokerage firms in China in 1995.

In the years following the promulgation and implementation of the Law on Commercial Banks in September 1995, the division of the financial industry into banking and securities was promoted along with bull and bear stock markets. GF Securities steadily moved forward with the capital increase and restructuring. After the publication of *On Investment Banking*, Dr. Chen Yunxian deepened research on the theoretical system of investment banking in light of his thoughts in management.

After the ups and downs of the stock market in 1996, the company recalled in the year-end meeting: "The situation of the securities market in 1996 was markedly seasonal, with four distinct seasons. The stock market was sluggish in the spring, with a sense of spring chill, gradually heating up in the summer, more brilliant in the fall, and ending more tragic at the end of the year." So, in the brokerage industry, which follows the stock market and has a strong cyclical nature, is there an inherent law in business management to avoid harm?

In June 1997, a sudden and severe punishment made GF Securities and a number of other securities companies suffer from the "1997 disaster."[10] While learning from the pain, the company seriously reflected on its business strategy and established a self-sustaining and self-improving development line. This profound experience also led Dr. Chen Yunxian to think deeply about a core question: what is the management axis of investment banking, which are the counterparts of commercial banks, in the context of separate banking and securities operation?

Dr. Chen began his analysis by writing an article in which he first reviewed the complex set of risks of investment banking in the broad sense:

> From investment banks' original primary market business of securities underwriting, project financing (including financing by means of bonds, stocks, and funds, as well as BOT and TOT), mergers and acquisitions, asset management (including client banking, fund management, and project custody), government or corporate consulting were gradually derived and extended. These businesses are exposed to various risks, such as the size of costs and fees and operational risks and market risks.
>
> The secondary market brokerage business of investment banks has also evolved from the early days of charging commissions on stock and bond transactions to the present-day trading of many types of products, including financial derivatives.... Here, investment banks are exposed to operational error risk, mechanical failure risk, disciplinary risk, default risk and market volatility risk.
>
> ...As far as proprietary business is concerned, investment banks are exposed to credit risk, operational risk, liquidity risk, settlement risk, policy risk and institutional risk.
>
> In the capital markets, investors, and intermediaries including investment banks and exchanges are exposed to risks, but investment banks bear the highest risk factor and face the largest variety of risks, and it is impractical to copy the asset-liability management theory of commercial banks for the management of their complex and risk-filled business.

10 For details, see Chapter VI of this book, "Rebirth through Trial and Error: The Road to Self-Reliance."

Dr. Chen pointed out that there are great differences between commercial banks and investment banks in terms of business origin, business scope, sources and applications of funds, financial functions, profit sources and composition, and management styles. The asset-liability management theory is the management axis of commercial banks, while the theory of risk-return correspondence is the management axis of investment banks.

In theory, there are four risk-return correspondences in investment banking: (1) high risk and low return; (2) low risk and high return; (3) high risk and high return; and (4) low risk and low return. Dr. Chen further discussed this as follows:

> Normal investment banking prefers low risk and high return. As a result, almost no investment banking wants (1); but everyone wants (2), but because of this, the competition is fierce and the relative return decreases, thus giving rise to (4), and the investment banking with low risk and high return becomes rare. Therefore, the investment banking forms category (3) with high risk and high return and category (4) with low risk and high return. Therefore, the investment banking provides the opportunity to choose between (3) and (4). High returns are accompanied by high risks, but investment banks are willing to take high risks without necessarily ensuring high returns. This needs the axis of business management of investment banks to ensure maximum return with minimum risk within a certain business time frame. Risk (with minimum risk) corresponds to return (with maximum return)...
>
> Risk-return correspondence management in investment banks closely links the three objectives of return, safety, and liquidity, and focuses the three objectives on different external environments and specific requirements at different stages. The theory of risk-return correspondence enables investment banks to strive for a dynamic balance and harmonization among the three objectives of return, safety, and liquidity.

Dr. Chen highlighted the "liquidity" requirement:

> Liquidity is one of the four main sources of profit for investment banks—the operating income of funds, which accounts for a large share (41 percent to 55 percent) of an investment bank's income and is achieved through a reasonable deployment of liquidity of liabilities, liquidity of assets, and liquidity to cope with contingencies. Therefore, investment banks are required to have a certain amount of cash assets (five percent to eight percent of total assets) or liquid assets from the perspective of asset stock. They should keep these assets in line with the expected liquidity needs, and be able to increase the sources of liabilities such as various borrowings and to recover the principal and interest portions of assets in a timely manner from the perspective of asset flow, in order

to effectively operate the funds and meet the necessary demands of investment and achieve returns.

Based on the theory of risk-return correspondence, Dr. Chen further elaborated on the specific application methods in the operation of investment bank funds, and classified the funds of investment banks into four categories: "stable" funds, "operating" funds, "adjustable" funds, and "high-risk" funds, and proposed different fund management methods and strategies for different funds.

Dr. Chen also proposed four principles for the theory of risk-return correspondence, namely, the principle of improving the asset structure and maximizing liquidity, the principle of portfolio investment and risk diversification, the principle of effective investment decision and economic cycle fluctuation, and the principle of rationalizing risk-return correspondence management and investment banks' organizational system.

In August 1998, Dr. Chen officially published his book *On Risk-Return Correspondence*. This book, which captures the key points and difficulties of investment banking management, is the theoretical result of Dr. Chen's years of exploration and the summary of his seven years of practical activities, and is undoubtedly innovative. As one of the earliest pioneers in the securities industry, he regards the theory of risk-return correspondence as the core value of investment banking management.

The "theory of risk-return correspondence" proposed by Dr. Chen Yunxian is recognized by GF Securities as the theoretical guidance of its long-term management, and is an important foundation of the firm's robust style and vitality. During the crazy speculative era of securities dealers serving as finance management agents, GF Securities did not do this even for a cent because it adhered to the basic principle of "theory of risk-return correspondence" and thus was spared from the disaster. Before Dr. Chen prepared to publish the thesis of "the theory of risk-return correspondence," he was opposed by some senior executives of GF Securities on the ground that, "How can we easily show the treasure of our company?" Many of the experiences and data in the book came from the real operating practices of GF Securities, for which the company had paid a price, to put it another way.

Dr. Chen Yunxian argued that any more valuable knowledge belongs to society and his company should lead an atmosphere of continuous exploration among the highly knowledgeable class and the aspiring and knowledgeable people in the capital markets. Dr. Chen concluded that the theory could and should be published.

On Risk-Return Correspondence highlights a particular thesis that investment banks should limit the size of their proprietary investment funds to less than five percent of their total assets. Twelve years after its publication, on July 15, 2010, the US Senate passed the Dodd-Frank Wall Street Reform and Consumer Protection

Act (commonly referred to as Dodd-Frank Act), a financial reform bill aimed at reforming US financial institutions, setting the standard for global financial regulatory reform. The Act's Volcker Rule explicitly requires that banks be allowed to invest in hedge funds and private equity in proprietary trading, provided that the size of their capital does not exceed three percent of their own capital. In contrast, the latter does not break through the theoretical framework proposed by Dr. Chen Yunxian in 1998, i.e. the theory of "risk-return correspondence" was more than a decade ahead of time not only in the industry, but also in the international academic community.

From the publication of *On Securities Investment* in 1991, *On Investment Banking* in 1995, and *Theory of Risk-Return Correspondence* in 1998, Dr. Chen's theoretical system in the field of investment banking was basically formed. The three books are called "Dr. Chen's 'three theories'" by GF Securities staff.

In seven years, Dr. Chen's theory and practice complemented and aided each other, and the GF Securities he founded had grown into one of the best securities firms in China. As the founder and chairman of the company, Dr. Chen Yunxian's dedication, sacrifices, and gains in theoretical research are no less than those of full-time academics. Bearing in mind the developments in the securities market in the 1990s, Dr. Chen, as a securities veteran, used his experience to identify problems, summarize laws, and create theories, making him a standard bearer of that passionate era.

3. The long road of knowledge and action

Securities veteran turns to politics

In early September 2000, Dr. Chen Yunxian, then chairman of GF Securities, went to the United States to study for a year. During this period, his two research projects "Theory of Risk-Return Correspondence as the Axis of Investment Banking Management" and "The Evolution and Development of the US Financial System as a Reference for China's Financial Regulation" were reviewed and approved by the experts of Harvard University, and he was appointed as a 2001 Fellow of the East Asian Research Center (now the Fairbank Center for Chinese Studies) at Harvard University.

At the end of March 2003, Dr. Chen came back to Harvard University again, but he was no longer the chairman of GF Securities. On March 21 of that year, Dr. Chen was appointed by the Organization Department of the CPC Guangdong Provincial Committee as a member of the Standing Committee of the CPC Foshan Municipal Committee. Dr. Chen was sent by the Central Organization Department to attend the SEF program at the Kennedy School of Government.

This sudden turn of events left many legends in the securities industry and the political and business circles in Guangdong, and there are many different opinions. But there is no doubt that after 12 years of hard work, Dr. Chen Yunxian left a very rich legacy for all the employees of GF Securities.[11] Just by financial data, from the start of the Securities Department of Guangdong Development Bank in 1991 with two million yuan in cash and eight million yuan in treasury bonds to the beginning of 2003, the total assets of GF Securities Co., Ltd. had total assets of 14.828 billion yuan and net assets of 2.41 billion yuan, ranking comfortably at the forefront of China's securities industry. The spiritual wealth beyond the financial data is more than what the data can express and a book is needed to reveal the details.

In May 2003, Dr. Chen was appointed as a member of the Standing Committee of the CPC Foshan Municipal Committee, executive vice mayor of the Foshan Municipal Government, and deputy secretary of the Leading Party Members' Group of the Foshan Municipal Government. After working in the academic and business worlds, he began his wonderful life in the political world.

He did a good job in his new positions. After serving as a local politician, Chen Yunxian continued the rigorous style of theoretical research, dedicated his knowledge to Foshan, a city of historical and cultural interest in Guangdong, and was called "scholar mayor," "PhD mayor," and "financial secretary" by the media.

During his work in Foshan, Dr. Chen Yunxian gave a typical impression to the outside world. One is his concern about people's lives, another is his talent, and still another is his honesty and uprightness. In the eyes of many people, he "was a very affable senior intellectual" and had a distinctive style as a government official. The staff around Dr. Chen found that he not only had a deep knowledge of finance, but also had a level of English comparable to that of professional translators. The former Harvard researcher, he often introduced Foshan to investors in English, catching reporters on the spot off guard, and he was even faster than the translators in translating certain professional terms. In public, Dr. Chen Yunxian was elegant and confident and answered all questions readily. He had a clear point of view and a good memory for numbers. He had all kinds of materials at his fingertips, and was very able in handling foreign affairs like a scholar official.

After being elected mayor of Foshan, in a collective interview with the media, Dr. Chen told a short story: An elementary school student once asked me at a press interview, "Uncle Mayor, are you the most powerful man in Foshan?" I answered him here: "At home, your parents are the most powerful; at school, your teachers are the most powerful; when you work, the people are the most powerful." Due to the yearly increase in investment in people's lives, Chen Yunxian was known by the public as the "mayor for people's lives" during his term as mayor of Foshan. He once said, "If we don't put money into the people's lives, we will fail to do justice to everyone."

---

11 For more details, see Chapter VII of this book, "At the Dawn of the New Century."

In Foshan, Dr. Chen Yunxian demonstrated his financial talents and proposed to "let the light of capital shine on the industrial heights." Soon after taking office as the mayor of Foshan, he proposed that Foshan should move forward in the direction of "four integrations to become an intelligent Foshan." In late 2008, Dr. Chen accurately predicted the V-curve of the global financial crisis, created the "Foshan segment" of the stock market, worked to develop rural areas, and proposed three financial plans. Together with Lin Yuanhe, then secretary of the CPC Foshan Municipal Committee, Dr. Chen led Foshan successfully in withstanding the impact of the global financial crisis and achieving an economic growth of over thirteen percent. As a result, Foshan was the first to break out of the crisis.

Based on the summary of the practice of Foshan and Shunde, the pioneer regions of China's reform and opening up, Dr. Chen Yunxian created the theory of guidance in advance in China's regional development, that is, giving full play to the regional governments' role of economic guidance, regulation, and early warning, and relying on market forces to organize technological innovation and other effective allocation of resources through price, taxation, and legal means. Later, Dr. Chen Yunxian authored a book entitled *Foresighted Leading: Theoretical Thinking and Practice of China's Regional Economic Development* in which he conducted an in-depth study and reflection on the functions of local governments in the stage of economic catch-up and their relationship with regional economic development.

According to Dr. Chen Yunxian, at the current stage of China's economic development, the government's functions included not only providing public services and managing public affairs, but also regulating, promoting, and guiding economic development. The so-called "guidance in advance" means regulating social and economic activities in advance, and using the invisible hand of the government to address the defects and failures of the market. *Foresighted Leading: Theoretical Thinking and Practice of China's Regional Economic Development*, which explores the path of China's economic transformation from a regional development perspective, was named the first practice-based book on regional economies in China.

In July 2011, Dr. Chen Yunxian was appointed vice governor of the Guangdong Provincial People's Government, assisting the governor in taking charge of finance, science and technology, education, culture, and intellectual property. He stood on a higher platform of working on finance, exploring, and leading regional economic development.

From August to September 2012, under the plan of the Central Organization Department, Dr. Chen Yunxian and his delegation went to Yale University to study the US handling of the financial crisis and its regulatory approaches and initiatives, and to think deeply about the future development of China's financial regulatory system. During his stay in the US, Dr. Chen read a lot of relevant literature and visited 12 senior financial scholars and legal authorities, including Senator Chris Dodd, the head of legal affairs of the US Senate who formulated Dodd-Frank Act of 2010, to discuss in-depth the causes and handling of the financial crisis, as well as the US financial regulatory system. In addition, Vice Governor Chen Yunxian also introduced the achievements of China and Guangdong's reform and opening up, economic development, livelihood improvement, and social progress to American friends on different occasions, and the response was enthusiastic.

Based on the experience and understanding of the study tour at Yale University in the United States, Dr. Chen published the book *The Disposition of Financial Crisis and Regulatory Evolution in the United States: A Report on the Study Tour at Yale University*, which makes relevant suggestions on the future development of China's financial regulatory system based on the development of the financial system and regulatory framework in the United States since the founding of the country.

Since 2012, the pace of developing finance in Guangdong has been accelerating, and the State Council has approved the construction of a comprehensive pilot zone for financial reform and innovation in the Pearl River Delta, and the CPC Guangdong Provincial Committee and Provincial Government have made important plans to accelerate the development of international finance, fintech, industrial finance, rural finance, and finance to improve the people's lives. In 2013, the Third Plenary Session of the eighteenth CPC Central Committee made a general plan for financial reform to "improve the financial market system," and a series of major financial reforms were accelerated. In 2014, the Guangdong Provincial Government issued the Guidelines on Deepening Financial Reform and Improving the Financial Market System, focusing on promoting financial reform and innovation in the new era.[12]

As financial reform entered the "deep water zone," Vice Governor Chen Yunxian called with urgency: "There are risks in reform, and there are big risks in not reforming." He proposed key reform directions worthy of attention: strengthening regional financial factor markets, actively promoting the reform and development of local legal person financial institutions, deeply promoting the integration and innovative development of finance, science and technology and industry, deepening rural financial reforms, and expanding financial cooperation and opening up.

In January 2016, at the age of 60, Dr. Chen Yunxian stepped down from his position as vice governor of Guangdong Province. In the following years, as a member of the provincial government's leading Party members' group, Dr. Chen continued to assist the governor in taking charge of finance, commerce, ports, free trade, and overseas Chinese affairs.

In Dr. Chen Yunxian's view, a true and more complete leader should have four

12 An interview report in *Nanfang Daily* on June 5, 2014.

competencies: insight, judgment, decision-making power, and driving force. He concluded, "It is important for officials, regardless of ranking, to do one or two practical things for the local people, so that the people can get benefits."

Staying true to the mission

> Sometimes your life changes because you heard one or two words or bumped into one or two persons.

In November 2017, with tears in his eyes, Dr. Chen Yunxian wrote this in a long essay in fond memory of his doctoral supervisor and patriarch, Professor Xiao Zhuoji.

Time flies. It had been a quarter of a century since Professor Xiao Zhuoji wrote a long foreword to his student Chen Yunxian's *On Securities Investment*.

On November 14, 2017, Xiao Zhuoji, a famous Chinese economist, a close friend of the CPC, a member of the Standing Committee of the tenth National Committee of the Chinese People's Political Consultative Conference (CPPCC), deputy director of the CPPCC Social and Legal Affairs Committee, professor at the School of Economics of Peking University, and PhD supervisor, passed away in Beijing at the age of 84 due to illness.[13] In the fields of the market economy, ownership, property rights, stock and securities markets, and on some key issues of China's reform and opening up, Professor Xiao Zhuoji left a deep research mark. His rich works such as *Biography of Karl Marx*, *Biography of Friedrich Engels*, *Marx in His Youth*, and *China's Economic Reforms and Economic Development* have influenced several generations of scholars.

"I have dedicated my life to education, and therefore, I am also the happiest person with the happiest life." This quote from his mentor had a profound impact on Dr. Chen Yunxian.

Dr. Chen had wonderful experiences in both business and politics, but what he always loved the most was being a scholar and giving lectures at school. Since 2001 when Dr. Chen became an expert receiving the special government allowance from the State Council, he has been the honorary director of the Institute of Advanced Finance of Sun Yat-sen University, the chief advisor of the Regional Management Innovation Research Center of Guangdong University of Finance and Economics, and the visiting professor and researcher of Harvard University, Hong Kong Polytechnic University, Peking University, Sun Yat-sen University, and Guangdong University of Finance and Economics.

Jinan University, located in Guangzhou, is the first government-funded overseas Chinese university in China, with a glorious history of operation and a rich humanistic connotation. On December 9, 2019, the campus of Jinan University was as calm as usual, but the academic lecture hall of the School of

13 News dispatch of Xinhua News Agency on November 20, 2017.

Economics was full of people, where Dr. Chen Yunxian started his two-week lecture.

Professor Liu Shaobo, dean of the School of Economics of Jinan University, who is an old acquaintance of Dr. Chen Yunxian, said this at the opening ceremony, "Chen will not be Chairman Chen again after he left GF Securities, and will not be Vice Governor Chen again after he left office, but Dr. Chen will always be Dr. Chen."

After leaving the Guangdong Provincial Government, Dr. Chen Yunxian did not enjoy a leisurely retirement, but lectured frequently and was busy as usual.

In fact, during his tenure as secretary of the CPC Foshan Municipal Committee, Dr. Chen returned to his alma mater, Peking University, to give a lecture on *Foresighted Leading: Theoretical Thinking and Practice of China's Regional Economic Development*; as vice governor of Guangdong Province, Dr. Chen Yunxian gave an English lecture entitled "The US Financial Regulatory System and Its Implications for China" to the faculty and students of Guangdong University of Foreign Studies. After leaving office, Dr. Chen again went to Guangdong University of Foreign Studies to give a lecture on "Financial Prospects of the Guangdong-Hong Kong-Macao Greater Bay Area." He also taught his economics books *Mesoeconomics* and *National Finance* to graduate students at Peking University, Fudan University, Sun Yat-sen University, and Jinan University.

"We, the intellectuals of this generation, have learned so much and have been in practice. In addition to doing practical things, we have the obligation to think about the development and breakthrough of economics." As an economist, Dr. Chen Yunxian gained an overview of the times with his unusual political and business resume. He was the first to propose the concept of "national finance." He believed that a country's financial system should be considered on the basis of the larger international financial system.

On the podium of Jinan University, based on the perspective of national finance, Dr. Chen Yunxian lectured on "financial regulatory model design," "national and local financial development," "offshore and onshore financial interaction," "examples of financial bending," "present and future network finance," "financial crisis prevention and disposal," and "international financial system building." He taught the six elements of the national financial system from the perspective of theory and practice, guiding teachers and students to think about the current problems of financial development of a country, thus providing guidance for deciphering the top-level design of national finance and other practical problems.

As a teacher, Dr. Chen Yunxian was fully engaged in every minute of the class. Each session lasted nearly two hours, and Dr. Chen almost always stood and finished his lectures in one breath, speaking with a clear voice and at a steady pace. His lectures flowed naturally and smoothly. The content of his lectures not only combined theoretical thinking with the current national and international developments, but also very cleverly included some real cases from his own business and political career, which always brought much realistic inspiration to the audience.

During the lecture, Dr. Chen Yunxian paid attention to engaging with his students. When taking questions from them, he always listened with a smile and gave answers seriously. When being asked questions, he was often given multiple identities by students; some called him Professor Chen, Mr. Chen, while others called him Vice Governor Chen and Dr. Chen.

GF Securities employees also attended Dr. Chen's lectures. The old employees often recall his words, "Recently the thought has often occurred to me: if possible, I can return to teaching at the university, so that my life can be calmer and more stable." They also remember when he confidently told his colleagues, "If I were to return to teach at Peking University now, my lectures would be well received by the students."

These memories of GF Securities employees have also become the common memories of the Chinese securities industry. The entrepreneurial journey of university intellectuals in China's securities market, typified by Dr. Chen Yunxian, is officially included in the China Securities Museum.

The China Securities Museum was inaugurated on December 22, 2018 at Shanghai Pujiang Hotel, and is the only national museum for the securities and futures industry in China. Jiang Yang, former vice chairman of the CSRC, when preparing for the establishment of the museum, suggested that the entrepreneurial journey of intellectuals from colleges and universities of GF Securities is part of the characteristics of Chinese capital markets and the relevant information is well worth being included in the museum.

On September 8, 2019, when donating a batch of securities history materials to the China Securities Museum, Dr. Chen Yunxian wrote the following passage:

> "The most valuable thing for a person is his life, and life belongs to a person only once." GF Securities is an important platform for us college intellectuals to realize the value of our lives in China's capital markets. Although we have had different life experiences after GF Securities, we always miss and cherish the years of working hard together there. Because of GF Securities, we have no regrets in this life.

The passage was written on September 8, the anniversary of GF Securities. The history of GF Securities from September 8, 1991 is the common memory of Dr. Chen Yunxian and the "PhD Legion."

Chapter II: The "PhD Legion" Sets Sail

Knowledge is indeed the great sun in the sky, it is a million rays of life, and casts a force.

—Dan Bost

1. Gathering talents for entrepreneurship

In Guangzhou in 1991, Tianhe North Road was just a flat construction site, Zhujiang New Town was still a green field, and Haizhu Square, where Guangdong Trade Center Building was located, was the city center of Guangzhou. It was an enviable thing to be able to walk into this building and go to work at Guangdong Development Bank. Within Guangdong Development Bank, the Securities Department, located on the fifth floor of the building, was a less desirable place to go.

After the official establishment of the Securities Department, Guangdong Development Bank organized a four-day securities business conference in Chaozhou. With chalk in hand, Dr. Chen Yunxian, the newly appointed general manager of the Securities Department, taught more than 50 securities professionals from the bank's Head Office and branches. For the majority of the staff, this was the first time they received training on securities business other than treasury bonds. Based on the feedback from the lectures, Dr. Chen was keenly aware of a problem: some personnel from other business lines seemed to be more interested in credit and other businesses than in securities. The reason for this was self-explanatory: in the banking business line at that time, credit business meant holding loan resources, occupying the seller's market, with little pressure on performance and guaranteed pay, while securities business required businesspeople to go out and compete and "actively seek others' help."

Unlike many people who look for various ways to work in the bank, Dr. Chen Yunxian was here to "work," but to "start a business." In his opinion, the most important and urgent problem in entrepreneurship was the shortage of talents. Dr. Chen wanted to find a group of people who shared his passion for entrepreneurship and believed in the great prospects of the securities market.

Personnel are selected from within the Bank and "willing oxen" struggle to pioneer the field

The Securities Department had a total of six employees at its inception. In addition to Dr. Chen Yunxian there was Hu Yousheng, who had just graduated from the Beijing Institute of Economics, Liu Lin, who had just graduated from Fudan University, and Li Weixiong, Zhang Hairong, and He Jianyu, who were in charge of the counter. The department had a modest office on the fifth floor of the Guangdong Trade Center building, but more often than not, everyone was working at the sales counter on the second floor.

The counter was made of ordinary linen stone and about 1.5 meters high. On the outside of the glass interval, a "Price List of Securities Transactions" with a black frame and white letters was hung facing the customers, listing the dates of issue, coupon rates, principal and interest due, and purchase prices of different treasury bonds. On the staff side, there were four dark red painted wooden stools with four tellers sitting side by side, where Dr. Chen often sat during busy business hours. The counter facing the customer was only 40 centimeters wide, densely packed with calculators, recording paper, and money counters, with the words "Development Bank" painted boldly on the desks, chairs, and equipment. The small counter was crowded with too many people inside and outside, and the space three meters away from the counter was the business space of sister company GF Gold and Silver Jewelry Co., Ltd.

Customers of all kinds came to do business. Dr. Chen was impressed by the Guangzhou people's idea that "wealth shall be not exposed." Once, a woman holding a child and dressed very ordinary came to the sales counter, and took out 200,000 yuan in cash from the child's swaddling clothes for buying bonds. Such a scene really took the counter staff by surprise.

Of course, a customer did not often come to spend a million yuan every day. The flow of people to the counter for business was not very stable: sometimes there was a long line, and sometimes there was no one. In the small space of the counter, Dr. Chen more often felt the difficulty of starting a business, and the gap between the ideal and the reality.

In 1991, a number of securities companies in Shanghai and Shenzhen had already made their first lot of money in the treasury bond business, with Wanguo

Securities' trading volume reaching 8.99 billion yuan and its profits reaching 13.17 million yuan.[1] The business network rapidly spread across the country. In Guangzhou, Guangdong Securities and Guangzhou Securities, which had been established for several years, also set up camp early. In order to realize the policy of "laying a good foundation, exploring horizontally and vertically, and leaning outward" and to prevail in the competition with local rivals such as Guangdong Securities and Guangzhou Securities, the first problem that had to be solved was the overstretched number of staff.

With the support of President Wu Chixin, Dr. Chen selected a group of key personnel from within Guangdong Development Bank, including Wang Hongmao, Wu Zhaoming, Chen Chunming, Su Yingbiao, and Li Mengjian, who came to the Securities Department one after another.

Wang Hongmao from the Trust and Investment Department was a talent that Dr. Chen Yunxian had been observing for a long time. Wang graduated from the School of Management of South China University of Technology. He was not only a solid employee who understood the financing needs of corporate clients, but also had a diligent attitude and an optimistic personality. As a veteran employee who joined Guangdong Development Bank in 1988, Wang Hongmao treated his colleagues, both old and new, with humility, and came to the department early every day to help clean up the premises. Another important reason Dr. Chen relied on him was that Wang, a Cantonese native, could speak Cantonese. On one occasion, when Dr. Chen paid for a pound of mandarin oranges on the street, he got only 0.7 pound from the vendor because he was speaking Putonghua. Wang Hongmao, who was well versed in business and knew the local customs, could help Dr. Chen solve many practical problems when the Securities Department was doing business with the outside world, especially when it came to communicating with corporate clients in Guangdong.

According to the regulations at that time, the Securities Department could not be allocated cars, and the means of transportation for external business contacts was bicycle. Dr. Chen rode bicycles and carried water bottles with his business officials, going from street to street under the scorching sun to various bank branches and trust companies to acquire bonds and sell treasury bonds. During the day, they searched for business opportunities and persuaded companies to issue bonds for financing, and at night, they came back to work side by side and stayed up all night to complete business proposals. Starting from the second issue of Guangdong Zhujiang Refrigerator Factory bonds and Rongsheng Rice Cooker bonds, the Securities Department began its initial investment banking business.

In 1992, the first full year of operation of the Securities Department, the Chinese capital markets also had a "spring story." Facing the Guangzhou citizens with high investment enthusiasm, the entire staff of the Securities Department hardly had a moment's rest during the peak period, and even after completing

---

1 Jin Liyang & Qin Yongheng. Wanguo Steps toward Investment Banking: An Interview with Mr. Ni Xinxian of Wanguo Securities [J]. *Securities Market Herald*, 1994 (11).

daytime transactions, they had to work overtime at night for manual settlement until 11:00 or 12:00 at night.

The busy schedule further aggravated the problem of manpower shortages, but Dr. Chen's thinking was very clear. According to the established plan of dealing with both equity and debt, both primary and secondary markets, and both domestic and international markets, he arranged the training direction for each employee, taking into account their characteristics and expertise. Among them, Wang Hongmao, as a manager, continued to dig deeper into the corporate bond business together with Dr. Chen and completed the Blue Ribbon Beer Bond and Huaying Fan Bond; Chen Chunming, who had a university degree and experience as a teacher in college, was consciously trained by Dr. Chen to be a risk investor in the bond market and stock trading; Wu Zhaoming, who had rich experience in accounting, was held further responsible for capital management; Hu Yousheng and Li Mengjian were in charge of the stock business. With the support of the leaders of Guangdong Development Bank, they secured one of the valuable 30-plus seats in the Shenzhen Stock Exchange. Su Yingbiao and Li Weixiong became the stock traders of the Securities Department in the Exchange. Liu Lin was in charge of fund business and followed up the issuance of the first "securities investment fund" in Guangdong Province.

Under the management policy of "laying a good foundation, exploring horizontally and vertically, and leaning outward," the Securities Department made progress in many areas in 1992. The agency issuance of financial bonds and corporate bonds made considerable achievements and the department formed a strong competitiveness in Guangdong Province, while the fund business and information consulting business in cooperation with the media also began to test the waters boldly.

A particularly notable achievement during the year was the addition of the Huanshizong Brokerage Branch with a high configuration. This branch, with computers and dedicated communication lines, allowed the Securities Department of Guangdong Development Bank to become the first securities institution in Guangzhou to start a proxy trading business for Shenzhen stocks, changing the competitive dynamics of the local securities market.

In October 1992, the office of the Securities Department was moved to the first floor of Provincial Sanjian Building in Huanshizhong Road, where the newly established brokerage branch was located. The gilded signboard of "Guangdong Development Bank Securities Department" and the "GF" inlay logo conveyed the new image of the Securities Department to people passing by in this busy place where people and traffic flowed incessantly. During the opening period, the eye-catching electronic stock quotation screen with red numbers pulsating attracted many people to come and watch the event, while uniformed economic police officers maintained order at the scene next to a powerful stone lion.

Dr. Chen appointed Hu Yousheng and Chen Chunming as the head of the Huanshizhong Brokerage Branch successively. Before joining Guangdong Development Bank, Chen Chunming had experience as a college teacher, and he was well-off and understood the locals well. In the process of developing business and analyzing the market, Chen Chunming often had unique insights and gave his colleagues some suggestions and reminders.

The Huanshuizhong Brokerage Branch of the Securities Department was called the "First Business Department," and the Haizhu Square Brokerage Branch was the "Second Business Department." These departments, together with the Business Development Department, Investment Department, Comprehensive Department, and Accounting Department, became the first six internal departments of the Securities Department. After continuous recruiting, the Securities Department was expanded to 35 employees by the end of 1992.

Dr. Chen used his staff to the best of their ability. Wang Hongmao, Chen Chunming, and Wu Zhaoming were repeatedly praised by him as "willing oxen." Appointing an official means raising a banner. The "willing ox spirit"—diligent, low-profile, and hard-working—brought valuable spiritual wealth to the Securities Department in the pioneering period.

There was no stock exchange in Guangzhou, and there was a certain gap with Shanghai and Shenzhen, which were at the forefront of the securities market at that time, but Dr. Chen Yunxian was keenly aware of the historical changes in the securities market in 1992. That year, in the stock market wealth effect attracted millions of people to gather in Shenzhen, resulting in the August 10th Incident, so the State Council leaders asked to speed up the establishment of a centralized and unified securities regulator. In October, the Securities Commission of the State Council and the CSRC were established, marking a new era in the regulation of China's securities market. In the same year, documents such as the Measures for Piloting Joint Stock Companies were issued, and large companies with significant economic benefits in Guangdong Province began to implement joint-stock reform on a trial basis, and the business space of the primary market was opening up. Also in the same year, three national securities companies—Huaxia Securities, Nanfang Securities, and Guotai Securities—were established, which had a great tendency to integrate the domestic securities industry.

Standing at the watershed of industry development, Dr. Chen felt very urgently that if the Securities Department wanted to become a securities company operating in a professional mode, if it wanted to seize the historic opportunities in the market, and if it did not want to be marginalized in the industry competition against the current, the bottleneck of talents, especially high-quality talents, was an urgent problem to be solved.

Recruiting from among old friends and recruiting PhDs for the core

After 1992, the Securities Department was still in the early stage of its business, and the conditions were relatively tough. What did it take to recruit highly qualified people? Dr. Chen recalled the talent strategy Cao Cao used during the Three Kingdoms period in the early stages of his political career—recruiting old friends, employing fellow townspeople, promoting people based on merits, and recommending each other, to successfully enlist a large number of strategists and military generals and quickly become the most talented force among different groups.

According to Cao Cao,

> Scholars, scholars, where are you?
> Years I have chanted the song of yearning—
> But would you ever come over to me?
> ....
> The mountain can never be too high,
> And the water never too deep.
> When an open-minded king calls for talent,
> It is him the world must stand by.

Cao Cao's sentiment of thirst for talents has been reverberating throughout the ages. In the early 1990s, when poetry and worldliness burst forth simultaneously, passion, romance, purity, and idealism were the spiritual undertones of a generation of intellectuals. Before finding a common career platform, they were moving forward on their own life trajectories. In 1993, the Chinese securities market continued the reform process that attracted the attention of millions of people, and in Guangzhou, under the entrepreneurial banner of Dr. Chen, a series of intellectuals' life trajectories intersected one after another.

In early 1993, a letter arrived unexpectedly, which made Dr. Chen Yunxian very happy. The writer of the letter, Dr. Ma Qingquan, was an old friend whom Dr. Chen had met in 1985 during his studies and with whom he had maintained a long friendship.

Ma Qingquan was studying for his PhD under Professor Wei Xinghua of Renmin University of China. Wei Xinghua was a renowned economist who was well known in the field of Capital research in China and elsewhere. Later, on the occasion of the seventieth anniversary of the People's Republic of China, President Xi Jinping personally awarded Wei Xinghua the honorary title of "People's Educator" with the approval of the CPC Central Committee. After receiving his doctorate in economics under the guidance of Professor Wei, Ma Qingquan was assigned to work at the Central Party School, where he served as secretary of the President's Council, director of the Research Department, associate professor, and professor. He was sent to Japan for a short visit as an outstanding young scholar, and then sent to the Soviet Union as a visiting scholar, so he was set to have a bright future. Dr. Ma's book *New Shortage Economics* received attention from the academic community and was regarded as a new exploration of the theoretical basis of socialist economic reforms. At the time of the dramatic changes in China's securities market in 1991, Dr. Ma was in the Soviet Union and witnessed another profound historical upheaval.

In October 1991, Ma Qingquan flew to the Soviet Union as a visiting scholar at the Central Party School. To his great surprise, on the day of his arrival, he was told by the Soviet education authorities who met him at the bottom of the gangway that he could not go to Moscow to study at the Plekhanov Institute of Economics as planned for his personal safety because of the serious crisis facing the Soviet Union. The Soviet Communist Party had just fallen from power and the political atmosphere in Moscow was very tense. For security reasons, Dr. Ma was sent to Volgograd (formerly Stalingrad) as a visiting scholar from the Central Party School, which was more remote. In December of that year, Eastern Europe changed dramatically and the Soviet Union collapsed.

It was still called the Soviet Union when Dr. Ma was on plane, but it was called Russia when the plane landed. During his year-long study abroad, he witnessed the whole process of the collapse of the Soviet Union, visited and studied many places in Russia, including Moscow, Leningrad, as well as Ukraine and the area around Volgograd. He was deeply impressed by the problems caused by the traditional planned economy of the Soviet Union. The extreme planned economy caused the Soviet Union's heavy industry to be abnormally excessive; the country overproduced heavy industrial equipment such as aircraft, tanks, and trucks, while the population lived in extreme material deprivation. Ma Qingquan was shocked by the huge historical suspense and felt that the traditional planned economy had to be reformed. (See Figure 2)

In October 1992, Ma Qingquan returned to China from Russia and was formally appointed professor of economics and director of the Economic Research Department of the School of Marxism at the Central Party School, but his focus was no longer limited to purely theoretical research. Back in his familiar circle of scholars, Dr. Ma was told by friends in Beijing that Dr. Chen had started a securities company in Guangzhou.

In the Spring Festival of 1993, Ma Qingquan wrote a letter to Dr. Chen, expressing his desire to get involved in the securities business in Guangzhou. Receiving the letter from his old friend, Dr. Chen was overjoyed and immediately called Dr. Ma's phone number, extending a generous invitation: "My Securities Department will soon become a professional securities company and is in urgent need of talents, so come over immediately, take a plane and I will pay for the airfare." Out of his understanding of Dr. Ma's academic attainment and character, Dr. Chen further said, "After you come, you will be the executive deputy general manager, ahead of other deputy general managers."

With this, Dr. Ma Qingquan resolved to go south. His veteran leader, Su Xing, vice president of the Central Party School, approved the request report of the

Organization Department of the Central Party School: "Agreed. But don't hold an actual official post; once you did, you can't come back." Dr. Ma's supervisor, Professor Wei Xinghua, also said to him with regret, "Ma, you are good at theoretical research, and it is a bit of a pity to run a company."

When Dr. Ma arrived in Guangzhou, the office space of the Securities Department had been moved to the guest house of Guangdong Province Materials Building. He was there just in time for the end of the day. He saw that the courtyard was poorly lit, with a light bulb hanging from the beam of the room and a few simple desks.

Dr. Chen warmly greeted his old friend, Dr. Ma, and after talking for a while, he took out a prepared envelope with 2,000 yuan inside. This was not a small amount at that time, and Dr. Ma was a bit surprised: "I just came to Guangzhou, and I haven't even started working yet. How can I ask for this money?" Dr. Chen insisted: "This is my personal money, not the company's money. You can buy some living supplies. If you don't take it, I won't be happy." Dr. Ma was touched in his heart. In fact, he really needed this money, and after getting off the plane, he only had one day's meal money left in his pocket.

In this way, Ma Qingquan, a professor at the Central Party School, became the forty-eighth employee of GF Securities, and for many years thereafter, he was the strongest supporter and practitioner of Dr. Chen Yunxian's entrepreneurial philosophy. Both PhDs believed that this tacit understanding was "an essential agreement, a heartfelt echo, which cannot be explained in a few words." The letter written by Dr. Ma at the beginning of 1993 had been treasured by Dr. Chen for more than 20 years. When Dr. Ma officially retired from Guangzhou, Dr. Chen took out this letter, which became his most precious retirement gift.

In 1993, Chen Yunxian's master's degree classmate Fang Jiachun was already the deputy general manager of Fujian Huafu Securities. After graduating with his master's degree, Fang Jiachun went to the Central Party School to study for his doctorate, then returned to Fujian and became one of the few PhDs in Fuzhou at that time. He was quite valued by the local provincial and municipal authorities. Going from theoretical research in colleges and universities to corporate practice, Dr. Fang's choice was similar to that of Dr. Chen.

As a classmate for many years, Dr. Chen knew Dr. Fang's feelings and career aspirations, and had already thought of inviting him to create a career together. However, Dr. Chen considered that Fujian Huafu Securities was an SOE under Fujian International Trust and Investment Corporation, and the pay was relatively stable, while GF Securities did not have any advantage over Fujian Huafu Securities in the early stage of development. This made Dr. Chen feel that the time was not yet ripe to invite Fang Jiachun to join.

Two years later, GF Securities already ranked among the top ten brokerages in China, and senior management talents needed to be further enriched, so Dr. Chen dialed Dr. Fang's phone number and formally invited him to come to GF Securities. Although Dr. Fang was willing, his career and life in Fuzhou were already stable and his family did not support his intention to develop in Guangzhou. Upon hearing this, Dr. Chen arranged for Dr. Ma Qingquan to go to Fuzhou, invited him again and tried his best to work with Dr. Fang's family.

When he came to Fuzhou, Dr. Ma talked about his own experience in GF Securities from the Central Party School. With his sincere persuasion, he dispelled the doubts of Dr. Fang's family and increased the confidence of Dr. Fang to join GF Securities. In this way, Dr. Fang Jiachun and his family came to Guangzhou from Fuzhou and started his career in GF Securities. The three PhD friends, who had been friends for many years, chose to support each other on a common career platform.

Since then, Dr. Fang Jiachun had been a practitioner of Dr. Chen's standardized management ideas and had also made significant contributions in several important M&A initiatives. In one of the conference speeches of GF Securities, Dr. Fang recalled the feeling of joining GF Securities: "Everyone is consciously and unconsciously looking for their own coordinate points in life. As Engels said, the progress of society is the result of the combined action of the parallelogram of forces. We are all at a certain point of the parallelogram, and this point is what we are constantly seeking, and the big attractive stage of GF is the inevitable result of my search for coordinates."

In 1993, Dr. Li Jianyong of Southwest University of Finance and Economics also received a call from Dr. Chen. As an old friend who met when applying for the PhD, Dr. Chen later did not share the same PhD supervisor with Dr. Li, but the friendship was deep during the doctoral study. This stems from the fact that the *Economist* magazine was cofounded by Mr. Liu Shibai and Mr. Xiao Zhuoji, the famous economists who were the mentors of the two PhDs. During Dr. Chen's doctoral studies, Dr. Li had already graduated as Professor Liu Shibai's student and served as the editorial director of Economist, and the two PhDs had very close communication and discussion about the emerging field of capital market research.

Li Jianyong became famous in the academic circle at a young age not only because of his own deep academic roots, but also because of his "obsession" when he was the editorial director of Economist. Some well-known economists' contributions, which no one else dared not eliminate, were eliminated by him. He could also stay up all night in the cold to revise an article that was written by someone he did not know and had originally been eliminated. In Southwest University of Finance and Economics, Dr. Li Jianyong, who liked long-distance running and was a keen bridge player, left many stories about his "obsession."

In 1993, at the age of 36, Dr. Li Jianyong was already rated as a professor and enjoyed the treatment of a deputy section chief. Faced with Dr. Chen's sincere invitation, Dr. Li frankly told him, "I didn't make up my mind and wanted to wait and see." Dr. Chen understood Dr. Li's enthusiasm for his academic career, but did not give up on his invitation. Dr. Ma Qingquan, also a good friend, kept advising Dr. Chen, "We must invite Dr. Li to come here from Southwest University of

Finance and Economics."

In mid-1995, Dr. Li Jianyong, who was already a deputy director of the School of Economics of Southwest University of Finance and Economics, was invited by Dr. Chen to observe a market analysis meeting of the self-supporting stock trading department of GF Securities. Dr. Li was deeply surprised that the breadth and depth of discussion in this meeting was even better than the professional research institutes in universities. The academic atmosphere of GF Securities immediately aroused his interest. Dr. Chen took this opportunity to send another invitation to Dr. Li Jianyong, and proposed that he could first not unlink with Southwest University of Finance and Economics, he would stay in Chengdu, and GF Securities would set up a business department in Chengdu, and Dr. Li would be in charge of it.

With this sincere invitation, Dr. Li Jianyong became the first general manager of GF Securities' Chengdu Brokerage Branch. A few years later, Li Jianyong formally decoupled from Southwest University of Finance and Economics and went to serve in the Guangzhou headquarters.

In the early 1990s, when doctoral talents were very scarce, Dr. Chen Yunxian, through his own network, introduced three doctoral friends into the core management team through his own connections. In the following years, Ma Qingquan, Fang Jiachun, and Li Jianyong served as the president of GF Securities successively. With their intellectual persistence and simplicity, they either laid the foundation of the company, opened up the territory or were appointed in the face of difficulties. With their outstanding contributions, the three doctoral friends promoted the entrepreneurial process of GF Securities and repaid the understanding of Dr. Chen. This also proved that Dr. Chen was farsighted in employing them. This phenomenon is unparalleled in the securities industry.

For the three PhDs themselves, joining GF Securities as entrepreneurs did not mean the end of their academic careers. Similar to Dr. Chen, all of them worked in the capital markets as part of the path of knowledge and action. Dr. Ma Qingquan had since published monographs such as *Theoretical Reflections on China's Reform*, *A History of Securities in China*, *A Brief History of China's Fund Industry*, and *Outline of New Capital Theory*. Dr. Fang Jiachun had published books such as *Leading Cases of Financial Trusteeship*. Dr. Li Jianyong had published books such as *Research on Non-Tradable Shares Reform* and officially returned to the university after stepping down from his post at GF Securities to continue his education and research.

Inspiring talents and developing business to improve destiny

The tide of the times and the undercurrents of social transformation were intertwined, and it was actually difficult for everyone in them to have a smooth sailing. From education to career, many people went through the process of suffering both mentally and physically, but they were not always able to have the opportunity of shouldering great missions. Because of this, when the light appeared for improving their fate, they all cherished the opportunity to fight and do their best to break new ground. In 1993, Dr. Chen recruited such a group of resilient talents.

In 1993, Ye Junying, a competent person who changed his career to join GF Securities, became the first head of the Business Development Department. Ye graduated from Peking University and Wuhan University with a master's degree in international economic law. Before joining GF Securities, he had worked in Nanhai Petroleum Joint Service Corporation and Guangdong Province Tobacco Corporation. He was a young man with outstanding legal skills and a history of working in large companies, which made him good at grasping key aspects in business development.

In 1993, the Business Development Department was tasked with transforming into investment banking such as equity underwriting, based on the idea of "developing investment banking and exploring new fields."[2] Based on the grasp of the transformation of the forms of the modern corporate system and company financing, Ye Junying made a great contribution to making the Business Development Department a brand name when it was first established. The Business Development Department made a great contribution to the establishment of the department. The substantial development of the primary stock market and the establishment of subsidiaries such as the Securities Consulting Company made Guangdong GF Securities Company "worthy of its name," which was approved at the end of 1993.

Ye Junying was a low-key person, always giving people the impression of a gentleman and a modest man. But in his initial career in investment banking, Ye was also once overwhelmed by the fact that he had to meet with different people every day, he got angry at every turn, and his subordinates in the department were under a lot of pressure. The primary market had sunk several times, and Ye gradually honed his mentality in the business, and his character became more and more stable. Dr. Chen once praised him by name at the year-end meeting for "being very clear-headed and dealing with big issues appropriately." The external evaluation of Ye Junying as pragmatic, plain, and low-key, just as his motto "manifesting plainness and embracing simplicity" suggested. This may come from his experience after choosing to join GF in 1993.

The battle to improve the business with the main underwriting of stocks as the breakthrough required both solid legal ability and excellent financial quality. It required both persistence when meeting customers and commitment when preparing materials, and it was impossible to make achievements in the Business Development Department observing the 9-to-5 work day. Dr. Chen repeatedly praised the eager beavers in the investment banking business for their outstanding dedication, one being Ye Junying and the other being Dong Zhengqing, who also joined GF Securities in 1993.

2 For more details, see Chapter III of this book, "Developing Investment Banking Nationwide."

Born in the economically backward rural area of Qianjiang, Hubei, Dong Zhengqing came to Hubei Institute of Finance and Economics to study accounting after years of hard study. When he was about to graduate, the government started to set up insurance companies, and the accounting class of the institute was changed into an insurance class, so he was assigned to work in an insurance company upon graduation. Dong Zhengqing soon became the backbone of the company and performed outstandingly. At that time, a colleague who graduated from a famous school saw that Dong Zhengqing's diploma was not as good as his own, but he was receiving almost the same pay, so he was rejected by him. Dong Zhengqing was so young and vigorous that he could not stand to be looked down upon, so he studied while working, and broke through the obstruction of his company, and finally received an interview notice from Shanghai University of Finance and Economics in 1988. Dong took a bus from Qianjiang to Wuchang, travelled by train from Wuchang to Zhengzhou, and then took a nine-hour green train ride from Zhengzhou to Shanghai. He became a master's student of the Finance Department of Shanghai University of Finance and Economics as he wished.

Near graduation, Shanghai University of Finance and Economics wanted Dong Zhengqing to stay in the university to teach, but Dong was determined to go to Guangdong, the frontier of reform, to make a breakthrough. So he gave up the opportunity to stay in Shanghai to his friend and went south to Guangzhou with his alumnus Chen Zhiying to find a job teaching in the Finance Department of Jinan University.

Dong Zhengqing taught insurance courses in the Finance Department of Jinan University and also served as a classroom teacher. Teaching required an environment of quiet reading and solitary reflection, but since the university did not solve the housing problem, Dong Zhengqing had to live with migrant workers. The long summer in Guangzhou, with its sweltering heat and rampant mosquitoes, had a serious impact on productivity. Dong Zhengqing could only endure it for a while. He taught, applied for research projects, and wrote a book on futures, hoping to get the title of lecturer and be assigned housing quickly.

However, fate played a big joke on Dong Zhengqing. Due to a change in policy, he was told by Jinan University that he could not participate in the lecturer selection, which was akin to a blow to the head. At this time, his wife had just been transferred to Guangzhou, and Dong Zhengqing, who had been hoping to be appointed as a lecturer and assigned housing, suddenly found himself unable to settle down in the face of reality.

In March 1993, Dong Zhengqing was introduced to two job opportunities: one was to go to Guangdong International Trust and Investment Corporation and the other was to go to the Securities Department of Guangdong Development Bank. Alumnus Chen Zhiying, who was already working in the Policy Research Office of the Provincial Party Committee, told him: "The development prospect of Guangdong Development Bank's securities Department is very good, and in particular, the general manager is a PhD graduated from Peking University, has ideas and vision, and is actively recruiting people. Were it not for the CPC Provincial Committee's reluctancy to let me go, I want to join him myself."

Under Chen Zhiying's recommendation, Dong Zhengqing rushed to Guangdong Province Materials Building and met the legendary Dr. Chen for the first time. This interview made Dong Zhengqing, who "had never obeyed anyone in his life," listen to him with fascination. When Dr. Chen talked about the development concept of the company, which was to take the road of "serving the country through industry" in the style of Tan Kah Kee, Dong Zhengqing was so excited that he chose to join GF without hesitation and made a vow to Dr. Chen to make a contribution.

At the beginning of his career, Dong was arranged to work as an accountant in the newly established GF Futures Clearing Company. With the full-scale shareholding reform in Guangdong Province, the Business Development Department was understaffed, and Dr. Chen, who had an eye for talent, soon transferred Dong Zhengqing to the Business Development Department to follow up on projects such as Baiyunshan and Macro. Since then, Dong Zhengqing became a legend in investment banking, growing into one of the most distinctive presidents in the history of Guangdong Development Bank with outstanding business ability. He also set a record for the fastest promotion within the bank, rising from employee to president in ten years.

In 1993, under the unified bank establishment, the Securities Department had no advantage over other departments of the bank in terms of office conditions and staff treatment. However, as the division of banking and securities became more and more obvious, Dr. Chen thought that he could attract more excellent talents from the bank by virtue of the bright future of the securities industry and the platform advantage of the securities company. Dr. Chen "boldly" issued an invitation to his sister Li Shuzhi, who had previously handled the procedures for him to join the bank.

Li Shuzhi was one of the earliest veterans of Guangdong Development Bank, who had been in the military when she was young, and had an upright and competent character. When the Securities Department was first set up, Dr. Chen invited Li Shuzhi to join him several times, hoping that she would take charge of a series of operational matters such as personnel and administration. However, considering that she did not know much about the securities business and that she was getting old, Li Shuzhi did not agree. In 1993, Dr. Chen Yunxian persuaded her for the fourth time, joking that he was "inviting Zhuge Liang to come out," and she was finally impressed by Dr. Chen's sincerity.

For the next ten years, she was in charge of many operational matters such as personnel, administration, CPC, and public affairs, and the trade union, and helped GF Securities to obtain more resources from the bank and the authorities in charge of the bank. Sister Li called her time at GF Securities the most memorable time in her career: "It was Dr. Chen who gave us a big stage on which to bring out the best in our lives."

Dr. Chen Yunxian's personal inspiration, as well as GF Securities' pragmatic and friendly atmosphere, has also attracted knowledgeable people from the same industry companies to come over. In 1993, Zhao Guiping from Guangdong Securities switched to GF Securities and became a powerful woman in the brokerage business.

After graduating with a master's degree, Zhao Guiping taught at South China University of Technology. For family reasons, she left the university and worked in the Rongyuan Brokerage Branch of Guangdong Securities, where she worked in computer technology.

Zhao Guiping, who studied automation, did not know much about securities at first, but had a strong interest in them. Just as she studied hard in school, she started from scratch, and while learning, she wrote a primer on stock investment in a few months.

While working at Guangdong Securities, Zhao Guiping found that the branch computer data was scattered, each business department had its own independent server, and management efficiency was extremely low. And she was under great pressure in maintaining computers and settlement finishing. She had worked too much overtime leading to hypoglycemia and fainted in front of the computer desk, but fortunately she was rescued by the economic police who found her in the monitoring room.

After deep thinking, she carefully drafted a report on the centralized trading solution of the business department and submitted it to the leaders of Guangdong Securities. Young Zhao Guiping hoped that the leaders would pay attention to the problems and recommendations mentioned in the report, but after a long time there was no feedback. She knew her report had been shelved.

At this time, the "state enterprise disease" of Guangdong Securities had become more serious, and there were many personnel arrangements that she could not understand. In 1993, Zhao Guiping wanted to change to another platform.

Wang Hongmao, an alumnus of Zhao Guiping's South China University of Technology, learned of Zhao Guiping's idea and immediately suggested to her: "Come to Guangdong Development Bank. We have a young Dr. Chen to lead us." Although the strength of Guangdong Development Bank's Securities Department was far from Guangdong Securities at that time, the "market-oriented and professional" atmosphere introduced by Wang Hongmao was refreshing and inspiring to Zhao Guiping.

So, Zhao Guiping also entered Dr. Chen's office in Guangdong Province Materials Building. Although it was an interview, the atmosphere was very relaxed and the process was very simple. Dr. Chen praised her after seeing the stock investment teaching materials and centralized trading solutions she had written and decided to hire her immediately.

Dr. Chen bluntly gave Zhao Guiping three positions to choose from: "We are preparing to build the Tianhe Road Brokerage Branch, and you can be in charge of it. The Computer Department will be set up soon, so will the Consulting Department, and you can also be in charge of one of them." Zhao Guiping thought for a moment and said, "I want to go to the Brokerage Branch to do business."

In August 1993, the Tianhe Road Brokerage Branch, with a business area of 800 square meters, was established; that was the Securities Department's Third Business Department, with 29-year-old Zhao Guiping as its first manager. Since then, the Tianhe Road Brokerage Branch has developed rapidly, and is still one of the most important brokerage branches of GF Securities. Zhao Guiping, together with several bold women, was hailed by Dr. Chen as GF Securities' "five golden flowers" (model women workers) and they grew into important brokerage and futures leaders.

2. Standardized management practices leading the industry

In 1993, Dr. Chen's talent strategy of recruiting old friends, inspiring talents, and recommending each other paid off remarkably, and there was a profound chemical reaction between this strategy and the development goal of "being based in Guangdong, radiating nationwide and expanding overseas."

In this year, Dr. Chen's alumnus from Peking University, Dr. Zhang Hongyi, joined GF Securities, and then introduced Kang Guohong and Qu Nianzeng, and the three of them became the first managers of the newly established Hainan, Shenzhen, and Beijing brokerage branches respectively. Together with Su Yingbiao's Shiquan Road Brokerage Branch in Shanghai, GF Securities' business radius expanded significantly in 1993.

By the end of 1993, Guangdong GF Securities Company, which was approved by the People's Bank of China and established on the basis of the Securities Department of Guangdong Development Bank, had already established a business network with the headquarters as the core. The company consisted of GF Futures Clearing Company, Guangdong Huayin International Futures Brokerage Company, Guangdong GF Securities Consulting Company, Hong Kong Guanghui Securities Co., Ltd. and the brokerage branches in Shanghai, Hainan, Shenzhen, and Beijing as well as the securities institutions of the branches of Guangdong Development Bank.

In addition, GF Securities took a cautious attitude toward opening more branches, which was an anomaly in the securities industry that was in full swing in 1993. Dr. Chen Yunxian's early theoretical research had given him a more objective understanding of financial risks, and his several years of personal experience within Guangdong Development Bank had also given him an intuitive sense of the difficulty of branch management and the burden of bad debts.

In Dr. Chen's view, "One more branch is one more crater."

Centralized and graded management of branches

In the first half of 1993, the price index of China's production materials rose over 40 percent, and the real estate and financial markets was extremely exuberant. Financial institutions began to speed up the establishment of securities business outlets, in order to quickly seize the market, and there was even a large number of institutions and businesses established without the approval of the competent authorities to expand the scope of business.

By the end of 1993, in addition to the two stock exchanges in Shanghai and Shenzhen and the two pilot exchanges in Beijing for the circulation of legal person shares, there were 18 securities trading centers and 36 securities companies, more than 1,200 securities business offices run by trust companies and comprehensive banks that also engaged in securities business, and more than 6,000 securities representative offices set up by various banks, and securities business organizations of all sizes spread across all provincial-level administrative areas in China.

From the 1990s to the beginning of the twenty-first century, the relationship between the headquarters and the branches of most securities companies was relatively loose, with the branches nominally under the control of the headquarters, but in actual operation, most of them could independently exercise the power of personnel, property, and material, like an "independent kingdom." Misappropriation of customer deposits for stock speculation, investment in the real estate industry, capital lending, and even shark loans appeared in many branches. Some branches issued bonds to raise funds without the knowledge of the headquarters, resulting in huge risk exposure.

This phenomenon seemed to be a problem that could hardly be avoided by the development mode of "crossing the river by touching the stones." There was a general lack of awareness of risk prevention among decision-makers of securities institutions, and a lack of experience in internal control management in practice. One more important reason was the lack of capital, resulting in "congenital deficiencies, acquired disorders."

The generally low capital not only made the securities institutions' foundation extremely weak for asset expansion, but also reduced their ability to withstand risks. Therefore, in the market downturn and customer assets outflow, securities companies generally turned a blind eye to the branches' variety of financial "tricks." In the end, it was proved that the branches' "tricks" only allowed liquidity to last a little longer, and in the end, often pulled the headquarters into a more dangerous risk abyss. Since 1993, when GF Securities set up brokerage branches in Shanghai, Hainan, Shenzhen, and Beijing, Dr. Chen Yunxian prescribed a targeted remedy—

centralized management of branches.

In an internal meeting, Dr. Chen stated that the necessity of unified management was self-evident, but that if the relationship between unified management and decentralized management authority was not handled properly, it was bound to frustrate the management enthusiasm of the brokerage branches. Therefore, he proposed: major matters are decided by the company, such as the development of new business varieties, the signing of major contracts, which should be agreed by the company before proceeding, but the daily operation is the responsibility of the branches themselves.

In the process of integrating the 26 brokerage branches of Guangdong Development Bank,[3] Dr. Chen started to implement grading management in the face of the uneven development of brokerage branches—in view of the differences in the business environment, profit and loss, capital scale, efficiency level, management quality and staff quality of each branch. He applied the index system to classify the branches into Advanced (A), Standard (B), Average (C), and Poor (D), and accordingly, the branches were authorized and guided in a graded manner. Branches of different grades were differentiated in terms of operation and management decision-making power, autonomy in capital utilization, business development rights, and self-determination of employee welfare, so that high-quality brokerage branches got more authority and resources.

Grading management played a very important role in rationalizing the resources of the whole system, promoting the optimal combination of assets, mobilizing and bringing into play the enthusiasm and creativity of branch operators, and controlling the risks of branches.

How to implement and execute such a complex management system? Dr. Chen Yunxian had the approach to taking one move that involves the whole system: "You don't need to do everything. Just keep an eye on three elements: personnel, finance, and materials."

Regarding personnel, it mainly refers to personnel appointment and removal. When holding on-site conferences in its early days, GF Securities of required three people of brokerage branches to participate, namely the manager, financial head, and computer head. From the second half of 1993, in addition to the head of the business department, the financial head and computer head are also appointed by the headquarters, and the rest of the personnel are recruited and used by the business department itself. This principle has been continued in the branches of GF Securities to this day.

The institutional management, planning and finance, and computer departments of GF Securities headquarters gradually increased the recruitment and training work from 1993, and sent experienced and skilled personnel to the grassroots on demand. It was not surprising that many managers and finance heads of brokerage branches were transferred to several jobs. Where there were employees with children going

3 For more details, see Chapter IV of this book, "M&A within Guangdong Development Bank."

to primary school, it was not surprising that children changed three or four schools. This arrangement also laid the foundation for the company's subsequent mergers and acquisitions and rapid expansion, and cultivated the cultural gene of GF Securities employees with strong ability and great dedication.

Regarding finance, it was mainly reflected in the management of both financial and capital of branches.

In terms of finance, the financial tools of China's securities at this time were backward and the bookkeeping practices lacked uniform regulation, which brought great difficulties to financial regulation and management.

First, it was difficult to ensure that the stockholders are the accountholders. Before the implementation of the Securities Registration and Settlement Management Measures in 2006, the procedures for opening an account at the counter of a securities company were very simple, and customers could open a stock account by filling out a duplicate account application at the counter, which only required the name and ID number to be filled in the account application, without audio and video recording, and without risk assessment, even if the fraudulent use of another person's ID number to open a stock account could not be identified.

Second, cash transactions were frequent, leaving more room for financial accounting. Old tellers of brokerage branches often told stories of shareholders placing orders at the counter with large bags of cash, which was surprising because Guangdong people believe that it is inadvisable to expose their wealth to others. In 1993 when there was an IPO fever, many plainly dressed large shareholders directly carried sacks of cash to buy shares in brokerage branches. Brokerage branch counters were often surrounded by numerous shareholders. Shareholders not in the line simply filled out account opening applications, wrapped them in ten yuan notes for processing fees, and directly threw them into the counters over glass barriers. At the end of the day, there was cash everywhere in counters. In the IPO of Baiyunshan, the finance head of the Huanshizhong Brokerage Branch counted so much money that he got an IV drip.

Third, the process of buying and selling stocks was basically done by hand, and the error rate was high. In a stock transaction, the shareholder had to fill out the purchase and sale application at the counter, and the teller then helped him or her to improve. After the shareholder signed the improved application, the teller would enter it into the brokerage branch trading system, or report it to the market representative ("trader") in the exchange. Then the market representative would enter the teller's order information into the exchange system to complete transactions. In the process, there were too many manual transfers, so errors were inevitable. In order to be able to smoothly settle accounts with the exchange, brokerage branches set up special accounts to record errors. Later, these gradually developed into "small accounts" that were separate from the brokerage branches' big accounts.

In addition, the full depository and three-tier settlement system also provided securities companies with the space for the misappropriation of customer margin.

The misappropriation of customer margin for industrial investment, applying for new shares, granting overdrafts to customers and other securities companies' for-profit projects for early primitive accumulation also made brokerage branches' accounts complicated. Coupled with lax account management and arbitrary items, this resulted in prevalent private coffers outside the big accounts of brokerage branches.

This also led to the huge workload of in finance when acquiring brokerage branches, because the vast majority of brokerage branches used manual accounting, vouchers, bookkeeping, registration books were all handwritten, and had to be calculated with abacuses or calculators. This was not only inefficient, but was also prone to error.

In terms of capital, most of the brokerage firms relied heavily on customer margin due to the inherent lack of capital, but after June 1993, the national financial situation took a sharp turn for the worse, and customer margin began to be lost in large quantities. In the period peak of 1994, the margin of GF Securities was lost at a rate of 10 million yuan per day.

Dr. Chen once discussed capital behind closed doors: "We have limited capital sources, but the use of capital is multifaceted, including the cost of opening institutions, seat fees for stock trading in various institutions, and the funds that need to be advanced when companies issue bonds for payment and self-managed treasury bonds. So, as long as we slightly mess up the position, it is easy to go wrong."

As for brokerage branches, in addition to their own operating expenses, self-dealing and overdraft business will not only take up funds, but also may bring greater risk exposure.

Overdrafts made things difficult for brokerage branches. In 1993, after the market began to fall, in order to compete for customers and stimulate trading, securities companies provided customers with overdraft services. This kind of overdraft in the form of "diverting client A's margin to client B" at first gradually developed into negative account balance overdrafts. Obviously, when the market is bad, the more overdrafts the greater the risk; but if you do not grant overdrafts, you will face the loss of customers.

The risk of self-dealing should not be underestimated. With the fluctuation of the market, the investment of securities companies in self-dealing increased, which became a common risk in the industry. By 1997, among 84 securities companies nationwide, 36 companies had self-managed securities exceeding 50 percent of their net assets and 17 companies exceeding 100 percent of their net assets, including Anshan Securities, Southern Securities, Guotai Securities, and Huaxia Securities.

In addition to the funds themselves, the settlement transfer of funds was also very risky. Due to the difficulty of the early bank payment system to support fast off-site transfer of funds after securities transactions, securities companies did not establish settlement relationships with Shanghai and Shenzhen stock exchanges' settlement institutions directly, but handled fund settlement through agents. Moreover, in terms of fund settlement, it was not divided by securities corporations as a whole, but by regions and by trading seats, so the transaction settlement of brokerage branches could be completed independently without going through the headquarters. It was often the case when there was a problem in the branches, the head offices were often kept in the dark. Under such circumstances, the entire settlement system was subject to considerable risk due to unclear settlement responsibilities.

What was to be done? In addition to actively generating revenue to enhance the overall financial strength of the company, it was also necessary to control the risk of capital. If brokerage branches stopped self-dealing and overdraft business, it was equivalent to suicide. If they were allowed to continue to do so, brokerage branches' management ability varied, and their professionalism and risk awareness fell far short of the requirement of the head office, and clearing irregularities also occurred from time to time. How could the risk be effectively controlled?

It occurred again to Dr. Chen Yunxian that he should try centralized management. At the end of 1993, GF Securities created the Fund Operation Department from the Planning and Finance Department. The new department operated independently in the unified management of stock transaction clearing of brokerage branches, the company's fund allocation, position utilization and proprietary investment, planned management of the company's funds, and the regulation and supervision of the use of funds of brokerage branches. Sun Xiaoyan, who graduated from Renmin University of China in 1993, left the Planning and Finance Department to become the chief of the Fund Operation Department. He became a personal witness of the important management reform in the early stage of GF Securities' finance.

For customer margin management, the company required branches to pay 70 percent of the customer margin to the headquarters, and later increased it to the full amount. This practice enabled GF Securities to greatly reduce capital risk. Since then, the "financial" rights of branches were gradually centralized, and the risk exposure was reduced step by step.

Regarding materials, it mainly refers to the fixed assets of the branches.

According to the existing concept, compared with financial assets, the fixed assets of securities companies should account for a smaller proportion. However, in 1993, under the call of the People's Bank of China to develop both finance and industry, securities companies were generally highly motivated to invest in industry.

Dr. Chen has made it clear many times within the company that industry was not the main business of securities companies and that his company should not be excessively involved in it. He said that securities companies should develop their business around the capital market in all respects. In 1993, he further made it clear that "all branches should submit their annual major fixed asset acquisition plans to the company at the beginning of each year, and the company will review and audit them before approving them for implementation. "

From 1993 to 1995, he was forward-looking in proposing and implementing the "centralized and graded management of branches," which not only directly established the pattern for the integration of branch brokerage branches, but also rationalized the management framework of branches from the top. This laid a solid foundation for the company's subsequent years of merger and expansion and standardized management.

Leveraging on information technology

The nascent Chinese securities market was actually no stranger to information technology, as the first transaction on the Shanghai Stock Exchange was completed by a computerized trading system on December 19, 1990. In a sense, information technology contributed to a significant "latecomer advantage" that enabled China's securities market to complete a development process in just 20 to 30 years that took a century for mature markets in the West to complete.

However, the adoption of computer equipment and information technology in the operation and management of securities firms in the 1990s varied greatly. For a long time, abacuses, calculators, and computers were used as coexisting production tools.

In the initial business expansion initiative of GF Securities, except for the business branch counters being equipped with computers because of business needs, there were few computers in other middle and back office departments. In 1993, there were only two computers in the Planning and Finance Department, which were equipped with the then advanced 386 processors, 64K RAM and DOS operating system, and were used by the whole department like a treasure.

GF Securities set up the "Computer Department" and related departments had "computer heads," which had the glory of being ahead of the times at that time. However, there were few talents who mastered computer technology, and the adaptability of computer hardware and software to the securities industry was low, which directly caused the computer heads to be overburdened, and more often than not, it was "manual work."

Zhang Shaohua, the earliest computer head of GF Securities, became a professional through self-examination. After joining in GF Securities, Zhang Shaohua often worked around the clock. Once, Zhang Shaohua was sick with a high fever, but no others in the company could handle the maintenance of computers, so he came to the computer room lying on a stretcher, directing colleagues to operate.

Zhao Guiping, who studied automation during her master's degree, did not choose the head of the Computer Department out of the three positions offered by Dr. Chen during the interview, but chose to prepare the Tianhe Road Brokerage Branch. This was partly because she liked to develop business, and it was also because when she was in Guangdong Securities, she was so tired that she fainted in the computer room. She really did not want to do that tiring job.

Dr. Chen Yunxian thought deeply about computers and information technology. He realized that in addition to making securities paperless, electronic transaction settlement can improve market efficiency and bring revolutionary changes to internal control management.

In the centralized and graded management of branches, the Planning and Finance Department of the company suggested using financial software to improve the efficiency of financial management, and this suggestion was adopted by Dr. Chen. Faced with the choice between stand-alone and network versions of financial computing software, Dr. Chen chose the most expensive network version of financial computing software in the market despite the financial constraints, which laid the earliest foundation for the centralized and unified management of "big finance" of GF Securities.

Based on the practice of the Finance Department, Dr. Chen Yunxian set the goal of developing IT applications throughout GF Securities at an early stage. As the company expanded, the need to develop a set of efficient, convenient, and tightly regulated technical tools to help standardize the management of the company became clearer and clearer. He was eager to find a person who could take up the burden of IT application for GF Securities.

He did not have to wait long to find this person. In October 1993, Li Shuzhi brought Yao Ruxin, who had just received his doctorate degree from Central South University (formerly Zhongnan Institute of Mining and Metallurgy), into Dr. Chen's office in Guangdong Province Materials Building.

Before meeting Dr. Chen Yunxian, Dr. Yao Ruxin had studied and worked at Central South University for more than ten years. During his studies of the master's degree, he developed a data processing and mapping system and promoted its application in the securities industry. In 1989, Yao Ruxin became a PhD candidate in an interdisciplinary program to conduct research on the development of computer control application systems for the production of non-ferrous metallurgical furnaces.

Soon after obtaining his doctoral degree, Yao Ruxin, with experience in computer application software development and securities trading LAN development, entered into the vision of Dr. Chen. Although Yao did not have much knowledge about finance and securities, such an interdisciplinary talent was what Dr. Chen particularly appreciated. The interview between the two PhDs was very cordial, and Dr. Chen immediately decided, "Dr. Yao should be hired to set up GF Securities' Computer Center."

In the small trading room, people were crowded around dozens of long-tailed and big-bellied electronic tube monitor screens, looking up at the intermittent red and green numbers. The counter was crowded with layers of stockholders holding cash for deposit, who had already filled out manually

> stock purchase and sale documents. Some of the back-office staff were busy with computer input of stockholders' account opening information, fund deposit or withdrawal vouchers, purchase and sale orders, and others were busy with telephone orders. The entire premise was busy and noisy.

This is the scene that Dr. Yao Ruxin wrote of the securities brokerage branch in 1993.

After joining the company, Dr. Yao further gained a better understanding of the securities industry. The technical strength of brokerage branches was weak, the trading system was paralyzed from time to time, and there were frequent trading interruptions. Networking used a T-head connection Novell network, and trading systems were not uniform, which also increased the difficulty of headquarters management and maintenance. Trading occupied too many reporting seats, and seats and communication costs were very high. More importantly, the headquarters of the securities company could not know the trading funds and their changes in time, and the funds were often misappropriated in violation of the law.

Dr. Chen Yunxian believed that computer networks and central databases were major infrastructure projects to improve the efficiency of trading business, reduce costs, and control risks. He clearly proposed that the Computer Center should have the three basic functions of centralized reporting, centralized trading, and centralized settlement. In Dr. Yao Ruxin's opinion, at that time, there was a general tendency in the industry to emphasize business at the expense of management and technology, and this layout of Dr. Chen was very much ahead of its time. According to Dr. Yao, not only was there no precedent in the Chinese securities industry, but also there was no applicable centralized trading system in the market.

At the beginning of the Computer Department, there were only four technicians. Dr. Yao and his colleagues proposed to cooperate with a computer company that had experience in network construction and large database development after many investigations and arguments. After the partner was selected, the two parties completed the industry's first company-level centralized trading system after nearly one year of closed development and debugging, which made an important step in the business development and trading security of GF Securities.

After the centralized trading system was put into operation, Dr. Yao's team communicated with the Southern Trading Center and related departments many times, and secured the extension of the Shanghai Stock Exchange order reporting terminal to the Computer Center of the securities company through a dedicated data line, thus realizing the groundbreaking transition from manual to automatic order reporting on the Shanghai Stock Exchange. This improved the efficiency of order reporting by more than five times and effectively avoided the risk of human operation caused by wrong input of buying and selling directions and stock trading units.

This significantly industry-leading approach also drew special attention from the technical department of the Shanghai Stock Exchange. Some people thought that it was unfair to other seat members by grabbing too many channel resources with lower seat costs. However, a leader of the Shanghai Stock Exchange personally visited GF Securities Computer Center and agreed that it was great technical progress. During further communication, it was found that the Shanghai Stock Exchange was also studying the introduction of an automatic order reporting terminal, so this "authorized technology" of GF Securities could continue to be used by default. About a year later, the Shanghai Stock Exchange started to promote the automatic order reporting system through two-way satellite data transmission and dedicated terrestrial data lines, and gradually eliminated manual order reporting. GF Securities also became the earliest beneficiary.

Due to the construction and operation of the centralized trading system at the company level, new brokerage branches no longer needed to add trading seats and purchase trading systems, and the network structure was relatively simplified, which in turn provided a boost to the rapid and low-cost expansion of GF Securities' brokerage business.

In order to ensure the security of trading and fundamentally solve the problem of unstable terrestrial communication, Dr. Yao's team proposed to establish GF Securities' own satellite station through multiple researches and arguments. Dr. Chen Yunxian decisively approved the proposal and invested in the construction of a two-way data transmission network by satellite. Since the rented site could not be used for that network, Dr. Chen also decided to spend a large sum of money to purchase permanent property to guarantee the long-term safe operation of the Computer Center. Compared with the industry's enthusiasm to expand the area of business offices and improve the grade of decoration, GF Securities' hardware construction idea was very unique.

After completing the construction of the new Computer Center and two-way satellite data transmission network, GF Securities had the experience with developing and operating the first-generation centralized trading system. After that, based on the application of database technology, the Computer Department designed and developed the second-generation of centralized trading system independently, which provided strong support for the rapid development of GF Securities' brokerage business.

Dr. Chen's concept was ahead of its time, and the process was difficult to put into practice. The construction of early information system in the Computer Center provided solid support for Dr. Chen's vision of "big finance," "big capital," and "unified clearing," which improved the company's management efficiency and level. The company's management efficiency and management level have been greatly improved. Yao Ruxin, Zhang Shaohua, and other experienced personnel of the Computer Department, who were praised by Dr. Chen as "willing oxen," became the "first-generation programmers" of GF Securities' information technology business.

Becoming the pioneer in setting up an internal control and supervision agency

In 1993, the person who suggested to Dr. Chen to use the web-based financial accounting software to improve management efficiency was Lü Ping, the first manager of the Planning and Finance Department. In 1994, he made another important suggestion to Dr. Chen: to set up a new audit department as a relatively independent internal supervision mechanism.

Lü Ping, who joined Guangdong Development Bank in 1993, graduated from Renmin University of China. Before moving south to Guangzhou, he had worked for several years in the Beijing Municipal Bureau of Statistics and the State Council's Office of Asset Verification as a deputy section chief, but Lü Ping always found it difficult to adapt to the prescribed routine of government agencies. At the home of his father-in-law, Professor Xiao Zhuoji, he often met Dr. Chen Yunxian, who came to discuss economics. Dr. Chen's *On Securities Investment* had a great influence on Lü Ping. In June 1993, he resigned from his government position in Beijing and joined Guangdong Development Bank. In response to the weaknesses in the management of brokerage branches, Lü Ping, who was good at statistics and data processing, made many suggestions to Dr. Chen.

In the first half of 1993, the hot market was accompanied by occasional incidents of irregularities in the industry. Some of them were irregularities at the ethical level. For example, a market trader sent by a securities firm in Guangzhou in 1993 cheated on the floor. He used the account numbers of his relatives and friends to buy and sell stocks on the floor, and traded with the tactic of filling orders after the transaction was made, causing clearing chaos. There were also securities institutions which, in their self-dealing business, they transferred their loss to their customers' accounts, or transferred the gains on their customers' accounts to their own accounts.

In early 1994, the vice general manager of a securities company in Shanghai and the manager in charge of the primary market were arrested for misappropriating public funds and overdrawing clients' margin, and seven or eight people were convicted and sentenced to prison.

In addition, there were substandard operations which gave rise to risk. For example, in 1993, an institution in Guangdong reported the number of shares as lots in the market, resulting in a loss of more than 17 million yuan in two to three hours; plus a fine of 300,000 yuan from the stock exchange, resulting in a loss of nearly 18 million yuan. Another newly opened securities institution reversed its operations when quoting the stock market, losing nearly 10 million yuan in less than an hour and failing to turn around its performance for a long time.

In the second half of 1993, along with the gradual decline in the stock market, the treasury bond futures market became increasingly active. The futures market with margin trading had a leverage effect and was very attractive to speculators. The year 1994 saw a total turnover of 2.8 trillion yuan in the national treasury bond futures market, accounting for 74.6 percent of the total securities turnover in the Shanghai securities market, a trend that continued into 1995, in stark contrast to the stock market downturn.

However, in February 1995, the 327 Bond Futures Incident, which shocked China and abroad, brought the hot bond futures market to an abrupt end. The once-prominent Wanguo Securities collapsed and was forced to merge with Shenyin Securities. On May 17 of that year, the CSRC announced the suspension of bond futures trading. The leaders of both the Shanghai Stock Exchange and Wanguo Securities paid a heavy price.

The headquarter of GF Securities did not participate in the sensational rivalry between the long and short sides in the 327 Bond Futures Incident, but the Shanghai branch of GF Securities was not spared. The branch lost 10.6 million yuan in the incident, and coupled with the previous losses in its self-dealing business, the Shanghai branch was forced to seek assistance from the headquarters. Like sounding an air-raid siren, this had a shocking effect on GF Securities, which was strictly guarding the risk of its branches.

Before the incident, Dr. Chen Yunxian proposed at a working meeting of GF Securities: "From 1995, the brokerage branches' self-dealing business will be brought under the unified control of the company, and the self-dealing limit of each brokerage branch can only be between 1 million and 2 million yuan, which is to be used to correct shareholder trading errors. Overdraft can only account for 20 percent of a brokerage branch's own funds and shall not exceed this amount, in order to ensure the safety of funds."

But the loss of the Shanghai branch in the 327 Bond Futures Incident made GF Securities realize thoroughly that in the fast-changing market, without effective execution of the company's decisions, the company will definitely pay the price with real money and even talents.

As Lü Ping said when he suggested the establishment of an audit department, "To operate properly, a modern organization must have three systems: a decision-making system, an execution system, and a supervision system. GF Securities has people who make decisions and execute them, but it does not have supervision." The huge loss of the Shanghai branch confirmed Lü Ping's concern.

At almost the same time, the British Bank of Bahrain, with a history of more than 200 years, was destroyed by a trader in one of its branches, triggering a shock in the world financial community. A high degree of risk prevention became an urgent priority for Chinese brokerage firms.

In early 1995, the Audit Department started to operate and Lü Ping became its manager. At the time of the 327 Bond Futures Incident in which the Shanghai

Branch incurred losses, the Audit Department had been in existence for less than two months. At this time, it was impossible to tell whether there were still cases of misapplication of the company's rules and regulations among the 25 branchers in the system.

With no established processes and experience to draw on, and only five or six people in the department, Lü Ping encouraged his department's staff to explore internal control experience in the face of the ecologically diverse branches. So, the Audit Department staff formed different teams to go around and started the first system-wide risk check.

Under the requirement of "100 percent coverage of on-site audits and exit audits for bosses leaving the company," the auditors gave full play to their diligent and responsible role. Although the audit was aimed at the beginning of the financial and internal control, the auditors went down to the brokerage branches not only to check the accounts but also to carry out effective supervision and correction of the management and legal awareness of the brokerage branches.

Based on the previous work experience, Lü Ping also attached great importance to the introduction of computer technology talents for the Audit Department, and gradually formed a characteristic of GF Securities auditing: attaching importance to computer system inspection and realizing the computerization of auditing earlier. Many off-site inspections were conducted through interface checks to analyze transaction data, identify some illogical data, and eventually discover problems.

Under the strict supervision and verification of the Audit Department, internal irregularities continued to surface. In 1995, GF Securities launched penalties one after another, such as criticism in public notices, performance deduction, removal from office, or termination of labor contract, and for some major violations, the company reserved the right to criminal prosecution.

The stormy disciplinary action was only an afterthought to fix the situation, and nipping the risk in the bud was the better regulation management. In May 1995, GF Securities set up a clearing center as a subsidiary of the Capital Department to manage the source and use of capital, margin and debit funds in separate accounts, and set up separate ratios for branch position funds, debit funds, and other funds.

After the implementation of a series of policies, Dr. Chen Yunxian was still worried by a big problem: were there any hidden risks in the brokerage branches of the bank's branches that had been acquired one after another?

In 1995, the after effects of the 327 Bond Futures Incident loss had barely subsided before a wave rose again. According to the mid-year statistics, the accumulated losses of the securities departments of the bank's branches that had been acquired one after another were more than 10 million yuan, and the problems caused by large capital costs, doubtful accounts, bad debts, overdrafts, and self-dealing once again aroused Dr. Chen's vigilance. On July 29, GF Securities set up three investigation teams to conduct a comprehensive investigation of capital, finance, and fixed assets starting from August. The Audit Department was responsible for special audits on the system-wide margin, self-dealing and overdraft funds. The vice presidents and managers of relevant departments led the inspection in order to thoroughly identify margin, self-dealing and overdraft funds.

To Dr. Chen Yunxian's relief, the inspection was quite effective and basically clarified the situation of self-dealing and overdraft in the system. The self-inspection of GF Securities was nearly a year and a half earlier than the successive documents issued by the national authorities since then to investigate and deal with illegal borrowing of funds, illegal overdrafts to customers and overdraft subscription of IPO shares. The financial investigation also solved some longstanding problems in the handling of accounts and closed the risk loopholes.

For securities institutions nationwide, which were generally losing money, 1995 was a year of difficult operation in a bear market, and a year in which both strengths and weaknesses were fully exposed. Although there was a significant drop in commission income and some of the former brokerage branches of the bank's branches had longstanding problems, GF Securities generally withstood the test and had smooth capital operation without major investment mistakes or being involved in "triangle debt" like other institutions due to the huge amount of treasury repo business. In that year, GF Securities achieved a net profit after tax of 23.14 million yuan, and achieved remarkable results in capital operation and many businesses.

In addition, the establishment and effective operation of the Audit Department in 1995 was quite symbolic. At a time when securities regulatory and supervisory systems were not yet quite in place, GF Securities took the lead in the industry in self-monitoring and self-regulation by setting up its own internal control body to protect the company's development, which is rare and valuable.

In March 1996, Lü Ping, the first manager of the Audit Department, published an article in *China Securities Journal* entitled "Improving the Internal Audit System of Securities Companies," emphasizing that "the internal audit body should be independent to ensure the objectivity and impartiality of audit conclusions. In addition, it should be authoritative, and once established, its supervisory power, prosecutorial power, recommendation power and punishment power should not be interfered with by other factors."

For a long period of time, the Audit Department became the main functional department of internal control supervision of GF Securities and cultivated a highly qualified audit team with financial, computer, financial securities, and legal knowledge. Lü Ping later assumed the position of chairman of supervisors of GF Securities and was the chairman of GF Futures, becoming a leading practitioner of internal control work in the securities and futures industries.

Based on the decision on centralized and graded management, the management systems of human, financial, and material resources, as well as the efficient operation of the information technology platform and audit and supervision mechanism, the early standardized practice of GF Securities was at the forefront of the industry, fully reflecting the sense of self-discipline of intellectuals during their entrepreneurship. In addition, it is also based on GF Securities' entrepreneurial collective understanding of the long-term development laws of the industry that the company should not pursue over-expansion but choose to win in the long run. As Dr. Chen Yunxian said, "Disciplined operation may seem to make GF Securities stand still at times, but the company is actually moving forward."

3. The strategy and policymaking

In January 1994, Mr. Li Yining, a famous economist known as "Li Stock," congratulated the newly established Guangdong GF Securities Company with the following message: "Contribute to the standardization and internationalization of China's securities market."

This economics mentor, who had given important guidance to Dr. Chen Yunxian at Peking University, inadvertently pointed out the "key words" of GF Securities in his message.

Thinking about market and industry trends and pondering GF Securities' own development strategies were the two paths Dr. Chen Yunxian always had in mind. During this period, Dr. Chen's principle and direction that "GF Securities should operate as an investment bank" had been established, but he was thinking hard about the specific operation and development path of GF Securities, which had just obtained the identity of a professional securities company.

Establishing a "four-fold" entrepreneurial agenda

The second book of Dr. Chen Yunxian's "three books on theory," *On Investment Banking*, had been written for nearly two years, and it had two fruits.

Based on his three or four years of work experience in the securities industry and his visit to the US in 1993,[4] Dr. Chen concluded that investment banks engaged in securities brokerage business had retained the name of banks, but they were actually securities companies, such as Merrill Lynch and Morgan Stanley in the US and Nomura Securities in Japan; however, as commercial banks continued to develop their investment banking business and further expand their business scope in their essence, investment banks had emerged with new characteristics of diversification, specialization, internationalization, and conglomeration.

While clarifying the essence from the perspectives of the industry, Dr. Chen became clearer about the business direction of GF Securities itself. In January

4 For more details, please refer to Chapter I of this book, "He Comes from Peking University."

1994, he made it clear that Guangdong GF Securities Company should "operate as an investment bank." In October of the same year, at an enlarged meeting held in Shenzhen, Dr. Chen Yunxian further proposed the development goals of "demutualization, internationalization, and conglomeration." In October 1994, at the expanded meeting held in Shenzhen, Dr. Chen Yunxian further proposed the development goals of "shareholding, conglomeration, internationalization, and standardization," and made the following statement:

Building on the past and embracing the future on the journey toward the goals of shareholding, conglomeration, internationalization, and standardization

1) Shareholding

From the point of view of establishing a modern corporate system and diversifying risks, we will consider absorbing powerful institutions as our shareholders when the time is ripe, so as to improve our capital strength and corporate reputation.

2) Conglomeration

On the basis of the parallel development of stocks, bonds, funds, futures, clearing, and consulting, GF Securities will further utilize its overall advantages of a large pool of talents, extensive information channels, and centralized capital utilization to develop business varieties with unique characteristics. In addition, we will continue to take over and manage the securities departments of each branch of the bank, and do a good job in unifying equity. We will make GF Securities a conglomerate with the densest outlets, the widest radiation area, the most complete business varieties, and the strongest strength in south China.

3) Internationalization

Internationalization means to go global from the geopolitical point of view, and to do international business in the business field. We should work to expand overseas business and come in line with international standards. At present, we are striving for or carrying out B-share underwriting, introducing overseas funds, and packaging companies for overseas listing. We expect to make substantial progress in 1995.

4) Standardization

We will continue to establish a sound management system and deepen internal standardized management. From the management style to the business operation procedures, we will strive to get closer to the international advanced model. Especially in financial management, accounting, auditing and inspection, capital utilization, and cost control, we will further refine the management rules so that the management of GF Securities will reach a new level.

These four development goals were different from the annual work policy, but were the strategic goals set for the first time in the history of GF Securities. They are of great importance to the long-term development of GF Securities and are also regarded as one of the most important contributions of Dr. Chen during his entrepreneurship period.

The goals are concise and catchy. Since their introduction in October 1994, Dr. Chen spoke about them at almost every meeting he attended, and was firmly committed to them. They still appeared frequently in important meetings and documents of the company until after the new millennium.

The securities industry has staged many cases of companies experiencing a sudden rise and fall. After enjoying the industry dividend and first-mover advantage to complete their primitive accumulation, many companies were confused about their development direction. The biggest effect of the four goals is to unify the understanding of the development direction of hundreds or even thousands of highly qualified talents.

It should be noted that at different times in the securities industry and at different stages of the company's development, the implementation of the four goals by GF Securities had different focuses and different projects, and the process was full of twists and turns. However, in general, a clear synergy was formed. This was also in line with the theory of "parallelogram of social progress," in which the progress of GF Securities is pulled by the convergence of the forces of different paths.

To attain the goal of conglomeration, different structural plans were made. According to Dr. Chen's original vision, different subsidiaries would be set up in different business sectors, and then listed separately after they became stronger and larger, while the conglomerate would manage them by holding a controlling share in them. This structure would not only take advantage of specialization, but also immune the conglomerate from the impact of one segment's business risks. Efforts to attain the goal of shareholding also faced the institutional divide in different times.[5]

Dr. Chen defined "internationalization" in terms of geography and business areas. Being located at the forefront of reform and opening up and close to Hong Kong, GF Securities opened up its international business horizon early. As early as 1992, the Securities Department co-organized the first seminar on the development of China's stock market and the comparison of Chinese and foreign stock markets with the Hong Kong Stock Exchange and Wanguo Securities. GF Securities also became one of the first securities companies to start B-share business by underwriting the issuance of Jinzhou Port B-shares to foreign investors. In the 1990s, GF Securities interacted frequently with financial institutions in the UK, Singapore, and Australia, and conducted in-depth discussions on setting up branches abroad.

5 For more details, please refer to Chapter IX of this book, "Going Public and Standing Proud in the South."

In addition, the trend of "internationalization" of investment banking was also the finding of Dr. Chen's research of several years. Around 1994, he wrote in an article that:

> Investment banking is moving toward internationalization. In recent years, the internationalization of capital has led to the internationalization of investment banking. Merrill Lynch's business not only includes organizing financing for transportation projects such as aircraft and railroads, large industrial projects, natural resources development projects, energy projects, and telecommunication projects, but also import and export trade financing. It not only provides commodity services but also provides consulting and research services for major companies in the world. It not only provides financing for governments and companies in the world's major capital markets, but also assists central banks of some countries in managing foreign exchange reserves and the transactions of stocks, bonds, and other securities.
>
> Japanese securities firms not only handle investments by foreign investors in their home countries (mainly stock brokers), but also deal with the issuance of foreign debt by Japan, and have set up business offices overseas on five continents.
>
> The uneven level of international economic development and the asymmetry of international capital supply and demand in time and space make the international flow of capital increasingly stronger and render the internationalization of investment banking inevitable.
>
> It can be said that in modern investment banking, due to the pressure of competition and the drive of interests, business diversification has first prompted the international development of business, and the international competition of business has accelerated business specialization and centralization. It is a trend worth noting and thinking about in the development of modern investment banking.

The goal of standardization was defined and worked for based on GF Securities' prior practice over the previous few years. From the concept to the plan, and to the information technology platform and supervision mechanism, GF Securities was one and a half to two years ahead of the industry as a whole. GF Securities generally smoothly survived the several early "devastating disasters" in the Chinese capital markets, such as treasury bond futures, treasury bond repo, and the real estate industrial investment fever. This was the result of the in-depth implementation of the standardization plan.

In the minds of GF Securities employees, the propagation, practice, and verification of the program for four goals further enhanced the prestige of Dr. Chen himself. When asked "why you joined GF Securities," many mentioned that "because Dr. Chen Yunxian has a good grasp of the laws of the industry."

In 1995, when Dr. Fang Jiachun first joined GF Securities, Dr. Chen gave him a manuscript of The GF Securities Development Strategy: Objectives and Plans. Studying this manuscript greatly shortened the process of Dr. Fang's familiarization with GF's work. From Huafu Securities to GF Securities, Dr. Fang's feeling was that "the business was not unfamiliar, but the difference was that the strategic objectives were clearer and the team was more professional." To this day, Dr. Fang still retains the manuscript on the four goals written by Dr. Chen in 1995.

Dong Zhengqing also recalled years later: "At that time, I did not fully understand the capital markets, but I trusted and admired Dr. Chen and regarded him as an authority. On this basis, I can do management. With this premise, there is good management. A group of people, such as Kang Guohong, Qu Nianzeng, and Zhang Hongyi, and I all came for a person who could lead everyone at that time."

Research puts the knowledge background to best use

After Guangdong GF Securities Company became a wholly-owned subsidiary of Guangdong Development Bank, Dr. Chen often laughed and said, "The biggest background of GF Securities is President Wu Chixin."

In the securities market, the rapid gathering of talents and the breakthroughs and innovations achieved in Guangdong and even in the whole country gave the young GF Securities a remarkable knowledge background. How to make good use of the knowledge background became a question that Dr. Chen Yunxian often thought about.

In the second half of 1993, in light of the demand for professional research on securities investment in primary and secondary markets, Dr. Chen began to plan for the establishment of a consulting department. On December 15, GF Securities officially decided to apply for the establishment of Guangdong GF Securities Investment Consulting Company (hereinafter referred to as the Consulting Company), which was to be set up by 30-year-old Ye Junying.

At this time, the main task of the Consulting Company was to serve primary market investment banking. When the Consulting Company was first established, it was actually the Business Development Department (the predecessor of the Investment Banking Department) with a different name. However, after the establishment of the Consulting Company, primary market research did not flourish immediately, but secondary market research developed faster than expected.

In April 1994, He Bing and Jiang Zuoliang joined the company to collect information on the secondary market. In September, the company established the daily magazine *GF Securities Express* to make full use of the advantages of GF Securities' wide distribution of outlets and many information channels to cultivate its own stock commentators.

In accordance with the idea of attaching importance to media and brand publicity, the Consulting Company established information networks with Shanghai, Shenzhen, and Hainan, and insisted on providing regular feature articles to newspapers such as *Stock Market Herald*, *Securities Weekly*, *Guangzhou Business*, *Stock Market Express*, and *Nanfang Daily*, providing information such as stock market dynamics and market analysis as well as stock market commentary articles, forming a unique professional style of GF Securities and expanding and improving its influence and reputation in all walks of life.

Roughly speaking, the responsibilities carried by the early Consulting Company were relatively similar to those of the investment advisory business years later, but in fact the differences were great. First, the sources of information at that time were limited, and there was no normal public access to a lot of information. Second, there was a shortage of macroeconomic analysis, and analysts with theoretical proficiency and professional competence were very rare. Finally, the industry regulation at that time was lagging, and the firewall of information was not formed. The first batch of the highest quality information of GF Securities came mostly from the personal contributions of the company's executives, which was an important reason why GF Securities could gather a group of highly loyal brokerage clients in the early days.

Dr. Chen visited brokerage branches from time to time, often even without notice. Whenever Dr. Chen appeared in the Tianhe Road Brokerage Branch, Zhao Guiping would rush to the branch's public addressing system to get the investors there to the big investor room to listen to Dr. Chen Yunxian's comments on stocks. Dr. Chen also never let stockholders down. He would discuss the latest information he learned, such as the latest national policies, and share his personal judgment of the stock markets in light of the current macro situation. Ma Qingquan, Ye Junying, and others also often visited brokerage branches to talk to stockholders face-to-face.

Compared with the booming secondary market consulting business, the relatively sluggish primary market research continued until 1995.

In 1995, Dr. Ma Qingquan, who was in charge of investment banking, often met with the investment banking team of Jun'an Securities. Dr. Ma was alerted to the fact that one of the Jun'an teams was very special, and their roadshows were refreshing from the form to the content as they not only included financial data analyses, but also industry analyses and solid material presentation. Back in Guangzhou, Dr. Ma quickly discussed with Dr. Chen whether to form a team independent of the investment banking team and dedicated to providing research support for investment banking projects.

This proposal prompted Dr. Chen Yunxian to give further thought to the positioning of research.

On July 29, 1995, Dr. Chen pointed out the weaknesses of GF Securities' research at the president's office meeting: "There is no real and feasible plan for the operation of the secondary market. The company now does not have a unified plan for development. The external publicity force is insufficient." GF Securities needed to form a new research department, and there were still chaotic areas in the naming and scope of responsibilities of the new department, as well as in the division of functions between the new department and the Consulting Company.

In August 1995, the Development Research Center was formally established, and relevant personnel were transferred frequently. After a period of exploration, Dr. Chen's position of the Development Research Center gradually became clear. In addition, he felt that one or two key people were still missing to put it into practice.

In April 1996, a reporter from the Guangzhou correspondent station of *Shanghai Securities News* approached Dr. Chen and recommended Dr. Wang Liangzhong, who had graduated from Shanghai University of Finance and Economics and worked for Guotai Securities. This was the first time the media recommended talent to Dr. Chen. Dr. Chen was interested and immediately made an appointment to meet with Dr. Wang.

Wang Liangzhong, a native of Hunan, and Dong Zhengqing, a native of Hubei, shared similar experience. His family was poor, and he was physically weak since childhood, meaning he failed the university physical examination several times after passing college entrance examinations. His family undertook a major change. Poverty-stricken, he entered university barefooted. After graduating as an undergraduate, he continued to study hard and finally obtained his doctorate degree from Shanghai University of Finance and Economics.

In 1996, Dr. Wang joined the Investment Banking Department of Guotai Securities, one of the top three securities firms at that time, and spent half a month writing the first research report on the electric power industry. Based on his observation of the innovation space of capital markets, he was determined to make a career in this industry. However, he felt that the working atmosphere of Guotai Securities was not suitable for him, so he had the idea of looking for another securities firm.

After the interview with Dr. Wang, Dr. Chen decided to let him stay on the spot and asked him if he had any other requirements. Dr. Wang hesitantly suggested that he would like to have a two-room apartment. Dr. Chen also agreed decisively.

When Dr. Wang came to GF Securities, Dong Zhengqing, who had been working in the company for less than four years, had already been promoted to the position of vice president of the company because of his outstanding achievements in investment banking.[6] At the end of 1996, Dr. Chen Yunxian assigned Dong Zhengqing to be in charge of the Development Research Center. Two months later, Dr. Wang Liangzhong, who had joined the company for less than six months, was appointed as executive vice president of the Development Research Center on Dong Zhengqing's recommendation and took charge of the overall work.

With two key people in place, the Development Research Center grew rapidly. In Wang Liangzhong's opinion, "Mr. Dong was very aggressive, active and business-

6 For details, please refer to Chapter II of this book, "Developing Investment Banking Nationwide."

minded. He treated his subordinates with clear rewards and punishments: He would never spare rewards for good work, but would ill scold for poor work, without being lenient." The first thing Dong Zhengqing did after taking charge of the Development Research Center was to ask about everyone's rank and income level. After learning that the income of employees of the Development Research Center was lower than the market average, he offered double salary to them. Around 1997, the center's outstanding researchers could earn about 30,000 per month, reversing the staff turnover problem in one fell swoop.

Wang admired Dong's business acumen, but when they first started working together, they disagreed because Wang thought Dong was "too commercial." Wang believed that from the perspective of research, in the future the Development Research Center should pay attention to macroeconomic research and make more external statements to make GF Securities better known. Dong Zhengqing, on the other hand, thought that the research purpose of the Development Research Center was to serve the internal departments and create direct economic benefits for the company, so to speak, "to make a fortune while staying silent."

The two of them argued about this and went to Dr. Chen Yunxian to report it together. Dr. Chen had already mulled over the positioning of the Development Research Center for a long time and set the tone on the spot: first, to make the company a brand; second, to serve the company's business; and third, to reserve talents for the company's development. This positioning covered the views of both Dong and Wang, but at the same time was high level and contained a more comprehensive top-level design principle.

Many years later, when Dr. Wang Liangzhong looked back on the work of GF Securities' Development Research Center, he concluded that many securities companies' research and analysis at that time focused on market operation, while GF Securities' positioning of research work at that time exceeded the industry's level of understanding of the functions of securities companies' research departments. The third positioning in particular made the Development Research Center a talent pool for GF Securities for a long time. Through in-depth research at the frontline of business, researchers were able to familiarize themselves with the market and various businesses of the company quickly and improve their overall quality in a relatively efficient manner. For a long period of time, after working in the Development Research Center for two years, the researchers were able to serve in the frontline of business, and many of them became business backbones and even department leaders.

After the positioning of the Development Research Center was clear, in accordance with Dr. Chen's instruction of "developing principles in a down-to-earth manner and promoting practical business from a high level," research work was divided into three major sectors: macroeconomic and policy research, industry analysis and value research of listed companies, and market operation analysis. Wang Liangzhong was also a very prolific "macro researcher" and "industry researcher," and during his ten years in GF Securities, he directly wrote papers, work reports, and books with more than four million words. There were even more reports and internal work statements he signed and published publicly as well as research reports he revised for other researchers.

Around 1996, *China Securities Journal* had a column entitled "Top 10 Securities Dealers on the Market." With the efforts of Dr. Chen Yunxian, GF Securities became a contributor to this column, but its articles were always ranked relatively low. One day after Wang Liangzhong took office, Dr. Chen happily approached Dr. Wang with a newspaper: "Your article was ranked first in the 'Top 10 Securities Dealers on the Market' column." Only then did Dr. Wang find out that Chen Yunxian had helped him to submit the article to the newspaper. Since then, GF Securities ranked top in "Top 10 Securities Dealers on the Market" for a long time. Later, *China Securities Journal* launched the column "21st Century Economic Forum," and GF Securities contributed to almost every issue.

In addition to contributing to external columns, the Development Research Center launched two highly privileged publications—*GF Securities Research* and *Market Research*—based on *GF Securities Express*.

The inaugural issue of the quarterly *GF Securities Research* was published on December 1, 1997, and the authors' remuneration at that time was 600 yuan per thousand words, almost the highest in the industry. Not only that, the journal had high requirements for manuscripts and strict peer review. If manuscripts did not meet the requirements, even if they were written by the company's leaders, Wang Liangzhong would not publish.

In May 1998, Chen Yunxian led Ma Qingquan, Fang Jiachun, Dong Zhengqing, and Wang Liangzhong to report to Wang Qishan, then member of the Standing Committee of the CPC Guangdong Provincial Committee and executive vice governor of Guangdong Province. Dr. Wang gave the newly published *GF Securities Research* to Wang Qishan. Vice Governor Wang carefully read it for ten minutes or so, retained it with great pleasure, and instructed his secretary to work with Dr. Wang, requesting that important research reports from the GF Securities Development Research Center should be sent over as soon as they were prepared in the future.

Since then, Wang Qishan also assigned several special research projects to GF Securities. The research on the impact of the Asian financial crisis was one of them. The vast majority of institutions predicted that the RMB would fall, while GF Securities' view was exactly the opposite. Afterwards, GF Securities' unique view was proved to be correct, and Wang Qishan specifically praised it: "GF Securities' view on the analysis of the Asian financial crisis is the most accurate."

Three systems to retain people by increasing their pay

As long as he had the opportunity to speak at the company's internal and external conferences, Dr. Chen Yunxian would definitely praise many employees, calling them "eager beavers," "willing oxen" or "five golden flowers." He always mentioned employees' deeds specifically and minutely with gratitude.

The management staff and key talents joining GF Securities would invariably go through Dr. Chen's personal interview. During the interview process, Dr. Chen seldom gave clear material promises, but the blueprint he painted to the candidates always made them feel excited.

Dr. Chen and his core team often got together to talk about the latest policy trends, macroeconomic developments, and the company's development plans. Dr. Chen described to everyone that they would make GF Securities an international time-honored company, and after retirement, they would live in a courtyard, play cards, drink tea, and chat. Such a vision seemed almost utopian at the beginning of the company, but it was really fascinating.

Dr. Chen Yunxian said on many occasions, "To rule a country is to manage officials. This is also true with a company and an organization. Therefore, people come first when it comes to entrepreneurship and development."

The 1990s was a decade of leapfrog economic development in China, and with it came an increasingly serious problem of corruption, with the financial circle becoming the hardest hit by economic crime. In response to the rising trend of crimes committed by securities practitioners, Dr. Chen Yunxian focused on the code of conduct of employees and advocated that "everyone should become an excellent practical operator and theoretical explorer of the Chinese securities market" and "become the owner of legal wealth and the possessor of high moral character." In Dr. Chen's view, "The vast majority of employees do not come only for the pursuit of money, and there is a value orientation in the pursuit of goals."

In 1994, Xiao Cheng graduated from Nankai University with a PhD and became the general manager of the Shanghai Brokerage Branch six months after joining GF Securities. In the post, the young Dr. Xiao Cheng completed a self-reflection and self-awareness of the value orientation of intellectuals.

According to the needs of his work, Xiao Cheng was allocated a beeper, a cellular phone, and a vehicle, which had just become popular in the market at that time. He kept calling his doctoral classmates, hoping that they would come to Shanghai as guests, and he would pay for them, with the intention of showing off. In Dr. Xiao's words, "My personal petty-bourgeois vanity was swollen to the extreme." But soon, Xiao Cheng saw the conduct of Dr. Chen, Dr. Ma, and many other leaders, and began to feel sorry for his failure to live up to the trust Dr. Chen had given him: "At the beginning, the pursuit of better living or working conditions is a basic need and there is nothing wrong about it, but is this the ultimate goal of an intellectual?" From then on, Dr. Xiao's understanding changed qualitatively and he was very diligent in different positions and completed several books on securities and futures. In 2016, Dr. Xiao officially retired, and GF Securities was his only workplace after graduation.

Based on his belief in the value orientation of the vast majority of employees,

Dr. Chen Yunxian had a simple wish in his heart—to fulfill the paternalistic promise to increase the income of his colleague and make the work, life, and career environment more comfortable for employees.

In 1994, the general manager of the Tianhe Road Brokerage Branch, Zhao Guiping's monthly income was about 600 yuan, and she received a few thousand yuan in bonus at the end of the year, basically at the average level of the employees on the job in Guangzhou. At that time, the brokerage branch had a frequent shareholder who came to the scene. He worked in Guangdong Guotuo Capital Management Co., Ltd. When chatting and asking about the income of GF Securities, he said somewhat smugly, "Your income at GF Securities is too little."

Dr. Chen used to work in the countryside and had done much cutting-edge research on the incentive mechanism of SOEs during his doctoral study. Before he joined the company, he had formed the concept of retaining employees by ensuring they had a good career and a well-paid job and had leaders and other colleagues who cared about them. He had realized that he would never be a leader who would only ask his employees to be dedicated without ensuring that they were well paid. In this period, he was determined to focus on staff welfare.

Lu Jinsheng, vice president of Guangdong Development Bank, was a native of Guangdong known for his pragmatism. He also took an extraordinarily enlightened attitude toward GF Securities' welfare:

> Unless employees are fired by you, as long as there is a contract in existence, you have to take care of their lives, health, and funerals in accordance with the Labor Contract Law. If their welfare is not as good as the branches of the bank for one to three years, where is GF Securities' superiority in management? If they have a bad time, where is the image of the company?

But in the start-up period of GF Securities, the company needed to improve its employee benefits rather than directly increase their wages to improve incentives.

First, there were more objective restrictions during the period transition from banking to securities. In the early days, as a former department and subsidiary of Guangdong Development Bank, GF Securities' salary payment standards were subject to the review of the provincial finance department and were not entirely up to its own discretion.

Second, the securities industry was very much cyclical. In the long run, the company had to have a sense of worry and build up a reserve salary to cope with big risks. Dr. Chen Yunxian proposed adopting the reserve strategy to avoid sizable fluctuations in employees' income on the one hand, and developing reserve funds for the long-term development of the company on the other. This feature later became a significant difference between GF Securities and its peers, and the grassroots employees also realized that "in a bull market, GF Securities' income may not be as good as other brokerages, but in a bear market, GF Securities will not lay off employees easily."

In 1994, GF Securities did three major things in internal management: personnel, salary, and housing reforms.

The personnel employment system of GF Securities was fully implemented on July 1, 1994, and all employees signed long-term, three-year or one-year contracts with the company according to the employment contract, thus providing the prerequisites for the implementation of the housing system and employee welfare system. To ensure that "the wage standard is adjustable," in early 1994, GF Securities applied to the Guangdong Department of Labor and Department of Finance through Guangdong Development Bank for the linking of wages with performance, i.e. the total profits and tax revenue in excess of the target would be retained according to a certain floating percentage, which enhanced the internal incentive mechanism and motivated the employees to work. The housing system solved the worries of the employees.

Although these three systems were implemented in response to the national policy, the overall speed of implementation exceeded that of the industry and was even ahead of the Head Office of Guangdong Development Bank. At the year-end meeting in 1994, Vice President Lu Jinsheng openly asked GF Securities for "experience."

The "transfer to the contract worker system" and "the linkage between wages and performance" were the choices made by GF Securities to adapt to the transition to a market economy and abandon the "iron rice bowl" and "big pot rice" under the planned economy. The housing reform was an "advance welfare" introduced by GF Securities, at least two years before the full implementation of "housing reform" by the state, which was a landmark event of GF Securities to improve the incentive mechanism through employee welfare.

In the early 1990s, when the market for commercial housing was not yet liberalized, the ability of an employer to provide housing was almost a yardstick by which society judged the value of a job. When the Securities Department was first established in 1991, the housing arrangement for its employees was under Guangdong Development Bank. When the separation of banking and securities began, all branches raised questions about the future allocation of housing, and Guangdong Development Bank had to emphasize in a document that the housing arrangement would remain the same. But after 1994, Guangdong Development Bank's housing itself was stretched to the limit, and in the face of complaint letters from many branches to the Head Office, Wu Chixin instructed, "Coordinate this issue if you can, but if it really comes to a difficult time, can we be determined to work on it ourselves?"

From 1993 to 1994, GF Securities achieved good returns. The expansion of the organization put forward higher requirements for talent recruitment. Especially in attracting talents from other places to join, housing benefits became more and more important, and it became feasible to solve the housing problem.

In order to let employees settle down with peace of mind, GF Securities adopted the method of housing allocation in kind and internal mortgage, with employees contributing 10 percent and the company contributing 90 percent. Housing of different sizes was allocated according to different job levels and working years of employees. Employees chose their own house location and paid for any part of the apartment that exceeded the specified area. Many employees thus bought apartments at their workplaces and solved their housing problems.

The solution of housing benefits significantly increased the level of talent recruitment and staff stability of GF Securities. Especially because GF Securities is located in Guangzhou, its housing availability greatly reduced the probability of talent flow to Beijing, Shanghai, and Shenzhen. This move had retained a large number of talents for GF Securities and even for the financial industry in Guangzhou.

Dr. Liu Zhengzhou joined GF Securities in 1998 after graduating from Shanghai University of Finance and Economics. He experienced the housing reform of GF Securities: "The company bought apartments and sold them to employees at internal prices, saving the employees a lot of money. In 1998, the company asked the employees to select from the best apartments in Guangzhou, such as Jinan Garden, Huagang Garden, and Junjing Garden based on their score and ranking. I obtained my apartment when the company bought apartments for its employees the last time. At that time, the vast majority of the leading employees were very satisfied and chose their new apartments. This was a very important landmark event for retaining and training these employees."

During this period, GF Securities also implemented many welfare policies closely related to employees' life, such as employees' medical insurance, children's study, communication, and transportation benefits, which greatly enhanced employees' happiness and sense of belonging.

In order to better motivate the leading employees, GF Securities also allocated cars to middle-level officials with outstanding performances. The first car Zhao Guiping had ever had was from the company: "It was an imported purple Toyota Camry, with the license plate. I became one of the four middle-level officials who were given a car at that time. In other words, in the 1990s, the company helped me to have an apartment and a car, which made me very proud."

The high level of identification with GF Securities made the company famous in the industry for its "stable senior management team and low staff turnover." The high level of recognition came from the guarantee of welfare, the strengthening of incentive policies, and, at a deeper level, from the unique talent growth mechanism. A large number of talents with different educational backgrounds, driven by the core layer, gradually realized the mutual achievements between them and their company.

Sun Xiaoyan, who joined GF Securities after graduating from university in 1993, first felt the conduct of the department heads during her work in the finance and capital operation departments. Li Suina, the manager of the Finance Department, who was loyal, professional, and bold enough to say no without losing her affinity, was affectionately called "Sister Suina." With her help, Sun Xiaoyan, a recent graduate, quickly integrated into the frontline of the post. Starting from the difficult manual bookkeeping operation and transaction clearing of five brokerage branches, she gradually participated in the groundbreaking "big finance" centralized and unified management of GF Securities. Likewise, the rigorous diligence of Wu Zhaoming, a "willing oxen," and Li Shuiquan's outspokenness also allowed the young woman to gradually understand the characteristics of financial work.

Even more significant growth of Sun Xiaoyan came from her being transferred to work in posts, which put her in the shoes of others. At the end of 1994, Sun Xiaoyan was transferred to the Investment Banking Department. On the first day she reported to work, Dong Zhengqing assigned her to "go on a business trip to Tibet in the afternoon to launch projects," but she was immediately reassigned elsewhere. In the Investment Banking Department, she had to do a good job in finance, but also to support securities business. She was often stationed at the project site during the day, and then worked overtime at night and on weekends to keep accounts and make statements. It was this seemingly contradictory work arrangement that made Sun Xiaoyan start to think about the relationship between management and operation which "complemented and conditioned each other," and grow rapidly together with Qin Li, Luo Binhua, Ouyang Xi, Jia Ziqiang, and other key personnel.

For departmental management, Dong Zhengqing once said, "Achievements, if not praised, cannot run away; problems, if not criticized, will only get more serious." This distinctive style of management philosophy made everyone dare not slacken off and feel as if they were walking on thin ice. At the company level, Dr. Ma Qingquan and Dr. Ye Junying's work requirements were equally strict. The most memorable experience for Sun Xiaoyan was when she and another female colleagues from the Investment Banking Department were criticized by Dr. Chen Yunxian in the sixteenth floor conference room of Huatai Hotel. Although she was embarrassed at the time, she had since "never dared to forget the discipline she must strictly observe as a financial officer, and always reminded herself that small mistakes may cause the company to miss some business opportunities." For her, this criticism would be of lifelong use.

When she first joined GF, Sun Xiaoyan did not have a clear concept of a "career." After the Finance Department, Capital Operation Department, and Investment Banking Department, she added the Self-Dealing Investment Department and GF Fund to her career history within GF Securities. With her extensive financial management experience in the broad investment banking, she grew to become the executive director, vice president, and chief financial officer of

GF Securities. After assuming the position of a top executive of the company, Sun Xiaoyan recalled:

> It is only now that I can feel how much responsibility the leaders had to bear back then. However, they did not directly transfer this pressure to us, but rather guided colleagues with different educational backgrounds to bring out their strongest strengths and move forward in the established direction of the company in a silent manner. The quality of GF Securities lies in the fact that as long as you are willing to learn and put your heart and soul into it, you will be able to find a suitable position for yourself in the company's continuous development."

The "PhD Legion," the birth of a name

Guangzhou in the 1990s was home to a group of top domestic news media with a collection of well-known journalists. People and events in the emerging securities industry were repeatedly reported as hot spots.

In 1994, Dou Wentao,[7] who was still young, did a TV news report on Guangdong TV about GF Securities and Dr. Chen Yunxian. The development momentum of GF Securities also caught the attention of Wang Zhigang, a reporter from Xinhua News Agency in Guangdong. After the interview, he found that there was a large group of highly educated intellectuals gathered here, and the first and second leaders of the company were also PhDs in economics graduated from Peking University and Renmin University of China, which made the company valuable to report. Thus, a TV special report called "A PhD Boss and His Legion" was launched. This was the first time the media used the words "PhD" and "legion" to describe GF Securities.

On May 27, 1996, Nanfang Daily, an authoritative media in south China and an organ of the CPC Guangdong Provincial Committee, published a front-page article entitled the "The 'PhD Legion' in the Capital Markets: A Report on GF Securities." Written by journalists Yang Xingfeng, Chen Guangteng, and Zhou Mingwu, the report was about the unique talent phenomenon of GF Securities, and the name of "PhD Legion" of GF Securities was quickly established in the domestic securities industry, becoming the most iconic and proprietary business card of GF Securities for many years.

The 3,000-word report begins by referring to Dr. Chen Yunxian as "a leading talent who plans and recruits talents," and states:

> There are 17 PhDs among the 800-odd employees of GF Securities. Some say that such a concentration of highly educated people is a wonder for a

7 Dou Wentao is a Chinese TV host, who currently works for Hong Kong Phoenix Satellite Television.

> securities company. What also surprised the reporters was that in GF Securities' "PhD Legion," there are not only those who studied economics, but also those who studied management, the history of thinking, and even those who studied geophysics and geochemistry, and some of them are returnees from abroad.... Although many of them have the titles of president and general manager, they still prefer to be called "Dr. so and so."

The name of "PhD Legion" given by the media was a great honor and recognition for GF Securities' talent team, and represented the people's thirst for "knowledge which changes fate" and their belief that "knowledge is power" under the background of the great reform and opening up at that time. However, as a public perspective, some of the media's usual thinking actually did not match or even differed from the feelings of the PhDs of GF Securities themselves.

During the interview, the Xinhua News Agency reporters once asked Dr. Chen and Dr. Ma successively, "What made you go into business?" Coincidentally, Chen Yunxian and Ma Qingquan both categorically denied the idea of "going into business" at different times and on different occasions without prior consent. Dr. Chen further clarified: "We, a group of intellectuals, are applying our theoretical knowledge to the practice of China's capital markets, using GF Securities as a platform to discuss and promote the development of China's financial industry." Dr. Ma, on the other hand, gave a more passionate definition: "We are not going into business; we are 'going north' by building a financial group in Guangzhou and marching to the north and to the whole country."

A number of media outlets reported a lot about the "PhD phenomenon" of GF Securities. When Dr. Chen Yunxian talked with reporters about the "PhD Legion" of GF Securities, he stressed again and again: "GF Securities has achieved what it has today, not only because of the efforts of this group of PhDs, but also because of a group of masters and bachelors who are in the frontline, and more importantly, because of the diligent and experienced staff." Dr. Fang Jiachun also recalled, "The growth of GF Securities from small to large could not be accomplished by only a few dozen PhDs."

There are more details about the reputation of the "PhD Legion."

Some of the PhDs recruited by GF Securities were not related to securities. At the beginning, many colleagues were puzzled by this, and Li Shuiquan from Huizhou Brokerage Branch had questioned, to his face: "What do we recruit so many 'professional mismatched' PhDs for?" Dr. Chen Yunxian said unhurriedly, "What I want is not only their doctoral degrees, but more importantly, their quality." Dr. Chen chose people based on their knowledge background and learning experience, and many of the people in his entrepreneurial team were not PhDs, but college teachers, masters or bachelors from well-known universities. Those who have studied hard and improved their knowledge for ten years can study in a certain field for a long time, at least have the spirit of perseverance, and can undertake projects and do a good job with strong willpower. They are just like horses that, as the ancient saying goes, "gallop without being whipped."

The reputation of the "PhD Legion" makes people imagine its appeal. However, in the early stage of the industry, recruiting PhDs in the name of a small securities department resulted in many costs beyond imagination, and the process of introducing a talent often had many twists and turns.

Once Dr. Yao Ruxin joined GF Securities, he almost got into a lawsuit. The reason was that when he left the original organization, he took away the laptop computer that had saved many personal research results. Finally, GF Securities compensated that organization on his behalf, and only then his worries were properly solved. Dr. Yao was in an average financial situation at the beginning of his stay at GF Securities, and Dr. Chen often helped him in any way he could, even giving him one of his own suits. However, soon after he joined the company, Dr. Yao found that its actual situation was too different from what he had expected. Not only did it have difficult conditions and weak foundations, but also the intensity of work in the Computer Department was too high. The tremendous pressure made Dr. Yao miss the days of teaching in university, so he had the intention to quit. When Dr. Chen Yunxian learned of this, he invited Mr. and Mrs. Yao Ruxin to his home and scolded them severely behind closed doors. In Dr. Chen's own words, the couple were successfully "scolded" back by him.

Wang Liangzhong's entry into the company, like Yao Ruxin's, was also full of twists and turns. As Guotai Securities had paid 24,000 yuan in training fees to Shanghai University of Finance and Economics for Wang Liangzhong, when he resigned, the leaders of Guotai Securities explicitly told Wang Liangzhong that if he resigned, he would not only return the training fees, but also that his Shanghai household registration and file would be revoked. Wang Liangzhong had little social experience and was at a loss, so he had no choice but to go back to Guangzhou and explain the situation to Dr. Chen. Dr. Chen did not hesitate: "Dr. Wang, it's okay. The training fee will be paid by GF Securities, and the company will solve all the problems of the household registration and file." Dr. Chen's words made Wang Liangzhong full of confidence, and he immediately returned to Shanghai and went through the resignation procedure with Guotai Securities. From then on, he devoted himself to the work of GF Securities.

As a matter of fact, the "cost" paid by GF Securities for recruiting Dr. Yao and Dr. Wang was more than paid back. Likewise, many PhDs such as Ma Qingquan, Fang Jiachun, and Li Jianyong, as well as the "eager beavers," "willing oxen," and "five golden flowers," contributed to the development of GF Securities, which is far more than a labor contract or a salary can cover.

The media focus on the academic halo of the "PhD Legion" was only a kind of attention to the surface. What was deeply inspired by Dr. Chen and GF Securities under the halo of education was the spirit of "scholars." Like traditional Chinese intellectuals, "scholars" do not necessarily have the highest education, but must be spiritual aristocrats who are willing to dedicate themselves to the cause.

As the expert of Chinese studies Qian Mu said:

> Scholars of vision are great in that they derive laws from all things. Their ambition and wish are to work for the entire humanity, their people, and their nation heart and soul. They consistently aspire to work for self-cultivation, put their family in order, govern their country, and bring peace to the world. People are all humans; they are unique in sharing the same culture and acquiring the cultivation as scholars of vision.

Chinese people are familiar with the sayings "a scholar of vision takes working for the world as his mission," "a scholar of vision will sacrifice his life for a friend who understands him," and "after even just three days' absence, a scholar of vision must be regarded with new eyes." In the "PhD Legion," the spirit of persons of virtue was mostly reflected in the return of the kindness, the self-study of academic and professional knowledge, the professional conduct of quiet and diligent dedication, the talent turnover rate far lower than the industry, and the recognition of GF Securities from the bottom of the heart.

Persons of virtue attach more importance to righteousness than profit. For a long period of time, the material treatment of the PhDs was not good. Dr. Ma Qingquan went south to Guangzhou alone, and his wife did not accompany him because of her work. When he first arrived at the Securities Department, Dr. Ma lived in Dr. Chen's apartment and shared the bank's dormitory with his colleagues. Later, GF Securities moved to Huatai Hotel, and in order to facilitate his work, Dr. Ma simply lived in the office. For three or four years, he worked in the office during the day and worked overtime there at night, and slept on the floor when he was sleepy. When asked about this, Dr. Ma Qingquan always said in a light-hearted way, "Anyway, my family is in Beijing, so it's convenient to sleep in the office." When it came to development goals, Ma Qingquan was full of enthusiasm: "My aim is to follow Dr. Chen, and what I have in mind is to 'assist him to build a financial empire in Guangdong.'"

Persons of virtue know what not to do. Li Shuzhi went to a branch on a business trip. When she was leaving, the brokerage branch gave her a small box, which Li thought was a small souvenir and accepted it without much concern. When she opened it, she found that it was a gold necklace. Li was very alert to this bad trend, and immediately reported it to the leading body. The gift giver and the head of the brokerage branch were dismissed and the whole company was informed. This incident shook GF Securities so much that a culture of resisting internal public relations was formed from top to bottom.

Persons of virtue often have a frank opinion. Regarding the positioning and graded management of brokerage branches, the head of the Beijing Brokerage Branch, Qu Nianzeng, wrote a letter to Dr. Chen with strong words: "Brokerage branches are setting up outlets everywhere and doing everything, while management departments are busy solving their problems. The problem-solving contingents are expanding (not just audit departments anymore) and the rank is rising to include the president. The shrinkage of business staff in the subordinate organizations, the deterioration of quality, and the expansion of problem-solving contingents form a vicious circle. It seems that it is time for someone to sit down and sort out the fundamental problems."

The company's leading body immediately made a sincere response: "Some issues need to considered, such as positioning, graded management, hierarchical authorization, institutional settings, and overall coordination of business; some issues need to be improved and demand attention; some conclusions and statements in the letter are too absolute, but there is no evil intention."

The company quickly arranged to propose measures for improvement. Li Shuiquan of the Huizhou Brokerage Branch criticized the company for "recruiting too many PhDs," but instead got Dr. Chen's trust and was later promoted to the company's chief financial officer.

Dr. Chen and Dr. Ma, the golden pair for cooperation, also had a story of criticizing each other frankly. Under the idea of "recruiting old friends and employing fellow townspeople," Dr. Chen long favored his friends and his fellow townspeople from Fujian and put them in different lines of training. After the gradual expansion of the company's outlets, several branch leaders came to realize that they had one or two Fujianese from the headquarters under them. They began to worry and even speculated, "Are they 'spies' arranged by Dr. Chen? Is it because Dr. Chen doesn't trust me?" When Dr. Ma Qingquan learned of this, he was somewhat at a loss of what to do. On the one hand, he wanted to alert Dr. Chen Yunxian, fearing that this such speculation would affect the internal unity of the company; on the other hand, he was worried about making things difficult for Dr. Chen, who was concerned about his hometown. So Dr. Ma put a note on Dr. Chen's desk which read, "Are the general and the commander united or disunited?" Dr. Chen read it, understood it, and quickly adjusted the relevant personnel arrangements.

The increasing internal cohesiveness of the the "PhD Legion" also made the friends and relatives of its members acquire a real and powerful appeal, forming a chain reaction which made the company more and more able to attract talent.

In addition to Zhao Guiping recommended by Wang Hongmao, Kang Guohong and Qu Nianzeng recommended by Dr. Zhang Hongyi and Lin Chuanhui and Liu Xiaoyan recommended by Dr. Ma Qingquan became the leading personnel of the investment banking and finance departments, and later grew to be important executives of GF Securities and E Fund respectively. Recommended by alumni, Dong Zhengqing joined GF Securities also "double-prongedly" introduced two batches of talents for the company. One of them consisted of alumni from Shanghai University of Finance and Economics, such as

Jiang Zuoliang and Yi Yangfang, and the other batch was comprised of graduates from Jinan University in Guangzhou, such as Qin Li, Ouyang Xi, and Luo Binhua. Many others joined GF Securities as they were inspired by Dr. Chen Yunxian's personality: Xiao Cheng, Xu Maoqian, Jiang Xurong, Xu Jianhua, and many other PhDs, Yan Xiaofeng, Luo Yonggang, Guan Tongwei, and a group of masters.

From 1995, GF Securities held a "Doctoral Symposium" and a "Master Symposium" every two years. The symposiums generally discussed two issues: first, their view of the market and the company; second, what position they wanted to take. Everyone could boldly talk about the problems, ideas, and suggestions, and those who wanted to transfer to other positions could step forward. The forums for PhDs and masters became a unique cultural tradition during the founding period of GF Securities, a platform for offering comments and suggestions and carrying out fair competition, and a symbol of respecting knowledge and profession.

In 1997, the President's Office launched an internal magazine, *GF Securities Express*, for reflecting the voices of employees, exchanging views, and promoting corporate culture. Among the articles published, many had distinctive views and were written in an incisive style. If you read them today, you can still feel the deep concern and thinking of GF Securities employees for the common cause.

For a long period of time, people were hardly called "Chairman Chen," "President Ma," and "Manager Zhao" within GF Securities, and superiors or elders were respectfully called Dr. so and so, Sister so and so, or Brother so and so. This made the efficient company more like a big family.

The "PhD Legion," a large family, was gathering under the same sail to start one more wonderful voyage to the vaster blue sea of investment banking, brokerage, and capital markets.

Chapter III: Developing Investment Banking Nationwide

The question of whether human thinking has the objective truth is not at all a question of theory, but a practical question.

—Karl Marx

From Guangdong GF Securities Company at the end of 1993 to GF Securities Co., Ltd. at the end of 1996, the change of names was not only a reflection of the evolution of the company, but also a reflection of its move from Guangdong to the whole country in just a few years.

In the context of the market economy, "going nationwide" seemed to be the rational choice of every company, and it seemed that financial companies should be like the Shanxi banks more than 100 years ago, which provided services nationwide. However, in the cases of "big failures" described by financial writers, many famous companies in the tide of reform and opening up unfortunately fell in the process of going nationwide. Going nationwide was a breathtaking leap in the development of companies. The wisdom and courage of decision makers, the development opportunities given by industry changes, and the most pioneering business sectors of the companies themselves were all necessary forces for the successful realization of this breathtaking leap.

1. The narrow concept of investment banking and the first investment banking department in China

In early 1993, Dr. Chen Yunxian drew up the 1993–1994 Development Plan, highlighting ten points for business expansion in these two years. "Consolidating and expanding the scale of bond issuance," "Shenzhen and Shanghai stock agency trading business," "handling fund transfer transactions with urgency," "developing futures and futures clearing business", and "grasping the development and management of securities outlets" were listed in second to sixth place. The following was in first place:

> Taking advantage of the opportunity of the current transformation of the corporate management mechanism to provide a series of intermediary services from mergers, restructuring, planning, consulting to securities financing, stock issuance and listing, financial management of listed companies, and achieving good economic benefits from them.

This means that, after achieving milestones in "laying a good foundation," in efforts to explore horizontally and vertically, and lean outward, the business for which Dr. Chen had the highest expectation was the primary-market business brought by the historical opportunity of company shareholding reforms. The primary market business, especially the stock issuance and listing business, was brought by the historical opportunity of restructuring, especially stock issuance and listing. Soon after, starting with GF Securities, this business was officially called investment banking in the Chinese capital markets.

Beginning and exploration

At the early stage, the Securities Department started in both the primary and secondary markets. It issued bonds for Guangdong Zhujiang Refrigerator Factory, which became its first investment banking project. In 1992, the Business Development Department was established under the Securities Department to underwrite stock and bond issues. Due to the objective environment of the Guangdong market, the focus of the Business Development Department during the year was still on the primary bond market in the province.

On April 25, 1993, the Interim Regulations on the Administration of Stock Issuance and Trading were issued, marking the formal establishment of the approval system for IPOs. The approval system mainly utilized the administrative power of the state to regulate stock issuance and listing. Under this system, the securities regulatory department of the State Council would first determine the total amount of issuance based on the actual situation such as the development needs of China's economy and the development of the capital markets. It would then further allocate the total amount according to the status and needs of each industry in China's economic development in each province. Finally, provincial-level governments or authorities in charge of industries would select and determine the companies that could issue shares and the size of the issuance.

In 1993 and 1994, the national stock issuance quota was 5 billion yuan and 5.5 billion yuan respectively. The approval system went in two stages: quota management and target management. Although it had characteristics of the planned economy, the system ensured the healthy growth of the stock market and improved the efficiency of the economic and market development to a certain extent when the market had yet to be improved.

For GF Securities, which had a firm foothold in the Guangdong market, this system also provided a valuable path to go nationwide in theory. The reason why it was "in theory" is that at this time, the companies with listing conditions were generally SOEs, and the overall strength of intermediaries was highly valued. The national securities companies such as Huaxia Securities, Nanfang Securities, and Guotai Securities not only had billion-yuan registered capital, but were also well connected with large state-owned banks, so they had the unique advantage of being awarded projects in the primary market. In addition, Wanguo Securities, Jun'an Securities, Haitong Securities, and Shenyin Securities had long been established and were very active in the primary market across provinces and regions.

Compared with the abovementioned securities companies, the primary market business of GF Securities was planned and started early, but the foundation was weak. At the beginning of its establishment, the Business Development Department was only a secondary department of Guangdong Development Bank's Securities Department. It not only lacked the resources to compete for quotas, but also had limited financial support needed for its underwriting business. In addition, GF Securities was generally defined as a "regional brokerage firm" at that time, and was often questioned about its business qualifications when seeking business outside Guangdong.

When first appointed to prepare for the establishment of the Business Development Department, Ye Junying, Zhang Li, and Li Xiangjun collected information on the primary market in many ways, and through systematic efforts, built the organizational structure of the department and actively secured several equity underwriting projects. Dr. Chen and Ye Junying also actively sought to facilitate the company's attendance at the Tianjin Conference and the Jiangmen Conference, which were of great importance to domestic stock offerings. These measures laid the organizational and operational foundation for the development of the Business Development Department in 1993.

At a time when the industry was "crossing the river by feeling the stones," the frontline employees were not sure of the specific business processes. Dr. Ma Qingquan, who was assigned by Dr. Chen Yunxian to be in charge of investment banking shortly after he joined the firm, felt a bit frightened. Although he was already a well-known scholar in the political economy, he admitted that when it came to new things like stock offerings, "When I first took over investment banking, I actually didn't know what to do. The main reason is that I couldn't understand the financial statements of companies, and did not know how to analyze cash flow, earnings, assets and liabilities. I don't know how companies make money and lose money. So I felt a little timid." Dr. Chen, however, fully trusted Dr. Ma: "If you do not understand, do not say anything first. After two or three months, you will feel better."

It was not uncommon for the leaders of securities firms not to understand investment banking. Shao Chun, who was the first president of Huaxia Securities, said in an interview with *Securities Market Weekly*, "The concept of P/E ratio was taught to me by your weekly reporter Liang Li in my office."[1]

According to the needs of the development of China's securities market, in June 1993, the Securities Association of China promptly organized a business training session for the leaders of securities companies to attend the "National High-Level Securities Managers' Foreign Study Course" in the United States, and began to make up for the lack of knowledge prevailing in China's securities market. Dr. Chen Yunxian participated in this business training session, which led him to think deeply about the nature of investment banking. Two years later, another of his monographs, *On Investment Banking*, was published.[2]

Dr. Chen stated there is investment banking in both a broad and a narrow sense, which was reflected in the specific practice of GF Securities: in January 1994, he proposed that "GF Securities should operate as an investment bank," referring precisely to investment banking in a broad sense. In the same year, GF Securities established the Investment Banking Department on the basis of the Business Development Department. The name of the Investment Banking Department referred to investment banking in a narrow sense, and the department further distinguished itself from stock trading in the secondary market, i.e. it took "underwriting and issuing bonds and stocks" in the primary market as its main business.

Although the term "investment banking" had long been used in China, there were various versions of how this imported term was understood. GF Securities was the first in the Chinese securities industry to use "investment banking department" as the name of its primary market department. A company leader once jokingly said, "It was Dr. Chen who named the primary market department of the securities company the investment banking department. The Investment Banking Department of a Chinese brokerage firm was actually not in line with the international market, but with Dr. Chen."

According to Dr. Chen Yunxian, "Without investment banks using bonds or stocks to help fundraisers raise capital, help investors open up new investment avenues, and underwrite the issuance of bonds and stocks, a country's microeconomy and even macroeconomy could not develop at a high and stable rate." Perhaps out of confidence in his theoretical thinking, Dr. Chen seemed

1 *Securities Market Weekly*, July 31, 2004.

2 For more details, see Chapter I of this book, "He Comes from Peking University."

particularly confident in carrying out investment banking in practice. Under his plan, from the Business Development Department to the Investment Banking Department, "underwriting the issuance of bonds and stocks" became the "test field" for GF Securities to clearly position itself in China's economic development, and also became the "vanguard" for GF Securities to go nationwide.

Beginning with Baiyunshan Pharmaceutical

In 1993, under the coordination of the Guangdong Provincial Government, Guangzhou Baiyunshan Pharmaceutical Holdings Co., Ltd. (hereinafter referred to as Baiyunshan Pharmaceutical) was lucky enough to be one of China's first companies to issue IPOs under the IPO quota system. It was a joint-stock company approved by the Guangzhou Municipal People's Government in November 1992 and established through the restructuring of five companies, including Guangzhou Baiyunshan Pharmaceutical Plant. Baiyunshan Pharmaceutical was a company of the Guangzhou Municipal Government and one of the most influential companies in Guangzhou at that time.

In the case of an undersupply of public shares, provincial governments could assign the main underwriter of the designated shares. At that time, there were already four professional securities companies in Guangdong Province competing for the main underwriting business for the issuance of corporate shares, including Guangdong Securities, Guangzhou Securities, and Guangdong International Trust and Investment Corporation, in addition to the Securities Department of Guangdong Development Bank.

From the second half of 1993, the depressed state of the secondary market greatly affected the primary market issuance. In August, the Securities Commission of the State Council issued the Guidelines on Offering and Subscribing to Shares in 1993, which were new regulations on the issuance of shares, i.e. allowing the issuance of shares to be linked to bank savings deposits, which meant that stockholders had to have a certain amount of capital. Due to the market downturn, shareholders' willingness to subscribe IPOs was greatly affected, and some companies might not be able to issue IPOs even though they had already received the issue quota. Therefore, the choice of a professional and reliable main underwriter was of great significance to Baiyunshan Pharmaceutical.

In the end, the Guangzhou Municipal Government made a forward-thinking decision not to designate, but to tender, a lead underwriter, on a level playing field, between two brokerage firms.

As a direct subsidiary of the Guangzhou Municipal State-Owned Assets Supervision and Administration Commission, Guangzhou Securities was logically selected for the tender. Of course, Guangzhou Securities was one of the earliest established securities companies in China and had considerable advantages in the regional market.

It was not easy for GF Securities to be shortlisted and compete with Guangzhou Securities, largely due to the favor done by Yi Zhenqiu, then director of the Guangdong Provincial Economic Reform Commission and director of the Guangdong Provincial Securities and Futures Regulatory Commission. Perhaps because he was keenly aware of the direction of change in the market, Director Yi Zhenqiu did not belittle the fledgling GF Securities when he reviewed the issuance qualifications of the brokerage firms and included it in the first batch of brokerages for issuing stocks in Guangdong Province. As a result, Dr. Chen Yunxian and the Business Development Department under his command were able to issue stocks and bonds.

Compared to its competitor, GF Securities was at a disadvantage not only because of its late establishment or lack of direct government connection, but also because the Business Development Department had not yet done a single equity underwriting project.

The bidding, which was of great significance to GF Securities, took place in the main conference hall of Baiyunshan Pharmaceutical. Dr. Chen Yunxian arrived early at the venue with Ye Junying and Li Xiangjun. The Baiyunshan Pharmaceutical management, Guangzhou Securities representatives, and GF Securities representatives each had a part of the conference hall. Although the air conditioning was on, the air in the conference hall was still filled with a touch of tension and burning. As a veteran brokerage firm, Guangzhou Securities brought an investment banking team from Hong Kong in order to win the battle, intending to impress the Baiyunshan Pharmaceutical management with its rich capital market experience.

In the competitive bidding site, GF Securities had only three people for the battle, so it looked weak. However, compared with the Hong Kong team of Guangzhou Securities, Dr. Chen, the "keynote speaker" of Guangzhou Securities, had a better understanding of the Guangdong securities market. Based on what he learned during his doctoral studies at Peking University and his solid research and thinking on the local market in his work, Dr. Chen made a strong presentation at the bidding site and systematically explained his views on the development trend of China's capital markets and the advantages of the modern corporate system. In addition, Dr. Chen also introduced the advantages of GF Securities' doctoral talents and promised to provide services by "concentrating the company's investment banking resources and putting in strong business backbone," which demonstrated a strong and competent project team for Baiyunshan Pharmaceutical's management.

Guangzhou Securities were also determined to win the Baiyunshan Pharmaceutical project. Dr. Chen Yunxian still has a vivid memory of the debate process: "Their project leader came from Hong Kong and was very familiar with the capital markets. At the last debate, the two sides were very aggressive and fought to the death. The other side talked about accounting, assets, and liquidity, and was very professional, but we were not afraid, and finally, based on our expertise, we won the project on the spot."

The Baiyunshan Pharmaceutical project gave Dr. Chen Yunxian a first taste of the power of "knowledge background" in the primary market, and strengthened GF Securities' determination to take the market-oriented road with its professional ability.

After winning the Baiyunshan Pharmaceutical project, GF Securities entered the underwriting stage, and it was at that time that Dong Zhengqing joined the investment banking team. Dong Zhengqing, who previously taught in the Finance Department of Jinan University, emerged successfully as soon as he got into the business. At that time, GF's investment banking team and several other underwriters found that the issuance plan determined by the government compressed the legitimate rights and interests of the lead underwriters. Because the Guangzhou Municipal Reform Commission was responsible for the issuance of Guangzhou companies' IPOs, the companies did not dare to bargain with the government authorities, and other brokerage firms chose to remain silent, but only the "inexperienced" GF Securities stood out and took the leading role in negotiating with the Municipal Reform Commission. GF Securities repeatedly reported the situation and demanded the protection of their legitimate rights and interests.

The Municipal Reform Commission reported the request of GF Securities to the Standing Committee member of the CPC Guangzhou Municipal Committee and Executive Vice Mayor Chen Kaizhi, who presided over the issuance work. Vice Mayor Chen investigated the relevant situation and agreed to hold a working meeting after the successful stock issue to put the issue of revenue distribution on the agenda.

At this meeting, which was a matter of vital interest for the brokerage firm, Dong Zhengqing, who was still a new employee at that time, made a wonderful presentation on behalf of GF Securities to Vice Mayor Chen and officials from the Municipal Reform Commission on the issue of earnings distribution. Dong Zhengqing was not condescending, his voice was loud, and his words were direct, which attracted the attention of the participants at the meeting. Considering that the demands of the brokerage firms were justified, the enlightened Vice Mayor Chen finally decided that the relevant departments would make concessions. Dong Zhengqing thus became famous with one battle.

On November 8, 1993, with the approval of the Z.J.F.S.Z [1993] No. 31 document of the CSRC and of the S.Z.S.Z No. 265 document of the Shenzhen Stock Exchange, Baiyunshan Pharmaceutical issued IPOs to the public and was listed on the Shenzhen Stock Exchange, becoming one of the first listed companies in Guangzhou with the stock code 000522.

The Baiyunshan Pharmaceutical project was the first shot of GF Securities' investment banking in the capital markets, which injected a shot of strength into the newly established, struggling investment banking team and greatly enhanced its confidence and energy. At that time, another encouraging project was also going on: the Macro project.

Macro: what makes families happy

In the 1980s, Cantonese songs and TV dramas were popular. The TV series *Love and Passion* was loved by many people, and the TV advertising slogan "Macro: what makes families happy" by the star of the series, Liza Wang, was popular, making the brand of Macro in the gas appliance industry as popular as ever.

Formerly known as Guangdong LPG Appliance Development Co., Ltd., Guangdong Macro Gas Appliance Co., Ltd. was registered in 1985. Its factory, which was put into operation in 1988, covered an area of more than 100,000 square meters and had 15 formalized production lines, with an annual production capacity of two million units of gas water heaters and 1.1 million units of gas cookers. The company is located in Shunde, Foshan, one of the Four Little Tigers of Guangdong. Since 1990, as a local company in Shunde, Macro has received many visits from CPC and central government leaders.

GF Securities entered into contact with this famous Guangdong company early. With the pilot work of shareholding reform in Guangdong Province, Dr. Chen Yunxian personally led the team to provide the plan and write the feasibility report and prospectus for the shareholding reform of Macro. Based on the relationship established in the early stage, Macro chose GF Securities as the lead underwriter when promoting the stock issuance and listing.

The Business Development Department had only six or seven people when they were appointed to the Macro project, and the business development manager Ye Junying sorted out the projects at hand and made the following arrangements: Dong Zhengqing and Dai Yunbai were in charge of the Macro project, Li Xiangjun was in charge of the Baiyunshan Pharmaceutical project, and Ye Junying and Shao Peidong were in charge of the Jiangmen Ganghua project.

At that time, the stock underwriting business had not yet formed a set of standardized operating procedures. In addition to preparing applications, there was also the printing of subscription certificates, the selection of collection outlets, notarization of the supervision departments, the announcements of the media, the allocation of various payments, the handling of the remaining shares, the prevention of fake lottery forms, and shareholder consultation. Each project team was faced with a shortage of hands, time constraints, heavy tasks, difficulties, and mounting pressure. The business team had to learn by doing without any experience and even without any standard guidelines.

Under the approval system based on quota management, the first thing to do to get approval for stock issuance was to prepare good materials, which became the most testing work for the professional strength of the securities company at that time.

Dong Zhengqing, the project leader, joined GF Securities not long before and did not know how to start with the material preparation. The industry-related regulatory document—Rules for Disclosure of Information by Companies Issuing Public Stocks—was released only a few months later, in June 1993. However, this man from rural Hubei had a unique focus on the primary securities market, and his previous unsuccessful work experience also aroused his high spirits. Dong Zhengqing found an issue of *Shenzhen Special Zone Daily*, and together with his colleague Dai Yunbai, studied the prospectus model in the newspaper as a reference. Based on the research on Macro, they worked continuously for about a week to "create" material on their own.

As a graduate of the Finance Department of Shanghai University of Finance and Economics, Dong Zhengqing was satisfied with the prospectus he had "created." At that time, Dr. Ma Qingquan, who just joined GF, started to take charge of the company's investment banking and came directly to the site of the Macro project. Dong Zhengqing handed over the new prospectus material to Dr. Ma as a highlight of his work. This prospectus had been finalized based on repeated revisions and deliberations. At that time, the CSRC had not yet issued the standardized format and requirements for prospectuses of listed companies. This practice of creating a prospectus by the imagination of frontline market employees was also a very interesting story in the early days of the Chinese securities market.

Dr. Ma Qingquan was exposed to the investment banking business of securities companies in the Macro project. Just as Chairman Mao said, he learned war from war: "At that time, investment banking was just available in China, and there was no prospectus paradigm for the issuance of IPOs. So before the Tianjin meeting of the CSRC in 1993, our prospectus structure was all thought out by ourselves. It was like reportage. We prepared things such as how to write about the basic condition of the company, its market share and its problems on on own. In my investment banking at the beginning, I was looking at deeds and materials one by one as Dr. Chen said. Dong Zhengqing studied financial insurance, and he was very familiar with finance. Although I was his leader, I often learned from his thinking when analyzing financial statements, and I slowly got it."

In addition to joint learning, Dong Zhengqing also boldly innovated the issuance method during the project's stock issuance phase. As a lot of lottery forms at that time could be bought at once, careful investors could calculate the winning rate after buying. Dong Zhengqing, who is well versed in statistics, then divided the lottery forms into many groups, and then numbered these groups for staggered sales. In addition, the Macro project also broke through the regional restrictions on the issuance of depository receipts, and realized the issuance of depository receipts in different places.

With tenacious inquisitiveness and rigorous professionalism, GF Securities finally came up with a wonderful prospectus and an innovative issuance approach.

In January 1994, Macro stock was successfully listed on the main board of the Shenzhen Stock Exchange with the stock code 000533.

As the first main underwriting projects of GF Securities in the primary stock market, the Baiyunshan Pharmaceutical and Macro projects accumulated valuable practical experience for the investment banking team and contributed hugely to the establishing of GF Securities, a professional securities company.

In 1993, GF Securities also acted as agent to issue six bonds, including the Xinhui Nylon Bond and Guangdong Provincial Sanjian Bond, totaling about 220 million yuan. The corporate bonds underwritten by GF Securities accounted for 80 percent of the corporate bonds issued in Guangdong Province, materializing Dr. Chen's vision of developing both shares and bonds. In the primary stock market, besides Baiyunshan Pharmaceutical and Macro, GF Securities also entered six companies, including Meiya and Guangdong Electric Power, to make public stock filings, and provided consulting services to Shenzhou Gas Appliance and other companies for shareholding reform.

Through business development in the primary markets of Hainan, Hebei, Jiangxi, and other provincial-level administrative areas, GF Securities actively explored the road to reach out to the whole country.

The newly established Business Development Department excelled in a series of projects, directly or indirectly bringing GF Securities nearly 20 million in revenue, while the department had been running efficiently with a staff of five or six employees throughout the year. From the Business Development Department to the Investment Banking Department, "high education level, high work enthusiasm, and high work efficiency" became the outstanding features of the department. The main underwriting projects represented by Baiyunshan Pharmaceuticals and Macro set a far-reaching spiritual benchmark for investment banking, which started in the midst of difficulties. This included the tireless curiosity of the PhD Legion and the indefatigable will to fight when solving problems. After 1993, under the inspiration of Dr. Chen Yunxian, Ma Qingquan, Ye Junying, Dong Zhengqing, and the famous GF investment banking team set their eyes on more distant places.

2. Innovation as the source of vitality of investment banking

After the Macro project, the authorities seconded Ye Junying to assist the local government in the organization and leadership of the stock issue, and Dong Zhengqing became the head of the Business Development Department. Unlike Dr. Chen Yunxian and Dr. Ma Qingquan, who were elegant and introverted, Dong Zhengqing was quick and flexible. As the head of the department, he started to recruit talents and grab projects.

When the team was short of hands, Dong asked people to find interns in universities. In Guangzhou at that time, only Jinan University had a finance department, and he had just left Jinan University. Ouyang Xi and Qin Li, students from the finance department, became the earliest interns of GF investment banking, and Luo Binhua joined a few months later. The interns were directly confronted with intense project work, and Ouyang Xi recalled this experience: "I went to see Dr. Ma Qingquan at nine o'clock in the morning, talked for half an hour, and started working at ten o'clock, and have been working until now. At that time, I was a full-time student, but when I joined GF, I became a full-time worker, and I went back to school at 11 o'clock every night. I had to climb the wall to go back to my university dormitory."

In 1994, GF Securities formally established the Investment Banking Department on the basis of the Business Development Department. When the investment banking team of GF Securities was about to open, the sluggish secondary market triggered a chain reaction and the stock issuance market fluctuated. The veterans and new recruits of GF investment banking needed to think about how to "break new ground" in addition to "working" intensely. Innovation is exactly the tool they found to break new ground.

Two words make a difference for the Star Lake MSG project

At the end of July 1994, the SSE index fell back to 325 points, after a 79.09 percent drop in the previous 18 months. In order to boost the extremely disillusioned market confidence, the securities market suspended the issuance of IPOs for a rare three times from 1994 to 1995, for a total period of nearly 15 months. In addition, the issuance of IPOs was extremely difficult, and there were numerous cases of failed stock issuance nationwide, with some companies only issuing about three percent of their shares.

The disadvantages of the stock issuance method were further highlighted in this market situation. In 1994, securities were issued by the "full prepayment, proportional allocation, and balance deposits" method, in which investors prepaid the full amount of funds required for IPO subscriptions, and the issuer and the lead underwriter determined the allocation ratio according to the proportion of investor subscriptions, the public lottery was then conducted, and the unsuccessful amount was transferred to deposit. In the absence of many rules, many companies adopted online pricing, online bidding and a variety of offline issuance methods. However, due to the sluggish environment, the results were not satisfactory, and most companies still could not escape the fate of being unable to sell more than half of their shares.

Even in such a situation, project resources still had to be strived for. Dr. Chen Yunxian and Dong Zhengqing made several trips to the Guangdong authorities for projects. Under the "balancing arrangement" of Guangdong Province, the

Guangdong Meiyan project was initially given to Guangdong Securities, while the Star Lake MSG project was given to GF Securities.

The predecessor of Star Lake MSG was an agricultural microbial pharmaceutical factory founded in 1964, which was converted to MSG production in 1981. In 1992, it was transformed into a joint-stock company on the basis of the former state-owned Zhaoqing MSG Factory, and was one of the first eight pilot joint-stock reform companies in Guangdong Province. When the news of the stock issue of Star Lake MSG was just released, the market was moved by the news and the then Zhaoqing Brokerage Branch of Guangdong Development Bank also actively strived for the right to issue company shares. Although both GF Securities and the Zhaoqing Brokerage Branch belonged to Guangdong Development Bank, at that time they were different business entities and competed with each other. In comparison, the Zhaoqing Brokerage Branch had local advantages, but GF Securities already had outstanding performance in the Baiyunshan Pharmaceutical and Macro projects, and with the advantages of professionalism and experience, it finally gained the trust of Guangdong Meiyan and stock authorities.

After securing the Star Lake MSG project, GF Securities had to face the great pressure of being unable to sell the shares. Dr. Ma Qingquan, who was in charge of investment banking at that time, recalled, "When Star Lake MSG was issued, the domestic issuance business was basically at a standstill, and the percentage of IPOs sold did not exceed 10 percent, mostly around 3 percent, leaving 90 percent unsubscribed." How to successfully issue the shares of Star Lake MSG was the biggest problem faced by the Investment Banking Department of GF Securities in 1994.

In Huatai Hotel, where the company was headquartered at that time, the investment banking staff and interns worked overtime to design the issuance plan, focusing on the "full prepayment, proportional allocation, and balance deposits" method. When the market was overheated, in order to curb the enthusiasm of individual investors and help the local government to keep all the money in the local area, issuance was designed to be linked to deposits: to buy shares, you must first deposit the full amount of money in advance to the bank; after winning the lottery, you will keep the winning money, and the rest of the money will be deposited for three months before it can be withdrawn.

Qin Li, Ouyang Xi, and other members of the project team found after research that the cost of capital occupation was the necessary cost for investors to apply for IPOs, and depended on two factors: the size and time of the capital occupation. If the amount of funds invested by investors in the subscription of IPOs was equal to the capital of the shares actually purchased in the end, then the occupation cost incurred could be regarded as effective cost, but if the amount of funds invested exceeded the capital of the shares purchased in the end, the occupation cost in excess could be regarded as additional cost. The "full prepayment, proportional allocation, and balance deposits" method shortened the subscription time and improved the efficiency of subscription, but due to the low winning rate, the balance of the prepayment to deposit would be locked for a period of time before it could be withdrawn. This invariably raised the occupation cost of investors, and caused a lot of pressure on their investment intentions. As a result, the already difficult situation of IPOs issuance snowballed.

Having understood the problem, they now had to find the right solution. They focused on the two words "balance transfer." After a fierce battle overnight, GF Securities designed a new issuance method—"full prepayment, proportional allocation, and refundable balance," changing the two words "balance transfer" to "refundable balance." This was the first of its kind in the country. In the new method, for investors, the unsuccessful prepayment would return to their own hands, greatly reducing the cost of capital occupation.

"We changed the two words to 'refundable balance,' and the money left over from the winning lottery would be refunded the same night." Dr. Ma Qingquan recalled the plan with excitement. This new IPOs issuance method of the Investment Banking Department of GF Securities received approval of the regulatory authorities. On June 25, 1994, Star Lake MSG published an IPO announcement and the IPO issuance officially began. The effectiveness of this issuance method depended on whether the market would accept it.

Most of the designated outlets for Star Lake MSG were in Zhaoqing and Guangzhou. When the announcement was published, Guangdong Province was hit by heavy rainfall that had not been experienced for decades. The water level of the Xijiang River and Beijiang River rose sharply, and the Pearl River Delta faced the threat of the biggest flood after the founding of the People's Republic of China in 1949, and Zhaoqing and Guangzhou were in the affected area.

The main leaders of the CPC Zhaoqing Municipal Committee and the Zhaoqing Municipal Government were members of the project issuance leadership team, who all went to the frontline of flood relief during this special period. The huge floods also discouraged investors in other parts of China, and the heavy responsibility of issuance work fell on the shoulders of the project team. In the face of great pressure, the project team actively worked with investors to dispel their concerns, and was busy with telephone inquiries.

The innovative issuance plan and the sincere service of the investment banking team triggered positive market feedback that greatly exceeded expectations, and funds from all over the country were poured into the Star Lake MSG project in a short period of time. GF Securities' Shanghai Brokerage Branch, as the distribution outlet for the Star Lake MSG, soon faced another kind of pressure.

At that time, stockholders not only had to line up to obtain application forms, but also had to line up to make orders and payments. If the bank account opened by the investor was not in the same bank as designated by GF Securities for issuing IPOs, the money had to be transferred to the designated bank by the

People's Bank of China after it was transferred from the investor's bank account to GF Securities. Many investors worried that the process would take a long time to complete so that they would not be able to apply for IPOs in a timely manner, so they brought cash to the business counters. To make it convenient, some people directly lined up at the counters for stock subscription procedures with simple packages of cash. The transactions involving large amounts of cash required a higher level of security at securities brokerage branches.

Dr. Xiao Cheng, the then general manager of GF Securities' Shanghai Brokerage Branch, remembered the subscription situation vividly: "At that time, many investors brought large amounts of cash directly to the counter. In order to prevent robberies, Dr. Chen Yunxian flew to Shanghai from Guangzhou and arrived at the brokerage branch in advance together with the leaders of the then CSRC and Zhang Ning, a deputy director of the Shanghai Securities Administration Office, to check the security of the IPO subscription on the following day. On the day of the IPO subscription, the Shanghai Public Security Bureau's Economic Investigation Brigade also specially deployed personnel to the site to maintain order."

In the midst of a sluggish market, Star Lake MSG hit an oversubscription rate of 15.13 times, shaking the entire industry. On August 18, 1994, Star Lake MSG was listed on the Shanghai Stock Exchange under the stock code 600866, and GF investment banking made a name for itself nationwide and once again experienced the great power of innovation with the changes of two words in the issuance method.

The "full prepayment, proportional allocation, and refundable balance" issuance method continued to be used in GF Securities' subsequent projects. In late 1995 and early 1996, when the market was in the doldrums and the securities media was discussing "how to issue 5.5 billion yuan of new shares," GF Securities became the lead underwriter for Guangzhou Steel, the first new stock after the Chinese New Year in 1996. Due to the special timing and coinciding with the Fourth Session of the Eighth National People's Congress, the relevant departments paid great attention to the offline offering, and the vice chairman of the CSRC in charge of the issuance work personally guided the issuance, with close cooperation from public security, supervision, and other departments.

After careful preparation, the offering was again made with the "full prepayment, proportional allocation, and refundable balance" method in six cities, including Beijing, Shanghai, and Guangzhou, and was a success. After that, GF Securities used this method again in the issuance of China United Construction and developed a series of improved tools such as network monitoring.

In December 1996, the CSRC issued the Interim Regulations on Stock Issuance and Subscription Methods, in which "full prepayment, proportional allocation, and refundable balance," "online pricing," and "linkage with savings deposits" were listed as the three major issuance methods, which were adopted by many companies for a long period of time.

The innovative issuance method proposed by GF Securities played a role in the change of stock issuance methods, and left a significant mark in the history of China's capital markets development.

The Guangdong Meiyan project

Under the quota management market system, issuance projects were mainly allocated by the government in a balanced manner, but the invisible hand of the market still played an important role. Aggressive brokerage firms regarded investment banking projects as the source of business to win corporate clients. Competition and fragmentation in the primary market were severe.

Pu Mingshu, former general manager of CITIC Securities, recalls that from 1994 to 1995, 614 companies were listed nationwide, but during this period CITIC Securities did not qualify as an IPO underwriter for even one of them and had to use the name of "China International Trust and Investment Corporation Securities Department" to serve as "distributor," "sub-underwriter" or "listing referee" in the prospectus documents of several IPO projects: "In the feast of stock issuance, CITIC can only get a small share of the pie at most when others eat meat in big chunks."[3] However, CITIC Securities and the CITIC Group attached great importance to the prospects of investment banking, and gradually achieved a breakthrough and rise in investment banking through projects such as Yaohua Glass.

In 1994, progress in GF investment banking was equally difficult. In addition to actively seeking projects from the government, the investment banking team made great efforts to explore corporate resources and actively contacted more than 10 companies such as Shaoneng, Yineng, Kelon, and Southern Airlines. However, Dong Zhengqing found that "the companies for which GF Securities became the lead underwriter through hard work could not go public, and for the companies that could go public, GF Securities could not become the main underwriter due to various factors." Coupled with its weak capital strength, GF Securities did not make significant improvement to its investment banking development.

The success of the Star Lake MSG project changed the situation. Under the market force and brand effect, GF's investment banking team achieved twice the result with half the effort in "grabbing projects." Previously, according to the government's allocation, the Guangdong Meiyan project underwritten by Guangdong Securities encountered difficulties in issuance, but thanks to the efforts of Dong Zhengqing, Guangdong Meiyan turned to GF Securities to help.

Guangdong Meiyan Enterprise (Group) Co., Ltd. was located on the Meijiang River in in Meixian District, Meizhou City, Guangdong Province, with

3 A report from *The 21st Century Business Review*.

hydropower energy as its main business. Both Meiyan and Star Lake MSG were the companies that carried out the shareholding reform in Guangdong Province early, but compared with the latter, Meiyan's issuance and listing were more difficult.

According to the issuance announcement of Meiyan, 16.1 million shares were to be issued from July 11 to 18, 1994. However, China's stock markets plummeted during this period, the Shenzhen index was about to fall below the 1,000-point mark, and the subscriptions in the primary market were also greatly affected. The issue period was about to end, but only a few million shares had been subscribed, which made the company and the local government desperate. If the issuance failed, it would not only be a loss for the company, but also a waste of the stock issuance quota of Guangdong Province. At that time, the news of the successful issuance of Star Lake MSG shook the market. As a project in the same province which was launched at the same time as Star Lake MSG, Meiyan regarded GF Securities as its savior in an emergency.

After accepting this uninvited occurrence, Dong Zhengqing led the investment banking team to quickly redesign the issuance plan and start looking for investors. Because the market was not good, they needed to look for "big investors" who had strong purchasing power. When communicating with the investors concerning Meiyan, the project team found that some large buyers expressed their wish to change the listing location from the Shenzhen Stock Exchange to the Shanghai Stock Exchange. Although the majority of companies in Guangdong would choose to be listed in Shenzhen, the Shanghai market was more active and the strength of the large investors in Shanghai was greater under the depressed market conditions at that time. According to the market reaction to the listing of new shares on both exchanges, the opening prices on the Shanghai Stock Exchange were generally higher than on the Shenzhen Stock Exchange. These investors said they would subscribe it if it were changed to Shanghai.

There was no precedent in the market for a temporary change of exchanges. The change was not made, the outcome would not be promising for the offering. With the issue deadline looming, the project team, after careful study and analysis, concluded that "it won't be easy, but it is not impossible." The project team first went to discuss with the Shanghai Stock Exchange, and then reported to the CSRC and the Guangdong provincial government that were in charge of the issuance of Meiyan. After some relentless lobbying, the Commission and the Shanghai Stock Exchange agreed to change the listing location, but the final decision on whether to change was left to Meiyan.

Compared with changing the issuance location, it was obvious that the success of the issuance was more important, so the pragmatic Meiyan immediately decided to change the issuance location. After some efforts, on September 12, 1994, Meiyan was successfully listed in the Shanghai Stock Exchange with the stock code 600868, and became the only company in the securities market that "announced the issuance in Shenzhen and was listed in Shanghai."

For various reasons, GF Securities did not assume the nominal role in the public materials of the issuance and listing of Meiyan. However, the good story of Meiyan was widely spread in the capital markets, and the role played by GF Securities in the project became a strong proof of GF Securities' professional standard.

The pragmatic, professional, and diligent investment banking team of GF Securities also left a deep impression on Meiyan. In 1995 and 1996, Meiyan issued 20 million SEOs on two occasions with the total underwriting amount exceeding 100 million yuan, both of which were done by GF Securities.

"We were able to issue Star Lake MSG successfully in a difficult environment and Guangdong Meiyan when other brokerage firms could not. These two projects established the leading position of GF Securities in Guangdong, as well as consolidated its status in the eyes of investors." The former interns Ouyang Xi, Qin Li, and Luo Binhua were already the backbone staff of the Investment Banking Department when the projects were completed, and they are deeply proud of the two representative projects in that year.

The Zhongshan Torch project and the expensive newspaper

On July 30, 1994, the front page of *People's Daily* published three heavyweight policies: "Suspend the issuance and listing of IPOs this year, strictly control the scale of rights offerings in listed companies, and encourage more funds to enter the market."

The market interpreted these policies as "three major measures to save the market," and investors in the secondary market seemed to see the light of day, but for GF Securities, it meant that the stock issuance projects of the Investment Banking Department would come to a complete halt. On the same day, Zhongshan Torch Hi-Tech Industrial Co., Ltd. (now Jonjee Hi-tech Industrial & Commercial Holding Co., Ltd., and hereinafter referred to as Zhongshan Torch), for which GF Securities was the lead underwriter, had just submitted its prospectus, and the prospect of the project was suddenly plunged into great uncertainty.

Three months later, the underwriting period agreed upon in the underwriting agreement between GF Securities and Zhongshan Torch had expired. According to the agreement, GF Securities had to strictly fulfill the agreed underwriting obligations, fully underwrite the 28 million shares originally to be publicly offered, and select the appropriate time for public transfer to the public in an appropriate manner. In this way, the pressure fell entirely on GF Securities to issue the shares.

The project team had to work on the "appropriate manner" because the "appropriate timing" was not available. Dr. Ma Qingquan believed that instead of waiting passively, the project team should take the initiative to break the deadlock in the market. The project team conducted an in-depth analysis of the lottery form issuance method in the issuance market at that time and saw the hope to break the deadlock. GF Securities' investment banking team came up with an idea to break the issuance deadlock in a way similar to a commodity pre-sale, where investors would make reservations through lottery forms and then make subscriptions with their reservation vouchers after the IPO was reopened, breaking the issuance deadlock based on a time difference, relieving the pressure on the company to advance funds while giving the subscribers real expectations.

In order to get the permission from the CSRC, Dr. Ma Qingquan and Dong Zhengqing flew to Beijing overnight to report to the relevant leaders of the Commission, and their report was finally approved. GF Securities then started all the work of booking the subscription immediately. Little did the project team know that their innovation would create a ripple in the capital markets.

On December 8, 1994, *China Securities Journal* published an announcement that GF Securities intended to resell 28 million public shares of Zhongshan Torch to private investors by means of "limited subscription, free reservation, lottery allocation, and payment upon lot." There was a reservation form attached to the announcement. Investors only needed to fill out the reservation form as required and mail it and other related materials to GF Securities to make a reservation for subscription. Then GF Securities would calculate the winning rate based on the number of reservations and the issue amount, and use the reservation form as proof for lottery and allocation. Zhongshan Torch became the first stock issued nationwide after the suspension of IPO for nearly five months.

The market, which had been quiet for months, suddenly stirred up after Zhongshan Torch announced the launch of the issue, which made GF Securities unprepared. And the market appeared to speculate on the *China Securities Journal* with the reservation form.

After careful investigating the situation, the investment banking project team found that the details of its approach overlooked a problem: the announcement's reservation form contained four words "Copies NOT Acceptable." According to the announcement, "No one is allowed to copy, reproduce, or falsify the reservation form," which means that the reservation form in the newspaper was the only proof of the investor's reservation. The circulation of *China Securities Journal* was sought at high prices, with one copy of the newspaper in some places even being sold at more than 10,000 yuan.

In order to prevent further developments, GF Securities urgently studied the situation and quickly provided a solution. On January 7, 1995, *China Securities Journal* published a new announcement stipulating that, based on the principle of "treating old and new reservation forms differently," the old reservation form sent to GF Securities before 16:30 on December 15, 1994 would continue to be valid and would be processed in accordance with the method of "limited subscription, free reservation, lottery allocation, and payment upon lot." The new announcement also said that the original and photocopies of the reservation form printed on January 7, 1995 would be considered as valid reservation forms, and the new reservation form would be processed in accordance with the "reservation with a form, full prepayment, subscription upon winning, and refund upon failure to win the lottery" method. A crisis that almost turned into a social incident was solved.

Reservation forms flew to GF Securities like snowflakes, and everyone from the company's leaders to the staff of the Investment Banking Department gathered in a humble office to manually assign numbers and make entries, working around the clock for more than half a month. Zhongshan Torch was ultimately 29.49 times oversubscribed.

To be a good pioneer who dares to break new ground, one must be both courageous and resourceful, and more importantly, must have a sense of responsibility. The episode of "making the newspaper expensive" reflected an ill-considered innovation of GF Securities, but the company took the responsibility and quickly remedied the situation. As a result, it was understood and pardoned by everyone for its courageous sense of innovation and spirit of commitment. This also made the whole capital markets look at GF Securities admiringly.

On January 24, 1995, Zhongshan Torch was successfully listed on the Shanghai Stock Exchange with the stock code 600872. This stock was not only the first stock in Zhongshan, but also the first stock in national high-tech development zones. As a representative project with long duration, large workload and wide external influence, the issue of Zhongshan Torch wrote a shining chapter in the early development history of GF Investment Banking Department.

3. Developing GF investment banking nationwide

In 1995, the Investment Banking Department was renamed as the Investment Banking Head Office. The head office's staff was expanded to more than ten people, and it has four departments, which were responsible for the primary market business both inside and outside Guangdong Province, as well as international business and comprehensive research. After the projects such as Star Lake MSG, Guangdong Meiyan, and Zhongshan Torch made a name for investment banking one after another, GF Securities officially blew the charge to go nationwide.

Going beyond Guangdong and entering the whole country meant facing directly the encirclement of large national and local brokerage firms at that time. Dr. Ma Qingquan recalled, "Strategically, there were some that we could not compete with, such as Huaxia Securities and Jun'an Securities, which often took away big national projects." Competition for big projects was already very fierce, and local government projects were bound to favor local brokerage firms, so GF Securities' investment banking needed to develop through fierce competition.

How to enter a new phase? Tactics was the key.

Business secured with the loudspeaker

According to its own resource endowment, GF investment banking found its own precise method: actively following up the project resources of the central government ministries and commissions, focusing on the development of the provincial-level administrative areas without large local brokerage firms, and striving to secure IPO quota from them. The idea of this method was that IPO quotas were generally in the hands of central government ministries and commissions and provincial-level governments, so if GF Securities could get the approval of ministries and commissions, it could break away from the limitation of provincial-level quotas.

Combining strategy and tactics, GF investment banking first set its eyes on northeast China.

In 1995, the state issued stock issuance quotas of 5.5 billion yuan. Dr. Chen Yunxian learned that Liaoning Province Knitted Cotton and Woolen Products Import & Export Corporation (the predecessor of Liaoning Cheng Da Co., Ltd.; hereinafter referred to as Liaoning Cheng Da) had been granted the quota for that year's stock issue. Dr. Chen was determined to approach the company quickly. At that time, he learned that the company had come to Guangzhou to attend the famous China Export Commodities Fair (Canton Fair).

In October 1995, the huge hall of Canton Fair was crowded with people, and Dr. Chen Yunxian was looking for a person in the hall—Shang Shuzhi, the general manager of Liaoning Province Knitted Cotton and Woolen Products Import and Export Corporation. At that time, cell phones were not yet popular, so Dr. Chen was in a difficult position to contact Mr. Shang in the crowded venue. However, the internal public addressing system of the venue suddenly caught his attention. In a short time, a beautiful female voice broadcasted in the venue: "Mr. Shang Shuzhi, general manager of Liaoning Province Knitted Cotton and Woolen Products Import and Export Corporation, would you please come to the service desk?"

In this way, the loudspeaker of Canton Fair facilitated the meeting between Dr. Chen Yunxian and Mr. Shang Shuzhi. Dr. Chen's sincerity and professionalism impressed Shang Shuzhi, and the two talked very well and reached a preliminary intention of cooperation. Mr. Shang initially agreed that GF Securities could "send two people to prepare the project."

At the end of October 1995, the Investment Banking Department arranged for Ouyang Xi and Chen Hui to go to Liaoning Cheng Da. At that time, the Investment Banking Department was seeking projects from all over the country, and the manpower was extremely tight. When they received the notice, they had just finished their last project. When they were suddenly assigned to Dalian, they were in a great hurry.

It was already evening when Ouyang Xi and Chen Hui arrived in Dalian, and the leaders of Liaoning Cheng Da enthusiastically arranged a reception banquet. However, the atmosphere was a bit awkward: "You guys talked quite well and said that all of you are PhDs, but finally only two youngsters showed up." At the dinner table, several company leaders of Liaoning Cheng Da were quite frank, starting from how Dr. Chen attached importance to the project when GF Securities was fighting for the project, focusing on how important the listing was to Liaoning Cheng Da, and then asking what projects the two had done, and worrying about "whether the young people can do it or not."

Ouyang Xi was allergic to alcohol and his whole body would be covered with red rash after each drink. However, this time he came to do the project on behalf of GF investment banking, so he could only try his best to toast to the clients. After the banquet broke up and they went home, Ouyang Xi and Chen Hui discussed that to prepare for the meeting to coordinate intermediaries the next morning, they must do their best in order to successfully complete the project that Dr. Chen had won. So, the two of them sobered up and organized the materials overnight. They worked until 3:00 a.m. when they put together a very detailed and targeted survey list, which included the information they had learned at the banquet.

The next day at the meeting of intermediaries, the two presented the listing plan, the division of labor statement, the due diligence checklist, and other materials. The leaders of Liaoning Cheng Da were impressed by the two young representatives of GF Securities when they saw how well organized the project had become overnight.

Before the Liaoning Cheng Da project, Ouyang Xi and Chen Hui had already done some corporate share listing projects for companies. They were quite understandable in the face of the clients' queries the night before. As Dr. Chen Yunxian had explained to them before the trip, "Investment banking should take the leading position in the process of corporate restructuring and listing. Although we have high and low positions and responsibilities within our company, once we go out on behalf of the company, we have to serve as the main coordinator in getting the company and other intermediaries to achieve the goal of corporate listing, rather than being led by the nose."

Liaoning Province Knitted Cotton and Woolen Products Import and Export Corporation was a state-owned foreign trade company with a history of more than 40 years. It had complicated business and the common problems of SOEs at that time; that is, it had unclear property rights and suffered a lack of separation between government administration and corporate management.

Ouyang Xi and Chen Hui spent a lot of time designing a reasonable shareholding structure, assisting the company in clarifying property rights, determining the number of shares to be raised, and planning the use of the fundraising. For more than four months, the two of them spent time in the company, communicating and coordinating with the company, the asset appraisal agency, and the accounting firm, working day and night, without even seeing what Dalian, a seaside city, looked like.

During this period, the clients' attitude to Ouyang and Chen also changed significantly, and their communication with GF Securities representatives gradually deepened. During the project communication, General Manager Shang Shuzhi, who was interested in the financial industry, often asked about GF Securities' business model and management structure. Ouyang and Chen made full use of the opportunity to dine with the company leaders in the evening to tell them about the Company Law and corporate governance, why the shareholders' meeting and the board of directors should be separated institutionally, and what risks might be caused if they were mixed together in management. All this won Liaoning Cheng Da's recognition.

In just five months, Liaoning Cheng Da initially completed the shareholding transformation and was successfully listed on the Shanghai Stock Exchange in June of the following year, becoming the first listed foreign trade company in Liaoning Province.

After the success of the Liaoning Cheng Da project, under the slogan of "developing GF Securities nationwide," all the investment banking team worked hard to deepen development in northeast China.

The difficulties in expanding investment banking from Guangzhou to northeast China were manifold. In order to get to know the leader of the Liaoning Province Reform Commission in charge of the relevant work, Dr. Ma and Dong Zhengqing braved the northeastern cold of more than 20 degrees below zero and waited at the door of the leader's house from 9 p.m. to 11 p.m. When the leader finally came home, they could only hand him their business cards and politely answered which place GF Securities was from and what they were there for. And then they made an appointment to meet at the leader's office the next day. They repeated this several times for a long time before slowly impressing the locals and developing a network of connection with them.

While impressing the locals with sincerity and persistence, Ma Qingquan and Dong Zhengqing also increased their clients' understanding of GF Securities through various channels. According to their recollection, "Customers would say in their internal discussions that, although this company was currently a brokerage in Guangdong, but the people they sent here were excellent; they had done Macro, Star Lake MSG, and Zhongshan Torch, and completed a representative project to turn around the situation in stock issuance. Slowly, the northeast customers came to know GF Securities. Moreover, they said that the so-and-so who came to do the project was a PhD or a Master, and he worked hard to prepare reports at weekends and during holidays in the hotel. Over time, companies and local leaders slowly accepted GF Securities."

GF Securities was not the only brokerage firm striving for projects in northeast China. At that time, many famous brokerage firms such as Shenyin Securities, Guotai Securities, Southern Securities, and Huaxia Securities, were fighting hard to replicate their "oligopoly" advantages formed in other regions in the northeast market. In the face of competition, Dong Zhengqing took a unique approach, looking for "allies" in the region to defend against powerful competitors. He sought the cooperation of Heilongjiang Province State Investment Corporation and opened up the client network step by step, erecting a solid barrier in front of the competitors.

The professional quality and elaborate service of GF's investment banking team won the heartfelt recognition of corporate clients. In the subsequent capital increase and expansion of GF Securities, clients who had become listed companies came to purchase the shares of GF Securities, hoping to participate in its long-term development. Liaoning Cheng Da, Jilin Aodong, and Zhongshan Utilities, the three GF related stocks, were the important clients GF Securities met in its early days of investment banking. Through their understanding of GF Securities' strategy and culture, they identified with the development prospect of the securities industry and finally chose to become shareholders of GF Securities.

Winning clients with sincerity and professionalism

In 1995, the business of the Investment Banking Department effectively broke through the limits of Guangdong Province and expanded to northeast, north and central China and other provincial-level administrative areas. Its international business also made substantial progress. At the end of that year, Dr. Chen Yunxian made a resounding statement in his internal summary: "At present, GF Securities has improved its primary market business capacity considerably so that it can effectively compete with the top three securities firms in China."

At the same time, as the business deepened, the inherent deficiencies of GF Securities' investment banking business became more obvious. In addition to the lack of resources and manpower, many projects were time-critical and stressful, and the newly recruited staff faced the dilemma of insufficient training, and the biggest obstacle to business expansion was the lack of a nationally influential brand. In response, the Investment Banking Department held several intensive training sessions to provide training on financial skills and material production from form to content. In addition, Dr. Chen Yunxian and Dr. Ma Qingquan visited important brokerages at the time, such as Shenyin Securities and Haitong Securities, to ask for face-to-face advice from outstanding brokerage leaders, such as Kan Zhidong and Wang Kaiguo, to exchange experiences with each other.

From 1994 to 1996, under the strategy of going nationwide, the Investment Bank Head Office had four internal departments besides two branches in Beijing and Shanghai. In addition to geographical expansion, GF Securities also continued to broaden its business scope by setting up the Rights Offerings Department and the Bond Department, and its business also expanded rapidly from IPO business to rights offerings, SEOs, and B-share underwriting and sponsorship projects.

The department was expanded to over 30 people. Under the unified command and hierarchical management of Mr. Ye Junying and Mr. Dong Zhengqing, not only the northeast region made a breakthrough under the responsibility of Ouyang Xi, but also Qin Li, who was in charge of the northwest region, completed projects such as Xi'an Tourism and Wuzhong Instrument, and Luo Binhua, who was in charge of rights offerings, completed the rights offerings projects of Wuhan Zhongbai, Power 28, and Guangdong Fenghua. After joining GF Securities, Zhang Shaohua focused on operating in Beijing and developing business in north China.

In order to strengthen the internal management, Sun Xiaoyan, who had experience in the Finance Department and the Capital Operation Department, joined the Investment Banking Department.

In the second half of 1996, CNNC Suzhou Valve Co., Ltd. (hereinafter referred to as CNNC Suzhou) planned to go public. As the first company under China National Nuclear Corporation (CNNC) planning to get listed, its restructuring and listing received a lot of attention from all sides. In selecting the lead underwriter, CNNC Suzhou set high standards and approached more than 20 brokerage firms. Yang Tongxing, the then deputy general manager of CNNC Suzhou, revealed afterwards that the reason for choosing GF Securities as the lead underwriter from among more than 20 brokerages was that they were impressed by the refined style and persistent dedication shown by GF Securities employees through their contacts.

The CNNC Suzhou project entered the market on December 23, 1996 and was successfully listed on the Shenzhen Stock Exchange on July 10 of the following year. The transformation and restructuring plan of the project was included in Plans for Carrying Out Shareholding Reform and Restructuring in Companies prepared by the National Reform Commission as an example of restructuring in the machinery industry. The reported materials of the project also received high evaluation from the CSRC. The P/E ratio of the market at that time was based on the standard of not more than 15 times, while the regulator gave a rare P/E ratio of 16 times for CNNC Suzhou, which shows the high quality of the project.

Through this project, Yang Tongxing said, "A sincere personal friendship was formed with GF people, and they became intimate friends." In the subsequent cooperation, such as in capital operation, GF Securities made full efforts to advise and give unconditional support to CNNC Suzhou many times.

When going nationwide and competing with large brokerage firms for projects, the GF Securities investment banking team paid extra attention to impressing clients with sincerity and professionalism, and the phrase "we will put our strongest business team in this project" became a very powerful promise. For the investment banking projects undertaken, GF Securities dispatched its resources to form the strongest team and gave their best effort sincerely. Dr.

Ma Qingquan recalled a time when he led a team to Chengdu to secure a main underwriting project: "The first time, Jun'an Securities sent more than 10 people, which surprised the client, while GF Securities came with only 4 or 5 people. However, the second time Jun'an Securities sent only one key professional and two interns, while GF Securities sent the same 4 or 5 people, indicating GF Securities' sincerity."

Under the quota management at this stage, the national market was limited, and the location and scale of the issuing companies also deeply affected GF Securities' business. It was a typical example of GF Securities' market-oriented awareness to promote investment banking to spread nationwide geographically and to focus on SMEs in terms of types of companies.

On May 27, 1996, *Nanfang Daily* published a front-page article entitled the "The 'PhD Legion' in the Capital Markets: A Report on GF Securities." GF Securities' "PhD Legion" rapidly gained a reputation in China's capital markets and became a brand name for the Investment Banking Department to expand its business nationwide. Dr. Chen Yunxian, Dr. Ma Qingquan, and a group of highly qualified talents made this brand more convincing by their "personal communications" during their visits to clients.

In addition to the high educational level of GF Securities' "PhD Legion," GF investment banking also had two advantages: firstly, it was fast in writing materials and could work overtime to produce materials on time; secondly, it had a strong pricing ability, and based on the macro situation, policy direction, and industrial development laws, its pricing was particularly accurate, satisfying clients and convincing the market.

During this period, GF investment banking's financial advisory business also made a big impact in the industry. In June 1996, with the approval of relevant authorities, GF Securities, as financial advisor, assisted Malaysia Ipoh Pty Ltd. to successfully acquire 20 million shares of non-state corporate shares from Guangdong Expressway Development Co., Ltd. at a price of 3.6 yuan per share. GF Securities ensured the successful completion of the acquisition through a lot of meticulous preparatory work, including the design of the plan, the determination of the acquisition price, and the coordination and negotiation between the two sides.

Analysts commented on this case: "As an early foreign acquisition case in the domestic securities market, the significance of this acquisition lay in the introduction of strategic investors through equity transfer, which laid a solid foundation for the stable operation and sustainable development of Guangdong Expressway, and also paved the way for the issuance of its B-shares. This transfer undoubtedly had an important guiding significance for the related business."

In 1996, the fourth year of the establishment of GF Securities Investment Banking Department, GF's investment banking made progress in the primary market in leaps and bounds: underwriting 13 IPOs and 2 rights offerings, serving as a sub-underwriter for three rights offerings, recommending 16 companies to go public, and being in the process of material production for six more, achieving both economic and social benefits. In December 1996, GF Securities was awarded the qualification of the first batch of principal underwriters of stocks by the CSRC as expected.

According to the statistics of China Securities Association, only 42 out of more than 500 securities management institutions in China were qualified as lead underwriters in 1996.

According to the statistics of the China Securities Association, in 1996, only 42 out of more than 500 securities firms nationwide were lead underwriters, and seven of them held 60 percent of the market share. By November 1997, the top five securities firms held more than 50 percent of the market share. During this period, GF Securities became one of the major securities firms in China's primary market by underwriting 30 companies, sub-underwriting 5 companies, and recommending 40 companies to go public, ranking fourth in the industry nationwide.

History of high-quality projects

If we look at the route of GF's investment banking expansion on the map of China, we can find that the route starts from Guangzhou, reaches Shunde, Zhaoqing, and Zhongshan around Guangzhou, and then extends out of Guangdong Province to reach Hubei, Beijing, Shaanxi, Liaoning, Tianjin, Jilin, Fujian, Shandong, and other provinces and municipalities. For GF investment bankers, this is a route of hardships and great success as well.

After Dr. Ma Qingquan, Dr. Ye Junying, and Dr. Dong Zhengqing (Ye Junying and Dong Zhengqing obtained their PhDs during their working years), Dr. Li Jianyong took over the leadership of the Investment Banking Department. He once described his career in GF investment banking as follows: "In investment banking, my colleagues and I once enjoyed a life of success. The investment banking career has turned the weak students and 'silly PhDs' on the campus and in the study into men who fought hard battles and would not stop without victory. From 'scholars' to 'war generals', this is exactly the transformation process of GF Securities' 'PhD Legion.'" This is also a reflection of the growth of GF's investment banking team.

In 1999, China's stock markets often did well, and the success of issuance was no longer the main problem in the primary market. However, this did not mean that the market was becoming less competitive. On the contrary, in Dr. Li Jianyong's view, the inflection point of the transition of China's capital market from a market with strong characteristics of the planned economy to a market fully based on market force began to appear, the polarization of brokerage firms became increasingly serious, the market was increasingly central, and a group of new investment bankers such as Southwest Securities and Shandong Securities were aggressive. This meant that GF Securities needed to be keenly aware of the investment banking crisis.

GF Securities focused its investment banking on the transformation from low-level competition to high-level competition. Accordingly, the investment banking team was expanded to about 70 people, and the Investment Banking Head Office was composed of the First Investment Banking Department with Ren Qun as general manager, the Second Investment Banking Department with Chen Yujie as general manager, the South China Business Department with Xue Ziqiang as general manager, the Beijing Business Department with Zhang Shaohua as general manager, the East China Business Department with Lin Chuanhui as general manager, the Northwest Business Department with Ma Sushuang as general manager, the Southwest Business Department with Zou Yunlong as general manager, and the Northeast Business Department with Yang Ming as general manager. It was crucial for the core professionals to further pass on their experience and bring the company's overall advantages into play.

Kelon Electric was a corporate client that GF Securities had followed up for many years. In this project, Cai Tiezheng, a new employee in investment banking, grew rapidly under the guidance of Dai Yunbai and others. In 1999, Kelon Electric, an H-share company, planned to issue A-shares and GF Securities became the lead underwriter. Since H-shares accounted for more than half of Kelon Electric shares, the issuance of A-shares meant more complicated shareholders' background and legal requirements. Cai Tiezheng and the project team resisted the pressure and communicated with and coordinated eight intermediaries during the whole issuance process, and finally assisted Kelon Electric to successfully complete the acquisition of Kelon Air Conditioner (a sister company of Kelon Electric), the acquisition of Huabao Air Conditioner and the operating assets of a large injection molding factory in Shunde, and to be successfully listed on the A-share market. The project not only set a new record in China's home appliance industry, but also helped Kelon to acquire a new company. The project not only set a record for the largest amount of M&A in the Chinese home appliance industry, but more dazzlingly, Kelon and GF Securities also applied the internationally accepted roadshow model to the issue presentation. Both parties decided to follow the international practice and make it a pure dialogue between investors and financiers, providing a more direct communication channel for investors.

On May 31, 1999, the event was successfully held in Beijing with the presence of Dr. Fang Jiachun, the then president of GF Securities, and the leader of Kelon Electric, making the roadshow model the first of its kind in the domestic securities market. This dialogue without officials' speeches drew great attention from the media. On the next day of the Beijing roadshow, a securities media even made a headline of "The Kelon Roadshow Moves Beijing."

Due to the good effect of the roadshow, a number of large companies held similar events for their IPOs. This spontaneous activity of GF Securities also attracted the attention of the competent authorities and was promoted through various forms such as experience debriefing sessions, so that "roadshows" were adopted by many companies for their IPOs and gradually became popular in the IPO work. In early 2001, the CSRC issued the Circular on Corporate Presentation of IPO Companies via the Internet, requiring all IPO companies to conduct at least an online roadshow, thus evolving from "why roadshow" to "why not roadshow" in just a few years.

In 2000, as the trend of IPO subscription grew, the focus of discussion from all walks of life gradually shifted to whether the "hot money for IPO" was reasonable and the allocation of IPO shares. Calls for changes in the way IPO shares were issued kept coming up. In this context, another boutique project created by GF Securities once again became the historic lucky winner.

Fujian Mindong Electric Power Co., Ltd. (Fujian Mindong Ele) is a company mainly engaged in the production and development of electricity. Its main sponsor, Fujian Mindong Old Revolutionary Area Hydropower Development Corporation, owned the Fujian Mindong Electric Grid, which was the only regional local power grid in Fujian Province that focused on developing small hydropower plants, and ranked second in scale and strength among the four major regional local power grids in China. In April 1999, Lin Chuanhui, a 36-year-old general manager of GF Securities' Investment Banking Head Office in East China, came to the small town of Fu'an, hoping to meet with the leaders of Fujian Mindong Ele.

Lin Chuanhui graduated from Jilin University with a degree in economics and worked at the Second Personnel Section of the Organization Department and at the Research Department in the Central Party School and as an assistant to Vice President Liu Haifan. His political future was promising, but he chose to go south to GF Securities, starting from the grassroots level as an investment banker. When he began to work on the Fujian Mindong Ele project, he had grown up to be the backbone of management in charge of the east China region based on his five years of investment banking experience.

The prepared Lin Chuanhui met with Yang Yibiao, general manager of Fujian Mindong Ele. They talked about using the capital markets to increase investment in the power industry in east China, and quickly reached a cooperation intention and signed an underwriting agreement soon after. After more than a year of efforts by Lin Chuanhui and his colleague An Yongbing, the Fujian Mindong Ele project entered the sprint stage in June 2000. At that time, Lin boldly proposed the idea of using the "Dutch bidding method" to let the issue price of Fujian Mindong Ele shares be determined entirely by the market.

The "Dutch bidding method" is one of the popular foreign market-based pricing methods, which is based on the principle that the lowest price of all bidders until the issue amount is raised is the final winning price, and all winning bidders subscribe for securities at this price. This was the "first crab" to try market-based issuance by using this competitive bidding method without a ceiling. On June 30, 2000, the prospectus of Fujian Mindong Ele was officially published in the newspaper and became the focus of the market.

In addition, the Fujian Mindong Ele project was also supported by GF Securities' resources. Vice President Dr. Li Jianyong was in charge of the project, Luo Binhua and Ouyang Xi, leaders of the Investment Banking Department, also joined the project team, and the number of participants increased from two to eight. During the roadshow in Shenzhen, facing more than 200 representatives of institutional investors such as funds and listed companies, Dr. Li Jianyong made it clear that GF Securities was ready to underwrite the full amount.

On July 7, the placement of corporate shares in Fujian Mindong Ele was completed and the issue price of Fujian Mindong Ele was officially set at 11.5 yuan per share, with a P/E ratio of 88 times, the highest P/E ratio for new issues in China's securities market. On July 14, the online pricing issue was well received by market capital, and the market-oriented practice of GF Securities in pricing new shares using the "Dutch bidding method" was a complete success. A few months later, *China Securities Journal*'s article "The Best of China's Securities Market in a Decade" made a proud entry for Fujian Mindong Ele: the highest offering P/E ratio.

4. Values and humanism of GF investment banking

Eager beavers inspired by personality

Throughout the 1990s, from the Business Development Department to the Investment Banking Department, investment bankers wrote their own chapter of "youthful ambition" in the development of GF Securities.

Looking for the reasons for the rapid rise GF Securities in investment banking, one can hardly ignore such a group—"an inspiring leader and a motivated management team." Since 1991, embracing the ideal of serving the country, Dr. Chen Yunxian had not only devoted himself to the development of the company and the creation of the investment banking theory, but also created the cultural notion of knowledge-based improvement, pragmaticism, and dedication. He was the first to teach GF Securities' investment bankers.

The leaders of GF investment banking were highly educated intellectuals. They formed a strong inspirational force with the spirit of inquisitiveness, and laid the foundation for entrepreneurship with the style of hard work, which led to the story of the subsequent investment banking team forging ahead and opening up new territories.

Behind the numerous investment banking projects, the journey of "intellectual entrepreneurship" was actually a mixture of brilliance and bitterness.

Someone once asked Dr. Ma Qingquan, "Did you have any psychological changes when you went from being an intellectual with a reputation to doing business and dealing with clients?" Ma Qingquan frankly admitted, "I used to be an intellectual, and I was relatively self-contained, so I seldom had to ask people for help. As an intellectual, I could publish a book and enjoy it myself. As a businessman, I suffer the most psychologically when I have to ask others for help."

During his previous work at the Central Party School, Ma Qingquan served as the secretary of Vice President Su Xing, with the title of professor, and also served as the director of the Economic Research Department of the School, so there was nothing that required him to come down off his high horse to beg others for help. But after he joined GF Securities, he found that "doing investment banking is to beg others for help. Without the quota, business just can't be carried out; business will be seized by rival brokerage firms if the business owner doesn't nod."

Dr. Ma had to come to terms with this huge psychological suffering. He had to be mentally prepared for asking others for help. He said, "I must have some Ah Q spirit. For example, before meeting customers, I must cheer myself up.... Before knocking on a client's door, I worked to control my emotions and tried to convince myself that: I am doing this not for myself." Looking back, Dr. Ma Qingquan himself feels it funny.

In addition to becoming mentally prepared, the PhDs, who used to be devoted to theoretical research, had to take into account the general sentiment amongst their clients to secure projects.

In the early days of the market, it was not uncommon to dine and drink with clients when competing for investment banking projects. When clients insisted that "people's wining behavior reflects their true disposition," the PhDs, the party B, often had no choice. Once, Dr. Wang Liangzhong from the Development Research Center invited Dr. Chen Yunxian to help the Investment Banking Department to win a project. After the formal meeting, they must invite their client to dinner. During the dinner, the client said half-jokingly and half-seriously, "If a PhD of GF Securities is brave enough to drink the chili oil on the table, GF Securities will have the project." Despite his health condition, Dr. Wang, a native of Hunan, picked up the red chili oil and drank it up. The client added: "If you can drink another big glass of alcohol, GF Securities will have another project." Dr. Wang froze for a second, and before Dr. Chen could dissuade him, he tilted his neck and drank again.

Of course, the main battlefield of the investment professionals was to make plans and prepare materials. In Dr. Ma's memory, in 1993, when he first joined the company, he started to develop primary market business together with Wang Hongmao, Ye Junying, and Dong Zhengqing. They often slept only two or three hours a day during the period when two projects, Baiyunshan Pharmaceutical and Macro, were going on simultaneously. When they developed on the NET system in Nanhai, it took only one week from beginning to work on the project to getting it listed, and all the materials were completed in only three days. At that time, a hardworking and efficient work style was formed.

Shi Xiu, a character in the Chinese classic *Water Margin*, is well versed in martial arts and exceptionally zealous, so he is known as an eager beaver in Jianghu. In 1995, Dr. Chen Yunxian mentioned the "eager beaver's" spirit of the investment banking team at internal meetings. Ye Junying, Dong Zhengqing, and Luo Binhua, who was in charge of the Investment Banking Department, were all representatives of the "eager beaver's" spirit that Dr. Chen praised. According to Dr. Chen, "They often spent no less time on the plane than they did at home."

During the Guangzhou Steel project, Mr. Ye was invited to Guangzhou Steel to discuss the main terms of the underwriting agreement with General Manager Chen Mingde and the chief accountant Chen Jialing. However, a long time after the meeting began, Ye had not shown up and he did not answer the phone. The client and Chen's colleagues of the project team were very anxious and did not know what had happened. Later, they learned that in order to keep up with the project, Ye travelled back and forth from Guangzhou to Shenzhen and was so tired that he had a road accident, though fortunately he was not seriously hurt.

The leaders of the Investment Banking Department were the first to do their best, which had a great effect on the working atmosphere of the department. Huang Xuhui, who was involved in the Guangzhou Steel project, recalled that during the National Day holiday in 1995, he and Dai Yunbai did not take any vacation in order to get the job done. They only slept for two hours almost every day. When they were too tired to work, they just connected the office chairs and lay down on them. It was hot in Guangzhou at night and the office's central air conditioning was turned off in the evening. One night, hot and sleepy Huang Xuhui really could not stand any longer, so he went to the company's business car and lay in it with the air conditioning on.

A veteran investment banker's diary truly reflects the work of GF investment bankers at the time. It goes like this:

> July 7, Slight Heat
>
> In the 168 hours from the early hours of July 1 to midnight on July 7, I wrote three reports, two project proposals, and four product presentations, and read a 365-page book on M&A due diligence in English.
>
> August 8, Start of Autumn
>
> Day after day, we faced a mountain of materials and a foot-wide computer, arguing endlessly with ourselves because we always felt our reports were not good enough; arguing with the clients because we could not possibly agree with their proposals; arguing with the lawyers because we always wanted to know their working papers. There was a map of China in the office, and that was our only recreation and fitness activity. For some reason, the four of us always competed to see who had been to the most provincial-level administrative areas. One week three months later, I travelled from Qingdao to Beijing, then to Tianjin, Shanghai, Sichuan, Chongqing, and Yichang in seven days, expanding my footprint by three more provinces and municipalities.

Luo Binhua, who joined GF Securities as an intern at the end of 1993, wrote a research report on the H-share offering of Guangzhou Shipyard at the request of Dong Zhengqing and soon became a full-fledged employee of the Investment Banking Department. He was thin, wore glasses, and looked very scholarly at first glance, so it was hard to imagine that this eager beaver had worked on three IPO projects at the same time and made them a success one after another.

In 1996, when the Guangdong Shaoneng project was in full swing, it was July and August when the heat was unbearable. Luo Binhua was preparing reports simply with his bare shoulders: "From the time the reports were submitted to the time they were approved, it took about 46 days, the shortest time for a project." The Guangzhou Nanhuaxi project and the Guangdong Baolihua project were also in progress, and only after doing three IPO projects in a row did Luo Binhua take leave from Dong Zhengqing: "I'm too tired and need a break."

After years of experience in investment banking, Luo Binhua and other investors growing up together have a similar view: "Having worked in the Investment Banking Department for so many years, I always think I am just its smallest potato, that is, an investment banking project manager." Speaking of the struggle, Luo Binhua could not hide his excitement: "The personal charm of leaders such as Dr. Chen, Dr. Ma, and General Manager Dong attracted a group of young people to develop our business in a wide world with our impetus, and finally GF investment banking gradually gained a firm foothold. A group of young people, except for the lack of time to rest, had no shortage of other things, and we were able to work tirelessly and with passion for entrepreneurship and a sense of responsibility. We didn't think about our pay and we just wanted to work for the company with a sense of accomplishment. We all relied on the spirit of 'eager beavers' to spread the seeds of GF Securities to all over the country and ensured that they take root in local areas. As a vanguard and model business, investment banking has laid the foundation for other businesses of GF Securities to go nationwide and make great achievements."

Improving efficiency by strengthening management

The book *Huawei Execution*, which attempts to decipher the secrets of Huawei's corporate management, documents Ren Zhengfei's thoughts on the contradictions between corporate scale and efficiency. Ren Zhengfei realized that a powerful measure to resolve these contradictions is to strengthen management, which is the only way to make the production and operation of the company more efficient and less costly. Good management can reasonably allocate the human, financial, and other resources of the company, and organize and mobilize the smallest input to get the biggest economic benefits.

As the investment banking of GF Securities gradually went nationwide, a shortage of hands, great workloads, heavy tasks, and mounting pressure became the norm of investment banking work. How to solve these outstanding tensions in real work became the primary concern of the investment banking managers who had long led the team in the frontline. While improving the investment banking operation mode and expanding the scale of investment banking, it was also necessary to improve efficiency and avoid the tendency of "emphasizing business but not management." This idea was already evident in the work summary of the Investment Banking Department in 1993, in which it was proposed that "internal management and external development should be given equal importance. We should not be reluctant to do things for corporate clients but not for internal employees."

In fact, in the rapidly expanding and unpredictable primary market, the enhanced internal management not only improved efficiency but also increased the invaluable awareness of decision-making risk in early investment banking.

In 1995, Changchun North China Wuhuan Co., Ltd. (hereinafter referred to as North China Wuhuan) received an issue quota from the State General Administration of Sports of China and was planning to go public. The GF Investment Banking Department was selected as the lead underwriter for North China Wuhuan after agreeing to provide a bridge financing. After working on the project for nearly two months, the project team found that it had more financial problems and false earnings projections. Ye Junying, Dong Zhengqing, and other members of the project team discussed the matter several times and concluded that there was a great risk. Ye Junying negotiated with the actual controller of North China Wuhuan to terminate the lead underwriter agreement, but North China Wuhuan did not agree. Ye Junying immediately called Dr. Chen Yunxian for instructions, and after hearing the report, Dr. Chen decided to withdraw from the project. After GF investment banking withdrew, North China Wuhuan found another underwriter and got listed. However, it was delisted soon after its share prices soared, causing quite negative impact to investors. In this project, although the staff of the Investment Banking Department worked for nothing for nearly two months, they were able to avoid the dangerous shoals that might affect the reputation of GF investment banking through professional judgment and decisive withdrawal.

As the saying goes, it takes a good blacksmith to forge good tools. In order to build a highly efficient executive team, Dong Zhengqing adopted three measures when he began to lead the Investment Banking Department: target management, full authorization, and clear rewards and punishments.

"Target management" is a management method to achieve business goals through employees' self-management by means of target setting and decomposition, target implementation, and inspection, reward and punishment of implementation.

According to Dong Zhengqing's requirements for implementing target management in investment banking, after confirming the target tasks, the project leader must complete the target decomposition and allocation, and based on this, work out a detailed and feasible plan and work progress schedule to master the pace of work progress and avoid blindness of work. In the work schedule, work progress should be determined based on a reasonable and feasible plan and according to the average time required for similar tasks in order to improve efficiency and reduce ineffective work. Care should be taken not to do anything without a clear goal, get busy but fruitless and ineffective, and stay disorderly.

"Fully authorization" is meant to mobilize the enthusiasm and creativity of employees and give them sufficient opportunities to work and grow. Veteran employees who have done investment banking have a deep feeling about this. When he did issuance projects, Luo Binhua was fully in charge of the project process as authorized by the department head, including staff assignment, program design, sales promotion, and order maintenance for payment. This management style was based on complete trust in subordinates.

Luo Binhua recalls that he was able to work and grow in the process of being independently in charge of projects, and that it was "very fulfilling" to help the company achieve its goals by coordinating all parties and solving problems.

"Clear rewards and punishments" means that people are measured strictly according to "what they have done and the results of what they have done," not according to "what they have said and how well they have said it." Qin Li recalls: "General Manager Dong was very clear in his thinking. The distribution was relatively fair without egalitarianism and commission. It was made sure that the enthusiasm of everyone for making the cake bigger is not affected because of the way the cake is divided. Everything was done to get things done." If the project was completed well, the bonus for the project team members would always be a surprise. Striving for fair and just rewards and punishments greatly enhanced the initiative of the staff for work.

These three measures for internal management can be said to be a summary of Dong Zhengqing's valuable experience in frontline command for many years. In a short span of ten years, Dong Zhengqing started as a basic-level GF investment banker and served as general manager, vice president, executive vice president and president of the Investment Banking Department. Looking back on Dong's investment banking career, he often surprised his colleagues with his skills and decisive and innovative moves, which attracted some criticism. However, as a company leader based on his business experience, Dong's thoughts on the frontline management of investment banking are quite valuable.

In 1993, in a 10,000-word report entitled "Building on the Past for Greater Success," Dong detailed to Dr. Chen Yunxian his management ideas and development goals for the Business Development Department. In 1994, in a "Request for Instructions on Certain Important Issues concerning the Establishment of the Investment Banking Department," he discussed his internal management ideas: "Efficiency first and hierarchical responsibility; unified deployment and clear rewards and penalties; being well versed in one area and pursuing comprehensive development; multiple assignments for each employee so that they each has his or her place; giving both demotions and promotions and ensuring that employees can be transferred to other jobs; achievement sharing and benefit sharing." This was agreed by Dr. Chen and Dr. Ma.

In 1996, when the internal and external environment of the Investment Banking Department changed significantly, Dong Zhengqing once again expressed his feelings about the management ideas and took the initiative to write a 8,000-word paper entitled "Management of the Investment Banking Department." Starting from the objectives, principles, and contents of management, the paper detailed personnel management, business management, decision control, risk prevention, and financial management, and even emphasized the value of information management and office automation.

In 1998, the Investment Banking Department took the lead in implementing the competition for management personnel, which became an innovative exploration of the management practice of GF Securities.

The constantly strengthened management mechanism ignited the enthusiasm of the investment banking staff. The exposure to different companies and industries through projects around the country also helped the investment bankers broaden their horizons and improve their knowledge. The stability of the middle-level staff and their courage to assume responsibility and the aggressiveness of the grassroots staff have made a difference in GF investment banking.

Humanistic investment banking

On July 24, 1997, the Investment Banking Department held the GF Securities 1997 Listed Company Seminar in Zhuhai, which was attended by more than 120 representatives of over 40 listed companies and experts and scholars. This created after-sales services by domestic primary market brokerage firms and marked the beginning of a new stage of formalization and regularization of GF Securities' after-sales services for listed companies.

During the seminar, a client said of GF Securities: "In the process of cooperation, we felt that GF Securities has strong talent advantages, and the 'PhD Legion' of GF Securities has not only quantitative advantages but also qualitative advantages, which is very familiar with business and has strong business ability.... Our restructuring process was extensive and there were many unforeseen difficulties and obstacles. Some of them were caused by laws and regulations and some were created by internal factors. When we encountered such a situation, GF Securities, whether it was the members of its project team or others, would have a very clear response immediately after a phone call back to their headquarters."

As capital market service providers, investment bankers must improve their professional services and become satisfied only after they help companies succeed, increased the profit of investors and the success of employees. But for intellectuals who have joined China's securities industry, these are not all the aspirations they had in the first place. Dr. Chen Yunxian and Dr. Ma Qingquan had deeper feelings about "making a contribution to society":

> One of the things I am proud of is the GF Hope Primary School in Yongchuan, Chongqing. When I was in the Investment Banking Department, I proposed that for every project we do in the future, we should set up a hope school where in the project is located. At that time, I also had an idea that I would be the headmaster of GF Hope School when we have more and more such schools in the future. We donated 300,000 yuan, which is not a big amount, to Yongchuan Hope Primary School, but the grandness of the donation site and the warm feelings of the school teachers are still very touching when I look back on it now.

It is a fond memory of Dr. Ma Qingquan, the first GF Securities leader in charge of the Investment Banking Department, to link "doing investment banking projects" with "building hope primary schools in the local areas." This is, perhaps, a unique sentiment of intellectuals in the investment banking world to serve their country.

The establishment of Hope Primary Schools was initiated by the Investment Banking Department, and since then it has become a public welfare tradition in which all of the departments of GF Securities. GF Securities' Fund Department financed Chunshui Hope Primary School in Guangning, Guangdong, and Beijing Jianhua South Road Brokerage Branch established two hope primary schools in Yongding District, Zhangjiajie and Wushi Town, Xiangtan, Hunan.

On May 31, 2000, the Hope Primary School donated by the Investment Banking Department to Ning County, a poor mountainous area in Gansu Province, was completed and its name was changed to "Ning County GF Hope Primary School." At the inauguration ceremony, Ms. Li Shuzhi, Vice President of the company, accepted the banner of "Love for education and the old revolutionary area" on behalf of the company. While expressing her gratitude, Ms. Li told the children that in the South of the country, there is a "PhD Legion" in GF Securities, which has many PhDs, masters, and bachelors. Li said that these people studied hard in the poor mountainous areas, and now they have left these areas and joined the business world. Li added that they are successful in their studies and careers, and they never forget to serve the country and make a contract to society.

The children gave wonderful performances, and Li Shuzhi gave them a smile and applause. Later, she wrote more of her feelings in an article and shared it in the company's internal magazine, *GF Securities Express*:

> To be honest, I watched the shows with a smile on my face and tears in my heart. A kind of shock that I had never had from other performances hit me straight to the heart: in front of me were innocent and lovely children singing and dancing, whereas behind me were the wheat fields with no harvest due to the drought. Under the blue sky, a poignant picture of fighting against poverty,

> fighting against disasters, and fighting against backwardness was fixed in my mind forever. What a tragedy! Where is hope? Hope grows in the green field; hope is placed in the new generation with knowledge.
>
> Loess has no water sources; peasants have to drive their donkeys to the mountains dozens of miles away to draw water. It is really "water is as expensive as oil." Seven or eight of us wash our hands with half a basin of water, and that is also considered a luxury thing to do. Standing in the yellow sand in the dusty Northwest, I thought of my fellow countrymen and women living by the South China Sea and of the Pearl River flowing day and night in front of our home. This made to realize that how rich we are. "We should not forget how we have prospered, and should make a contribution." What should and can the people who got rich first do for their compatriots in the poor and backward areas?

Around 2000, GF Securities donated 22 hope primary schools in Sichuan, Shaanxi, Shanxi, Fujian, Qinghai, Yunnan, and Guangdong. Public welfare undertakings became another evergreen cause that the Investment Banking Department and all GF Securities employees have been working hard to maintain.

Many years later, the Hollywood movie *The Wolf of Wall Street* showed the gobsmacking richness and extravagant life of American investment bankers. Probably in the eyes of some people, this is how the life of an investment banker should be, flying first class on business trips, living in five-star hotels, enjoying limousine service, wearing handmade suits, high-end ties, and brand-name shoes, and moving hundreds of millions of dollars of assets at will while laughing.

However, unlike most people's understanding of investment banking, extravagance is not what GF investment bankers work for. In the internal theatrical performances of GF Securities, GF investment bankers sang a song "Hardships of Investment Bankers," describing the life of investment bankers in its entirety:

> I thought investment banking life would really be great, but on day one I start with grassroots work. If all the drafts I made are lined up, they can go around the globe several times. I have to be well versed in accounting, law, and finance. Travelling by subway standing, I ask how many billions of yuan the deal will be worth. When the train arrives to my subway station, I say "excuse me" and feel I am privileged. What do investment bankers do this for? For our dreams.

The numerous "firsts" and "mosts" GF Securities created in the history of Chinese securities in the 1990s were the efforts and sweat of generations of GF investment bankers. The last listing gong in China's capital markets in the twentieth century was sounded by GF Securities' Fushun Special Steel project, and the first listing gong in the new century was sounded by GF Securities' Yantai Wanhua project. For GF's investment bankers who were heading for the whole country and the new century, these were precious and happy sounds.

Chapter IV: Acquisition and Expansion of GF Securities

Deciding on a problem requires wisdom and patience in its implementation.
—Homer

For securities investors, the red and green K-line image with overlapping ups and downs is an examination paper; for securities firms, the cyclical securities market is more like an examination paper with multiple meanings. The decision makers of securities firms need to make investment decisions according to market fluctuations, and also make decisions to enter, stay or withdraw according to the ebb and flow of the industry and the game of peers. The history of the securities industry in Europe and the United States over the past hundred years is a history of M&A and restructuring of securities firms.

In the 1990s, Chinese brokerage firms emerged in large numbers, and were then divided and restructured under the impact of several industry waves. A small number of brokerages survived the competition, while an even smaller number of brokerages seized the opportunities presented by the industry cycle to develop or expand when the market was not good. GF Securities, which has been sizing up the situation, has established its scale and experience advantages through many M&As in the early stage of its establishment, and has blazed its own path of knowledge-based development in the Chinese securities industry.

1. Dividing business based on developments and seeking intensive development in Guangdong

Seven core brokerage branches take the lead in development

Agent trading business has always been a very important source of income for securities companies. In the live trading model in the early stages of the industry, the number of brokerage branches meant cash flow and market share and represented the breadth and depth of the companies' access to customers. The establishment of brokerage branches were subject to strict approval by the regulatory authorities, and license resources were very valuable, so brokerage branches can be said to be the core competitiveness of securities companies in this period.

The First Business Department's Huanshizhong Brokerage Branch, the Second Business Department's Haizhu Square Brokerage Branch, the Third Business Department's Tianhe Road Brokerage Branch, as well as the brokerage branches newly established in 1993 in Shanghai, Beijing, Shenzhen, and Hainan were the core brokerage branches called by GF Securities people. Dr. Chen Yunxian, who helped establish these brokerage branches, still remembers the difficulties encountered in opening them.

In 1992, when the Huanshishong Brokerage Branch opened, it was autumn in Guangzhou, whereas at the opening ceremony of the Brokerage Branch on the first floor of Sanjian Building, No. 321 Huanshizhong Road, Guangzhou, it was a hot summer-like festive scene. Yi Zhenqiu, chairman of the Guangdong Provincial Reform Commission, Ding Lisong, executive vice chairman of Guangdong Development Bank, and other leaders were invited to deliver speeches at the opening ceremony, and together with many citizens, they witnessed on the spot the birth of the first securities branch in Guangzhou to open the business of off-site Shenzhen stock trading.

It was a latecomer, and the time was opportune. The Guangdong Development Bank Securities Department was established two to three years later than Guangdong Securities and Guangzhou Securities in the same city, but after just one year of establishment, it boldly set up a business office in a prime location in Guangzhou and successfully secured the "first bite" of the off-site securities trading business. For the establishment of the first branch, Dr. Chen and the Securities Department staff were busy for more than three months, spending their time on site decoration, computer installation, and dedicated line installation. All their efforts were made only to ensure that the Huanshizhong Brokerage Branch became the first in Guangzhou to open the business of off-site stock trading in a competition with its stronger rivals in the same city.

From the beginning of GF Securities, Dr. Chen had in mind that GF Securities was not a "local brokerage." After setting up its Guangzhou offices and achieving a good start, the Securities Department did not focus on the struggle with its local rivals in opening branches. With not much capital in hand, Dr. Chen set his sights on the forefront of China's capital markets, actively preparing to open business offices in Shanghai, Beijing, Shenzhen, and the newly established province of Hainan.

But to Dr. Chen's surprise, the regulatory authorities had a very different understanding of the function of "local securities institutions."

After opening the stock trading business of the Shenzhen Stock Exchange, Dr. Chen started to apply for the qualification of stock trading business of the Shanghai Stock Exchange as planned and prepared to set up a brokerage branch in Shanghai. However, the application was rejected by the Guangdong branch of the People's Bank of China on the grounds that "local securities institutions trading Shanghai stocks would drain Guangdong's capital to other places." Hearing such a reason, Dr. Chen Yunxian felt angry and dismissed it as absurd that it was already 1992 when the local regulators still distinguished between capital circulation in and outside Guangdong Province. But if he could break through this unreasonable confinement, it would mean that GF would take the lead in the competition with its local rivals.

So, Dr. Chen patiently communicated with the leaders of the Financial Management Division of the People's Bank of China, but the other side could not defeat Dr. Chen theoretically and simply avoided him, and every time Dr. Chen visited him, he would look for opportunities to avoid him. After several trips, Dr. Chen saw that the other party did not want to talk to him, so he left a note to the leader, the content of which was to the effect that "in the general environment of reform and opening up, Guangdong's finance is lagging behind to such an extent that if you do not really use the thinking of reform and opening up to promote the relevant policies in this area, in the future, you will become an obstacle to Guangdong's financial reform." The bookish Dr. Chen wrote down his name and work unit at the end of the note, put it directly on the desk of the leader of the Financial Management Division, turned around and left.

After Dr. Chen left, the leader returned to the office, saw the note and did not get angry, but commented on the note, "This is the opinion written by Dr. Chen Yunxian of the Securities Department of Guangdong Development Bank. I hope all in my division will discuss it." The leader deliberately marked out the title of Dr. Chen Yunxian.

Afterwards, Dr. Chen learned that the leader of the Financial Management Division was a veteran college student graduated from Renmin University of China and that it was not true that "he did not know what he was doing" but in fact, he could not but had done what he had done for the sake of government policy. As a market regulator, there was still a debate within the PBOC on whether there were boundaries for funds in the market, which also reflects the conflict between the management model at that time and the exploration of reform and opening up. However, as a practitioner in the market, GF did not have the excuse to stay conservative. Dr. Chen persistently broke through the resistance and finally obtained the qualification of stock trading business in the Shanghai Stock Exchange.

GF Securities' successful entry into Shanghai also left a beautiful story in the high-level exchange of reform and opening up between Guangdong and Shanghai unexpectedly.

In March 1993, when the sessions of the National People's Congress and the CPPCC National Committee were held in Beijing, the Shanghai delegation said that Guangdong was at the forefront of reform and opening up and had advanced in development, but it had never come to Shanghai to guide its work and for exchange purposes. Zhu Lin, governor of Guangdong Province, was a native of Shanghai, and in the face of the Shanghai delegation's "call by name" at the sessions, he immediately made a statement of "learning from the people of Shanghai."

In preparation for the exchange in Shanghai, Guangdong Province tried to find out whether the province had financial institutions doing business in Shanghai, and found that the Guangdong Development Bank Securities Department had stationed traders in the Shanghai Stock Exchange, and was preparing to establish its Shanghai Brokerage Branch. So, after the two sessions, Guangdong Development Bank President Wu Chixin and General Manager of the Securities Department Chen Yunxian were immediately recruited into the Guangdong delegation and accompanied Governor Zhu Lin to Shanghai for a study tour.

When the Guangdong delegation arrived at the Shanghai Stock Exchange, Governor Zhu Lin and his entourage paid a visit with the company of Wei Wenyuan, general manager of the Shanghai Stock Exchange. During trading hours, the busy hall of the Shanghai Stock Exchange was filled with traders from various financial institutions, who were methodically tapping on the keyboard, or answering the phone, or staring at the ever-changing securities market display in-between, and the atmosphere was tense and orderly. Governor Zhu suggested that he would like to see the traders of GF. But in the face of the crowded traders, even the accompanying Dr. Chen Yunxian could not identify which seat was GF's. Seeing this, Wei Wenyuan suddenly shouted, "Where is the trader of GF?" The noisy trading floor was suddenly quiet, and everyone stopped what they were doing and stood up to see what was going on. Hearing the shout, Su Yingbiao and Li Weixiong, the representatives of GF, waved their hands vigorously in the crowd, immediately attracting the attention of the Guangdong delegation. Governor Zhu Lin quickly walked toward GF's seats to shake hands with them, and reporters at the scene also swarmed to surround GF's traders and Governor Zhu, and even squeezed Dr. Chen Yunxian out of the crowd. The flashing lights recorded this vivid historical moment, and several years later, securities veterans who had witnessed this moment laughed about it, saying that Wei Wenyuan's shout brought the stock market to a halt for a minute.

In June 1993, GF Securities' Shanghai Brokerage Branch opened, with Su Yingbiao as its first leader; in August, the Guangzhou Tianhe Road Brokerage Branch was established with Zhao Guiping as its first leader; in September, the

Shenzhen Brokerage Branch started its trial operation with Kang Guohong as its first leader; and in October, the Hainan Brokerage Branch opened with Zhang Hongyi as its first leader. At the end of the year, Dr. Chen Yunxian returned to Beijing, the capital where he studied for three years, to witness the birth of GF's seventh brokerage branch.

On December 28, 1993, in the middle of winter, the entrance to Building 6, Hepingli West Street, Chaoyang District, Beijing, was filled with flower baskets to congratulate the opening ceremony, and Dr. Chen Yunxian and Qu Nianzeng, the first head of the Beijing Brokerage Branch, were busy greeting the guests. Dr. Chen's heart was warmed by the fact that this mentor, Mr. Xiao Zhuoji, as well as economist Mr. Han Zhiguo and Guangdong Development Bank consultant Mr. Qiu Yongyi were invited to the opening ceremony. To Dr. Chen's great surprise, thanks to the good office of his colleagues in the Beijing Office of Guangdong Development Bank, Mr. Liu Hongru, chairman of the CSRC, was also invited to the opening ceremony. Chairman Liu Hongru had a casual demeanor, but Dr. Chen felt the "disparity in status," and he accompanied Chairman Liu with anxiety until the end of the ceremony.

The opening ceremony of the Beijing Brokerage Branch welcomed leaders of regulatory authorities and famous scholars to present their congratulations, which made the company's employees feel proud and also caused good reactions in society and media. The scholars and media reporters who knew Dr. Chen Yunxian laughed and said, "Dr. Chen Yunxian, who went to Guangdong, has made his way back to Beijing."

It is imperative for companies to seize strategically important places. The five brokerage branches established in 1993, together with the previous Guangzhou Huanshizhong Brokerage Branch (with Chen Chunming in charge) and Haizhu Square Brokerage Branch (with Zhang Min in charge)—these seven core brokerage branches became the "starting point" for GF's layout in China's securities industry. The start was remarkable; it not only brought more stable customers and cash flow for Guangdong GF Securities Company, which was newly born at the end of 1993, but also helped it quickly become strategically important in terms of capital flow, information flow, and talent flow in China's capital markets.

The Huatai Hotel Meeting on the eve of the establishment of the company

In 1993, the headquarters of GF Securities was moved from Guangdong Province Material Building Guest House to the ninth floor of Huashan Hotel on Huanshidong Road, and then to the sixteenth floor of Huatai Hotel on Xianlienan Road. The interior of the office space was relatively simple, with a 60-centimeter-wide bronze plaque hanging next to the yellow wood-grained door in the aisle of the floor, inscribed with the eight traditional characters for "Guangdong GF Securities Company," indicating that this was the headquarters of the securities company, which had seven brokerage branches and more than 200 employees in those days. In contrast, the outdoor signboard hanging from the roof of the building is particularly eye-catching. When night fell, the three-meter-high signboard lit up with golden lights, and the dignified six Chinese characters for "GF Securities Company" brightened the sky, attracting the attention of traffic and pedestrians on Xianlienan Road and the Quzhuang Flyover.

Xianlienan Road is rich in history, and many terms that shine in China's modern history can be seen everywhere on the road signs. This seems to be a marvelous place for business. Three years later, when the headquarters of GF Securities moved out from here, it was already ranked among the top ten brokerages in China, with more than 1,000 employees and net assets increasing from 28 million yuan to 1.214 billion yuan. Correspondingly, the brokerage branches of GF Securities surged to 37 in three years, quickly ranking among the top in the industry.

New brokerage branches increased rapidly, but they were not mainly set up by Guangdong GF Securities Company itself; they were acquired in the context of separation China's banking and securities. This represented a successful merger and acquisition of the securities business within Guangdong Development Bank. Before 1993, "the brokerage branches of Guangdong Development Bank's Securities Department" and "the securities brokerage branches of Guangdong Development Bank's branches" were two concepts that could easily be confused by outsiders, but on December 30, 1993, with the arrival of a document, the two concepts gradually became one.

For GF Securities, the Yinfu [1993] No. 432 document of the People's Bank of China, which was finally issued at the end of 1993 after nearly two years of waiting, was significant at least on two levels. First, Guangdong GF Securities Company was established on the basis of the former Securities Department, which became a professional securities company;[1] second, the document stipulated that, "In accordance with the principle of separating banking and securities, the Head Office and branches of Guangdong Development Bank will no longer operate securities business, and its existing securities departments will be under the management of Guangdong GF Securities Company."

Established in 1988, Guangdong Development Bank's early operations were limited to Guangdong Province, with branches set up in various prefecture-level cities in the province and a portion of its equity funded by the local governments. This shareholding structure was conducive to the expansion of capital scale and facilitation of development for the early branches, but it also resulted in excessive autonomy in the operation of local branches, and the management of the Head Office was susceptible to interference by local factors.

Specifically for securities business, the Head Office of Guangdong Development Bank established a securities department in 1991, and local

1 For more details, see Chapter I of this book, "He Comes from Peking University."

branches set up their own securities brokerage branches and securities representative offices from 1991 to 1993. The Securities Department of the Head Office was hardly "managing" the securities businesses of the local branches, but it was in essence a "cooperative" relationship. In this relationship, the prefecture-level cities in Guangdong Province, except Guangzhou and Shenzhen, were actually regions inaccessible to the Head Office Securities Department. Because of the lack of unified management, the level of development of securities business in each branch was also very uneven, and irregular business practices under the mixed banking and securities model began to appear in some branches.

At the end of December 1993, after Dr. Chen had completed the layout of seven core brokerage branches, the PBOC's Yinfu [1993] No. 432 document gave Guangdong GF Securities an easterly breeze of policy for its development goal of "being based in Guangdong." One month before the issuance of this document, at its Third Plenary Session, the fourteenth CPC Central Committee adopted the Decision of the CPC Central Committee on Several Issues concerning the Establishment of a Socialist Market Economy, which became the masterplan for the establishment of a socialist market economy in China. When it comes to "accelerating financial reforms," the Decision stated that "the banking industry and the securities industry should be managed separately." In order to implement this decision and ensure that finance plays a better role in exercising macro-control and improving resource allocation in the economy, the Decision of the State Council on Financial Reforms in December 1993 further stipulated that "state-owned commercial banks will be delinked from the insurance, trust and securities industries in terms of personnel, finance and materials, and these industries will operate separately."

However, these policies did not necessarily mean that everything was successful; on the contrary, painstaking, pioneering efforts still needed to be made in the reform process, and with every single progress, came hard work. In early 1994, Dr. Chen was faced with the People's Bank of China's request for the separation of the banking and securities industries. On the other hand, there were doubts and even resistance from local branches about the policy of banking and securities separation. Being under the same roof of Guangdong Development Bank, Dr. Chen knew the operation of each branch well. The branches with better securities business naturally regarded their brokerage branches highly and were unwilling to give them up; the branches with poor securities business and even those that had invested more real money wanted to make up for the loss.

After the issuance of Yinfu [1993] No. 432 document and before the overall resistance of dozens of branches, Dr. Chen was determined to seize an opportunity to further "leverage" the situation and seek to "set the tone" for the separation of banking and securities in the banking system. This opportunity was the Securities Conference held every spring in the Guangdong Development Bank system and attended by the heads of all branches.

The 1994 Guangdong Development Bank Securities Conference, which was initially scheduled for the end of February, was eventually postponed by a full month. This was because the meeting was linked to the formal establishment of Guangdong GF Securities Company, and there was still a controversy within Guangdong Development Bank as to what system should be used for Guangdong GF Securities Company. Some people proposed to "establish the company first, and then straighten the relationship," suggesting to postpone the work of unifying the equity. However, Dr. Chen insisted that this would lead GF Securities to follow the old path of Guangdong Development Bank, and the subsequent unification of equity would be extremely difficult. This view was finally approved by the leaders of Guangdong Development Bank and People's Bank of China. The meeting was held at Huatai Hotel, South Xianlie Road, the new headquarters of GF Securities.

As the meeting was approaching, Dr. Chen carefully prepared his presentation materials. In the previous year's Guangdong Development Bank Securities Business Conference, Dr. Chen Yunxian's report on investment banking was closely related to the business plan and was relatively concise and practical. On March 27, 1994, at the Huatai Hotel Conference, Dr. Chen presented a long 10,000-word report titled "Separating the Management of Banking and Securities to Develop GF."

Delivered to the leaders of the supervisory department, the leaders of the Head Office, and the managers of the securities departments of each branch, Dr. Chen's report fully reflected the thinking of "taking advantage of the situation." Starting from "business," the report emphasized that "the businesses of Guangdong Development Bank and GF Securities Company are businesses in line with the trend of the development of market economy." It also analyzed from three perspectives why the management of securities and banking should be separated. Although the focus was on taking advantage of the situation, Dr. Chen did not rigidly "convey the guiding principles from the document of the People's Bank of China," but started from the two major development trends of commercial banks in the world and from the difference between investment banking in the narrow and broad senses, and compared the development trends of J.P. Morgan and Morgan Stanley, as well as Deutsche Bank, Merrill Lynch, Nomura Securities, and a series of other financial giants with those of GF. The first half of the report was more like for high-level professional theoretical training.

The second half of the report moved on to "how to view the current GF Securities team" and "concrete steps for GF Securities to implement management." These contents were related to the system and management of Guangdong GF Securities Company, but also to the most important issues of personal interest. Dr. Chen stated candidly:

> On the issue of straightening out the relationship of the securities business of each branch and bringing it under the unified leadership of the Head Office's securities company, there is also a dilemma: the branches may not be

willing to give up their business to unified leadership and may have various disagreements. To be honest, we have also had our own considerations. Up until now, GF Securities business has developed more or less successfully. Originally it planned to take this year as a year of benefits to provide better benefits to the Head Office. This will make it possible for us not only to report good news but also take a break. However, we cannot do that anymore as the historical task of "exercising unified management of the securities business of all the branches" has objectively fallen on our shoulders. Undertaking this heavy responsibility has both advantages and disadvantages.

The advantages are that we can form a larger scale and gain stronger strength, and we can also use local advantages in the counties and cities in Guangdong to unify our business. The disadvantages are that this management is bound to be accompanied by certain risks, as long as one branch has problems, it will affect the brand and reputation of GF Securities; and moreover, after each branch securities institution passes the capital verification, part of the capital will be incorporated into the capital of GF Securities Company, and the rest will be transformed into working capital, enjoying the same authority of benefit distribution as the Head Office. For the more efficient branches, we will try to protect their earnings, which is not a problem, but for the less efficient branches, the part of the funds allocated to the company as capital will also have to receive the same benefits from the company. If we get it wrong, it is likely to become a burden on the securities business of the entire bank.

But objectivity does not allow us to think more for ourselves, and unified management is indispensable. We must formally establish GF Securities Company with the support of the People's Bank to carry on GF's securities business.

Before Dr. Chen's speech, copies of the Certain Decisions Guangdong GF Securities Company on the Establishment and Management of Branches (Draft) had been distributed to the participants, with a preliminary management plan in terms of human, financial, and material systems. The discussion of the three-day meeting was very heated, and everyone expressed their views on the way branch leaderships would be created, margin management, and staff stability. Dr. Chen carefully categorized the questions raised by the other participants and answered more than 20 questions in four categories one by one in an open and honest manner.

President Wu Chixin, who had just returned from a study tour of the securities industry abroad, attended the meeting. He strongly agreed with Dr. Chen's series of views on "developing GF's business," and in his speech and group discussion, Governor Wu pointed out in a clear voice:

When we consider our own development and growth, we should stand higher, think farther and expand our mind. We can no longer be like the early reform period during which we only talked about opening up and invigoration, without talking about modern operation... We must reach a standardized

> management through the formation of the securities company, so that our business management reaches a high level... Now we will see whether we are using the small peasant economy vision to develop rural-urban credit cooperatives, or truly use an international perspective to expand our GF securities business.

Responding to some branch representatives stating that "we do not want to have our securities business brought under unified management," Governor Wu stated categorically that:

> Those who are unwilling to be brought under unified management have two options, either to change their brands, or to do less business.... Now that we have we set the principle of unified management, under this premise, for how to manage and operate our business, we can say whatever we want. But we'd better not say we do not want unified management.

Many years later, mentioning this meeting, Dr. Chen said with emotion, the mergers of the brokerage branches of the branches were made possible thanks to the support of Boss Wu.

At the end of the three-day meeting, the representatives of several branches expressed their views and suggestions from their own perspectives, and basically reached a consensus on the understanding of "integrating securities business into the system of Guangdong GF Securities Company."

The last item on the agenda of the meeting was the celebration of the establishment of Guangdong GF Securities Company. Dr. Chen delivered a speech in formal attire with great vigor and calmness.

For the securities business of the whole Guangdong Development Bank, this meeting was a watershed; for the new Guangdong GF Securities Company, it was a meeting of victory similar to Mao Zedong's Red Army reorganization meeting at Sanwan.

Absorbing the brokerage branches of Guangdong Development Bank

To promote the implementation of the policy of separating banking and securities was to "take advantage of the situation"; to hold a Guangdong Development Bank meeting to clarify the industry trend to branches was to "clarify the way"; to absorb the 19 branch brokerage branches afterwards was to test the wisdom and courage.

After the securities business conference, Guangdong GF Securities Company issued the Certain Decisions of Guangdong GF Securities Company on the Establishment and Management of Branches to all Guangdong Development Bank branches and began the takeover work in earnest. Although there was the policy background of the People's Bank of China for separating banking and securities and the support from the Head Office of Guangdong Development Bank, in the specific absorption process, due to the equity issue of each branch's securities brokerage branches, it was still necessary to follow the law of market value in order to achieve a smooth merger between the two sides. Therefore, GF Securities negotiated with one branch after another, as well as the shareholders and government departments behind them.

Based on the observations made during the discussion at the securities business working conference, Dr. Chen categorized the branches in different situations. First, branches with a good securities business that had opened a stock agency business with the Shenzhen Stock Exchange or the Shanghai Stock Exchange; second, branches that did not have a stock business but had launched a bond business; and third, branches that did not have a securities business. Among the branches that had opened stock business, not many of them were large and efficient, and had set up separate accounts for margin positions and savings funds. The Shaoguan and Zhaoqing branches had mixed operation of margin and savings funds, while the Dongguan Qingyuan branches had just opened their stock business not long before without significant benefits.

For the excellent management personnel who had emerged from the branches' securities business, such as the Huizhou branch's Li Shuiquan, the Dongguan branch's Luo Peiqiang, the Zhaoqing branch's Cui Xia, the Foshan branch's Li Shurong, the Shaoguan branch's Li Hong, and the Zhuhai branch's Liang Linzhu, Dr. Chen gave extra attention. He believed these officials were smart, capable, and responsible, and were well connected locally for the company's business development in Guangdong's prefecture-level cities.

However, these excellent branch talents in Dr. Chen's mind had different feelings and different observation perspectives about their being brought under unified management. Li Shuiquan, who was the manager of the Securities Department of the Huizhou branch at that time, was impressed by this experience:

> At that time, Dr. Chen Yunxian was very shrewd.... In order to smoothly acquire the branches' securities departments, he adopted two different sets of tactics. For the Head Office, he implemented the technique of leveraging the situation, that is, he used the pretext that the central government would launch the policy of separating banking and securities to convince the bank leaders to transfer the securities departments of its branches to GF Securities; for the securities departments of these branches, he used the tactic of letting them off first in order to capturing them later: he pretended that he did not want them, but he had to take them over as he was told to the decision of the Head Office. In addition, in the staffing and management, he implemented a step-by-step approach. This move really worked: the acquisition of 19 security departments were acquired and integrated without any deviation.

In order to promote the acquisition and unified management of the branches' securities departments, Guangdong GF Securities Company established the Institutional Management Department, and the first person in charge was Chen Wenzhan from the Personnel Department of the Head Office of Guangdong Development Bank. The first and foremost task of the newly established department was to go to each branch's securities department to conduct asset assessment and exchange views with local leaders in order to get as much information and understanding as possible. Chen Wenzhan's research results were basically the same as Dr. Chen's prediction: a few branches with good business performance were reluctant to hand over their securities business and their demand was excessive; branches with poor securities performance were willing to be merged, but in fact they were "hot potatoes," and needed Guangdong GF Securities Company to take over their original losses; and most branches' securities departments had a mono business model and were not very profitable.

Subsequently, GF Securities hired Guangdong Asset Appraisal Company to evaluate the assets of the branches' securities departments, calculated the salvage value and net value of various fixed assets according to the financial accounting method, drafted the acquisition agreements on this basis, and then negotiated based on the specific conditions of each branch. It finally acquired them only when conditions were ripe.

In August 1994, GF Securities and Guangdong Development Bank's Jiangmen and Foshan branches signed agreements on the transfer of securities departments, and they became the first two branches' departments to be absorbed. By the end of that year, the transfer of securities departments of the Zhuhai and Zhanjiang branches was also completed.

In order to ensure the smooth implementation of the absorption work, Guangdong Development Bank further issued a document stipulating that branches, offices, and relevant departments of the Head Office must not change the business personnel of the existing securities departments, especially those in charge of the securities departments, finance, and computers, without the consent of GF Securities. The document said that those key securities personnel who were eligible for housing allocation should be temporarily allocated housing by their respective branches and that the existing equipment and business sites of the securities departments of the branches must remain unchanged.

With the support of the Head Office, GF Securities carried out a lot of meticulous work in accordance with market-oriented means. For the repeated sudden price increases by the branches, Dr. Chen and the management of GF Securities made specific studies and judgments, and did not dwell too much on details, reflecting their ability to keep the big picture in mind. One of the most popular stories is the story of "taking over the Securities Department of the Zhaoqing branch with a price increase of 800,000 yuan."

The Securities Department of the Zhaoqing branch was one of the most profitable departments of a branch at that time. Cui Xia, the business manager of the department, was famous in the securities system. With her daring business impetus, she expanded securities business in the less economically developed areas of Zhaoqing and Yunfu, and led her colleagues to attract a large number of customers and achieved a high conversion rate of her consumers' savings deposits to margin. In 1995, entering the negotiation stage for acquiring the Zhaoqing branch's Securities Department, Dr. Chen specially dispatched Wang Hongmao to Zhaoqing to talk to Cui Xia, hoping she would join GF Securities. But when it came his department with excellent performance and his key staff member, the Zhaoqing branch's president expressed firm opposition, trying to persuade Cui Xia to simply go back to the branch. In the final stage of negotiations, the Zhaoqing Branch demanded "an additional 800,000 yuan" on the basis of the total assets of its Securities Department, which was undoubtedly sheer robbery.

In 1995, the securities industry was in a bear market, and GF Securities had a very difficult time, and the sudden increase of 800,000 yuan was equivalent to several months' profit of a profitable brokerage branch at that time. Some people in the company could not accept the unreasonable offer of the Zhaoqing branch, but Dr. Chen was very courageous, he said, "We should try our best and pay 800,000 yuan; Cui Xia is worth it."

The facts proved Dr. Chen's vision was right; Cui Xia said, "After joining GF Securities, I heard how I joined GF Securities. To save Dr. Chen's face, I worked hard." In many years, the economic efficiency of the Zhaoqing Brokerage Branch ranked in the forefront of all branches of GF Securities and became a star brokerage branch known inside and outside Guangdong Province. Cui Xia, who was inspired to develop a strong career spirit, became one of the "five golden flowers" of GF's brokerage business. She served as the general manager of the Zhaoqing Brokerage Branch, general manager of the Guangzhou branch of GF Securities, assistant to the president of GF Securities, and chairperson of the GF Securities Trade Union, and devoted her youth to GF Securities.

On May 10, 1995, the Commercial Bank Law of the People's Republic of China was promulgated and came into effect on July 1 of that year. Article 43 of this law stipulates that, "Commercial banks shall not engage in trust investment and stock business in the territory of the People's Republic of China." This established by law the financial model of separation of the banking industry from the trust and securities industries in China. At this time, GF Securities, which had worked to separate banking and securities early, had already signed agreements with 15 branches to transfer their securities trading offices.

On May 30, 1997, with the signing of the agreement between the Taishan branch and GF Securities, all 19 securities departments of Guangdong Development Bank were handed over, and the separation of banking and securities between GF Securities and Guangdong Development Bank finally came to a successful conclusion after more than three years.

GF Securities leveraged this development for a rise. The 19 brokerage branches were gradually taken over, so GF Securities significantly enhanced its network scale and capital strength, becoming one of the top ten brokerage firms in China early. Established early in Guangdong, the Shaoguan Brokerage Branch, the Zhongshan Brokerage Branch, and the Meizhou Brokerage Branch were the first brokerage branches in the prefecture-level cities and had established a significant advantage for GF Securities to develop in Guangdong and obtain local high-quality customer resources.

2. Responding to the first wave of impact

In 1995, when Cui Xia and a group of key personnel of the branch Guangdong Development Bank chose securities, some of her colleagues and subordinates chose to return to the bank because they "did not see the prospect of securities industry." In fact, there were not a few such cases, and individual branches even threw their "problematic" employees as a burden to Guangdong GF Securities Company when they handed over their securities departments.

The mindset of the employees was a reflection of the industry at that time. In that year, the Chinese securities industry, with 97 securities firms, was shrouded in the gloom of a market downturn.

Around 1995, the brokerage industry, which earlier had had a strong impulse to survive and expand, suffered a severe market impact while the policy of separating banking and securities catalyzed M&A restructuring. Culminating in the "327 Bond Futures Incident" in 1995, individual leading brokerages collapsed or underwent policy-based restructuring, while some companies did not collapse but experienced operational difficulties. Dr. Chen Yunxian later referred to this period as "the first wave of impact on the brokerage industry."

The industry's first market-based M&A

The contradictory opposites of business expansion and prudent restraint in management decisions have been with GF Securities since its inception, forming a standardized management practice that leads the industry. In a depressed industry atmosphere, the value of standardized management to GF Securities began to emerge.

In January 1995, Dr. Chen put forward three concise priorities for the annual work: "revitalizing capital," "strengthening management," and "moderate development." As for "moderate development," in addition to developing new products and international business, GF Securities needed to increase a number of business outlets. A plan for expansion was implemented in a sluggish market in secret.

This year, signs of the economy ebbing from rapid development were appearing in several industries and cities in China, and Hainan Province, which experienced the bursting of the real estate bubble, was becoming a sad place for many real estate companies, financial firms, and speculators. As one of GF Securities' top staff members in developing the Hainan market, Dr. Zhang Hongyi had spent three years in Hainan.

In 1993 the Hainan Brokerage Branch in Yilong Road, in Haikou, had a business area of 422 square meters. In the speculative atmosphere at the time, the general manager of the Brokerage Branch Dr. Zhang Hongyi and his colleagues took this land as a base for hard work.

The staff dormitory of the Hainan Brokerage Branch was a dilapidated bungalow in Haifu Road, Haikou. Due to the remote location, the dormitory was robbed by gangsters. At that time, a demobilized serviceman employee wanted to rush out to subdue the robbers. Just he opened the door, he was hit on the head. Afterwards, although the brokerage branch reported the incident to the police, they still failed to recover the staff's belongings. This incident caused a great blow to the staff from other parts of China who had created the brokerage branch. Coupled with the initial operational difficulties, everyone's mood was inevitably low. In order to boost morale, Dr. Zhang Hongyi organized an activity to strengthen the organization of the Communist Youth League of China. He led his colleagues to plant three banyan saplings in Wanlü Garden in Haikou, expressing GF Securities' determination to take root in Hainan and persevere in the face of adversity. These three banyan trees have since grown into deep-rooted trees that have become the mental support of GF Securities employees in Hainan.

At the end of 1995, Dr. Zhang Hongyi heard news from the industry: Zhejiang Securities' Haidian Island Brokerage Branch in the north of Haikou was not operating well and suffering business losses. Zhejiang Securities wanted to give up the brokerage branch. Dr. Zhang Hongyi was keenly aware this was an opportunity, and immediately reported it to the headquarters, suggesting that the company fund the acquisition. But in the face of the long bear market and the local economic situation in Hainan, GF Securities was divided over the acquisition.

In this year, GF Securities' Hainan Brokerage Branch had just turned around, and at this time Hainan Province had 33 brokerage branches, with 30 in Haikou alone, so the network density ranked in the forefront of the country. The city of Haikou only had a population of a little more than 500,000 people, the number of stockholders was limited, the secondary market was too small, and securities institutions in the bear market in general were operating with difficulties. In order to gather popularity and increase income, the Hainan Brokerage Branch of GF Securities even turned the VIP trading lounge on the second floor of its building into a karaoke hall and a dance hall at night, and invited singers and professionals from Beijing to take care of it. The "first wave of impact" in Haikou, where the sound of waves can be heard all year round, seemed to be particularly violent.

In such a situation, acquiring a brokerage branch inevitably met internal opposition in the company. Dr. Zhang Hongyi insisted that "the bear market will always go away. What others do not want is just what we want. A successful acquisition will also greatly enhance the strength of GF Securities in Hainan."

His view was supported by Dr. Chen Yunxian. With the prediction of the market cycle, Dr. Chen believed that this was indeed a good opportunity for a low-cost acquisition of business offices. He then arranged for Dr. Fang Jiachun, who had just joined GF Securities, to take charge of the acquisition project.

In order to understand the situation on the spot, Dr. Fang flew to Hainan immediately with Zhao Guiping and other key personnel. Together with Zhang Hongyi, they investigated the situation. After evaluation, the project team found that the loss of Zhejiang Securities' Haidian Island Brokerage Branch was not too serious, and this was the only brokerage branch on Haidian Island at that time and had certain geographical advantages. In addition, the brokerage branch had some real estate properties to sell at low prices.

In accordance with market principles, the project team of GF Securities had formal communication with Zhejiang Securities. For Zhejiang Securities, which was eager to get rid of its burden, the lower purchase price offered by GF Securities was not so difficult to accept. After several negotiations, the two sides finally reached an agreement on the intention to entirely transfer to GF Securities Zhejiang Securities' Haidian Island Brokerage Branch, including the relevant properties for more than 10 million yuan. GF Securities soon submitted a request for acquisition to the People's Bank of China Hainan Branch.

After the New Year's day in 1996, GF Securities' Haikou Yilong Road Brokerage Branch sent the acquisition team into the Haidian Island Brokerage Branch. According to Ding Chengkun, a member of the acquisition team who was in charge of financial work at that time, the acquisition was unexpectedly fast and smooth. The other side actively cooperated with GF Securities in providing accounts, balance sheets, and customer information.

According to the negotiation between the two sides, as long as the personnel of the former Haidian Island Brokerage Branch were willing to stay, GF Securities would accept them. At the beginning, the employees of the former Haidian Island Brokerage Branch felt confused and uneasy about entering GF Securities, so Dr. Zhang Hongyi called a meeting to explain the development prospects of GF Securities and the management and culture of the company, which soon settled their mind.

What is particularly worth mentioning is that, in order to establish the image of GF Securities as a "strong and reputable" company among Hainan shareholders, the acquisition project team also invested resources and made full use of local newspapers, TV stations, and other public opinion tools to publicize the acquisition in a high profile. At the end of March 1995, *Hainan Daily*, the local mainstream newspaper, published a full-page article about GF Securities' acquisition of Zhejiang Securities' Haidian Island Brokerage Branch. On the top of the page was a bold headline, "Buying Cheap and Selling High Means That There Is No Such Thing That the Bear Market Has No End." In the middle of the page, the Logo of GF Securities was printed with red ink. This is like a torch in the mist, announcing GF Securities' distinctive attitude toward the market trend and industry trend, which became a unique viewpoint in the industry at that time.

On March 18, 1996, the Haidian Island Brokerage Branch of Zhejiang Securities was renamed as the Haikou Haidian Island Brokerage Branch of Guangdong GF Securities and was officially opened for business. That morning, everyone at the entrance to the Brokerage Branch was ready to take a group photo. While Yilong Road Brokerage Branch employees had posed for the picture, some female employees of the original Zhejiang Securities seemed to be a bit shy, remaining on the sidelines watching. When Dr. Zhang Hongyi saw this, he immediately called them to come over and they all stood in front of the steps, glowing and smiling, leaving a group photo of the employees of the two brokerage branches of GF Securities in Hainan. Under the banyan trees at Wanxiangyuan in Haikou, there have been more GF people since then.

Three months after the completion of the acquisition, with the arrival of a new round of an improved market and the end of the long bear market, the Haidian Island Brokerage Branch made its first profit after the opening, and in that year created a net profit of four million yuan. It was not long before it recovered the merger costs and entered a positive track of performance.

What is more symbolic is that, GF Securities' acquisition of Zhejiang Securities' Haidian Island Brokerage Branch did not follow the common "government-led" models of M&A in China's securities industry, such as administrative takeover, bank refinancing, policy injection, and insurance fund restructuring. Occurring in late 1995 to early 1996, the acquisition was the first case of China's brokerage firms using market-based means for the M&A of business offices, creating a "market-led" model for the first time.

"Buying cheap and selling high" is the ancient business wisdom recorded by Sima Qian more than 2,000 years ago in his *Economic Commentary Records of the Grand Historian*. Making decisive decisions based on rational judgment to achieve low-cost expansion by market-based means has become the core strategy of GF Securities in many M&As since then.

Another valuable gain of the Hainan acquisition project was that GF Securities, which had already steadily dominated the Guangdong market, found a new path to march into the whole country. At that time, in Beijing, the capital city, a large-scale acquisition that GF Securities had not experienced before was already underway.

Participation in the acquisition of BOC Trust

On October 5, 1995, the People's Bank of China issued the Decision on Taking Over BOC Trust and Investment Company, announcing the takeover of BOC Trust and Investment Company. This was the first such case in the 46-

year financial history of the People's Republic of China. The serious problems of irregular operation and insolvency of BOC Trust gradually surfaced.

The BOC Trust and Investment Company, established in 1988, had a very well-connected shareholder. At the beginning, BOC Trust was created based the United States mixed business model. Its organizational structure included banking, trust, securities, industry, and real estate and it has business outlets throughout China. It almost amounted to a full license "financial supermarket." However, such a Chinese trust giant collapsed after its head Yang Xiufang's case of cashing in on treasury bonds broke out. According to information, in 1995, the assets and liabilities of BOC Trust and Investment Company amounted to four billion yuan and there was a huge backlog of overdue loans.

The PBOC handled this incident with particular caution to ensure overall financial stability. In view of the serious fact that BOC Trust was insolvent at that time, it was no longer practical to restore normal operation by improving management and making additional investments. It was relatively feasible for a commercial bank with good asset quality to merge and acquire BOC Trust and take over its debts and liabilities. Guangdong Development Bank caught the attention of the decision-making leadership. Located at the forefront of reform and opening up, Guangdong Development Bank had been playing a good role as a "local economic booster" since its establishment, and had been branded as a "local commercial bank" for a long period of time due to various factors. In 1995, after integrating its shareholding and legal entity, Guangdong Development Bank was eager to move beyond Guangdong and expand its scope of development. By acquiring BOC Trust, Guangdong Development Bank could contribute to the resolution of financial risks and stabilization of public order, and would thus gain the opportunity to move from a local to a national bank.

In order to accomplish this task, which concerned the future of Guangdong Development Bank, Chairman Wu Chixin named the person in charge of the acquisition internally. Based on great trust and recognition, he first selected Dr. Chen Yunxian, who was also the assistant to the bank's president at that time.

Around the Chinese New Year in 1996, when the spring cold invaded his bones, Dr. Chen spent three months in Beijing in a closed office. Faced with a large amount of information research and complicated coordination work for the BOC Trust project, he only had four assistants to help him with business, accounting, legal, and general affairs. Without the knowledge of the other employees of GF Securities, the five-member team worked hard in a closed hotel room in Beijing with extremely high efficiency: "I was responsible for the coordination and communication of the whole project for banks, securities and trust, and I reported all the progress directly to Chairman Wu, who in turn reported to the Head Office of the People's Bank of China." Dr. Chen Yunxian became the lead person for the entire project at the executive level.

During the closed work period, the Head Office of the PBOC suddenly sent an official surnamed Liang to the hotel. The project team members initially thought he was there to guide the work and hoped he would provide some advice on how to move the project forward. Strangely enough, after a few days, the official did not give any guiding advice, but just stood by and watched the work they were doing from time to time, which made the project team members very surprised.

"In fact, he was silently observing how well we were doing," Dr. Chen later recalled. It was this detail that made Dr. Chen and his colleagues appreciate the confidentiality and importance of the BOC Trust project.

On September 17, 1996, as the BOC Trust project entered the acquisition stage, a special mobilization meeting was held in the conference room of Guangdong Development Bank Head Office. Bank leaders, heads of departments, and branch managers, as well as a number of key personnel from across the bank, were seated to listen to Chairman Wu Chixin's rallying speech. With an encouraging attitude, the helmsman of Guangdong Development Bank talked about the bottlenecks of the bank's development and the significance of the acquisition of BOC Trust. The speech was not only blood-curdling, but also slightly tragic. Wu Chixin stressed, "Guangdong Development Bank must have a broader position to train our team." The mobilization meeting was followed by a solemn flag ceremony, where the project team members received the bank flag and departed from Guangzhou to fly to the capital. Upon arrival, the project team was arranged to stay at the guest house of the Central Organization Department to wait for orders.

"Before receiving the notice, I had not thought at all that GF could participate in the acquisition of BOC Trust, which was unthinkable for both Guangdong Development Bank and GF Securities with our strength at that time. On the night the acquisition project team arrived in Beijing, my heart was full of pride." Talking about their departure that day, the excitement still shone in the eyes of Dr. Ma Qingquan, then president of GF Securities. "It was only on that day that my colleagues and I learned that Dr. Chen had been secretly doing the BOC Trust project for several months in Beijing. When we received the notice, we kept exclaiming that GF could take such a big project, and that Dr. Chen was really something."

On September 24, 1996, one year after the People's Bank of China took over BOC Trust, Guangdong Development Bank formally signed an acquisition agreement with BOC Trust and Investment Company. On the same day, Guangdong Development Bank set up a leading group for the acquisition, headed by Li Ruohong and vice headed by Chen Yunxian, with Ma Qingquan, Wang Guizhi, Liang Jianhua, Kang Guohong, and Nan Ping as members, and the office of the leading group located in Beijing. GF Securities and its subsidiary Guangfayuan Corporate Trustee Company acted as financial advisors for the project.

"Because it was urgent and it was feared that confidential information could be leaked, when we arrived in Beijing we all still did not know what the acquisition was about until the leadership team assigned the task and each of us was issued a copy of a government document and a list of institutions BOC Trust had in each place, and then let us set off..." Zhong Xiongying, who had participated in the Shenzhen regional acquisition, said with emotion: "At that time, in China there had not been such a large financial institution that had been acquired so there was basically no experience to learn from." Back then, this key employee, who graduated from Wuhan University's law department, had just been seconded from a brokerage branch to the Institutional Management Department of GF Securities, and was involved in the acquisition project of BOC Trust on the first day.

Zhong Xiongying still clearly remembers in the autumn of that year, as soon as he landed in Shenzhen from Beijing, he took the government document and single-handedly moved to a dozen subsidiaries and their subsidiaries of BOC Trust in Shenzhen, and even a greyhound racing track: "First taking over the legal person official seal and financial seal and taking charge of the money and people was the formal control, and it will be a process before the actual control was realized." Because of no notice from BOC Trust, some legal persons did not know what had happened and the Shenzhen company's personnel found various excuses for malicious boycott. In desperation, Zhong Xiongying could only reason with them to lay out the facts and find ways to take charge of people, property, and materials. After the situation was under control, he asked the Head Office of Guangdong Development Bank to send people over to clarify which was industrial business and which was financial business. The banking business was merged into Guangdong Development Bank, and the industry was allocated to the industrial holding company established by Guangdong Development Bank to digest, and the securities business was delivered to GF Securities.

The acquisition team members who went to other cities also encountered varying degrees of malicious boycotts, and the asset quality and financial position of BOC Trust was unsurprisingly problematic, with much confusion in management. A key participant in the acquisition project recalled that she was in charge of taking over a newly established exchange under BOC Trust, and when she checked the accounts, she found that the head of the exchange had given some employees arbitrary salaries without any approval process.

Taking people as a mirror, one can learn from mistakes. Having participated in the entire acquisition of BOC Trust, the management of GF Securities spontaneously sorted out the reasons for the collapse of the trusteeship and used it as a lesson. In his year-end speech in 1996, Dr. Chen Yunxian noted:

> The lessons of this company are threefold: First, it started with connections and was destroyed by them. Second, there was an internal division: the split in thinking led to the split in leadership, and finally led to the division of assets. Third, there was no scientific decision-making mechanism and no feasibility analysis, and major projects were decided arbitrarily. The collapse of BOC Trust had a huge impact on its employees, many of whom were excellent talents, but now face many problems such as the way out and future.

As a result, Dr. Chen cautioned GF Securities employees:

> This case has inspired me with three main points: one is that when drinking water, we should not forget who dug the well. Our main support is Guangdong Development Bank. No matter what friction there is, this basic idea should be adhered to. Two is unity, which is the basis of a company's survival and development. Three is to adhere to prudent operation and appropriate decision-making.

To understand the inside story of the BOC Trust acquisition, Hu Shuli, a famous media personality who founded the *Caijing* magazine, interviewed Dr. Chen. But Dr. Chen knew that the background of the acquisition was very complicated, and he did not disclose any single piece of "effective information" in the interview. Hu Shuli had to go to interview Chairman Wu Chixin. Dr. Chen later learned that Hu Shuli spoke highly of him in his interview with Chairman Wu, mentioning repeatedly that "Dr. Chen Yunxian is very prudent."

"The background of this project of BOC Trust is indeed very complicated!" This is what Dr. Chen mentioned most often when recalling this acquisition.

The successful acquisition of BOC Trust by Guangdong Development Bank set a precedent for the acquisition of a non-bank financial institution by a bank, leaving an important impact on several levels in the history of the development of the financial industry. One media source once commented on the acquisition, "The acquisition of BOC Trust was not only a commercial act, but also a major political task." In order to pay off the debts of BOC Trust, Guangdong Development Bank paid a high economic price and was also thus able to establish branches in Beijing, Shanghai, Nanjing, Hangzhou, Kunming, and Dalian, thus laying the foundation for Guangdong Development Bank's nationwide development. The new branches also brought lasting and significant benefits to Guangdong Development Bank.

As the main force of Guangdong Development Bank, GF Securities assumed part of the debt to resolve financial risks and maintain social stability, and also took the opportunity to acquire five brokerage branches in Beijing, Shanghai, Hangzhou, and Shenyang, further strengthening its network outside Guangdong Province. What is more important was the brand effect that came with it: many in the industry were surprised to see that a local brokerage firm had taken over a central company.

Making quick moves to develop in many more cities

The takeover of BOC Trust in 1995 further alerted the People's Bank of China to the chaos of the trust industry's blind development.

On July 2, 1996, the People's Bank of China issued the Circular on Issues Related to the Abolition or Transfer of Securities Brokerage Branches under Trust and Investment Companies of Wholly State-Owned Commercial Banks, requiring the four major commercial banks, ICBC, Agricultural Bank, Bank of China, and Construction

Bank to delink from their trust and investment companies and to abolish the securities brokerage branches with poor operating conditions and irregular business practices and transfer other securities brokerage branches to qualified securities companies and trust and investment companies. On September 5, the People's Bank of China issued another document, further clarifying that except for securities companies and trust and investment companies, other financial institutions were not allowed to set up securities trading departments and that those that had been set up must be abolished or transferred by the end of the year.

M&A opportunities had emerged, and the curtain had opened on the struggle between powerful brokerage firms. GF Securities, which had accumulated more experience in acquisition, reacted quickly and immediately sent several groups of people to Chengdu, Wuhan, Dalian, and Chongqing to negotiate with the targeted brokerage branches.

As soon as Dr. Fang Jiachun learned that CCB's Fuzhou sales office was ready to be transferred, he immediately went to contact it. When he arrived in Fuzhou, he found out that another well-known Chinese brokerage firm had already moved first and reached an acquisition intention with CCB, just short of signing the transfer. Faced with the sudden competition from the top management of GF Securities, the representatives of the competing brokerage firm were also in a bit of a hurry. When Dr. Fang and the head of the brokerage branch of China Construction Bank talked inside, they sat outside waiting. In a hurry, the other competitor also presented a power of attorney from the president of their company, to the effect that no matter how much GF Securities offered, they would add another 1 million yuan on top of that. But after three days and many rounds of negotiations, it was GF Securities that left with a smile on its face. Dr. Fang recalls:

> In fact, we did not offer a sky-high price, let alone take any crooked path, but we inspired the other party with GF's dedication. We put forward a whole set of detailed proposals, including proposals on the future development of this brokerage branch and the future multilevel cooperation with CCB. This finally attracted the other party, and this was what our competitor was not prepared for.

In addition, GF Securities people in expeditions to Chengdu, Wuhan, Dalian, and Chongqing such as Li Jianyong and Lin Zhihai also had good news. They successfully took over those cities' brokerage branches of the China Life Insurance Company, the Industrial and Commercial Bank of China, the Agricultural Bank of China, and the Bank of China.

In the era of scarcity of brokerage branch licenses, cyclical market factors, administrative factors for crisis relief, and the policy factors of separating banking and securities gave the industry a rare opportunity to acquire brokerage branches. In the securities industry that fell and rose, whoever seized an opportunity quickly would be more able to compete in that industry. From 1995 to 1996, GF Securities, which experienced the impact of the first industrial crisis, increased the number of business offices to 37 through M&A when the market was not doing well. The newly added brokerage branches were located in many major cities in north, southwest, central, southeast, and northeast China, and GF Securities successfully entered the regions outside Beijing, Shanghai, and Guangdong Province to reach the whole country. During this period, under the cooperation of GF's investment banking of "developing nationwide," GF Securities emerged from the image of a "local brokerage" in the eyes of its brokerage peers and became a fast-growing "rising horse."

3. Debut in the midst of an international financial event

The crisis of Guangdong International Trust and Investment Corporation

In the mid- and late 1990s, when the national financial system was undergoing great changes, the trust industry, which started earlier than the securities industry, once again fell into the weird circle of "development-irregularity-rectification." In February 1997, China Rural Trust and Investment Company was shut down for failure to pay its debts as they fell due. In June 1998, China High-Tech Venture Capital Company was shut down for operating illegally and becoming insolvent. In October 1998, the news of the administrative closure of Guangdong International Trust and Investment Corporation (GITIC) drew a lot of attention from the national financial community and foreign investors.

The reason why GITIC had attracted attention at the international level was firstly because of its sheer size and its significant influence in the international financial markets.

In the early 1980s, when large banks such as the Industrial and Commercial Bank of China, Agricultural Bank of China, and China Construction Bank were not allowed to operate foreign exchange business, GITIC enjoyed the right to operate foreign exchange and was subsequently identified by the national authorities as the "window" for foreign loans and stood at the forefront of China's overseas financing. Since 1983, it had signed loan agreements with dozens of banks in Japan, the United States, the United Kingdom, France, and Switzerland, with a credit line of over US$300 million. In the international bond market, between 1986 and 1988, GITIC issued large bonds almost every year to China's Hong Kong, and Europe and other places. In the 1990s, GITIC was awarded credit ratings by Moody's and Standard & Poor's, and the ratings were equivalent to sovereign bonds at that time.

In more than ten years, on the strength of its creditability as a window company, GITIC supported and established a number of key projects in Guangdong Province by issuing bonds, granting loans and guarantees, equity participation, investment, and leasing in the international market. In addition, GITIC also developed from a single trust business to a company group mainly focusing on financial and industrial investment, with investments in dozens of fields such as finance, securities, trade, communications, energy, high technology, and real estate, with a total of more than 3,000 investment projects, owning a number of high-quality assets such as the Guangdong International Building, Jiangwan New Town, and Guangzhou Fari Complex, and its real estate companies held the largest amount of land to be developed in Guangdong Province at that time. The real estate companies under it possessed the largest amount of land to be developed in Guangdong Province. With its scale, assets, influence, overseas connections, and government background, GITIC became the largest business kingdom in Guangdong at that time, known as the "GITIC aircraft carrier sailing to the ocean."

In May 1994, Huang Yantian, president of GITIC, was pictured on the cover of the US *Business Week*, with an article by a foreign journalist commenting that GITIC was "almost unique in China's fastest-growing region."[2]

Among the hundreds of trust and investment companies in China at the time, GITIC was second in size only to China International Trust and Investment Corporation (CITIC Group's predecessor), the first trust company in China established in October 1979. CITIC, which served as a window on China's opening up and later developed into a large, comprehensive multinational conglomerate with both financial and industrial operations, described GITIC as follows in its book *Brilliance in the Face of Hardship: 30 Years of CITIC*:

> Second in size only to CITIC, Guangdong Trust and Investment Corporation (GTIC) was founded in 1980, and in October 1983, with the approval of the People's Bank of China, GTIC became a state-run financial company and received a license from the State Administration of Foreign Exchange to operate foreign exchange business. In December of the same year, GTIC changed its name from "Guangdong Trust and Investment Company" to "Guangdong International Trust and Investment Corporation," and became a "window company" designated by the state to allow foreign borrowing and debt issuance. This treatment was fully comparable to that of CITIC.
>
> In 1986, GITIC received an "AA-" credit rating from the Japan Bond Research Institute and successfully issued 20 billion yen of samurai bonds in Japan in September of that year. In August 1987, it issued a $50 million Asian dollar bond in Hong Kong. In May 1988, a 20 billion euro and yen bond was issued. The years from 1989 to 1991 were the most exceptional three years since China's reform and opening up, when the Western embargo on China kept all foreign investment out of the country, but GITIC still received a $70 million loan from Japan. In July 1992, GITIC entered the Japanese samurai bond market

2 Some of the materials are cited from Fei Handing, "The Era Represented by a Bankruptcy Case: On the 15th Anniversary of the GITIC Bankruptcy," and Tian Bingxin, Chen Bingfeng, Wang Qi, and Ling Guangzhi, "GITIC, an Aircraft Carrier Sailing to the Ocean."

again, issuing 15 billion yen in bonds.

After 1995, the Chinese government made it clear that local governments could not issue foreign bonds on their own, and the government would no longer provide guarantees for window companies, and decided to implement full-caliber management of foreign debt. However, relying on its existing government credit, GITIC continued to raise debt, bypassing regulation. By the end of 1997, GITIC's overseas financing totaled more than $5 billion, ranking second in the Chinese trust industry.

Corresponding to the speed and scale of its borrowing, over the previous decade or so, GITIC's investments swelled rapidly; it was involved in more than 3,000 projects in dozens of fields of industrial production, including transportation, energy, communications, raw materials, chemicals, textiles, electronics, medical care, and high technology, and also entered the fields of finance, securities, trade, hotels and tourism, and real estate development. GITIC poured huge sums of money into real estate to become the largest "real estate king" in Guangdong Province. A large number of these thousands of projects were connection-based loans and impulsive investments.

However, GITIC's massive investment in the manufacturing sector yielded almost no revenue. A Guangdong government spokesman told reporters three months after GITIC was shut down that unrecoverable investment, loan and interest losses amounting to 9.6 billion had been identified.

The Asian financial crisis finally put GITIC on the road to collapse, and 1998 was the peak year for its debt service, which reached $1 billion, a huge payment pressure that finally overwhelmed it. It again planned to issue bonds or loans overseas to borrow new money to pay off old ones and short ones to pay off long ones. In addition, the company's commissioners were ordered to go around the country immediately to collect the money owed, but by this time, GITIC's subsidiaries were also piling up bad debts and could hardly protect themselves, so they had no power to save their master. The media described, "In August, the fund scheduling meeting became the most important, urgent, and frequent high-level meeting of the company."

I'm sure the above scenarios will be familiar to a good portion of CITIC's veteran staff. Even the management itself was not sure how many subsidiaries and their subsidiaries' subsidiaries were under its jurisdiction, where they were located, and who their legal representatives were.

In October 1998, GITIC was finally administratively closed down because it could not pay its huge debts. At the time of closure, the entire group owed nearly $3 billion in foreign debt.

CITIC faced the same situation, except that Wang Jun realized the seriousness of the problem earlier and set out to solve it.[3]

---

3 Wang Weiqun, *Brilliance in the Face of Hardship: 30 Years of CITIC* (CITIC Press Group, 2010), p. 234.

Once known as the "unsinkable aircraft carrier," the company suddenly hit the rocks in the middle of its journey.

In the second half of 1997, the Asian financial crisis broke out, hitting Japan and other countries where GITIC's major creditors were located. The creditors contracted their foreign investments and demanded that GITIC pay its foreign debts as they fell due.

In addition, another window company in Guangdong Province, Guangdong Yuehai Investment Holdings Co., Ltd., was also unable to pay its huge foreign debts as they fell due, and there was a run on small and medium-sized financial institutions in Guangdong, especially rural credit cooperatives. Guangdong's financial institutions were in crisis.

In order to prevent and resolve financial risks, in November 1997, the central government held a financial work conference, deciding to spend about three years to establish a financial institution system, a financial market system, and a financial regulation and supervision system that were compatible with the development of the socialist market economy, significantly improve the operation and management of the financial industry, and basically achieve a marked improvement in the national financial order. The meeting also clarified the responsibility mechanism of financial institutions, which, according to the market interpretation, means "each is held responsible for its own loss and profit."

On October 6, 1998, the People's Bank of China issued an announcement, officially shutting down GITIC. After an in-depth investigation into the black hole of its debt, the central government made a painful decision to let GITIC go into complete bankruptcy and, in accordance with the internationally accepted bankruptcy practice, to treat all creditors equally and not to give priority to overseas creditors in repaying their debts. This meant that the huge amount of money loaned to GITIC by more than 100 foreign creditors would be lost. After this decision was announced, the world was in an uproar, the Guangdong provincial government and even the central government faced unprecedented international pressure, and many foreign creditors were so upset that they even threatened to sue the Chinese government. A crisis concerning the creditworthiness of the Chinese government began to spread around the world.

In order to deal with the special situation of Guangdong Province at that time, thanks to the efforts of the GITIC Disposal Leading Group, a specific GITIC Trust Liquidation Group was established in Guangdong Province, with Wang Qishan, then Standing Committee Member of the CPC Guangdong Provincial Committee and Executive Vice Governor of Guangdong Province, as the leader, and Wu Jiesi, assistant to the Governor of Guangdong Province, and Chen Yunxian, Chairman of GF Securities, as the vice leaders, with Wu assisting the leader in coordinating all work and mainly taking charge of the cleanup and consolidation of trust and investment companies in the province, and Chen focusing on assisting the leader in the cleanup and consolidation of securities business divested from trust and investment companies in the province.

Looking back to 1991, GITIC erected its 63-story headquarters building, Guangdong International Building, on the busy Huanshi Road, which became the tallest building in south China at that time and was called the "63 stories" by Guangzhou residents; while on the same road in the same year, Dr. Chen Yunxian, who had graduated not long before, was preparing to build GF Securities' first street-level securities office here. The same year, on the same road, Dr. Chen Yunxian, a recent graduate, was preparing to build GF's first brokerage branch facing the street. Seven years later, in the midst of the changing storm, GF Securities was appointed to take the stage of the first bankruptcy case of a non-bank financial institution in China, which shocked both China and those abroad.

The dramatic change of the "63 stories" venue

One day at the end of September 1998, Dr. Chen Yunxian, who had just returned to Guangzhou from a meeting in Beijing, called Zhao Guiping, the head of the Institutional Management Department, to his office. Before she could sit down, Dr. Chen handed over a sheet of notes from the Tianzi Zhuangyuan Hotel in Beijing. The notes were written in Dr. Chen's handwriting and had obviously been revised several times. The title of the notes clearly read: "GF Securities' Trusteeship of ...'s Funds Department and Securities Departments," but the name of the institution under trusteeship had been blacked out. Under the heading were the main points of the trusteeship:

> The main points to be addressed are: (1) shareholder runs; (2) incomplete accounts and fund transfers; (3) computer and communication failures; and (4) accidents caused by psychological panic among shareholders and employees.
>
> To this end:
>
> (1) Organizing a team of 40 people and assigning four people to the Funds Department and to each of the securities departments, including one leader, one treasurer, one computer clerk, and one in charge of the counter.
>
> (2) Assigning people to the Funds Department and each of the securities departments in different areas on October 3.
>
> (3) 300–500 million yuan of contingency funds to be prepared by GF Securities by October 5.
>
> (4) As soon as the market opens on October 5, the financial information will be sealed, computer passwords will be changed, and the trusteeship coordination will be organized.
>
> (5) From October 7 to 17, a Guangzhou accounting firm will be engaged to conduct a capital verification, and the acquisition will be completed by October 25 according to the net assets.
>
> (6) Publishing an announcement in *China Securities Journal* and *Securities*

Times by October 25 to change the names of the Funds Department and securities departments.

(7) Reporting to the public security department where each securities department is located from October 5 to the end of October to assist in maintaining law and order.

(8) Doing internal and external explanation work for the purposes of stability.

(9) The original remaining issues (including the issue of illegal buildings of securities departments) will be postponed until after October 25 through negotiation.

The manuscript, totaling just 350 words, presented Dr. Chen's clear thoughts on the highly complex trustee liquidation work. It also became a precious collection of Zhao Guiping. She only made a personal guess about the name of the institution to be placed under trusteeship that had been blacked out on the paper: Dr. Chen went to Beijing to attend a meeting held by Vice Governor Wang Qishan to study how to resolve the risks in Guangdong's financial reform, and a financial institution with great influence in Guangdong Province would be disposed of.

Dr. Chen instructed Zhao Guiping: "We have something big to do soon, but keep it secret!"

In addition, Dr. Chen also instructed Li Shuiquan, who was then the general manager of the Capital Operation Department. Dr. Chen simply explained, "Shuiquan, would you please make 300 million yuan of funds for me? Don't ask why!"

On the eve of the National Day, Zhao Guiping felt that the whole company was busy with an extraordinary event, while she, with a little excitement, worked overtime with the institutional management team to refine the trusteeship plan according to Dr. Chen's sheet of paper. The Institutional Management Department thought of various scenarios, even bought rice paper and printed many seizure slips, but they never knew which company was about to be placed under their trusteeship.

On September 29, 1998, Dr. Chen Yunxian called Dr. Fang Jiachun, the then president, from Beijing to lay out the task: GITIC might have to close down, and GF Securities would accept the commission from the Guangdong provincial government to organize a strong team to place the business and funds departments belonging to GITIC under their trusteeship to ensure social stability.

The mission was clear and the responsibility was very big. GF Securities immediately organized a leading group consisting of heads of relevant departments to coordinate this work. In addition, in accordance with the trusteeship plan previously laid out by Dr. Chen and the number of GITIC's brokerage branches, a working group was proposed to be assigned to each brokerage branch, with each working group having a leader, plus three staff members for finance, computers, and the counter. According to this configuration, plus the staff assigned to the securities headquarters of GITIC, the company needed to organize a large trusteeship work team. So, led by the Institutional Management Department, more than 50 staff members were urgently selected from various departments and notified to report to the company's headquarters on October 1 without fail on the grounds that the company had an important task. Fang Jiachun, Ye Junying, Li Xuzhi, Cui Xia, Zhao Guiping, and many other key employees from outside Guangdong Province joined the trusteeship team.

At 9:00 a.m. on October 1, 1998, when Dr. Chen Yunxian and the main leaders of the president's team walked into the headquarters conference room and saw more than 50 employees who had been temporarily drawn back from all over the country, they were in an unusually excited mood. Many of them had already bought their air tickets and been ready to go on vacation with their families, and some had even prepared to hold their weddings during the National Day holiday, but after receiving an urgent notice from the company, more than 50 of them did what they were called to do and reported to the company at the set time.

At the mobilization meeting, Dr. Chen Yunxian announced the decision of GF Securities to be entrusted by the Guangdong provincial government to take over the securities departments belonging to GITIC, and at the same time briefly emphasized the great significance of this work. The president's team made the following arrangements on specific trusteeship matters.

1. The guidelines of the trusteeship: be highly responsible, internally strict and externally relaxed, and ensure success.
2. Organize the leading group and executive group of the trusteeship, and transfer the heads of relevant departments to form a regular task force, and rely on the unified leadership and command of the institutional Management Department of the corporation.
3. Formulate the work flow and conduct training on hosting matters by each professional department temporarily.
4. On the evening of October 4, each trusteeship team secretly arrives at its trusteeship place, finds a nearby guest house to stay, and investigates the basic situation of the brokerage branches of GITIC.
5. Bring the bulletins and other promotional materials printed by the higher authorities and standby in each place.

In the days leading up to the trustee team's departure, everyone worked overtime to prepare the trustee materials to ensure that the 40 sets of materials were complete and ready, while attending intensive training. Compared with the previous acquisition of BOC Trust, GF Securities made a lot of preparations for this trusteeship program, and the Institutional Management Department led a "Crash Course on Trusteeship Business," which focused on: How to deal with the resistance of the other side after entering their premises? How to use man-to-man tactics to control computers and finance? How to prevent the computers' super passwords from being changed? How to ensure financial security? How to win the cooperation of the other side's employees? How to appease the stockholders?.... These details were considered with the the focus on controlling the situation in the shortest possible time, straightening out the relationship between people, money, and materials, and ensuring a smooth transition.

At 8:00 p.m. on October 4, members of the trusteeship teams arrived in Shanghai, Tianjin, Xi'an, Puning, Shenzhen, and Guangzhou as scheduled. They were carrying a full set of trusteeship information, laptops, and various seals in their hands and stayed in the designated hotels around brokerage branches. Soon, the top secret document of the People's Bank of China on the closure of GITIC was officially issued, and GF Securities urgently prepared the announcement and authorization letter, which were immediately sent to the trusteeship teams in various cities. These members were waiting for the order to enter the brokerage branches to place them under trusteeship.

On October 6, 1998, the first day of work after the National Day, the white-collar workers on Huanshidong Road in Guangzhou did not know that a historical event was about to happen in Guangdong International Building that would shake the financial world. At 2:30 p.m., as notified by the General Office of the Guangdong provincial government, the leadership team of GF Securities attended a meeting to close down GITIC. When the group arrived at the famous "63 stories" of GITIC headquarters, the large conference hall was already full of people in charge of all GITIC departments. On the podium were the leaders of the General Office of the People's Bank of China who had come all the way from Beijing, the Guangdong provincial government, and the main officials of GITIC. What aroused people's speculation of the stage was that there were also the president of the Bank of China Guangdong Branch and the chairman of GF Securities on the podium. Because many people present did not know what the meeting was for, the atmosphere in the conference room was not really gloomy, some people were still chatting in a relaxed manner, and others might have foreseen something, so they were silently waiting for the meeting to start.

The meeting was presided over by the leader of GITIC. First, the head of the People's Bank of China read out the Decision on the Closure of Guangdong International Trust and Investment Corporation and formally announced that GITIC would be closed down and liquidated, the People's Bank of China would organize and set up a liquidation team in accordance with the law, and during the liquidation period, its debts and liabilities would be under the trusteeship of the Bank of China, and its securities brokerage branches would be entrusted to GF Securities for management. Then, the People's Bank of China, Bank of China, and GF Securities read out the relevant trusteeship announcements, while the head of the liquidation group made a statement on the relevant situation of the closure of GITIC. Finally, the person in charge of GITIC made a statement on behalf of the board of directors and the leadership team.

Zhao Guiping attended the meeting with the trusteeship team, and it was an unforgettable image for her: after a moment of silence, the venue immediately became lively again, some people shook their heads and sighed, some people were indignant, and some people shed tears on the spot, and the sudden change was difficult for many people to understand and accept. At this time, hundreds of employees from the liquidation and trusteeship groups of Junxin Law Firm and KPMG had also been stationed in the headquarters building of GITIC, and with their suits and serious expressions, the liquidation and trusteeship battle was officially started in the hub of this financial giant ship. On the other side, there were employees of GITIC who were in tears and could not accept the fact that the company had been closed down. Most of them were the proud graduates of famous universities at home and abroad, and some of them had just joined GITIC and should have had a very bright future, but with the collapse of GITIC, they instantly experienced a huge change of fate.

In order to ensure the smooth trusteeship of brokerage branches, GF Securities trusteeship team directly found the leader of GITIC responsible for securities business at the meeting place, and asked him to cooperate to call each brokerage branch to inform the trusteeship matters. After every call made by the GITIC leader, the GF trusteeship team, which had already been on standby in the area, immediately moved in to take over. At this time, it was already the stock market closing time. In accordance with the previous plans, the trusteeship teams quickly moved in to take control of all financial seals, accounts, and asset information and take over all computer rooms, databases, and servers, to ensure that the transaction business were controllable, while posting announcements to stabilize customers.

With that, came the unknown test of the complex situation from the frontline of the brokerage branch trusteeship.

Three years of trusteeship and successful bidding

The next day following the trusteeship, that is, October 7, many investors learned the news of the closure of the GITIC. Most investors behaved calmly, and customers of the Shanghai Xietu Road Brokerage Branch even said after seeing the announcement, "It is good that GF Securities took over; it is much better than the original company and we are relieved."

However, as the inspection and verification of capital deepened, many of the brokerage branches under trusteeship began to reveal problems, coupled with other brokerage branches sending people to win over their customers, and there appeared unstable factors. The investors gathered either asked for cash withdrawals or transfers, causing great pressure on the trusteeship groups. In the trusteeship network, the trading self-service machines of the Guangzhou Jiangwan Brokerage Branch were posted with the slogan "Return my hard-earned money," the Shenzhen Brokerage Branch had a liquidation fund crisis, the Tianjin Brokerage Branch had a crisis in the payment of treasury bonds, and the Xi'an Brokerage Branch had its trusteeship blocked.

In response, the Guangdong provincial government, the liquidation teams, and the Guangdong Securities Regulatory Bureau coordinated all parties to actively support the trusteeship of GF Securities. GF Securities fulfilled its responsibility to protect the normal operation of the brokerage branches.

"GITIC brokerage branches had complex and incredible problems. Although we had made all kinds of mental preparations before the takeover, we found a large number of non-compliance behaviors in the operation of the brokerage branches after entering them. Some of their leaders had complicated backgrounds, chaotic management and reckless behavior, which were shocking," Zhao Guiping recalled. She added during the days of trusteeship that she received calls from colleagues almost every day to report all kinds of unbelievable things, and some were even serious enough to endanger their lives.

For example, the Tianjin Brokerage Branch of GITIC illegally issued securities trusteeship certificates worth nearly 50 million yuan off the books for self-use and external lending. Due to serious losses, the risk of payment emerged, involving more than 4,000 small and medium-sized investors, so the impact would be huge. This could lead to social unrest if not handled properly. In order to conceal this fact, the original leader of the brokerage branches used social connections to intimidate and threaten the trustees of GF Securities. Wang Junhe, the head of the Tianjin trusteeship team at that time, had to change hotels every day, carrying the official seal and keys with him everywhere he went. One day he drove his van back to his residence, but when he went out the next day, he found that the windows of his van had been smashed. The pressure of intimidation came over him, and even a strong man like him could not bear it for a while, and he sobbed uncontrollably when he reported the matter to Zhao Guiping by phone.

As the deputy head of the trusteeship group, Zhao Guiping also received a message for the trusteeship team of the Jiangwan Brokerage Branch of GITIC to "stop." The team found IOUs worth hundreds of thousands of yuan in the safe of the Jiangwan Brokerage Branch. There were serious overdrafts, and overdraft information was missing in large quantities, making it quite difficult for investigations. When the former leader of the GITIC Shenzhen Brokerage Branch was in criminal detention, he even shouted that he would "settle accounts with you after I come out."

The complexity of the blocked trusteeship of the Xi'an Brokerage Branch of GITIC had not been expected. Years later today, as the head of the Xi'an team, Zhong Xiongying is still vividly aware of the twists and turns in the process of the trusteeship on the spot.

After the market closed on the afternoon of October 6, the Xi'an trusteeship team entered the brokerage branch, but the head of the brokerage branch refused to hold a middle-level meeting and hand over. The trusteeship team tried to negotiate several times without success, so they had to leave the brokerage branch that night. In accordance with the company's instructions, Zhong Xiongying and other members of the team tried every means to investigate, and finally found out why the trusteeship work was blocked. It turned out that the brokerage branch was a joint venture between GITIC and an influential local real estate company. The real estate company actually had control of the brokerage branch, including its personnel recruitment, and the investor's margin had illegally been misappropriated.

After the Xi'an trusteeship team reported the situation, the Head Office of the People's Bank of China notified its Shaanxi branch by phone and internal fax in the early hours of October 7 to help advance the trusteeship. Just when the matter was expected to be resolved, there was another sudden twist when the Shaanxi Provincial Higher Court suddenly issued a ruling on October 7 to enforce the sale of GITIC's Xi'an Brokerage Branch and seized the relevant documents and all vehicles of the brokerage branch. For safety reasons, the trusteeship team of GF Securities decided to leave. But at this time, the shareholders of the brokerage branch who did not know the real situation began to take action against the brokerage branch, and the internal personnel of which also began to deal with financial and computer data accordingly. The Zhong Xiongying-led trusteeship team constantly received the threat of intimidation from local interest groups, and their trusteeship work was in a dilemma.

When the situation was difficult to be solved, Premier Zhu Rongji gave two important treasure to the Shaanxi provincial government, the Xi'an municipal government, the Shaanxi provincial securities authorities, and the People's Bank of China to cooperate in the trusteeship of GITIC, and to investigate the illegal facts and the forces behind them. On October 14, the Shaanxi Provincial Higher Court suspended the enforcement procedure. On the early morning of October 16, after 10 days of obstruction, the Xi'an trusteeship team of GF Securities officially entered the brokerage branch, defusing another incident that could have triggered social unrest.

Years later, Zhong Xiongying, general manager of the Zhuhai branch, recalled the situation at that time and said he was not too afraid and worried, remarking, "Maybe it has something to do with my previous work experience, but more crucially, we got the evidence of the violation of the law, and our report was solid and justified, so that it was reported to all levels and got the approval of the Premier. In the face of difficulties, we always believe that GF people will accomplish our mission."

Zhao Guiping is also deeply proud of the successful trusteeship of GITIC Business Department: "The point I am most proud of is that our trusteeship program, as well as the margin calculation caliber formula created with KPMG, were groundbreaking. The trusteeship program later became a model for the China Securities Regulatory Commission to conduct risk disposal, while the margin calculation caliber formula entered the textbook for the securities qualification examination." As the project progressed, through cooperation with KPMG and other international accounting firms, GF Securities' staff grew in many ways, and the company's international perspective and management level were enhanced.

According to the initial plan of government departments, the nine brokerage branches of GITIC were to be placed under the trusteeship of GF Securities and could be directly transferred to GF Securities at a lower price subsequently. However, due to the extremely complex legal issues of debts involved in the bankruptcy liquidation of GITIC and the huge international impact, the government required that they should be handled strictly in accordance with the law. Upon the recommendation of KPMG, the firm responsible for this liquidation, it was finally decided to dispose of these assets by competitive bidding in accordance with international practice to show fairness to creditors. The trusteeship, which had lasted nearly three years, was about to end with an auction.

On July 18, 2001, Dr. Fang Jiachun took Dong Zhengqing, Li Shuzhi, Zhao Guiping, and Cao Gang to the auction site. Dr. Chen Yunxian, chairman of the board of directors, who was far away in the United States, was also concerned and instructed in advance that the nine brokerage branches of GITIC should be bought as long as there was no malicious bid-raising.

Before the bidding started, Zhao Guiping briefed Dr. Fang Gachun again on the previously conducted due diligence, the acceptable price according to the margin calculation caliber, the premium of the customer value, and the profit forecast for the brokerage branches. During the more than two years of arduous trusteeship, GF Securities had paid too much, but had also come to very well understand the value of the brokerage branches' customers. For the auction, GF Securities was determined to win.

According to the rules of bidding set by the GITIC bankruptcy liquidation team, the bids would be opened in the form of dark bids on the basis of the reserve price of 136 million yuan, and after the participants had quoted the highest price, they would then seek advice from GF Securities, which enjoyed priority. If any company offered a higher price, and GF Securities waived the exercise of priority, the company that offered that price must bid to buy it, otherwise its deposit of 30 million yuan will be forfeited. Therefore, most of the bidding securities companies gave up the bid at the last minute. The two companies, GF Securities and Guangdong Securities, paid deposits as requested. In the end, Guangdong Securities offered 153 million yuan, but GF Securities said it was willing to pay the same price. So GF Securities took possession of all the nine brokerage branches with priority rights, with an average price of 17 million yuan each. At this point, the trusteeship of GITIC brokerage branches, which had caused a sensation, came to a successful end.

From July 9 to 20, 2001, many authoritative newspapers in the securities industry published successive commentary articles, affirming the positive effect of GF Securities' trusteeship and acquisition of GITIC brokerage branches. The main business of GITIC was in the trust industry, but its bankruptcy process also exposed many problems in the management of securities institutions, providing a negative example for the standardization of China's securities market. In addition, GF Securities' successful trusteeship and acquisition created a classic example of a successful trusteeship in China's financial industry.

"If the acquisition of GITIC is successful, I will buy three jars of wine, rush to the top of Mount Huangshan, invite my colleagues who have fought together, get drunk first, and then pour out my sorrows and bitterness to the fullest possible extent." This is a grand wish made by Li Shuzhi before the acquisition. But after the successful bid, she and Zhao Guiping left only a group photo at the auction site, and then moved on to more follow-up work. For the trusteeship and acquisition of GITIC, she wrote in a recollection article, stating that, "We have reason to celebrate, but have no time to stop; there is still a lot to do."

Working to clean up local small and medium-sized trust companies

GF Securities completed the trusteeship and acquisition of GITIC's brokerage branches, but outside of the securities assets, the disposal of GITIC's bankruptcy estate and the collection of external claims stretched over a long period of time until March 22, 2019, when China's first liquidation bankruptcy case of a non-bank financial institution was finally settled with full payment of all claims, as ruled by the Guangdong Provincial Higher Court in accordance with the law. The curtain finally came down on a 20-year-long bankruptcy case.

The case of GITIC brought about an important change in the concept of domestic financial regulation. When Wang Qishan first took office in Guangdong, he faced the "threatening lawsuit" from foreign creditors. He firmly stated that "the Chinese government's handling of the bankruptcy of GITIC is fully in line with international practices, and the Chinese government should not and will not repay the debt for GITIC.... If the creditors outside the country are willing to fight, we will fight to the end." In addition, Wang Qishan repeatedly explained to the creditors: "GITIC's credit is neither sovereign credit nor general corporate credit. This kind of transitional credit between government and company can be called 'window company credit,' but, as China's reform deepens, the connotation of 'window company credit' has long since quietly changed, and the government background has long since been diluted to near zero." Moreover, the Chinese government imposed bankruptcy on GITIC in accordance with the law precisely to rectify the credit environment, to take the financial order seriously, to truly play by commercial rules, and to create a better financial environment for foreign investors. This attitude became an important basis for finally reaching a consensus with European and American creditors.[4]

The GITIC case also made central regulators and local governments feel deeply about the dangers of trust institutions operating securities businesses in violation of the law. After years of overheated development, the trust industry was in disorder, with international trust and investment companies founded by the central and provincial governments (e.g. GITIC), wholly-owned affiliated trust and investment companies set up by various specialized banks (e.g. BOC Trust), and trust and investment companies founded by various industry sectors and local governments. Most of these companies suffered from high operational risks, poor asset quality, unclear main business, and irregular operation. In 1999, after the bankruptcy and liquidation of GITIC and the restructuring of Yuehai Group, the cleanup of local small and medium-sized trust and investment companies and other financial institutions in Guangdong Province began.

In July 1999, the Securities Law, which was newly promulgated and implemented, clearly stipulated that the securities, banking, trust, and insurance industries shall be operated and managed separately, and that securities companies shall be established separately from banking, trust, and insurance business institutions.

On November 23, 1999 came the Plan for Handling the Financial Risk of Local Small and Medium-Sized Financial Institutions and Institutes of Rural Finance in Guangdong Province. To "solve the regional and systemic financial risks that have been formed and consolidate the achievements of Guangdong's 20 years of reform and opening up," with the plan delineating responsibilities in accordance with the principle of "whoever run these institutions and name their leaders shall be held responsible." The many outlets of urban credit cooperatives, trust companies, rural institutes of finance, urban commercial banks, and rural credit cooperatives societies in Guangdong Province were included in the risk disposal plan. Wang Qishan was head of the disposal coordination group, with Dr. Chen Yunxian as a key member.

Subsequently, according to the instructions of the CSRC and Guangdong provincial government, GF Securities set up a trusteeship and acquisition working group and an outbound trusteeship team to become the main force on the trust company cleanup front. Dr. Chen appointed Dong Zhengqing as the leader and Cui Xia and Zhao Guiping as the deputy leaders to draw up a detailed plan and launch several rounds of negotiations to take trusteeship of 42 brokerage branches (including seven brokerage branches of Zhuhai International Trust and Investment Corporation and Zhuhai Special Economic Zone Trust and Investment Corporation) under 14 small and medium-sized trust and investment companies in Guangdong Province.

The previous successful trusteeship of GITIC's brokerage branches had demonstrated to the local government and regulatory authorities the advantages of GF Securities' trusteeship work. However, when applying this experience to the brokerage branches of trusteeship of small and medium-sized trust company, trusteeship was again met with their lack of cooperation. Although the trusteeship was carried out in accordance with a high-profile administrative order, the specific acquisition had to be done in accordance with the laws of the market, and the final acquisition prices had to be negotiated between the GF Securities project team and the local governments and trust investment companies.

In order to complete the acquisitions quickly, Dong Zhengqing took Zhao Guiping and Cui Xia on tours around the province. In order to resist the acquisitions, many trust and investment companies tried every possible way to get the local government to back them up. In response, Dong Zhengqing and others persistently chased the provincial leaders. When the vice governor of Guangdong Province Song Hai was delivering a speech in Shunde, they chased to Shunde; when he gave a speech in Shenzhen, they chased to Shenzhen. When they met him, Dong Zhengqing cut to the chase and said that, "Vice Governor Song, you must give us this opportunity."

During this period, Dr. Chen Yunxian was also often personally involved in negotiations. On one occasion, Dr. Chen and Cui Xia came to Foshan to start acquisition negotiations. The other party's representative was a government official in charge of financial work in Foshan, and the negotiations were exceptionally hard because they did not want to hand over the brokerage branches. Faced with the other party's erratic and unreasonable offers and attitude, Cui Xia was so angry that she directly slapped the table, and even Dr. Chen, who was always gentle and elegant, was also annoyed. The two sides parted on bad terms. But in order to complete the trusteeship, GF Securities finally gave in and took over the brokerage branches Foshan International Trust at Investment Corporation at the cost of an extra two million yuan.

Interestingly, years later, Dr. Chen Yunxian's first stop in politics was in Foshan when he served as its executive vice mayor in charge of financial work. Because of the quarrel with Dr. Chen, the government official was embarrassed to report his work to the new executive vice mayor face to face until Dr. Chen took the initiative to invite him to dinner, and only then did they make peace. The extra five million yuan he received that year was quietly returned to GF Securities without the knowledge of Dr. Chen.

In June 2000, after more than six months, GF Securities finally succeeded in acquiring 11 more brokerage branches on the basis of trusteeship work, and once again contributed to the resolution of financial risks in Guangdong Province.

4. Growth through the industry cycle

Following the first wave of impact on the securities industry, the second wave from 1997 to 1998 caused several brokerage firms to suffer severe damage. The important reason for this round of impact was the strengthening of national macro-control and regulatory management. Some brokerages continued to survive, but their expansion rate slowed down significantly; some brokerages' asset quality deteriorated and their image was greatly damaged.

In order to respond to the second wave, GF Securities, on the one hand, seized the favorable factors of the upward market movement, which greatly enhanced its asset scale and profitability, and on the other hand, assumed social responsibility in the big events such as the bankruptcy and liquidation of GITIC, maintained a rational and calm mind without craving for greatness and success, and completed acquisitions in accordance with market-oriented principles to the maximum extent. After the second wave, GF Securities achieved the metamorphosis from a "local brokerage firm" to a national brokerage firm, and had a certain influence in the international financial market.

In 1994, the number of brokerage branches in the industry was 2,262, and from 1997 to 1999, the number of brokerage branches in the industry was maintained at 2,142 due to the control of licenses,[4] while GF Securities increased the number of its brokerage branches in the system from seven to 53 in 2000 (excluding service departments and brokerage branches under trusteeship) through several rounds of M&As since 1994.

Looking back, the first decade of China's securities industry had seen a number of leading brokerages with scale advantages, and different leading brokerages had taken different paths. After the 327 Bond Futures Incident, Shenyin Wanguo Securities was established by merging the former Shanghai Shenyin Securities and the former Shanghai Wanguo Securities. After the related risk incident in 1998, Guotai Jun'an was established by merging the former Guotai Securities and the former Jun'an Securities through capital increase. Under the background of separating banking and securities, Yinhe Securities was established by merging the brokerage branches under the five companies—China Huarong, China Great Wall, China Eastern, China Cinda, and PICC—wholly owned respectively by ICBC, Agricultural Bank of China, Bank of China, China Construction Bank, and PICC. CITIC and local governments also created leading brokerage firms by integrating their own brokerage branches. In the 1990s, GF Securities always adhered to a high degree of autonomy and market-oriented principles on the road of M&A, maintaining and continuing its mainstream culture in the midst of rapid development and growth.

M&As can make a securities company bigger, but only M&As that follow market-oriented principles can make a securities company stronger, which is the deep experience of GF Securities and its successful experience. One after another M&A constructed expanded GF Securities, generating great value in terms of outlets, capital, customers and brand, and laying the foundation for the strong rise of GF Securities in the Chinese capital markets.

Looking back at the history of GF Securities' M&As, some may say, "GF Securities was lucky to catch the fast train of several policy adjustments." In this regard, Hou Wailin, former director of the Guangdong Securities Regulatory Bureau, specifically pointed out that some of GF Securities' acquisitions were indeed mandatory in nature, but their operations followed the laws of the market, and it was even not accidental that GF Securities was chosen for

4 *China Securities and Futures Statistical Yearbook.*

mandatory acquisitions. For example, when looking for the trustee of Guangdong International Trust and Investment Corporation's brokerage branches, the relevant authorities wanted to find a strong securities institution that had no longstanding problems, had high-quality staff and standardized management, and had leaders who were forward-looking. GF Securities had obviously comparative advantages, so it was selected. If a cone is in a bag, its end is immediately visible. As GF Securities adhered to standardized operation and market-oriented principles, it naturally gained the favor of many and prevailed in the market.

"Strategic vision and market awareness were the important factors contributing to the development and growth of GF Securities," Song Hai, former vice governor of Guangdong Province, commented.

Dr. Chen Yunxian repeatedly talked about the fact that GF Securities did not have a strong governmental and financial background, and its M&As were more a matter of following the laws of the market: buying cheap and selling high.

Dr. Ma Qingquan saw the acquisition work as a very important lever for the development of GF Securities: "Without these large and small M&As to complete capital accumulation, the company could not survive and develop rapidly."

Dr. Fang Jiachun said in an interview that failed cases of "alliance between giants" in economic life told us that we must not engage in "loose alliances." Therefore, GF Securities continued to stress its dominance in alliances.

At the beginning of the new millennium, the third wave of impact on the brokerage industry came. The long bear market that lasted for several years after 2000, as well as the major changes such as the separation of credit and securities, the comprehensive governance of securities companies, the reform to make non-tradable shares tradable, and the implementation of the policy that the number of fund management companies in which an institution or a number of institutions controlled by the same beneficial owner shall not exceed two, of which the number of controlling fund management companies shall not exceed one, refined the changing industry repeatedly. However, over the years, the road of knowledge-based improvement of GF Securities, which grew through M&As, continued.

In July 2001, GF Securities restructured and took control of the former Jinzhou Securities, increased its capital to 100 million yuan, and changed its name to GF Northern Securities Brokerage Co., Ltd. This move pushed GF Securities' M&A path to a new level, not only creating the first securities company group, but also initiating M&As of the whole securities companies.

At the end of the same year, entrusted by the People's Bank of China and the CSRC, GF Securities began to put 10 brokerage branches belonging to the former Hainan Huayin International Trust and Investment Company under its trusteeship. Against the background of the national regulatory policy of stopping the establishment of new brokerage branches, the company was approved to establish five new brokerage branches in Zhengzhou, Changchun, Xiamen, Lanzhou, and Nanning due to its contribution of the Hainan Huayin trusteeship.

In April 2003, GF Securities took control of the former Huafu Securities, increased its capital to 550 million yuan, and changed its name to GF Huafu Co., Ltd.

In August 2005, GF Securities took trusteeship of 25 brokerage branches and four securities service departments owned by Wuhan Securities, and completed the formal acquisition of them in September 2007.

In January 2006, GF Securities took trusteeship of 38 brokerage branches and 31 service departments belonging to Hebei Securities Co., Ltd. and completed the acquisition of four of them in September 2007.

In GF Securities acquired 16 brokerage branches and four securities service departments owned by First Securities Co., Ltd.

In June 2006, GF Securities took trusteeship of five brokerage branches belonging to Zhuhai International Trust and Investment Corporation and Zhuhai Special Economic Zone Trust and Investment Corporation, and completed the formal acquisition of them in February 2007.

In September 2006, GF Securities acquired the Jilin Hunchun Street Brokerage Branch (including the Panshui Service Department) and Jilin Beijing Road Brokerage Branch of Changcai Securities Brokerage Co., Ltd.

In December 2006, GF Securities absorbed and merged 14 brokerage branches and four securities service departments belonging to GF North Securities Brokerage Co., Ltd.

By the end of 2007, GF Securities had 169 brokerage branches (including GF Huafu), 54 securities service departments, and a total of 223 outlets, ranking among the top three in China.

"I really can't remember how many M&A negotiations GF Securities has conducted over the years. We have been doing this non-stop for more than a decade." Zhao Guiping, who participated in the vast majority of GF Securities' acquisitions, said this when recalling this long journey.

GF Securities' success in all waves of M&A is inextricably linked to its internal organization, action ability, and team spirit. When the Institutional Management Department first started an M&A, several employees could not come up with a decent proposal even after several days of work, but after the battles of taking trusteeship of GITIC, GF Securities could come up with a complete acquisition proposal after an all-nighter. And its brokerage, legal, audit, finance, IT, and other professional talents can be called upon to fight.

In the hot weather of August 2005, with the assignment of taking trusteeship of Wuhan Securities, nearly 100 employees of GF Securities' trusteeship team quickly assembled and boarded the train. On the green train from Guangzhou Railway Station to Wuhan, they were neatly dressed, carrying laptops and sitting among the woven bags and chicken cages. Although their clothes were soon drenched with sweat, they persevered on the hard sleeper all the way to Wuhan, the "furnace," and then put themselves into the battle of taking trusteeship of 25 brokerage branches and four service departments.

During the snowy and icy season in January 2006, GF people in the South suddenly received the order to take trusteeship of Hebei Securities. Many of them had never been to the north in the harsh winter, and their luggage still included spring and summer clothes. Zhao Guiping immediately called colleagues in the Beijing Brokerage Branch to prepare trench coats, gloves, hats, and other cold-weather supplies for them. After changing clothes in Beijing, they found the highway to Hebei was closed for ice, and even the truck drivers were simply stopped working for the weather. But the order was there, and the GF Securities' team still tried every possible way to arrive at the trusteeship site on time.

The complex twists and turns, hardships, and difficulties in the middle of trusteeship are hard to understand without being there. Some employees were sent out for several months or even years, separated from their families, and some even stayed to work at local brokerage branches. They were misunderstood, intimidated, and even had their lives endangered during the trusteeship. It is also because of the training of one trusteeship acquisition battle after another that GF Securities built a strong "iron army" on its own talent high ground, and a large number of grassroots employees stepped up to the stage of managers because of the experience in this.

During the acquisition negotiations with Huafu Securities, 30-year-old young lawyer Zhong Yunbo worked overtime for years for the acquisition, often staying up all night until he had nosebleeds. The leader urged him to go to the hospital for a physical examination, but he insisted on finishing the project before going. Later, when he went to the hospital, he was found to have nasopharyngeal cancer. After Zhong Yunbo's death, Dr. Fang Jiachun went to visit his family on behalf of the firm. In Zhong Yunbo's diary, all he wrote were his plans for the life of his child to be born and his work at GF Securities. The death of Zhong Yunbo became the eternal pain of GF Securities' leaders and his colleagues of the trusteeship group.

The acquisition was a training course for GF Securities on many levels. External negotiations were exhausting, and the arguments in internal decision-making were intensive. In a long list of acquisitions, GF Securities actually "worked selectively." In 2005, when its former rival Guangdong Securities in the same city of Guangzhou faced restructuring, GF Securities gave up its trusteeship attempt after repeated consideration. In the same period, concerning the acquisitions of Wuhan Securities and First Securities, GF Securities had a full internal debate, which gave play to the interaction and accumulation of management wisdom of the management team. Before Wuhan Securities and First Securities were acquired, there was a lot of disagreement within GF Securities' management due to doubts about the quality of their assets and the possibility of subsequent improvements, and at one point, some members of the management were close to walking out of the meeting room. However, after the final agreement was reached, the effective execution resulted in tangible benefits. The financial projections for the Wuhan Securities acquisition projected a loss of 47 million yuan in 2006, but with the implementation of cost-cutting measures and a quiet turnaround in the market, the company was able to turn around by March 2006. However, after the final agreement was reached, the effective execution resulted in tangible benefits. For the Wuhan Securities acquisition, the financial estimates expected a loss of 47 million yuan in 2006, but with the implementation of measures to cut costs and the quiet warming of the market, by March 2006 the company had turned around. The assets acquired in the three years from 2006 to 2008 brought a total profit of 817 million yuan, and the acquired business outlets almost became the "money printing machine" under the bull market.

Acquisition was also a way of spreading GF Securities' corporate culture. When acquiring assets with money, it is more important to uphold the culture to win popular support. Since 1994, GF Securities has formed a set of effective integration measures from personnel training and institutional arrangement to corporate culture in its acquisitions. As early as in the process of acquiring brokerage branches of the branches of Guangdong Development Bank, considering the staff's problems brought by the industry's downward spiral and unbalanced business development, GF Securities' management repeatedly summoned the staff of brokerage branches to hold mobilization meetings to introduce the company's cause and prospect, and at the same time, implemented unified management in capital operation, financial audit, training and education, and business assessment. Unlike the common "collective dismissal" in the securities industry, after Jinzhou Securities, Huafu Securities, and Wuhan Securities were acquired by GF Securities, a large number of their local officials were retained and had a good development history in GF Securities, and the placement of ordinary employees also showed the "people-oriented" concept. The placement of ordinary employees also shows the "people-oriented" concept. After the acquisition of several brokerage branches of BOC Trust, Dr. Chen Yunxian went to Beijing and Hangzhou to interview and communicate with employees, promising that "GF Securities will not easily let any employee fall behind." After Wuhan Securities was acquired, half of the original 450 employees on the rolls chose the buy-out offers, while those who remained were also apprehensive and anxious. In order to dispel their doubts, Assistant to the President Zhao Guiping, Human Resources Director Chen Wenzhan and General Manager of Hubei Headquarters Li Zhongwen repeatedly shared with them the entrepreneurial history of GF Securities, showing the simple, efficient, and pragmatic company style. Years later, retired Ms. Chen Wenzhan was still able to casually find the handwritten sentiments of Wuhan Securities employees after attending the training: "I have seen hope and got to know where my career is: it is in GF Securities!"

Different brokerage firms are struggling in a securities market with many competitors, temptations, and dark currents. Every M&A is a reminder of the defeat of industry cases. For the fall of such giants as BOC Trust and GITIC, Dr. Chen Yunxian paid much attention to analyzing the causes from the cultural level and passed the culture of "knowledge and strength, truthfulness and dedication" to every employee. This is the way that GF Securities has been able to overcome the industry cycle and rise in the midst of M&As.

Chapter V: The Flourishing Brokerage Business

It is only in marriage with the world that our ideals can bear fruit.

—Bertrand Russell

In March 1995, Dr. Chen Yunxian received a letter from Xiao Xuesheng, a young employee in the Beijing Brokerage Branch. After reading it, he offered a public reward to the writer. In this letter, Xiao Xuesheng, who graduated from Renmin University of China and joined the Beijing Brokerage Branch of GF Securities (hereinafter referred to as GF Beijing) only nine months earlier, offered rational suggestions on risk prevention of the company and also talked about the competitive environment of the Beijing securities market:

> I am now often with my clients and have learned a lot from them. They talk about the competition among brokerage firms. For example, one client talked to me about the three major disadvantages of GF Beijing:
>
> (1) In terms of information, Huaxia Securities, as the big brother in Beijing, has a network of connections in all areas and a very wide source of information. As a broker from outside Beijing, we are at a disadvantage in this respect.
>
> (2) In terms of the environment, GF Beijing has a small business area and its computer equipment is not fully utilized.
>
> (3) In terms of financing, Huaxia Securities can use securities as collateral for financing, which provides a lot of convenience, whereas we cannot compete with it in terms of capital strength and financing for clients.
>
> But why can GF Beijing keep them? The main reason is that our people here are very enthusiastic. As long as there is some investment information, we will

> call them after work to inform them, which makes them very touched. They think that GF Beijing is the best among all the brokerages in Beijing in terms of service. Of course, there are some other reasons. Our clients here are all making money now, and they feel that GF Securities has brought them good luck.

The competitive environment faced by GF Beijing was actually a common phenomenon in the brokerage business of GF Securities in the 1990s. With the background resources, hardware environment, and capital strength lagging behind the rivals in the industry, the brokerage business of GF Securities had to pursue not only "quantity" in network expansion, but also "quality" in professional service, fine management, and low-cost operation. Under the label of so-called "licensed industry" and "regional monopoly," the brokerage business had been in fierce and even cruel market competition for a long time. Through trials and tribulations, the brokerage business had always played the key role in the development of GF Securities with a large customer base and a high revenue share.

1. Differentiated marketing in the initial period

Close combat with each other

The establishment of the Shanghai Stock Exchange and the Shenzhen Stock Exchange in December 1990 and July 1991 respectively marked the shift of China's stock markets from over-the-counter decentralized trading to on-counter centralized trading, and as a result, the secondary market developed rapidly. However, GF was still in the pioneering period in 1991, and before starting the proxy trading business in Shenzhen, the Securities Department had very few businesses that could generate stable income. Dr. Chen and his colleagues rode bicycles to acquire treasury bonds and promote corporate bonds. Earning the difference in price by buying and selling treasury bonds in different places also became a common memory of GF Securities' earliest group of employees, including Li Weixiong. They often rode on slow green trains to financial institutions in other provinces to "escort bonds." The whole process was often as follows: both sides first negotiated the price, drew up a contract, stamped it, and confirmed it by fax, and then GF people took the original to the localities, made the payment, and escorted the bonds back to the company accompanied by the police. Due to the small face value of the bonds and the large total amount, the treasury bonds shipped back were often huge packets. The escorting people were careful not to keep the treasury bonds out of sight all the way. Even when they stayed overnight outside the province, two or three people would stay in the same room to ensure the safety of the escort. The key to this business was "to be diligent" and "ensure safety." With hard work, the Securities Department made its first profits in the secondary market of treasury bonds.

In 1991, there were only 14 companies listed on the stock exchange in China, with a total market value of 10.919 billion yuan and a turnover of 4.337 billion yuan. At the end of 1996, there were 514 A-share listed companies and 85 B-share listed companies, with a market value of 984.237 billion yuan and a cumulative turnover of 2.13 trillion yuan for the year. The rapidly developing market environment gave rise to the booming development of securities intermediaries, and the scarcity of stock resources on the one hand and the rising investment enthusiasm of stockholders on the other brought to the fore the phenomenon of oversupply. In Shanghai, a 30-yuan stock warrant was speculated to be 10,000 yuan. In Guangzhou, in order to open an account early, the stockholders would rely on various connections to get to a brokerage branch through the "back door," and they were even so crowded that the glass of brokerage branches' trading halls was crushed.

Old employee Liang Yanxin still clearly remembers the common trading scene in the Huanshizhong Brokerage Branch: the not spacious trading hall was crowded, a long line extended from the Securities Department the road across its gate, and the enthusiastic stockholders patiently waited to fill out the order. Stockholders needed to manually fill out the order. After the counter received cash, it then opened a margin deposit. After customers bought shares, they had them delivered. The purchase window, sale window, delivery window, inquiry window, and margin window were lined up and surrounded by stockholders almost all day. In order to effectively respond to the demand of stockholders, the staff at the counter of the Brokerage Branch had developed solid basic skills. Some of them were fast in entering stock codes and could memorize all the stock codes in a short time. Some people were able to memorize all the stock codes within a short period of time, and some people were so fast and accurate in counting money. Counting money until your hands cramped actually happened.

In the hot environment from 1992 to 1993, securities operating institutions were in the sellers' market, and the overall marketing thinking of the brokerage branches was in the stage of "sitting in the business location to do business." Unfortunately, the bull market was short and the bear market was long. In 1994 and 1995, the market entered a period of downturn. The regulator took a variety of measures for developing the market. It introduced some new trading varieties, and at one point, it used the T+0 trading clearing, which was rare even in developed countries, but the wealth effect of investors was gradually declining. In order to enliven their brokerage branches, many brokerage firms provided free lunch to the stockholders and gave them movie tickets and other "additional services." In addition, they invested heavily in their trading halls' luxury decoration. But the bear market lasted longer than most people had expected, the stock trading volume was low, and the area of the trading site was too large and brought higher operating costs. With decision-making power in marketing in their hands, brokerage branch bosses racked their brains on how to smoothly make it through the bear market.

Due to the seasons of founding time and geographical location, GF brokerage branches did not fully enjoy the first wave of the bull market dividends, which also made the first batch of brokerage branch general managers begin to face the cruelty of the market very early. Chen Chunming, Zhang Min, Zhao Guiping, Su Yingbiao, Zhang Hongyi, Qu Nianzeng, Kang Guohong, and others not only had a highly educated knowledge background, but also had the impetus to think, act, and innovate, and fought bravely with regional rivals.

The GF Hainan Brokerage Branch let out its VIP trading lounge in the afternoon after the market was closed. It closed its computer settlement port, used its computers with internet connectivity, and transformed the lounge into a karaoke room in order to amortize its operating costs. Behind all kinds of "strange tricks" was the strong desire of the brokerage branch to survive, which also let it to better survive the market downturn than its rivals in the same city and create the industry's first market-oriented M&A.[1]

In 1993, the newly established Tianhe Road Brokerage Branch is located in Tianhe East Road in Guangzhou. The surrounding land had just begun to be developed. Next to the Brokerage Branch was farmland and it was a sparsely populated area. The Brokerage Branch started business from scratch and accumulated its customers from scratch. That was a very difficult process. How to develop customers and how to support the normal operation of the Brokerage Branch became the first problem of its young general manager Zhao Guiping. After the Brokerage Branch was opened for a period of time, she was a bit at a loss. Due to the previous work in Guangdong Securities' Rongyuan Brokerage Branch for a year, she remembered its VIP customers.

So, Zhao Guiping contacted an "opinion leader," Wu Huanming, encouraging him to bring other VIPs over to the GF Securities Tianhe Road Brokerage Branch for stock speculation. In order to lobby Wu, Zhao Guiping cited several advantages of her own Brokerage Branch: "Our Brokerage Branch is relatively large with an especially spacious and well-lit VIP trading lounge with new computers for every VIP with internet connection uninterrupted." But Wu also immediately raised the problem:

"We mostly live in Beijing Road in Yuexiu District, but your Tianhe Road Brokerage Branch is located far away; it is already in the suburbs. It is impossible for customers to walk to you." Zhao Guiping immediately calculated an account silently in her heart: this batch of customers were professional shareholders, and with their amount of capital and the commission their trading volume contributedd, even renting a car for them was cost-effective. So she promised: "The distance is not a problem. I can find a car to pick you up every day to come to the Brokerage Branch and give you VIP treatment." Wu was impressed by Zhao Guiping's sincerity and boldness, and promised to lobby other VIP to transfer to

1 For details, see Chapter IV of this book, "M&As within Guangdong Development Bank."

the Tianhe Road Brokerage Branch.

When making this promise, in fact, Zhao Guiping did not know whether that would work: "Will Dr. Chen agree?" Only Dr. Chen could help her solve the problem of the car. Surprisingly, after Dr. Chen listened to her face-to-face report, without a moment's hesitation, he immediately arranged for the administrative department to borrow a van from Guangdong Development Bank. He told Zhao's Brokerage Branch to hire a driver, to seize the opportunity to organize a site visit and further mobilization through meals. In this way, the newborn brokerage branch had the first group of VIP customers. These customers from the old city of Guangzhou took the shuttle bus to speculate on stocks every day, just like commuting to work. In the face of sudden competition, rival brokerage firms criticized GF Securities in the media for tempting customers with food and paralyzed them with vehicles, but as that was done for the survival of the new Brokerage Branch, colleagues dismissed it with a smile.

After winning over the first group of VIP customers, the employees of the Tianhe Road Brokerage Branch continued to cast the marketing net. With limited funds, in order to expand the impact, they oil printed colorful leaflets, reading "Good news, good news, the Huangpu Avenue Brokerage Branch has opened. Whoever opens an account with it in its first month will have a big gift. We have a spacious trading hall...." After the market was closed, everyone rode a bicycle to the community to hand out leaflets, using "visiting every building," "mailing marketing leaflets," and other customer marketing models to expand the market. With the full development of the Tianhe CBD, the Brokerage Branch moved to Huangpu Avenue in time. With the unremitting efforts of the staff, the Huangpu Avenue Brokerage Branch's customer resources grew increasingly rich.

Established in 1993, the GF Securities Hongbao Road Brokerage Branch also faced fierce competition from rivals in the same city. Located at the forefront of China's securities market, Shenzhen had more than 200 brokerage branches, and most of them were concentrated in Luohu and Futian districts. As the first brokerage branch of GF Securities in Shenzhen, the Hongbao Road Brokerage Branch had a business area plus office area of only 700 square meters without a trading hall when it was first established; and next to it was the luxuriously decorated Guoxin Securities Brokerage Branch with 6,000 square meters of business area, as well as more than a dozen brokerage branches of Jun'an Securities, Dapeng Securities, Haitong Securities, Luoyang Securities, and other large and small brokerage firms. They were staggered in the area of the 150 square meters around the GF Securities Hongbao Road Brokerage Branch. The branch did not have advantages in terms of financial strength, research power, and business scale. In addition, under the GF Securities strategy of standardized business, it could not, like small and medium-sized brokerages, use rebates, overdrafts, and other means. As a result, the general manager of the branch Kang Guohong was faced with the dilemma of survival in the cracks.

To find a way out, the Brokerage Branch conducted an in-depth market survey. They found, in the floor trading mode, more than 200 brokerage branches in Shenzhen could provide 60,000–100,000 positions (with each having an average of 500 customers). The total number of stockholders in Shenzhen should be about 600,000 (with each brokerage branch having an average of 3,000 customers). That is to say, about 500,000 stockholders could only enjoy services of "using stock machines to watch the market and using the telephone to buy and sell stocks" because of their work or lifestyles, and could not get the effective services of brokerage branches. This showed that there was a huge potential for development.

Through an analysis of the industry, customers, and competitors, the Hongbao Brokerage Branch decided to take the road of virtualized services, aiming to provide "remote services" for the customers who could not be present at the branch to operate. In addition to telephone commission and other traditional ways, after years of development and technology upgrades, the brokerage branch launched services such as "Stock Trading Secretary," "Family Remote VIPs," "Online Stock Trading," and "Good Manages" services, which established the unique service image of GF Securities and won over more customers from competitors. With technical advantages, the Hongbao Road Brokerage Branch Securities formed a unique landscape in the field of brokerage business and was awarded the title of "Excellent Securities Brokerage Branch" in Shenzhen for many years. The team of the Hongbao Road Brokerage Branch also kept close contact with telecommunications, media, and other institutions for a long time, actively tracking the latest technological developments, and had Kang Guohong, Yang Long, Peng Jianping, and other management talents with keen perspectives.

Word-of-mouth marketing of dedicated service

After 1994, through a series of initiatives such as the acquisition of the brokerage branches of the branches of Guangdong Development Bank and the acquisition of BOC Trust Securities Department, GF Securities' brokerage business expanded rapidly and the bosses of its brokerage branches were able to display their management talents on a broader platform.

The Beijing Brokerage Branch of GF Securities was one of the first batch of securities institutions that were established in Beijing by institutions outside the city. It had a difficult start and tight expenses. Ms. Li Shuzhi visited the staff during her business trip in Beijing, but found that the staff dormitory was a simple housing in Tong County in a suburb with very difficult conditions, and most of the people living next to it were peasants wearing white goat belly towels. The dormitory was chosen here just to save some rent.

Under the leadership of General Manager Qu Nianzeng, the Beijing Brokerage Branch figured out its own advantages. In addition to what the letter from the new employee described above, "our people here are very enthusiastic," the Beijing

Brokerage Branch also created the first commissioned night market in the capital, shareholder evaluation, stock index quizzes, and a series of service activities. It was the first in north China to achieve "point-to-point" communication. In 1996, GF Securities was the first brokerage firm in Beijing to provide a series of services, such as night market, shareholder evaluation, and stock index quiz, and was the first in North China to realize "point-to-point" communication and was highly praised by investors and regulators, while its turnover entered the top ten of brokerage firms in Beijing.

In 1996, GF Securities restructured the two loss-making brokerage branches of BOC Trust in Beijing and integrated them into the Beijing Business Headquarters. So GF Securities had three brokerage branches in Beijing: the Jianhua South Road Brokerage Branch, Fuchengmen Brokerage Branch, and Tiyuguan Road Brokerage Branch. The Beijing Business Headquarters added a financial center, used bulletin boards to provide investors with trading information, daily memos, and market forecasts, held investor salons from time to time, and used various media to distribute investment analyses to enhance the influence of analysts and effectively increase investors' understanding and trust of GF Securities. In 1997, the Beijing Business Headquarters not only made up for the loss of 35 million yuan of the former BOC Securities Department, but also made a profit of 44.84 million yuan.

The Zhaoqing Brokerage Branch, which had been acquired with a price increase of 800,000 yuan during the process of acquiring the brokerage branches of the branches of Guangdong Development Bank, became the representative of marketing ability within GF Securities for a long time. It was not only rated as excellent within the company, but also recognized as an Excellent Securities Brokerage Branch by the Guangdong Securities Association in 1997. In the economically underdeveloped western region of Guangdong, the achievements of the Zhaoqing Brokerage Branch were hard to come by.

Zhaoqing Brokerage Branch General Manager Cui Xia made "diligence" the basis. It would offer to do what other brokerage firms were not willing to do; it carried through to the end without a letup, which other brokerage firms could not do. Cui repeatedly stressed to the staff: the competition of brokerage firms is like a tug-of-war. Your side will be pulled over by the other side if you do not persevere, so at no time can we relax; we must make something out of diligence.

In the 1990s in Zhaoqing, the Brokerage Branch of GF Securities was not only the longest one in operation, but also provided various agency services for customers within the company's business scope, including opening shareholder accounts, subscribing to new shares, and handling dividends and interests. In order to take care of different levels of shareholders, the Zhaoqing Brokerage Branch also opened a daily stock commentary, afternoon salon, and evening night school for shareholders.

Moreover, the branch used holidays to carry out frequent securities consultation stall activities. In addition to the expansion in the city, in accordance with the fact in the mountainous areas, Zhaoqing did not have easy access to traffic and information, the branch also organized its staff to hold roadshows in all counties and cities in the region to provide one-stop service for local stockholders to invest in securities. This not only made it greatly convenient for remote stockholders, but also expanded the group of investors of the Zhaoqing Brokerage Branch.

From the end of 1996 to the beginning of 1997, the securities market was booming. It was inconvenient for stockholders to have on-site trading, so the Zhaoqing Brokerage Branch introduced computer telephone commission and remote terminal business in a timely manner. This timing was very accurate. Customers were very enthusiastic in requesting the installation of the machine, the Brokerage Branch saved costs and space, and this part of the new customer base was very stable.

In 1997, another brokerage firm entered the city of Zhaoqing, with computer hardware and a superior site environment, which diverted some customers of GF Securities. Considering that it was difficult to compete with it in terms of hardware for a while, Cui Xia thought of impressing the shareholders with service and sincerity, so she specially invited back the shareholders who had left GF Securities, and used the form of seminars to solicit comments and suggestions and listen to criticism, hoping that the shareholders would understand some problems that existed before. For this group of customers, she also took measures to provide personalized services. This touched them and some returned to GF Securities.

When the stock market was in the doldrums, the account opening rate of remote VIP accounts dropped sharply, and the conventional marketing services could not reverse the trend. In order to stabilize customers, Cui Xia made opening remote VIP accounts a task for employees, and linked the performance with the benefits. This mechanism made the Brokerage Branch's remote account opening rate rapidly increase, with some employees even over-achieving their task by a big margin. The Zhaoqing Brokerage Branch's remote terminal customers reached more than 300, ranking among the top domestic brokerage firms. In the 1998 Shanghai shareholder account designated trading business battle, Cui Xia again used the "task to person" strategy, so that the Zhaoqing Brokerage Branch won a large number of customers in a short period of time. And in many battles in the Brokerage Branch, Cui Xia herself was always the one who received the most tasks and took the lead to complete.

In 1998, GF Securities implemented the policy of fixing posts and staffing and overstaffed brokerage branches faced layoffs. Having developed a love for her subordinates, Cui Xia did not like the idea. After repeated thoughts, she decided to take the margin collection business as a bargaining chip, as she wanted to transfer some employees of the Zhaoqing Brokerage Branch to banks. She had repeated consultations with the Agricultural Bank of China, Industrial and Commercial Bank of China, China Construction Bank, and Guangdong Development Bank, and finally, Guangdong Development Bank agreed to receive the eight employees of the Zhaoqing Brokerage Branch in return for its margin deposits. With these people having a way out, the Zhaoqing Brokerage Branch's work of fixing posts and staffing basically met GF Securities' requirements.

In 1999, GF Securities leaders received a letter from Zhaoqing, which reads:

> We are the Zhaoqing Brokerage Branch's loyal stockholders. Over the years the leadership and staff of the Zhaoqing Brokerage Branch is very trustworthy. General Manager Cui Xia, in particular, often works with us and tries to communicate with us, creating a comfortable investment environment for us. In addition, General Manager Cui fully understands Zhaoqing's local customs and popular sentiments and the concerns of local stockholders. Whenever anything happens, she would inform her stockholders, so that we have reduced losses in several market shocks.

This letter caused the executive vice president in charge of brokerage business, Dong Zhengqing, to think a lot, and he commented on the letter:

> Investors trust Cui Xia for four reasons: first, she works with them and tries to communicate with them; second, she creates a comfortable investment environment; third, she understands local customs and popular sentiments; and fourth, she reduces investors' losses. To obtain such trust, we must have a sincere heart to serve investors, a keen market judgment, and a high degree of responsible dedication. Some of our brokerage branches' objective conditions are not worse than Zhaoqing's, but their performance is not good. Why? Compared with Cui Xia, the leaders of these brokerage branches are not poor in terms of personal ability, but they are poor in terms of professional dedication and pioneering spirit.
>
> I hope the general managers of the brokerage branches whose business volume is languishing will learn from Cui Xia in terms of service spirit, dedication, and pioneering spirit.

Zhaoqing's Cui Xia took the initiative and assessed the performance of all her staff to win, while the general manager of the Huizhou Brokerage Branch Li Shuiquan's concept that "rendering services is not for the purposes of making money, but good services will definitely make money" is a more straightforward expression of popularity-based marketing. This locally based concept explains clearly which comes first in frontline operation and is deeply appreciated by Dr. Chen Yunxian.

The reason why such a point of view could be put forward is because when Li Shuiquan first arrived in Huizhou, he found two small conflicts in his brokerage branch in serving customers:

(1) The shareholders needed to go to the Brokerage Branch for on-site speculation. When they bought vegetables or passed the brokerage branch, they would stop their bikes or motorcycles to see the market. For security reasons,

the brokerage branch hired two security guards who took care of their bikes or motorcycles in return for payment. Some customers might only look at the market for a few minutes, but they still had to pay for parking. They complained about this a lot.

(2) As computers were costly, many stockholders would print quotation sheets from the counter in the afternoon after the close of business. Despite the limited number of stocks on the market, they still needed to print two to three pages of quotation sheets. The brokerage branch charged one yuan per sheet; that was still a lot of money for the stockholders.

Most of the brokerage branch bosses would not take these trivial issues to heart, but Li Shuiquan calculated an account: in the T+0 transaction clearing at the time, the brokerage branch would collect a commission of three thousandths of the turnover; the turnover of one million yuan of stocks bought and sold would generate 6,000 yuan for the brokerage branch. The bike storage and quotation sheet printing would not generate substantial income, but would interfere with the stockholders' trading experience. He boldly proposed to waive the cost of bicycle storage and quotation sheet printing for stockholders, in order to attract and retain customers.

In the then loss-making Huizhou Brokerage Branch, this initiative met with resistance, because the bicycle storage fee could cover the security guard's salary, and the quotation sheet printing fee could also make up for the cost. The brokerage branch's staff could not understand it for a while.

Li Shuiquan repeatedly instilled in the staff: the basic income source of the brokerage branch is the entrustment transaction fee and the margin spread of customers. Without customers, there will be no income, and then the economic basis of our employees will be lost. If we serve the customers, our source of food and clothing, well, it will inevitably bring higher commission.

In order to attract shareholders, he not only spent dearly on hiring well-known stock critics to the brokerage branch for roadshows, but also provided shareholders with mineral water free of charge. His careful and thoughtful services not only retained customers, but also attracted more investors to come to his brokerage branch.

In Huizhou, Li Shuiquan constantly created new services, developing from the most primitive counter trading method, to telephone commission, magnetic card commission, self-service terminals, remote terminals, stock BP machines, and telephone automatic transfers. The brokerage branch also analyzed and interpreted abnormal stock price movements and offered daily after-hours stock reviews through radio, newspapers, telephone consultation hotlines, newsletters, and other information media to expand its influence among local citizens.

In the internal management, the Huizhou Brokerage Branch did not emphasize the notion of the "task to person," but focused on improving services. This was like a magnet which attracted customers. From 1995 to 1997, the Huizhou Brokerage Branch shifted from the loss of more than 1.8 million yuan to a profit of nearly 100 million yuan. Due to the sudden increase in stockholders, the Huizhou Brokerage Branch once raised the threshold for stockholders to open accounts, becoming one of the two brokerage branches in China forced to restrict the opening of accounts, which can be seen as evidence of the popularity of the Huizhou Brokerage Branch in the local area.

Low-cost operation creates "hidden advantages"

The policy of fixing posts and staffing which was resisted by Cui Xia and the leaders of brokerage branches was an internal management policy GF Securities began to implement in the mid-1990s. After the bull market from 1996 to 1997, there was a strong desire to expand the brokerage branches, but in Dr. Chen Yunxian's opinion, the booming brokerage business was experiencing "growing pains."

With the completion of the acquisition of the brokerage branches of Guangdong Development Bank, the acquisition of BOC Trust, and the orderly progress in the trusteeship GITIC brokerage branches, GF Securities' brokerage branches reached 37. For the cost control of brokerage business, this was a large "multiplier." If a brokerage branch expanded the recruitment of five or ten people, this would not seem to be much of a problem, but if all the 37 brokerage branches of GF Securities were to do the same, the management and cost problems would be very serious, and thus the development of business would give rise to new problems. And from the lessons of BOC Trust and GITIC, the excessively fast speed of expansion and too many redundant employees were common problems, and GF Securities must not repeat the same mistake.

The calm thinking in the bull market made Dr. Chen put forward the requirement of "fixing posts and staffing" at the beginning of the market downturn in 1997, ahead of the rest of the industry. The headquarters of the company implemented the total salary management for each division, and the total salary was approved once a year with the staffing, and would not increase or decrease due to the increase or decrease of staff. The company adjusted the staff structure of each brokerage branch and it was strictly prohibited to increase the staff without approval. Taking into account the individual circumstances of different brokerage branches in the context of growth, the policy of fixing posts and staffing took into account commonality and individuality, and the organizational structure and post design of brokerage business became more reasonable. The headquarters of the company implemented unified management of labor cost, training and education and business assessment for each brokerage branch, and the staffing of the business headquarters and the subordinate brokerage branches was limited to about 20 people. For example, the long-established Huanshizhong Brokerage Branch had 33 people at the end of 1997, and the approved staffing level was 22 at the beginning of 1999. The structural salary system based on job value and performance assessment as the basis for adjustment let salaries play a better role in staff motivation and management.

For GF Securities' brokerage business, which was destined to survive in the market cycle, the policy of "fixing posts and staffing" in 1997 was like a preventive injection, which had a short sting but accumulated management experience in the face of the bull-bear transition early. After the short bull market in 2000, GF Securities once again reinforced the requirement of "fixing posts and staffing" in the whole company. With customer relationship management at the core, the brokerage branches finely set post groups, forming groups of management personnel, groups of back office business personnel, groups of front office account managers, and groups of front office financial advisors. They took measures to take into consideration business transformation and to ensure that people took jobs based on competition. They also implemented regional centralized trading and other methods. All helped the company better realize "cost efficiency" in the bull-bear transition. In the M&A expansion, the cost management advantage also became a useful instrument for GF Securities to turn the acquired brokerage branches profitable.

What many people do not know is that the GF Securities brokerage business had a hidden and deep low-cost advantage—its own property.

Brokerage branches live trading often requires a larger premise, and its costs were high. But GF Securities had a poor foundation to start with, and the brokerage branches it opened were all not designed to win based on the area of their premises. After having a certain amount of capital accumulation, Dr. Chen Yunxian proposed to buy property in the name of the company or brokerage branches to support the long-term low-cost expansion plan.

In the 1990s, Wanguo Securities, Huaxia Securities, and Southern Securities, which had strong capital levels, made large direct investments in real estate, but most of them were involved in speculation in the real estate industry and were not only not used for business or offices, and they also became non-performing assets. With local support, securities firms generally owned their own properties in the cities where they were headquartered, but they were rarely willing to acquire properties outside these cities for long-term development. In contrast, Dr. Chen Yunxian's decision to purchase a large number of properties cheaply during the real estate downturn seemed to be quite "different."

From 1997, GF Securities purchased properties in Meizhou, Foshan, Zhuhai, Huizhou, Dongguan, Zhaoqing, Shantou, and other places in Guangdong Province for the upgrading and long-term development of its brokerage branches. Take the Meijiang Second Road Brokerage Branch in Meizhou as an example. The company purchased from the local public security bureau a property located in Jiangnan Shizi Qi Lane, Meijiang District in Meizhou, with a floor area of 3,764 square meters and a usage right of 50 years.

Outside Guangdong Province, the Heping Avenue Brokerage Branch and Yilong Road Brokerage Branch in Haikou owned properties of 1,482 square meters in the Blue Sky Building and 800 square meters in the Huayin Building, respectively. With the expansion of business outlets, GF Securities' brokerage branches in Hangzhou, Hefei, Jinzhou, Shenyang, Liaoyang, and other places also had their own properties.

Further, GF Securities not only purchased properties for its local brokerage branches in Beijing, Shanghai, and Shenzhen, but also purchased its own properties in key areas such as Beijing Financial Street, the same building of the Shanghai Stock Exchange, and the same building of the Shenzhen Stock Exchange. In Beijing, for example, GF Securities' Beijing Jianhua South Road Brokerage Branch had a 412-square-meter property with a floor area of 1,881 square meters in Fuchengmen South Street in Xicheng District, and GF Securities had 2,128 square meters of office space in Financial Street. In Shanghai, in addition to properties of 3,372 square meters in Yulan Road and 1,521 square meters in Shiquan Road, GF Securities bought 1,246 square meters of office space in Shanghai Securities Building in Pudong South Road, where the Shanghai Stock Exchange is located. The company also purchased commercial properties in some cities according to its work needs.

It was once jokingly said that "McDonald's, which sells burgers, and IKEA, which sells furniture, are actually real estate companies." This is because, under the business models of these two multinational business giants, they both had the secret of buying a large number of their own properties, with the McDonald's real estate rental business even contributing nearly half of its operating profit and IKEA becoming one of the largest foreign-owned "landlords" in China. In the commercial real estate sector, GF Securities could hardly compete with these two smart multinational giants, but before the Chinese real estate market started to soar, GF Securities seized the valuable window to acquire more properties, a move that led to the low-cost expansion and steady growth of its brokerage business in several first- and second-tier cities. Even without considering the appreciation in real estate value (e.g., the average price of a commercial property purchased in Shenzhen's Jingpeng Mansion in the 1990s was only about 3,600 yuan per square meters), the savings in operating costs for local branches from owned properties over a 20-year period alone were significant.

Behind the fierce marketing competition, the strict control of labor cost and low cost of property acquisition became the "hidden advantage" of GF Securities' low-cost brokerage business operation, and injected the sense of prudent operation and intensive development for the whole company from top to bottom. Many years later, when the Securities Association of China ranked the national securities companies by "cost management ability," GF Securities ranked first with obvious advantages.

2. Transformation and development under the new business model

New proposition in the law-based era

After many years, while the brokerage business was hit by the market waves in turn, laws and regulations and regulatory policies were constantly pushing brokerage firms to make profound changes. Before the introduction of the Securities Law, margin management of brokerage business became a major focus to test the management wisdom of each brokerage firm.

In the face of the short bull and long bear market, it was difficult for the brokerage branches to increase revenue, while business expenses were very high. Some of the brokerage branches also needed to underwrite IPOs and treasury bonds, as well as handle rights offering for listed companies and promote their self-dealing business in the secondary market. All this stretched their capital, and the misappropriation of margin became a more common practice of them, driving the brokerage business into the grey area.

In 1993 GF Securities began to centralize the branch hierarchy management,[2] continuing to tighten institutional construction and the management processes. Dr. Chen also repeatedly told the heads of brokerage branches: "The heads of brokerage branches are young, lack financial work experience, and to some extent are too bold, so they should especially pay attention to the use of funds to prevent problems before they occur. " However, the risk of margin management was still not completely kept out of the company, and the brokerage business paid the price for this in its rapid growth.

In the acquisition of the brokerage branches of the branches of Guangdong Development Bank, the Jiangmen Brokerage Branch was absorbed early, but its original customer margin debit, investment and other longstanding problems failed to be thoroughly solved. In January 1997, the GF securities headquarters received complaints from Jiangmen Brokerage Branch employees, saying that General Manager Li Weiyue borrowed funds from other financial institutions, and misappropriated customer margin without authorization to lend Xinhui CTS Corporation a huge amount of money. The leader of Xinhui CTS Corporation used the money for real estate speculation in Macao. The property he bought did not have clear property rights, so he could not repay the debt.

After the headquarters of GF Securities learned of this incident, they immediately sent a task force led by Li Shuzhi to Jiangmen to investigate. As the investigation progressed, the team found that the matter was far more complicated than previously expected. Given the amount of money and complexity of the case involved, GF

2 For details, see "Standardized management practices leading the industry" in Chapter II of this book.

Securities reported the case to the judiciary and took out a huge insurance policy for the members of the task force. Upon receiving the report, the Jiangmen judicial and law enforcement authorities set up a task force in a hurry, with Ye Meilu, the chief of the Guangdong Provincial Procuratorate's Major Cases Guidance Division, as the task force's leader, to arrest Li Weiyue and the middlemen. Through examination, the task force learned that Xinhui CTS had converted HK$81 million into nearly 100 million yuan for real estate speculation in Macao, and that a Portuguese businessman was involved. After clarifying the relationship and the amount of money involved, GF Securities embarked on a long road to recover the debt, and the task force's leader Wu Yuemin went to Macao, which had not yet been returned to China, several times with the prosecutor's office to recover the debt. The houses, the BMW car, and more than HK$400,000 in cash under the name of the head of Xinhui CTS were seized, but the Portuguese businessman had long since fled Portugal and was nowhere to be found.

The case was further complicated when the land in question came to the attention of Macao's 14K triad, which wanted to claim the land for themselves due to confusion over the title. In April 1998, the Guangdong Provincial Procuratorate, GF Securities' Li Shuzhi and lawyer Cao Gang negotiated with 14K triad boss "Broken Tooth" Wan Kuok Kui over the land in question. They were unsuccessful. A few days later, "Broken Tooth" was arrested, and the company continued to maintain contact with his brother. One day, the team leader, Wu Yuemin, received a phone call from the then secretary of the Guangdong provincial government and learned from the president of the Macao Chamber of Commerce that if GF Securities agreed to pay HK$50 million to the gangster society, it would get the land in Macao.

After careful consideration, the company's top management did not agree to the above request under the dazzling series of "casino fiasco" scenarios. Because GF Securities had no experience in dealing with such triads, it was likely that the company would not get the land even if it paid for it. After that, the company still maintained communication with the judicial authorities, but never obtained the ownership of the land. Fortunately, the company recovered more than 30 million yuan worth of assets including cash and properties as compensation.

The Jiangmen special case sounded alarm for GF Securities. In order to strengthen the fund management of the company and enhance the ability to fend off risks, the Fund Management Measures of GF Securities Co., Ltd. were officially promulgated in March 1997. This document clearly pointed out that: branches shall not have any overdraft; branches shall not use the reserve or their own funds for their self-dealing business without authorization; branches shall not borrow funds from each other; branches shall not lend their funds to borrowers outside GF Securities; in principle, the company's headquarters shall not lend its money to outsiders; branches are not allowed to set up securities trading seats in various trading centers without authorization; and if necessary, the company's headquarters will set up such seats in a unified manner.

Dr. Chen Yunxian said emphatically in the 1998 year-end work conference: "As the head of the company, I often warn myself that regulation is the foundation and development is the driving force. In this process, I should grasp three points: First, I should grasp my own integrity, do practical work and have professional ability. Second, I should grasp the leadership team, including middle-level officials, to fully understand the reality of China's historical stage. Third, I should grasp the team's institute building."

In July 1999, the Securities Law was officially implemented, marking the establishment of a centralized and unified regulatory system for the securities market, and also marking a new stage in the law-based construction of the securities market, where brokerage business would compete in a regulated context. In the law-based era, the grey space for soliciting customers by improper means had been greatly reduced, and the focus of brokerage business had shifted to high-quality consulting services and efficient and safe trading services, and continuous business innovation had become the key to the sustainable development of brokerage business.

On the road of transformation

With the intensification of competition, the marketing method of "fighting for venues" was declining, and the traditional brokerage business was accelerating its transformation into modern brokerage business. In an internal report, "Research on the Innovation of China's Securities Brokerage Business," the Institutional Management Department of GF Securities made the following judgment:

> The connotation of traditional brokerage business is the transactional business in the capital markets. Because of the continuous innovation of brokerage business, the connotation of traditional brokerage business has been profoundly changed. First, modern brokerage business is investment service, including intermediary agent buying and selling as a trading channel for investors to make investment. Second, modern brokerage business provides financial service of different degrees from general financial information to complete expert financial service. Brokerage firms provide customers with comprehensive personalized information and consulting services by virtue of highly qualified investment advisors or brokers, and provide high value-added financial services through service innovation. Finally, with the development of financial markets and the deepening of financial innovation, new derivative financial instruments have emerged, and large investment banks have developed into financial supermarkets and financial department stores, providing investors with financial products with a variety of risk-return portfolios and a full range of personalized financial services.

A more intuitive and profound change was the subsequent floating commission system. In the early development, commission income from brokerage business accounted for more than 50 percent, or even 80–90 percent, of the total income of brokerage firms. Prior to 2002, commission discounting was considered a "cheap and vicious" competitive tactic in the industry. In April 2002, the CSRC, the State Planning Commission, and the State Administration of Taxation jointly issued the Circular on Adjusting the Commission Charging Standard for Securities Trading, which stipulated that the former fixed commission should be changed to a floating system with a maximum ceiling, and the commission charged by securities companies should not be higher than three thousandth of the amount of securities trading, and should not be lower than the supervision fee for securities trading and the commission of securities trading. This marked the shift from the fixed commission system to the floating commission system. This, coupled with the lifting of restrictions on opening new brokerage branches, the liberalization of the brokerage system, and the development of online brokerage business, made the competition in the industry more and more intense. If there was no effective weapon, the loss of stockholders' accounts, the reduction of commission, and the shrinkage of assets would surely follow, the brokerage business and even the main source of profit of all securities companies would face overall decline. The transformation of the brokerage business of the whole industry was inevitable.

The floating commission system was implemented very quickly after it was promulgated, and many brokerage firms had difficulty coping with it for a while. In the era of channel services, the number of brokerage branches determined the strength of brokerage business. In 2001, GF Securities had 71 brokerage branches and 19 remote service outlets and the number of various business outlets was leading in the country, taking into consideration factors such as trusteeship and acquisition. But Dr. Chen Yunxian had made an analysis before the arrival of floating commission system:

> The brokerage business is in the midst of transformation, but at present, we still have to rely on the number of business outlets to win, because there is not much difference in the service means and service quality among the top-ranking securities companies in terms of trading volume. However, GF Securities still lags behind other brokerage firms in terms of diversification of trading varieties in brokerage business, such as in bond and treasury repo trading.

Breaking the homogenization of brokerage business became an industry proposition, and various securities companies carried out reform. Fuyou Securities fully implemented the brokerage system with the help of online trading, and Dapeng Securities learned from Merrill Lynch's FC system, which had attracted attention in the industry. The "Top Ten Model Window" brokerage branches launched by Shanghai securities industry at that time demonstrated the new developments of brokerage business of brokerage firms. Guotai Securities' Yanping Road Brokerage Branch launched a "securities supermarket," and Hainan Hong Kong and Macao International Trust Investment Co., Ltd.'s Nanpu Road Brokerage Branch established the "securities investment square," Hubei Shangzheng advocated "family-type securities services." These brokerage branches sublimated the content and items of regular and special services into a new business concept by reviewing, planning, and packaging them carefully.

In the face of the transformation, the GF Securities' Institutional Management Department fully invested in innovative research. After many days of research and analysis, GF Securities released its service system after customer segmentation: company-level CRM system (customer relationship management system), VIP customer service system, and IPTV video broadcasting system. It gradually implemented regional centralized trading and established the company's unified information service platform. In particular, as the first securities company to introduce a CRM system and implement a system for assigning a manager for each stockholder, GF Securities received widespread attention from the industry.

What had a more profound impact was the advancement of the bank securities express business ahead of schedule. In 2001, GF Securities signed cooperation agreements with Industrial and Commercial Bank of China, Pudong Development Bank, and China Merchants Bank, and the bank securities express business was launched in depth. By the end of 2003, the number of accounts opened at GF Securities had reached 14,074, with a total trading volume of 940 million yuan. In particular, the bank securities business in Guangzhou achieved good results, and made preliminary preparations for exploring new operation modes of brokerage business and expanding new development space. After that, the bank securities express business became a strategic breakthrough in the transformation of the brokerage business, and achieved extraordinary development, creating the backbone of a marketing team.

Likewise, e-commerce research was incorporated into the innovation of the Institutional Management Department, and GF Securities became one of the early securities companies to promote transformation with the advancement of internet technology.

The rule of law and floating commission system rewrote the pattern of brokerage, and the innovation of GF Securities' brokerage business in products, technologies, financial industrial cooperation, and internal management gradually unfolded in-depth.

The customer service system forged the brand of "Golden Housekeeper"

The focus of market development of brokerage business gradually turned to "attracting more customers," and brand building could enhance the company's popularity, which in turn helped product sales and customer services in brokerage business.

On July 10, 1999, at a secondary market business development meeting, Dong Zhengqing, executive vice president of GF Securities, made a judgment on development direction of the brokerage branches, proposing that "the brokerage branches should serve investors while creating profits and the company's brand and image." After years of development, GF Securities' brand promotion and public relations work were still in the initial stage, and it had not made a professional plan for its overall brand in the secondary market. Attendees at the meeting believed that brand awareness and super chain store awareness should be enhanced, the unique service concept and business characteristics of GF Securities should be formed to reach a universally unified standard, and the nationwide outlets could magnify their publicity effect, truly reflect the style of GF Securities, and enhance its popularity.

In addition, GF Securities invested only 0.09 percent of its revenue in branding, which was a very incongruous ratio figure when compared with multinational companies and leading financial companies. How to shape its overall image? GF Securities began to focus on exploration in the secondary market.

In 2000, the Institutional Management Department began to implement the system of assigning a manager for each customer in all brokerage branches, and launched brokerage service brands for different levels of customer needs. These included the "GF E-to-One Service System" for off-site trading customers and the "GF VIP Customer Service System" for high-end customers. For the CRM system, under the guidance of "being professional and dedicated to provide what you want," GF Securities brokerage business formed five major service systems.

(1) The VIP customer service system

The VIP customer value-added service system provided different customers with truly personalized services. The VIP customer service system was established by integrating the resources of the company's Investment Banking Department, Asset Management Department, and Development Research Center to provide value-added services for customers with assets of over five million yuan at GF Securities: securities experts' analyses of industry investment strategies; special research reports on various investment products; specialized and personalized investment programs; and annual securities market visits and exchanges.

(2) The core customer service system

The system used a company-level customer relationship management platform to track and analyze all the core customers of GF Securities in a comprehensive manner. It also relied on the manager teams of brokerage branches to provide more individualized and professional investment services for core customers. The main services included assigning a dedicated manager for each core client; when a client encountered difficulties in trading, he or she could contact the manager so that the problem could be solved immediately; when a client was uncertain about an investment decision, the manager would provide valuable reference advice. In addition, the system provided all customers with 24/7 consultation on stock exchanges and individual stocks, GF Securities information interpretation, and dynamics information on other financial markets.

(3) The E-to-One service system

At the GF website (www.gf.com.cn) and the E service centers brokerage branches, all customers could, through cell phones and the network, enjoy personalized information push services related to customers and information customization services. They could also enjoy the rich online resources of the GF network through the very analytical gem version of the online trading analysis system, just like "online VIPs." The main services included: it provided E-to-One services for off-site trading customers of GF Securities; customers could commission transactions through the network and telephone; they could also enjoy online stock commentary, live comments during trading, and online consulting; they had access to market announcement information related to their stock positions; they provided information on bonus shares, dividends, and rights offering; they were provided with information on subscription, placement of shares, and successful subscription of new shares; and they had expert seats in the E service center. In addition, the company provided early warning information tips, popular data analysis, and online securities video programs to all customers.

(4) The IPTV video broadcasting system

The gathered the best possible securities analysts to provide six hours of daily video investment tips live to clients through the satellite communication system, making the interactive communication with investors more intimate, intuitive, and timely.

The IPTV video broadcasting system mainly provided the following services: instant market commentary during market opening by senior analysts of GF Securities; special live coverage of major financial policies and events; interpretation of GF Securities' industry research reports; replay of live broadcast of China's securities experts' seminars; training on investment techniques of new trading products and business promotion; annual and quarterly investment strategy reports; research reports on key listed companies; and face-to-face communication with fund managers.

In addition, the company also provided its clients with exciting contents such as intraday dark horses, main capital movement, online video on demand, industry investment portfolio, and information mines.

(5) The fund management service system

As an important bridge between fund management companies and fund clients, this system delivered fund investment information in a timely manner, allocated fund assets for different needs of clients, and provided personalized services of fund product consultation and analysis. The main services included fund product consultation, fund net value tips, fund investment briefing, fund manager meetings, and quarterly fund finance salons.

In addition, the company also provided clients with fund investment operation ideas, knowledge training on other financial products, and personal investment and financial planning.

In April 2003, GF Securities' Golden Manager customer service brand was created, and the brokerage business began to obtain value-added service income through brand marketing. Based on the previously launched E-to-One service and other systems, GF Securities began to form a service system on the basis of multifaceted customer relationship management—the GF Securities "Golden Manager" customer service system, which was oriented to meet customer needs, with IT technology as the platform, information service as the breakthrough point, and the division of labor and cooperation for internal resources at the core.

The "Golden Manager" customer service system included nine kinds of trading methods, 26 kinds of investment information products, 20 kinds of value-added investment services, a variety of affectionate services, and a team of professional financial advisors, which could provide personalized and comprehensive services tailored to different customers. It gained high recognition among customers upon its launch.

In the subsequent development, GF Securities further established the status of "Golden Manager" as the main brand of brokerage business, and launched three sub-brands of "Finance & Economics," "Investment Interviews," and "Wealth Management" for different clients as supporting customer brand systems. The launch of "Golden Manager" laid a solid foundation for GF Securities' brokerage business to gain the first-mover advantage, and won such industry awards as "China's Best Brokerage Business Service Brand."

The three-level management structure and brokerage talent echelon

In January 1994, GF Securities established the Institutional Management Department, with Chen Wenzhan as the first head. The initial task of the department was to "ensure that Guangdong Province GF Securities Company operates and manages the securities business of the branches of Guangdong Development Bank." In 1995, the Department of Institutional Management was renamed as the Department of Planning and Management, and the scope of its functions was expanded to include "research and study of major development plans of the company" and "staff education and training." "In 1997, the name of the department was restored and it no longer had the function of development planning and began to focus on the branch-oriented management functions. Zhao Guiping succeeded Chen Wenzhan as general manager of the department, starting her 13-year career in brokerage business management. In many important acquisitions, the Institutional Management Department also played a function similar to that of an operational command.

In 1999, as the change of GF Securities' brokerage business management system deepened, the functions of the Institutional Management Department also underwent a series of adjustments, and the newly added functions included secondary market information exchanges and services of the former Development Research Center; guidance on premise change and business equipment acquisition in the former Administration Department and Business Department; guidance on the assessment and appointment of personnel below the middle-level officials in the brokerage branches, except for those in charge of computers and finance; statistical analysis and reporting of secondary market business data in the former Asset Management Department; and secondary market business regulation and verification.

This period was also the transition stage during which the Securities Law was about to be promulgated and the industry was facing a new task of becoming law-based. The Institutional Management Department, with only three people, was responsible for the institutionalization of the company and the establishment of rules and regulations for branch management. In September 1999, the Institutional Management Department submitted to Dr. Chen Yunxian a 5,000-word report on "Thoughts and Suggestions on the Work of the Institutional Management Department."

Based on the department's functional positioning, the report put forward the functions of communication and coordination, management guidance, evaluation, and incentives and made a quantitative analysis of key tasks such as "improving the network of brokerage branches," "improving the variety of agency business of brokerage branches," "promoting the process of business standardization," "improving the hierarchical management system of sales departments," "guiding the innovation of agency business" and "developing customer networks and subdividing customer groups."

The report reflected the frontline issues of brokerage business management at that time, such as the assessment system of the brokerage branches, and was approved by Dr. Chen Yunxian, Dong Zhengqing, and Cui Xia.

The positive thoughts and suggestions of the Institutional Management Department actually coincided with the work being promoted by GF Securities from top to bottom. During this period, GF Securities held several forums on brokerage business. In addition to strengthening relevant management functions, the leaders of the company, the Institutional Management Department, and regional business headquarters focused on the important issue of the "three-tier management structure."

In 2000, GF Securities cooperated with Arthur Andersen & Co., Ltd. in the "Internal Risk Control System Enhancement Project." In 2001, according to the three-tier management plan formulated by the project, all brokerage branches gradually transitioned to a unified three-tier management structure, with the brokerage branches in Guangdong being managed in conjunction with the administrative region, and those outside the province being managed across provinces and regions.

The specific structure was based on the three basic principles:

(1) to centralize the management of subordinate branches;

(2) to change the current coexistence of the second and third levels of brokerage branch, eventually bring all brokerage branches under the the three-tier management system, and ensure that the company's head office managed the regional headquarters and the regional headquarters managed all their subordinate brokerage branches; and

(3) to fully share the resources of the branches to achieve the "brokerage branch + regional service support" model.

Through three-tier management, GF Securities strengthened support for the regional business headquarters' brokerage business innovation and information service, so that the brokerage branches had faster and more direct access to the extension of the head office resources.

Under the three-tier management structure, the Institutional Management Department also set up a refined management orientation, including planning and development, integration of resources, strengthening assessment, and cost control. It further strengthened the service and innovation functions, focusing on information sharing and technical support. In February 2002, the Institutional Management Department was transformed into the Brokerage Business Headquarters, responsible for the overall management and coordination of the company's brokerage business, with Zhao Guiping as the general manager.

As an important talent base of GF Securities, the brokerage business line continuously provided backup manpower support for its development. Many of the managers in the headquarters departments had worked in the frontline positions in the brokerage branches and knew the market well. The brokerage business cultivated talents in various ways. In addition to ensuring they received training in trusteeship acquisition projects and other major projects, it also persistently held professional training courses and career development training courses in marketing, investment consulting, customer service, and other areas.

In order to have sufficient reserve officials, GF Securities held the "Brokerage Business Operation and Management Talents Training Course" at an early stage. The course enhanced the sense of identity and loyalty of employees through the development and training of management-level staff teams and to maintain the stability of backbones, so it was internally known as the "Whampoa Military Academy of Brokerage Business." The main goals of this course were to enable participants to better understand the products, processes, and customer service system related to the brokerage business, and to comprehensively improve their personal management skills and team building ability, and to enable the general managers of the brokerage branches to master the basic skills required in human resources, finance, marketing, and risk management. After the course was launched in 1998, more than one hundred talents emerged to take up management positions in the brokerage business system.

After 2003, in order to match the transformation of the company's brokerage business, GF Securities shifted the goal of talent training to wealth management. With the goal of cultivating wealth management talents with international vision, GF Securities held five wealth management training sessions in cooperation with the Canadian Securities Institute in the five years from 2007 to 2011, and sent more than 100 key business officials to study abroad in total. The advanced wealth management concepts and business models from abroad brought unprecedented inspiration to GF Securities' brokerage business, which played a significant role in promoting the company's subsequent transformation and development. During the training period, 78 trainees passed the professional examination and comprehensive defense of Certified Wealth Manager and obtained the CSWP certificate, reserving a number of high-end talents for the transformation of brokerage business, which can be said to have far-reaching impact.

Product development with customer demand as the core

In 2000, GF Securities made fruitful achievements in secondary market product development, and launched "Pay Plus Pay" and "Savings Accumulation Accelerator" in some regions. In 2003, these two businesses were very fruitful and achieved a multi-win situation for customers, brokerage firms, and banks, and in some areas there were even lines of customers willing to participate.

The "Pay Plus Pay" business was a financial management business launched by GF Securities in cooperation with Guangdong Development Bank, which mainly concentrated customers' daily idle funds and various incomes into one account for regular repurchase of treasury bonds, and the balance of the funds could also be used for daily cash withdrawal or consumption. "Pay Plus Pay" was flexible and secure, and was a relatively safe and low-cost way to manage money.

The 2003 brokerage business summary data showed that GF Securities launched the "Pay Plus Pay" cooperative treasury bond repo product in the market downturn, and nearly half of its brokerage branches carried out this business, bringing new assets of 706 million yuan and 9,158 customers. In just six months, the Hangzhou Brokerage Branch alone developed more than 4,000 customers and assets of more than 200 million yuan, and customers lined up to subscribe in all branches of the Guangdong Development Bank Hangzhou Branch.

In 2003, the brokerage business took the distribution of fund products as an important work of transformation and carried out extensive and in-depth cooperation with fund management companies, and the number of fund seats of GF Securities reached 20. In particular, during the offering of the GF Jufu Fund, GF Securities sold 1.27 billion shares, ranking first in the total number of funds sold by domestic brokerage firms, breaking the record of fund distribution by brokerage firms, and for the first time, the number of shares sold exceeded that by banks, which made all staff excited.

On October 14, 2003, knowing that the fund offering was about to be approved, the leading bodies of GF Securities convened a special meeting in advance to make a plan for making the offering of the GF Jufu Fund a priority of the company's business work of the year. The success or otherwise of the fund launch would have a significant strategic impact on the company's business development. The fund launch leadership team sent a strong task force consisting of the president's team and some middle-level key personnel. On the same day, GF Securities sent a document to the whole system, requesting them to do a good job in selling GF Fund Company's Jufu Fund, making a plan for matters such as tasks, implementation, and incentive measures for fund distribution.

On October 27, 2003, the GF Jufu Fund was officially approved for offering, and the staff of the Brokerage Business Headquarters came up with a complete sales plan within two days. Facing the tight capital and sluggish market environment at the end of the year, in order to better mobilize the enthusiasm of the whole system, the company held a mobilization meeting for the GF Jufu Fund on November 3 at the IPTV Studio. Fang Jiachun, president of the company, Dong Zhengqing, executive vice president, and Lin Chuanhui, general manager of GF Fund Company, delivered mobilization speeches at the meeting, which greatly encouraged the morale of GF people in fund sales.

On October 31, 2003, more than 100 business branches of GF Securities from Shanghai in the east, Hainan in the south, Gansu in the west, and Jilin in the north launched a simultaneous charge, and at 9:30, the first order was received at the Fengqi Road Brokerage Branch in Hangzhou, where Ms. Lu, a customer of the branch, bought 5,000 units of the Jufu Fund, firing the first shot of the battle. In the days of the offering of the Jufu Fund, all GF Securities people worked for its marketing. Zhao Guiping called the general managers of the brokerage branches every day to ask about the situation, and the Brokerage Business Headquarters also compiled the "Daily Sales Report." As the frontline forces, the brokerage branches set up fund sales working groups in advance, decomposed sales tasks, organized relevant training, and prepared promotional materials, as their marketing planning proceeded in an orderly manner.

During the fund sales period, the bosses of the brokerage branches and the staff worked side by side and shared the hardships. They gave up the weekend, disrupted the normal commuting time, and set up sales battlefields of GF Fund in all corners of factories, mines, schools, communities, and banks. Some employees spent the night in the field because they went to visit customers at night and it was too far away to go home without a car, and some employees even postponed originally scheduled surgery till after the fund sales.

On November 7, 2003, the Chongqing Keyuan Road Brokerage Branch completed the sales task of four million units of the Jufu Fund in only one week, which was exciting and encouraged other sister brokerage branches. On

November 24, GF Huafu Securities Company exceeded the total sales task of the Jufu Fund with a total sales volume of 50.42 million units six days ahead of schedule, becoming the first distributor of the company to successfully complete the task. On the same day, GF Northern exceeded the sales task with a total sales volume of 30.01 million units. Meanwhile, the business headquarters and brokerage branches under the Brokerage Business Headquarters also successively delivered the good news of exceeding the sales task, with 70 out of 71 brokerage branches under the Brokerage Business Headquarters exceeding the sales task.

In this fund offering battle, the strong brokerage network and the vast retail customer base became the important extension force of the GF Fund. The subsidiaries and branches of the brokerage business system, together with the newborn GF Fund, created a classic case of complementary resources and close cooperation within GF Securities.

3. Client growth in GF

Explaining investment concepts to clients

Li Xueben, a shareholder client of GF Securities and a native of Nanhai, Foshan, recalls his early experience of stock speculation:

> I joined the market in 1997, when I was a self-employed businessman with a small workshop dealing with wooden molds and wooden ware processing. Some time before entering the market, I paid attention to the stock market quotes published in the newspaper. I thought it was better to buy stocks than to save money in the bank, but I did not know which stock to buy. There were no computers to check stock movements, so I just cut out the daily stock quotes published in *Yangcheng Evening News*, and connected them with glue, and they amounted to 20 to 30 meters long several months later.

Many of those who joined the stock market early had studied it hard. Those like Li Xueben who invested a small amount of money and lacked information channels of individual investors were commonly known as "retail investors." This customer group was different from the "VIP investors" and was more different from the market forces such as institutional customers that emerged later, but they were an important force that had existed in the capital markets for a long time. During the development of its brokerage business, GF Securities always paid extra attention to its shareholder customers. As the saying goes, "Helping customers is helping the company."

When GF Securities had only seven brokerage branches, Dr. Chen Yunxian often visited them in the afternoon after the close of trading. Over time, if stock investors who knew him met him, they would certainly ask him to interpret the market trend. Dr. Chen's market interpretations were often based on macroeconomic and monetary policy, which also influenced the style of the GF Securities research department. In 1994, the stock Hainan Jinpan's price was in the vicinity of seven yuan per share. Through the analysis of its financial statements and market performance, the Tianhe Road Brokerage Branch predicted that this stock might become Hainan's leading stock. The brokerage branch had a discussion and alerted its stock investors. Only two weeks later, Hainan Jinpan rose to 19.48 yuan per share.

Of course, GF Securities was not the only one to help the shareholders in the market make money. If a securities company could help the shareholders fend off market risks based on research and judgment, it would undoubtedly establish a greater degree of professional prestige, and even make shareholders become loyal customers.

In the second half of 1996, GF Securities issued an internal notice to thoroughly clean up financing and prevent risks. Luo Peiqiang, general manager of the Dongguan Brokerage Branch, strictly implemented the notice and did a good job in communicating with the customers. In just three days, all the financing was quickly cleaned up with a resolute attitude. The shareholders in Dongguan soon became aware of GF Securities' initiative, but some shareholders saw that other brokerages were still offering financing and expressed their incomprehension of GF Securities' behavior.

At the end of 1996, the stock index fell to the ground, and the customers who still held financing-based stocks in other brokerage firms suffered heavy losses. The stockholders who listened to the advice of GF Securities' brokerage branches and operated cautiously at the beginning were naturally thankful and expressed their gratitude to the brokerage branches, saying "I'm glad I listened to you. GF is still reliable."

At the beginning of 1997, the bull market started again. In just over five months, the Shenzhen index rose from near 3,000 points at the beginning of the year to 6,103 points, and the leading stock, Shenzhen Development, soared from 15.17 yuan per share to 49 yuan per share, up 2.23 times.

In the midst of the bull market, GF Securities remained vigilant. On May 12, 1997, after 10:00 a.m., Dr. Chen Yunxian finished his work at hand and suddenly instructed Dr. Fang Jiachun to inform Zhao Guiping, head of the Institutional Management Department, to advise stockholders to sell their shares. Dr. Fang came directly to the office of the Institutional Management Department and urged, "Call the heads of the brokerage branches quickly. Today is Monday, and advise the stockholders to sell their shares before Wednesday." Zhao Guiping had not fully understood it and was thinking of assigning this task when Dr. Fang added, "Don't let others call. You call them personally." Realizing the seriousness and urgency of the matter, Zhao Guiping started to call 37 brokerage branches one by one from 11 o'clock, and even missed her lunch. In the process of calling, Dr. Chen personally came to her office, and re-ordered, "Do not wait until

Wednesday. Tell them to sell all today." He also deliberately added: "Call those again you have already called."

After receiving the notice from the headquarters, the bosses of each brokerage branch immediately notified their stockholders. The incident was sudden, and the shareholders naturally thought differently. In the exhilaration of the rising stock market, they would not necessarily follow the advice. The then general manager of the Zhongshan Brokerage Branch Lin Qing adopted a very wise approach. He ordered three tables of food at noon that day, and invited his stockholders to dinner during which he solemnly suggested that they sell stocks. Although they were full of doubts, out of their trust for GF Securities and their brokerage branch, most them sold their stocks the day they received the advice.

On May 12, the share price of Shenzhen Development hovered at 45–49 yuan per share, but from May 13, this starry-eyed leading stock started to fall non-stop, and the share price fell to about 19 yuan per share in a short period of time, and then continued to go down in a long process before bottoming out. A phone call from GF Securities helped the shareholders in the brokerage branches to dodge the crisis and keep the fruits of victory. Afterwards, many shareholders asked their brokerage branches' bosses how GF Securities was so great that it could foresee the decline in stock prices. After learning that this was a proposal from the headquarters, some further stated that they "really want to see Dr. Chen."

Out of the same curiosity, Zhao Guiping couldn't help but ask Dr. Chen afterwards why he could accurately instruct stockholders to sell their shares. Dr. Chen talked lightly about the logic of his judgment: as the bull market went on, the regulatory authorities were strengthening the constraints on irregular market behavior. At that time, large brokerage firms were fined for their self-dealing business. And at this time, the securities market basically only had retail investors and brokerage firms' stocks. Institutions were punished, so they would certainly clean up their trading positions, which in turn would inevitably trigger a decline in the market, and leading stocks were bound to bear the brunt.

Of course, despite the bull market's momentum, the stockholders listened to GF Securities' advice and sold their stocks in time also because of their trust of the professional value of the "PhD Legion." This precise guidance also won a group of loyal fan-level clients for GF Securities.

With the "quality" and "quantity" of its brokerage business, GF Securities rose rapidly in the secondary market: in 1996, GF Securities ranked first in the ranking of the Shenzhen Stock Exchange in terms of total trading volume. In 1997, GF Securities entered the top 10 in the ranking of trading volume of the Shanghai Stock Exchange for the first time.

Consistent investor education

In 1998, the international financial situation became increasingly severe and the competition in the domestic market intensified, so GF Securities put forward the idea of "thinking of danger in peace and seeking progress in stability," and launched "the cross-century GF Securities and quality services" program in the secondary market. GF Securities organized client representatives to visit listed companies, a move that pioneered secondary market shareholder education. In July 1998, GF Securities organized the "Beijing Tour for Rational Investment," and in 1999, it again organized the "Century Tour for Rational Investment in Shanghai and Shenzhen for GF Clients."

In November 1999, the "Century Tour for Rational Investment in Shanghai and Shenzhen for GF Clients" took place in Shanghai and Shenzhen at the same time. More than 140 investor representatives from GF Securities' brokerage branches in various places and 20 journalists visited five listed companies with restructuring concepts, namely, Longtou, Shanghai Auto, Shenneng, Shanghai Belling, and Shanghai Pharmaceutical in Shanghai, and five high-tech listed companies, namely, Shenzhen Konka, Shenzhen Hongkai, Haiwang Bio-pharmaceuticals, Shenzhen Seg, and Shenzhen Fangda in Shenzhen. This innovation was also welcomed by the listed companies. Among the ten listed companies visited, except for one which was received by the secretary of the board, the other nine were personally met by the chairman or general manager with a number of senior executives, and these leaders answered their questions.

In addition to visiting listed companies, GF Securities also invited experts, scholars, and government officials to give a number of lectures on high-tech industrialization, asset restructuring, fund management, investment and speculation, and other issues. As many as 21 news media participated in the event, including CCTV, China's National Radio, three major securities newspapers, *Economic Daily*, and other nationally renowned media. CCTV made a series of special reports on the event seven times in the program "China Finances," *Shanghai Securities News* and Securities Times made more than 20 reports on the event, and two websites—www.hexun.com and www.stockstar.com—also set up columns for the event and followed the whole event. The tracking reports of the whole process of the event from a wide range and with a high frequency made this event leave a very good impression on local governments, industry authorities and listed companies. Zhang Ning, deputy director of the Shanghai Securities Regulatory Office, said, "This event organized by GF Securities drew investors' attention from computer screens to listed companies, which is a good way to promote the healthy development of China's securities market."

No one cherished this face-to-face exchange opportunity more than the investor representatives from all over the country. The "exchange" included both the information and emotion exchange between investors and listed companies and the investment experience exchange between investors. At the investor-media meeting held on the evening of November 18, an investor from Dalian thought that such activities provided an opportunity for ordinary investors to understand the listed companies where they were located, and made him "feel the respect he should receive as a shareholder for the first time." Another investor from Beijing believed that in judging whether a listed company had investment value, besides studying its financial statements, it was also very important to study its boss, and what kind of manager would run what kind of business. He said, "The biggest gain during the trip was to get a general impression of the company's development prospect through face-to-face communication with its boss." There was also an investor from Chengdu who was interested in the opportunity to discuss investment skills with "fellow investors" from all over the country, and he said that this kind of communication was generally difficult to carry out between investors in the same brokerage branch.

After that, GF Securities organized similar large-scale customer events every year, dedicated to promoting investor education and advocating rational investment in a clear-cut manner.

After participating in the events, Liu Beirong, a shareholder from Meizhou, Guangdong, said in a thank - you letter, "Market participants have given me high praise for my vision of 'being rationally bullish on the stock market' at the most difficult time of the stock market. I was overjoyed by this. When I think of the source of my vision, the first thing I think of is GF Securities, which nurtured my growth. If GF Securities had not given me the opportunity to participate in two study tours of listed companies, I, an ordinary investor with an engineering background, would not have been able to achieve what I have today."

Spreading the right ideas to investors also became a calling card for GF Securities as it conducted business in an entirely new region. In 2000, GF Securities entered Lanzhou and Taiyuan. The Lanzhou Brokerage Branch was newly established for GF Securities' trusteeship of Hainan Huayin International Trust. The Taiyuan Brokerage Branch was formerly the Shantou Brokerage Branch relocated from Guangdong Province. Although it was "relocated," but the original staff and customer resources were not relocated with it. Compared with the new brokerage branch in Guangdong, the Lanzhou and Taiyuan brokerage branches in the Northwest found it more difficult to start, as the local stockholders were very unfamiliar with GF Securities. Experienced the previous "securities black market," the local people even thought that GF Securities was a fraudulent company. For this reason, the staff of the brokerage branches took to the streets to visit every building, dividing into groups to distribute leaflets in the nearby communities, and actively using the platform of TV stations to produce investment popularization programs, so that the shareholders, while understanding B-shares and online trading, could identify with GF Securities. Hard work pays! The Lanzhou and Taiyuan brokerage branches achieved the initial accumulation of customers and also improved the popularity and reputation of GF Securities in the Northwest.

From the headquarters to the grassroots level, from large-scale investor exchange activities to the day-to-day shareholder lectures in the brokerage branches, GF Securities carried out investor education. Entering the new millennium, investor education became important for regulatory authorities and industry associations.

In 2001, Laura Cha Shih May-lung, vice chairwoman of the Securities and Futures Commission in Hong Kong, was invited by the then State Council leader to be the vice chairwoman of the CSRC, becoming the first vice-ministerial official appointed by the central government from Hong Kong since the reform and opening up policy was introduced. Dr. Shi formally introduced the concept of investor education, saying in an interview, "I want to build up investor education. We have such a huge number of stockholders, and they really need to have a good understanding of the market and of the market economy."

In the same year, in order to implement the guiding principles of "protecting investors' interests and strengthening investor education" from of the National Securities Work Conference and the speech of Zhou Xiaochuan, chairman of the CSRC, who said, "Protecting investors' interests is the top priority," GF Securities' Xiamen Brokerage Branch actively applied to be the teaching point of *Shanghai Securities News*' shareholder school after it was established and cooperated with *Xiamen Business News*, a local mainstream newspaper. The shareholder school in Xiamen attracted an overwhelming response, with an endless stream of investors inquiring and enrolling, with more than 800 people enrolled in just one week.

The first class of the school was taught by Zhuo Wen, deputy general manager of the Xiamen Brokerage Branch. He explained the basic knowledge of securities, the operation mechanism of joint stock companies, the listing process, and the issuance mechanism of stocks, which were of concern to shareholders. This kind of education, which aimed to help investors better understand the market, learn to invest rationally, and enhance risk awareness, was welcomed by all sectors of society, including investors. The opening of the shareholder school not only enhanced the service image of the Brokerage Branch, but also conveyed the information of the special service of the Brokerage Branch to the shareholders in the lectures, which expanded the popularity of GF Securities in the Xiamen market and became another special service of GF Securities.

During this period, GF Securities had an important way of developing investor education—by strengthening the secondary market analyst team. In January 2002, Dr. Fang Jiachun, president of GF Securities, pointed out in a GF Securities seminar that strengthening the ranks of secondary market analysts was "to act as a real practitioner of investor education and enlightenment." The analyst team of GF Securities made their customer services professional in a real sense, and applied professional services to practice, so as to resist the commission war in the market by enhancing the value of customers. In addition, the team helped to establish the concept of "value investment." Under the culture of prying information of market makers and keeping pace with others, the team of analysts of GF Securities was the first to propose the concept of "value investment." On the other hand, it helped to establish the concept of "value investment." Under the trend of prying information of bankers and following bankers' operation, GF Securities was the first to put forward the concept of "value investment" and guided stockholders to establish the correct investment concept, so that stockholders had a preliminary understanding of asset allocation.

As a pioneer in the field, the analyst team of GF Securities cooperated with the Securities Association of China in recording investor education courses and participated in many of its research projects. After years of accumulation, the GF Securities Investor Education Base became one of the first national securities and futures investor education bases named by the CSRC. In terms of monographs, Zhao Guiping authored the book *Investor Education: International Experience and Chinese Practice*, which became a model for investor education in the securities and futures industry. The book *Improving the Investor Education System and Constructing the Long-Term Investor Education System*, coauthored by Dr. Cai Shifeng, Di Yongzhong, and Zhao Guiping, was also awarded the third prize for key research projects by the Securities Association of China and was incorporated into the book *Research on Frontier Issues of the China Securities Market.*

Bringing customers to the E era

After 2000, the reform of information technology rapidly penetrated into every corner of economic life. In the 1990s, the Chinese securities market became an outstanding representative of timely and full application of information technology in various industries, and securities companies took information technology as an important means to reduce transaction costs and improve core competitiveness. GF Securities' brokerage business repeatedly came to the forefront of the industry in promoting the integration of finance and technology, and made efforts to advance its own technological revolution around the new millennium.

In 1994, GF Securities became the first domestic brokerage firm to have a corporate wide area network.

In 1995, GF Securities established a two-way satellite information transmission network, brought into play the functions of the Computer Center for unified order reporting, transaction, clearing, fund operation, and information consultation, and built its counter trading system.

In 1996, GF Securities implemented centralized order reporting nationwide using the terrestrial network and the satellite network of the exchanges.

In February 1997, GF Securities completed and put into use www.gf.com.cn, becoming one of the earliest securities firms in China to build a professional website for securities.

In November 1997, GF Securities invested in building its own two-way satellite master station covering all its brokerage branches nationwide, which greatly improved the reliability of securities trading.

In November 1997, GF Securities established two company-level online trading platforms for trading through the Guangdong Wuyangjin network.

In 1998, GF Securities unified counter trading software.

In July 1999, GF Securities took the lead in fully opening cell phone stock speculation services in more than 50 brokerage branches.

In 2000, GF Securities fully upgraded the ground DDN wide area network, which ensured the backup of trading as well as the use of an office system, information system, and financial system.

In November 2000, the GF E-to-One service center software was installed and put into use in all brokerage branches of GF Securities.

In December 2000, the company's new website was officially launched.

In January 2001, the IP satellite multimedia broadcasting system of GF Securities was launched.

In February 2001, by the document Z.J.X.X.Z. (2001) No. 3, the CSRC formally approved that GF Securities was one of the first securities companies to be qualified for online commission business.

In June 2001, GF Securities completed the centralized trading monitoring system, which provided a platform for off-site aggregation of trading behavior and enhanced the company's risk control capability.

In July 2001, GF Securities completed the company-wide customer data warehouse system, realizing a higher level of personalized customer services and providing decision-making support for brokerage business marketing.

In June 2002, the GF Securities ERP system was put online.

In August 2002, the CRM system of GF Securities was put into operation, providing a unified comprehensive service platform for customer service personnel of all brokerage branches of the company and bringing the customer service of brokerage business to a higher level.

In December 2002, the GF Securities Exchange Backup Center was established, which made the company's ability to resist sudden disaster risk rank in the forefront of domestic securities companies.

In terms of trading means, GF Securities shifted from on-site to off-site brokerage service as a whole; from telephone to network and mobile securities, it realized the leap from wired to wireless brokerage service. After launching unified online trading software and web page trading in 2000, GF Securities' total online trading volume reached 31.2 billion yuan in 2001, ranking among the top domestic brokerages. From 2001 to 2003, GF Securities' online trading grew 10 percent, 16 percent, and 24 percent respectively, while the growth rate of national online trading volumes were 4.38 percent, 8.99 percent, and 14.90 percent respectively, leading the market growth rate by nearly 100 percent.

Take GF Securities' Western Guangdong Brokerage Headquarters for example. With a rich tradition of marketing services, the headquarters actively expanded its business scope and built its service system in Zhaoqing after 2000.

By the end of 2002, the headquarters had 14,823 online trading clients, set up nine technical service stations, and had an online trading volume of 269.89 million yuan, accounting for 13.9 percent of the total volume. Due to the vast territory and inconvenient traffic of western Guangdong, the application of online trading opened a brand new picture of brokerage business.

In 2000, GF Securities took the lead in building the E-to-One e-commerce customer service model, which pioneered the integration of the brokerage firms' information and consulting systems through the internet, and once became one of the standard models for the business. President Dr. Fang Jiachun analyzed that E-to-One service focused on three major areas: the GF network, the Brokerage Branch E service center, and the analyst team.

On the basis of E-to-One service, GF Securities further established a team of nearly 20 full-time analysts in 2002 at its headquarters who specialized in the production of high-quality professional information products. Together with the company's R&D and postdoctoral staff, the analysts produced different media and different levels of information products for different levels of customers, and delivered them to different customers through the four service systems that had become mature. These included *GF Express* (daily and weekly), VIP Investment Strategy Reports (weekly, monthly and quarterly), annual reports, various media including websites, newspapers, TVs, the IPTV, and information of various investment reports, realizing the professional production and delivery process of products and services on the company's unified information platform.

Witness of the IPTV

On February 24, 2001, the GF Securities IPTV satellite multimedia broadcasting system was launched. Through this system, the headquarters could send stock commentary, training and video programs such as teleconferencing directly to any desktop computer in each brokerage branch, which brought an immediate innovation to the means of serving stockholders in brokerage business.

In March 2002, a six-hour-long daily securities information channel was launched. GF Securities' programs were transmitted via satellite and synchronized with the securities trading hours. From 9:00 to 15:30 on each trading day, GF Securities continuously broadcasted real-time securities information programs with multiple columns, mainly about market trend and strategy analysis, instant commentary as trading began, commentary as trading closed, hotline stock commentary, each day's operation strategy, and research reports. Especially when the market fluctuated, IPTV invited nationally renowned senior experts to make special reports and arranged excellent securities analysts from the GF system to be the main speakers, which was well received by customers.

During the years, the IPTV multi-functional broadcasting system, which was upgraded and renovated, had become a leader in the brokerage industry and a window of communication between the secondary market analyst team of GF Securities and stockholders all over the country, and a group of star analysts, such as You Wenfeng, Wang Xiaoping, Gong Guilin, Zhang Danqun, and Wen Fu, had become the market flag bearers in the eyes of GF's veteran stockholders.

In 2003, the market style changed, and retail investors who used to like "inquiring about insider stories and following corporate restructuring" found that corporate performance and growth gradually became the main basis of investment market. With the increase of institutional investors, the market investment grew more rational.

In June 2003, the IPTV studio of GF Securities was brightly lit and two stockholders, Ms. Lin and Ms. Shi, accompanied by GF Securities hosts Chen Qiuwei and Ji Xingyu, described their growth path in the stock market.

Ms. Lin, who joined the market in 1997, was an accountant and initially joined the market only to do primary market subscriptions. As the number of participants in the subscriptions at that time was small and the winning rate was high, Ms. Lin's received an annual 30 percent return on her 300,000 yuan of capital, making her realize the benefits of the capital markets.

In the early days, there was a lack of information on stocks in the market, and there was even no information on individual stocks. After the May 19 market price soar in 1999, Ms. Lin found that the supply of information in the market was greatly enhanced. Her proudest achievement was to buy Shanghai Belling (600171) with a profit of 20 yuan per share and a book profit of nearly 200,000 yuan at the peak of the market. But after the May 19 market price soar, they was a sharp fall in market prices, eroding much of her profit. After deep reflection, Ms. Lin felt that she had not really understood the stock market.

Starting in 1999, she paid extra attention to the information provided by GF Securities and the night school for stockholders, researching every day until 4:00 or 5:00 p.m., and rushing to the night school to listen to classes every time in spite of the weather. As an accountant, she started to study financial statements of listed companies and took a long position in a technology stock in 2000. The reason she dared to take a long position was that the listing underwriter of the technology company was GF Securities. Later, the stock lived up to Ms. Lin's trust and rose tremendously. In 2000, Ms. Lin read a report entitled "The Last Gold Mine: B-shares" from in GF Securities Zhaoqing Ruizhou Fifth Road Brokerage Branch. The brokerage branch also opened a special night school lecture on the topic: "That day was very cold, and very few came for the lecture, but I listened to it very carefully." In order to confirm the investment value of B-shares, Ms. Lin also communicated with Dr. Liu Yunzhe, the head of the brokerage branch at that time. "Dr. Liu gave me important reference advice," for which Ms. Lin is very grateful. Subsequently, Ms. Lin opened a B-share account.

In March 2001, along with the news of market opening, B-shares surged and Ms. Lin gained 200 percent profit. In June of the same year, she saw a commentary on the "bubble theory" from GF information, and she sensed the risk and sold all her B-shares immediately.

When asked about her views on other investors, Ms. Lin was quite impressed: "Nowadays, the vast majority of investors do not value the large amount of information provided by brokerage firms. They do not make efforts to study properly. They are very blind and have a gambling mentality. The stock market is a cruel place, and the thing everyone has to do is to make sure they are not eliminated."

In contrast to Ms. Lin, who had a relatively mature operating mentality, Ms. Shi, another shareholder who had been in the market for a short time, had a very different experience.

"Before I entered the market, I didn't think the stock market was difficult. Others said it was difficult, but I thought I could do it!" Ms. Shi, a teacher by profession, entered the B-share market in the first half of 2001, but it was not long before she got hung up. After a period of uncertainty and reflection, she felt it was important to choose a good brokerage firm.

So Ms. Shi switched to GF Securities in May 2002 and discovered the great value of IPTV:

"It was on IPTV that I watched the best programs, such as 'The Stocking Trade Platform,' 'The Art of Money Management,' 'New Ideas of Investment,' 'The Secrets of Market-Makers' and 'Four Series of Technical Lectures,' which were really beneficial. I took detailed notes every day."

Through the study, Ms. Shi's investment philosophy changed tremendously. At the beginning, she did not understand how to stop loss. She thought that as long as she kept stocks, and as long as she did not sell a stock, it would be possible for it to rise in value. After learning the stop-loss theory from expert lectures, she half-heartedly chose two stocks that were making a loss at the time. She kept one of them and applied the loss-stop theory to the other. After learning and practicing, comparing and summarizing, Ms. Shi's feeling was "You can trust the experts at GF! Not only did I not lose money, but I was starting to make profits."

In front of the camera, Ms. Shi's notebook with dense content in beautiful handwriting also presents the learning experience of an individual investor: "I have also experienced the process from focusing on individual stocks to focusing on investment philosophy and methods. The investment philosophy and financial experience of experts is a resource that can be translated into wealth. In order to take fewer detours and make fewer mistakes, we investors can put the resources of experts to our own use and find the door to wealth."

The securities market is the "barometer" of the economy, and the brokerage business seems to be the "barometer" of the securities market. The expressions of stockholders in the trading rooms of the brokerage branches often become a vivid picture for the media to report the latest trend of the securities market. In the IPTV studio in 2003, two individual investors talked about the changes in their mentality, which became the testimony of GF Securities' philosophy of growing together with customers. As the backbone of brokerage business and host of the IPTV column, Chen Qiuwei and Ji Xingyu also felt a lot of emotions after hearing the experience of two clients, and then wrote an article to record their feelings of growing together with clients:

> In the securities market today, the majority of small and medium-sized investors have lost a lot of time and money. They have made important contributions to the development of the securities market, but what they often get is often failure and disappointment. Fortunately, more and more investors have made great progress in investment methods through learning, practice, and summing up, and have found their own survival space in the thrilling game of the market.
>
> As a securities firm, it makes us proud to be trusted and relied on by investors. In the next transformation of our brokerage business, our goal is to become a "five-star" service provider, professional secretary, product manager, and financial expert for our clients.
>
> We know that our clients' success is our success.
>
> We promise that every member of GF will provide you with professional, dedicated and specialized services.
>
> We hope that every client of GF grows with GF.

From the traditional channel service during the establishment period to the wealth management in the new era, GF Securities has left solid footprints on the development of technology, products, brand and customer service systems in the brokerage business. On the premise that the fundamentals of brokerage business are firmly established, GF Securities effectively explored proprietary investment and innovative business.

Chapter VI: Rebirth through Trial and Error: The Road to Self-Reliance

The sea of danger, doubt and denial around man's little island of certainty challenges him to dare the unknown.

—Rabindranath Tagore

1. The rise of GF Securities in the secondary market

The formation of the Investment and Finance Department

In the three years before 1995, Dr. Ma Qingquan worked in the office during the day and slept in it at night; he traveled when he had investment banking projects outside Guangzhou and he worked and rested in his small office when we returned from trips. In the second half of that year, his daily activities in Guangzhou changed. In addition to attending to work at Huatai Hotel on South Xianlie Road, where the firm was then headquartered, he began to spend more time with five or six young people in a low-key business hotel near Tianhe Road, discussing the business ideas, investment philosophy, and investment strategies of the self-dealing team of GF Securities, which was about to get involved in the securities market.

In mid-1995, under Dr. Chen Yunxian's well thought out new business layout, Dr. Ma switched from GF's prestigious investment banking to the company's proprietary business and set out to open up a new front. He led young team members such as Zhan Hongsheng, Wang Weizhen, Liu Xiaoyan, Jiang Zuoliang, Kang Guohong, and Yang Dongmei in forming the Investment and Finance

Department of GF Securities, officially declaring the presence of GF Securities in the secondary securities market. Among these young people, Jiang Zuoliang, the famous investment director and deputy general manager of E Fund, Liu Xiaoyan, the general manager of E Fund, and Kang Guohong, the general manager of the Shenzhen branch, who was once an high-ranking official of GF Securities, became prominent. Among them, Jiang Zuoliang was a master's degree student of the Department of Finance whom Dr. Chen Yunxian hired as talent by breaking the rules and paying the training fee to his graduation institution, while Liu Xiaoyan was a master's degree student of economics who was admitted after Dr. Chen's personal interview.

In 1995, GF Securities was ranked by the Securities Association of China as one of the top ten securities firms in China for the first time in terms of total stock transactions, total assets, and total profits. Guided by the strategic goal of developing GF nationwide, the investment banking of GF Securities expanded rapidly from Guangdong to Northeast, North, Central China and provinces and cities in other areas in just a few years. The company's primary market business capability was gradually achieving full coverage of the domestic stock issuance market, and the company became comparable with Guotai, Nanfang, and Jun'an, China's leading brokerage firms. The Company's primary market business capability was gradually achieving domestic stock issuance market coverage and assuming a position where it could compete with Guotai, Southern, Jun'an, and other top brokerages.

The company's brokerage business formed a strategic layout of occupying Guangdong, radiating the whole country and facing overseas markets after taking over and managing the brokerage branches of all branches of Guangdong Development Bank.[1] In contrast, the performance of GF Securities in the secondary market was somewhat staggering. Although as the earliest securities operating institution in China to manage more than two funds at the same time, the first and second phases of its GF Investment Fund achieved good investment returns and social benefits, the company only obtained management fee income. In terms of proprietary business, as a basic system of risk control for securities companies, GF Securities was the first securities company in the industry to stipulate that "proprietary accounts are under the unified control of the Head Office" throughout the company. Therefore, when the company reached a new stage of development, how to coordinate the company's business resources in the secondary market under this risk control system required a new vision and a new strategic arrangement.

Dr. Chen Yunxian, the head of GF Securities, gave this task to his deputy, Dr. Ma Qingquan. To this day, "self-dealing by brokerage firms" is still a slightly mysterious market force in the minds of ordinary stockholders. In some contexts, it is indistinguishable from such terms as "main force" and "manipulation." The self-dealing team of each financial institution in the whole securities market was destined to go through the test of wind and rain, so as to become a mature

1 Guangdong GF Securities Company 1995 year-end work summary.

investor in terms of standardized systems, investment philosophy, and investment art, and grow into a qualified institutional investor.

The GF Securities Investment and Finance Department was hastily set up at the time when it was urgently needed for the company's business development, when the entire Chinese securities market was not sufficiently regulated, and on the eve of the upcoming bull market. It had the spirit of GF, which is bold, aggressive, and vigorous, and at the same time bore the marks of naivety, sloppiness, and immaturity that prevailed in the early stage of the whole industry in many areas such as institution construction, investment philosophy, and compliance awareness. These marks laid the groundwork for the first major test in the development history of GF Securities soon after.

The inevitability of the bull market in China's securities market in 1996

In the second half of 1995, due to the follow-up of the 327 Bond Futures Incident, the investment atmosphere in the capital markets was light, and the Shanghai Stock Exchange Index went down from 792 points to 552 points in half a year, with the average daily turnover of the Shanghai and Shenzhen markets being about two billion yuan. During this period, the buying targets of the Investment and Finance Department were mainly the first and second phases of GF Investment Fund listed in the market. The department began to buy them at a low level of about 0.7 yuan, successfully formed a hot spot in the market for closed-end funds, and sold them for profit before the end of the year.

This success did not let the investment team's anxiety alleviate too much. This anxiety came from the market. In the last two months before the end of the year, the SSE index accumulated a decline of 22.5 percent. In addition, it was because the team's own investment philosophy had not matured. The self-dealing mode of work was undoubtedly very different from the previous business area of providing services to clients; it required real money in hand and the wisdom of the team to play in the high-risk market. In the event of a major investment mistake, one would not only face a loss of money, but could also be held responsible for affecting the company's development.

Years later, Dr. Ma Qingquan stated, "Faced with more than 300 stocks in the market at that time, we did not know what to buy."

At the beginning of 1996, the Investment and Finance Department held several market validation meetings, but no consensus was reached. During the Chinese New Year holiday, Dr. Ma returned to his home in Beijing and sat down at the desk where he had been working on economic theory a few years earlier to try to change his thinking and reexamine the direction of the Chinese stock market over the previous few years and possible investment opportunities from the macroeconomic perspective.

Dr. Ma noted that, due to the macroeconomic control that started in 1992, the

GDP growth rate dropped from the super high growth rate of around 14 percent, but remained high overall. More importantly, the overall growth rate of M2 remained above 30 percent from 1992 to 1995. In contrast, from 1993 to 1995, the stock market was in a state of shrinking trading and stock prices were seriously undervalued. Among the listed companies on the Shenzhen Stock Exchange in early 1996, stocks priced below their net assets abounded. The average price-to-earnings ratio was as low as eight times, and investors lost a lot of money.

This serious paradox of high macroeconomic growth, a very loose monetary environment, and a sluggish stock market seemed to make Dr. Ma, who had a strong background in economics, feel something. He had some hazy feeling, but was not very clear and sure what it was. The market trend before Spring Festival was very sluggish, and the turnover of the Shenzhen Stock Exchange was even less than 100 million yuan for several trading days, which also made it difficult for him to make up his mind for a while.

Spring Festival was about to pass, and the stock markets were near resuming trading. Was the Investment and Finance Department to "sow in spring" in the market, or continue to "stay inactive as it did in winter"?

During the rare days of vacation, Dr. Ma locked himself in his study and pondered hard, hoping to connect the macroeconomy, money supply, stock market trends, and price performance of the two markets in Shanghai and Shenzhen to find out the regularity of performance. Finally, in the early morning of the first day after the holiday, his mind was clear and developed a clear judgment like lightning and fire: a round of bull market was imminent; having declined for a long time, the stock markets would develop fast; the deeper the decline, the stronger the reversal; making the Shenzhen Stock Exchange listed stocks whose prices were below the net assets as a breakthrough would be a completely risk-free investment opportunity.

Shooting the first shot of the bull market

On the first trading day after the Chinese New Year in 1996, Zhan Hongsheng, the head of the Investment and Finance Department, received a call from Dr. Ma from Beijing at 5:00 a.m., requesting a morning meeting for all department staff. After arriving in Guangzhou on the earliest flight, Dr. Ma briefly exchanged views with the relevant officials in the conference room and immediately decided on a course of action and organized its implementation: invest all the positions allocated by the company and buy stocks with prices below NAV in the Shenzhen market on a selective basis.

Based on the previous research and analysis of the fundamentals of individual stocks, after some intensive operations, the Investment and Finance Department completed the buying in one morning.

The market's signals were keen, and this buying began to make waves in the market as traders began to examine the market situation. The volume of the Shenzhen market increased significantly that day. In the first week after Chinese New Year 1996, the turnover of Shenzhen Stock Exchange reached 2.138 billion yuan, which was 2.33 times of the week before the festival. After the agitation in March, the Shenzhen market in April was like a fire fueled with dry firewood, the Shenzhen Stock Exchange index rose from 1,029.84 points to 1,525.54 points, a one-month increase of 48.13 percent. This opened the curtain of the bull market for more than a year.

About the market game, Dr. Chen Yunxian said a pithy sentence: "What is the market? When you are in the market, you are the market." The GF team, which dared to invest with firm confidence against the market at this low level, is the illustration of this saying. Dr. Ma Qingquan derived from the macro-level analysis of the inevitability of the arrival of the bull market, a profound understanding the stock market "barometer" function: short-term deviations will inevitably be corrected in the long run.

In addition to confidence, there was also strategy. The reason why the department targeted the Shenzhen market stocks was because its valuation was lower, the trading volume was lighter, and was more in a state of "value depression." In addition, Shenzhen is close to Guangzhou, so it was convenient to go there for research purposes. The investment team had the confidence that it held "high-quality assets, at least in the future, it can also have access to dividends." The amount of capital invested by GF Securities Investment and Finance Department was only a drop in the ocean in the capital markets, but the big buying decision in March 1996 flapped the wings of a butterfly in the extremely low market sentiment, which not only ignited the market sentiment, but also caused the butterfly effect that the Shenzhen market was more sought after by the capital.

At this time, China's securities market operating rules had many "characteristics of the times." Not only was there no ceiling on how much shares could rise or fall but the stock exchanges in Shanghai and Shenzhen were still managed by the local people's banks of China. In the context of regional competition, indicators such as trading volume and price increase of the two markets were not only closely tracked by the market, but also related to the image of the two markets in building financial centers, and even linked to the performance evaluation of local leaders. In April 1996, the Shanghai Stock Exchange Index rose 22.42 percent, falling far behind the 48.13 percent gain in the Shenzhen Stock Exchange Index. In the long bull run that followed for more than a year, the Shenzhen market as a whole maintained a prominent position with stronger gains. The gap between the turnover of Shanghai and Shenzhen also gradually widened. There was a single day turnover of 4.246 billion yuan in Shanghai while the turnover of Shenzhen reached 14.713 billion yuan on the same day, forming a sharp contrast. Shenzhen outperforming Shanghai led to resulting discussions in the media and among shareholders.

Shenzhen outperforming Shanghai once was only a temporary stock market atmosphere in early 1996. This started a majestic and treacherous bull market for the entire Chinese securities market. The problems and irregularities that emerged afterward in the second half of the bull market cannot negate the inevitability and legitimacy of the first half of the bull market, which was rooted in macroeconomic development and the inherent laws of the market. And just as many grand events were often triggered by a fuse, realistically speaking, it was GF Securities' proprietary business that fired the first shot in the spring of 1996, when the Chinese stock market started a bull market, performing the historical drama of Shenzhen outperforming Shanghai.

As the market gradually went bullish, the thinking of GF Securities' investment team also changed. There were more small and medium-sized listed companies in the Shenzhen market, and the change of individual stock fundamentals was very important for investment risk control. The team's research energy was limited and it was difficult to diversify investment. The department meeting decided to focus on a few "bull stocks" to gain income by combining their capital strength and positions.

After the meeting, team members went to Shenzhen to conduct field research, and one stock gradually became the focus of the investment team at this time.

Shennan Property A (000046, later renamed Oceanwide Holdings) was a stock listed on the Shenzhen Stock Exchange in September 1994. It was the listed platform of the property subsidiary of the then famous Shenzhen Oceanwide (Holdings) Ltd. In light of the economic trends, market hotspots, and housing reform policies at that time, the investment team finally set its eyes on Oceanwide Holdings. From the second half of 1995, the Investment and Finance Department had already bought a small amount of shares of Oceanwide Holdings. After determining the strategy of concentrated shareholding, the investment team of GF Securities decided to close the funds withdrawn from other stocks to Oceanwide Holdings and buy the stock step by step based on the research and analysis of its location advantages and property value, as well as on the judgment of the long-term future good performance of real estate stocks.

Under the established strategy of increasing holdings, GF Securities' investment team avoided frequent buying and selling on Oceanwide Holdings. Although Oceanwide Holdings received more and more attention from market participants as the stock price gradually moved higher, its stock price amplitude was not significant relative to the broader market and leading and popular stocks during the same period, and the market maneuver of baiting short and baiting long did not appear for it. In the second quarter, Oceanwide Holdings' share price rose from 3.30 yuan per share to 5.27 yuan per share, a 59.70 percent increase, which was lower than the 120.9 percent increase in the Shenzhen market during the same period.

The bull market was getting stronger and stronger, and the "distorted" data in the whole stock market had a strong recovery. At the beginning of 1996, the average P/E ratio of the Shanghai and Shenzhen markets was only 16 times, 2with the P/E ratios of leading stocks Sichuan Changhong and Shenzhen Development at 3 and 7 time, respectively. With the arrival of the bull market, the ultra-low P/E ratio and the 512.82 point of the SSE at the beginning of the year became historical lows that appeared again. The average P/E ratios of the two markets continued to approach the median line, driven by the market chasing the top-performing stocks at the time, Sichuan Changhong and Shenzhen Development in the second quarter of 1996 rose 215.6 percent and 92.82 percent, respectively, the highest single-day turnover of Shenzhen Development reached 1.842 billion yuan, and one after another value pits were filled by funds.

As it was hard to correct the phenomenon of "a hot primary market and a cold secondary market," the securities market had significantly repaired the function of improving resource allocation. The State Council made the instructions on "steady development and appropriate acceleration" for the securities market in April 1996. On May 1, the People's Bank of China announced an interest rate cut, and on August 23, it cut interest rates again by 1.5 percent for deposits and 1.2 percent for loans. Market sentiment was further ignited.

As a market participant, GF Securities decided to further increase its proprietary investment efforts. After consolidation, the company formed the Investment and Finance Headquarters based on the former Investment and Finance Department, Treasury Bonds Section of the Capital Department, Guangfayuan Corporate Custodian Company, and GF Securities Consulting Company. Four departments were set up, which were responsible for stock market operation business, treasury bonds business, research on listed companies, and market information analysis. GF Securities' investment and finance team was further strengthened.

In May 1996, in commemoration of the centennial of the Dow Jones Industrial Average Stock Price Index, Dow Jones & Company launched Dow Jones China Indexes. This was the first index series compiled by a global index compiler for stock markets in China's mainland, and the booming Chinese stock market gradually began the process of being integrated into the world's mainstream capital markets. Stock price indices are a digital representation of the level of activity in the market. In late autumn and early winter of 1996, Chinese stockholders' appetite for the wealth gradually became fierce. In addition, the stock market was about to enter its second half in an accelerating surge as a sign of the immaturity of the early Chinese securities market.

Inauguration of GF Securities Co., Ltd. in the spring of the bull market

At the beginning of the New Year in 1997, the entire GF Securities team was immersed in celebration. On January 16, the inauguration ceremony of GF Securities

2 www.p5w.net, "1996: The Correct Understanding of 1258 Points," accessed March 1, 2021.

Co., Ltd. was held at the Garden Hotel in Guangzhou. Ren Zhongyi, the former first secretary of the CPC Guangdong Provincial Committee, as well as veteran leaders such as Wang Quanguo and Liang Lingguang, Wu Chixin, president of Guangdong Development Bank, and other leaders and guests attended the celebration. Dr. Chen Yunxian, chairman of GF Securities Co., Ltd. raised his glass frequently to thank the many guests who came to congratulate his company.

GF Securities took three big steps in six years: the establishment of the Securities Department of Guangdong Development Bank in 1991, the establishment of GF Securities Company at the end of 1993, and the further increase of capital at the end of 1996 to become GF Securities Co., Ltd.

In December 1996, the first meeting of the Board of Directors of GF Securities was held, at which Chen Yunxian was elected as chairman, Ma Qingquan as vice chairman and president, Fang Jiachun appointed as executive vice president and Wang Hongmao, Ye Junying, Li Shuzhi, and Dong Zhengqing as vice presidents. The inauguration of GF Securities Co., Ltd. marked the abandonment of the geographical characteristics of GF Securities. GF Securities, the young pine born in the land of South China, had grown into a large tree and become one of the large comprehensive securities companies in China.

At this time, the company headquarters had moved to the fourth floor of GF Financial Building on Nonglinxia Road. Members of the first leadership team stood side by side for a photo. The seven members of the team were dressed in formal attire and smiling. Dr. Chen, in the center, was wearing a red and blue tie, with his elegant face overflowing with love for the securities business. Dr. Ma Qingquan and Dr. Fang Gachun were in their prime, and were steady and serious in their easy and amiable manner. Vice presidents Wang Hongmao, Ye Junying, and Dong Zhengqing were sharp-eyed and had a pioneering spirit. The only woman in the leadership team, Li Shuzhi, as the vice president who assisted the chairman in the administration of the company, carried a natural elegant lofty temperament and was confident and resolute, elegant and generous.

At this moment, GF Securities had 1,033 employees. Over the previous year, it had made a net profit of 260 million yuan and achieved solid milestones in the goal of "demutualization, conglomeration, internationalization, and standardization."

The day after the ceremony, GF Securities held a work summary meeting in 1996. Dr. Chen Yunxian made a comment in the annual work report that was very encouraging to the Investment and Finance Headquarters:

> The relatively weak situation of the company's secondary market was changed, and the self-dealing business became one of the company's new main sources of profit. The company achieved its goal of having the primary and secondary markets develop together. While creating good benefits, we have gained certain lessons of operating large capital. Our project research, analysis

and planning, and operation ability have been greatly improved.

As a recently established department, the performance of the investment team was appreciated by colleagues from other departments. As the stock market was nearing the end of its consolidation at the beginning of the year and the general market was showing signs of an upswing again, the Investment and Finance Headquarters was full of expectations for the new wave of the market and ready to add more impetus to the development of GF Securities after the restructuring. (See Figure 3)

2. The first regulation of China's securities market

Causes of the subhealth of the second half of the bull market

Starting from late autumn and early winter of 1996, the dramatic bull market, which was originally rooted in the macroeconomy of China and the intrinsic laws of the development of the securities market, entered its second half. The speculative atmosphere in the market became more and more intense and the irregularities became more and more serious, which finally aroused the vigilance and anger of the highest decision-making level and led to the first heavy-handed regulation of the Chinese securities market in the autumn of 1997.

At the end of 1995, when the securities market began to show signs of spring and the beginning of a bull market, the highest decision-making authorities had high hopes for the function of the securities market in improving the allocation of resources. In accordance with the instructions of the State Council leader on "steady development and appropriate acceleration" for the securities market, the People's Bank of China took a series of interest rate cuts starting from May. These policy initiatives demonstrated the central government's positive attitude toward the development of the securities market.

However, the fledgling Chinese securities market was not yet ready for a standardized bull market, both in terms of institutional development and market participants. The first securities law was enacted only three years later, on December 29, 1998, by the Standing Committee of the National People's Congress, and came into force in July of the following year. From the perspective of market participants, regulated institutional investors such as securities investment funds had not yet emerged, and natural persons and short-term arbitrage capital became the dominant force in the market. The competition between the Shanghai and the Shenzhen Stock Exchanges and the local governments' tolerance or even tacit support for the corresponding irregularities in market operations and funding sources out of support for this competition also became one of the main factors contributing to the abnormal second half of the bull market. Under the combined effect of these factors, the development of the market gradually deviated from the correct direction it should have followed.

Irregularities in the securities market at that time were mainly manifested in the following areas.

First, bank funds entered the market illegally. For example, the Hefei branch of ICBC and the Jinan branch of CITIC Bank lent 11.759 billion yuan and 4.8 billion yuan respectively to non-bank financial institutions to speculate on stocks during the stock issues of two companies, Anhui Gujing Distillery and Jinan Diesel. A large amount of bank funds flowed into the stock market, driving up stock prices.

Second, securities institutions had illegal overdrafts. For example, securities operators such as Zhongshan Securities Company, Guangdong Development Bank Jiangmen Branch, and Hainan Hong Kong and Macao International Trust and Investment Co., Ltd. illegally overdrew 1.65 billion to purchase stocks during the issuance of stocks by Jiangsu Sopo and Qinghai Gelatin.

Third, the irregularities and even violations of market participants, such as price manipulation and arbitrage, became the dominant pattern of market behavior. These participants influenced and competed with each other, and their behavior was much talked about by the public.

By now the stock market had entered a bubble state. The SSE index climbed from 914.06 points on January 2, 1997 to 1,510.18 points on May 12; the SZSE index rose from 3,195.52 points to 6,103.63 points.

The first heavy-handed regulation of the securities market was inevitably written into the history of Chinese securities in the 1990s.

Severe regulations on stock trading

Prior to the regulatory storm in late 1996 and early 1997, the regulators had also introduced some milder regulatory initiatives and penalties against certain brokerage firms in the hope of alerting all market players and keeping the situation under control.

Since October 1996, the regulators issued a series of severe regulations on stock trading, including the Measures for the Administration of the Self-Dealing Securities Business of Securities Operators, the Circular on the Prohibition of Securities Market Manipulation, the Circular on Further Strengthening. The Legal System, Supervision, Self-Discipline and Regulation became the working policy repeatedly emphasized by the leaders of the regulatory authorities on many occasions. Article 19 of the Measures for the Administration of the Self-Dealing Securities Business of Securities Operators stipulates: "Securities operators engaging in securities business shall have liquid assets accounting for no less than 50 percent of their net assets or securities working capital." Article 20 details that, "The total amount of equity securities held at cost on the securities proprietary business accounts of securities operating institutions shall not exceed 80 percent of their net assets or securities working capital." In addition, with regard to the prohibited conduct of brokerage firms' proprietary operations, the Measures clearly stipulate that securities operators are prohibited from "buying and selling a certain type or class of securities frequently and continuously in large quantities over a period of time to cause abnormal changes in market prices." However, these mild tips had not attracted the full attention of market participants. In the context of the Shanghai-Shenzhen competition, the scale of self-dealing of individual securities companies was inevitably pushed up. For example, the total scale of self-dealing of Shenyin Wanguo Securities exceeded 3 billion yuan,[3] which greatly exceeded the provisions of the Measures for the Administration of the Self-Dealing Securities Business of Securities Operators. Elsewhere, the consistent and ferocious market making by a famous brokerage firm in Shenzhen was well known in the Chinese securities market at that time.

In addition to strengthening the management of listed companies, stock exchanges, and the media, regulators also prioritized securities operating institutions. In November 1996, the CSRC seriously investigated the cases of Haitong Securities and Shenzhen Development Bank for illegally providing financing to their clients in stock trading, and gave warnings and fines to the two securities operators. In December, the media announced that the CSRC had punished Jun'an Securities, Shandong International Trust, Guangdong Securities, Huayin Trust, and 31 other institutions for illegal subscription of new shares. During this period, new regulations on proprietary business, credit business, and equity underwriting business were also issued one after another.

Judging from the market reaction, the severe regulations on stock trading had a deterrent effect, but did not fully achieve the purpose of controlling the overheated market. As mentioned earlier, the intensifying Shanghai-Shenzhen competition in the market at that time was one of the factors contributing to market irregularities. According to the disclosure afterwards, the rise of Shanghai and Shenzhen indices and stocks was regarded by Shanghai and Shenzhen as an important work to compete for the position as China's financial center. Under the strong will of the local government, the local exchanges, media, listed companies, and securities companies passively participated in the competition between the two cities. The representative stocks of Shenzhen Development, Lujiazui, and Shanghai Petrochemicals of the two cities alternately rose. The popular voice among stockholders, such as "it is not as profitable to speculate in Shanghai stocks as in Shenzhen stocks," reflected this situation.

Conversely, irrational market behavior hastened the process, putting the stock market on a standard and legal track. The crackdown by regulatory authorities made history pay a price at the cost of market participants.

---

3 Kan Zhidong, *Twenty Years of Glory and Disgrace: My Life in the Stock Market,* Chapter 5 (CITIC Press Group, 2010).

On November 11, 1996, *People's Daily* published an editorial entitled "Resolutely Punishing Violations and Consciously Safeguarding Financial Order," which stated in stern terms that:

> The purpose of developing China's securities market at this stage is, first, to help speed up the pace of company reform and promote the change of the way businesses operate; second, to develop direct financing in an appropriate manner, transform a portion of idle social funds into production and construction funds, and provide new financing channels for company development. However, the government will never allow the use of the securities market for speculative activities and profiteering, and will not allow bank credit funds to make their way into the stock market for speculation, thus disrupting the normal financial order. Therefore, we must be determined to cut off the channels of bank credit funds speculation in stocks, and severely punish violations. Leaders who are directly responsible for state banks shall all be transferred from their jobs in the banks for their violations and be given administrative sanctions, and they are strongly advised not to violate the law. All commercial banks should strictly implement the Commercial Bank Law of the People's Republic of China, consciously maintain the financial order, be a model of operating in accordance with the law, and promote the healthy development of the socialist market economy.

This editorial made it clear that the focus of this securities market rectification was to make investigating and dealing with the irregular entry of bank credit funds into the stock market the main thread, and also to rectify various irregularities in the securities market.

On May 14, 1997, *China Securities Journal* published a commentary calling on stockholders to "invest wisely and prevent risks":

> Recently, the evolution of the stock markets in Shanghai and Shenzhen has aroused widespread concern throughout the country. The regulatory authorities issued a series of cooling measures, but the two market indices have risen to record highs due to market hot spots.
>
> The headlong chase of stocks whose prices have kept rising is breading a growing risk. This trend is worth seriously thinking about by investors, and they should stay calm and take real action to prevent risks.
>
> Therefore, during the recent period, the regulatory authorities introduced a series of regulatory measures, such as increasing the supply of stocks, cracking down on irregularities and increasing the stamp duty, designed to ensure the overheated market cools down and guarantee the stable and healthy development of the securities market. Investors should have a comprehensive and correct understanding of the meaning of these policies and make sensible choices. In the current situation

> of high stock prices, it is important not to blindly follow the trend, but investors should always pay attention to controlling risks and make positive efforts for the risk prevention year activities advocated by the regulatory authorities this year.

On June 6, 1997, the People's Bank of China issued the Circular on Prohibiting the Inflow of Bank Funds into the Stock Market in an Illegal Manner, making seven provisions such as "Commercial banks and their branches are strictly prohibited from engaging in trust investment and stock business" and "All branches of the People's Bank of China shall strictly manage the lending and borrowing business between commercial banks and trust and investment companies, securities companies, and non-bank financial institutions." The Circular strictly required that:

> After 10 days from the date of issuance of this document, if it is found that commercial banks under its jurisdiction are still engaged in equity securities transactions in a direct or indirect manner, and if they provide funds for the economic entities they run to engage in equity securities transactions, their presidents, vice presidents in charge, and the personnel handling these matters shall be removed from their positions. For each securities operating institution that engages in securities transactions with funds borrowed from commercial banks, the People's Bank of China shall disqualify the head of the institution from the post of senior management of financial institutions. For commercial banks colluding with securities operating institutions to lend funds for securities trading, the president, vice president in charge, and the staff handling the matters should be removed from their office.

The rapidly warming speculative market atmosphere and increasingly stringent regulatory environment meant that the impending penalties for banking financial institutions and brokerages might exceed expectations.

Heavy-handed regulation of the securities market and regulatory punishment of financial institutions

After a period of investigation and evidence collection, in June 1997, the national financial regulatory authorities made administrative results against a number of offending banks, securities companies, listed companies, and their leaders. Xinhua News Agency reported on June 12, 1997:

> Recently the Securities Commission of the State Council, in conjunction with the People's Bank of China, the State Audit Office, the CSRC, and other relevant departments, after thorough investigation and evidence collection, seriously punished a number of violating institutions and their leaders in the

securities market in accordance with the law.

Shenzhen Development Bank used a huge amount of 311 million yuan to speculate directly on its shares for more than a year from March 1996 to April 1997, making an illegal profit of 90.34 million yuan. This act violated the provisions of the Commercial Bank Law that commercial banks shall not engage in stock business, and also violated the state regulation that listed companies shall trade in their stock. More seriously, until April this year, Shenzhen Development Bank continued to speculate in its shares, which seriously interfered with the normal market order, misled investors, and had a bad impact. The relevant authorities decided to punish Shenzhen Development Bank President He Yun by dismissing him as president and banning him from the financial and securities market for five years; to record a major demerit for Li Wei, former head of the Shenzhen Development Bank Securities Brokerage Branch; to impose a fine on Shenzhen Development Bank and confiscate its illegally held shares of Shenzhen Development Bank as well as sell: ... as well as sell them all, turning all profits over to the state treasury.

From September to December 1996, the Shanghai branch of the Industrial and Commercial Bank of China gave huge loans and overdrafts to some securities companies for stock speculation. It lent a total of 910 million yuan to Haitong Securities Company and 6.31 billion to Shenyin Wanguo Securities Company; meanwhile, it gave an average daily overdraft of 1.2 billion yuan in late October and 1 billion yuan in November, while giving an average daily overdraft of 580 million yuan in September, 830 million yuan in October, and 910 million yuan in November to Shenyin Wanguo Securities Company. After the publication of a special commentator's article in *People's Daily* on December 16, 1996, it still gave overdrafts to relevant securities institutions, which amounted to 395 million yuan on December 25. The actions of ICBC Shanghai Branch seriously violated the national regulations that any financial institution should not lend funds or give overdrafts for stock transactions, which encouraged speculative activities in the stock market and had a bad impact on the standard and stability of the stock market. For this reason, the authorities decided to punish the president of ICBC Shanghai Branch, Shen Ruolei, by dismissing him from this role.

The chairman of Guangshen Railway Co., Ltd., a company listed in Hong Kong, Ge Wen'an, without the decision of the board of directors, entrusted 300 million yuan of the funds raised in December 1996 to Jun'an International Finance Co., Ltd., which was not qualified to engage in financial business in China's mainland. The latter transferred the funds to Jun'an Securities Company to speculate in stocks, making an illegal profit of 40 million. These actions seriously violated the relevant national securities regulations and accounting system. The relevant authorities punished the company's chairman Ge Wen'an and its chief accountant Zeng Xianzhao by removing them from their posts and giving them a record of major demerit through legal procedures, and instructed the company to recover 300 million yuan of the illegally used fundraising funds.

It has also been found that in recent years, Haitong Securities Company, Shenyin Wanguo Securities Company, and GF Securities Company illegally obtained huge amounts of bank funds and manipulated the prices of Shanghai Petrochemical, Lujiazui, and Oceanwide Holdings stocks respectively by means of continuous buying and selling and massive contra trade, causing abnormal fluctuations in the share prices of the above companies, disrupting the normal order of the securities market, harming the interests of other investors, and promoting excessive speculation in the stock market. The relevant authorities decided to remove Li Huizhen, chairman and general manager of Haitong Securities, Kan Zhidong, president of Shenyin Wanguo Securities, and Ma Qingquan, general manager of GF Securities, from their positions and to give them a record major demerit. Each of the three securities companies was fined and suspended from stock proprietary business for one year. Jun'an Securities Company was also suspended from stock proprietary business for six months for violation and had its illegal income confiscated.

The state financial and securities regulatory authorities decided to further increase law enforcement efforts to combat all kinds of illegal and unlawful acts in the financial and securities markets. They decided that where state-owned banks provided funds to other institutions and individuals to speculate in stocks, and where listed companies, securities companies, and institutional large investors used bank credit funds to speculate in stocks and manipulate the market, the main responsible person will be removed from office and identified as a person without access to the securities market without failure. For serious circumstances constituting a crime, they will be held criminally responsible in accordance with the law. [4]

At this point, the administrative penalties for institutions and leaders in China's securities market had been meted out for the first time. Its positive significance is that it urged and accelerated the development of the legal system of the securities market. A year and a half later, the Securities Law of the People's Republic of China, the first of its kind in China, was promulgated and formally implemented the following year.

3. Rebirth: the establishment of a self-sustaining and self-improving course

Nirvana of the phoenix: responsibilities and reflections

Based on the recommendation of the regulatory authorities for punishment,

4 See *Shanghai Securities News*, June 13, 1997; see also Kan Zhidong, *Twenty Years of Glory and Disgrace: My Life in the Stock Market*, p. 185.

GF Securities accepted the then president of the company, Dr. Ma Qingquan, and appointed Dr. Fang Gachun as the new president of the company. The company encountered the biggest test since its establishment, which was the "1997 crisis" in the hearts of GF Securities and GF people.

According to the document issued by the CSRC on June 11, 1997, the administrative penalties imposed on GF Securities were mainly based on: (1) opening self-dealing accounts in the names of 153 individuals to speculate in the shares of Oceanwide Holdings; holding 29,541,742 shares as of March 9, 1997, accounting for 25.95 percent of the total share capital of Oceanwide Holdings, and failing to fulfill its obligations to report, disclose, and announce relevant documents and information in accordance with the regulations; (2) using different accounts to make transactions of similar price and quantity but in opposite directions on the shares of Oceanwide Holdings to increase the price of the stock, which rose from 8.55 yuan per share to 20.49 yuan per share, an increase of 1.4 times; (3) misappropriating customer margin and using bank funds to speculate in stocks, and raising 260 million yuan in over-the-counter financing from Guangdong Development Bank for stock speculation from April 1996 to January 1997.

Objectively speaking, the direct personal responsibility involved in the basis of the above penalties was actually divided into two levels. One level was the responsibility of the leader in charge of stock investment in the Investment and Finance Department for irregularities in some periods and in some practices; the other level was the responsibility of the company's headquarters' Funding Department and the vice president in charge for irregularities in the sources of funds provided to the Investment and Finance Department. Dr. Ma Qingquan had a degree of leadership responsibility for the first level of violations. The Investment and Finance Department was hastily established to meet the urgent need of the company's business development. While its organization, understanding, investment philosophy, and risk control construction were all still very weak, it encountered a sudden bull market and responded to it hastily.

Dr. Ma's consistent leadership style of "trust the person in position" made him particularly liberal. Although the investment project of Oceanwide Holdings was under the full responsibility of one of the vice presidents of the Investment and Finance Department at that time, the failure to do a good job of building the rules and regulations of the Investment and Finance Department and discussing and defining the prohibited acts of investment when the department was established was certainly an important reason for the irregularities in the operation.

However, Dr. Ma Qingquan was not directly or indirectly personally responsible for the second level of irregularities in fund raising. The day-to-day operations of the company's capital department were the concern of another vice president at the time. However, since GF Securities was a wholly-owned company of Guangdong Development Bank at that time, in fact both the relevant person in charge of

Guangdong Development Bank and the vice president in charge of the Funding Department of GF Securities probably perceived that it was proper for Guangdong Development Bank to provide funding support to GF Securities. This special relationship between a shareholder and its wholly-owned subsidiary was indeed different from the relationship between other brokerages that had also been subject to administrative penalties and their sources of funding. For example, Shenyin Wanguo and Haitong, two brokerages that were also subject to regulatory penalties at the time, did not have such a controlling shareholder relationship with ICBC, which financed them. Of course, despite this controlling relationship in terms of equity, the irregular nature of the bank's credit funds entering the stock market was established. Moreover, in the absence of a strict third-party custodian system, the head of the capital department and the vice president in charge of it at the time may have considered it logical for the Head Office to call on clients' margin.

GF Securities implemented a strict system of division of responsibility under the leadership of the chairman. The leaders in charge had their own duties. The president and vice presidents had their own areas of responsibility and cooperated but did not interfere with each other; even the chairman of the board of directors did not interfere with the daily work of the team members within the scope of their division of labor in general. Even the chairman of the board of directors did not interfere with the daily work of the team members within the scope of their division of labor. In the day-to-day investment activities or financing activities as described above, if it was within a certain authorized amount, it would not be interfered with by or made known to the chairman. The 260 million yuan loan from Guangdong Development Bank was the total amount of financing that occurred within a span of seven months.

Under normal circumstances, a company's liability for negligence is generally attributed to the person directly responsible. But the second half of the 1997 bull market was a special case, an exception to the usual logic: with the regulatory authorities' severe regulations losing their deterrent effect, it was difficult to reverse the market's madness without extreme measures. Measures must be excessive in order to make corrections. In this special historical condition, the "one size fits all" approach to pursuing the leadership responsibility of the main person in charge of the company became the inevitable option of the regulatory authorities at that time.

In fact, the specific penalty clauses of GF Securities and other brokerage firms had already reached the competent departments of the relevant companies in the form of consultation through some informal channels before the official text was formed. Coincidentally, one morning at the company's reception desk, Dr. Ma Qingquan happened to overhear a phone call from a section chief of the CSRC, surnamed C, to one of the company's vice presidents, and clearly heard the section chief tell the vice president that no matter what, one of the key leaders of GF Securities must be held responsible.

Hearing this call, Dr. Ma was deep in thought.

If the company's administrative punishment had to be borne by the main leader of the company, then he could not help but be responsible. This was the only right choice he could make. It was not only the way to behave in return for Dr. Chen Yunxian's kindness, but also an unshirkable responsibility to protect the company. "If I don't go to hell, who will?!"

With his mind made up, Dr. Ma Qingquan flew to Beijing. He met with a vice chairman of the CSRC in charge of the matter and the director of the Department of Non-Banking of the People's Bank of China in Beijing and made it clear that he was the president of GF Securities and was willing to take the leadership responsibility for this administrative punishment of GF Securities. Considering that the administrative punishments of the brokerage firms involved were determined and inevitable under the objective circumstances at that time, Dr. Ma Qingquan also thereafter declined the hearing arranged by the Institutional Department of the CSRC because he did not see the need to go through the motions.

The final result was the penalty decision announced in a press release issued by Xinhua News Agency on June 12, 1997. In addition, the proposed punishment of a bank-level head of Guangdong Development Bank was avoided because GF Securities took the initiative to assume responsibility for the bank's credit funds. At that time, in a meeting room of the Guangdong provincial government, Secretary General You Ningfeng convened a meeting with the leadership team of GF Securities, and Zhang Gaoli, Standing Committee member of the CPC Guangdong Provincial Committee and executive vice governor, extended his thumb to Dr. Ma Qingquan and said: "You are a good official trained by the Central Party School, and you have protected our financial institutions in Guangdong Province. We Guangdong Province will not forget you."

Dr. Ma has no regrets about his choice in the "1997 crisis" of the company except that he did not expect that the personal punishment of the executives of the Chinese securities industry would be broadcast in the evening news broadcast and brought great anxiety, panic, and worry to his mother, who was nearly 80 years old. This is the eternal guilt and sorrow in Dr. Ma Qingquan's heart: his mother originally took the greatest honor that her humble family had one of the earliest PhDs and professors of the People's Republic of China.

Perhaps due to the concern of the leaders of the provincial government, less than a month after Dr. Ma Qingquan resigned as the president of GF Securities Company, he resumed his job as the legal representative and general manager of the Fund Department of GF Securities according to the deployment of Dr. Chen Yunxian and the suggestion of Guangdong Branch of the People's Bank of China, and started to embark on a new journey in the strategic layout of Dr. Chen Yunxian.

At the end of 1998, when GF Securities was involved in the preparation of Harvest Fund Company, Dr. Ma Qingquan officially became the first chairman of Harvest Fund Company under the care of Zhou Zhengqing, the chairman of the CSRC, and with the trust of Dr. Chen Yunxian, and started a new journey on the road of development of the regulated fund industry in China's securities market.

Establishment of a self-sustaining and self-improving course

In 1997, events such as the return to the motherland of Hong Kong triggered the emotion of all Chinese sons and daughters for the magnificent historical scroll of vicissitudes and changes. A famous popular song, "1997 A.D.," expressed the feelings of Chinese people about this special year:

> 1997, I call you with affection
> Let the whole world jump for you
> Let this fabulous name live forever in the heart
> There were long, dark nights
> There was a painful parting
> In many dreams we embraced you
> Your heart and mine will never part

In the second half of 1997, a number of significant changes took place in the Chinese capital markets.

In August, the State Council put the Shanghai Stock Exchange and the Shenzhen Stock Exchange under the direct management of the CSRC, with general managers and deputy general managers of stock exchanges appointed by the CSRC, the chairmen and deputy chairmen nominated by the CSRC, and the board of directors elected. This made it impossible for local governments to restart the competition between the Shanghai and Shenzhen stock exchanges.

In November, the central government held a national financial work conference and decided to reform the management system of the national securities industry, straighten out the securities regulatory system, put local securities regulators under the vertical leadership of the CSRC, and transfer the securities operators formerly supervised by the People's Bank of China to the CSRC.

The previously bubbly Chinese stock market, under the effect of severe regulation and control policies such as the increase of stamp duty and the increase of issuance quota, gradually consolidated and fell from the high point in May 1997. On December 31, the Shanghai Stock Exchange Index closed at 1,194.10 points, up about 30.21 percent for the year, achieving the goal of stable growth.

China's securities market was on a regulated development track and was ushering in greater opportunities for development as the new century approached.

Meanwhile, the capital increase and shareholding reform of GF Securities, as well as the delinking from Guangdong Development Bank, were being carried out in an orderly manner in accordance with the requirements of the Commercial Bank Law on the separation of banking and securities. In accordance with the requirements of the modern financial company system, the shareholding structure and shareholders' background of securities companies were crucial. The choice of the equity structure of GF Securities after surviving the "1997 crisis" was the choice of its own fate. What kind of shareholder was the most suitable for the development of GF Securities?

On the eve of a new stage of development of the securities market, at the time of separating banking and securities, preparing to introduce new shareholders and establishing a new shareholding structure, GF Securities, a rising star in the securities industry, attracted the attention of several institutions in society with strong strength and some special background. Some of them started to contact and reach out to the leaders of the company, expressing their strong desire to enter GF Securities as shareholders.

At this time, GF Securities was at a historical juncture when it had just stood up from the heartbreaking pain of 1997, and the company was working together to heal itself and welcome new development. Did GF Securities want to open up its equity to such shareholders?

During their many years of operation, from the primary market for underwriting projects to the secondary market, Dr. Chen and Dr. Ma had a deeper sense of the importance of the "resources" of securities companies than many others. How many times had market opportunities been lost because of the last "missing force"?

In the capital markets where opportunities and risks coexist, who is not eager to stay away from the dilemma of "getting into trouble at every turn"? After the company paid a heavy price by losing a president, would it want to be like a peer who was said to find a strong supporter from shareholders?

The memory of the 1997 crisis in the securities industry was still fresh in the minds of GF Securities people: the presidents or legal representatives of three major securities companies, Haitong, Shenyin Wanguo, and GF, fell together and none of them was spared. A company with a recognized fierce style in the securities industry escaped severe punishment because of the background of its shareholders, and the company was only financially penalized. Was GF Securities going to go the same way?

"When you stare into the abyss, the abyss stares back at you."

Brokered by connections, Dr. Chen and Dr. Ma experienced several similar trysts.

In a major city, the receptionist arranged for a car to drive directly to the plane ramp to meet them, after which they drove all the way to their destination The implication is self-explanatory: this was to show their strength to the two PhDs from GF Securities. After that, from Macao to Hong Kong, a small private plane was used, and in these two places, from dining to entertainment, all the reception was extremely luxurious, of which two "silly" PhD intellectuals had never heard.

But it was this ostentatious act that made the two PhDs toss and turn. From the company's perspective, could these people really bring a broader and smoother development prospect to GF Securities? If the equity approach was used to seek the shelter of the "powerhouse," what other price would the company pay? Individual brokerage firms certainly had a momentary glory, but was this model suitable for GF Securities?

What was the original intention of the "PhD Legion"?

At 4 a.m., Dr. Ma knocked on the door of Dr. Chen's room next door and said what he thought: "We can't agree. We are not the same as them after all."

Once again, Dr. Ma, as the first mate of the ship GF Securities, coincided with the thoughts of Dr. Chen Yunxian, the captain of the ship.

Dr. Chen Yunxian refused the request of such institutions to join the company. As a Confucian businessman, Dr. Chen, through his good offices and games, with his wisdom and art, "did not offend them in the end."

The soul-level gazing and pondering is a rebirth in another sense. Perhaps it was at this time that GF Securities really stepped over its "1997 crisis" and established its choice of its own destiny: not to blame God, not to seek "umbrellas," but to adhere to the nature of intellectual entrepreneurship and to steadfastly follow the development path of self-sufficiency and self-improvement.

The real supporter is self-confidence based on norms

After the "1997 crisis," GF Securities deeply realized that the only real supporter for the company to be invincible was self-confidence based on norms. Were the administrative penalties imposed on GF Securities too light or too heavy? It is meaningless to complain about the administrative penalties that GF Securities had received. If the company had been free of errors and violations in all aspects of its operations and management, would those administrative penalties have occurred? In addition, even if the company threw into the arms of a supporter that could be relied on for a period of time, could this supporter guarantee long-lasting stability? If there was no standardized management of the company as the foundation, would the company end up in failure due to its supporter? As a matter of fact, didn't the company that had been lucky enough to escape from the "1997 crisis" that had hit GF Securities fall in the hands of its supporters more than a year later and become merged by another company, with its leaders ending up in jail? GF Securities must take the path to self-centered, independent, and self-improving development.

After the route was determined, Dr. Chen Yunxian began to plan for the next step of the company's development. In his article "The Germ of the Third Wave Has Appeared in China's Securities Industry," he wrote that:

> The common problems faced by the Chinese securities industry are: the securities industry are in the primary stage of development; securities laws and regulations are not sound; securities dealers have little self-regulatory behavior;

> and the solution of problems such as business layout, management, investment decisions, accident prevention, and poor performance and efficiency requires the joint efforts of the regulatory authorities and securities dealers.
>
> However, as far as the securities firms themselves are concerned, they should use the current efforts to separate banking and securities and seek mergers and cooperation, and seize the opportunity of the second wave of China's securities industry, which is generated by forming economies of scale and standardizing operations for the Chinese securities market and the international securities market, to realize placement or take the path of mergers and cooperation to form economies of scale. They should deepen institution building and standardize management to prevent all kinds of securities risks, make full use of the domestic and international securities market, and develop various securities business to turn around.

In order to achieve this goal, Dr. Chen carried out a series of reforms to the organizational structure, business structure, and management mechanism of GF Securities.

First, in accordance with the requirements of laws and regulations at that time, the company's irregularities were investigated and comprehensively reviewed, including the strict separation of the company's own funds and customer deposits, the resolute elimination of misappropriation of customer deposits, and the comprehensive cleaning of off-book accounts and unauthorized coffers.

Second, the company reshaped its organizational structure. With a focus on centralizing unifying management and strengthening risk control, it set up a clearing center and a development research center. The company strengthened the function of the Audit Department, established an audit system of ex ante risk research, interim risk monitoring, and ex post supervision, as well as created a new accounting system and strengthened the supervisory function of the Finance Department.

Third, in terms of business structure, the company comprehensively cleaned up and disposed of non-securities business and changed the company of multi-industries into a professional investment bank. In addition, the main business segments were adjusted.

Fourth, the company established a centralized and unified management mechanism. According to the business characteristics of investment banking, a brand-new accounting system and financial system were designed, drawing on the experience of large international investment banks.

In addition, the company issued a series of normative documents one after another, such as the Circular on Reviewing Unified Securities and Funds in the Company, the Decision on Implementing the Greater Financial Management System, the Measures on Funds Management of GF Securities Co., Ltd., the Measures on Funds Transfer Management, the Regulations on Statistical Management of GF Securities Co., Ltd., and Certain Provisions on Implementing the Dispatch System for Treasurers, which creatively established a management mechanism compatible with the characteristics of investment banking and the future development of securities market.

In view of the fact that standardization was a systematic and long-term work, Dr. Chen Yunxian put forward the requirement of "thorough standardization" for the president's team and all management officials. In 1997, GF Securities issued the Circular on Further Strengthening Standardized Management and Stable Operation, and issued the Internal Audit System of GF Securities Co., Ltd. in early 1998. The company was the first securities company in China to creatively establish the internal audit system and risk firewall system. These two systems preceded the relevant requirements of the CSRC by six years.

The entire company felt the change in the pace of the company's work: from June 1997 onwards, the company successively held the interim board meeting, the meeting on standardized management and risk prevention in the company, and the meeting on financial work in the company, and decided to review the institutional business of the company.

Subsequently, the company further strengthened the hierarchical management. It resolutely implemented the rules and regulations that had been promulgated on prohibiting brokerage branches from lending funds and making overdrafts. It reaffirmed the abolition of brokerage branches' self-dealing power and set up its investment decision-making group. It established risk monitoring and early warning systems. It kept the primary and secondary market projects under control. It established a unified management system for its greater finance, capital, and computer systems. It set up an internal monitoring procedure for hierarchical authorization with clear responsibilities, and seriously investigated and dealt with irregularities.

With the implementation of a series of management measures, GF Securities strengthened its internal control system and improved checks and balances, becoming an early brokerage firm in the industry to improve the overall structure of internal control. Later, the internal control improvement measures after the "1997 crisis" were also widely used in many acquisitions and mergers by GF Securities, effectively solving the risk disposal and internal control problems of the acquisition targets.

"What is lost in the morning is made up in the evening." Based on thinking, adjustment, and sublimation in 1997, GF Securities stepped over this most important hurdle in its start-up stage. In January 1998, Dr. Chen Yunxian, chairman of the company, announced to all employees that, "Today, GF Securities has entered a benign development stage."

Chapter VII: At the Dawn of the New Century

Everything is changing, everything is changing, only the whole is the same. The birth and death of the world is endless. Every moment it is destroyed, there is no exception and there will never be any exceptions.

—Denis Diderot

1. Reflections over response to China's accession to the WTO

The thought in Songyuan Hotel

The Baiyun Mountain in Guangzhou is full of trees, which clean the air, and is therefore called the "northern lung" of Guangzhou. Located at the foot of the mountain, Songyuan Hotel is a place rich in "oxygen." Every time Dr. Chen went there for a meeting, he often recalled what Ding Lisong, the deputy secretary-general of the Guangdong provincial government, had said when he was soliciting him in Beijing before defending his doctorate at Peking University: "The north is short of oxygen, so I hope you can come to Guangdong, which is at the forefront of reform and opening up."

Guangdong was at the forefront of reform and opening up, but the north was not short of oxygen. On August 28, 1998, Wang Qishan, who was transferred from Beijing to Guangdong, brought a whirlwind of wisdom to GF Securities at the Songyuan Hotel, where the mid-year working meeting was being held.

The sudden appearance of a "big leader" Wang Qishan at the company's internal meeting and his participation in the group discussions was a surprise to

Dr. Chen Yunxian, Dr. Ma Qingquan, Dr. Fang Jiachun, and other GF Securities officials, who, of course, were no strangers to Wang Qishan and his unique style of work. When Wang Qishan served in the People's Bank of China, he signed his first approval document for the establishment of a financial institution, which was GF Securities. After he became the Standing Committee member of the CPC Guangdong Provincial Committee and executive vice governor of Guangdong Province, Wang Qishan also asked the leadership team of GF Securities to report directly to him at his office several times in order to grasp the situation of Guangdong's financial industry quickly.

At this moment in Songyuan Hotel, Wang Qishan picked up many business cards that were just handed to him, and after carefully examining them, he smiled and said to the PhD Legion at the scene: "I actually don't approve of printing the title 'doctor' on business cards. Chinese culture has a big culture and a small culture, and printing PhD on the business card is a small culture. Education and social culture are not the same thing, I don't think we should take academic title too seriously."

After the light-hearted opening remarks, Wang Qishan began to talk about the international and domestic financial situation. The thoughts of the participants on the floor jumped out of their own company affairs and they started to think about the big events in the world financial field at that time: the Asian financial crisis, which started in Thailand the previous year, had reached a white-hot stage in August 1998, when the conference was held, and international financial speculators and the Hong Kong Monetary Authority were engaged in a fierce battle in the exchange, stock, and futures markets.

Wang Qishan, who had deep roots in economic theory and a broad historical perspective, shared his views on the Asian financial crisis with the officials of GF Securities: "The management and restraint of hedge funds and derivatives are generally lacking in the international community, including the United States, and many of the phenomena experienced by Southeast Asian countries are difficult to explain by traditional economic theories. In addition, at this turn of the century, humankind has caught up with a technological revolution tipping point, and the world has entered a new phase, encountering problems never encountered before, which may lead to big losses, even in the United States."

As it suggests today, Wang Qishan's 1998 comment on derivatives which "may lead to big losses, even in the United States" is very prescient, considering the US subprime mortgage crisis that erupted years later. But at the turn of the century, Wang Qishan focused on guiding the officials of GF Securities on the spot to think about what changes internet technology would bring to human life. He talked about his several encounters with Bill Gates of Microsoft and his feelings about the "tipping point of the human technological revolution." His question to Bill Gates about the information technology revolution also made the officials of GF Securities think deeply: "What will the business you are engaged in and pursuing bring to humankind?"

Based on his previous experience working at China Construction Bank, Wang Qishan also continued to discuss his weighty thoughts in light of the topic of business management at the mid-year meeting: "I have been thinking deeply about this for the past two years and found that one of the problems must be solved, namely the asymmetry between the consequences and benefits we bear for making mistakes now... Our management will be strengthened in the midst of experience and lessons learned, but the management philosophy and guiding thought must change first... I hope that the GF Securities people will explore and make a demonstration of organizational and institutional innovation in the Chinese securities market. I think there will be a very prosperous period in China in this regard, and it is coming."

These meaningful words echoed in the meeting room of Songyuan Hotel. On the same day, less than 200 kilometers away in Hong Kong, a big event that would go down in the world's financial history was taking place. August 28, 1998 was the day of the decisive battle for the defense of Hong Kong's finance, in which international financial speculators lost a lot of money on the settlement day of the HSI futures, and the HKSAR government finally defended Hong Kong's economic security and stability.

Wang Qishan's words, from the academic title on his business card, to his thoughts on the information technology revolution, to the historical role of the securities industry, opened up a new depth of thought for Dr. Chen, who Wang affectionately called "Brother Yunxian": small culture should be integrated into big culture, PhDs with high education "must realize that to understand things thoroughly, one must engage in practice," and capital markets should be promoted in accordance with Chinese reality first.

In another internal meeting, also held in Songyuan Hotel, a wise elder gave GF Securities another perspective of "reflecting response to China's accession to the WTO." He suggested that the Chinese capital markets could only be further standardized and matured by actively aligning with international practices. This time, the elder speaker was Professor Xiao Zhuoji, who called Dr. Chen his "disciple."

It was January 2000, when China and the United States had completed the difficult negotiations and reached an agreement on China's accession to the WTO. With the lighting of the sacred fire at the China Century Altar in Beijing, China entered the new millennium with boundless expectations. In the occasion of taking stock of the harvest and planning for the new year, GF Securities grandly appointed five highly respected persons, including Professor Xiao Zhuoji, Wu Chixin, former chairman of Guangdong Development Bank, and Lu Jinchang, former vice president, as GF Securities' advisors. Upon receiving the appointment letter, Professor Xiao Zhuoji took the stage to lecture on the economic situation and capital markets trends to 140 managers of GF Securities.

With the calm mind of an economist, Professor Xiao Zhuoji analyzed the basic ideas of China's economic development and summarized the macroeconomic situation in 2000 in three sentences: "The economy is moving at the same level, stability is improving, and the difficulties should not be underestimated." He unapologetically pointed out a series of problems at that time: the lack of effective demand, the large increase of the unemployed population, the impact of WTO accession on the domestic economy, the difficulties in promoting SOE reform, and the diminishing space for proactive fiscal policy.

A year before that, Mr. Xiao Zhuoji had pointed out in his speech "Suggestions on Financial Development and Financial Security" at the Second Session of the Ninth National Committee of the Chinese People's Political Consultative Conference that financial development should be given top priority, and that non-development was the greatest insecurity. In this internal meeting of GF Securities, Mr. Xiao reminded everyone to be prepared for danger and change their understanding. He analyzed and judged from several levels that China's capital markets, which had a major task in the operation of the economy, were "at an important turning point": regulation and development go hand in hand; retail investors and institutional investors should go hand in hand; policy impact and company performance should come together; intermediaries were moving away from fragmentation to centralization.

Faced with the irrational phenomenon in the capital markets at that time, Mr. Xiao highlighted the need to come better in line with international practices. "The most important feature of the domestic capital markets is that the equity structure is extremely unreasonable, and state-owned shares and legal person shares are not tradable. Only by actively aligning with international practices can China's capital markets be further regulated and mature... China is in the stage of transition from a planned economy to a market economy, and policy uncertainty is inevitable... Some things cannot be done now, but that does not necessarily mean that they cannot be studied, and there are many businesses that can be studied and considered from now on."

In the blue sky of the academic world, compared with the "casino theory" and "theory of the Shanghai Composite Index falling back to 1000 points" which were prevalent in the same period, Professor Xiao Zhuoji's guidance and admonition to GF Securities at this time reflected his consistent wish to move the securities market from immaturity to maturity. Under the historical background of the imminent accession to the WTO, the securities industry, which had only 10 years of growth, was encountering the situation that "our position in the domestic market is being seriously threatened by foreign capital," as Mr. Xiao said. What kind of thinking, layout, and action should GF Securities, which was basking in the dawn of the new century, have?

It was necessary to "take the actual situation in China into account" and "come better in line with international practices." Songyuan Hotel, rich in "oxygen," had inadvertently become a forum where GF Securities employees had the honor to learn from high level experts from Chinese politics and academia. China's accession to the WTO meant that it would be fully integrated into the world through the WTO and that its reform and opening up had entered a new stage. As the torrent of the times rolled forward, GF Securities should be more active in integrating its "small culture" into the "big culture" of the country and history.

At this time, after nearly ten years of rapid growth, the total assets of GF Securities had increased 200 times and the net assets 220 times, and it had become one of the first comprehensive securities companies with a registered capital of 1.6 billion yuan in China. Its headquarters was moved to Metropolis Plaza on Tianhe North Road, starting a new career journey in this representative senior office building in Guangzhou.

By this time, Dr. Chen Yunxian had completed his three theory books and his theoretical system in the field of investment banking had been basically formed. However, in his "reflections over response to China's accession to the WTO," Dr. Chen still maintained the same vigilance he had had at the beginning of his career. He has written many articles judging that the Chinese capital markets were about to have the "third wave of impact." The previous two waves were not only directly reflected by the rise and fall of the stock market, but also washed away many brokerage giants and changed the industry pattern. According to him, the third wave of impact arising from the transition of the capital markets from the rough stage to the mature stage would be much greater than the first and second waves. For this reason, he repeatedly remind his company:

"We still have a lot to do."

The high ground of talents of the first financial company in China to have a postdoctoral R&D base

To embrace the new century and respond to China's accession to the WTO, the Chinese securities industry had different thoughts.

In December 1999, the Securities Association of China held its second general meeting. On December 17, *China Securities Journal* published a special edition on "Strengthening Self-Discipline and Embracing the 21st Century with a New Posture," reporting on the newly elected leadership of the second council of the Securities Association of China. CITIC Securities Chairman Chang Zhenming was appointed as the chairman, Dr. Chen Yunxian and Beijing Securities Chairman Lu Kequn, Guangda Securities Chairman Nie Qingping, Industrial Securities Chairman Lan Rong, China Merchants Securities President Niu Guanxing, Guotai Jun'an Chairman Jin Jiandong, Dapeng Securities President Chen Yuping, Guoxin Securities President Hu Guanjin, Huatai Securities President Wu Wanshan, Xiangcai Securities Chairman and President Chen Xuerong as vice chairmen, and Dr. Ma Qingquan as vice chairman and full-time secretary-general.

In the special edition article, the leading figures of each brokerage firm gave different perspectives on "Opportunities and Challenges in the New Century."

Dr. Chen Yunxian expressed his thoughts on strengthening capital strength, enhancing information technology, and improving market variety. Dr. Chen also appealed to the industry in terms of talent:

> The quality of brokerage firms includes not only the quality of leadership and management, but also the comprehensive quality of employees; it includes not only the professional quality of the team, the quality of corporate culture, but also the quality of the application of technical means and foreign languages. To participate in international competition, the cultivation and use of multiple types of talents is a basic requirement for Chinese brokerage firms.

In 1999, Dr. Wang Liangzhong, head of the Development Research Center of GF Securities, was somewhat anxious when he was confronted with the topic of "talent."

This task was to expand the "PhD Legion" through the platform of the Development Research Center. The task also clearly required the recruitment of people from every province and city in China and from every famous university in the world so that there would be more than 100 PhDs in the Development Research Center.

Dr. Wang Liangzhong, a native of Hunan, acted with great enthusiasm at the very beginning of the assignment, going with the HR department of the company to interview PhD students at Peking University and other prestigious universities in China, and releasing recruitment information at several international universities through various channels. Although Dr. Wang knew the importance of the task, doctoral talents were undoubtedly a scarce resource, and it was quite difficult to expand the company's original 20-odd PhDs to achieve the goal proposed by Dr. Chen in just one year.

In 1999, a new opportunity came to this work. The Ministry of Personnel was considering the establishment of postdoctoral stations in the financial industry.

In 1984, Professor Tsung-Dao Lee suggested to Deng Xiaoping in person that the postdoctoral system should be implemented in China and the suggestion was appreciated by Deng and the system was implemented in China. However, the early postdoctoral R&D bases were mainly in natural science fields such as science and engineering. In 1999, after being informed of the relevant policies of the Ministry of Personnel, Dr. Yunxian Chen immediately realized that it was not only an opportunity for the company to promote the established idea of "expanding the 'PhD Legion,'" but, if a postdoctoral R&D base was established in GF Securities as early as possible or if GF Securities became the first to have such a station, it would also have a great significance to the talent gathering effect and brand effect of the company.

The Guangdong Provincial Personnel Department also understood its importance and actively helped GF Securities to apply for the policy from the Ministry of Personnel. On December 16, Dr. Liu Zhengzhou, who was in charge of the application in the HR Department of the company, finally got the RF No. [1999] 140 approval document from the Ministry of Personnel, and the postdoctoral R&D base of GF Securities was approved, and GF securities became the first financial company in China to have such base. (See Figure 4)

Thereafter, the "PhD Legion" "moved to the next higher level." One morning in the following spring, a simple but solemn inauguration ceremony was held at Metropolis Square under the golden glass, with leaders from the Ministry of Personnel, the CSRC, provincial and municipal departments present at the ceremony. Professor Xiao Zhuoji and Professor Liu Shibai, the leading scholars in the field, also appeared at the ceremony. Professor Lu Zhonghe, the vice governor of Guangdong Province, who was a scholar, pulled the red silk with Dr. Chen Yunxian, and in the warm applause, the postdoctoral R&D base of GF Securities was like a pearl, adding the light of knowledge to the practice of serving the country with finance.

Metropolis Square is adjacent to Tianhe North Road, which is full of traffic. The inauguration ceremony was held by the roadside, which seems to mean that GF Securities' postdoctoral R&D base had chosen the road of "grounding" from the very beginning. The core idea of GF Securities' postdoctoral R&D base was "to be both a theoretical explorer and a practitioner in the capital markets," and to closely link the research with the company's operation and management. At the atmospheric postdoctoral R&D base symposium, Professor Xiao Zhuoji said, "We must apply what we learn and train a group of domestic leading financial talents. We look forward to the results." Professor Chen Zheng said, "This is a big event for GF Securities, for Guangdong Province, and for the national financial industry." Professor Cao Fengqi said, "We have to choose the right research topics and the right problems that we need to solve urgently."

At this time, the Asian financial crisis was almost over, the Chinese securities industry was becoming more aware of the importance of financial innovation products, and China's imminent accession to the WTO had put forward higher requirements for its brokerage firms to expand the variety of securities.

Dr. Chen Yunxian and Dr. Wang Liangzhong decided to make a "first move" by determining the research direction of the postdoctoral R&D base, and took quantitative research, financial product innovation research, and online trading as the important direction of the research projects. When recruiting the first and second groups of researchers, the postdoctoral R&D base examined and recruited a considerable number of PhDs in mathematics and engineering, and arranged for them to focus on financial product design, data mining, and high frequency data analysis.

Dr. Gu Juan was one of the first group of postdoctoral fellows recruited into the base. She distinctly felt the difference of GF Securities from the beginning of her stay: in addition to doing research, she had to participate in the daily work of the company as much as possible; from the company-level management meetings to the working meetings of brokerage branches, she could break the constraints of her position and rank to attend them. The R&D base not only held a special seminar once a year, but the company chairman Dr. Chen Yunxian also had many discussions with the postdoctoral fellows. In two years, Gu Juan was able to quickly and comprehensively understand the business and nature of the securities company, and grew from a PhD of science to a postdoctoral fellow in finance.

Dr. He Rongtian, who had a background in mathematics, was one of the second group of postdoctoral researchers trained jointly by GF Securities and Peking University in 2001. Before entering the base, Dr. He had studied in the UK and taught at a university for two years, which was a good match for the base's English proficiency and academic background requirements. Similar to his senior Peking University student Dr. Chen Yunxian, He Rongtian also had a strong dream of serving his country in finance. The cordial research and working environment within the base had allowed Dr. He to take advantage of the fact that the researchers who had joined the base had their own areas of expertise. Dr. He learned mathematical modeling from Dr. Bi Qiuxiang and programming from Dr. Zhang Yongdong. They all learned from each other and improved their research together.

Dr. Xu Jianhua from the Institutional Management Department, who was previously the backbone of the company's GITIC Bankruptcy and Liquidation Group, participated in the postdoctoral interview session as an internal mentor. In order to further catalyze the effective combination of scientific research and practice, Dr. Chen Yunxian proposed, after reflection, to give some of the research projects to people who were more familiar with both the company and the business. To this end, a selection process was conducted among the middle-level officials of GF Securities, and Dr. Xu Jianhua and Dr. Jiang Xurong from the Investment Banking Department joined the first group of postdoctoral researchers as working postdocs. As they were working employees of GF, they had more advantages in understanding the business logic and acquiring relevant data, and the postdoctoral research of their projects went more smoothly.

In terms of living conditions, GF Securities took great care of the postdoctoral researchers who came from all over the country, arranging a two-room dormitory with full appliances for each person, and a transportation car to and from the dormitory. Twelve doctoral supervisors, namely, Professor Xiao Zhuoji, Professor Liu Shibai, Professor Chen Zheng, Professor Zhang Weiguo, Professor Cao Fengqi, Professor Chen Yongchuan, Professor Wang Qiwen, Professor Xi Junyang, Professor Chen Yehua, Professor Chen Jianliang, Professor Li Jianping, and Professor Guo Tiemin, from many universities became the members of the magnificent expert steering committee of GF Securities' postdoctoral R&D base.

In addition to formally employing well-known university professors in the academic field, more members of the leadership team and middle-level officials of GF Securities also became internal mentors of postdoctoral fellows, including Fang Jiachun, Li Jianyong, Yao Ruxin, Zeng Hao, Wang Liangzhong, Qin Li,

Ouyang Xi, Zhao Guiping, Liu Jianzhou, Wu Xinqun, Liu Zhengzhou, and Jiang Zuoliang. Zhao Guiping, general manager of the Institutional Management Department, was surprised at first: "I only have a master's degree myself. How can I be an internal mentor for postdocs?" However, she soon understood Dr. Chen's intention: this was a mutual "training" and mutual promotion process, and the middle and senior officials of the company should also combine theory with practice and not relax their pursuit of academic ability.

During the two years of training, the postdoctoral fellows also received in person several research instructions from Dr. Chen Yunxian, the "academic director" of the R&D base. When hearing Gu Juan's comment that she was "unfamiliar with a series of concepts" and Jiang Xu Rong's comment that "investment banking basically has no theory at present in China," Dr. Chen cheerfully encouraged them: "To be honest, the best job of GF Securities is to do research. Look at Ouyang Xi. He is so busy all day that he looks worried. Why? Because the actual operation department is too risky. In contrast, the research of universities is too theoretical, and the practical department is too busy to do research. Only in the interface between the two is the easiest place to produce academic results: this is the research institutes of large institutions and large companies."

As Dr. Chen said, "We should not regard the R&D base merely as GF Securities' own postdoctoral R&D base, but also as an innovation in the history of China's financial development for financial institutions to create postdoctoral R&D bases. We should stand at the forefront of the financial industry and view our own strength, research topics, and research results from the height of commitment to participate in international financial competition." Dr. Chen even asked the fellows to have the ambition to "apply for the Nobel Prize in Economics if possible."

In 2002, when the first batch of postdoctoral fellows were discharged, GF Securities announced the research achievements of the previous two years in the Postdoctoral R&D Base Research Achievement Exhibition: The fellows published 91 academic papers in *Social Sciences in China*, *Journal of Financial Research*, and other national authoritative newspapers and journals, presided over and participated in eight scientific research projects, including projects funded by the Postdoctoral Science Found of China, the National Social Science Fund of China, and the China Securities Regulatory Commission, published two papers in international conferences, published, edited or helped write five monographs, and won the Second Outstanding Financial Research Achievement Award, the Second Prize of the Guangdong Finance Society, and the Third Prize for the Outstanding Research Results of Members of the Shenzhen Stock Exchange. In terms of internal contribution to GF Securities, they completed 54 papers for GF Securities in two years, and undertook 31 research reports and project reports for GF Securities' Third Five-Year Plan, Self-Dealing Department, Investment and Finance Department, Development and Research Center and other departments, providing effective intellectual support for GF Securities' operation and management.

Beginning in 2002, a number of high-end talents with dreams entered GF from the R&D base and society at large. After leaving the base, Dr. Gu Juan went to the Chinese University of Hong Kong to do research, and then officially joined GF Securities, where she became the head of the Investment Department, and an early business expert in the field of quantitative and derivatives in China, playing an important role in the design and practical operation of the first warrants, stock index futures, and options products in China. Dr. He Rongtian continued his research on the operational theory of risk-return correspondence in investment banking and became a member of the Fixed Income Expert Committee of Securities Association of China. After a long period of responsibility for fixed income business of GF Securities, he left GF to found an investment management company to continue his dream of serving the country with finance. Dr. Xu Jianhua later worked as a vice president of a large real estate group and made great achievements in domestic and international equity financing and trust financing.

With the reform and innovation in China's securities industry in the following years, the postdoctoral R&D base of GF Securities, as the cradle of high-end financial talents and the intellectual engine of market innovation, refreshed the industry's perception.

The "leader" went to the US for research

Dr. Chen Yunxian, who pioneered the comparative study in this field with his doctoral dissertation "A Comparative Study of Chinese and Foreign Portfolio Investment," kept his attention on the foreign securities market after graduation, especially on the separation of banking and securities industries and their management. Dr. Chen formed a mature understanding during his entrepreneurial practice in GF Securities, and wrote a paper on "Trans-Century Reform of China's Financial System."

However, on November 4, 1999, the US House of Representatives and Senate passed the Financial Services Modernization Act (FSMA), which proposed that commercial banks, insurance and securities industries could operate in a mixed manner. At this point, after 66 years of separation, the US financial industry reentered the era of mixed industries. Japan and the United Kingdom also carried out the same reform to introduce mixed operation.

Two months later, Dr. Chen Yunxian began his year-end meeting at GF Securities by asking this question: "What should China do now that the founders of separation have gone back to the path of mixed operation? Should China go back to the path of mixed business?" He then spent nearly half an hour answering this question to all participants through the logical framework of a comparative study between China and foreign countries: "Immediate mixed operation in China is not yet possible."

This institutional change in the US on the eve of the new century, and the corresponding reform of the financial regulatory model, were very attractive to Dr. Chen Yunxian at the academic research level. In addition, facing the "third wave impact" of China's capital markets and the inevitable trend of international integration after joining the WTO, what path should GF Securities take in the new century? Should it be like Merrill Lynch, which had developed its own characteristics mainly in investment banking and wealth management, or like Morgan Stanley, which had developed its own characteristics in proprietary operations in the secondary market, or like Goldman Sachs, which had won in its main core business? How had the industry landscape of US investment banking changed in the information technology era? Thoughts on academic research and choices in business decisions had added to Dr. Chen's interest in the changing US financial industry.

At the age of 45, Dr. Chen decided to be a student again, this time in the United States.

On September 1, 2000, Dr. Chen Yunxian, chairman of GF Securities, was dispatched by the Organization Department of the CPC Guangdong Provincial Committee to attend a one-year training program for management talents from Guangdong Province to study at the University of Massachusetts, Boston, USA.

Driven by a strong desire for knowledge, Dr. Chen took courses on US monetary policy (U.S. money, banking, and financial markets), US corporate finance, contemporary global economy, US personnel management, US economic overview, US fiscal policy (public budget), US business, government, and society, English professional writing, and US strategic business management during his one-year stay in the US. While studying in the Advanced Management Program (AMP) at Harvard Business School, which was designed to train senior executives in the world of business, he studied and worked on an average of three cases per day and read up to 500 pages of material per week. During this valuable year, he received several honors. In December 2000, he applied for two research projects: "Theory of Risk-Return Correspondence as the Axis of Investment Banking Management" and "The Evolution and Development of the US Financial System as a Reference for China's Financial Regulation," which were approved by relevant Harvard University experts, and he was appointed as an Honorary Fellow of the Year 2001, Fairbank Center for East Asian Studies, Harvard University.

During his intensive study, Dr. Chen also visited many commercial banks, securities firms, fund management companies, insurance companies, accounting firms, stock exchanges, and associations in Boston, New York, and Washington D.C., and attended two international conferences. On May 6, 2001, at the China Forum held at Harvard University, Dr. Chen presented "China's Stock Market and the Challenges of Globalization" in English at the Finance Group in front of over 400 entrepreneurs, government officials, and researchers from the US, UK, Germany, and China. On August 29, Dr. Chen was awarded a certificate of completion from the University of Massachusetts at Boston at the end of his year-long study.

Before returning home, Dr. Chen bid farewell to his landlord, the renowned Boston composer and pianist Mr. Rick Kuethe and his wife, Ms. Florri Aversa. Kuethe had been nominated for an Emmy Award, the highest honor in the American music industry. After visiting GF Securities in China at the invitation of Dr. Chen, Mr. Rick Kuethe and his wife were inspired to compose a melodious piece, "Find Your Dream with Me." An important crystallization of the corporate culture, the piece has been widely sung at GF Securities for many years since then.

After returning from the US, Dr. Chen was "dragged" into the meeting room of GF Securities by President Dr. Fang Jiachun to have a warm discussion with his colleagues after a year's absence, even though he had just got off the plane with jet lag. In September 2001, GF Securities was celebrating its tenth anniversary with many important meetings, and there were many invitations from inside and outside the company for Dr. Chen to share his study experience in the US. However, Dr. Chen still squeezed in a lot of time to work on the final stage of his monograph on his study in the US.

He hoped that through this monograph, more people would be able to grasp the entire evolution of the US financial system and that the book would serve as a reference for the reform and development of China's finance. He hoped to discover the practicality, effectiveness, and foresight of the "theory of risk-return correspondence" as the axis of investment banks management through his analysis of the core operating data of three famous investment banks, Goldman Sachs, Merrill Lynch, and Morgan Stanley, and even further practice the capital operation of investment banking. He also hoped to feel the huge impact of online trading on traditional brokerage business in advance through Merrill Lynch's cross-century competitive strategy adjustment after being challenged by Charles Schwab.

He summarized his year of study in the United States in his book:

> My awareness of the United States has returned from fantasy, legend, and with a bit of conjecture, to reality. First, with regard to the economic development of the United States and its rules, there are many problems, but there are indeed many areas worth learning and learning from. Second, as Chinese, the most critical thing is that we must have national pride and a sense of historical responsibility. Building a rich and strong and prosperous country is our unshirkable responsibility; doing a down-to-earth job is our necessary requirement.

On September 8, 2001, a series of activities to commemorate the tenth anniversary of the founding of GF Securities brought the atmosphere of Guangzhou Metropolis Square to a climax. In the printing house of a publishing house in Beijing, a monograph, *A Study on the American Financial System*, had just come off the press. The book's title page bears a bold line: "For the tenth anniversary of GF Securities."

Mr. Ezra F. Vogel, a professor at Harvard University and former director of the Fairbank Center for East Asian Studies, who is known as "Mr. China," had already started writing an important book, *Deng Xiaoping and the Transformation of China*, but he gladly took the time to write the preface to Dr. Chen's *A Study on the American Financial System*. He wrote:

> The devastating effect of the Asia finance crisis of Indonesia, Thailand, Malaysia, and other countries illustrates how serious the risks can be as countries are increasingly open to the global markets. It also illustrates how much countries must prepare before they open their markets. And yet China cannot avoid opening its markets and it is therefore vitally important that as its equity markets expand rapidly that far more Chinese understand these developments.... I believe it is very much in the interest of the United States to have more Chinese who understand developments in other countries, including our country.

Based on his monograph *A Study on the American Financial System*, Dr. Chen Yunxian began to fully estimated risks and find areas of weakness for development from the perspective of the chairman of GF Securities and a ten-year veteran of the securities industry. In early 2002, after internal company discussions, Dr. Chen summarized the serious challenges facing Chinese securities firms after China's accession to the WTO into six major areas.

> The first is the impact of competition for major clients. International securities firms, with their advantages in cross-regional and cross-market operations and cross-investment varieties, will certainly have a strong attraction to the clients in China, especially institutional clients.
>
> The second is the impact from the competition for large projects in China. International investment banks often amount to tens of billions of dollars in capital and hundreds of billions of dollars in total assets, so they have notable competitive advantages in mega fixed asset investment projects in China.
>
> The third is from the competition in terms of the high-technology-supported management process. The entire management tools and business processes of foreign first-class securities companies are built on high-technology-supported operation systems.
>
> The fourth is the competition in terms of development strategy and professional experience. Foreign first-class securities companies have accumulated rich experience in deepening services and making them more detailed.
>
> The fifth is the impact of talent. Localized professionals will be the focus of competition among overseas securities companies.
>
> The sixth is the impact on the property right system and distribution system. China's incentive mechanism is restricted by the property right system

and distribution system, so foreign securities companies will attract a group of key professionals with favorable treatment.

Dr. Chen Yunxian repeatedly called for responses to the "six challenges" in interviews with *China Securities Journal*, *Securities Times*, and *Securities Market Weekly*, and then proposed that time should be taken to prepare in six areas, namely, "preparation for capital strength," "preparation for multi-species and multi-market development," "preparation for technical means," "preparation for high-quality staff," "preparation for institutional innovation and improved corporate governance structure," and "preparation for quality and comprehensive services to improve overall competitiveness." He especially called for supporting the development and growth of Chinese securities companies with equity structure policies.

It is worth mentioning that Dr. Chen's "six challenges" and "six preparations" were taken seriously by *China Securities Journal* and reported to the leaders of the State Council in the form of an internal reference after revision. According to the feedback from those in charge of *China Securities Journal*, Zhu Rongji, who had been in charge of China's economic work for many years, gave instructions for the issue of the internal reference and the document was referred to officials at the vice minister level and above nationwide.

"For those who are unprepared, the challenges are greater than the opportunities; for those who are prepared, the opportunities are greater than the challenges." Thereafter, Goldman Sachs and other international investment banks entered China and dominated many of its large projects. This shows that Dr. Chen Yunxian's call for reform and development of the securities industry in 2002 had an insight beyond academic research itself. In addition, it was also an answer to the top-level design of GF Securities based on reflections over responses to China's accession to the WTO.

2. The best gift of standardized development

Transformation to the modern corporate system

Guangzhou-based GF Securities and Shenzhen-based Vanke Real Estate seemed to have little intersection, but if we take Harvard University in the United States as the lead, we can observe a comparison spanning ten years. In 2001, Dr. Chen Yunxian returned from a visit to the United States; ten years later, in 2011, Wang Shi, the star entrepreneur and founder of Vanke, entered and started a longer study tour in Harvard University, which employed Dr. Chen as a researcher.

In 2011, Wang Shi's move attracted a lot of interest from the Chinese media and the corporate world, and one of the major concerns was, "Why is Wang Shi able to go on a study tour? How is Vanke managed and run internally now?"

In 2001, a decade before that, the modern corporate system and management concepts were far from popular in China, and peers in the securities industry had the same logical question about GF Securities: "Dr. Chen is taking classes in the US, how else can he 'manage 'you?"

In fact, Dr. Chen had called a meeting with his team before going to the US, explaining the two reasons why he "dared" to go to the US to study. First, the company's development direction was very clear; second, he was very assured of the president's team: "Whether GF Securities can do well depends on you. You should have a sense of urgency and more importantly, feel pressure." For the individual members of the team who were full of pioneering spirit but impatient, Dr. Chen also talked to them individually many times before the trip.

In Dr. Chen Yunxian's full year of stay in the US, GF Securities seemed to have entered the situation of "the master is in seclusion to practice his kung fu" in a martial arts novel. On New Year's Day 2001, President Fang Jiachun, Executive Vice President Dong Zhengqing, and Secretary Yan Xiaofeng went to the US to visit Dr. Chen, who was busy with his studies, and reported on the company's "work" in the first year of the new century. According to the financial data at the end of the year, GF Securities' revenue was expected to increase by nearly 70 percent and net profit by more than 80 percent.

After the "1997 crisis," as a result of after a series of far-reaching adjustments such as equity adjustment, delinking from Guangdong Development Bank, and placement, GF Securities' corporate governance structure was relatively sound, and GF Securities Limited Liability Company would soon be changed to GF Securities Co., Ltd. This laid a good foundation for the transition of GF Securities to a truly modern corporate system.

In the first year of the new century, the company achieved marvelous results without Dr. Chen's personal "leadership," which seemed to confirm the success of the company's transformation, the company's management coming in line with international standards, and the 1,313 employees becoming free from the reliance on the "rule of man." However, this was far from the truth.

The growth in 2000 was due in large part to the upswing in the market (the Shanghai Stock Exchange saw an 84.9 percent year-over-year increase in turnover). From the establishment of an idea of becoming thoroughly standardized and self-sustained after the "1997 crisis" to the basic establishment of a modern corporate system, GF Securities was actually a self-transformation which was full of arduous discussions and arguments, leaving a lot of puzzling details at the turn of the century.

At least at the moment of "moving into the new century," GF Securities was not too harmonious. On December 31, 1999, the company held a lively "Millennium Night" party, inviting guests including the former chairman of the Hong Kong Securities and Futures Commission, Mr. Leung Ting-bong, and the staff and their families in Guangzhou. However, for some reasons, the key employees of an important business department of the company were not present at the "family dinner" of GF Securities.

This big disharmony confirms the Leo Tolstoy's saying that, "All the variety, all the charm, all the beauty of life is made up of light and shadow." The focus of light and shadow at this time is the idea of "thorough standardized development."

At the 1999 year-end work conference, Dr. Fang Jiachun, the president, took the stage to make a report, and the theme of this annual report was "Deepening Management Comprehensively and Seeking Standardized Development." When it came to the details of "increasing standardization and adjustment," many participants started to exchange ideas, and they disagreed with it in group discussions. Strictly controlling the proportion of the company's proprietary positions, thoroughly standardizing the management of financial funds, and strictly eliminating the overdraft of shareholders' deposit margin, which have become the industry norm today, were greatly questioned internally at that time. Of course, the questioning was not about the requirements per se, but about the "timing" of their introduction: in an environment of vicious competition among many securities firms, was it appropriate for GF Securities to start the thorough standardization first? In the case of undertaking investment banking projects, there was a widespread practice of bridge financing in the industry as a result of policy loopholes, so was GF Securities "tying its own hands" by taking the lead in promoting thorough standardization and abandoning the projects?

Faced with the controversy of the business departments on "thoroughly standardizing development," President Dr. Fang Jiachun, on the one hand, was determined on implementation, and on the other hand, he undoubtedly felt a lot of pressure.

On July 1, 1999, the Securities Law of the People's Republic of China came into force. The capital markets, which had been developing for many years in the reckless era, finally had its own industry law, and further transitioned to the direction of standardization and strict management. Regulatory effects came from several areas. From the primary market point of view, in 1996, GF Securities took only more than 40 days to complete the Guangdong Shaoneng project, while in 2000, it might take two to three years for an investment banking team to complete an IPO project.

The brokerage business, which was known as "living at the mercy of elements," not only had a long period of slow trading after the last bull market, but also had to deal with the situation of declining spread income and rising business venue costs. Brokerage branches in Jiangmen, Shantou, Wuhan, and other places had been found to have irregularities by the Audit Department.

At this time, GF Securities had expanded from six employees to more than 1,300. The staff expansion required the promotion of M&As, the integration of teams, and the synergy of investment banking and brokerage business lines, which made management more difficult. As one of the key managers, Dong Zhengqing was also keenly aware of some of the company's phenomena, and he even once said, somewhat reluctantly:

> If it is a rule that a big company brings bureaucracy, all we can do is to take measures to mitigate the negative impact of this rule on business as much as possible. We do not expect to achieve seamless cooperation between departments, but we should try to achieve coordination among departments in implementing major decisions of the company, to further improve the cooperation between business departments and management departments, to reduce tug-of-war and to improve efficiency.

Several rounds of the securities market surge not only opened up the performance gap between securities companies, but also opened up the gap between the company's internal bars. The rumors of how a certain company does its business and how a department shares its bonuses are always able to quickly stir the hearts of people. The primary market and the secondary market created wealth respectively for entrepreneurs and stockholders. Although the employees of securities brokerages as intermediaries also have rewards, in contrast, they inevitably have the feeling of "making wedding clothes for others."

In 2000, the famous director Ang Lee shot *Crouching Tiger, Hidden Dragon* the first Chinese film to win the Academy Award for Best Foreign Language Film. A classic line of the film goes like this, "Giang Hu is a world of tigers and dragons, full of corruption." This seemed to be very applicable to the securities practitioners at that time.

Dr. Chen Yunxian was always wary of such "tigers and dragons," based in large part on his observation of the chaos of the industry giants. Before 1998, he found that many people of GITIC were very "active." They had strong business ability, so they established the fourth and fifth levels of subsidiaries under GITIC. Their head office found it difficult to detect their specific business initiatives. This finally became the source of the trouble. As for the problem of customer margin, which eventually caused the collapse of Southern Securities, GF Securities had strictly guarded against it in the financial system since early on, separating its own funds and customer margin into separate accounts and managing them separately.

However, GF Securities did not avoid "tigers and dragons." When reviewing the achievements in 1999, Dr. Chen commented on two highlights. One was the "stock reform" and the other was the "housing reform." The "housing reform" allowed most of the employees of GF Securities to enjoy the benefits within the scope of the national policy, while the "stock reform" not only brought about a significant transformation of the company's mechanism, but also made the employees desire to "become the owner of material wealth under the protection of the system."

As early as in 1994, GF Securities applied for linking wages with work efficiency, but for a long time, the total salary of GF Securities was strictly controlled by the Guangdong Provincial Labor Department. During the rapid development stage, it was often necessary to make great efforts to fight for the total salary. Obviously, the concept of "wage ceiling" should not appear in a modern corporate system in the true sense of the word. In addition, the post establishment inherited from various historical reasons was also not reasonable. For example, when the company was first established, the Institutional Management Department of the headquarters had only three posts, whereas some overstaffed business departments had more than 40 people.

Beginning in 1997, Chen Wenzhan, head of the Personnel Department, changed her priorities several times. One day Dr. Chen called her and Dr. Lan Wenbo to his office and asked, "Do you know why a financial institution cannot retain talents?" Chen Wenzhan was stunned, and Dr. Chen replied for himself, "Because they don't pay attention to employee welfare. You have to think about this problem."

In 1998, GF Securities embarked on a reform of its distribution system, diluting the concept of monthly income and strengthening the concept of annual income. Annual income was determined by the company's revenue and employees' performance, and a link between bonus distribution and performance evaluation was also established. Staff promotion was divided into four brackets: management positions, technical positions, researchers, and ranking divisional officers.

In 1999, the system linking wages and performance continued to be implemented and the salary system was further revised.

At the beginning of 2000, the Personnel Department was reestablished as the Human Resources Management Department, and the person in charge, Ms. Chen, no longer had to run to the Guangdong Provincial Labor Department for the total amount of wages. The functions of the department under her jurisdiction were expanded to include human resource allocation, quality assessment and performance evaluation, employee career development guidance and talent cultivation, wage and benefit management, and a series of systems such as the Regulations on Employee Performance Management were then introduced.

During the same period, GF Securities also conducted several internal competitive recruitment, a pioneering selection system by the Investment Banking Department, which was later promoted. The company selected a number of middle management staff from all its departments, causing a great shock among ordinary employees. A series of initiatives such as official exchange, mandatory leave, self-reporting began to be implemented. The Development Research Center and several major brokerage branches gradually expanded the staff. Individual brokerage branches in the Shenzhen Special Economic Zone began to take the initiative to try out the elimination system.

In the face of the industry downturn, some securities companies were operating in difficulty and their expenses were stretched to the limit. GF Securities, however, began to make great efforts to organize groups of business officials to go to the United States and Hong Kong, China, for studies in 1998. This cost was regarded as an investment in human capital by the management team of the company, which not only introduced new knowledge and expanded the influence and popularity of GF Securities abroad, but more importantly, the outbound training allowed a group of middle-level officials to go to Goldman Sachs, Merrill Lynch, Morgan Stanley, and other first-class international investment banks for personal observation and intensive training, so that they had an intuitive understanding of the importance of the modern corporate system before they had the opportunity to take up the leadership position of GF Securities.

Among the four groups of trainees from 1998 to 2000, many executives emerged, including Li Jianyong, Lü Ping, Lin Zhihai, Luo Binhua, and Chen Liming. As one of the first cohort members, Dr. Li Jiangyong has deep feelings when he talks about his 1998 visit to the United States: "At that time, I introduced to my American counterparts that the registered capital of GF Securities was 800 million yuan, but I was so dumbfounded when they revealed their wealth that I was embarrassed to talk about the 800 million yuan later in the presentation." Back then, data showed that the assets of all Chinese brokerage firms combined were probably less than one tenth of those of Merrill Lynch.

Before Dr. Chen went to the United States to study in September 2000, a change was taking place that focused on reversing the concept of human resources and improving the talent pool. As China's WTO accession was approaching, the "big culture" of domestic thinking was also repeatedly focused on the topic of corporate management. The best-selling management book *A Message to Garcia* had just been introduced to China, and was recommended by Dr. Chen to be reprinted in the company's internal publication *GF Securities Express*.

Huawei in Shenzhen not only had a team of highly educated and qualified talents, but also kept exporting profound Chinese company management ideas, which made GF Securities "want to align with it," and the Huawei Basic Law and "The Huawei Winter" caused continuous discussions and reflections among GF Securities employees.

Dr. Chen Yunxian had a clear understanding of his company's management level at this time, and he positioned it as "the transition from inefficient to intensive management." He began to think boldly about how to significantly improve the efficiency of internal management and whether there were better tools.

ERP: the industry's first "new cheese" project

On June 21, 1999, Zhou Zhengqing, chairman of the CSRC, called a meeting with 28 brokerage firms, and GF Securities was among them. The upcoming implementation of the Securities Law in ten days and the related preparatory work were undoubtedly the focus of the meeting.

Dr. Chen Yunxian was invited to be the first to speak at the meeting. In addition to introducing GF Securities' experience in regulatory management, he also mentioned the "cat and mouse" joke circulating in the industry about the relationship between the regulator and the regulated.

Chairman Zhou Zhengqing interjected at this point: "I do not agree with the cat and mouse argument. We are colleagues in the same Chinese securities market. We just have different divisions of labor, but we all have the responsibility to jointly push the Chinese securities market to a new stage of standardized development."

Chairman Zhou Zhengqing's rebuttal of the "cat and mouse theory" with the "colleague theory" made Dr. Chen feel keenly that it was a straightforward confirmation of the identity of securities companies as the main force of the market. This was one of the major purposes of the implementation of the Securities Law: securities companies, like commercial banks and insurance companies, are equal members of the financial system, and are under different authorities.

Of course, the full significance of a serious law for securities companies cannot be equated with the happy news about the industry's status. Zhou Zhengqing concluded his speech at the conference by identifying the business problems of brokerage firms: don't overdraw, don't misappropriate shareholders' deposits, don't use private accounts for proprietary accounts, and review off-book assets and other irregularities and violations quickly.

To be the main force, regulation is a prerequisite.

Thanks to the "four-pronged" approach (shareholding, conglomeration, internationalization, and standardization) established in 1994, GF Securities was always about two years ahead of other brokerages in terms of standardized operation and risk management practices. In August 1999, after the implementation of the Securities Law, GF Securities launched two major projects after careful examination of several foreign consulting companies: Arthur Andersen was hired to strengthen its internal risk management system, and Bridge was hired to assist in building integrated network services. GF Securities became the first company in the Chinese securities industry to promote Enterprise Resource Planning (ERP).

However, in the first spring of the new millennium, Dr. Chen Yunxian found that the technological advantage of this standardized practice was being surpassed by its peers.

It was in March 2000 when Jiang Yang, director of the Institutional Department of the CSRC, led a team to several securities companies in south China for field research. Dr. Chen learned during the briefing that several peers in Shenzhen had put a lot of resources into the central real-time monitoring system and had actually achieved real-time monitoring of the daily operation of their branches around the country, and furthermore, had started to attract large institutional clients by means of network trading.

Compared with the praise from the Institutional Department of the China

Securities Regulatory Commission for the effectiveness of several projects in Shenzhen, it was clear that the two major projects that GF Securities had rolled out at that time needed to be accelerated.

Dr. Chen Yunxian knew exactly what the sticking point was. Previously, Dr. Yao Ruxin and a group of key professionals of the Computer Center had a good accumulation in the construction of the company's information system, and had also participated in the construction of industry standards for many times. And at this time, GF Securities looked to Andersen, a multinational consulting company, in the hope that with its relatively mature thinking and experience, it could significantly improve GF Securities' management efficiency, risk management and internal control systems, significantly adjust the internal organizational structure and business processes, and then realize the program through procedures and systems. However, it was easy to put computers on every employee's desk; it was difficult to get employees to accept the "office automation" mindset and habits.

In 2000, the headquarters had a full-time position of "typist," and prior to that, company documents were printed on paper and delivered weekly by courier to all branches. The drawbacks of this way of communicating management information were obvious, and there were even cases where a department manager locked the company's documents in his own drawer, so that his subordinate employees were not aware of the company's policies for a long time. In the headquarters' back office departments, there were still more people who thought that "information technology is the concern of the computer post," and the difficulty could be imagined to make information technology projects cover the business line and high-level decision-making. This required a thunderbolt action.

The Andersen project did not go well at first. The young employees of this multinational organization found that many employees of GF Securities were not accustomed to using emails, had no awareness of process traceability, often did not bring their notebooks to project meetings, and listened to their unfamiliar process management lectures without taking notes. The Brokerage Branch managers of GF Securities were not polite to the consultants, thinking that they "do not understand the securities industry."

At Baiyun Hotel in Guangzhou, the Andersen project team scheduled five working days of intensive training starting in early April 2000, but management-level employees were late from the start. A company briefing was issued for the latecomers, and the president's office and training center, which did organizational work poorly, were also criticized. To this day, this early-21st-century criticism of tardiness can still be found on GF Securities' OA system, which has been in use for many years.

As the Andersen project was rolled out, a series of management reforms with far-reaching effects on the company's development began to move from the consulting program to the various parts of GF Securities. Xiao Fenglei, general manager of the Finance Department, was responsible for the comprehensive budget system; Wu Zhaoming, general manager of the Audit Department, was responsible for performance assessment; Yan Xiaofeng, secretary of the Board of Directors, was responsible for business management processes; Chen Wenzhan, general manager of the Human Resources Management Department, was responsible for individual employee appraisals; Zhao Guiping, general manager of the Institutional Management Department, was responsible for the three-tier management system; and Chen Peixiong, general manager of the Clearing Center, was responsible for the computerized integrated business network. Each department formulated monthly project plans and summarized them for the project team regularly.

In August 2000, when the Arthur Andersen project reached the midway point, Dr. Chen adjusted the team's division of labor before his departure for study in the US. Executive Vice President Dong Zhengqing, who had been in charge of investment banking and brokerage business, was put in charge of the Computer Center and worked with Vice President Li Suina and CFO Li Shuiquan to advance the project. This accelerated the fast process.

In November, the project wrapped up. In the following year, the company held a formal meeting to summarize and evaluate the Andersen project in retrospect. The introduction of management concepts and methods such as total budgeting, three-tier management, and performance evaluation was approved, and the business "firewall" structure proved its value in the new regulatory policies introduced during this period. On this basis, the meeting made an in-depth analysis of the shortcomings of GF Securities and Arthur Andersen in the project, and focused on the management application of IT technology, the experience of dealing with international consulting companies, and the experience of large-scale project management.

This retrospective summary was timely, and the minutes were quickly read to all members of another project team at the request of Dr. Fang Gachun. Around the time of his return to China in 2001, Dr. Chen Yunxian was determined to add another push to the company's information system construction.

This was because a sudden call from the management team on the other side of the ocean during a busy and quiet period of further study of Dr. Chen gave him a new thought about the company's risk management process structure.

At that time, as the domestic market suddenly heated up and the business department proposed to expand the scale of entrusted wealth management, Dr. Fang Jiachun strongly disagreed at first. However, seeing the market getting hotter day by day, and encouraged by the head of the department, Dr. Fang and the Risk Control Committee also began to hesitate. Finally, they suggested asking Dr. Chen for advice by phone.

On the other end of the phone, Dr. Chen firmly said no and asked the Risk Control Committee to strictly implement the previous judgment on the "entrusted wealth management fever" and strictly control the scale of entrusted wealth management. The subsequent evolution of the market proved that this decision enabled GF Securities to avoid a catastrophic loss in that year.

From the advice of "strictly controlling the scale" before going to the US to the calm decision in the hot market, this phone call became another legend that made many GF people more convinced by Dr. Chen. At this time, Dr. Chen, based on his study of the risk control model of the first-class investment banking in the United States, was thinking how to better overcome the defects of the traditional decision-making process with the power of technology, and stop the practice of halting risky moves by any individual as much as possible.

The ERP system became the project he was determined to develop.

In a July 2001 email reply to a consulting company executive, Dr. Chen wrote in a rare and blunt way, "I've been in a very bad mood lately. In the case of very competitive business, other companies' ERP implementation is progressing fast, while our company has been proposed more than two years earlier than others, but now it is still where it was. I really want to go back and punish someone."

In August 2001, a scholar from Boston University, Pan Haidong, visited GF Securities headquarters and gave a lecture on the ERP project. In September 2001, Dr. Chen was accompanied by Dr. Zhang Mengyou, an intern at the headquarters of Fidelity Investments, and Shen Hao, a master from Harvard University, who returned to GF Securities. Dr. Zhang wrote an article, "A Few Thoughts on Studying in the US," which was soon forwarded throughout the company, with an impressive statement: "I want to emphasize here: in the world's top 500 companies, there is none which has not implemented ERP, because ERP can help companies save costs and improve efficiency."

With the latest thinking of the modern corporate system in the United States, the ERP project began to be fully rolled out within the company. At the time, a management book, *Who Moved My Cheese?*, was widely discussed in China, and the company's ERP project was figuratively named the "New Cheese" project. In addition, the CRM (brokerage business) project team, headed by Dr. Zeng Hao and composed of staff from the Institutional Department and Computer Center, also started to operate to accelerate the transformation of the brokerage business.

On the basis of Andersen's work, more multinational organizations hired with the task of transformation came into GF Securities, PricewaterhouseCoopers Consulting (PWC) entered to carry out employee competency model design and job evaluation, and Deloitte International Human Capital Consulting (DELOITTE) was hired to improve the compensation system and performance management system. As one of the pivotal departments for the project project, the Computer Center was renamed as the Information Technology Department, and along with the name change, there was a rapid transformation of the department's functional direction and work pace.

When the ERP project entered the selection and demonstration stage, the project team was caught in a debate and torn between the two types and paths of SAP from Germany and ORACLE from the United States. After Dr. Chen's judgment, the German SAP seemed to be complete, but it had limited the system's levels 1–4 sub-subjects. In light of the development trend of China's capital markets for a period of time, this ERP system, which was generally applicable to the German mechanical industry, would restrict the space for GF Securities' business development. Dr. Chen resisted the "advice" of individual experts in the Information Technology Department and finally decided to use ORACLE.

In June 2002, the ERP system was officially launched. After the in-depth planning and implementation of the main modules and core application functions of finance, human resource management, as well as procurement and asset management, GF Securities' standardized practice and management level had a more solid technical foundation. With the integrated information system supporting the three-tier management system of headquarters and branches, the achievements of the previous management consulting had been consolidated. Using data warehouse technology, the ERP system provided the necessary data and system support for decision analysis and risk prevention of company management.

From the Andersen project to the ERP project, the previously unsettled policies on posting, compensation system and performance management had been implemented. The previous posting system based on the Guangdong Development Bank "banking staffing system" was changed to align with international investment banks. From the basic staff to the company leaders, there were eight "job grades," supplemented by "job grades" reflecting the difference of job value and "job equivalence" reflecting performance. The human resource management policy closely related to each employee effectively broke through the limitations of the previous "system of linking wages with performance" and was continuously improved in practice. There were advanced policies and information platform guiding all employees to find "new cheese."

At a deeper level, the ERP project with the name of "New Cheese" actually brought about a change in the concept of many people. Dr. Chen once emphasized that the "Dr. Army" is just a flag, and the whole GF Securities is really a multilevel team. At the beginning many of the middle-level officials who grew up in the business were resisting the ERP project, and spirited arguments occurred repeatedly between employees trained in China and those trained abroad, but with a sense of modern corporate management, they finally took the initiative to find their own "new cheese."

One of the leaders of the ERP project even lamented in his later memories: "Dr. Chen was quite good at placing people. I actually did not understand technology; I hated it. At first even I did not want to use it. Dr. Chen told me to urge others to use it. But in the end, we all did it together in a thunderous manner. In the end, after the collapse of Jun'an Securities, we were alerted to the fact that standardization is not possible without technology to support it. Dr. Chen was able to see the trend through the fog and worked hard to align with top international investment banks."

The best gift

Dong Zhengqing remembers the date of March 21 very well.

On March 21, 1993, Dong Zhengqing, a teacher at Jinan University, walked into Dr. Chen's office from the pulpit of his class and, after a cordial interview, became a GF Securities employee.

On March 21, 2003, Executive Vice President Dong Zhengqing saw on the TV news on Friday night that the US and the UK had started an undeclared war against Iraq, and what shocked him even more was another piece of news: the Organization Department of the Guangdong Provincial Party Committee announced that Chen Yunxian had been transferred to the Standing Committee of the Foshan Municipal Party Committee.

"It felt like the sky was falling!" Dong Zhengqing and many employees described their mood of that night like this.

The seriousness of the announcement issued by the organization department could not be doubted, but many employees still called Dr. Chen himself that night to ask for confirmation. Dr. Chen Yunxian confirmed the news one by one, and his tone on the phone was calm and he did not explain too much.

Subsequently, Dr. Chen Yunxian was dispatched by the Central Organization Department to Harvard University in the United States to participate in the Kennedy School of Government SEF program. After returning to China in May of that year, he began to officially serve as a member of the Standing Committee of the Foshan Municipal Party Committee, executive vice mayor of the Foshan Municipal Government, and deputy secretary of the leading Party members' group of the Foshan Municipal Government.

Many employees still could "react" to the fact that Dr. Chen Yunxian, as the chairman and founder of the company, officially said goodbye to GF Securities.

The reasons for Dr. Chen's sudden departure from GF Securities and his turning to politics have been said to be many.

Some people analyzed the trajectory of Dr. Chen, and concluded that "good scholars tend to do business" and then "good businessmen tend to become officials." As it is a traditional tendency of Chinese Confucian intellectuals to actively pursue a career, people believed that Dr. Chen's departure for politics after 12 years of entrepreneurship was a reflection of this tendency. They even further analyzed Dr. Chen's previous "traces," such as his study at the provincial Party school in 1995 and his study trip to the United States in 2000 arranged by the organization department, suggesting that Dr. Chen had been thinking about the path to politics for a long time.

Some people, in conjunction with the long bear market around 2003, believed that Dr. Chen became pessimistic about the operation of the securities market in the long-term bear market, and especially after the extraordinarily difficult 2002, he became tired of the bottleneck in the development of GF Securities under the impact of the third wave. They concluded that "the one who knows the time is the best," and he then accepted another path.

Some people recalled the company's difficult start-up, believing that GF Securities lacked a strong government background and often withdrew from the competition at the last moment when the company was trying to "fight" for a project for various reasons, giving up the project to other peers with rich resources. They speculated that "Dr. Chen finally believes that the best platform in China to fight for his financial ambitions is the government."

Others believed that Dr. Chen had been deeply affected by the punishment suffered by his entrepreneurial partner Dr. Ma, and that the road to politics was a relatively better path in the face of the "institutional traps" that kept appearing in the process of capital markets development and improvement.

In the face of all the speculation, Dr. Chen Yunxian himself rarely responded. He did not comment on the appointment order issued by the government organization department, either.

"There are always many choices that you have to make in life."

Those who analyzed Dr. Chen's motives for turning to politics often overlooked one of his identities: after the decoupling of Guangdong Development Bank from GF Securities, Dr. Chen Yunxian no longer served as vice president, but was still a provincial government official. Facing the transfer order from the organization department, as a provincial government official, he had only one choice.

People also tended to overlook another situation of GF Securities at that time: as a "PhD Legion" known far and wide in Guangdong Province, GF Securities had formed a center of talents like a water tower, sending talents to local governments, People's Bank of China offices, and other emerging financial institutions.

For a long time, the top team of GF Securities had been very stable, while the middle-level officials had been transferred elsewhere repeatedly. Many of the aforementioned units either directly transferred the talents they needed from GF Securities, or set out high-standard "talent exchange" requirements for GF Securities, specifying that they must have a doctorate degree and rich operational experience. A middle-level official in the Investment Banking Department, one of the few people selected by the company for medium- and long-term training in the US at its cost, was later transferred to a local state-owned management department. The head of the Hainan region from GF Securities was later transferred to a state-owned financial institution. A junior of Dr. Chen's from Peking University came to Guangzhou to "warmly visit" Dr. Chen when he was transferred from a government department to head a securities company in Shanghai, but he quietly persuaded several key employees of GF Securities to move to Shanghai. In order to meet the "talent exchange" requirements of the regulatory authorities, GF Securities had to send an employee who had just finished his doctorate.

Dr. Chen, who attached great importance to the value of talent, had been struggling to maintain the team. As the leader of the "PhD Legion," it is also a self-evident fact that he himself was selected by the government organization department early.

In early June, government agencies and the company's board of directors began an exit audit of Dr. Chen Yunxian. In late November, a team of more than 30 auditors left GF Securities with a fairly positive assessment of the company's key operations.

At the end of 2003, after the successful completion of the placement of GF Huafu Securities Company, Dr. Fang Jiachun also left GF Securities to become vice chairman and CEO of HeungKong and later chairman of Topsperity Securities. Together with Ma Qingquan, Ye Junying, Wang Hongmao, and Li Shuzhi, who had left the company in the previous years and had already established to own businesses, Dong Zhengqing was the only member of the first collective leadership of GF Securities who was still with the company.

On December 5, 2003, the board of directors and shareholders' meeting of the company passed the resolution appointing Wang Zhiwei as the chairman, Dong Zhengqing as the president of the company, and Li Jianyong as the executive vice president of the company.

The initial illusion that the sky was falling did not become a reality for many employees. Dr. Chen's departure had a significant impact on GF Securities, especially his previous series of big plans around placement, which had been close to success at the board meeting on the morning of March 21, that could not be realized because of the sudden transfer order that night. In the many years that followed, Dr. Chen, the executive vice mayor, Dr. Chen, the mayor, Dr. Chen, the secretary of the municipal Party committee, and Dr. Chen, the vice governor, were regarded as the spiritual leader by the new and old employees of GF Securities.

The trajectories of early securities companies such as Wanguo Securities, Shenyin Securities, Jun'an Securities, Dapeng Securities, and Southern Securities show a prominent phenomenon: the development of the companies and the fates of their respective entrepreneurial leaders were closely related. These companies often fell after experiencing major personnel changes, and their development had since degenerated into a downhill slide, or even disappeared from the securities industry.

The exceptions were GF Securities and Dr. Chen Yunxian. These "exceptions" were, in fact, what Dr. Chen himself had been pursuing for a long time. This was evident from "standardization," which was emphasized in the four-pronged approach in 1994, to the series of control systems for "thorough standardized development," to the characteristic shareholding structure in the industry, to the strongly promoted ERP system. Facing a key business employee resisting the ERP system, Dr. Chen asked him a question: "Who do you think ERP has limited to the maximum? It is the company's first in command! ERP removes any room for him to abuse his power."

The theoretical system represented by the "three theories" of the capital markets, the practice pattern based on the four-pronged approach left by the entrepreneurial team, as well as the transformation of GF Securities to introduce the modern corporate system and come line with first-class international investment banks at the turn of the new millennium enabled GF Securities to achieve the transition from the reckless era to a standardized company, forging the will and experience to resist the waves in the capital markets, and cultivating a management team to pass on the spirit of entrepreneurship.

This is just like Li Bing's water management in the Warring States period. When he was in office, he made it a rule to "remove silt and keep the weir low" to solve the raging floods of the Min River. He left behind an exquisitely designed and enduring Dujiangyan Irrigation System, which laid the foundation of Chengdu Plain as the land of abundance.

So, although the incident occurred suddenly and GF Securities' spiritual leader left, GF Securities itself grew steadily in 2003 and for a long time afterwards.

The entrepreneurial sleepers pave the way and the train whistles forward, which is the best gift of standardized development.

3. Advancement and pioneering: GF investment banking at the turn of the century

Achieving two firsts in the sponsor examination

In January 2004, after getting the operation data of the previous year, the new leadership made a collective decision before the cold Spring Festival: all the leaders of the company would not be paid year-end bonus, and the bonus resources would be given mainly to the frontline business and grassroots staff.

The net result of "-72 million yuan" was the only annual deficit in the history of GF Securities. If we only look at the absolute data, this loss seems not too serious, but its impact is both "deep" and "far." We say "deep" because behind this negative figure, the overall performance was supported by the high-risk and high-yield proprietary business, while the company's investment banking in 2003 consisted of only two A-share underwriting projects, one share placement, and three listing recommendations, and also bore the losses brought by a previous underwriting business. You can imagine how morale had been eroded. We say "far" because the deficit set the stage for important decisions.

GF securities' loss haze was actually the background of the entire securities industry at that time. From 2001 to 2005, the total market value of China's stocks as a percentage of GDP was 44.6 percent, 35.6 percent, 35.3 percent, 25.8 percent, and 19.8 percent respectively, showing a decreasing trend year by year. The continuous industry-wide losses and disorderly operation of some brokerage firms led the media to declare that "the brokerage industry has gone technically bankrupt" and that "more than half of the brokerage firms will exit the market."

The ship of GF Securities was caught in high waves. At this time in the ship "cockpit" were Wang Zhiwei from Meizhou, Guangdong, Dong Zhengqing from Qianjiang, Hubei, and Li Jianyong from Langzhong, Sichuan. The differences in origin, upbringing, and personalities allowed them to complement each other in the management of the business, starting a period of executive tenure with "giving up the year-end bonus."

In terms of practical effect, the policy of "no year-end bonus for leaders" actually did not allow a large number of grassroots employees of GF Securities to receive much payment in the industry winter, but it was more of a spiritual warmth: in the face of operating losses and competitive dilemma, the new leadership will continue the humanistic tradition of showing concern to employees and sharing good and bad times with them.

The new chairman, Wang Zhiwei, had worked at Guangdong Development Bank for 15 years before he was transferred to GF Securities. Although the president of the management team, Dong Zhengqing, and the executive vice president, Li Jianyong, had very different personalities, they had similar resumes of teaching at universities and being in charge of investment banking before and after joining GF, and had a high degree of tacit understanding of modern investment banking. Dr. Li Jianyong, a mature and prudent man, repeatedly stated that "there was no sense of harmony in the cooperation with other leaders." The pairing of Dong and Li at the operational level was later described by GF as "just like Li Yunlong and Zhao Gang in *Drawing Swords.*"

After the important personnel changes, the first task of the new leadership was to get GF Securities out of the mire of the industry downturn quickly. On the material of the company's general meeting that year, there was a striking flow chart of "great platforms, great collaboration, great systems." This diagram explained the new leadership's business ideas for the next three to five years: through the centralization of information, customer resources, marketing systems, capital management, and human resources, the company would achieve the purpose of sharing resources (the network, human resources, information, and customer resources).

In this blueprint, the ERP system and CRM system that had been put into use had become important basic platforms, and the expansion of the new generation of mainframe rooms had been carried out, while the customer call center and the new generation of large centralized trading system had also been quickly put on the agenda after the demonstration. Meanwhile, in a series of business department structure adjustment, GF Securities decided to start with the Investment Banking Department. In response to the slow development and lack of innovation in bond business and M&A business, the former Investment Banking Department was split in early 2004, and the new Investment Banking Department specialized in IPO and refinancing business, with a new M&A Department established.

The original bond underwriting business was first merged into the Fixed Income Department, and then was given to the new dedicated Bond Business Department. Internal names of "small investment bank" and "big investment bank" were created at this time.

In addition, the management of the company also made a special task very clear: to grasp the sponsor examination, to maximize the number of sponsors, and to study and formulate the sponsor management system.

It was January 9, 2004. Most of the investment bankers sitting in the conference hall on that day did not foresee what kind of changes would be brought to the whole ecology of investment banking by this examination to be held in more than two months.

Even the term "sponsor system" had been officially introduced in the Chinese capital markets for less than two weeks at that time. On December 28, 2003, the CSRC announced the Interim Measures on the Sponsor System for Securities Issuance and Listing, and the first sponsor examination would be held on March 20, 2004.

In the early years, the "quota system," which was characterized by quota allocation, target management, and government recommendation, had a strong color of the planned economy, and its confining effect on the primary market was becoming more and more obvious. The regulatory authorities had established and implemented the approval system for securities issuance and listing in March 2001, and directly determined the number of companies each brokerage firm could report according to its strength and performance. This was known as the channel system with the securities industry.

At that time, GF Securities was in the "first camp" of investment banks and had made outstanding contributions to the industry's cleanup and consolidation. It had "8+1" channels in its investment banking, the most in the industry. On the one hand, the channel system changed the previous problem of excessive administrative intervention and improved the influence of market mechanisms on stock issuance. On the other hand, the channel system inhibited the effective competition among brokerage intermediaries and the policy guidance on the quality and responsibility of practitioners was not clear enough.

In the new competition under the sponsor system, despite its "PhD Legion" and its good professional reputation in the industry, GF Securities did not dare to take this examination lightly. According to the new rule that "every company must have two sponsors to sign for listing," the management of GF Securities was determined to maximize its advantage in the number of sponsors and fully support the preparation for the examination.

For the first time, the competence examination for sponsors set the requirement of "having worked in investment banking for three years and having done at least one main underwriting project." There were more than 3,500 applicants nationwide, but only 1,549 of them were qualified. As the examination approached, excluding some of the key personnel who were in the critical moment of the project and could not get away, the GF Investment Banking Department gathered dozens of qualified people and organized them for "off-the-job intensive study" in Guangzhou, Beijing, and Shanghai.

The young employees in the Investment Banking Department spent a month of intense preparation in Hongbo Hotel in Guangzhou, which was probably their most memorable learning experience since graduating from university. To help them read through more than ten thick reference books in the hotel room, the company organized senior professionals to train them in financial accounting and laws and regulations as priorities for the examination, arranged people to help organize the materials, and provided three meals a day including fruit. During the intense study, the colleagues had the books taken from them during meals and "answered each other's examination-related questions."

What made them dare not slack off was that many members of the management team also appeared from time to time with books among the young employees. The news that "the leaders are also preparing for the exam" spread throughout the Investment Banking Department and the rest of the company. The high enthusiasm for exam preparation also inspired the other business departments. Ms. Cui Xia carried a fruit basket to Hongbo Hotel to visit the investment banking "talents" preparing for the exam, and some "enthusiastic" colleagues even sent the "internal reference materials" they had obtained.

On March 20, those who walked into the examination room and saw the exam papers found that the "examination training" was of limited help to the exam, and the "internal reference materials" were quite irrelevant. The content of the sponsor examination was not about memorizing knowledge, but obviously examined the candidates' investment banking ability and business experience. In "the first exam of China's sponsors," the type of questions was very different from what was envisioned before the exam. Single choice and multiple choice questions being even mixed together without hints; and the total number of questions and case material reading were extremely large. After three hours of an intense, long, and brain-racking exam, GF investment banking employees, like the vast majority of candidates from other divisions, did not finish answering the exam paper. After exchanging opinions outside the examination room, most of them even sighed, stating they "are sure about the results."

On March 25, the CSRC "released the results." In the "List of Qualified Persons in the First Sponsor Examination," 33 people from GF Securities passed the examination, ranking first among 81 institutions. Among the 614 people on the list, He Kuanhua from GF Securities ranked first.

GF investment banking proved the professionalism of the team with the fairness of the examination, and this demonstration of knowledge inspired the whole company. On March 25, the company's board of directors was holding a meeting, and the shareholders of the company were also very excited after learning the news. Soon, those who passed the exam received a letter of encouragement from the company and a bonus of 100,000 yuan. After the subsequent qualification screening and registration certification, 609 people from GF Securities and other institutions became China's group of sponsors.

In December of that year, the CSRC organized the second sponsor examination. Attracted by the halo of the first group of sponsors and encouraged by a series of measures of the company, many GF investment bankers who missed the opportunity to sit the first exam actively prepared for it and entered the examination room. In the process, they witnessed an inspiring story: although Executive Vice President Dr. Li Jianyong failed the first examination by two points, he reappeared in the examination room at the age of 47 after serious revision.

The results of the second examination were announced. GF Securities once again had the largest number of successful candidates, and Dr. Li, as the oldest candidate with the highest position, became one of the second group of sponsors. Compared with the young grassroots investment bankers, the "promotion" brought to Dr. Li's career was not obvious, but he showed his persistence in studying under Professor Liu Shibai of Southwest University of Finance and Economics, and inspired the whole investment banking team under his supervision to prepare for the exam. Through the examination, a group of "technical" staff members who had been working on grassroots projects for years further strengthened their professional advantages, and had since continued to train in the company's management and multiple business positions.

Like the college entrance examination, the results of the sponsor examination reflected the professional ability of individuals with a certain degree of randomness, but the aggregation of the number of sponsors after the two examinations greatly affected the pattern of brokerage sponsor institutions and opened up the imagination for the number of reported companies. Only three candidates from an important national brokerage firm with eight channels which had underwritten many large projects passed the first sponsor exam. The 26 brokerages, including Guangzhou counterparts, were facing the dilemma of losing their underwriting qualification because less than two people passed the exam.

The new leadership of GF Securities was satisfied with the result of "stressing the exam." The company was actively preparing to implement the sponsor management system when the climate of the industry changed beyond expectation.

On January 1, 2005, the "channel system" was formally abolished. The "channel system" was officially abolished, and the market price of about 1,000 sponsors and "quasi-sponsors" went up in the "poaching war" launched by many brokerages. In the headhunting information circulated among the public, many small and medium-sized institutions easily offered "transfer fees" of more than one million yuan to the sponsors. By May 2005, according to the registration information, 112 of the first 609 sponsors had changed to other institutions, with a flow rate of 18.39 percent in one year, and one agent even changed jobs four times in one year.

In the war of "poaching" and "being poached," a brokerage firm in Shenzhen took the lead in introducing "sponsor allowance" and implementing a more thorough "project-based" assessment for investment banking. This further pushed up the daily income and project income of the sponsors. In contrast, GF Securities, which had the largest number of sponsors, would be lagging behind if it only gave a 100,000 yuan bonus to those who passed the exam.

In the previous years of investment banking management, GF Securities was known for its fair distribution and incentives, and the primary principle of its management in performance allocation was to "assess by team first." At this time, GF Securities was initially unconcerned about the phenomenon of "high price poaching" and excessive incentives among peers. When individual sponsors in the Investment Banking Department submitted their resignations and were ready to change jobs, the management once showed a tougher attitude, emphasizing the role of the company platform in nurturing individual sponsors and repeatedly persuading them to stay during individual talks.

However, it is advisable to let nature take its course. As the phenomenon of job-hopping gradually increased, GF Securities started to face the real climate of the sponsors and followed up with the introduction of the sponsor allowance, which started at a low level and gradually approached the average level in the industry. The allocation principle of "assessing by team first" continued to be used in GF investment banking management for many years.

Dr. Chen Yunxian's prediction before the turn of the century that "knowledge-based industries will become more and more valuable" was very intuitively reflected in the sponsor system that started in 2004. As one of the most representative positions in the securities industry, sponsors had long been regarded as a "mysterious golden-collar class" by the outsiders, and there were even many speculative exaggerated descriptions, and "the exam for sponsorship" had become a way for many young people to change their fate and realize their personal value. As a sponsor institution, GF Securities' primary definition of "sponsor value" was not personal income, but the content of practice level and the professional honor of diligence and responsibility. It is the purpose of the modern corporate system to let the scarce talents get the market-based material rewards. However, under the legal system environment, the securities industry will not be able to use equity incentives and other ways to manage talents for a long time. In the general environment of rising salaries, the increasingly "quantitative" incentive policies of the industry would inevitably bring a short-term tendency, which was a new management and cultural test for GF Securities.

Overtaking at curve in the reform of non-tradable shares

On April 22, 2005, a large white passenger ship sailed out of Chongqing passenger port. The red banner of "GF Securities System Client Seminar" hung on the side of the ship was particularly eye-catching. The whole management team of GF Securities attended the seminar and had a good discussion with 60 institutional and individual clients in the cabin conference room.

The passenger ship went downstream along the Yangtze River and started its journey to the Three Gorges. The majestic scenery on both sides of the Yangtze did not distract the clients, as the hosts and guests were enthusiastically focused on a major institutional change coming to the Chinese capital markets. During the previous six months, the high profile importance attached to the capital markets by Chinese leaders, as well as the regulatory authorities' statements on related policies, had constantly been the focus of market participants' attention.

- In November 2004, Huang Ju visited the Shenzhen Stock Exchange and chaired a symposium on capital markets reform and development, calling for the effective implementation of the Guidelines of the State Council on Promoting the Reform, Opening Up and Stable Development of the Capital Markets.
- During the two sessions of the NPC and the CPPCC in March 2005, Premier Wen Jiabao expressed the country's determination to develop and improve the capital markets.
- On April 12, 2005, the leader of the CSRC publicly stated for the first time in an interview with reporters on eight sensitive issues in the stock market that, according to the guidelines of the State Council, "Conditions are in place to start a pilot program to solve the problem of non-tradable shares."

The change was coming, with which came opportunities. At this GF Securities Client Seminar in the Yangtze River Three Gorges, the reform of non-tradable shares was the only theme. The management team of the company painted a passionate picture of the investment opportunities during the market turnaround to the VIPs, while Zhou Wei of the M&A Department and Zhu Ping of the GF Fund Management took turns to share the research results of GF Securities on the reform non-tradable shares and the situation of the securities market. In front of the Kui Gate, under the Goddess Peak and on the Three Gorges Dam, until April 24, before disembarking from the passenger ship terminal in Yichang, the management team and the key employees of GF Securities departments kept seizing the opportunity to communicate with the clients one by one, discussing the research experience and negotiating more cooperation intentions.

"Despite the incessant cry of apes from the banks, the swift boat has already sailed through thousands of hills." Five days later, the CSRC issued the Circular on Issues Related to the Pilot Reform of Non-Tradable Shares of Listed Companies, officially starting the reform of these shares.

Creating warrant consideration for the China Yangtze Power Project

In 2005, GF Securities was destined to have a deep relationship with the Yangtze River. After the client surname on the Three Gorges Passenger Ship, GF Securities seized China Yangtze Power and then Wuhan Iron and Steel in the pilot reform of non-tradable shares. The reform of two major blue chips of the central government was successfully completed, which was a sensation in the industry.

In the second half of 2005, GF Securities successfully acquired Wuhan Securities, adding 25 business offices and four service departments nationwide, including 15 business offices and four service departments in Wuhan.

Behind this profound fate, there was no matchmaker, and the GF people relied on themselves to design and develop these relationships.

In 2005, the reform of non-tradable shares was decisively pushed forward under the boldness of the chairman of CSRC, Shang Fulin, who said, "Once you've shot the arrow, there's no way of getting it back." The problem of non-tradable shares had been there for many years before their reform began, and the previous explorations of making them all tradable by government departments were hardly successful, and many brokerage firms were still hesitant in 2005, fearing to "pay tuition fees." In addition, the sponsors' income from the share reform business was not high at that time. Keen on underwriting for listing large projects, leading brokerage firms did not think work for the reform of non-tradable shares was profitable.

The management of GF Securities studied the huge business opportunity behind the reform of non-tradable shares share reform. Although the sponsors' income from a project on reforming non-tradable shares was less than one million yuan, there were more than 1,300 listed companies in the market to be reformed, and after the reform, there would be projects in share trusteeship, corporate refinancing, and innovation services, and the "invisible income" would be very substantial. GF Securities started a top-down mobilization for the business for reform of non-tradable shares in advance.

The reform of non-tradable shares had gone far beyond the concept of "investment banking business" in the eyes of GF Securities. Members of the management broke the boundaries of the division of work. Whether it was Zhao Guiping of the brokerage business, or Chen Wenzhan of the Human Resources Department, all the company leaders above the assistant to the president claimed their own part in the work on reform of non-tradable shares. Each of them worked to make use of their townsmen, alumni, and other social connections and seek corporate reform targets together with their employees. Ms. Chen, who had seldom done investment banking projects, secured the January Ganyue Expressway project for reform of non-tradable shares.

Under the background of the "great platforms, great collaboration, and great systems" advocated by the company, investment banking and brokerage not only operated through the business information, but also deeply integrated their personnel to jointly undertake projects. The team of less than 100 people in the Investment Banking Department, as the backbone of the reform of non-tradable shares, was sent to the frontline of each administrative area at the provincial level to secure projects for reform of non-tradable shares. At the peak of this reform, the company organized an emergency "non-tradable shares reform business training course for non-investment bankers" and assembled about 100 employees from headquarters departments, brokerage branches, and subsidiaries outside the Investment Banking Department to "arm" them with investment banking knowledge through intensive training before throwing them into the market to obtain projects. In addition, more than 20 staff members were seconded to the Investment Banking Department from all other parts of the company and became prominent in the practical operation of reform of non-tradable shares. Many of them were "borrowed" by the Investment Banking Department and made a career transition from the Information Technology Department and the grassroots brokerage branches to the Investment Banking Department.

In addition to pursuing the market share of the non-tradable share reform business, the management of GF Securities was also determined to make up for a shortcoming that had existed for many years, taking advantage of this historical opportunity. They advocated in person an important signal to the business team to grasp big projects. In the capital markets at that time, there were very few industry leaders with private company background, and the so-called "big projects" referred to SOEs, especially the central government companies. These companies were often at the departmental or even ministerial administrative level, and the high threshold was self-evident. With GF Securities' resource endowment, how could it get their favor and realize the dream of developing big projects?

After reform started in the first group of four companies, including Sany Heavy Industry, the second group of 42 listed companies for the trial reform of non-tradable shares was announced on June 19, and two large blue-chip stocks, China Yangtze Power and Baosteel, which were representative and influential in the securities market, appeared. Among them, China Yangtze Power was the largest listed hydropower company in China at that time, and China Yangtze River Three Gorges Project Development Corporation was the major SOE shareholder holding 63 percent of its shares. Becoming one of the second group of pilot units was not only the result of Yangtze Power's own efforts to become a model for SOE stock reform, but also reflected the regulator's principle of "pilot first, coordinated advancement, and step-by-step solution" and the intention to test investor acceptance and market tolerance through large blue-chip projects.

GF Securities, which advocated the "big project" strategy, was naturally very interested in the China Changjiang Power non-tradable share reform project. After Niu Huaming, head of the Investment Banking Department, learned of China Yangtze Power's intention to reform its non-tradable shares, he sought opportunities to secure the project through friends. CITIC Securities was the host broker for China Yangtze Power's IPO in 2003, so it was natural for CITIC Securities to enjoy privileges in this project at that time. CITIC Group, the central government parent company of CITIC Securities, had officials working at the Three Gorges Corporation at the time, so it had deep connections. Niu Huaming learned that CITIC Securities was already preparing for the reform of non-tradable shares in China Yangtze Power, but he did not give up. After a period of continued follow-up, he reported a change to the company: there was still an opportunity for the China Yangtze Power Project.

China Yangtze Power's non-tradable share ratio before the reform of non-tradable shares was 70.39 percent, and the state needed to hold absolute control because it was a key industry related to the country's livelihood. And the first group of companies had reformed their non-tradable shares mainly through rights offerings, with the average level of consideration of three shares for every 10 shares. If China Yangtze Power still used a single approach of rights offerings, at least nine percent of the company's total share capital must be paid out to tradable shareholders, which was certainly not the most appropriate approach. According to Niu Huaming, CITIC Securities submitted a "10 for 2" rights offering plan, which did not break the requirement for state minimum holding of shares in China Yangtze Power, but its leaders still said "the plan is too simple, so let's find another securities company to see if it can come up with another."

GF Securities' investment banking team realized that this was a fleeting and valuable opportunity to achieve a breakthrough in securing a large project of a central government company.

When GF Securities saw an opportunity, it went for it. The Investment Banking Department and M&A Department sent a team of more than ten leading professionals, including Liu Xuyang, He Kuanhua, Zhou Wei, Fang Hong, Zhao Yuan, Zhang Lijun, and Zhang Jinyang, to prepare for the project, and also "secretly included" many financial derivatives research experts, including Dr. Wang Liangzhong and Dr. Gu Juan from the Development Research Center. China Yangtze Power's pilot reform was so significant that, in accordance with confidentiality requirements, the project team from GF Securities was required to conduct closed management at Daxianghu Hotel in the outskirts of Beijing, during which they were not allowed to go out, their cell phones were turned in, and landlines only had access to internal services.

Rarely, in order to provide direct leadership and come up with the most technical solution, President Dong Zhengqing and Executive Vice President Dr. Li Jianyong were also stationed in the hotel in Beijing and participated in the closed discussion for more than two weeks, becoming the de facto project team leaders. The project team led by Liu Xuyang, the publicity team led by He Kuanhua, and the team members responsible for model measurement and material arrangement were frequented Dong Zhengqing's room to participate in the discussions. The research and judgment of the client's needs and the modification of the non-tradable share reform plan were pushed forward at an intense pace.

The basic logic of the reform of non-tradable shares was that the non-tradable shareholders of the listed companies should pay "consideration" to the tradable share shareholders in order to make their own shares tradable. More than 1,300 listed companies had their own characteristics and difficulties. The level of "consideration" depended to a large extent on the game between shareholders of non-tradable shares and shareholders of tradable shares. In the China Yangtze Power Project, state-owned shareholders had doubts about a single rights offering approach. If rights offerings were less than desirable, the worry would be that the plan would not be passed by vote; if rights offerings were excessive, the worry would be that "state-owned assets would be lost" and that the plan would be approved by the State-owned Assets Supervision and Administration Commission. In addition, the total number of shares exceeded 7.8 billion yuan, so the "cash consideration" method alone was not appropriate.

Fortunately, China's reform of non-tradable shares was wise because it fully combined Chinese characteristics and fully reflected Chinese wisdom. With "consideration" as the legal basis and the principle of "decentralized decision making," the reform allowed sponsors to give play to their value of "product managers" in the non-tradable share reform projects of different companies. If the market only existed in the "share consideration" and "cash consideration" models, the magnificent reform would be discredited and even unsuccessful.

The project team of GF Securities communicated with China Yangtze Power for many times and concluded that under various constraints, it might not be possible to satisfy the balance of interests of all parties by adopting any one simple payment method for the consideration, and only a combination of methods could be chosen to pay for the consideration. The main measures of the comprehensive plan proposed by the project team included six items:

- use capital reserve fund to increase the share capital and rights offerings;
- use the Three Gorges Fund replacement to raise the electricity price of Gezhouba;
- share increase plan and share repurchase plan;
- long-term shareholding commitment;
- increase power generation and improve the cash dividend ratio; and
- the plan to issue warrants.

In the whole reform of non-tradable shares, the reform plan for China Yangtze Power was one of the most complicated plans.

Compared with the previous slightly "simple" plan, the plan that GF Securities came up with was favored by China Yangtze Power Chairman Li Yong'an and other leaders. In fact, as clients, the professional and rigorous leaders of China Yangtze Power and Three Gorges Corporation were also contributors to this highly technical proposal, and the instructions of Li Yong'an, Bi Yaxiong, Fu Zhenbang, and other leaders on the non-tradable share reform project gave GF Securities' project team many valuable inspirations. The final scheme introduced had a positive effect on the long-term development of the listed company itself, as well as on the balance of interests of all parties and the smooth promotion of the reform of non-tradable shares.

The warrant plan in the proposal was the result of institutional innovation in the reform of non-tradable shares. Warrants are internationally mature financial derivative products, but they were a "new weapon" used for the first time in the Chinese capital markets. As a tool to pay consideration in the reform of non-tradable shares, warrants had natural advantages. They could relieve the pressure of cash payout and rights offering of listed companies, better realize the marketization of consideration, and provide investors with a tool to control risks and lock in interests. In order to launch warrants securely, GF Securities mobilized more than 30 employees from all over the country to Daxianghu Hotel in one day to conduct innovative and pragmatic research around warrants. Dr. Wang Liangzhong, Dr. Gu Juan, and others repeatedly calculated the complex warrant model, often overnight.

In addition, as an innovative financial instrument in the Chinese market, the communication cost of the warrant consideration for all parties was very high. After the intentional proposal was introduced, the project team reported the feedback of the proposal to the SASAC and CSRC respectively on a daily basis as required, which was approved by the director of the market Supervision Department of the CSRC, Xie Geng, and other leaders. After the warrant design work was completed, the project team suddenly received instructions from the senior leadership that the warrants must be theoretically interpreted. The project team received the assignment at about 10:00 p.m. and immediately worked through the night to summarize and sort out the comments. By 6:00 a.m. they had completed a 3,000-word theoretical interpretation of the warrants, which was passed to the State Council leader in charge of the reform of non-tradable shares at the time and was finally approved, and the warrant plan was incorporated into the plan for the reform of non-tradable shares in China Yangtze Power.

The bear market environment in 2005 put tremendous pressure on this pilot project. Many people's one-sided view was that the reform of non-tradable shares would only increase market supply and would lead to a further plunge in the stock indexes. In the early days after the draft reform was plan promulgated, a number of media outlets continued to report individual scholars and market participants questioning the Chinese Yangtze Power project and even the entire reform process. Their views included the "theory of competition with the people for profits," the "public scourge theory," the "theory of warrants collecting money illegally," and even the "theory of the culprit causing the stock indexes' decline." They advocated that once the non-tradable share reform proposals of China Yangtze Power and Baosteel were passed, the stock index would fall below 900 points. They incited investors to oppose the reform. In early July, a financial media outlet in the south published an eye-catching article, "China Changjiang Power's Non-Tradable Share Reform Plan Is

Difficult to Develop: Two Major Sponsors Have Differences," which directly exposed the project team's discussions at the business level.

Under heavy pressure, China Yangtze Power's general manager Bi Yaxiong and other leaders gave full trust to the project team. In 60 days, China Yangtze Power held four rounds of large-scale investor communication activities in Beijing, Shanghai, Guangzhou, and Shenzhen, and maintained close contact with 161 fund companies, insurance companies, strategic investors, and other institutions. In order to communicate sincerely with small and medium-sized shareholders, the the China Yangtze Power Project also innovated with IPTV meetings, where leaders from China Yangtze Power, GF Securities, and CITIC Securities interacted online with investors from more than 200 brokerage branches nationwide. Throughout the communication process, GF Securities followed up with investors holding more than 1.3 billion shares.

The publicity team of the project team arranged a number of professional and theoretical officials to "guide public opinion positively." He Kuanhua, Yang Jinghui, and others wrote columns in authoritative media such as *Securities Times* and *Shanghai Securities News* to introduce the concept of large-cap blue chips' non-tradable share reform and knowledge about warrants, and took the initiative to write articles on the intrinsic value and highlights of the non-tradable share reform plan of China Yangtze Power. A number of articles such as "The Value Pivot of China Yangtze Power in the Context of Making All Its Shares Tradable" were objective, positive, and easy to understand, helping more and more investors to "settle their accounts," and the long-term investment value of China Yangtze Power, as an undervalued power stock, was gradually recognized by the market.

On August 5, 2005, the non-tradable share reform plan of China Yangtze Power was successfully passed with a voting result of "99.18 percent of all shares and 96.76 percent of tradable shares in favor." As one of the most complicated non-tradable share reform proposals, the China Yangtze Power reform plan not only achieved a high participation rate and high approval rate, but also balanced immediate interests and long-term development, achieving a win-win situation for both controlling shareholders and small and medium-sized investors, became a market benchmark at once, and was highly recognized by the CSRC, SASAC, and other government departments.

For GF Securities, the China Yangtze Power Project was a victory of innovation, a victory of efforts to secure "big projects," a victory of "great platforms, great collaboration, great systems." At the end of August 2005, GF Securities issued the Decision on Commendation of Relevant Departments and Personnel of the China Yangtze Power Project, saluting the 38-member Joint Operation Collective, including the Investment Banking Department, M&A Department, Development Research Center, Institutional Clients Department, General Office, Brokerage Business Headquarters, Beijing Business Headquarters, and Wuhan Brokerage Branch.

Completing the Wuhan Iron and Steel Project

The Yangtze Power Project was not without regrets. As a member of the project team said, "It would have been nice if GF Securities had been ranked in front of another one in the ranking of the co-sponsors of the Yangtze Power Project."

This is because, although the China Yangtze Power Project used GF Securities' non-tradable share reform plan with the highlight of warrant consideration, which was also highly recognized by the company, GF Securities ranked second as a co-sponsor for various reasons, and was still regarded as a token sponsor by some peers who did not know the inside story.

The investment banking projects at the beginning of the company in the 1990s repeatedly brought spiritual motivation to the young business staff. The company's leaders taught them by citing its history. Leading cases such as Macro, Zhongshan Torch, and Star Lake MSG, the investment banking team learned the importance of "willpower" in business development:

First, they had to be persistent and never give up until they achieved their goal.

Second, they had to be able to endure hardships others could not and suffer what others could not bear.

Finally, they must not be taken in by fallacies or tremble in the face of danger or difficulties.

Although China Yangtze Power was a rare large central government project secured in the history of GF Securities, and the first warrant consideration also established a brand effect in the whole market, the investment banking team of GF could only look forward to a new opportunity to do better in a larger project to wipe out its regret about its lower ranking in the China Yangtze Power Project.

In September 2005, based on the overall success of the first two groups of pilots, China's reform of non-tradable shares entered a full-scale, focused phase. In late September, four listed central government companies, including Wuhan Iron and Steel, appeared on the list of companies to carry out reform of non-tradable shares.

Wuhan Iron and Steel was the first iron and steel conglomerate built in the People's Republic of China, a key construction project of the First Five-Year Plan with the assistance of the Soviet Union in the 1950s. It produced the first molten iron in the People's Republic of China. At the beginning of the new century, Wuhan Iron and Steel Group had a complete steel production process and its production scale was second only to Baosteel and Anshan Steel in China. Wuhan Iron and Steel, as an absolute state-controlled company, was one of the top ten listed companies in Shanghai and Shenzhen at that time, and its total share capital reached 7.838 billion shares after the share issuance was completed in 2004. In terms of project volume, brand effect, and social influence, Wuhan Iron and Steel's non-tradable share reform was even better than the China Yangtze Power Project, which was undoubtedly a big project that GF Securities could only dream of.

But all market participants, including GF Securities, were well aware that in the previous year, CITIC Securities was once again the main underwriter for Wuhan Iron and Steel SEOs.

The investment banking team of GF Securities respected the service standard of CITIC Securities to Wuhan Iron and Steel and took its 2004 SEOs project as a classic case. In addition, GF Securities' planning and involvement in Wuhan Iron and Steel's reform of non-tradable shares was actually much earlier, and it gained a valuable head start in 2005. The first reason was that the management of GF Securities had an earlier and better prepared overall layout for the reform of non-tradable shares, and the second reason was that one of Dong Zhengqing's classmates from the Central Party School many years ago, Mr. Deng, was already an important leader of Wuhan Iron and Steel at that time.

In the Spring Festival of 2005, Dong Zhengqing came to Wuhan early to pay a visit to Mr. Deng. Although there was a close classmate friendship, at this time Mr. Deng was different from what he was before. As the leader of Wuhan Iron and Steel Group, he was more cautious in the exchange.

Wuhan Iron and Steel had just finished a huge refinancing project in 2004. Mr. Deng told Dong straightforwardly that it was unlikely to have a big financing project in the short term. He only briefly introduced Wuhan Iron and Steel's ideas in capital management and in its development.

A few months later, on April 21, 2005, the day before the GF Securities Client Seminar on the Three Gorges passenger ship, the GF investment banking team came to Wuhan again. At this time, the domestic discussion on the reform of non-tradable shares had begun, and the official policy was on the verge of being introduced, so the investment banking team hoped to get a head start before the introduction of the policy by virtue of the old classmates' relationship. However, everybody knew that the classmate relationship between Mr. Dong and Mr. Deng was just a stepping stone to do business. The non-tradable share reform project which was supervised by the regulatory authorities, was tracked by the media, and caught the attention and shareholders. If GF Securities lacked professional ability and understanding of its customer, this stepping stone would come to nothing.

Before the formal meeting with Wuhan Iron and Steel's leaders, GF Securities' project team drafted a 60-page proposal for Wuhan Iron and Steel's reform of non-tradable shares in accordance with industry standards. However, at Dong Zhengqing's request, the thick project proposal was reduced to two pages, and later condensed into one page. This surprised the project team members who were responsible for preparing the materials overnight: how could one page impress such a big company?

In the conference room of Wuhan Iron and Steel Hotel, the GF investment banking team had a formal meeting with the leaders of Wuhan Iron and Steel. During the communication, Mr. Deng, who started from the grassroots level of the steel mill, said nothing but steel jargons and had no idea of what "P/E ratio" was, let alone "consideration," so the short half-hour meeting was basically straight to the point:

what will be used as the consideration? How much will the consideration be? Only then did the GF investment bankers at the scene came to understand, and they were very impressed by Dong Zhengqing's grasp of the client's psychology.

During the meeting with the leaders of Wuhan Iron and Steel, the investment banking team of GF also keenly found that, compared with "non-tradable share reform" and "capital operation," Mr. Deng was more concerned about "strategic development" and "accelerating development and improving growth efficiency." He had far-reaching ideas in industry M&A and internal integration. This meant that Wuhan Iron and Steel's reform of non-tradable shares was a complex task that required "multiple birds be killed with one stone."

Mr. Deng was probably attracted by the sharp talent of GF's young people, or heard of GF Securities' high performance in the China Yangtze Power Project, so he asked Peng Chen, the chief accountant, to contact GF Securities and examine its proposal.

Although this meeting did not clarify the partnership between the two sides, GF Securities had finally set one foot in Wuhan Iron and Steel. After coming out from the meeting room, Li Zhongwen, as the project leader, was stationed on the spot and booked a long private room in Wuhan Iron and Steel Hotel. He asked all GF Securities departments for personnel support with the assistance of Jin Bo, the president's secretary. Xu Youjun, who was in charge of the south China region of the Investment Banking Department, and Fu Zhu from the M&A Department soon moved in to the hotel and started to work on the project day and night.

During the six-month-long period when they stayed in Wuhan Iron and Steel Hotel, they could only take a walk for exercise in the courtyard after dinner every day, and the days they went home were few, subject to the approval of the company. Dr. Li Fenghua, deputy general manager of the Development Research Center, Dr. Liu Baoyao and Dr. Cai Shifeng, researchers, as well as Chen Zhi and Yao Jun from the Institutional Clients Department, were ready to support the project according to its progress, while General Manager Li Qin and Cheng Hui of the Wuhan Brokerage Branch, were responsible for all support services.

The team members worked hard to analyze the materials and think through the ideas, and made draft after draft of the proposal. With the full rollout of the pilot reform of non-tradable shares, a number of prominent brokerage firms were already present at Honggangcheng in Wuhan's Qingshan District. CITIC Securities, which had served Wuhan Iron and Steel's SEOs project, also sent a team to Wuhan Iron and Steel. The situation suddenly became tense, and all the GF Securities project personnel on site were under pressure, and began to have the same concern as "Chinese style contractors" in other industries: they had done a lot work, but Wuhan Iron and Steel was late in signing the project sponsor agreement with GF Securities, which meant that the identity of GF Securities in the project was not yet clear, and it might be replaced at any time.

Li Zhongwen repeatedly expressed his intention to the relevant leaders of Wuhan Iron and Steel, but did not get a clear answer, so he reported to the company headquarters for support. After Dong Zhengqing learned of this, he soon left for Wuhan and once again made a face-to-face effort with Wuhan Iron and Steel's top management.

Mr. Deng was still not available. On the day the meeting between the two sides was scheduled, an emergency occurred within Wuhan Iron and Steel, and Mr. Deng hurried to several places. The GF Securities project team drove to follow the car of Mr. Deng from early in the morning, but never found the opportunity to talk to him. By the afternoon, Mr. Deng went into the Yangtze River Hotel for a long meeting, while the GF Securities project team simply rented a room in the hotel and stared through the window at the door of the conference room.

Li Zhongwen still remembers the scene: after this meeting, Mr. Deng drove back to the Wuhan Iron and Steel headquarters quickly. They had to follow him again to Wuhan Iron and Steel Building No. 1. When another meeting was over, they seized the opportunity to run fast from the long outdoor corridor and squeezed through Wuhan Iron and Steel's entourage. Although he realized that Mr. Deng was still frowning and serious, Dong Zhengqing handed over the latest revised project proposal to his previous class monitor with a smile. Mr. Deng had one foot in the car door, but Dong Zhengqing briefly introduced the selling points of the proposal and expressed his strong desire to provide services. Mr. Deng patiently listened for a while, and finally said to the people around him, "Let the two of them do it together," and then hurriedly drove away.

As two companies would do it together, it was still a "co-sponsorship." Although the GF Securities project team had basically obtained the qualification to serve Wuhan Iron and Steel, this result still made it a bit disappointed after moving around a day. Since it was a co-sponsorship, it would give rise to the problem of "who ranks first and who ranks second," the same problem that had occurred in the China Yangtze Power Project. It was clear to the investors that who ranked first in the co-sponsorship was not a matter of saving face, but a matter of substantive dominance of the whole project and who could take the lead in long-term cooperation with the client thereafter.

With the fait accompli, GF team quickly adjusted its mentality and strategy: respecting the rival, learning from it, and competing with it with professional services. The seventh floor of Wuhan Iron and Steel Hotel was occupied by more than ten people from GF Securities and CITIC Securities at the same time. This would be a process of advancing the plan together and also the process of improving the plan in the process of discernment. The difficult part of the plan was to grasp Wuhan Iron and Steel's development ideas, bottlenecks, and specific needs.

In 2005, Wuhan Iron and Steel was in the midst of a strategic transformation from its original "quality goods strategy" to a "bigger and stronger iron and steel business on the basis of quality goods" in the steel industry, having gone through waves of changes. In the face of various securities companies, many Wuhan Iron and Steel officials often said "Wuhan Iron and Steel is not short of money."

The project team of GF Securities repeatedly went to work at various departments of Wuhan Iron and Steel and after due diligence and comprehensive research, they selected the strategy of "aiming high and developing fast." According to the strategy, based on the acquisition of main industry assets through private placement in 2004, Wuhan Iron and Steel would issue rights offering warrants during the reform of non-tradable shares. It would integrate its resources and acquired six auxiliary assets closely related to the main steel industry, namely oxygen, coking, gold, energy and power, transportation and international trade, so as to build a complete steel industry chain and create core competitiveness.

This meant that what GF Securities hoped to provide for Wuhan Iron and Steel were three major investment banking projects of reform of non-tradable shares, refinancing and asset restructuring, and a series of financial advisory services such as merger and expansion, internal integration, and strategy implementation. In order to design this complex plan, the project team spent six months of time and effort between the preliminary contact of the early period of the reform of non-tradable shares and the announcement of the preliminary plan by the board of directors, which was significantly higher than other short and quick projects to reform non-tradable shares.

Xu Youjun led the project team and was in a "round-the-clock" situation for a long time: he came up with a revised proposal during the day, was criticized in meetings during the day, continued to think about improvement at night, and changed it again until late at night. Fu Zhu, who was in charge of the warrant design, revised the project proposal into 19 editions, not including countless schedules and memos. The project team often had to catch an early flight to the SASAC in Beijing or the Shanghai Stock Exchange the next day after pulling an all-nighter. The publicity and institutional communications teams, of which Li Fenghua and Chen Zhi were members, were constantly following up on media monitoring, making publicity releases, and organizing communications with institutional investors in step with the project's progress. While the frontline team was working hard, they also called for support from the headquarters from time to time.

Key investment bankers, such as He Tao, Cheng Yan, Zhou Wei, and Ao Xiaomin, went to Wuhan from time to time to provide support. A large number of employees from routes such as the company's senior management, the Development Research Center, the Proprietary Department, the Brokerage Business Headquarters, the Wuhan Brokerage Branch, and the Shanghai Headquarters worked in concert under the principle of "great systems, great platforms, and great collaboration."

Under heavy pressure and as a result of a high sense of responsibility, a beautiful "butterfly" hatched on the seventh floor of Wuhan Iron and Steel Hotel: Butterfly Warrants made their debut as an innovative product in the Wuhan Iron and Steel Project.

As a central government company in the national key industry, Wuhan Iron and Steel Group had a high demand for absolute control from its major state shareholders. GF Securities' proposal included "Subscription + Put" two-way warrants, which better reduced the influence of the majority shareholders' holding ratio and took into account the interests of shareholders of tradable shares. Under GF Securities' proposal, investors who were bullish on Wuhan Iron and Steel's share prices could keep the subscription warrants and sell their warrants to gain maximum profit when Wuhan Iron and Steel's share prices rose. Investors who were bearish could reverse the operation and gain profit when the share price fell. Bearish investors could operate in the opposite direction and take profits when the share prices fell.

The "new weapon" warrants, which exerted market influence in the China Yangtze Power Project, were "upgraded" in the Wuhan Iron and Steel Project. The final implementation of this proposal would allow the Wuhan Iron and Steel Project to achieve a number of innovations in the Chinese capital markets and further build GF Securities' expertise in the derivatives field.

As the proposal was approaching maturity, the ranking of GF Securities in the co-sponsorship of the project once again became an urgent issue that needed to be resolved and clarified by the project team. After several thoughts, the project team worked one more night shift and finally condensed the key points of GF Securities' proposal and confidence in winning into one page. The next day, after the page was circulated within Wuhan Iron and Steel, Wuhan Iron and Steel leaders finally took a pen and drew a thick horizontal line on the ranking order.

This line gave the project team the coveted right to lead the project, and established GF Securities' position to serve Wuhan Iron and Steel for the next ten consecutive years.

In late September, the project team received an urgent notice that the materials originally planned to be submitted after the National Day on October 1 would be submitted on September 26. During the three-day countdown, the project team worked through the night to complete and finalize the five documents for publication and 11 documents for posting on the website, and almost everyone was stretched to their physical limits.

On November 10, 2005, Wuhan Iron and Steel's non-tradable share reform plan was approved with 97.76 percent of all shares and 84.65 percent of tradable shares in favor. The shareholders of tradable shares received a "share bonus+butterfly warrants" consideration, i.e. 2.3 shares for every 10 shares, 1.5 subscription warrants and 1.5 put warrants, as well as a commitment from the major shareholders on the minimum shareholding ratio, the advanced dividend distribution ratio, and the minimum selling price. After the reform of non-tradable shares, Wuhan Iron and Steel Group maintained a 69.76 percent state controlling stake, rationalized its shareholding mechanism, and used the capital markets to achieve strategic development step by step.

The "win-win" Wuhan Iron and Steel non-tradable share reform plan is still a classic case for finance majors in many universities in China. Its comprehensive design idea and its use of the derivative product function and financial engineering technology have been the subjects of many academic articles.

Following the China Yangtze Power Project, the GF Securities finished the Wuhan Iron and Steel Project. Coincidentally, GF Securities worked with CITIC Securities' teams in both projects, gaining valuable experience from excellent peers and learning from the dedication of CITIC Securities' teams. The two companies alternated in ranking first in their co-sponsorship of the projects. In the Wuhan Iron and Steel Project, although different positioning of the project eventually led to the selection of the client, victory and defeat were commonplace in securities competition. CITIC Securities' withdrawal from the Wuhan Iron and Steel Project did not affect its frequent victories in other large projects, let alone its growth into the best modern investment bank in China. GF Securities has always regarded the Wuhan Iron and Steel Project as a classic case because, to some extent, it cherishes this valuable experience of growing with its excellent peers.

In January 2006, during the "President's Award Fund Presentation" session of GF Securities' year-end work conference, Li Zhongwen's presentation on behalf of the Wuhan Iron and Steel project team left a deep impression on all participants. Li Zhongwen once took a sleeper train with Mr. Dong to visit clients on the first the night of the new millennium. He was too nervous to turn over in the upper berth. And several years later, on behalf of the Wuhan Iron and Steel project team, he passionately reviewed the arduous journey of the previous six months, and finally said about the competitor: "Thanks to our competitor. Competition and games also proved our strength, tested our shortcomings and prompted us to grow and improve, which became our lifetime wealth."

It must be noted that GF Securities' victory in the Wuhan Iron and Steel Project was a victory in an "asymmetrical war," which was achieved by the company's main leaders directly working on the frontline of the business and directing the whole process based on the company's strength. The company invested much more composite resources than its rival and made great efforts to achieve a breakthrough in a large project of a central government company and obtained the follow-up cooperation opportunity of the project. In the company's history, after Wuhan Iron and Steel, there were no more similar projects for GF Securities. This also shows that this project was an opportunity arising from the special background of the reform of non-tradable shares and similar cases of securing big projects of central government companies under the direct leadership of the president himself have not appeared again since then. GF Securities' overall strength is still in high-quality SME projects, and its experience in large projects has not been replicable in general.

Innovation emerges and the dawn of light is ahead

From 2005 to 2006, the reform of non-tradable shares continued in full swing. During the same period, the State Council made a decisive decision to carry out a three-year comprehensive rectification of the securities industry, implementing regulation by category, attaining a full understanding of the industry, cleaning up and rectifying irregularities in financial management, and better resolving longstanding risks. From 2004 to 2006, 31 securities companies were closed or restructured. The securities industry took on a new look after the cleanup and consolidation and risk disposal, and was brought onto a benign development track, with industry-wide operating income reaching 23.1 billion yuan and profits of 12.3 billion yuan in the first half of 2006.[1]

Just after the Spring Festival in 2006, Zhuang Xinyi, vice chairman of the CSRC, led a team to GF Securities for research. After reviewing the team foundation, financial foundation, and market foundation of GF Securities, Vice Chairman Zhuang Xinyi also affirmed the management foundation of GF Securities: "The achievements of GF Securities were made without major detours, without major mistakes, without haphazardness, and without laziness."

Vice Chairman Zhuang was known for his stern and decisive work style and such a verbal comment made the management of GF Securities deeply pleased. As an important leader in promoting the comprehensive governance of the industry, Vice Chairman Zhuang spoke out his views on comprehensive governance: curbing irregularities, resolving historical burdens, and reversing losses in the industry, and carrying out the three criteria to the letter.

Regulatory leaders had been concerned about the financial situation of the industry for a long time. After 2005, the securities industry had been losing money for four consecutive years. Discussions on brokerage firms' pooled wealth management, securities margin trading, asset securitization, refinancing and other businesses had become increasingly heated, and the industry was in urgent need of new profit growth areas.

Both in 2004 and 2005, GF Securities made a net profit of over 100 million yuan. The brokerage business became the "pillar" for the company to overcome the rapids, and some brokerage branches were transformed faster, so that the situation of "living on the mercy of the elements" was greatly reversed. The investment banking made a great impact in the non-tradable share reform projects of China Yangtze Power, Wuhan Iron and Steel, COSCO Shipping, and Guangdong Electric Power. However, some employees were surprised that the non-tradable share reform business only achieved "overall break-even" at the financial level of the company. In the case of the primary market IPO "closed" due to the reform of non-tradable shares, the investment banking wasn't that profitable.

1 Statistics of the Securities Association of China.

More employees did not know that the sponsorship of Wuhan Iron and Steel's non-tradable share reform, which was a milestone of the company's big project, required the efforts of dozens of officials for more than sixth months, but the project's sponsorship income was only three million yuan, which was several times that of other non-tradable share reform projects. The final bonus package of the whole team was only 500,000 yuan. In the market with low income, the primary target of the GF Securities management team for the non-tradable share reform sponsorship business was to increase market share. By the time the market-wide reform of non-tradable shares was completed in 2007, GF Securities had completed the non-tradable share reform sponsorship of 108 listed companies, ranking second in the industry, and its 7.96 percent market share was also the highest in the history of its single business. With its fame in the Wuhan Iron and Steel Project, GF Securities successively secured the non-tradable share reform projects of Jinan Iron and Stee and Laiwu Iron and Steel, accumulated high-quality customer groups, and laid a solid foundation for the subsequent refinancing and broker-related businesses.

GF Securities people were not wrong in forecasting "follow-up project opportunities" from the Wuhan Iron and Steel Project. With the efforts of the Xu Youjun-led inter-departmental team, GF Securities completed the 7.5 billion Wuhan Iron and Steel share-traded convertible bond project in 2007, the 8.345 billion Wuhan Iron and Steel rights offering allotment project in 2011, and the 7.2 billion Wuhan Iron and Steel corporate bond project in 2012. Among them, the 2007 share-traded convertible bond project set several market records, including the lowest interest rate, the largest amount of frozen capital, and the highest exercise prices of related products, and has become the largest refinancing project in the history of Chinese securities to date. In addition, the project's sponsorship income also set the record of underwriting income of GF Securities.

In the rights offering project of Wuhan Iron and Steel, Dr. Li Jianyong, the most senior sponsor in the industry, personally served Wuhan Iron and Steel as the project sponsor. For a long period of time, GF Securities established a strong relationship with Wuhan Iron and Steel, leaving no room for other top brokerage firms to compete for business opportunities.

The success of the reform of non-tradable shares deeply activated the basic functions of China's capital markets during the "emerging plus transition" period, and the wealth effect gradually emerged. Under the effect of comprehensive industry governance and business competition, the concentration of the securities industry increased significantly. As a pilot innovation brokerage since 2004, GF Securities had been actively raising and integrating internal and external resources over the previous few years, and had been stepping up its efforts to reap innovation dividends when the industry spring came.

The Bond Business Department, which was set up in early 2005, became another professional main force for securing big clients and large projects for GF Securities. It became a main profit-making department in the year of its establishment. Each member of the leading bodies of GF Securities led a team to secure projects. In 2005, GF Securities completed the main underwriting of two corporate bonds of two billion for Fujian Expressway and 1.5 billion for Guangdong Transportation Group, achieving a breakthrough of "zero" in the main underwriting business after the State Council approved the corporate bonds in 2000. It also set a number of records in corporate financing in two large business provinces, which was highly evaluated by local leaders and related institutions.

In 2006, the Bond Department completed projects in many more cities, including the issuance of 1.5 billion corporate bonds of Zhongyuan Expressway. After doing other projects in many places, such as Qinghai Investment and Changsha City Investment, GF Securities started to gain fame in the field of corporate bond underwriting. All this was done by old and young GF investment bankers, such as Huang Xuhui, Zuo Yaxiu, Zhang Xinqiang, Chen Dong, Ye Peng, and Li Qingwei. They experienced the twists and turns in the primary and secondary markets of bonds, the tortuous competition with China Development Bank, CITIC Securities, and CICC, and even the exhaustion to the point of fainting at the project sites, nosebleeds, and drips on the loess slope, but time and again welcomed the various questions of large corporate customers with a smile.

The derivatives research team, which was highly acclaimed in the industry for its "new weapon" warrants in the reform of non-tradable shares, was brought together in the firm's new New Product Department at the end of 2005. This department was responsible for the creation and trading of covered warrants, issued the first structured product in the industry, and combined financial engineering and investment trading to launch the first quantitative trading and alternative investment business in China. The department had He Kuanhua, Gu Juan, and Fu Zhu as its team members and was both based on the Development Research Center, Postdoctoral R&D Base, Investment Banking Department, M&A Department, and Corporate Innovation Group and supported by new members from society. It once close contacted with Societe Generale Group for technology consulting and transfer in order to lead China's derivative products market.

When Fu Zhu was on duty for the Wuhan Iron and Steel Project, she received a call from an investor on the verge of despair. With a raspy, low voice, the investor said, "Will the warrants go up tomorrow? If not, I will jump from a high building." Under the shock, Fu Zhu quickly realized that the Wuhan Iron and Steel warrants had not been listed yet. After asking, she learned that the investor had bought warrants from another steel company at high prices, but the call went to the Wuhan Iron and Steel project team by mistake. Fu Zhu patiently explained the concept of warrants, the more appropriate operation strategy after buying warrants, and cautioned the other party not to invest in financial products he was not familiar with. The investor finally hung up the phone, but the GF Securities derivatives expert fell into a pensive mood. "We must be responsible to investors" has since become an important principle in her career and that of her team members.

Driven by the trend of industry innovation, the charm of derivatives business was fully reflected in the creation of such products as China Southern Airlines warrants, China Yangtze Power warrants, and GD Power warrants. Many securities companies, including GF Securities, gained profits of hundreds of millions and billions of yuan, and the media once called the warrant business a "money printing machine for brokerage firms." However, as a high-risk investment product, investor education around warrants also attracted more attention. The GF Securities project team for the Wuhan Iron and Steel's non-tradable share reform carefully designed butterfly warrants. In the first day of the opening, due to the speculation with a large amount of money, both subscription and put warrants reached the upper level of the daily trading limit.

Afterward, the development of the derivatives business such as warrants was once frustrated by market doubts, but the team of the New Product Department did not disappear but continued to undertake the innovation mission in the Derivatives Business Department, Fixed Income Department, Investment Banking Department, Asset Management Department, and Counter Trading Market Department.

The fixed income business, which was a mainstream segment of modern investment banking, also "emerged" in GF Securities during this period. In 2006, the Fixed Income Department seized the investment opportunity of convertible bonds, tried the warrants portfolio, LOF fund arbitrage, and other low-risk, large capital arbitrage opportunities. The annual self-management yield increased more than 30 percent and the profit was over 100 million yuan. The department not only provided strong support for large projects in the primary bond market, but the team led by Dr. He Rongtian also achieved several "firsts": the first to do ETF arbitrage in GF Securities system, the first to be the main trader of LOFs in the market, the first to price and provide two-way quotes for ABS on the exchange, the first to hold simulation trading with the Shenzhen Stock Exchange, the first to invest in segregated bonds, and the first to design exchangeable bond product solutions.

As the wave of innovation rose, the term "fission," a term used in the field of nuclear physics, was frequently repeated by GF Securities' management.

Starting from the Andersen Project in 2000, GF Securities' brokerage business began to implement and improve the three-tier management structure. On the eve of the reform of non-tradable shares in early 2005, GF Securities foresaw the impending transformation of business network functions and conducted a pilot business model transformation in Shanghai. The newly established Shanghai Headquarter in Pudong New Area attracted the attention of the whole business system from the very beginning. The biggest significance of the Shanghai Headquarters was that it could engage in all business except for the investment business in proprietary business and asset management. The headquarters had the Investment Banking Department, Product Sales and Trading Department, and middle and back office departments. In the subsequent general mobilization of the reform of non-tradable shares, the Shanghai Headquarters reaped effective results in "breaking down departmental and regional boundaries," and made a breakthrough in the investment banking in Shanghai, which had not been carried out effectively for many years. The headquarters secured Pudong Construction and Shanghai Xinmei's projects to reform their non-tradable shares sponsorship.

At the beginning of 2006, the GF Securities Fission Plan was launched with a focus on institutional adjustment, and 13 regional headquarters were formally established. They were the Beijing headquarters, Guangzhou Headquarters, Shanghai Headquarters, Shenzhen Headquarters, Jiangsu Headquarters, Shandong Headquarters, Zhejiang Headquarters, Hebei Headquarters, Henan Headquarters, Hubei Headquarters, Northeast Headquarters, Southwest Headquarters, and Northwest Headquarters. The headquarters were headed not only by Cui Xia and other veteran brokers who had been fighting in the frontline of brokerage branches for years, but also by veteran investment bankers and sponsors. "The establishment of the regional headquarters, together with GF Securities' trusteeship and acquisition of Wuhan Securities, FIRSTTRADE, and Hebei Securities, highlighted GF Securities' quality and quantity of business network advantages.

The company's management's initial layout of "market share first" for the non-tradable share reform business also reaped significant rewards through the custody of restricted tradable shares. At the end of 2006, based on the success of the non-tradable share reform business, the tradable shares under GF Securities' trusteeship reached 17.4 billion shares, and the market share of equity fund trading reached 5.16 percent (including GF Huafu), fulfilling the five percent market share target of the Fission Plan ahead of schedule. Just like the expansion effect brought by sponge storing water, from the grab of the market share in the reform of non-tradable shares, to the trusteeship of large numbers of tradable restricted shares, and to the M&A and fission of business outlets, the brokerage business of GF Securities fully seized the dividends of this wave of capital markets reform, and the scale of clients was greatly expanded, which further built the foundation for the enhancement of the company's industry status.

On January 9, 2007, the SSE index touched 2,800 points for the first time, and the turnover of Shanghai and Shenzhen exchanges reached 120.8 billion on that day. *The Wall Street Journal* of that day described the Chinese capital markets as follows:

> With the SSE Composite Index, widely regarded as the market's yardstick, hitting a record high, China's stock markets are finally showing the kind of prosperity befitting the world's fourth-largest economy in full take-off, and it is really starting to play a real role in the economy's rapid growth.

The daily rising K-line chart, like a bull's horn raised high, signals that China's stock market is about to reach an unprecedented high; it is also like a steep mountain, reminding ambitious climbers of the risk of losing their footing midway.

The bull market was on the way with the spring breeze. After all the ups and downs at the beginning of the century, GF and the 82,000 employees in China's securities industry were entering a "better era."

From the "1997 crisis" to the eve of the bull market in 2007, it was a decade of self-reliance and entrepreneurial practice of intellectuals in GF Securities. From theoretical exploration, to management institution building, and to business innovation and development, Dr. Chen Yunxian and his entrepreneurial team laid a rich and solid foundation for GF Securities. The melody of "Find Your Dream with Me" echoed for a long time. GF Securities employees pursued the future glory legacy.

The ten years before and after the new century were also a period when the industry was gradually reshaped. With the dawn of the new century, GF Securities' efforts during this period were largely focused on another "main thread" of the securities industry. In May 2000, Zhou Xiaochuan, chairman of CSRC, pointed out at a symposium on the development of financial companies and capital markets that, "On the basis of developing the securities market and reforming the issuance system, financial companies are welcome to issue and list their shares." The first-tier brokerage firms in the industry then competed to go public. A few years later, CITIC Securities, the first to achieve IPO listing, became the envy of the industry's "third wave of impact," with an increasingly clear lead.

By staying true to its founding mission and choosing the path of self-reliance and self-improvement, GF Securities steadily moved forward in the reform of non-tradable shares and comprehensive governance of the industry with its professional advantage of "gaining strength with knowledge," and also showed its true strength in the competition with its outstanding peers. Before the projects to reform non-tradable shares in China Yangtze Power and Wuhan Iron and Steel in 2005, GF Securities and CITIC Securities had already competed with each other at another level. The game of acquisition and counter-acquisition in September 2004 was recorded in the history of Chinese securities industry

Chapter VIII: In a Show of Courage: A Market-Based Counter-Takeover

Courage, then, would be a kind of patience; and since it is patience that enables us to practice forbearance and self control.

—Arthur Schopenhauer

1. A survival game

From the lead underwriter to the target of a takeover

With the listing of CITIC Securities on the Shanghai Stock Exchange on January 6, 2003, the first securities company in China's securities industry was born in the form of an IPO. As the representative of the lead underwriter of CITIC Securities, Dr. Chen Yunxian attended the bell ringing ceremony that morning and witnessed the birth of the "first stock of a Chinese brokerage firm" together with many leaders of CITIC Group and CITIC Securities. A reporter from *Shanghai Securities News* who was covering the event pressed the shutter of his camera and published a photo of the event in the next day's newspaper.

This photo inadvertently witnessed the division between the two securities firms: the leaders of CITIC Group and CITIC Securities, such as Kong Dan and Wang Dongming, were staring intently at the quotation screen, discussing their work in a focused manner, as the financing platform of the stock market listing had provided the listed CITIC with a huge imagination for its expansionary development; Dr. Chen Yunxian was smiling as he witnessed the glorious moment of his outstanding peers, with some anxiety in his eyes.

In the year that followed, GF Securities' listing process was once slowed by sudden and important personnel changes, and the company even suffered an annual loss. CITIC Securities, after frequent interactions with the Qingdao municipal government, paid 678 million yuan of the 1.8 billion yuan raised from the listing to acquire Wantong Securities. With the remaining amount, CITIC Securities added 190 million yuan from a series of CITIC Securities' assets in Shandong to acquire a 73.64 percent stake in Wantong Securities in a capital increase restructuring. Wantong was renamed CITIC Wantong Securities Co., Ltd.

From 2003 to 2004, the securities market was still in a long bear market and most securities companies were in a quagmire, while CITIC Securities, backed by a mega state-owned conglomerate, and with a financing platform as a listed company and ample cash flow in hand, was able to appear all mighty after its successful takeover of Wantong Securities.

In the several waves of the securities industry, brokerage firms including GF Securities staged a number of takeovers in a bearish market. This time, who would become the next takeover target of CITIC Securities after Wantong Securities?

The answer was revealed. GF Securities, born in September, suffered the biggest crisis of its survival in September of 2004.

On September 2, *Shanghai Securities News* and many other media reports about "CITIC Securities' takeover of GF Securities" suddenly struck a thunderbolt to the hard-working employees of GF Securities.

Shanghai Securities News published a report titled "CITIC Intends to Buy Equity in GF in a Shocking Move for the Securities Industry in a Harsh Environment," with the opening line "A new round of structural restructuring in China's securities industry is about to begin," announcing the resolution of the previous day's CITIC Securities board of directors' meeting on "the proposal to acquire part of the equity in GF Securities Co., Ltd."

A year before, GF Securities had been the underwriter of CITIC Securities' IPO; a year later, GF Securities became the target of CITIC Securities' takeover. This is a rare phenomenon even in the history of the global securities market.

However, as a listed company, CITIC Securities' takeover intention was based on its own business decisions, complied with laws, regulations, and regulatory requirements, and fulfilled its information disclosure obligations by way of an announcement. This report in *Shanghai Securities News* gave the following judgment:

> CITIC Securities' takeover of part of GF Securities is different from the government-led M&A model, and is a completely market-oriented act.

"Market-based takeover" had become the most prominent "label" of this takeover. In the maturing capital markets, two representative securities companies were in the spotlight of the whole industry under the "market-oriented" rules. The shocked group of employees of GF Securities could not be as "neutral and objective" as the media. According to the previous agreement between the two parties, the listing of GF Securities was conducted by CITIC Securities as the lead underwriter and due diligence had been completed by CITIC Securities, which meant that the asset quality, shareholding structure, and even the strengths and weaknesses of GF Securities at many levels were not secret to CITIC Securities. The vast majority of GF employees were previously unaware of the CITIC Securities takeover, and on September 2, they were shocked, bewildered, and then more than a little emotional.

On the same day, there were a lot of emotional messages on the company's internal "Say Something" forum. A fund manager of GF Fund posted a post on the forum with the theme of "seven sins," expressing his views on the takeover in a heated text of about a thousand words, in which "original sin," "deception," "robbery," "deception," "robbery," "jealousy," "betrayal," "unscrupulous," "ignorance" and other judgments both presented the author's mood in the heat of anger and represented the true attitude of many of his colleagues at the time.

This post reads:

> The value of GF Securities lies not only in its net assets of 2.4 billion yuan, nor in its nationwide business network, and the first group of the largest number of sponsors in China, but also in the sound business style, the united, realistic, hardworking, and innovative corporate culture and the unique pioneering spirit that we have accumulated and built over the years. The value of GF Securities can be calculated in tangible terms, but the intangible part of goodwill is immeasurable.
>
> ....
>
> Once CITIC Securities comes in, how would it handle the relationship between CITIC investment banking and GF investment banking, between CITIC brokerage branches and GF brokerage branches, and between CITIC Fund and GF Fund? How would it treat the two integrated brokerages fairly and how would it not harm the long-term development of the two companies? If it is a transfer of benefits, and if improper transactions occur, it would be nothing but a robbery of the interests of our employees and the interests of other shareholders.
>
> ....
>
> CITIC Securities has a larger registered capital and net assets than GF Securities, but its net profit in the first half of 2004 was only 56.52 million yuan, which was lower than GF Securities' first-half results of 59.48 million yuan. What is the sin of GF? It is its wealth.

The sentence "What is the sin of GF? It is its wealth" reflects very clearly the true feelings of the employees including the poster toward GF Securities: they had deep identification with the culture of their own company, they believed that GF Securities was better than its rival, and they would never be willing to be acquired.... More deeply, they believed that the market-oriented platform of GF Securities could protect their rights and interests, but if it was acquired by CITIC Securities, they would have a great sense of insecurity.

Within a day, a counter-takeover campaign was quickly launched within the company. On September 3, internal public opinion continued to ferment as employees spontaneously expressed their resistance in a variety of ways: some employees went directly to the Guangdong Securities Regulatory Bureau to "present their will" against the takeover, while the labor union led a company-wide campaign to sign a petition against the CITIC Securities takeover.

The September 4 issue of *Securities Times* reported in vivid detail on this "presentation" by employees of GF Securities:

> Employees of GF Securities and its subsidiaries, who are in the center of the "takeover vortex," went to the offices of the Guangdong Securities Regulatory Bureau, the local regulator, yesterday afternoon to express their position and attitude to the regulator against the entry of CITIC Securities into GF Securities.
>
> A group of 22 GF employees came to the Guangdong Securities Regulatory Bureau at around 2:30 p.m. The Guangdong Securities Regulatory Bureau, in accordance with the regulations on the number of petitioning visitors, allowed five of the employees to make a statement directly to the person in charge of the First Regulatory Section. The reporter requested to be present, but was politely refused by the Regulatory Bureau.
>
> The remaining 17 employees of GF Securities gathered in the conference room of the Guangdong Securities Regulatory Bureau in an orderly manner and talked about the matter.
>
> An employee from the brokerage business of GF Securities said, "CITIC Securities suddenly made this matter public unilaterally and in a high profile, without any goodwill at all. Now that it wants to acquire GF Securities, why doesn't it take care of GF Securities? Instead, it greatly hurts GF Securities."
>
> According to reports, after CITIC Securities made public the news of its proposed takeover of GF Securities, GF Securities' business was negatively affected to a certain extent, and many business offices saw customers withdrawing their deposits; there were many customers who called to ask if GF Securities was in trouble.
>
> Another employee added: "The behavior of CITIC Securities has caused too much damage to GF Securities. Today the general market trend is not good. Many brokerage companies are in trouble. After the news of the takeover was made public, many investors think that GF Securities also cannot survive, which can easily lead to margin runs, which in turn leads to instability and chaos in the financial industry."
>
> "We do not welcome such a hostile takeover. In terms of the quality of assets,

GF Securities is not worse than CITIC Securities; in terms of the number of business offices, GF Securities is more than twice that of CITIC Securities; in terms of the number of sponsors, GF Securities is also the most." He went on to say.

....

After about 20 minutes, the five employees who directly presented their attitude came out. One of them said, "We mainly expressed three points to the Securities Regulatory Bureau: First, the two cultures are different, and CITIC Securities' forced entry would only hurt both sides, and would not achieve the purpose of the union of strong securities firms as CITIC Securities wishes. Second, CITIC Securities' unilateral and sudden public announcement has caused the market to misunderstand GF Securities, and this kind of hostile takeover should not be encouraged. Third, we are worried about the fate of GF Securities after CITIC Securities comes in. If CITIC Securities became the largest shareholder of GF Securities, it would not be able to step over the hurdle of intra-industry competition. How to coordinate the business of CITIC Securities and GF Securities in the future, such as brokerage, investment banking, asset management, subsidiaries? Should profitable business be given to CITIC Securities or GF Securities?"

The reporter also found out that the Guangdong Securities Regulatory Bureau listened to the opinions of the employees very carefully and said they would pay attention to the matter.

Not only did *Securities Times* follow up on the 22 employees, but on the same day it also published a counter-takeover statement signed by 2,230 employees of GF Securities, summarized as follows:

The case of CITIC's takeover of GF has made waves again. Yesterday, a website published a statement of employees of GF Securities strongly opposing the hostile takeover by CITIC Securities. The statement, signed by "2,230 employees of GF Securities," says that GF Securities "strongly oppose the hostile takeover by CITIC Securities and would fight to the end." The statement uses the word "shocked" to describe the reaction of GF Securities employees to the takeover. In addition, GF Securities employees made it clear that they were strongly indignant and resolutely opposed to this undeclared hostile takeover. They believe that the takeover is "not a win-win situation, but a lose-lose situation." GF Securities' 2,230 employees issued a statement firmly opposing the hostile takeover bid by CITIC Securities.

....

CITIC Securities and GF Securities have such different corporate cultures and management models that there is no such thing as "complementary strengths and similar cultures," so how can we achieve "integration" with such a serious cultural conflict? Moreover, how can a "win-win" situation be achieved when the hostile takeover leads to such strong resistance from both sides?

> The statement also said that if CITIC Securities is bent on acquiring GF Securities, a well-managed company with a good brand and unique culture and a dynamic and excellent company in China's securities industry would be seriously harmed and a large number of high-quality securities talents would be lost. A hostile takeover would only be a lose-lose situation, which would only end in "1+1 < 1."

The employees' outrage intensified, with GF Securities' internal forum even chanting the slogan "It is better to die when life is a disgrace." Some employees logged on to CITIC Securities' website to comment on and denounce the takeover, so much so that they dominated the website's comment column on September 4. GF's investment bankers had some knowledge of the foreign M&A market and had creatively proposed a "plan for countering the takeover poison pill" within the company.

CITIC Securities seemed to be surprised by the strong opposition from the employees of GF Securities. As its previous relatively smooth takeover of Wantong Securities suggested, communication with the government and authorities and shareholders was the focus, and the "opinions of the employees of the target company" did not seem to be a consideration in its takeover plan.

In 2004, GF Securities had over 200 PhDs in its workforce and 60 percent of its headquarters staff had a master's degree or higher, which was unique in the securities market at that time. What's more, under the leadership of Dr. Chen Yunxian and others, this group of intellectuals and professionals with the name of "PhD Legion" had to go through many difficulties and struggle in the market for more than ten years to build GF Securities into a securities company with distinctive characteristics. GF Securities was a company, but it was also the fruit of this group of intellectuals' efforts and a platform for the employees to put their future and hope on. In this sense, if one wanted to do a "comprehensive study" of GF Securities, one had to face the cultural characteristics and legitimate demands of this workforce.

It was not until September 7 that CITIC Securities issued an announcement with the intention of appeasement, stating that "the purpose of the takeover of part of the equity interest in GF Securities is to seek to leverage the business and resource advantages of the two companies to grow bigger and stronger. The result of the takeover would not lead to a change in the domicile of GF Securities, a change in the legal entity, or a significant adjustment in the operation and workforce." In addition, CITIC Securities also emphasized in its announcement on September 7 that it "has a good experience of cooperation with GF Securities, which has an excellent management team and talent team. This is an important basis for joint development and a win-win situation."

However, the voice of opposition from the employees had not abated, and in most people's view, the announcement was merely "fulfilling the obligation of full and timely information disclosure." The merger was bound to produce real problems such as intra-industry competition, which could not be solved by promises alone. If GF Securities was left with its hands tied, it could only fall into a passive situation step by step.

Until September 7, the media reporters gradually found that the employees of GF Securities were in an uproar in the face of CITIC Securities' takeover, but the management of GF Securities had not yet made a public statement.

Not a surprise attack

The famous Battle of Chibi in Chinese history left a famous dialogue about the pre-battle decision in historical books such as *Records of the Three Kingdoms* and *Comprehensive Mirror for Aid in Government.*

> Lu Su said to Sun Quan: "Now I can surrender to Cao Cao, but you cannot. Why do I say so? If I surrendered to Cao Cao, he would send me back to my hometown and evaluate my reputation, so I would not lose my position as a minor official, and I would be promoted step by step by riding in a cart with officials and soldiers, and would still not lose my position as a governor of a county. What do you want to get when you surrender to Cao Cao? I hope you would make up your mind early and not take the advice of those people." Sun Quan sighed and said, "I am very disappointed by the opinions held by those people. Now you have enunciated the right course, which is exactly what I think."

After receiving Cao Cao's announcement that he would "fight with Sun Quan in the State of Wu," Sun Quan, the decision maker, and Lu Su, the supporter of a war, had different statuses and different considerations about whether to fight or surrender. Sun Quan had doubts that there were different voices among his subordinates, but Lu Su put himself in Sun Quan's shoes and eventually contributed to the latter's decision to go to war.

Objectively speaking, the more than 2,000 employees of GF Securities were not universally opposed to the takeover when the company's survival was at stake. After the initial shock, there were some mid-level and junior employees who watched and speculated about the personal benefits of a CITIC Securities takeover, but these were, after all, very few. From September 2 to September 7, the outpouring of resistance from the staff was not only unexpected by CITIC Securities, but also by the media and, in fact, by the GF Securities management.

The presentation, the joint statement, the forum statements, and the counter poison pill plan, all these real responses of employees gave the new GF Securities management the greatest courage to make decisions. They were in the eye of the storm, and before making a public statement, they were making a comprehensive research and judgment of various information.

On September 2, while the financial media were reporting on the CITIC Securities takeover decision, *China Securities Journal* of that day further detailed the whereabouts of CITIC Securities executives:

> On September 1, Capital Airport at sunset is extraordinarily beautiful. The heat is already receding in the autumn evening. Zhang Youjun, managing director and general manager of CITIC Securities, who has just finished a board meeting in the morning, hurriedly boards a flight south to Guangzhou. We have found that Zhang Youjun's trip to the South is designed to negotiate the takeover of equity with GF Securities and the shareholders concerned. If it goes well, he would be authorized by the board of directors to sign a letter of intent to transfer with the transferor on the spot. Before leaving, Zhang and related personnel clinched fists to wish each other good luck, and his relaxed smile seemed to indicate that the trip is guaranteed to be a success.

The gesture of "guarantee success" undoubtedly indicated that CITIC Securities had made sufficient preparations for the takeover. What many people did not know was that CITIC Securities had not only advanced the takeover process before September 1, 2004, but had also communicated its intention to the GF Securities management through a number of channels. The market takeover on September 1, seemingly launched suddenly, was not actually a "surprise attack." It can even be said that CITIC Securities was somewhat "courteous before launching the setback."

Chairman Wang Zhiwei had already received a personal message from the leadership of CITIC Securities, who said: "CITIC Securities has already obtained the intention to sell the shares in GF Securities held by Zhujiang Investment (10 percent), Yunda Technology (3.83 percent), Zhongshan Public Utilities (15 percent), Xiangshan Investment (6.17 percent), and Guangdong Meiyan (8.4 percent)." CITIC Securities had even made plans for Wang Zhiwei's personal future: "After the completion of the takeover of equity by CITIC Securities, if Chairman Wang is willing to change GF Securities into the Southern Headquarters of CITIC Securities, he can continue to be the head of the Southern Headquarters; if he still wants to go back to the banking business, he would be arranged by CITIC Group to be the vice president of CITIC Bank." Chairman Wang Zhiwei probed, asking the other side, "Has the Guangdong government's opinion been sought?" CITIC Securities leaders replied, "The chairman of CITIC Group has been asked to write a letter to the Guangdong provincial government and entrusted the Guangdong Provincial Finance Office to forward the letter to the governor."

President Dong Zhengqing had also previously received a personal message from CITIC Securities' leaders, who approached him privately at an industry meeting held by the CSRC at the Xijiao Hotel in Shanghai in June 2004 to "seek" his opinion on CITIC Securities' proposed takeover of a stake in GF Securities. The other side said, "If you oppose the takeover, we would stop; if you agree, we would continue to move forward. Likewise, the other side also offered Dong some jobs."

However, in an informal exchange, it was impossible for Wang Zhiwei and Dong Zhengqing at that time to give CITIC Securities a formal answer. In terms of corporate governance, the takeover of a company's equity was mainly through negotiation with shareholders, and the operating management had limited say. In terms of personal experience, the two main leaders of GF Securities had just assumed their new positions for less than a year, and were suddenly faced with being acquired, the attitudes of the local government, regulators, major shareholders, and other members of the leading body had not yet been clear, and even the business ideas between the main leaders were in the process of integration, so how could they make a clear statement on the sudden takeover?

In August, news came from different sources that CITIC Securities was negotiating with several shareholders of GF Securities to acquire their shares, and the pace of work had a tendency to speed up.

At this point, the management of GF Securities could judge that CITIC Securities had not only completed due diligence on GF Securities' assets, but also contacted major shareholders and executives, and prepared for the takeover from the government public relations level, taking advantage of its previous sponsorship agreement. The first loss of GF Securities in 2003, the shaken confidence of shareholders, and the run-in process of the new leadership after Dr. Chen entered politics all contributed to CITIC Securities' determination to acquire GF Securities. The abundant capital flow after the listing of CITIC Securities, the motivation to make excellent performance statements, and the regional complementarity of the southern market all meant that CITIC Securities was determined to win this takeover.

Under heavy pressure, the management of GF Securities "made a decision before making a move."

In August, during several management meetings, the leaders of GF Securities communicated among themselves that CITIC Securities was preparing to acquire their equity, and hoped that everyone would focus on unity, communicate in a timely manner, and prepare to face the crisis.

Early on the morning of September 2, while the media was in an uproar, President Dong Zhengqing covered up the newspaper and walked out of his office, when he ran into Chairman Wang Zhiwei in the corridor. Dong Zhengqing asked Wang Zhiwei, "What do you think?" Wang Zhiwei said, "I strongly oppose the takeover." Dong Zhengqing then replied, "I have the same attitude." The two key leaders further formed a consensus.

At 9 a.m. on September 2, the GF Securities management held an emergency meeting to study and deploy the counter-takeover effort. The meeting analyzed CITIC Securities' previous initiatives, emphasizing the need for stability in mentality, personnel, and business, and for enhanced communication with customers. The leaders discussed a series of matters such as contacting the heads of shareholders, and then took action according to the division of labor. At this meeting, an important plan that had been in the works for several months was formally incorporated into the counter-takeover effort.

On the afternoon of September 2, the company held a company-wide IPTV conference to inform all employees about CITIC Securities' proposed takeover of part of the company's shareholders' equity, and to convey and emphasize the basic attitude of the company's major shareholders toward GF Securities, which is "a strategic investment, not a financial investment." The company's management issued an internal announcement that "no matter what the outcome is, we will do our best to protect the interests of our employees."

On the morning of September 5, GF Securities held a meeting with middle-level and above officials at its headquarters and solemnly announced the implementation of the counter-takeover plan.

On the morning of September 6, GF Securities formally reported to the Guangdong government on the CITIC Securities takeover, emphasizing that "the ultimate goal of the takeover is to merge and write off GF Securities" and "the takeover is not conducive to strengthen finance in Guangdong," and requesting the provincial government to "coordinate with relevant authorities and companies to keep the shareholders of GF Securities in Guangdong Province stable.... If equity must be transferred, please transfer it to a non-securities company, and give priority to companies in Guangdong Province, so as to prevent the malicious takeover by CITIC Securities from adversely affecting Guangdong's capital markets."

On the afternoon of September 6, the company held another company-wide IPTV conference to announce specific actions to be taken. A platform named after the initials "GF" of Guangfa would take up the mission of counter-takeover on the basis of what it had, and this decision aroused great reactions from the staff.

On September 7, the main leaders of GF Securities jointly issued an internal open letter to all employees, stating that "the company has encountered the biggest crisis in its history," praising the employees for "their unprecedented unity, high morale and high loyalty," and firmly stating that "from the current situation, the major shareholders of GF Securities are stable and the controlling interest of GF Securities is also stable, so it is hoped that the employees can work with peace of mind. As employees, the best way to deal with the takeover and cooperate with the company's counter-takeover is to stick to their jobs."

On September 9, the management of GF Securities made a formal statement to the public. Guangdong mainstream media, *Yangcheng Evening News*, reported a solemn statement against the takeover with an interview with Dr. Li Jianyong:

> For the first time, GF's senior management stated: we oppose CITIC's takeover. With CITIC insisting on acquiring GF's equity and GF employees firmly opposing the takeover, Dr. Li Jianyong, executive vice president of GF Securities, gave an exclusive interview to our reporters yesterday, disclosing for the first time to the outside world the

distinct attitude of GF's top management toward the takeover battle.

Li Jianyong said that Guangdong, as an economically strong province, is trying to become the financial center of South China. And there are only a few excellent securities companies in Guangdong Province (excluding Shenzhen). CITIC has proposed to acquire GF, its goal will definitely be to hold the controlling share of GF, and the result of doing so would make GF, the excellent brand of the securities market, no longer exist.

Li Jianyong said that CITIC's takeover is a market behavior and there is nothing wrong about it. The transfer of shares is also a matter of shareholders. As the manager, GF Securities cannot and do not have the right to oppose. But GF's management felt that CITIC did have several problems in this takeover that were not solved well or were difficult to solve well. He analyzed that in such a large-scale takeover, as two strong companies, the two sides should fully communicate and basically agree on the way forward before the takeover, which is an important premise. This is an area where CITIC has not done enough. Because while CITIC had some communication with some of GF Securities' shareholders prior to this, there was no communication with the vast majority of shareholders, especially the largest shareholder. There was also not an adequate communication with GF Securities' executives, and CITIC only mentioned the matter rather casually on some informal occasions.

Li Jianyong revealed that the bosses of the first- and third-largest shareholders very much trusted the current management and staff of GF Securities. They categorically stated: if 10 yuan a share were offered, they would not sell GF Securities. Because they were very optimistic about this industry, and optimistic about GF Securities' leadership.

Finally, Li Jianyong said that the company's executives and employees had great respect for CITIC in many respects. As the first listed company in the industry, CITIC's outstanding performance in the securities industry was also evident to all. However, out of recognition of GF's corporate culture, optimism about the sustainable development of GF in the future, and eagerness to protect GF's brand, GF employees really did not want CITIC to make this takeover.

This official statement was well-reasoned with constraint and contained a rich strategy:

First, it highlighted the special role of GF Securities in the context of Guangdong Province's development policy of "building a financial center in South China" at the time, in the hope of gaining the support of the local government and shareholders in Guangdong.

Second, it emphasized that it had "great respect for CITIC in many respects" and said that as the manager, GF Securities could not and did not have the right to oppose, establishing the tone of counter-takeover by market-oriented means.

Third, it disclosed to the market the attitudes of the first and third-largest shareholders to establish GF Securities' position to counter the takeover by market-oriented means.

Fourth, it analyzed the purpose of the rival was to hold the controlling share of GF and summarized some problems in the rival's takeover work, so as to maximize public opinion support.

When the management of GF Securities officially stated its attitude to the public, it still left a question unanswered. Dr. Li Jianyong said in the interview, "The transfer of shares is a matter of shareholders. As the manager, GF Securities cannot and do not have the right to oppose." So what was the biggest support for GF Securities management's counter-takeover strategy? Was it only through communication with shareholders that they could block the takeover by CITIC Securities? Even if the first- and third-largest shareholders stuck to their promises, did GF Securities' management have the initiative over the other shares of equity?

The answer to this huge question was discussed and deployed at the management meeting on September 2, and and the plan was announced to all employees at the company's IPTV meeting on September 6. A plan that would bring together the determination, wisdom, and wealth of more than 2,000 employees of GF Securities had officially moved from backstage to the front stage, and was about to burst forth in the fierce market-based counter-takeover battle.

The birth of GF Venture Capital

In GF Securities' 1999 Corporate Culture Program, one of Dr. Chen Yunxian's ideas was included: "Employees should become the owners of material wealth under the protection of the system." This memorable phrase represented one of the long-cherished wishes of the founding team, which was to realize employee stock ownership. In accordance with the progress of the reform of the national policy, GF Securities started to explore the employee stock ownership plan early on, which allowed employees to hold part of the equity. After the new leadership took office, the company continued to make great efforts to promote the plan in order to further improve the incentive mechanism of the company.

In an internal meeting in May 2004, the company's leadership announced the idea of employee stock ownership: as a first step, the employees would set up a new company to acquire 17 percent of Liaoning Cheng Da's shares held by GF Securities' labor union, becoming the second-largest shareholder of Liaoning Cheng Da, which was also the largest shareholder holding 25 percent of GF Securities' shares; as a second step, the newly established company would acquire the shares transferred by other shareholders of GF Securities. In the second step, the newly established company would be used to acquire part of the equity interests transferred by other shareholders of GF Securities. This idea was approved by the company's major shareholders.

In two working meetings in June, the working group of the employee stock ownership plan came up with a plan to register the company in Shenzhen, discussing the distribution ratio and principles of the share options and focusing on the funding sources. When it came to "naming" the new company, He Kuanhua, a member of the working group, named the proposed company "GF," the harmonious sound of the initials "Guangfa."

On June 27, 2004 and July 30, 2004, the company held two staff meetings to formally review the employee stock ownership plan company-wide and to inform the employees about the preparation for company GF Venture Capital. The Working Group on the Employee Stock Ownership Plan met three times in July to further refine the share subscription plan and discuss employee feedback.

The so-called "employee feedback" was actually very simple and realistic: some employees said they "couldn't afford it."

Employee stock ownership was a great tool to improve the incentive mechanism, but also a risky area at the time. The regulator was most concerned about the legality of the source of funds in the employee stock ownership plan. The working group was well aware of the stakes and strictly ordered that no department or subsidiary could fund employee contributions or give abusive bonuses. This meant that employees had to contribute "real money."

In the internal plan in early July, employees at level 1 were eligible for 100,000 shares, those at level 2, 150,000 shares, and so on. The higher the rank, the more shares must be subscribed. In 2004, when the securities industry was in the doldrums and employees were earning average incomes, this amount was not a small sum for many of them. Some employees had difficulty in coming up with the full amount over time because of the short time they had been in the company or because they had large expenses to purchase, for example, a house or a car.

In addition, the employees' contribution in the stock ownership plan was for the company's equity, which could theoretically share the great appreciation brought by the company's development, or might suffer losses due to the company's poor development. As the management said at the mobilization meeting of employee shareholding, "Now it is a test to see if you are bullish on the development prospect of China's capital markets, and if you are bullish on GF Securities."

There were many employees who were "bullish," and once the "prospectus" of GF Venture Capital came out, more employees in the investment banking and investment parts contributed to the subscription in the first place, and poked around among colleagues for more investment. Individuals from financially stressed families borrowed money from all over the world to come up with the money.

There were also many employees who were "not optimistic." In the feedback, most of them expressed the objective difficulties of family income and expenses, but some people privately believed that "there are investment risks, so one should be cautious in buying stocks." After all, CITIC Securities, the "No. 1 brokerage stock," was listed on January 6, 2003 at 5.53 yuan per share and was not sought after by the market for a long time, and hit its lowest share price of 5.79 yuan in July 2004. As a simple analogy, some employees naturally had a question in their minds.

From May to July, the topic of GF Venture Capital had been hotly debated among the employees. At this time, the establishment of GF Venture Capital had been promoted with the goal of employee shareholding, and the mission was more to help employees with investments in return for higher returns under the principles of voluntary participation, transferred rights, and investment.

The work of GF Venture Capital gradually converged with the counter-takeover work.

In August, according to the news from different channels, the management of GF Securities gradually confirmed that the progress of CITIC Securities' takeover of GF Securities was accelerating. While they were studying the situation and preparing for defense, they focused on GF Venture Capital, which was halfway through the process.

At this time, CITIC Securities' announcement had not been issued and GF management could not publicly convey this information to its employees. On top of the previous subscriptions, there was still a small shortfall of funds to prepare for GF Venture Capital. However, if GF Venture Capital was to play a role in a possible counter-takeover battle, it was necessary to accelerate the "loading of bullets."

The company's key leaders put up millions of dollars to subscribe to GF Venture Capital equity, and on various occasions "strongly recommended that people buy GF Venture Capital." Under the premise of ensuring the legitimacy of the funds, there were some "mandatory requirements" in the subscription work. After quantification and decomposition, addressing the shortage of funds from top to bottom became a task that had to be completed. Individual mid- and lower-level officials felt relatively greater pressure in the subscription not only from paying a large amount of money but also from the "attention" of the company's management. For the previous feedback on the "purchasing power" problem, the management simply calculated an account, using "the money that has been paid over the last five years" to measure the disposable income of employees. For the mid- and lower-level officials, this was obviously having them "pay to keep their place in the company."

The candidates for preparing for GF Venture Capital were also on the agenda, and the requirement of "being passionate, motivated, capable, and loyal to the company" was put forward in the internal meeting.

After hearing the news, Jia Ziqiang, who was working in GF Futures at that time, volunteered to take charge of the preparatory work. Within a short period of time, employees from the Audit Department, Finance Department, brokerage business, the company's labor union, and various subsidiaries became directors, supervisors, and management candidates for GF Venture Capital.

On September 2, with the official announcement of the takeover by CITIC Securities, the revolt of GF employees was quickly ignited. On the company's internal forum, some employees posted: "We set up GF Venture Capital because from now on, we want to control our own destiny." "Buy GF Venture Capital" was given the meaning of "living and dying with the company," and the enthusiasm for subscription was renewed. To raise funds, one of the company's drivers even mortgaged his only two-bedroom property and took out a loan of 100,000 yuan to subscribe to GF Venture Capital's shares. The company's internal counter-takeover mobilization meeting also became the founding meeting of GF Venture Capital.

Thus, 2,126 natural shareholders, including GF Securities, GF Huafu, GF Northern, GF Fund, and GF Futures, contributed 248 million yuan, and Shenzhen GF Venture Capital Co., Ltd. was born.

The September 8 issue of *The Beijing News* made a public report on the establishment of Shenzhen GF Venture Capital:

> We have learned that GF Securities implemented its employee stock ownership plan through the establishment of Shenzhen GF Venture Capital Co., Ltd.
>
> According to the prospectus of GF Venture Capital, the company would directly or indirectly hold a considerable number of shares of GF Securities, thus realizing the indirect shareholding of employees in GF Securities.
>
> An employee at the office of GF Securities told us reporters that so far GF Venture Capital has raised 248 million yuan in employee subscription funds. She added, "Our company is doing quite well, and not very bad, why should it be acquired?"

These rather southern-style words sounded "full of energy." The employees of GF Securities finally had their own shareholding platform. When GF Venture Capital was born, it was not greeted by flower baskets, lion dances, and applause, but by a counter-takeover battle that had already been underway. In the eyes of GF people, GF Venture Capital, with 248 million yuan contributed by GF Securities people on September 7, 2004, was like the strong army of the Soviet Red Square parade on November 7, 1941, which went straight to the battlefield while boosting the morale of employees.

2. Culture, morale, fighting spirit, and market-oriented competition

Behind the high-profile takeover

"The transfer of shares is a matter of shareholders. As the manager, GF Securities cannot and do not have the right to oppose." The establishment of Shenzhen GF Venture Capital reversed this dilemma, and the management and employees of GF Securities could play the game with the acquirer and shareholders through the shareholding platform. However, it was not easy to take control of the situation quickly and win in the end.

Whoever acquired the equity of GF Securities from the shareholders first would have the initiative; whoever acquired the share of equity to reach the controlling requirement would be able to achieve the final victory.

A detailed table of the shareholding structure was presented to the management of GF Securities. The equity structure of GF Securities as of the time of the 2004 counter offer was shown in the table below.

Table 1
Shareholding Structure of GF Securities

No	Shareholders	Shares	Ratio (%)
1	Liaoning Cheng Da Co., Ltd.	400,000,000	20.00
2	Zhongshan Public Utilities Group Co., Ltd.	300,000,000	15.00
3	Jilin Aodong Pharmaceutical Group Co., Ltd.	275,000,000	13.75
4	Guangdong Zhujiang Investment Co., Ltd.	200,000,000	10.00
5	Guangdong Meiyan Enterprises Group Co., Ltd.	167,945,584	8.40
6	Heong Kong Group	123,469,109	6.17
7	Liaoning Wanheng Group Co., Ltd.	86,236,500	4.31
8	Kunming Yunda Science and Technology Industry Co., Ltd.	76,621,130	3.83
9	Jiuquan Iron and Steel (Group) Co., Ltd.	62,500,000	3.13
10	Hengtong Group Co., Ltd.	50,000,000	2.50
11	Anhui Huamao Textile Co., Ltd.	50,000,000	2.50
12	Guangzhou Gerui Industrial Co., Ltd.	48,960,773	2.45
13	Guangdong Fenghua Advanced Technology Holding Co., Ltd.	43,118,250	2.16
14	Guangdong Xinhui Meida Nylon Co., Ltd.	34,494,600	1.72
15	Liaoning Foreign Trade Property Development Company	25,383,095	1.27
16	Jilin Aodong Pharmaceutical Group Yanji Co., Ltd.	24,622,164	1.23
17	Guangzhou Iron and Steel Enterprise Group Co., Ltd.	10,779,562	0.54
18	Fujian Fufa Co., Ltd.	7,933,759	0.40
19	Shenzhen Zhongke Venture (Group) Co., Ltd.	6,467,737	0.32
20	Guangdong Zhaoqing Star Lake Biotechnology Co., Ltd.	6,467,737	0.32
Total		2,000,000,000	100
Registered capital: 2 billion yuan			

The shareholding structure showed that GF Securities shares were dispersed, and its largest shareholder, Liaoning Cheng Da Co., Ltd. (hereinafter referred to as Liaoning Cheng Da) only had 20.00 percent equity interest. At that time, China's economy was in a downturn, and some shareholders had a strong desire to cash out their equity in GF Securities due to their own business difficulties or the adjustment of their own business structure. The year 2003 saw the first loss of GF Securities, which also shook the shareholders' confidence in their shareholdings to a certain extent. CITIC Securities' sense of the market was very keen, its grasp of the timing of the takeover was very smart, and its execution of the takeover was very strong. At this point in time, the 20 shareholders were inevitably of different mindsets.

According to CITIC Securities, it had completed its contacts with GF Securities' shareholders without the market noticing, and had obtained the intention to sell more than 30 percent shares. Many media reports had followed up on the attitude of the shareholders.

On September 3, *Securities Times* made the following reports:

> **Liaoning Cheng Da: No intention to transfer for now**
>
> Regarding the announcement of CITIC Securities' intention to acquire equity interest in GF Securities, Liaoning Cheng Da, the largest shareholder of GF Securities, said that the takeover of GF Securities is a unilateral intention of CITIC Securities and has nothing to do with Liaoning Cheng Da. At present, Liaoning Cheng Da has no intention to transfer the equity of GF Securities.
>
> The secretary of Liaoning Cheng Da, Yu Zhanyang, said that the company knew in advance that CITIC Securities has the intention to acquire the equity of GF Securities, and CITIC Securities has communicated with the company on this matter, but the company has no plans to transfer the equity of GF Securities at present. As for the announcement of CITIC Securities, Yu Zhanyang believes that it is a market behavior and it is appropriate for CITIC Securities, as a listed company, to release such an announcement.
>
> We, the reporters, have found out that Liaoning Cheng Da is still optimistic about GF Securities, and some senior people of the company said that if CITIC Securities really becomes the largest shareholder of GF Securities, it may be beneficial to the development of GF Securities, but Liaoning Cheng Da will not give up its shares of GF Securities.
>
> **Guangdong Meiyan: ready to sell at a good price**
>
> Meiyan holds 8.40 percent of the equity of GF Securities, and is its fifth-largest shareholder. The person in charge of the company said that CITIC Securities had not yet expressed its willingness to the company to acquire its equity of GF, but if the price was suitable, the company would consider transferring the equity.
>
> The person said that the company intended to transfer the stake, mainly because its main business was currently transforming to hydropower, and after

the transfer of equity in GF Securities, they could concentrate their energy and capital on the development of hydropower.

After the establishment of GF Venture Capital, the September 8 issue of the *International Financial News* also reported on the movement of shareholders and the progress of the counter-takeover:

> We, the reporters, found out that relevant people from both GF Securities and CITIC Securities are now in an intense stage of work. People from GF Securities have been working outside for several days. And CITIC Securities has also sent staff to actively fight for the shareholders of GF Securities. Apparently, the takeover and counter-takeover war between CITIC Securities and GF Securities has gradually entered the mid-stage of a strength competition.
>
> We learned that GF Securities should had already secured the support of a significant number of shareholders, and its largest shareholder, Liaoning Cheng Da, would definitely support GF Securities' existing management due to years of mutual participation. Another favorable factor is the establishment of GF Venture Capital in early September, which was funded by employees of GF Securities. It will contribute to winning over Liaoning Cheng Da or other shareholders.
>
> For CITIC Securities, its financial strength and background is even better. According to CITIC Securities' 2004 interim report, it has 269 million yuan in unused proceeds. In addition, with the support of CITIC Group, China's top financial conglomerate, CITIC Securities has an unquestionable ability to secure financing. According to another source, Heong Kong Group and Zhujiang Investment have basically confirmed their intention to transfer. It The second- and third-largest shareholders Zhongshan Public Utilities and Jilin Aodong have also begun to be moved, and have now become the main battleground for both sides.

It should be pointed out that the intention of each major shareholder listed in the report had a certain basis, and there were also elements of "psychological description" by media reporters. And based on the willingness of some shareholders to cash out, as well as the previous successful takeover of Wantong Securities, CITIC Securities had reason to believe it had a good chance of winning.

As the attitudes of all parties gradually emerged, the media, which had been observing for days, also found some clues, and public opinion began to be divided.

The September 9 issue of *Securities Times* published a report, "The CITIC-GF M&A Case Intensifies, Three Major Doubts Emerge," asking three questions: Why is CITIC making a high-profile takeover? Why are GF employees strongly opposed? What are the prospects of the takeover? In light of the strong opposition and public statements of more than 2,000 GF employees, the article argued that all this "makes this incident seem somewhat unusual." Citing market speculation, the article that noted that, "CITIC Securities' high-profile takeover is likely a 'tactful' approach, i.e. putting pressure on the parties involved." In terms of speculation about the prospects for the takeover, the article offered a very different view from previous media reports:

> As for the takeover prospects, it is certain that CITIC Securities should have no major problems acquiring part of the stake. As for whether CITIC Securities can become the largest shareholder as it wishes, it remains to be seen. We, the reporters, have found out that in addition to Liaoning Cheng Da's clear indication that it will not transfer its equity, another major shareholder outside Guangzhou is also likely to not transfer its equity, and the combined equity of these two amounts to about 40 percent. In addition, GF Venture Capital has acquired up to 20 percent of the equity. CITIC Securities may not actually be able to match about the 60 percent or so of the equity.
>
> However, the advantage for CITIC Securities is that GF Securities' equity is quite fragmented and there are no local government-controlled stakes, so it's not impossible that the original shareholders can be swayed if the price is attractive enough. This is undoubtedly what CITIC Securities will like to see the most. However, some industry insiders point out that if GF Securities uses all available resources, CITIC Securities' power of action may be compromised. After all, among the shareholders of GF Securities, except for Liaoning Cheng Da and Jilin Aodong, the rest are mainly local companies in Guangdong.

The different public opinions all made a judgment on the intention of shareholders based on the established shareholding structure. On the whole, GF Securities' counter-takeover was still in an extremely unfavorable position. With the attitude of major shareholders such as Liaoning Cheng Da basically clear, the small and medium shareholders with fragmented shareholdings had instead become the relatively dangerous party. In particular, if Meiyan, Yunda, and other shareholders, who had obvious willingness to sell, were once won over by CITIC Securities, this would quickly influence the choice of other shareholders, and the balance of the initiative would be tilted in CITIC Securities' favor.

In the face of the possible "loose chips," which side of the game had more chances to win? Which party could make first good moves?

The newborn company wins

When CITIC Securities seemed set to win and the public was adopting a wait-and-see attitude, the eighth-largest shareholder with 3.83 percent of the shares, Yunda, was first to disclose their choice to the market.

On September 10, Yunda announced that it would transfer 76,621,130 shares of GF Securities to Shenzhen GF Venture Capital. This part of shares accounted for 3.83 percent of the total share capital of GF Securities, and the total price of the transfer was 88.88 million yuan. The transfer was priced with reference to the audited net asset value per share of GF Securities at the end of 2003. Shenzhen GF Venture Capital would pay 60 million yuan by September 10, and the remaining amount would be paid within two working days after Yunda had completed the procedure of releasing the pledge of shares.

GF Venture Capital, which had been established just three days previous, successfully took a 3.83 percent stake in GF Securities in the competition with a powerful rival, which was a shock to the market.

The success of GF Venture Capital's first battle was both unexpected and logical. Jia Ziqiang, the founder of GF Venture Capital, recalled that GF Venture Capital had more than 2,000 shareholders in many parts of China. According to the regulations at that time, the establishment of a joint stock company in Shenzhen required the approval of the Shenzhen Municipal People's Government, which was a huge workload. In order to acquire the equity of GF Securities quickly, in the process of preparing GF Venture Capital, GF Securities had arranged for special persons to contact Yunda on the equity transaction. In early September 2004, Shenzhen GF Venture Capital, while applying for the business license, reached a preliminary agreement with Yunda that the other party would hold a board meeting to consider the relevant transaction matters quickly, which meant that the counterparty, Shenzhen GF Venture Capital, had to be borne on time. On September 6, the personnel of Yunda rushed to Shenzhen in advance to wait for the seal, and on September 7, Shenzhen GF Venture Capital got the business license issued by the Shenzhen Industrial and Commercial Administration as expected, which made it possible for the board of directors of Yunda to consider the motion of equity transfer of GF Securities as scheduled on September 8 to finally complete the meaningful equity deal.

After the first shot of the takeover war, the newly established GF Venture Capital immediately set off waves of speculation. In the market there appeared comments such as "it is uncertain whether CITIC Securities will succeed in its takeover attempt at GF Securities."

In media reports, CITIC Securities reacted strongly, directly questioning the legitimacy of Shenzhen GF Venture Capital. The September 12 issue of *The Economic Observer* reported that:

> CITIC Securities also "bombarded" GF Venture Capital, arguing that out of the 248 million yuan of capital raised by GF Venture Capital from more than 2,000 employees, 6 or 7 million yuan was contributed by some individuals, and that they did not know where some GF people got such a huge amount of money, suspecting that the funds came from bank loans for emergencies, and claiming that they should ask the securities regulator to investigate the source of

the funds. And GF Securities said the details could not be disclosed.

....

In addition, CITIC Securities released the news that it has reached a transfer intention with some shareholders of GF Securities and will soon disclose the progress. The insiders said that the current chips in hand are above 20 percent.

The bottom line of "legitimacy of funds," which had been abided by in the process of employee share subscription, had become a source of strength for GF Venture Capital to accept the scrutiny of all parties. Whether it's the 248 million yuan of registered capital or the "surprising 6 or 7 million yuan of individual contributions" mentioned in the report, outside "concerns" would not interfere with GF Venture Capital's actions.

GF Securities won the first round of the counter-takeover battle, and Shenzhen GF Venture Capital achieved the first success, which also completely woke up CITIC Securities.

3. The last-minute decisive victory

Guangdong Meiyan: ready to sell at a good price

After Yunda, the choice of several shareholders in Guangdong Province would undoubtedly determine the balance of the battle. While making fierce attacks and putting up defense in accordance with the market-oriented rules, the two sides also did not give up their attention to the "visible hand." The media repeatedly speculated that the takeover and counter-takeover battle could be declared over as long as GF Securities could win the support of the Guangdong provincial government and call on the relevant shareholding companies in Guangdong Province to declare their support for GF Securities, or at least "stay silent."

In fact, GF Securities did want to hold on to the last straw, but the public relations with the government had little effect. Before CITIC Securities made its official announcement, GF Securities' management reported to the director of the Financial Work Office of the Guangdong Provincial People's Government, and the province's vice governors and governor through different channels. On September 6, the company requested the provincial government's support in a formal written report (see previous section). The company also communicated with Zhao Wei, the head of the Guangzhou correspondent station of *China Securities Journal*, and asked him to draft an internal report to the relevant leaders of Guangdong Province, suggesting that Guangdong Province should support GF Securities, but there was no response.

The provincial government's attitude was certainly somewhat disappointing to GF Securities, but under the market economy, the government did not interfere with the legal and compliant business practices of market players, which was also a reflection of Guangdong Province's enlightenment and progress. The GF Securities management continued to focus its efforts on the fight for shareholders.

As the matter progressed, the takeover battle entered a tug-of-war phase. CITIC Securities increased its efforts to work with shareholder units, focusing particularly on contacts with those in Guangdong. As early as September 7, Guangdong media reported that "shareholders such as Zhongshan Public Utilities and Heong Kong Group are inclined to transfer their stakes to CITIC Securities, which is basically certain to acquire more than 30 percent of GF Securities."

However, the management of GF Securities had not given up the fight for each shareholder unit, and had been working to win them over according to the established division of labor in several routes.

The fifth-largest shareholder, Meiyan, held 8.40 percent of the shares of GF Securities and is headquartered in Meizhou, Guangdong. GF Securities has the advantage of being located in Guangdong as Meiyan is, and also had the good cooperation story of helping list Meiyan on the Shanghai Stock Exchange. However, in 2004, Meiyan was in the critical period of transformation to the hydropower industry, and the huge investment required made Meiyan feel the pressure, so it was an important choice to guarantee the investment of hydropower project and relieve the pressure of cash flow by selling the equity of GF Securities. Mayan was well aware of the fight between CITIC Securities and GF Securities, and its basic attitude was to sell at a good price.

According to *Southern Metropolis Daily*, CITIC Securities' offer price to Meiyan was 1.25 yuan per share, a high premium. CITIC Securities also predicted that, "Once Meiyan sells to whoever offers the higher price, CITIC Securities will have a higher chance of winning than GF Securities, because GF Securities' employee-owned GF Venture Capital is unlikely to acquire the equity at an excessive premium."

Similar to the fight for Yunda, GF Securities' fight for Meiyan began before the establishment of GF Venture Capital, and it made a more generous offer to it in advance. Although Meiyan showed interest, it had not finalized the matter. Chao Guanghua, head of the company's Brokerage Branch in Meizhou, took advantage of being located in the same city of Meiyan, long acted as a liaison, and usually communicated a lot with Chairman Yang Qinhuan of Meiyan. After the anti-takeover campaign was launched in early September, Chao Guanghua even went to Chairman Yang's office every day to have tea and talk about the market.

On the afternoon of September 12, Chao Guanghua once again finished drinking tea and walked out of Chairman Yang's office. Just before he reached the staircase, he was called back by Chairman Yang. The other party handed him a fax, Chao Guanghua took a look at it, realizing that it was about CITIC Securities' intention to acquire the equity of GF Securities, and asked Chairman Yang "to make this happen." It was sent by an important person. Yang Qinhuan said to Chao Guanghua, "It seems that we can only sell to CITIC Securities." Chao Guanghua was shocked and felt that the situation was serious. After saying goodbye hurriedly, he immediately reported the development to GF Securities' management.

On the same day, another piece of news also reached the GF Securities' management: Zhang Youjun, the managing director and general manager of CITIC Securities, who was about to negotiate with Chairman Yang Qinhuan and sign the equity transfer agreement the next day, was in Meizhou.

CITIC Securities' move was like an imminent war, and at this moment, the survival of GF Securities hung in the balance based on the equity "chips" available to both sides.

The reversal night of September 12

CITIC Securities seemed set to secure Meiyan's shares in GF Securities. At nightfall on September 12, the management and informed employees of GF Securities almost all had this helpless thought.

On the evening of September 12, several former leaders of GF gathered in Foshan and had dinner together amidst bright laughter.

On this day, Wu Chixin, former chairman of Guangdong Development Bank, and Lu Jinchang, former vice president of the bank, were returning to Guangzhou accompanied by Chen Wenzhan of GF Securities. When driving through Foshan, "Uncle Wu" and "Uncle Lu" proposed to get together with Dr. Chen Yunxian, who was the executive vice mayor of Foshan. When Dr. Chen heard about it, he was very enthusiastic to arrange a dinner gathering.

The cordial meeting with "Boss Wu" made Dr. Chen take a break from his busy government work. They happily reminisced about their years in GF. Halfway through the dinner, former leader Wu Chixin took the initiative to ask Dr. Chen, "What do you think about the current takeover of CITIC Securities?"

Although Dr. Chen Yunxian had been following the progress of the takeover battle in the media since early September, he was not at liberty to take a position on GF Securities' affairs due to his key government position. During this period, it was also true that no officials or employees of GF Securities came to consult Dr. Chen for his opinion. Hearing the former leader's question at this time, Dr. Chen immediately expressed his opinion in this non-public communication occasion: "Fight back."

Although he had left GF Securities for a year and a half, Dr. Chen's memory of the company's shareholding structure was still very clear. He casually reported the shareholding ratio of the top shareholders, and after a slight analysis, he said to Wu Chixin, Lu Jinchang, and Chen Wenzhan: "Now Meiyan is critical. We have to find a way to win its support, and see who is in a position to convince it."

After dinner, Wu Chixin and the others continued to rush back to Guangzhou by car. The atmosphere in the car was somewhat silent in the dusky night. After listening to Dr. Chen's analysis, Wu Chixin vaguely felt that CITIC Securities was bound to win the shares of Meiyan, and that GF Securities would probably be in a disadvantageous position, or even move step by step toward the situation of being controlled by CITIC Securities.

In 2004, Guangdong Development Bank started its restructuring, and the Guangdong provincial government no longer controlled it. Many Chinese and foreign strategic investors, including Citibank, participated in the bidding. As the first chairman and president of Guangdong Development Bank, Wu Chixin had an "attachment" to Guangdong's local financial companies. After Guangdong Development Bank, GF Securities was one of the few well-known financial companies in Guangdong. If it lost the battle for equity.... Wu Chixin had an indescribable feeling about it.

When he was about to return home to Guangzhou, former leader Wu Chixin asked Chen Wenzhan, who was in the same car, "Do you still need my help in your company?" Chen Wenzhan said without thinking, "Yes, very much so." Wu Chixin said, "Then I'll try to find someone who can I hope can convince Meiyan. I'll do my best, and you also contact the company's leaders and ask them to get ready."

Under the efforts of the former leader, the main leaders of GF Securities set off from Guangzhou overnight, traveling 500 kilometers overnight, arrived at Meizhou at about 6:00 a.m. on September 13, and rejoined Chao Guanghua of the Meizhou Brokerage Branch who had been waiting there for a long time. They then went straight to the residence of Yang Qinhuan, the chairman of Meiyan.

At 7:00 a.m., after opening the door and seeing the people from GF Securities, Chairman Yang Qinhuan was very surprised. He then waved his hand and said, "If you enter my home, people would think there is something fishy in the transfer of equity. Let's go to the office to talk about it."

Visitors from GF Securities knew very well that this window of time was very valuable, and it was important to negotiate the transfer of equity before the leader of CITIC Securities arrived. As soon as they entered Chairman Yang's office, they all started to discuss the advantages and disadvantages from all levels, analyzed to the chairman the benefits gained by Meiyan in its investment in GF Securities, and expressed GF Securities' sincerity. Taking advantage of Yang Qinhuan's somewhat changed attitude, they started the negotiation on the transfer price, and finally an agreement was reached. And then the agreement of transferring the equity of GF Securities to Shenzhen GF Venture Capital was signed.

When Chairman Yang Qinhuan sent visitors from GF Securities out of the office, he ran into the leader of CITIC Securities who had come as promised. Chairman Yan Qinhuan said with both hands stretched, "There is no way out."

According to the agreement reached between the two sides, Shenzhen GF Venture Capital took 8.40 percent of the equity of GF Securities held by Meiyan at a price of more than 200 million yuan (with a first payment of 140 million yuan). At this point, Shenzhen GF Venture Capital's stake in GF Securities had reached 12.23 percent, making it the fourth-largest shareholder of GF Securities, behind

Liaoning Cheng Da (20.00 percent), Zhongshan Public Utilities Group (15.00 percent), and Jilin Aodong (13.75 percent).

On the occasion of Meizhou's success, Zhongshan Public Utilities, the second-largest shareholder located in Zhongshan, also stabilized its attitude toward its equity holdings. The former leaders of GF Securities contacted through their personal relationship, and finally convinced the major shareholder of Zhongshan Public Utilities who decided not to consider transferring the equity of GF Securities for the time being.

Was the reversal that happened on the night of September 12, 2004 a coincidence or an inevitability? Was the fate from Meizhou to Guangzhou, Foshan, and Zhongshan intentional or unintentional? Was it the visible hand or the invisible hand that finally tipped the scales? Perhaps this was a heavenly reward for hard work.

4. The establishment of the shareholding structure for long-term stability

The white knight increases its holdings

The third-largest shareholder of GF Securities, Jilin Aodong, held 13.75 percent of shares. In the takeover battle that lasted for many days, Jilin Aodong, headquartered in the northeast, had attracted the attention of both sides. CITIC Securities had made use of its strong public relations power to contact Jilin Aodong several times for the transfer its equity.

Where to go? There were heated debates within Jilin Aodong. The main view at that time was that Jilin Aodong's main business was very profitable and it should cash out its equity in GF Securities to focus on its main business.

After 6:00 p.m. on September 14, Dr. Wang Liangzhong, general manager of the GF Securities Development Research Center, who was working overtime, suddenly received a message from the company's management: "The Development Research Center must come up with a research report tonight to fully explain the future development prospects of China's securities market and the investment value of securities companies. I will be downstairs at the headquarters building tomorrow at 6:00 a.m., and I must have the report."

Dr. Wang Liangzhong immediately contacted Chen Xuebin, deputy director of the Development Research Center, and researchers Chen Xiaoshun and Yu Xiaoyi. The four met in the office and immediately went to work. By the time a complete study was printed out, it was 4:00 a.m. The four of them took a nap in the office. At 6:00 a.m., Dr. Wang opened his eyes and went downstairs to deliver the research report to the company leader who was waiting in the car. The streets were deserted in September, and Dr. Wang watched the car drive toward the airport and disappear in an instant.

On September 16, Jilin Aodong, whose attitude had not been clear before, made an announcement that stirred a burst of admiration in the securities market.

Jilin Aodong announced to the market that it had acquired 2.16 percent shares of GF Securities Co., Ltd. held by Guangdong Fenghua High-Tech Group Co., Ltd., totaling 43,118,250 shares, with a transaction amount of 50,362,116 yuan; and acquired 1.23 percent shares of GF Securities held by Jilin Aodong Pharmaceutical Group Yanji Co., Ltd. for a total of 24,622,164 shares, with a transaction amount of 28,758,687 yuan, for a total payment of 79,120,083 yuan for the two takeovers.

Not only had Jilin Aodong not transferred its shareholdings, but it also unexpectedly increased its holdings. After the completion of the transaction, Jilin Aodong's stake in GF Securities rose from 13.75 percent to 17.14 percent, surpassing Zhongshan Public Utilities to become the second-largest shareholder of GF Securities.

In Western M&A cases, the investor who saved the company from being taken over in bad faith from an unfavorable situation was called a "white knight." In the face of external interference and internal dissent, Jilin Aodong finally supported GF Securities, which did not have the upper hand, with its actions.

The cooperation between GF Securities and Jilin Aodong began in 1998. At that time, Jilin Aodong's had its first rights issue. As 8.62 million legal person shares gave up their eligibility, the lead underwriter GF Securities bought more than eight million legal person rights issue shares. In 2001, these shares were allowed to became tradable, but GF Securities did not liquidate them because it was optimistic about the prospects of Jilin Aodong. After two rights issues, GF Securities still held more than 12 million tradable shares of Jilin Aodong in 2004. Jilin Aodong participated in the placement of GF Securities, thus forming a mutual shareholding situation.

The reason for choosing to be the "white knight" was not only the emotional factor accumulated through years of cooperation, but also the decision-makers' awareness of the development prospect of the securities industry and their recognition of the value of GF Securities as an excellent company.

CITIC Securities' best move: making a high premium offer

With the clear attitude of several shareholders, GF Securities was out of the most dangerous area, but still did not fully obtain the controlling initiative.

In the midgame, CITIC Securities quickly took a strong countermeasure: a tender offer. This strategy was decided by September 15 and sent to all GF Securities shareholders on September 16. On September 17, *China Securities Journal* reported in detail the adjustment of CITIC's takeover strategy in the form of a "Q&A":

Q: As the first case of market-based M&A of a securities company in China, CITIC Securities' takeover of part of GF Securities has received widespread attention from all walks of life, and people are very concerned about the progress of the takeover. What is the progress of the takeover so far?

A: CITIC Securities held a board meeting on September 1 and passed a proposal to acquire part of the equity interests of GF Securities Co., Ltd. Under the authorization of CITIC Securities' board of directors, its management has made extensive contacts with the shareholders of GF Securities in strict accordance with laws and regulations, and has disclosed necessary information.

In accordance with the principles of openness, fairness, impartiality, and market orientation, CITIC Securities has issued a tender offer to all existing shareholders of GF Securities to acquire equity interests on September 16, and plans to reach a unified equity transfer agreement with shareholders that intend to offer equity interests in GF Securities, so as to improve the operational efficiency of equity transfer and smoothly achieve CITIC Securities' goal of acquiring part of the equity interests in GF Securities.

Q: The audited net asset value per share of GF Securities as of December 31, 2003 was 1.168 yuan. How was the takeover price determined in the offer issued by CITIC Securities to all shareholders of GF Securities?

A: The takeover price will be based on the evaluated net asset value per share of GF Securities and on the premise that the acquirer will bear certain risks and fully reflect the interests of the existing shareholders of GF Securities. In addition, the preliminary transferee price and a reasonable premium were determined.

The initial price of the equity transfer was determined to be 1.25 yuan per share, and a price adjustment mechanism was designed on this basis. According to this adjustment mechanism, CITIC Securities will ensure a 10 percent to 14 percent premium on the appraised value of the equity interest of the transferring shareholders of GF Securities, regardless of the final appraised value of GF Securities.

Q: The transfer price and the method for paying it are the two issues of most concern to the transferring shareholders. What kind of payment method will your company adopt for the takeover price?

A: The purchase price of the equity transfer will be paid in cash. As the equity transfer needs to go through a series of legal procedures, the equity takeover price will be paid in three installments, namely, 20 percent of the total transfer price as advance payment after signing the transfer agreement; 50 percent of the total transfer price (including the aforementioned advance payment) after the equity transfer agreement is approved and effective; and the remaining amount will be settled immediately after the completion of the equity change registration procedures.

Q: After the offer, the shareholders that are interested in the offer will have to express their intention to CITIC Securities to transfer their equity interests.

How are these arrangements made in terms of operating procedures?

A: According to the takeover target, specific takeover conditions were set out in the tender offer. The shareholders that intend to transfer their equity interests are required to deliver the original "Letter of Intent to Transfer Equity Interests" within the prescribed time limit, expressing their intention to transfer their equity interests in accordance with the takeover conditions set forth in the offer. My company will determine the transferring shareholders and the shares to be transferred in the order of delivery as determined by the notary, and will stop accepting new letters of intention when the total shares intended to be transferred reach 51 percent of the total share capital of GF Securities. Subsequently, my company will sign a formal equity transfer agreement with the transferring shareholders in accordance with the agreed time frame.

Q: Why did CITIC Securities adopt the tender offer approach and what are the characteristics of this takeover?

A: We believe that there are three outstanding features in this takeover process, namely the innovation of the tender offer method, market-oriented operation, and adequate information disclosure.

In the process of steadily advancing the equity takeover, we have adopted the takeover method of tender offer, which is a targeted invitation of tender offer to all existing shareholders of GF Securities. The offer invitation is consistent in terms of equity transfer conditions, such as the price and payment method, thus reflecting the principle of equal shares and equal rights. We also hope to complete the transaction in a fully market-oriented operation.

The "tender offer" was a wonderful takeover tactic that GF Securities did not anticipate at all, and it was also a major innovation for listed companies to acquire the equity of non-listed companies. From the perspective of the development of China's securities market, it was also a contribution to this market-oriented takeover and counter-takeover.

From the announcement, it could be seen that in the face of Shenzhen GF Venture Capital's swift action, CITIC Securities promptly adjusted its strategy from a one-to-one contractual takeover to a one-to-many tender offer, disclosing to the market the terms, price, duration, and other elements of the takeover. This not only helped CITIC Securities to cut the communication and time costs in the fierce takeover battle, but also demonstrated its strength to the shareholders with a more favorable price, which compressed the space for GF Securities and GF Venture Capital to negotiate with the shareholders separately.

Moreover, the takeover price of 1.25 yuan per share was quite attractive. In a sense, in addition to the shares pocketed by Shenzhen GF Venture Capital, other shares of shareholders had the possibility of accepting this tempting condition. The clause that CITIC Securities "will stop accepting new letters of intention when the total shares intended to be transferred reach 51 percent of the total share capital of GF Securities" not only clearly declared CITIC Securities' intention to take a controlling share in GF Securities, but also intended to create a gaming effect among the shareholders.

Obviously, CITIC Securities was convinced that with its resource background, capital advantage, and brand influence, it could acquire the remaining shares of GF Securities to the largest extent and win the market-based takeover.

The "Iron Triangle" lays the foundation of victory

After the offer of CITIC Securities was issued, the management of GF Securities did not respond publicly, but was actually in a "fearful" situation. Executive Vice President Dr. Li Jianyong recalled years later, "If CITIC Securities had raised the price a little bit more, we would have lost."

For more than a week, there was still no response from shareholders willing to sell their stakes in GF Securities.

Perhaps the shareholders had realized that the takeover and counter-takeover had evolved so intensely in just two weeks that CITIC Securities had gone out of its way to offer a high premium, wasn't that just another reflection of the intrinsic value of GF Securities' equity?

Of course, at this time, GF Securities did not dare to slow down for a moment, and its leaders continued to contact each shareholder according to their division of work.

In this rare "firefight interval," various financial media also continued to explore hot spots for coverage. After Jilin Aodong increased its holdings and CITIC Securities issued an offer announcement, a reporter from *Shanghai Securities News* interviewed Chairman Li Xiulin of Jilin Aodong on September 22. In the face of the reporter's assumption that "if Jilin Aodong transfers its stake to CITIC Securities, it can gain several million yuan of investment income," Li Xiulin's reply again drew the market's appreciation: "Jilin Aodong will not be moved and will not consider transferring its stake in GF Securities. If CITIC Securities withdraws, Jilin Aodong will take the opportunity to increase its stake in GF Securities to 20 percent."

In this interview, Chairman Li Xiulin further disclosed the important information that Jilin Aodong had communicated with Liaoning Cheng Da, hoping to increase its stake so that it, too, could become the largest shareholder of GF Securities. CITIC Securities and Jilin had also communicated on the phone, but the latter believed that the securities market had just seen an improvement and it would not be moved by the takeover price of 1.25 yuan per share and would not consider transferring the equity of GF Securities.

The attitude of "hoping to increase its stake so that it, too, can become the largest shareholder of GF Securities" meant that Liaoning Cheng Da, Jilin Aodong, and Shenzhen GF Venture Capital were conducting concerted actions. The equity held by this "iron triangle" at this time was close to absolute control.

On September 28, the "iron triangle" made the final blow to lay the foundation for victory. Liaoning Cheng Da and Jilin Aodong released an announcement at the same time to increase their stake in GF Securities again.

The announcement of Liaoning Cheng Da disclosed that on September 24, 2004, the company signed a share transfer agreement with Meida, in which Meida transferred all of its 34,494,600 shares of GF Securities to Liaoning Cheng Da, whose shareholding in GF Securities increased from 51,169,600 shares to 54,614,200 shares, accounting for 27.31 percent of its total share capital.

Jilin Aodong announced that, following the announcement on September 16 to increase its stake in GF Securities by 3.39 percent, on September 24, 2004, it signed a share transfer agreement with Guangdong Zhujiang Investment Co., Ltd., acquiring the latter's 200 million shares in GF Securities, or 10 percent of the total. After the completion of the transaction, Jilin Aodong held 27.14 percent of the shares of GF Securities.

By now, Liaoning Cheng Da and Jilin Aodong had become the first- and second-largest shareholders of GF Securities, respectively, with a large shareholding advantage, and the shares held by the two companies amounted to 54.45 percent of GF Securities. Together with the shares held by Shenzhen GF Venture Capital, the "iron triangle" controlled 66.68 percent of the equity. The situation in this high-level takeover and counter-takeover battle in the Chinese securities market was completely clear.

On October 14, CITIC Securities announced that the company's offer to acquire the equity of GF Securities had not reached the expected target of 51 percent, and the offer was therefore cancelled.

The employees of GF Securities, who had been nervous for more than a month, were finally relieved. They were all hands-on participants in this classic case that would remain in the history of China's securities development. When they met with a powerful rival on a narrow road, more than two thousand people showed their courage.

After the crisis was lifted, GF Securities then took stock and reflected. Long-term inherent weaknesses in the shareholding structure had not previously attracted sufficient internal attention, and the counter-takeover was perhaps a "war that could have been avoided." After the market-oriented counter-takeover experience, the equity relationship of strategic investment in Liaoning Cheng Da and Jilin Aodong was strengthened, and the pattern of relatively concentrated holding by major shareholders was formed, laying the foundation of long-term stability in the equity structure.

The market-oriented mechanism and care for the employees were the important advantages of GF Securities in the long run. Throughout the takeover battle, the acquirer failed to indicate the post-takeover development prospects to the employees of GF Securities, and the firm opposition of GF Securities employees to the takeover could be said to have exceeded general expectations. In contrast to the employees in other securities firms and other industry takeovers, the cultural traits of GF Securities were very distinct. The victory of the market-based counter-takeover was also a victory of values that highly valued the vital interests of employees. After this battle, GF Securities' management gained a deep understanding of the concept that "people are the most valuable asset of a securities company." This experience has been inherited in the management of GF Securities for many years since then.

During the takeover war, many mainstream financial media had a high degree of excitement for the news that kept coming out, but also generally remained neutral and objective. While the winner had already been decided, the financial press, which had been watching for a long time, seemed to be still not satisfied, "helping" both sides to make many levels of summaries.

Securities Times commented in "The Case of CITIC Securities' Purchase of GF Securities Ends Calmly with Three Major Reasons for the Loss":

> GF Securities was blessed by the disaster. For GF Securities, another major victory in the shareholding battle was that employee shareholding has been launched naturally and the company was expected to gain more understanding and recognition from various parties. For the establishment of GF Venture Capital, GF Securities had been quite low-key, and the secrecy had been well protected, and no media disclosure had been made before that. One of the main reasons was that employee shareholding in financial companies was still a sensitive topic at the moment. With the outbreak of the shareholding battle, the establishment of GF Venture Capital Corporation could be said to be justified, and to have given full play to its positive role in maintaining the stability of the shareholding structure and improving the corporate governance structure. Of course, for the management of GF Securities, after the employees took out hundreds of millions of yuan of "real money," employee shareholding also meant greater pressure.

China Securities Journal, focusing on "marketization," analyzed the deeper implications:

> From the moment the battle between takeover and counter-takeover began, a term had repeatedly appeared in the rhetoric of the two opposing sides: "marketization." Both sides had tried to boast that they were operating on market-based principles, while each seemed to suggest, consciously or unconsciously, that the other side had a non-market-based bias. And so far, market-oriented was the most significant feature of this merger war. Unlike the administrative trusteeship and mergers that were common in previous brokerage industry consolidations, this merger and purchase was about strength-based standardized market operations. GF Securities, which had grown up completely

by exploring in the market for more than a decade, had seven successful M&As and a clearer judgment of its own strength and the condition of its shareholders; while CITIC Securities, a listed company, had made it clear from its opening statement that it wanted to operate in a standardized and transparent manner according to market-oriented rules, emphasizing that the merger and takeover was a matter at the shareholder level, and that the idea of "whoever offers the higher price wins" was the minimum market principle. It should be said that this was a reciprocal game with common rules, and this is the direction that the Chinese management had been advocating:

A thousand-mile journey starts with the first step. The textbook of China's market-oriented securities industry is being written in practice, chapter by chapter. From this perspective, the CITIC Securities-GF Securities case, no matter how it ends up, has significance far beyond the case itself. We expect it to be a complete case of market-oriented operation, as it will provide a benchmark for the future, offering valuable experience and lessons in various respects, thus contributing to the healthy development of China's securities market and Chinese brokerage firms.

CITIC Securities' leader had said more than once that the company's goal was to become "a Goldman Sachs in China." After the setback in acquiring GF Securities, CITIC Securities quickly beat the drum again, and in the following two years, it acquired Jintong Securities, Huaxia Securities, and Huaxia Fund with a high degree of execution, establishing itself as one of the leading securities firms in China and setting an example for the securities industry in many ways.

During the bull market in 2007, the overall performance of the brokerage stocks, with CITIC Securities as the leader, was spectacular. And "in a bull market, hold on to brokerage stocks" became the "belief" of many stockholders. The intrinsic value of securities company shares had also been re-examined by the entire capital markets. After a deep understanding of the stock market was required, the ultra-low valuation of the brokerage industry similar to that around 2004 was no longer possible. CITIC Securities, Liaoning Cheng Da, and Jilin Aodong, which had predicted the development trend of the securities industry in advance in 2004, had reaped huge dividends since then.

GF Venture Capital has evolved since then and is no longer a platform for employee shareholding, but it has still brought great wealth rewards for the loyalty and wisdom of its 2,126 employees, some of whom had gained nearly 20 times their investment. GF Venture Capital has also left many topics of conversation for employees of different ages of GF Securities: "How many shares of GF Venture Capital did you buy back then?" This has become a unique salutation to greet the old employees of GF Securities. Of course, everyone also enjoys the beautiful legend of "being forced to subscribe at that time, and finally being forced to get rich."

Chapter IX: Going Public

The spirit of persisting in a great cause requires unswerving spirit.

—Voltaire

1. "Shareholding" as part of the four-pronged approach

Forward-looking thinking of the shareholding structure

The dream of going public of GF Securities should be traced back to 1994, when Dr. Chen Yunxian formally put forward the four-pronged approach of GF Securities, namely "shareholding, conglomeration, internationalization, and standardization." The "shareholding" was the starting point of GF Securities' dream of going public.

Although "shareholding" was a common term in today's economic activities, it was still a controversial and fashionable term in China at the early stage of reform and opening up. The economics world in China knows "Shares Li," "Stock market Xiao," and "Market Wu." The "Shares Li" refers to Mr. Li Yining, an economist known for his active promotion of the shareholding economy.

In the 1980s, Li Yining saw with a keen eye the important role of the shareholding system in promoting China's economic development. He called for it in many important conferences and published an article in *People's Daily*, suggesting that the best means of economic reform was to use the shareholding system to transform existing SOEs and large collective companies. Mr. Li Yining's shareholding theory later became an important theoretical support for China to promote the development capital markets and the reform of SOEs.

Of course, Mr. Li Yining was not the only one who actively promoted the shareholding economy during this period. Economists such as Dong Fureng, Xiao Zhuoji, and Jiang Yiwei all conducted more in-depth studies in this regard. It was under their active promotion that the shareholding economy was gradually unfolding amidst the argument of whether a shareholding economy was capitalist or socialist.

In November 1993, the Third Plenary Session of the 14th CPC Central Committee discussed a number of important issues concerning the establishment of a socialist market economy and issued the Decision of the CPC Central Committee on Issues concerning the Establishment of a Socialist Market economy (hereinafter referred to as the Decision), in which it was clearly stated that "China should establish a modern corporate structure with clearly established ownership, well-defined power and responsibility, separation of government administration and enterprise management, and scientific management to meet the requirements of the market economy."

On shareholding, the Decision proposed, "In qualified large and medium-sized SOEs, a single investment body can be restructured into a wholly-owned company, multiple investment bodies can be restructured into limited liability companies or joint-stock companies in accordance with the law. Only a few joint-stock companies can go public subject to strict review." It could be seen that in the environment of the early 1990s, the start of "shareholding" was not an easy task.

As a disciple of the famous economist Xiao Zhuoji, Dr. Chen Yunxian had an early contact with the idea of shareholding and further deepened his understanding of the advanced nature of shareholding in the process of GF Securities' management practice. Especially for solving some practical problems of GF Securities, "shareholding" was a must.

The securities business needed sufficient capital support, such as for underwriting business and new business outlets. In the case of limited inherent resources, seeking capital support was undoubtedly a path that could quickly improve development efficiency. In turn, investors wanted to make their shares tradable and increase their wealth. Thus, shareholding was a win-win option for both the company and the investors.

In addition, the Chinese capital markets in the 1990s was like a newborn baby, with no sound external regulations, no sound internal systems, and no rich practical cases. Talent was essential for securities firms to stand out from the competition and achieve sound development. How to gather talents at the top of the industry pyramid and make these senior talents actively dedicate to the company? Dr. Chen believed that exploring employee stock ownership on the basis of shareholding was an important way to seek the common development of individuals and the company.

Dr. Chen had more ideas about shareholding in GF Securities.

First, how should "shareholding" be implemented at the group level? How to ensure that the capital injection does not affect the management decisions and the established development direction of the company? In the market cases, the injection of capital and the change of shareholding structure may have a significant impact on the management of the company. In 1994, the famous "Jun'an-Vanke dispute" staged a malicious takeover of capital.

GF Securities must not only introduce bold capital to promote the company's steady development, but also not let the introduction of capital affect the existing management process and structure: "The ideal shareholding framework should be that the group level, where the management hub is located, does not go public, but instead it should split all the business into subsidiaries and then lists all the subsidiaries." In Dr. Chen's opinion, if the group was not listed, the capital could make an impact on the group's management; and the listed subsidiaries could be restrained and supervised with the help of regulatory laws and regulations and the power of the market to prevent their operational risks and avoid their risks from affecting the whole group.

Second, how would the equity structure be set?

The company's equity structure is the cornerstone of corporate governance, and the property rights basis of corporate governance, and plays an important role in the long-term sustainable development of the company. Dr. Chen understood the importance of this, so he had carefully designed the equity structure from the beginning to maximize the advantages of a balanced equity structure.

There are three main types of equity structures in the market: the "major shareholder control model" with a controlling shareholder or an effective controller, the "insider control model" with no dominant shareholders and a large number of minority shareholders, and the "no effective shareholder control model" with a small number of significant shareholders and a certain number of minority shareholders (note: many people generally classify the "no effective shareholder control model" as the "insider control model," which is inaccurate. To avoid confusion, the "no effective shareholder control model" will be referred to as the "balanced control model" below).

If the equity structure of a joint-stock company is different, the behavior of shareholders will be different, too, and the impact on the functioning of the corporate governance structure will also be different, so the appropriateness of the equity structure will directly affect the efficiency of corporate governance. The major shareholder control model is characterized by a major shareholder holding more than 50 percent of the shares, or more than 30 percent of the shares and having actual control. This is true with subordinate companies whose controlling shares are held by SOEs or that are controlled by SOEs, or subordinate companies whose controlling shares are held by private enterprises or that are controlled by private enterprises. The members of the board of directors of such companies are basically all directly decided by the major shareholder, and the management of the company is also indirectly decided by the major shareholder.

The advantage of this governance model is the high efficiency of decision making, the disadvantage is the high risk of loss. The more concentrated the equity, the higher the cost of risk. In addition, there will be a situation where the major shareholder usess up all the funds of the controlled company in order to encroach on the interests of small and medium shareholders. An important condition to take advantage of this governance model and prevent its disadvantages is to have good external governance and monitoring mechanisms for the whole market or economy. In the case of a state-controlled model, there is also a situation where the chain of governance is too long and efficiency is compromised.

Dr. Chen was keenly aware that if the major shareholder control model was adopted in the prevailing Chinese market environment, the company would be subject to the major shareholder while the external governance and monitoring mechanism of the market was weak, making it difficult to sustain the development in the long run.

The insider control model is characterized by the fact that the shareholders of the company are basically financial investors who have a "free-rider" mentality toward the development of the company, while the management of the company is the core part of the corporate governance structure and is most familiar with the business, has the most say in the development strategy of the company, and is most concerned about the development of the company.

After carefully studying this equity model, Dr. Chen concluded that a full insider control model was also difficult to ensure the company sustained development in the long run. According to Chen, this model would make it difficult for shareholders to act on the governance efficiency of the entire company through internal control mechanisms, and operators might make adverse selections and have moral hazards.

The balanced control model is characterized by the balance of forces. Under this model, no single major shareholder can have the exclusive right to speak, but several important shareholders can unite to have the right to decide. This also avoids the situation in which the major shareholder uses up the funds of the company or encroaches on the interests of the company. The management has the right to decide on the daily management, but if there are matters beyond the scope of authorization, it is necessary to obtain the consent of important shareholders. This mechanism can largely prevent the management's adverse selections and moral hazards.

According to the characteristics of the securities industry, how could the arrangement of the equity structure balance supervisory power and operational efficiency? How should the shareholding proportion of the company's shareholders be reasonably set? How should the historical development of GF

Securities be balanced with its future development? In the process of such forward thinking, GF Securities embarked on the shareholding reform.

Implementation of shareholding reform

In December 1996, with the approval of the People's Bank of China, Guangdong GF Securities Company underwent the first shareholding reform and conducted placement. After the placement, the registered capital of the company increased to 800 million yuan, of which 600 million was newly raised. The number of shareholders also increased from one to 18, and Guangdong Development Bank became the largest shareholder with a capital contribution of 200 million yuan, holding 25 percent of the company's shares.

With the approval of the General Office of the Guangdong Provincial People's Government, Guangdong Provincial Economic and Trade Commission and CSRC, Guangdong GF Securities Company was restructured and renamed as GF Securities Co., Ltd., which was free from the local title and meant that the status of GF Securities as a major national brokerage firm was clarified.

In August 1999, GF Securities Co., Ltd. was decoupled from Guangdong Development Bank and conducted placement. Subsequently, the registered capital was increased to 1.6 billion yuan. In the same year, the CSRC approved the company as a comprehensive securities company.

In July 2001, GF Securities Co., Ltd. completed the change of registration and increased its registered capital to two billion yuan. When GF Securities completed the change of registration, it had 20 shareholders.

Liaoning Cheng Da Co., Ltd., the largest shareholder at that time, held 400 million shares of GF Securities, accounting for 20 percent. Liaoning Cheng Da was established in 1993 and listed on the Shanghai Stock Exchange in 1996. At that time, Liaoning Cheng Da was mainly engaged in the import and export business of cotton knitted products, wool knitted products, home textiles, and garments, as well as the business of pharmaceutical chains, financial investment, commercial investment, and foreign trade. In 2001, Liaoning Cheng Da achieved a main business revenue of 1.487 billion yuan and a main business profit of 188 million yuan (source: Liaoning Cheng Da 2001 annual report).

The second-largest shareholder at that time, Zhongshan Public Utilities Group Co., Ltd., held 300 million shares of GF Securities, accounting for 15 percent. The company was the controlling shareholder of the listed company Zhongshan Utilities Science and Technology Co., Ltd. The scope of business of Zhongshan Public Utilities Group Co., Ltd. was to invest, manage, and provide services to companies it was authorized to operate (source: Zhongshan Public Utilities Annual Report 2001).

Jilin Aodong Pharmaceutical Group Co., Ltd., the third-largest shareholder at that time, held 275 million shares of GF Securities, accounting for 13.75 percent of the shares. Jilin Aodong was established in 1993 and listed on the Shenzhen Stock Exchange in 1996. At that time, Jilin Aodong was a large national Class II company with pharmaceutical industry and deer breeding as its basic industry, and engaged in a combination of printing, commerce, and breeding industry. The main products of the company, "Anshen Bunao Syrup" and "Linaoxin," were awarded "Chinese Famous Brand of Traditional Chinese Medicine" by the State Administration of Traditional Chinese Medicine. "Anshen Bunao Syrup," "Linaoxin," "Xuefu Zuyu," "Yixuesheng," and "Xinnao Shutong" were put under state protection. In 2001, Jilin Aodong achieved a main business income of 360 million yuan and a main business profit of 219 million yuan (source: Jilin Aodong 2001 annual report).

The other 17 shareholders were Guangdong Zhujiang Investment Co., Ltd., Guangdong Meiyan Enterprise (Group) Co., Ltd., Heong Kong Group Co., Ltd., Zhejiang Xinlian Co., Ltd., Kunming Yunda Science & Technology Industry Co., Ltd., Jiuquan Iron and Steel (Group) Co., Ltd., Hengtong Group Company, Anhui Huamao Textile Co., Ltd., Shenzhen Special Economic Zone Real Estate (Group) Co., Ltd., Guangdong Xinhui Meida Nylon Co., Ltd., Liaoning Foreign Trade Property Development Company, Jilin Aodong Pharmaceutical Group Yanji Co., Ltd., Guangzhou Iron and Steel Enterprise Group Co., Ltd., Fujian Fufa Co., Ltd., China Venture Capital (Group) Co., Ltd. of Shenzhen and Guangdong Zhaoqing Star Lake Biotechnology Co., Ltd. At that time, these 20 shareholders from all over the country were all leaders in various industries, and most of were listed companies or high-quality private companies.

Thus, under Dr. Chen's plan, GF Securities completed the equity structure under the "balanced control model." In this model, there was "no single major shareholder," "three significant shareholders are independent and hold about half of the total shares," and there were "numerous minority shareholders." The final picture of the early equity structure was that "Liaoning Cheng Da has 20.00 percent of the shares, Zhongshan Public Utilities, 15.00 percent, and Jilin Aodong, 13.75 percent, totaling 48.75 percent, and 17 other shareholders have 51.75 percent of the shares."

It can be seen that these 20 shareholders not only had relatively dispersed shareholdings and were located in very different parts of China, but also were mostly clients or important partners of GF Securities. In the history of GF Securities, the shareholder structure under the "balanced control model" had remained unchanged despite changes in the shareholding ratio and ranking of major shareholders.

Dr. Chen had also given a lot of thought to the structure of the board of directors. A scientific and reasonable board structure enables the board of directors to efficiently exercise its business decision-making function and evaluate and supervise the management, which is related to the long-term development of the company and the protection of shareholders' interests.

The board of directors of GF Securities maintained a stable structure of three thirds, i.e. one third for shareholder directors, one third for executive directors who were substantially responsible for management, and one third for independent directors who were outside professionals.

This structure of the board of directors was not only a concrete implementation of the balanced control model, but also a balance achieved by the game of forces. In this structure, no one type of directors could have the exclusive right to speak, but the majority of directors could have the right to decide when they reached consensus, thus avoiding the situation of using up the funds of the company or encroaching on the interests of the company under the control model of shareholder directors; the executive directors of the company could observe from the perspectives of major shareholders, small and medium shareholders, the company and employees; and the independent directors of the company could express their opinions in a more independent and transcendent role.

The quality of the board of directors was an important indicator to determine the future performance and development of the company. After the shareholding reform, GF Securities had maintained a relatively balanced equity structure and board composition, which had built a superstructure of close cooperation and sound operation for the future development of the company. In particular, the setup of independent directors of GF Securities was a leading practice of the independent director system of China's brokerage firms. With an eye on "high starting point and high configuration" and to better improve the corporate governance structure, GF Securities had invited a group of experts with high reputation both at home and abroad to join the board of directors. Professor Chen Xiaoyue, vice president of Beijing National Accounting Institute, Professor Jiang Ping, PhD supervisor of China University of Political Science and Law, Professor K. C. Chan, acting dean of business and management at the Hong Kong University of Science and Technology (who became secretary for Financial Services and the Treasury of the Hong Kong Special Administrative Region in 2012 and Finance Secretary at the end of 2016), Professor Li Yang, director of the Center for Financial Studies of the Chinese Academy of Social Sciences, Professor Lu Zhiyang of University of Southern California, and Mr. So Chak Kwong, chairman and chief executive officer of the Hong Kong MTR Corporation were appointed as independent directors of GF Securities.

Of course, shareholding reform both established an important superstructure and was closely related to the company's history and realistic development, and a flawless equity structure did not exist. In the early days of the industry, GF Securities benefited more from the "balanced control model," but also had a crisis of equity being taken over in the evolution of the securities industry because of the absence of controlling shareholders. Even today it is not completely free from this problem. What's right here may be wrong elsewhere. This was perhaps another practical experience that GF Securities has provided for the industry.

2. Exploring employee stock ownership

Being careful in the dark tide

As a foresighted institutional arrangement, Dr. Chen included management shareholding and employee shareholding when considering the implementation path of shareholding. The "shareholding" in the four-pronged approach proposed in 1994 not only refers to the establishment of a modern corporate system and the absorption of powerful institutions into the company, but also implies the possibility of making employees shareholders. Further, in the Corporate Culture Program of GF Securities in 1999, one of Dr. Chen's ideas was included: "To let employees become the legal owners of material wealth under the protection of the system."

Shortly before or after this event, there had been a dark tide of employee share ownership in the Chinese securities industry. In 1997, Jun'an Securities made a secret attempt at management stock ownership, but was investigated for irregularities in the operation, and the company and its leaders were doomed, becoming a lesson for the industry.

Although there was a tide of employee stock ownership in the industry, the thoughtful Dr. Chen did not take any chances.

On September 17, 1999, the second annual extraordinary shareholders' meeting revised the company's articles of association, which added to the article on shareholders' fulfillment of obligations: "As soon as permitted by law and policy, shareholders shall transfer not less than 10 percent of their capital contributions to the company's employees or employee shareholding associations at a preferential price not higher than the net assets." In July 2001, when GF Securities Limited Company was changed to GF Securities Co., Ltd., in order to further clarify the arrangements for the establishment of the long-term mechanism of GF Securities, it was specified in the articles of association adopted by the founding meeting of the company that the shareholders shall transfer to the employees of the company or the employee shareholding association at a price not higher than the audited net assets per share of the company in equal proportions. In comparison with the long-term incentive mechanism arrangement in 1999, the arrangement of "equal proportional transfer by the founding shareholders" and "a total of 10 percent shares" was more clearly defined. This provision was maintained until February 2010 when GF Securities was listed through a shell of delisted company, i.e. until the legal entity of the former GF Securities was cancelled. The relevant arrangement in the articles of association reflects the far-reaching consideration of GF Securities shareholders about the establishment of a long-term mechanism.

In addition, in the 1999 Articles of Association, it was stipulated that a fund for employees' entrepreneurial contributions would be set aside from the company's after-tax profits to reward employees who contributed to the company's performance. In that year, GF Securities began to set aside 5.88 percent of its after-tax profit as a contribution fund for employee entrepreneurship, laying the foundation for employee stock ownership thereafter.

In October 1998, GF Securities became the second-largest shareholder of Liaoning Cheng Da by acquiring 25.6 million shares (18.61 percent of the total share capital) held by the Liaoning Provincial State-Owned Assets Supervision and Administration Commission. The cross-shareholding between the two companies was both a check-and-balance arrangement and paved the way for GF Securities' employee shareholding two years later, providing an alliance for the subsequent counter-takeover battle.

The buyback plan received the approval of major shareholders, but the policy environment did not allow this and there was a lack of successful precedents, and this made it difficult to clarify the specific operational plan of the employee stock ownership plan for some time. After the abovementioned preparations, the early employee stock ownership plan of GF Securities was finally partially launched in 2000. In preparation for the IPO, the regulator advised GF Securities to liquidate its stake in Liaoning Cheng Da. In June 2000, GF Securities transferred its 46,828,800 million legal person shares of Liaoning Cheng Da (from a placement of 25.6 million shares in that year) to the Trade Union Committee of GF Securities at a price of 1.5 yuan per share, for a total price of 70,243,200 yuan. GF Securities Trade Union in essence became the second-largest shareholder of the company's first-largest shareholder.

The source of funds for the equity takeover by GF Securities' labor union was mainly the Employee Entrepreneurial Contribution Fund, which was withdrawn from 1998. The fund had a different percentage of withdrawal and the amount withdrawn varied from year to year. In 1999, with the approval of the shareholders' meeting, the fund received a high bonus due to the significant profitability of the year.

Although the shareholding of GF Securities' labor union could be regarded as a form of employee shareholding and an incentive mechanism mainly for the company's management, the labor union, as a social rights group legal person, had an ambiguous owner. The value of Liaoning Cheng Da's legal person shares held by the labor union was high, but under the legal system at that time, it was difficult to specify which individual held the shares.

Therefore, the idea of "shareholding," which had been implemented for many years and in essence, alternated with the work of shareholding reform, listing, and employee share incentive, had become an important part of the top-level design of GF Securities and had also established the market-oriented advantages for many years afterwards.

Among the earliest financiers in China's securities market, Dr. Chen Yunxian had both professional theories and business management experiences. Among the earliest securities companies, GF Securities also had the inherent advantage of shareholding practice. The long and careful planning around "shareholding" was expected to reach a consensus with major shareholders at the board meeting on March 21, 2003, which would lead to a further step of shareholding and employee stock ownership. However, history was full of uncertain coincidences. With a job transfer order on the same night, Dr. Chen turned to politics and became the executive vice mayor of Foshan. The results of the negotiation with shareholders on the equity structure were not implemented, which became the biggest regret left by Dr. Chen in GF Securities. From the perspective of shareholding layout, this may also be the biggest loss of GF Securities in its development stage.

GF Venture Capital's mission

At the beginning of 2004, the market environment was gradually relaxed, and there was no legal prohibition for employees of securities companies to become their shareholders. In addition, in August of that year, the plan of 75 percent shareholding by executives of the newly established Gaohua Securities was approved, so there seemed to be a breakthrough in the policy. After careful planning, GF Securities decided on a plan to set up a company to hold shares of Liaoning Cheng Da instead of the trade union.

Shenzhen GF Venture Capital Co., Ltd. (hereinafter referred to as GF Venture Capital) came into being. With the mission of developing employee shareholding, GF Venture Capital had been originally in an internal state of preparation, but with the sudden intervention of CITIC Securities and the outbreak of the "battle for the equity of GF Securities," efforts had to be accelerated to found GF Venture Capital, which was made public. In September 2004, the company was set up in the midst of the crisis and eventually became famous in the counter-takeover battle.[1] When the tender offer of CITIC Securities was repelled, the employee shareholding of GF Securities also received attention from all walks of life.

The company was established by 2,126 natural shareholders with a registered capital of 248 million yuan, all of whom were employees of GF Securities and its four subsidiaries. The per capita contribution was about 100,000 yuan and 12 people contributed more than one million yuan.

Those holding more than five percent of the shares of a securities company were subject to the approval of the CSRC according to the law. However, GF Venture Capital was established in the midst of a life-and-death takeover crisis, and there was no opportunity to seek regulatory advice on its holdings in the securities company. Thereafter, in 2006, when GF Securities was moving forward with its IPO, the regulator explicitly required GF Venture Capital to be rectified prior to the IPO.

---

1 For details, see Chapter VIII of this book, "In a Show of Courage: A Market-Based Counter-Takeover."

Another mission of GF Venture Capital during the preparation period was the transfer of 10 percent of the shares by the shareholders of the company in equal proportions in 2004, three years after the establishment of the joint stock company, in accordance with the provisions of the articles of association regarding the buy-back of the shares. GF Venture Capital was going to complete the plan in two steps. The first step was the transfer of Liaoning Cheng Da's shares held by the GF Securities Trade Union, and the second step was the takeover of the shares from the shareholders of GF Securities.

There was a conflict between the employee stock ownership plan and the IPO process and a choice had to be made. In April 2006, GF Venture Capital held a shareholders' meeting in Guangzhou and decided to sell all the shares of GF Securities at a price not lower than the net asset value of GF Securities at the end of 2005 of 1.25 yuan per share. This marks the end of GF Venture Capital's mission as a platform for GF Securities' employee shareholding.

On September 26, Yanbian Highway issued a report on going public on the strength on the strength of its shell, announcing that the shares of GF Securities held by GF Venture Capital had been transferred to four companies, including Hedy Holding. In addition, according to the report, Liaoning Cheng Da and Jilin Aodong would transfer five percent of their respective equity interests in GF Securities to GF Securities employees for the purpose of the employees' equity incentive.

It was unexpected that just after GF Venture Capital announced the transfer of all the shares of GF Securities, on May 23, 2006, at the China Economic Summit, Zhou Xiaochuan, the governor of the People's Bank of China, said that although there had been great confusion about the employee stock ownership plans proposed by some financial companies in the 1990s, international experience showed that "the employee stock ownership plans help to mobilize high-quality employees, help to improve and utilize the ability of employees to participate in management, and also help to give full play to the role of employees in monitoring and alarming the management of the whole company in terms of compliance and preventing malicious incidents such as fraud."

A leader of the CSRC even said clearly to the media: "In fact, the establishment of the employee incentive mechanism is a clear direction, but how to regulate the operation is a problem that we have been studying. The employee share incentive plan of each brokerage firm needs to be implemented gradually according to the regulations of the regulatory authorities, instead of being implemented in a variety of other ways."

On September 6, 2006, CITIC Securities seized the historical opportunity of the reform of non-tradable shares and implemented the plan for the first batch of incentive shares. The main content of the plan was: the total number of first incentive shares was 30 million shares, temporarily deposited under the stock account of CITIC Group. Of these shares, 22,163,116 shares were the source shares of the company's plan for the first batch of incentive shares, which would be transferred to the incentive recipients from the account of CITIC Group after the board of directors of the company reviewed and approved the Decision on the Implementation of the Plan for the First Batch of Incentive Shares of CITIC Securities. After the transfer was completed, the shares were, in nature, shares which would become tradable within 60 months from the date of transfer. The remaining 7,836,884 shares were the shares of SOEs managed by the national and local State-Owned Assets Supervision and Administration Commissions in the same proportion. The board of directors of CITIC Securities would review and approve the implementation plan after obtaining the approval of the SASAC. Pending the approval of the SASAC, the shares would continue to be temporarily deposited in the account of CITIC Group.

After the first stage, CITIC Securities said that the implementation of the company's equity incentive mechanism provided the company with a good tool to improve the management model and fully mobilize the motivation of the incentive recipients, and also encouraged other employees.

After CITIC Securities, a number of brokerages including GF Securities submitted their equity incentive or employee stock ownership plans to the regulatory authorities, but no new cases emerged in the industry for a long period of time.

As a long-term effort, GF Securities did not abandon the equity incentive plan. On March 17, 2010, the Extraordinary General Meeting of GF Securities unanimously passed the motion to amend the Articles of Association and other motions. The revised articles of association provide for four cases in which the company "may acquire shares of the company in accordance with the laws, administrative regulations, departmental rules and regulations and the provisions of these articles of association," which included the case of "awarding shares to employees of the company." Article 25 of the Articles of Association also stipulated that, "The shares of the company acquired by the company in accordance with the provisions of Article 23 (3) shall not exceed 5 percent of the total number of issued shares of the Company. The funds used for the takeover shall be paid out of the company's profit after tax. The acquired shares shall be transferred to the employees within one year."

According to the Articles of Association of the company, the 99.98 million shares of GF Securities, which increased to 120,457,800 shares following the stock-to-stock scheme, were held by Guangdong Yuecai Trust Co., Ltd. as entrusted by 15 GF Securities shareholders, including Liaoning Cheng Da, Jilin Aodong, Zhongshan Public Utilities, and Heong Kong Group, with the corresponding shares derived from the company's share dividend or capital increase to be transferred, as the source shares for the company's employee equity incentive plan, to the company's equity incentive recipients at the price agreed in the relevant trust agreement in accordance with the relevant laws, rules, and regulations and after the company's equity incentive plan was approved by the CSRC.

3. The ordeal of going public

From the mutual sponsorship to the counter-takeover

Throughout the 1990s, securities companies felt like they were just helping other succeed in the market: they pushed a number of excellent companies in various industries to the capital markets through their underwriting skills, but they were unable to raise funds through listing due to the temporary policy restraint.

At the turn of the century, the need for securities companies and financial institutions as a whole to replenish their capital became more and more urgent. After China's accession to the WTO, although there was no clear timetable for the opening of the securities market, this had been a general trend, and joint venture funds and joint venture brokerage firms had gradually approached. With financial consortia such as Merrill Lynch, Goldman Sachs, and Morgan Stanley with equity capital of tens of billions of dollars, Chinese securities companies were facing tremendous competitive pressure both in terms of operational quality and capital scale.

In 1999, Dr. Chen Yunxian pointed out in his paper "Chinese Securities Firms Are Facing the Third Wave of Impact" that, "The Chinese capital markets are facing the third wave of impact in the transition process from the beginning of the rough stage to the mature stage, i.e. the impact of market transformation, which is a much larger wave than the first and second waves." He predicted that "brokerage firms may be allowed to be directly listed. The leading stocks in foreign securities markets started with real estate stocks, and then there were financial stocks, and only later there were technology stocks. I personally believe that sooner or later, the development of China's securities market will require financial stocks as the leading stocks. Among the financial stocks, according to international practices, there are not only stocks of commercial banks, stocks of trust and investment companies, stocks of fund asset management companies, but more importantly, stocks of securities companies and investment banking listed on the stock exchange."

In the new century, as the competitive landscape continued to change, the securities industry had begun to show a gradual trend of concentration in major securities companies. The diversification and integration of securities business also required brokerage firms to increase their capital to meet the needs of their business. However, the sluggishness of the secondary market sentiment had made the process of conducting placement and improving the asset structure of securities companies difficult. In this context, listing had multiple practical implications for the long-term development of securities companies: it was conducive to expanding capital strength and business expansion; improving corporate governance and establishing a sound modern financial corporate system; meeting the challenges of internationalization; and accepting supervision and upgrading the level of standardization.

In May 2000, Zhou Xiaochuan, chairman of the CSRC, delivered a speech on welcoming the listing of financial companies at a symposium on the development of financial companies and capital markets. The CSRC subsequently issued the No. 1–6 Rules for the Preparation and Disclosure of Information by Companies That Publicly Issue Securities to commercial banks, insurance companies, and securities companies that intended to publicly issue securities. The Rules clearly stipulated the special requirements related to information disclosure of securities companies applying for public offering of shares: securities companies could not act as their own counseling institutions and underwrite their own public offering of shares.

The listing layout of GF Securities had already been laid out before that. After the preliminary discussion, its 1998 work report formally proposed that "improving the share system is the foundation of the company's long-term stability," and combined shareholding reform with listing for a clearer path:

> First, the company's equity structure should be rationalized. It should be regulated according to the Company Law and the Securities Law, so as to form a group of stable shareholders with strong strength and standardized operation, who can cooperate with the business development of the company, and ensure the long-term stability of the company.
>
> Second, we will take the restructuring of the brokerage firm as an opportunity to strive for placement, with a recent target of 1.5 billion to 2 billion yuan.
>
> Third, during the placement, we will take advantage of the opportunity of sectoral management and classification management to merge, gain the controlling share of, or participate in a number of securities companies with good asset quality.
>
> Fourth, on the basis of further standardization and convergence with international standards, we will actively strive to raise shares from the public and become a joint stock company listed on the stock exchange.

In November 1999, the CSRC approved the placement plan of GF Securities and classified it as a comprehensive securities company. GF Securities' registered capital increased to 1.6 billion yuan.

In March 2000, the annual board of directors of GF Securities passed a resolution to approve the listing of the company. At the end of March, when the Institutional Department of the CSRC visited GF Securities for research, the company's leaders reported on the operation and management of the company after the placement and its classification as a comprehensive securities company, as well as the idea of using the stock market to raise capital and go public. In early April, when the leaders of GF Securities reported to the leaders of Guangdong Province on the acquisition of GITIC's brokerage branches, they also reported on the company's intention to go public, which was approved by the provincial leaders. At the end of July, GF Securities set up a preparatory committee for restructuring, with Chen Yunxian, Fang Jiachun, Dong Zhengqing, Ye Junying, Li Jianyong, Li Suina, and Li Shuiquan as members.

In June 2001, the CSRC approved the change of the company to GF Securities Co., Ltd. with a registered capital of two billion yuan in the Z.J.J.G.Z. [2001] No. 86 document. GF Securities Co., Ltd.'s founding meeting was held in the form of a written motion, and the shareholders of the company converted all their respective interests they held in GF Securities Co., Ltd. as of December 31, 2000 into ordinary shares at a ratio of 1:1. In accordance with the needs of the listing process, GF Securities also established a secretariat for the Board of Directors.

After the symposium on the development of financial companies and capital markets in May 2000, securities companies with the conditions to go public accelerated the pace of listing. In accordance with the requirement that "securities companies cannot act as their own counseling institutions and underwrite their own public offering of shares," GF Securities and CITIC Securities actively approached each other, and a "mutual sponsorship" plan was reached, i.e. the two brokerage firms became each other's counseling institution and lead underwriter for the initial public offering of shares.

This cooperation between the two parties was based in large part on their relatively close industry positions at the time. In 2001, the total profit of CITIC Securities and GF Securities were 823 million yuan and 740 million yuan respectively; GF Securities and CITIC Securities ranked eighth and ninth respectively in terms of the value of brokerage business; and CITIC Securities and GF Securities ranked third and seventh respectively in terms of underwriting capital raised.

In November 2001, CITIC Securities, the lead underwriter, officially started the IPO counseling for directors, supervisors, and executives of GF Securities after the approval of the company's board of directors.

The title of "the No. 1 listed Chinese brokerage firm" had an undeniable glow and became the target of competition among brokerage firms. At the end of 2001, it was not yet clear which would win the title.

Under the media spotlight, CITIC Securities, a subsidiary of CITIC Group, and Guotong Securities (i.e. China Merchants Securities), a subsidiary of China Merchants Group, were making an all-out sprint with the support of their parent companies as newcomers in the industry; Shenyin Wanguo, Haitong Securities, and Guotai Jun'an, with more seniority, also included listing in their short-term plans; Guoxin Securities, Dapeng Securities, and Xiangcai Securities also launched their listing competition. Similarly, the listing of GF Securities also attracted a lot of attention. The November 29, 2001 issue of the *Southern Metropolis Daily* even reported that GF Securities was expected to overtake CITIC Securities to become the No. 1 listed Chinese brokerage firm.

However, all things considered, CITIC Securities was clearly in a better position to go public first. Lü Zhequan, secretary of the board of directors of CITIC Securities, told the media that, "We have been preparing for the listing for many years, and the pace of work has been significantly accelerated recently." Senior investment bankers analyzed the advantages of CITIC Securities, pointing out that it was established late, with a high starting point and a light burden; it was restructured early and benefited from the development of the securities industry after restructuring. While the old brokerage firms were actively working to clear up the thorny issues left over from their history, CITIC Securities' leading edge in the race for listing was becoming more and more obvious.

From March to September 2001, during the six-month counseling period for CITIC Securities' IPO, the Investment Banking Department of GF Securities, under the command of Li Jianyong and Luo Binhua, appointed a project team including Liu Xuyang, Liu Binhai, Zhou Zhilin, and Zhao Ruimei to prepare the application documents for the IPO. On September 28 of the same year, GF Securities formally recommended CITIC Securities to apply for public offering and listing, and submitted the documents to the CSRC for review.

It coincided with a severe winter in the securities market and an unfavorable external environment, and the offering had many twists and turns. CITIC Securities, as the first securities company to apply for a public offering and listing, had many difficult issues to deal with in the prospectus documents. CSRC had issued two pre-screening inquiry letters, two pre-screening feedback outcomes, two review opinions of the issuance committee, and several oral review opinions on CITIC Securities' stock issuance application documents. The project team of GF Securities always maintained good communication with the regulator and obtained the understanding of prospectus document disclosure and the innovation of the plan, so that CITIC Securities' disclosure on many issues such as business and internal controls complied with the relevant regulations of the CSRC and the lead underwriter's diligence requirements, while maintaining the issuer's commercial secrets.

On September 25, 2002, CITIC Securities' IPO application was approved by the CSRC by a unanimous vote. On January 6, 2003, CITIC Securities was successfully listed on the Shanghai Stock Exchange with 400 million tradable shares, raising 1.8 billion yuan. The IPO project of CITIC Securities was one of the largest and most challenging underwriting projects for GF Securities around the new millennium.

GF Securities recommended the listing of CITIC Securities as planned, and the dedication and professionalism of the GF Securities project team was praised by the management and Investment Banking Department of CITIC Securities. Unfortunately, GF Securities' own listing process was repeatedly hindered. While trying to communicate with the regulator about its own history, there was a change of core management personnel in 2003 and an annual operating loss, which put the listing on hold.

CITIC Securities led the securities industry in both "IPO" and "M&As" with its excellent strategic layout. In 2003, CITIC Securities acquired and increased its capital to establish CITIC Wantong Securities, exploring a path to expand its scale and increase its competitive advantage in regional markets. A year after its successful IPO, in September 2004, CITIC Securities held the twelfth meeting of its second board of directors and voted on the Proposal to Acquire a Portion of the Equity Interests of GF Securities Co., Ltd.[2]

From 2001 to 2004, the cooperation between the two securities firms of "mutual sponsorship" failed to realize the beautiful vision of "blooming together." After the successful listing of CITIC Securities and the failure of GF Securities, it turned into a fierce fight between market-oriented takeover and counter-takeover. CITIC Securities' takeover intentions were not successful due to the will of GF Securities' shareholders and the strong opposition of GF Securities' management and employees. In terms of the development of China's securities industry, an opportunity for a "strong alliance" between a North and a South brokerage firm disappeared. For GF Securities, the successful counter-takeover strengthened internal cohesion and continued the "traditions" and culture of GF Securities. After the crisis, GF Securities continued to search hard for the way and time to go public.

The innovation and variation of shell listing

In January 2005, the leading bodies of GF Securities held a meeting on principles at Dongguan Yujingwan Hotel, in which important matters such as GF Venture Capital, the counter-CITIC Securities takeover, and the planning of the company's listing were discussed in depth, and the types of shareholders to be introduced and the proportion of the equity structure were openly discussed.

Entering the second half of 2005, with the continued advancement of the reform of non-tradable shares, brokerage firms finally ushered in the market turnaround. Significant growth in business revenue and operating profit, lucrative returns brought about by innovative businesses such as warrant creation bringing, good performance and optimistic expectations became direct drivers for brokerage listings.

On a more macro level, China's capital markets were undergoing the reform of non-tradable shares and were about to enter a golden era of development. At

2 For details, see Chapter VIII of this book, "In a Show of Courage: A Market-Based Counter-Takeover."

the end of 2005, the total market capitalization of Shanghai and Shenzhen was 3.65 trillion yuan, the SSE index fell 8.33 percent, and the securitization rate was 19.8 percent. At the end of 2006, the total market capitalization of Shanghai and Shenzhen was 10.74 trillion yuan, the SSE index rose 130.43 percent, and the securitization rate was 51.3 percent. With the gradual completion of the reform of non-tradable shares, increasing the proportion of direct financing in the economy had become one of the main directions of the government's financial reform.

Along with the development of securities market, GF Securities' performance had increased significantly and its competitive advantages had been strengthened. In the primary market business, GF Securities had been ranked among the top 10 in the industry in terms of the number of IPO underwriters and underwriting value for a long time. In 2006, the total number of registered sponsors of GF Securities reached 42, ranking first among all sponsor institutions, which had laid a good foundation for further development of investment banking.

In terms of secondary market business, GF Securities' business network had been reasonably distributed in economically developed regions such as the Pearl River Delta, Yangtze River Delta, Bohai Bay, northeast China, and north China, and its brokerage business system ranked among the top of domestic brokerage firms.

GF Securities also had a controlling stake in GF Northern, GF Huafu, GF Futures, and GF Fund, had a stake in E Fund, and had been approved to establish GF Holdings (Hong Kong) Corporation Limited.

All this had created favorable conditions for GF Securities to expand its securities business, carry out financial innovation, and move into the international market.

However, the registered capital of GF Securities was two billion yuan and its net assets were 2.848 billion yuan, so there was a certain gap compared with the large securities companies in the industry, and the capital size also limited GF Securities' innovative business.

In July 2005, the CSRC issued the Measures for the Administration of Risk Control Indicators of Securities Firms and the Circular on the Issuance of Standards for Calculating Net Capital of Securities Firms, which established a risk control regulatory system with net capital at the core. The leaders of the CSRC expressed their support for compliant securities firms to enrich their capital through listing and financing, directed placement, and introduction of strategic investors.

GF Securities soon put listing on the agenda again. In the context of the reform of non-tradable shares, in order to improve the effect of M&A and restructuring of underperforming companies, one of the "policy combinations" studied and formulated by the regulator was to take the opportunity of the shareholding reform to improve and restructure underperforming companies. This innovative consideration could bring hope to the company itself, as well as to the shareholders of non-tradable and tradable shares, and was therefore of great value.[3] This also provided a new path for securities companies to go public

3 Li Jianyong et al. *Research on the Reform of Non-Tradable Shares* [M]. Beijing: Economic

through shell listing in addition to IPOs.

Although the advantages of IPO listing were obvious in terms of time cycle, transaction costs, and operational procedures, for brokerage firms that were eager to go public and had just passed the industry downturn, the "three-year profitability requirement for IPOs on the main boards" was a challenge to most.

GF Securities was facing this situation when it wanted to launch another IPO attempt. In 2003, GF Securities suffered its only loss since its inception, and if it were to go public through the IPO, it would have to wait until after the 2007 financial results were released. In addition to the timing issue, due to the strict IPO audit and the great uncertainty of the audit cycle, and the "after-effects" of GF Venture Capital, the main executor of the employee stock ownership plan, after careful consideration, the GF Securities management decided to promote the listing on the strength of a shell.

After many rounds of selection, GF Securities finally determined to make Yanbian Highway its shell. Yanbian Highway was listed on the Shenzhen Stock Exchange on June 11, 1997 and its total share capital increased to 184,109,986 shares through the implementation of the plans of making rights offering, using the provident fund to increase the share capital and delivering bonus shares. In 2005, the performance of Yanbian Highway declined significantly and became a poor performing stock.

For GF Securities to go public on the strength of the shell of Yanbian Highway, several important issues needed to be resolved: first, how to reform the non-tradable shares of Yanbian Highway in the process? Second, the main business of Yanbian Highway was road construction and operation whereas the main business of GF securities was securities-based financial business. How to dispose of all the business and assets of Yanbian Highway? Third, GF Securities was much larger than Yanbian Highway. After the injection of GF Securities' assets and the disposal of GF Securities' assets, could it meet the requirements of the ratio of tradable shares? Fourth, there were many parties and stakeholders involved. How to ensure the fairness of the pricing?

Against this complex background, GF Securities leveraged its expertise and experience in investment banking to coordinate all parties and designed a plan to go public on the strength of the shell of Yanbian Highway. It innovatively solved the above important issues. This model and operation plan also became the operation case and model for the subsequent shell listing of many companies.

The core point of the transaction plan was: the targeted share repurchase and the share exchange and absorption of GF Securities would be inseparable as a whole. Yanbian Highway would repurchase its non-tradable shares held by its major shareholder in consideration of all its assets and liabilities to reduce its share capital, and at the same time, dispose of the existing assets lacking sustainable profitability, thus creating conditions for the share exchange and

Science Press, 2008: 125.

absorption of GF Securities.

Through the share swap and absorption of GF Securities, Yanbian Highway accepted all the existing assets and business of GF Securities, completely changed the situation of insufficient profitability of existing business and difficulties in sustainable operation, and successfully transformed into a comprehensive securities company, with its main business changing to securities-based financial business.

On September 26, 2006, Yanbian Highway publicly disclosed documents such as the Prospectus of Yanbian Highway Construction Co., Ltd. for the Reform of Non-Tradable Shares Share and the Report Yanbian Highway Construction Co., Ltd. on the Targeted Share Repurchase and the Absorption and Merger of GF Securities Co., Ltd. by Additional Shares, announcing the details of the operation.

In short, the plan was for Yanbian Highway to buy back and cancel the non-tradable shares held by and to be transferred to the former major shareholders (the total number of both was 84,977,833,000 shares, accounting for 46.15% of the total share capital) with all assets and liabilities, and the total share capital would be changed from 184,110,000 shares to 99,132,167,000 shares. The non-marketable shareholders other than those of the major shareholders would be reduced from 99,132,167,000 shares to 97,407,178,000 shares in the ratio of 10:7.1. Finally, the shares of GF Securities would be exchanged for new shares at a ratio of 1:0.83, i.e. the shares would be changed from 97,407,178,000 shares to 250,704,5732,000 shares. This is called the "trilogy of share exchange and merger" by the market.

Before GF Securities announced its shell listing plan, there were only two listed brokerages in Shanghai and Shenzhen, CITIC Securities and Hongyuan Securities. In 2006, a number of brokerages such as Changjiang Securities, Everbright Securities, and Haitong Securities publicly expressed their intention to go public. Among them, except for China Merchants Securities, Guoxin Securities, and CICC Securities, which explicitly stated that they would be listed through IPOs, all other brokerages might choose to be listed through shell listing. According to the incomplete statistics of the market at that time, there were more than 30 listed companies related to the shell listing of brokerage firms. The shell listing proposal of GF Securities was considered by the market to be the first to break the deadlock and had a great impact, and the call for batch "replication" of brokerage firms' shell listing was growing day by day.

Sinolink Securities then also announced its shell listing plan, but in a slightly different way than GF Securities' shell listing. Sinolink Securities' path was to have its major shareholder go public first, and then the equity held by Sinolink Securities would be replaced into the shell company, and finally, when the time was ripe, Sinolink Securities would be listed as a whole by way of absorption and merger or overall takeover. This was somewhat similar to the previous traditional restructuring model for listing by injecting high-quality assets into the shell. And for the industry's leading large brokerage firms, they would prefer the GF

Securities shell listing path. The market speculated that, "If Haitong Securities, Guotai Jun'an Securities, Orient Securities, and other brokerage firms want shell listing, they might prefer the GF Securities model."

At this time, the market response to the shell listing began became prominent. Liaoning Cheng Da, Jilin Aodong, and other companies related to the brokerage concept were vigorously pursued by market capital, and the share price was also soaring, all up by more than 200 percent.

In addition, some institutions and listed companies began to take advantage of the "shell concept" to engage in malicious speculation, raising the share prices for profit. For brokerage firms interested in shell listing, excessive market speculation due to leaked news led to high share prices, which also caused various variables. A brokerage firm had to reconsider the cost of shell listing precisely after the news of shell listing was leaked, which led to the over-priced shares of the shell company and too much premium in the agreement transfer and directed issuance.

In the face of malicious speculation by some institutions and listed companies, the CSRC, out of the consideration of protecting the interests of small and medium-sized investors and promoting fair trade, made the presence or absence of significant fluctuations in the share price of the proposed shell company before the shell listing as one of the regulatory criteria. As the first case of shell listing by a brokerage firm, the stock price fluctuations caused by the shell listing of Yanbian Highway by GF Securities inevitably received focused attention.

Since May 2005, the share price of Yanbian Highway had been maintained at a range of two to three yuan per share, with low turnover. From February to March 2006, the volume showed signs of further shrinkage. After the second half of March, the volume of Yanbian Highway gradually expanded. At the end of April, the share price started to rise sharply, from 2.92 yuan per share at the close of trading on April 25 to 5.08 yuan per share at the close of trading on May 10, and the volume also increased sharply.

On May 10, the media reported that GF Securities would soon be listed on the shell of Yanbian Highway, and its stock reached its upper level of the daily trading limit on the same day. On May 11, Yanbian Highway clarified the media's shell report, saying that the major shareholders and management had not had any contact with GF Securities on the shell listing and that the reform of non-tradable shares was still in the preliminary preparation stage. On June 5, after a two-day suspension of trading, Yanbian Highway admitted that its controlling shareholder "is communicating and discussing with GF Securities on shell listing." In the meantime, its stock reached the upper level of the daily trading limit for six days.

On July 31, the Market Supervision Department of the Shenzhen Stock Exchange sent a formal letter to GF Securities to investigate all the accounts of S Yanbian Highway [note: S means failure to reform non-tradable shares] held by GF Securities' clients. GF Securities was asked to provide information about the relevant accounts, including the actual controllers and funding background. In

October 2006, the CSRC's Inspection Bureau sent another team to Guangdong to investigate, with the cooperation of the Guangdong Provincial Securities Regulatory Bureau. The case investigation continued until around May 2007.

According to the media at the time, "A source with knowledge of the situation said that the CSRC had already had the results of the investigation and considered that the incident was a personal act and would not affect the listing of the company, which led to the subsequent announcement of the shell listing plan."

On October 31, 2006, the share swap plan received 96.81 percent of the votes in favor of S Yanbian Highway shareholders, but the stock had not been able to resume trading. On March 16, 2007, Yanbian Highway released its 2006 annual report. For the progress of the GF Securities shell plan investors were concerned about, the annual report did not clarify this, only stating that the relevant materials had been submitted to the CSRC.

Insider information leakage case

On May 30, 2007, the total number of accounts in the Chinese stock market exceeded 100 million in history, reaching 100.27 million. The indelible memory of this day for all Chinese stockholders was the heavy news on the CCTV 2 "Economic News Broadcast" at 00:00 am about the increase of the stamp duty rate on securities transactions. This caused more than 900 stocks to reach the lower level of the daily trading limit on that day. The lack of confidence in the market at the policy level led to huge shocks in the stock indexes in the following trading days. A few hours before the stamp duty news arrived, GF Securities had already been involved in a deep shock by more news on the evening of May 29.

At 7:00 p.m. on May 29, CCTV News broadcasted a message that "the CSRC has proposed punishment for alleged insider trading and information-disclosure violations by parties related to GF Securities' shell listing based on Yanbian Highway. Some parties suspected of insider trading and other forms of crimes and evidence and clues of suspected crimes have been transferred to public security organs, and the judicial organs have asked to pursue their criminal responsibility in accordance with the law." The CSRC also pointed out in the same day's briefing, "As the GF Securities shell listing based on Yanbian highway is the first case of brokerage shell listing involving several listed companies, Yanbian Highway's reform of non-tradable shares, and major restructuring matters, the CSRC has strictly examined the matter in an objective and impartial manner and in accordance with the law."

On the evening of the same day, leaders of GF Securities in Guangzhou rushed back to the company and met overnight to discuss how to deal with the unexpected event.

On May 1, during an internal meeting of GF Securities to brief on major matters, President Dong Zhengqing announced his resignation. He explained the reasons for his resignation: firstly, he did not achieve the expected work target of GF Securities' shell listing; secondly, he was mainly responsible for the negative impact caused by GF Securities' shell listing based on Yanbian Highway and the process of equity change. This was the last time that GF Securities employees saw Dong Zhengqing on the IPTV meeting screen.

On June 5, GF Securities issued an internal "Circular on Requesting All Employees to Help Maintain Stability." It called on them to make every effort to maintain the stable operation of the company and ensure normal business and management activities.

One month later, Dong Zhengqing was criminally detained on suspicion of leaking insider information. On March 27, 2009, the Guangzhou Intermediate People's Court issued a final verdict that Dong Zhengqing was guilty of leaking insider information and he was sentenced to four years of imprisonment and a fine of three million yuan. The court rejected the insider trading charges brought by the procuratorial authorities due to insufficient evidence.

While Dong Zhengqing was serving his sentence, Dr. Chen Yunxian, the founder of the company and mayor of Foshan, sent him a copy of *Tao Te Ching*, exhorting him to cultivate his mind and nurture his character. Dong Zhengqing, the youngest member of GF Securities' first leadership team, later said, "It would had been good to read this book earlier. 'They grow, and there is no claim made for their ownership; They go through their processes, and there is no expectation of a reward for the results. The work is accomplished, and there is no resting in it as an achievement.' If I had not gone through this process, it would have been difficult for me to have this wisdom."

As a glimpse of history, the case from the legal point of view had been concluded. GF Securities, which had suffered a major setback, also made profound reflections and improvements in its corporate governance model and other areas. And from the perspective of reason, in fact, there are still some events that the parties are reluctant to mention again, and will always be sealed in history.

During the abrupt suspension of the GF Securities shell listing, other brokerage firms rose to prominence. In July 2007, Haitong Securities was successfully listed based on a shell, and quickly completed a directed issue in the A-share market. By the end of 2007, Haitong Securities' net assets had reached 36.9 billion yuan. In September 2007, CITIC Securities successfully implemented a public offering, raising 25 billion yuan in total. In November 2008, Southwest Securities was conditionally approved by the M&A and Restructuring Committee of the China Securities Regulatory Commission for listing based on the shell of *ST Chongqing Changjiang. In August and November 2009, Everbright Securities and China Merchants Securities were good latecomers, completing their first rounds of capital raising in the capital markets at record issue prices. In addition, several brokerages that were not listed at that time also posed a direct challenge to GF Securities. At the end of 2009, the net assets of GF Securities were only

16.4 billion yuan, which was significantly lower than that of its outstanding counterparts, and the pressure of competition had increased.

The securities industry's trends were becoming clearer. With the rapid rise of capital intermediary business and buy-side business, capital strength directly determined the competitiveness of brokerage firms. The long road to going public, which was the expectation of all employees, was difficult but efforts had to continue and were still continuing.

4. Successfully going public and rising to the next level

After 48 days of efforts, the A-shares resume trading

The turnaround finally came in late 2009. In late December 2009, a leader of the CSRC instructed GF Securities by phone to restart the shell listing.

GF Securities had gone through a lot of difficulties to wait for this moment.

In 2009, the listing project was led by Chairman Wang Zhiwei and President Li Jianyong, while the executive team was led by Vice President and Secretary of the Board of Directors Luo Binhua. GF Securities involved six A-share listed companies at the shareholder level, and together with Yanbian Highway, it involved seven listed companies in terms of information disclosure and board of directors and other decision-making procedures.

After sorting out the various constraints, Yanbian Highway announced on December 28, 2009 that in order to implement the plan of Yanbian Highway to reform the non-tradable shares and restructure the company to absorb GF Securities with additional shares, the company intended to further communicate with GF Securities on related matters. The shares of Yanbian Highway would continue to be suspended, and the shares of six companies related to GF Securities would also be suspended at the same time.

On January 8, 2010, Yanbian Highway Construction Co., Ltd. announced the implementation of the restructuring working plan to reform its non-tradable shares and absorb and merge GF Securities with additional shares. The transaction structure, trading method, and pricing method would be basically consistent with the plan adopted in 2006.

On the same day, Liaoning Cheng Da, Jilin Aodong, Zhongshan Public Utilities, and three other listed companies holding equity interests in GF Securities also published their respective boards of directors' resolutions, agreeing to the absorption of GF Securities with additional shares by Yanbian Highway and other related matters.

As of September 30, 2009, the net assets of GF Securities increased by more than 12 billion yuan compared with June 30, 2006, an increase of more than four times. The 2010 plan's share exchange ratio remained unchanged, which would enable the old shareholders of Yanbian Highway to enjoy the rapid increase in net assets due to the rollover of GF Securities' operating results over the previous three years of suspension of Yanbian Highway, with their opportunity cost of liquidity of public shareholders being compensated and their interests being protected. (See Figure 5)

After the resumption of the shell listing efforts, GF Securities was praised for its efficiency, securing the approval of the SASAC, shareholders' general meeting, and CSRC in less than one and a half months, and the share swap merger plan was officially implemented.

On February 6, 2010, Yanbian Highway announced that its application for the targeted share repurchase and merger with GF Securities with additional shares was approved by the CSRC.

As one of the leaders of the CSRC said on a private occasion, "After such a big event, if it were any other company, it would had collapsed long time ago; and GF Securities could continue to operate and develop steadily, which shows that the company was extremely resilient, so we agreed to restart the shell listing of GF Securities."

After 48 days and nights of efforts, at 9:24 a.m. on February 12, 2010, Song Hai, vice governor of the Guangdong Provincial People's Government, and Wang Zhiwei, chairman of GF Securities, jointly rang the listing bell at the Shenzhen Stock Exchange, adding a heavyweight member to the Chinese stock market, with the resumption of trading of "GF Securities" under the code 000776.

GF Securities opened at 54 yuan per share, up 411.8 percent, and closed at noon at 50.5 yuan per share, up 374.4 percent, corresponding to a dynamic P/E ratio of 27.6 times. GF Securities completed its shell listing in the securities market, with its total market capitalization exceeding 100 billion yuan, and becoming a new spotlight in the legion of blue-chip stocks. In 2010, GF Securities ranked third in terms of total revenue and net profit.

The shell listing of GF Securities was a special case in the history of Chinese securities. For the A-share market and the brokerage sector as a whole, the listing of GF Securities was of great significance. One of the most direct effects was that it added another high-quality listed brokerage firm to the A-share market, with a total market capitalization of 125.4 billion yuan on the first day of listing, surpassing Vanke as the new "No. 1" stock in the Shenzhen market in terms of market capitalization. In addition, the successful listing of GF Securities also helped raise the overall valuation of the brokerage sector.

Soon after the successful listing of GF Securities in early 2010, securities firms such as Huatai Securities, Shanxi Securities, and Industrial Securities also completed their financing in the capital markets through IPOs. While a group of listed securities firms continued to expand their capital and strive for business development opportunities by means of issuing additional shares, placing shares and raising debts, CITIC Securities and Haitong Securities in the first tier proposed to raise funds through IPOs in Hong Kong, taking further steps toward internationalization.

After the shell listing of GF Securities, how it should raise funds through the platform and replenish capital had become an issue that had to be faced and pondered.

Selling Huafu to address intra-industry competition

At the shareholders' meeting in March 2010, the net capital of GF Securities aroused the concern of the participants: could the existing net capital of GF Securities meet the development needs of various businesses?

The management of the company said that the purpose of the shell listing was to develop and expand GF Securities. Moreover, the development of the company's businesses had an increasing demand for capital, and refinancing was one of the necessary means to address the demand. The choice of how and when to refinance was subject to further study.

Numerous brokerage research institutions compared GF Securities with Haitong Securities and believed that the two were similar in terms of industry positioning, company size, and business strength, but GF Securities was far inferior to Haitong Securities in terms of capital strength. Capital bottleneck was still a realistic problem GF Securities could not avoid. The primary prerequisite for capital replenishment was to solve the increasingly prominent problem of intra-industry competition.

Since the second half of 2007, the Regulations on Supervision and Administration of Securities Companies, Trial Regulations on Establishment of Subsidiaries by Securities Companies, and Interim Regulations on Approval of Business Scope of Securities Companies had been issued one after another, requiring securities companies to solve the problem of intra-industry competition. Under the mandatory requirement that "the same shareholder or beneficial owner should only hold the controlling share in one brokerage firm and participate in another brokerage firm at the same time," GF Securities and its holding subsidiary GF Huafu were facing the problem of intra-industry competition.

Founded in June 1988, GF Huafu Securities, formerly known as Fujian Huafu Securities Company, was one of the first securities companies established in China. In January 2003, GF Securities contacted the relevant parties in Fujian Province to discuss the possibility of GF Securities' participation in Huafu Securities Company. On March 7, important legal documents such as the Capital Contribution Agreement of Guangfa Huafu Securities Co., Ltd. and the Net Assets (Equity) Transfer Agreement were officially signed to allow GF Securities to hold the controlling share in Huafu Securities Company. On March 12, GF Securities sent five people to attend the first meeting of the preparatory group of GF Huafu

Securities Co., Ltd.

In April 2003, with the approval of the CSRC, Huafu Securities increased its capital, adopted the shareholding system, and changed its name to GF Huafu Securities Co., Ltd. GF Securities held 60.35 percent of its shares, becoming its controlling shareholder. With a registered capital of 550 million yuan, GF Huafu Securities was headquartered in Fuzhou, Fujian Province and had 34 securities branches in Fujian Province and Shanghai, with 686 employees.

The establishment of a controlling stake in GF Huafu Securities Company had a positive effect on forming GF Securities' leading position in the Fujian securities market and further increasing its market share in developed regions such as the Yangtze River Delta.

However, GF Securities had to transfer its equity in GF Huafu Securities according to the policy that "the same shareholder or beneficial owner can only hold the controlling share in one brokerage firm and participate in another brokerage firm at the same time." On February 5, 2010, in the process of the shell listing, the Second Extraordinary Shareholders' General Meeting of GF Securities in 2010 reviewed and approved the Resolution on the Transfer of All Equity Interests of GF Huafu Held by GF Securities to Address Intra-Industry Competition and the Resolution on Authorizing the Board of Directors to Deal with Intra-Industry Competition. The company promised that it would not apply to the CSRC for new businesses, new products, and new outlets until the intra-industry competition was resolved and that it would strive to resolve intra-industry competition with GF Huafu within the year.

The existence of intra-industry competition greatly affected the business expansion of GF Securities, as the company's new brokerage branches and new pooled financial products were not approved, and most of all, its qualification as one of the first pilot companies for securities margin trading business was also affected. In addition, under the "special attention" of supervision, GF Securities was under instant pressure from being communicated with or warned by the regulator.

Initially, GF Securities considered to directly absorb and merge with GF Huafu, but there were many influencing factors, the process was extremely complicated, and the decision-making process was not easy. A person in charge of the project at that time recalls, "The whole process was extremely difficult and could even be described as unbearable." After weighing all pros and cons, GF Securities made the decision to sell its entire stake in GF Huafu.

On November 7, 2010, the sixteenth Meeting of the Sixth Board of Directors of GF Securities reviewed and passed the Decision on Transferring 60.3519 percent Equity Interests in GF Huafu Securities Co., Ltd.

On the evening of December 8, 2010, GF Securities announced that it would transfer 60.35 percent equity interests in GF Huafu for 2.49 billion yuan to a consortium of three companies. With a capital contribution of 332 million yuan,

GF Securities reaped a profit of more than 6.5 times.

A brokerage research report pointed out that the brokerage share of Huanfu Securities in GF Securities was 0.72 percent in 2009. After the transfer, the market share of GF Securities by equity would be reduced from 4.42 percent to 3.99 percent. However, according to the market price, GF Securities would get about five billion yuan in cash. Considering the yield of this cash, the comprehensive impact of the transfer was -3 percent to -4 percent. However, some brokerage firms calculated that the share of brokerage business in GF Securities would not change significantly after the divestment of Huafu. Ouyang Xi, then vice president in charge of brokerage business of GF Securities, responded: "In terms of Fuzhou, where the brokerage business of Huafu Securities is located, its local market share and profitability are in the leading position. However, due to the fierce competition in the market, its commission rate is even lower than the average commission rate of the company, and its overall position in the company is not very prominent."

After the transfer of equity interests in GF Huafu, the issue of intra-industry competition was completely resolved. Although the market share of GF Securities' brokerage business had decreased, the income generated from this equity transfer would help increase the size of its net capital, which was conducive to the expansion and development of businesses such as securities proprietary trading, securities margin trading, and direct investment. In particular, after fulfilling the commitment to solve the problem of intra-industry competition, GF Securities could apply to the China Securities Regulatory Commission for new products, new businesses, and new outlets, further improve the layout of securities business outlets across the country, and increase the market share of its brokerage business. In addition, GF Securities could also apply for developing pooled wealth management products and expanding the scale of asset management.

The sale of GF Huafu also became a catalyst for GF Securities' share price at that time. From October 8, 2010 to December 8, 2010, its share price rose by more than 66.14 percent, outperforming all other brokerage stocks.

Raising 12 billion yuan building on previous success

After solving the problem of intra-industry competition, the issue of capital replenishment was quickly put on the agenda by the management of GF Securities.

Among the financing options available in the capital markets, a non-public offering was the best choice for GF Securities. The pricing of the additional issue was the key to the non-public offering of shares, and the lower the price lock, the better the success of the issue. The non-public offering of shares of GF Securities was considered and approved at the thirteenth meeting of the sixth board of directors held on July 31, 2010, which marked the official launch of the non-public offering of shares of GF Securities.

July 2010 was the most sluggish period of 2010 for the stock market, with the Shanghai Stock Exchange Index falling to 2,319.74 points on July 2. The share price of GF Securities also reached the lowest price of 27.78 yuan per share on July 16, 2010. GF Securities made the right judgment and decisive decision in time to seize the best time to determine the price of the issue.

When GF Securities started the issuance project, it set strict requirements for the project team to ensure the progress: firstly, the progress of the project must not be delayed due to the decision time of GF Securities' senior management; secondly, the progress of the project must not be delayed due to the related reasons of intermediaries. Under these two prerequisites, all the work related to the issuance was arranged according to the tightest schedule.

After obtaining the regulatory comments issued by the Institutional Department of the CSRC, GF Securities took only one working day to submit the full set of filing materials to the CSRC. After the Issuance Department of the CSRC gave its comments, GF Securities took only one working day to submit the complete feedback materials to the pre-examiner. In the end, because of the company's full preparation for pre-diligence investigation, material production, roadshow at the Stock Issuance Review Committee of the CSRC, coupled with the good performance of GF Securities' leaders and sponsors at the Stock Issuance Review Committee, GF Securities' non-public offering was unconditionally approved.

It was already early June when GF Securities received the approval document from the CSRC, and the issuance had to be completed within one year after the approval of GF Securities' Fourth Extraordinary General Shareholders' Meeting in 2010, i.e. by September 1, 2011. This meant great time pressure.

In addition, the total amount of the non-public offering was not more than 18 billion yuan. According to the regulations, it had to be issued to no more than ten investors, so the average amount of subscription per investor was about 1.8 billion yuan. This meant that the amount of funds required to subscribe for the shares was large. Few investors would had so much cash on their books, and most of them needed to raise funds through various structured financing or mobilize funds from other sources, which in turn led to differences in investors' fund preparation.

In 2011, the continuous tightening of monetary policy by the People's Bank of China, the deepening of the sovereign debt crisis in Europe, the second bottoming of the US economy, and the declining growth rate of the domestic economy led to an extremely severe stock situation in the domestic secondary market. This posed a great challenge to GF Securities' issuance efforts.

Under the double constraints of time pressure and the differences in investors' capital preparation, GF Securities took into account as much as possible the various situations of investors and assisted them in solving their problems. GF Securities initiated the implementation of the non-public offering of shares at the right time to in order to raise as much capital as possible.

With the close cooperation of GF Securities' leadership, Development Research Center, Investment Banking Department, and other relevant departments and the directed issue project team, GF Securities successfully raised a total of 12,179.5 million yuan, with net financing amount of 11,999.9 million yuan after deducting issuance expenses.

After the fund raising, the capital strength of GF Securities was significantly enhanced. At the end of August 2011, its net assets reached 31 billion, rising to fourth place in the industry (after CITIC Securities, Haitong Securities, and Huatai Securities), and the net capital of the parent company reached 23.7 billion yuan, reaching the third place in the industry. This achievement was extremely difficult and hard to achieve.

According to WIND statistics, GF Securities was among the top issuers at that time in terms of the amount of funds raised:

> In 2011, the GF Securities project ranked first in terms of the A-share financing scale (including IPO and refinancing, excluding strategic capital injection by major shareholders) was the only project with more than 10 billion yuan.
>
> The GF Securities project ranked tenth among nearly 690 public and private issuances (excluding asset swaps, but including strategic capital injections by major shareholders) in the history of A-share financing in China.
>
> The GF Securities project ranked fourth in the history of A-share financing of listed securities companies in China (including IPO and refinancing).

GF Securities successfully raised 12 billion yuan through a non-public offering of A-shares based on previous achievements. This greatly enhanced the company's capital, established its position in the first tier of the industry, and laid a solid foundation for its long-term sustainable development.

Listing H-shares on the international capital market

With the development of capital markets and the diversification of brokerage business, especially the rapid development of capital-consuming business such as securities margin trading, and direct investment, the demand of brokerage firms for capital was increasing.

In 2011, GF Securities formulated the Five-Year Strategic Development Plan (2011–2015), which clearly stated that "in the next five years, GF Securities will continue to narrow the gap with its leading peers and aim to reach the top three in the industry in the nine business indicators of operating income, net profit, net capital, client assets, brokerage business, investment banking, asset management business, large buy-side business, and research." The internationalization strategy, one of the six key strategies, also clearly stated that "we will strive to increase the proportion of overseas business income and the number of overseas institutional clients."

In 2013, there were three mainland securities firms listed on the Hong Kong Stock Exchange: CITIC Securities (October 6, 2011), Haitong Securities (April 27, 2012), and China Galaxy Securities (May 23, 2013). CITIC Securities and Haitong Securities were listed on the Shanghai Stock Exchange before they were listed on the Hong Kong Stock Exchange. At that time, Guotai Jun'an, Guoxin Securities, and other first-tier mainland brokerage firms were also gradually advancing in their A-share listing process. The competition in the brokerage industry, especially among the first-tier brokerage firms, was fierce.

In the competitive environment of the brokerage industry where GF Securities wanted to overtake others and avoided being overtaken, GF Securities had been exploring how to achieve listing in Hong Kong since 2013. The leadership of GF Securities had the foresight to realize that listing in Hong Kong would be more conducive to the enhancement of the company's capital strength and the expansion of its international financing channels than continuing to raise capital in the mainland A-share market. Listing in Hong Kong would be more conducive to the enhancement of the company's visibility, international branding, and reputation; it would be more conducive to the development of its international business and institutional clients; and it would be more conducive to the enhancement of its overall competitiveness. (See Figure 6)

Due to China's regulations regarding the reduction of state-owned shares for overseas listing, GF Securities had conducted a lot of exploration of Hong Kong listing methods, including the IPO method of directly issuing H-shares, the introductory listing method of converting some A-shares in the mainland into H-shares in Hong Kong, and the shell and absorption merger method of first listing GF Holdings Hong Kong Co., Ltd. or purchasing the net shell of a listed company in Hong Kong, and then absorbing and merging through share swap. Either way, there were significant challenges. Of course, the IPO method of direct H-share issuance was generally the best, but also the most difficult.

From the experience of the peers going public in Hong Kong, CITIC Securities, Haitong Securities, and China Galaxy Securities, as well as other financial institutions, all involved the tricky issue of transferring billions of yuan of capital and shares to the Social Security Fund. GF Securities had a relatively fragmented shareholding, and most of the shareholders' shares were non-state-owned legal person shares. Who would pay this part of shares or funds to the Social Security Fund ? If the issue of transferring and reducing state-owned shares could not be solved, the IPO method of directly issuing H-shares would not work.

In 2014, as the state promoted the mixed ownership economy, the state-owned assets authorities changed from "managing assets" to "managing capital." The third-largest shareholder of GF Securities, Zhongshan Public Utilities, promoted the mixed ownership reform. As Zhonghui Group transferred part of its shares to Fosun Group through an agreement, Zhongshan Public Utilities became a listed company not absolutely controlled but relatively controlled by state capital. Under the comprehensive environment at that time, the problem of transferring shares to the Social Security Fund faced by GF Securities to directly issue H-shares through an IPO was solved.

Then, GF Securities quickly launched and precisely executed the H-share IPO program, namely the Future Glory Project. The project took only 141 days from the formation of the board resolution to the successful listing, and was completed to the day in accordance with the initial timeline.

On April 10, 2015, GF Securities was successfully listed on the Hong Kong Stock Exchange. The iconic large screen prominently displayed the "GF Securities Co., Ltd." and "Stock Code: 1776" logo in traditional Chinese characters. Chairman Sun Shuming and HKEx CEO Charles Li Xiaojia smiled and shook hands, announcing the successful debut of GF Securities in the international capital market.

GF Securities H-share's global offering was 1.48 billion shares, and the issue price was HK$18.85 per share. After the full exercise of the over-allotment option on April 13, the number of H-shares issued by GF Securities reached 1.702 billion, raising a total of HK32.079 billion.

According to Goldman Sachs, the sponsor, this was the largest IPO of any brokerage firm in the world at that time, and the largest IPO in Asia and the second-largest IPO in the world at that time), the highest valuation (diluted P/N ratio of 1.61 times for GF Securities, 1.28 times for CITIC Securities, 1.30 times for Haitong Securities, and 1.25 times for China Galaxy Securities), the most efficient execution (4.5 months, compared to the normal 6–8 months), and the most enthusiastic subscription (50 percent lock-up for Cornerstone, 15 times subscription for the international placement, 180 times for the Hong Kong public offering).

GF Securities' H-shares opened at HK26.50 per share and closed at HK25.40 per share, up 34.75 percent from the offering price on the listing day. From March 31, when GF Securities finalized the pricing of its offering, to April 10, the H-shares of CITIC Securities and Haitong Securities rose 25.22 percent and 34.20 percent, respectively. GF Securities' stock price fluctuated between 30 percent and 40 percent on the listing day, the pricing of the H-share offering was reasonable and fair, and the increase was reasonable and normal compared to the increase of comparable brokerage stocks in the same period.

The successful issuance and listing of H-shares was an important milestone in the development of GF Securities and another new starting point for GF Securities. The H-share IPO of GF Securities was significant from multiple perspectives. The HK32.079 billion raised by the IPO, supplemented by the leverage that meets regulatory requirements, had strongly supported GF Securities' capital needs in the following years and had greatly benefited businesses such as securities margin trading. With the combined benefits brought by the A+H listing, the overall debt capacity of GF Securities was significantly enhanced. According to the regression analysis of the development of the securities industry in the post-2015 period, capital strength showed a very high positive correlation with the ranking of brokerage firms, which confirms the importance of the H-share listing in 2015 for GF Securities to maintain its top position in the industry.

Around 2014, many international investors still had a rudimentary understanding of China's securities industry, with stereotypes such as "a high degree of state control, a lack of vitality, single business, and living at the mercy of the elements." Through communication with international investors, GF Securities and other organizations had gradually refreshed the understanding of the Chinese securities industry by international capital and public media. During the international roadshow, GF Securities' senior management publicized and explained the laws and prospects of China's economic transformation and capital markets development, prompting international capital to change their understanding and increase their confidence, and successfully reversing international institutional investors' ambiguous understanding of China's capital markets. The project issuance results confirmed that international capital cast a vote of confidence in China's economic development and capital markets.

The H-share offering enhanced GF Securities' capital strength and international visibility, while helping GF Securities to gain access to a large number of international investors and partner resources. The listing in the international capital market was also conducive to further standardization of GF Securities' operation and improvement of management level and corporate governance structure, enabling GF Securities to move forward toward its strategic goal of "becoming a modern investment bank with international competitiveness, brand influence, and systemic importance."

With hardships and difficulties, GF Securities was able to achieve success. From "shareholding," which was proposed in October 1994 as part of the four-pronged approach, to February 2010, when GF Securities rang the listing bell at the Shenzhen Stock Exchange, to April 2015, when the company was listed on the H-share market, GF Securities used the successful listing to make the best explanation of its the development process and to bring the best return to shareholders, employees, and stakeholders. With the successful listing, GF Securities, the third A+H share brokerage company in China, continued its dream-chasing journey in the capital markets.

Chapter X: The GF Phenomenon in the Fund Industry

The right path is this: learn from what your predecessors have done, and move forward.

—Leo Tolstoy

If you look at the geographical distribution of Chinese fund companies, you would find that almost all large fund management companies with a scale of more than 100 billion yuan have their headquarters in Beijing, Shanghai, and Shenzhen, but there are two companies that have chosen to settle in Guangzhou. They are E Fund and GF Fund launched by GF Securities.

It was these two fund companies that, in a rare case, ranked among the top ten in the industry soon after their establishment. They explored and adhered to the concept of value investment early in the industry. They always grasped opportunities and promoted development regardless of the market ups and downs, and moved in the forefront of the industry quickly and steadily despite difficulties and hardships. They became a unique GF phenomenon in the fund industry.

What made them able to turn danger into success in every crisis they faced? What made them resist the temptation of the market and always stay true to their established policy? What made them make the right strategic choice again and again in the wave of the times? What made them develop further? To answer all these questions, we have to begin with GF Securities, which was in the spring tide of reform.

1. Starting securities investment fund business

Originating from "old funds"

In Western countries, investment fund is a type of financial investment organized in the form of shareholding after the securities market developed to a certain extent. However, in China, the development of investment funds and the securities market started almost simultaneously. What we now know as "funds" in China are originally called "new funds," but before that, there was a little-known "old fund" era.

In January 1991, the People's Bank of China issued the Circular on Strict Management of Overseas Securities Investment Approval, which clearly stated that "Chinese securities companies and other financial institutions that can operate securities business are allowed to start investment fund business in China."

A group of pioneers with a keen sense of the market took action and investment funds, an "imported product," began to spring up all over the country, bursting into vigorous life. Most of these initial fund products were not really securities investment funds, as they were mainly industrial funds, or a mixture of industrial investment and securities investment funds, in terms of investment direction, and thus these funds were also called "old funds."[1]

At that time, few people in China really knew what funds were for, and there were not even any books on the subject. But the word "fund" was not new to Dr. Chen Yunxian. As early as 1991, in his doctoral dissertation "A Comparative Study of Chinese and Foreign Portfolio Investment," he had forward-lookingly proposed that "stock investment should be realized by an improved market mechanism, and the relationship between primary and secondary markets should not be artificially cut off." This means that securities companies not only engage in primary market business as investment bankers, but also carry out secondary market investment business at the same time. After joining the capital markets and founding GF Securities, Dr. Chen Yunxian realized more and more clearly that "funds" were an indispensable part of securities companies in the development of secondary market business.

At the end of 1991, in the first year-end summary of the Securities Department of Guangdong Development Bank, Dr. Chen Yunxian formally included "developing securities investment funds" in the work plan of the following year. In 1992, with the approval of the Guangdong Branch of the People's Bank of China, the Investment Fund Management Department of Guangdong Development Bank was established with independent legal person status under the supervision of Dr. Chen Yunxian. Its first general manager was Mr. Wang Hongmao, who was later called "Uncle Mao"

1 It was customary to refer to funds established after the implementation of the Interim Measures for the Administration of Securities Investment Funds in 1998 as "new funds" and to those established before 1998 as "old funds." See Ma Qingquan and Liu Zhao, *A Concise History of China's Fund Industry (1998–2013)* (China Financial Publishing House, Beijing, 2014).

by GF people. In October of that year, the Fund Department issued the first closed-end fund product, GF Investment Fund, also known as "GF I," with 50 million units in a targeted offering. The product was listed on the Southern Stock Exchange on August 18, 1993, becoming the first "securities investment fund" listed in Guangdong Province.

It was not always easy for a new business to be finally recognized, understood, and accepted. Just between 1992 and 1993, a professor teaching finance at Jinan University in Guangzhou and serving as a counsellor to the Guangdong Provincial People's Government seriously refuted Dr. Chen's views on the development of fund business at a conference. His reasoning was that "the various mutual funds at the grassroots level in rural areas have already messed up the financial market enough, and you are here to start a 'fund.'" Undoubtedly, this professor equated the new fund business with the underground bidding associations that engaged in private lending.

Dr. Chen recalls, "Although he was a university professor of finance, he unleashed a critical accusation that left us speechless when he did not know much about the new fund business." For the questioning and criticism, GF people did not retreat and falter, but insisted on following the established direction to do a good job in fund performance and reward investors as the best answer.

Due to the shortage of supply, the highest price per unit of "GF I," which was offered at 1, once reached 5.40 during its existence, and the fund was hardly available on the market. Not only was the fund popular in the secondary market, it also achieved an average annualized return of more than 15 percent during its duration and paid dividends every year, which was widely recognized by investors. After the success, the subsequent GF II product sold out in half a day, making GF Securities the only asset management institution managing two funds at the same time in China.

This achievement was not only sought after by investors, but also recognized by the industry. At the annual meeting of Securities Association of China in 1995, Dr. Chen Yunxian was invited to introduce GF's experience to the whole industry, and his views on "how GF Securities understands and expands the fund business" attracted the attention of the whole audience. Dr. Chen Yunxian proposed that fund investment should adhere to the principle of "portfolio investment, risk diversification and comprehensive return," and management must adhere to the idea of "managing wealth on people's behalf and making it appreciate in value," and should implement "sound management" The management must adhere to the origin of "managing people's money and making it increase in value," and should implement the policy of "sound management." These GF experiences from old funds became the basic guidelines for the development of public funds in the future, and provided valuable experience for the establishment of a standardized management system in the fund industry.

From the very beginning, Dr. Chen Yunxian envisioned not merely issuing one or two fund products. In the four-pronged approach of GF Securities, namely "shareholding, conglomeration, internationalization, and standardization," conglomeration consisted of investment banking, brokerage, and asset management business, and fund business was an important part of the asset management business of the "conglomerate."

GF Securities was able to introduce the GF experience to the whole industry because it was always two or three steps ahead of others. The employees of GF Securities summarized it bluntly as "I have what no one else has, I am doing especially well in what others are also doing, and I am doing better when others are doing especially well." On May 30, 1992, the Guangdong Development Bank Securities Department became one of the first off-site members of the Shenzhen Stock Exchange. On September 8 of the same year, it became a member of the Shanghai Stock Exchange.

On September 8, 1992, it became the first agent in Guangzhou for stock exchange at the Shenzhen Stock Exchange.

October 1992, it issued the first fund in Guangdong.

In March 1993, it became the first agent in Guangzhou for stock exchange at the Shanghai Stock Exchange.

In April 1993, it became the first to conduct listing and trading of NET corporate shares.

In May 1993, it became the first to operate futures clearing business.

In May 1994, when underwriting Guangdong Zhaoqing Star Lake MSG, it created the issuance method of "full prepayment, proportional allocation, refundable balance, and payment." The CSRC made this method one of the main methods of stock issuance for the country as a whole.

In December 1994, in the issuance of public shares of Zhongshan Torch, it created the issuance method of "free reservation, limited subscription, and lottery allocation."

At the end of 1995, it acquired the former Haidian Island Brokerage Branch of Zhejiang Securities, which was the first acquisition and merger among domestic brokerage firms.

It can be said that from the time when GF Securities was established to 1995, almost all the innovations of securities business in Guangdong Province came from GF Securities. Among them, the pioneering development of fund business during the "old fund" period with the accumulation of valuable experience, was not isolated innovation, but the fruit of innovation in the overall planning of the capital markets at that time.

The first crab eater in the "new fund era"

The rapid development of "old funds" was accompanied by the lack of a unified regulatory framework, multiple management, unclear product investment, and substandard management, making the fund market during this period inevitably characterized by a transitional period.

Recognizing the current situation and drawbacks of the domestic market, which was dominated by retail investors, the regulators drew on the successful experience of international markets and studied domestic practices, and a regulated regulatory system for the fund industry gradually took shape. In November 1997, the Securities Commission of the State Council promulgated the Provisional Measures for Securities Investment Fund Administration, which put an end to the previous situation of unregulated and disorderly development of fund business and further clarified the procedures of fund companies and fund establishment. The underlying regulatory framework for the fund business in the new era was also already completed. This gave a rebirth to the fund business and ushered in the new fund era.

GF Securities firmly carried out the planning and development of the new fund business, and treated fund business as the core segment of its conglomeration effort.

What kind of people should be chosen to explore this unknown blue ocean? Dr. Chen Yunxian set his eyes on his old partner Dr. Ma Qingquan.

Dr. Ma Qingquan still recalls his first experience with funds: "In mid-1997, after I stopped serving as president of GF Securities, Dr. Chen Yunxian gave me a copy of the newly published Interviews with Nine Major International Investment Fund Managers with a message. Since then I have had a close relationship with the fund industry."

In 1998, under the guidance of the competent authorities to "legislate first and pilot later," GF Securities, as the main sponsor, together with three other companies, initiated the establishment of Harvest Fund, which was opened in March 1999. Dr. Ma Qingquan became the first chairman of Harvest Fund. GF's fund business set sail again. (See Figure 7)

In parallel with the establishment of the "old ten" funds, the liquidation of the "old funds" was also in full swing. In March 1999, the China Securities Regulatory Commission started to restructure and clean up the original securities investment funds. However, most of the "old funds" posed a huge challenge to the cleanup work due to the irregularities in the initial establishment. The idea of "using market means to bring in external parties to participate in the cleanup of 'old funds'" gradually became clear when the cleanup work was at a deadlock.

At the end of 1999, in order to cooperate with the transformation of "old funds" in Guangdong Province, Ye Junying, then vice president of GF Securities, convened the first Guangdong Province "Old Funds" Clean-Up Meeting in a small conference room on the forty-third floor of Metropolis Plaza. The participants at that time became the members who later participated in the establishment of the "E Fund Preparatory Group."

Liu Xiaoyan, who is now the president of E Fund, was one of the main members of the preparatory group at that time. As a "veteran GF employee" Liu Xiaoyan had worked in GF Securities' Investment and Finance Department, Fund Department, and other departments, and had witnessed a scene in a brokerage branch that changed her life: an elderly couple sitting on the steps of the brokerage branch hugging and crying because they had lost money in stock speculation.

"I saw this scene at that time and was shocked and felt sad. I went to ask Dr. Ma Qingquan if there was a business that could help not only brokerage firms make money for themselves but also for ordinary people?" Liu Xiaoyan still remembers Dr. Ma's reply: "You should do funds. Funds manage the money of the general public."

It was with her enthusiasm for her work that Liu Xiaoyan participated in the establishment of E Fund, serving as E Fund's inspector and general manager of the Supervision Department, assistant general manager, general manager of the Marketing Department, marketing director, vice president of the company, and executive vice president of the company, before taking over as president in 2011.

Initially, there were only six people in the E Fund Preparatory Group, all of whom were veterans of the securities industry. They gave up their jobs at brokerage firms and other relatively mature platforms to join the new industry of public funds. Facing new things, this group of young people's perception of the fund industry was also very vague, and most of them entered the industry with the simple idea of "doing something and helping ordinary people make money." The preparatory work was not as smooth as expected, cleaning up and standardizing "old funds." For them communicating with the regulatory authorities, and finding shareholders of other provinces in accordance with regulatory requirements—everything was like feeling the stone in crossing the river.

Many years later, Liu Xiaoyan still had a vivid memory of the first preparatory meeting of E Fund: "There was no ceremony, no record, no photo. We didn't know that after that day, we would come together, work together, explore together, create together, argue together, laugh together, look forward to the future together, and look back on the past together. Nor did we think that it would be the beginning of an era of passion, growth, and splendor." In that year, the size of the fund industry was 60.32 billion yuan, less than the size of an average asset management company today.

In 2001, when the internet concept was at its peak, the English name of E Fund carried the expectations of the founding team for this "new fund" to bravely embrace the new era. After giving the fund its English name, the idea of having a Chinese name was very simple: "The names of the funds established before us were all very big: Guotai, Fuguo, and Huaxia, so we thought we'd just had a three-word one." Old colleagues recalled, "So there was Yifangda. It just so happened that it also sounds like Yifada (easy to get rich). It sounds very Cantonese; it is auspicious." The more we use this unconventional company name, the more we like it. After a market test, it gives it a richer and deeper connotation such as "turn the difficult into the easy and achieve success if you put your heart into it."

In April 2001, GF Securities, together with five other institutions, established E Fund in accordance with regulatory requirements, with a balanced and equal shareholding of shareholders within and outside Guangdong Province. Ye Junying was the first general manager of E Fund. With the joint efforts of the shareholders, the board of directors and the management of E Fund, a balanced and stable shareholder structure was formed to ensure that the business philosophy of "sustainable and steady growth through professional operation and teamwork under the premise of integrity and regulation" was adhered to and implemented.

After the "old ten" funds, E Fund was the first fund of the second group of funds established in the industry. E Fund was also the first fund established after the transformation of the "old funds," and it happened to be the first fund in the industry to be established in a place other than Beijing, Shanghai, and Shenzhen, with the dual mission of transforming the "old funds" and issuing "new funds." In December 2001, six "old funds," including GF I and II, were transformed and merged into E Fund's Fund Kexiang, Fund Kehui, and Fund Kexun, which were each listed on the Shenzhen and the Shanghai Stock Exchanges and completed their expansion soon after listing. These three products had become the basis for E Fund's subsequent development, and while promoting the transformation of "old funds" in Guangdong Province, they also provided useful reference for the transformation of "old funds" elsewhere.

During the pilot period of "new funds," GF Securities launched and established two companies in succession, namely Harvest and E Fund, and deeply participated in the transformation of fund products from "old funds" to "new funds," which also proved GF Securities' firm confidence in the long-term development of fund business.

With the establishment of funds becoming normalized, the requirements of the competent authorities for the equity of funds had gradually changed from equal equity to the policy that the number of fund management companies in which an institution or a number of institutions controlled by the same beneficial owner would not exceed two, of which the number of controlling fund management companies would not exceed one. GF Securities could finally set up a holding fund company in accordance with the established goal of conglomeration and participate more deeply in the historical process of deepening reform of China's fund industry.

However, according to the regulatory requirements, GF Securities needed to solve the problem of its own participation in two funds first. To this end, GF Securities held several meetings to repeatedly study the issue of transferring equity interests in either Harvest Fund or E Fund. Finally, GF Securities decided to transfer the equity of Harvest Fund and launch a new fund, GF Fund, as the controlling shareholder.

To establish the new fund, it was necessary to appoint its chief first. Dr. Chen Yunxian first thought of Lin Chuanhui, then executive vice president of

Investment Banking Department of GF Securities, who was looking for a "general" who was good at developing new business and had a long-term strategic vision for the GF Fund in the making.

Lin Chuanhui recalled that he was on a business trip when he suddenly received a call from Dr. Chen Yunxian who hoped that Lin could participate in the preparatory work of GF Fund. Lin was very surprised, "I really didn't expect to be me. I'm really not familiar with the fund business." But since the leaders trusted him so much and entrusted him with the important task of opening up the business, Lin Chuanhui resolutely said goodbye to the familiar investment banking and devoted himself to the fund industry.

In fact, it was not only Lin Chuanhui who was facing an important life decision. For many others, going from the booming securities industry to the fund industry with an unknown future was a risky venture. At that time, many funds were faced with the dilemma of not being able to find people when they were established. Fortunately, GF Fund received strong support from GF Securities. In order to select talents for GF Fund, GF Securities directly conducted internal selection from all its departments, and at one time, application materials came from all over the country.

During this period, the stock market had experienced more than two years of continuous downturn, and 2002 was a rare year of adjustment. In addition, in the A-share market at that time, "speculation based on hearsay" and "buying on the upswing, and selling on the downswing" was the norm of stockholders' investment. As a result, the ordinary investors who knew little about financial investment often suffered heavy losses. Faced with such a situation, a group of young people from GF Securities, with the disbelief of their friends and relatives and the pressure of the long bear market, were ready to join the fund industry which GF Securities was exploring continuously.

At the beginning of the preparation, employees from all over the country applied, but the selection was very strict, requiring both youthfulness and high quality. The reasons were: firstly, the essence of fund investment was "to manage money on behalf of others," so it was necessary to always keep integrity as the basis, and to always "bear in mind others' entrustment" in order to be faithful to others; secondly, only with very high professional quality could one achieve the goal of helping clients to defuse risks in both bull and bear markets and improve profits; and finally, as the fund industry was full of temptation, practitioners must be highly self-disciplined, have outstanding character, and maintain respect for the market. With these stringent requirements, the preparatory team selected 24 individuals through various levels of selection. As the preparatory work progressed, the team gradually expanded to 32 people, and a vigorous entrepreneurial team was formed. Kong Weiying, the current head of the Human Resources Department of GF Fund, recalls, "When selecting people, we had to look at both professionalism and talent, as well as quality and personality, and we put more emphasis on the latter. We finally selected spirited and capable elite individuals."

In November 2002, the SARS epidemic came unexpectedly, and this period was also the most critical for the preparation of GF Fund. At that time, the drafting of the Securities Investment Fund Law had already entered its final stage, and the public fund industry was undergoing crucial regulation, with a more standardized top-level system design bringing a historic development opportunity for the industry. This undoubtedly was the best opportunity for GF people to move into the fund industry. But SARS was raging, some companies and factories were closed, and the usually lively office buildings were silent. Lan Huiyan, a member of GF Fund's start-up team, was anxious.

As the person in charge of preparing materials for submission and approval, she often had to travel to several cities a day to visit company directors and independent directors to solicit and collect their comments and signatures on the filing materials. Beijing was the city she visited most often. She vividly remembers how she went to Beijing to deliver materials during the SARS outbreak: "At that time, almost no one traveled to Beijing or did business there, and there was almost no one in the hotels. At that time, the office of the China Securities Regulatory Commission was under quarantine for the epidemic, and visitors were not allowed to enter. The receptionist asked us to put the filing materials on a tray, and then carefully took them out with tweezers wearing gloves and sent them to the approval office." Lan Huiyan recalls the working condition of everyone at the start-up stage, saying, "No one in the preparatory group took leave, staying up late and working overtime was the norm, everyone did their best full of emotion." Even during the extremely severe situation of SARS, the preparatory work of GF Fund was not delayed.

On August 5, 2003, GF Fund was officially established, with Dong Zhengqing, then executive vice president of GF Securities, as chairman and Lin Chuanhui as general manager. GF Fund became the thirtieth new fund in China and one of the third group of "new funds." (See Figure 8)

Looking back at the development of the two "GF" funds—E Fund and GF Fund, the reason why they were able to gain a firm foothold at the beginning was due to the factors of the times of the great development of the Chinese fund industry, as well as some unique advantages.

First, the two funds both had very good governance structures. GF Securities, as their shareholder, had a deep understanding of the asset management industry, attached importance to the standardized management of the funds, trusted their professional management teams, and did not interfere too much in their specific operations.

Second, GF Securities' accumulation of expertise, clients, and experience and its advantages in investment banking had laid a good foundation for value investment for the two funds.

Third, the backbone of GF Securities became the mainstay of the initial teams of the two funds, and formed two excellent teams with professional ability and courage to fight.

The ocean is boundless for fish to leap at will and the sky is unlimited for birds to fly at ease. During the transition period of fund business between old and new funds, GF Securities transferred a large number of professionals to the fund industry, such as Ma Qingquan, Ye Junying, Yu Liping, Lin Chuanhui, Liu Xiaoyan, and Jiang Zuoliang. During the preparation period, Dong Zhengqing, Sun Xiaoyan, and others also contributed a lot to the management structure of the funds. They firmly bore in mind and implemented the professional, hardworking, and pragmatic spirit of GF people and became the fund industry's early pioneers and wrote their own wonderful stories in their subsequent careers.

Beginning with the end in mind and integrating "standardization" into the DNA

In the four-pronged approach of GF Securities proposed by Dr. Chen Yunxian, "standardization" was an important prerequisite for the company's conglomeration. Similarly, the two funds of GF Securities also made standardization their goal.

During the preparation of the open-end fund of E Fund, a foreign expert group asked during the inspection, "Why do you attach importance to the professionalization of corporate governance management?" Then President Ye Junying replied, "I have been involved in China's capital markets since the early 1990s at GF Securities. We have experienced many risky events in the industry, and have seen some examples of securities companies being liquidated and bankrupt or restructured and reorganized due to mistakes in compliance issues, so we know very well that integrity and standardization are the foundation stone for the long-term survival and development of a fund."

In 2000, media coverage of fund practices raised many concerns and even questions about the functional role of funds in stabilizing the market. Against this backdrop, E Fund, which was in the process of being established, as a new force in the industry, had an even greater need to think deeply about the issue of continuous standardization and blaze a new path for the Chinese fund industry. With the questions, Ye Junying studied in depth the legal relationship of China's fund industry, and wrote an article, "Discussion on Some Basic Legal Issues of Securities Investment Funds." The article elaborated that the core of the legal nature of funds was the fiduciary relationship, and pointed out clearly the essence of funds was "managing the money of others on their behalf." Therefore, the cornerstone of the fund industry and the development of funds was integrity and performance. Only by being honest and standardized can we gain trust and be entrusted, and only by giving investors stable and good returns can we continue to develop and grow. Based on the in-depth understanding of the essence of the industry, E Fund established the early business philosophy of "sustainable and steady growth under the premise of lawfulness," which had been continuously improved in the subsequent development.

In order to make the newly established E Fund strong, in terms of its governance, Ye Junying led a team to conduct in-depth research and analysis, and write an article entitled "Fund Governance Arrangements to Avoid the US Mutual Fund Scandals." Starting from the regulatory measures of the US mutual fund industry, the article prospectively concluded that mandatory external governance is important as an institutional arrangement, including fund managers' admission standards, practitioners' practice standards, mandatory trusteeship of fund assets, investment ratio prohibition and restriction systems, and strict internal control systems. These valuable studies have provided important references for E Fund to develop a scientific and effective compliance system since then.

The entrepreneurial team's pursuit of "standardized management" drove the entire company's passion for fund management. The staff of E Fund studied and researched from foreign experts and international audit and consulting institutions, and wrote more than 50 papers in their spare time, from which nearly 20 papers were selected to become a book titled *Securities Investment Funds: Theory and Practice*. Edited by Ye Junying, the book was published in 2002 and received a lot of attention and good comments from the industry. Some of the research and analysis on foreign fund industry was not only the earliest in China at that time, but also still has considerable reference value even now.

By studying the governance structures of model fund companies in different countries and creatively combining them with China's reality, E Fund became the first in the industry to introduce the system of independent directors, forming a balanced and stable governance structure. In addition, it innovatively designed a four-level internal control system, including articles of association, internal control principles, basic systems, and departmental systems based on the requirements of the China Securities Regulatory Commission. In this way, it formed a risk management-oriented, top-down and bottom-up pragmatic and effective system for internal control. The company also conducted in-depth and comprehensive research on the principles, risks, and responses of each aspect of open-end fund operation, which laid a solid foundation for the company to establish a fund business operation management system in line with international standards, and provided a strong guarantee for the standardized and sound operation in the future. An employee, who was involved in the process of establishing internal control systems, laughingly said, "Years later, when we exchanged and cooperated with world-class capital management institutions, we felt that we were actually very close in cognition, philosophy, and framework, mainly due to the company's early forward-looking research and study."

In addition, the system had its own process to improve and update. Each part of the company such as investment research and risk management would review and update their systems. Ye Junying wrote a 10,000-word-long article "The Process" for all staff, explaining the importance of institutional processes for a company's continued sound and innovative development. He argued that process was a long-term dynamic process that unifies institutional development and implementation and integrates robustness and innovation. For a sustainable company, designing and improving the process was a continuous process of "standardization-innovation-standardization," which would enable the company to maintain a solid and stable foundation while sustaining the vitality of development. The core competitive ability of an excellent company was derived from this internal process improvement based on continuous sublation and upgrading.

It was in such an atmosphere of constant review and learning that norms were integrated into the business process and became the starting point of what E Fund did. It was because of these systems and norms that the business could achieve steady development and realize the long-term goal of "winning in the long run."

After GF Fund was established, it also attached great importance to the requirement of "standardization," drawing on domestic and international experience to institutionalize its business and make it process-based. In its subsequent years of operation, it always took compliance as its lifeline and firmly established the risk control concept of creating value through compliance. A veteran employee who had been working on risk control at GF Fund for many years once lamented: "GF Fund has always been operating in a stable and steady style. We will not do anything that is not in line with the principle of the asset management industry, and our culture has been like this since GF Securities was established, and it has never changed over the years." This sense of mission to live up to every trust of investors drove every employee of GF Fund to always have the word compliance engraved in their hearts.

"People are careful when crossing the Jingxi River with dangerous reefs and rapid waves. No one is heard falling into the river and drowning all year round." It was because they paid great importance to compliance and risk control that the two companies always focused on standardized operation, bore in mind the essence of the fund, faithfully fulfilled their fiduciary duties, abided by their fiduciary obligations, and took care not to cross bottom line for industrial risks. As a result, they won the trust and support of more and more investors.

Everyone works together to make their first fund sales a success

As one of the second and third batches of fund companies in China's fund industry respectively, E Fund and GF Fund did not have a "first mover advantage" in a sense. When E Fund was first established, its three closed-end fund products were all derived from restructured old funds. After 2002, open-end funds started to emerge and relied heavily on sales channels, but the market at that time was characterized by low market awareness and customer trust in public funds, and the sales team had no experience in how to sell open-end funds. How to ensure the establishment of the first open-end fund under heavy difficulties became a common problem for both companies.

An open-end fund is a fund whose total amount of fund shares is not fixed and whose shares can be purchased or redeemed at the time and place agreed in the fund contract. It is the mainstream product of the global mutual fund industry. Compared to closed-end funds, open-end funds give investors the right to "vote with their feet" and can force managers to improve performance and services, which is more in line with the long-term development of the securities investment fund industry. Open-end funds are a major innovation for the fund industry.

Through previous investigation and research, E Fund was optimistic about the development prospect of open-end funds and believed that its advanced scientific governance and operation model and more effective investor interest protection mechanism represented the development direction of the public fund industry and would be the mainstream model for the development of China's fund industry. Therefore, the newly established E Fund made great efforts to prepare for and develop open-end funds.

But issuing open-end funds was a big test for a fund management company's comprehensive ability. In product design, system preparation, personnel capacity, crisis management, and sales organization, fund companies must meet the standards in all respects, in order to be able to control and manage such type of products for which investors could "vote with their feet." Compared with other peers who were included in the pilot and had been preparing for more than six months, E Fund was a latecomer at that time. In order to catch up and seize the opportunity, E Fund completed all the preparations within six months and passed the on-site inspection by the CSRC and the Panel of Overseas Investment Fund Experts on December 15, 2001, and was granted the approval to issue the first group of open-end funds.

After passing the issuance qualification hurdle, the real test would follow: sales.

Closed-end funds were mainly sold to investors who had accounts with securities companies, and the target customers were retail and institutional investors of securities companies. While open-end funds were mainly designed for low and medium risk bank counter customers, the sales channels and modes were completely different. How to do a good job of open-end fund sales was a difficult problem facing E Fund.

In the market at that time, retail customers had limited knowledge of the fund. "Is this new thing risk free?" "Is it definitely profitable?" This type of question was the most heard by the sales team. Not only the end customers, but also the banks were not familiar with the intermediate business of fund distribution, and the thinking that "deposit is king" prevailed. To do a good job in investor education was to do a good job in fund sales, ensuring that channels and customers fully understood the characteristics of open-end funds and E Fund's investment philosophy, which became the core work policy of E Fund's first open-end fund sales team.

During a visit to Germany, Ye Junying met with a company whose average age of clients was significantly older, and which provided services to its clients mostly for decades. He believed that when doing sales, E Fund should look for people who shared the same ideas as the fund managers and would go on together because of trust, work together until old age because they harbored a common philosophy, and do something long-lasting together.

This vision, which still seems a bit idealistic nowadays, was practiced by the sales team of E Fund since the first open-ended fund was sold.

E Fund's first open-end fund, "Steady Growth," was issued in partnership with Bank of China. Bank of China had branches in major cities across the country, featuring foreign exchange and import and export business and having high-caliber staff and customers, making it an ideal partner. Since open-end funds were also an important and innovative business for Bank of China, it gave strategic input and support.

Thus, led by Ye Junying, E Fund's sales team of less than ten people at that time, with an average age of less than 30, passionately ran around the country with a group of young people from Bank of China's Trusteeship Department, organized top-down activities such as bank-wide meetings and training, financial planner training at major outlets, and direct presentations to key customers. To make frontline sales staff and key customers have a correct understanding of the open-end fund concept in a short period of time, each person had to do four or five training sessions in a day according to the high coverage requirement to reach as many customers as possible at that time.

Through such intensive training, the young sales staff of E Fund conveyed the features of open-end funds, product return characteristics and the company brand of E Fund to the frontline of bank branches.

The high-intensity work trained the team of E Fund, and a group of young new employees grew up rapidly and became the backbone of the team who could take charge of their own business. Later, Chen Tong, vice president in charge of domestic market, was a member of the sales team of the first open-end fund "Steady Growth."

After hard work, on August 23, 2002, E Fund's "Steady Growth" open-end fund was established, with an initial launch size of 4.67 billion yuan. The fund size managed by E Fund took a big step to reach the new level of more than 10 billion yuan, ranking the company among the biggest in the industry.

In its second year of operation, in a market environment where the stock market was all the way down, E Fund achieved rapid development with a scientific, serious, and demanding work attitude. At the celebration banquet at the end of the "Steady Growth" issue, Jiang Zuoliang, who was the general manager of E Fund's Investment Management Department, said with a smile, "In the future, we will not just drink porridge anymore, there is some meat in the pot." That celebration party left a deep impression on many veteran employees of E Fund, and they all remembered that the celebration party was by Luhu Lake in Guangzhou, and the moon was very round and bright that night, reflecting on Luhu Lake.

If the sale of E Fund's "Steady Growth" was a "wealth missionary" journey led by investor education in a market where open-end funds were not fully understood, then the fundraising of GF's first product, GF Jufu Fund, was a "desperate battle" that tested faith and courage.

GF Fund was established in 2003 at a time when the number of fund companies and fund products in China's fund industry was growing rapidly. In that year, 29 new fund companies were established and approved for preparation, more than the total number of companies established in the previous four years. A total of 39 open-end funds were launched in the year. However, the distribution channels and industry resources were disproportionately tilted toward the old fund management companies, making the situation for new companies quite difficult.

If the first fund failed, the start-up team of GF Fund might even fail to make ends meet. The newly established GF Fund, without the support of performance and brand, was unknown in the channels. For the market development staff of GF Fund, they were facing a big test that they could not afford to lose.

Yang Jingyuan, who was in charge of channel development in Beijing at that time, had previously worked in the Trading Department of GF Securities, and it was a new test for her to develop the market. During the SARS outbreak in Beijing, the roads were empty, and Yang was running around the headquarters and branch offices of ICBC. At that time, many people did not know GF Securities, so she knocked on the bank's door with GF Securities' business license: "It was not uncommon for her to wait outside for hours to meet and communicate with the other party's leaders. Following many visits, she got familiar with her clients, so she worked at the bank's fund agency office and ate in their cafeteria. As a result, she was mistaken by the bank satisfaction for their new colleague." The trust was built up through visit after visit and communication, and some of her bank branch managers even said, "I had never heard of GF Fund before, but I know you, so I am willing to cooperate with you."

Relying on the "stupid method" of running through the soles of everyone's shoes and on their hard work, GF Fund gradually opened up the channels for selling funds through banks.

In addition to the strong support from the trusteeship bank ICBC, the parent company GF Securities played an important role as the main distribution broker. "Dong Zhengqing, who was also chairman of GF Fund, asked GF Securities to give full support and cooperation when selling the fund. He made full mobilization in GF Securities. In the end, the total distribution amount of our GF Securities and its subsidiaries even exceeded that of the trusteeship bank. When GF Securities wanted to do something, it mobilized all its strength," Zhao Guiping, who was in charge of GF Securities' brokerage business at that time, remembers it well.

In bank channels, quality customer resources were in the hands of client managers. In order to make them recognize GF Securities, a fledgling company, GF Securities spent a lot of effort to train them and help them improve their sales skills: "Our training courses were also very popular in banks." Xiao Wen, then deputy general manager of GF Fund, recalls, "At that time, GF Fund's marketing team had only about 20 people, but we always asked everyone to strive to be at the forefront of the industry. For example, for the training of bank client managers, when many companies were still doing work in the first-level bank branches, we had already reached the second-level branches; when others started to work on the second-level branches, we had already penetrated into the key outlets."

With the great efforts of all the people in the company, GF Fund had withstood the severe test of no historical performance and no brand effect at the beginning of the first product launch, and achieved success. Among the four funds launched at the same time, the first product of GF Fund, GF Jufu, topped the list with a fundraising amount of 3.138 billion yuan. Industrial and Commercial Bank of China, with two funds being distributed at the same time, distributed a total of 1.15 billion yuan for GFJIF, while GF Securities and its subsidiaries distributed a total of 1.27 billion yuan, creating a new model of fund sales in which brokerage firms and banks distributed almost the same amount.

The success of the first shot in the market was only the first step of a long march for E Fund and GF Securities, because at the beginning of the twenty-first century, Dr. Chen Yunxian set a goal for them "to become 100 billion yuan funds."

"We were shocked that this goal was a little too big." Lan Huiyan, the first inspector general of GF Fund who attended the meeting, could not believe this "100 billion yuan target." Would it be a myth for the latecomers E Fund and GF Fund to become 100 billion yuan funds in just a few years?

In fact, Dr. Chen Yunxian's goal, which seemed unattainable, was set only after careful consideration. As a pioneer in the study of investment theories in overseas capital markets, he firmly believed that, compared to overseas markets, China's capital markets had just started and there was a lot of room for future development.

Faced with this ambitious goal, his old partner Dr. Ma Qingquan showed great confidence: "The market trend is going up in the long run, the market capacity is changing, and the scale of funds will be enlarged accordingly. In addition, the fund industry has been developing for seven or eight years, and the scale of management is too small. How can it be brought in line with the international market? Chinese fund management companies should have the courage to manage big funds." Having studied political economy, he said at that time with foresight: "The emergence of a large fund group in the Chinese fund industry is inevitable; it was a historical necessity." (See Figure 9)

In the following years, the fund industry developed rapidly, public funds truly every household, and the power of "inclusive finance" erupted. In May 2006, GF Celüe Youxuan, the sixth fund managed by GF, was launched with an initial offering of 18.4 billion yuan. It became the fund with the largest initial offering, the shortest initial subscription period, and the largest number of effective initial subscriptions in the Chinese fund industry at the time. In April 2007, E Fund's "Jiazhi Chengzhang Honghe" was announced to be closed one day early, valid subscription applications reached 19.5 billion yuan, and the effective subscription amount was confirmed after the implementation of the proportional placement was approximately 11 billion yuan. In June 2007, "Dapan" sold out in one day, raising more than 27.3 billion yuan on the same day of issuance, and the final confirmed effective subscription amount was about 15 billion yuan after proportional allocation, with more than 600,000 effective subscribers. In September 2007, "GF Jufeng" was split into shares and opened for subscription on October 11, resulting in a one-day collection of over 60 billion yuan. In order to protect the interests of shareholders, the company decided to confirm the subscriptions at 25 percent, and the final confirmed subscription was 15 billion yuan.

From 2005 to 2007, E Fund and GF Fund also developed rapidly along with the public fund industry. The management scale of E Fund jumped from 40.2 billion yuan to 196.4 billion yuan, and GF Fund jumped from nine billion yuan to 137.7 billion yuan, both breaking the "100 billion yuan" mark. At this point, only four years had passed since Dr. Chen Yunxian proposed the strategic goal of "100 billion yuan."

Exploring value investment based on principles

Now it seems that, for the funds with professionalism, value investment is both a choice and a necessity. As a professional institutional investor, fund companies can only provide long-term and steady returns to ordinary investors through value investment by discovering companies with competitive advantages and allowing projects and companies with market potential to emerge.

However, at the beginning of the establishment of E Fund and GF Fund, the concept of "value investment" had just been introduced to China, and the A-share market was characterized by a culture of "banker stocks" and "news" from unknown sources. The market was full of speculation, and many people were pursuing the so-called "insider information." In the market environment at that time, adhering to the concept of value investment instead became a lonely move against the trend.

"We are obsessed with winning in the long run." Such a simple slogan that had been shouted for many years was also a reflection of the values behind E Fund's investment research. "Good companies are worth investing in, and we should try to find them." Jiang Zuoliang, then manager of the fund Kehui, summed up in one sentence the cornerstone of E Fund's pursuit of specialized investment capabilities.

The practice of value investing in China was not easy. In order to find really good companies, Jiang Zuoliang and other key members of E Fund's early investment and research team carried out a series of institutional innovations. They took the lead in the industry to build a "trinity" system of the investment decision making committee, the alternative pool, and the joint investment and research conference system. They formed a mechanism of close interaction and complementarity between investment and research. They made sure that behind each investment decision, there was full professional research support. They followed the simple investment truth that "investment decisions are based on the intrinsic value of the company."

The seemingly simple concept of "research-driven investment" E Fund pursued at that time was against the mainstream of the market. True gold still needed to be refined by fire, and professional investment philosophy and practice needed to withstand the test and questioning of the market.

In 2001, China's securities market was booming, with the Shanghai Stock Exchange Index on the rise. The investment research team of E Fund realized that a market bubble had emerged and that, against the backdrop of China's rapid economic growth, superior companies would continue to emerge and value-oriented companies with low P/E ratios and high dividend returns had emerged. Generating solid returns for investors should mainly rely on "deep research on fundamentals and long-term long position in individual stocks." Based on the judgment of the situation, E Fund clarified its investment strategy at that time: to take heavy positions in "double low" (low P/E ratio and low price) investment targets, fully consider liquidity, and hold stocks for a long time, and pursue stable growth under low risk level.

However, there was a lot of discussion in the market about this investment strategy. In particular, the heavy position in "double-low" investment targets led to questions about the risk of concentrated holdings. However, in the eyes of value investors, blind diversification without adequate research was the biggest risk. Jiang Zuoliang attributed the reasons for the concentration to structural problems. He argued that since most companies in the Chinese stock market at that time had high valuations, if diversification was done, the probability of the portfolio covering low investment value companies would increase and the probability of loss would be high. On the contrary, the probability of loss was small if the concentrated investment could be well investigated and well researched.

When the tide goes out, the value of investment increases. Since its inception, the funds Kehui, Kexiang, and Kexun had been the top performers for three consecutive years, with the highest cumulative return of over 40 percent and the lowest close to 20 percent, while the market index fell by almost half from 2,200 points in the same period. The professional value investment concept had led the investment research team of E Fund to get out of the market fog and make its own performance brand.

E Fund also carried the banner of value investment in the industry: "Other funds followed our joint investment and research conference system, and our institutional innovation soon became the industry standard." Talking about the impact of E Fund's value investment philosophy on the whole industry, a member of the investment team back then recalled this.

While E Fund achieved impressive results with its professional operation, the newly established GF Fund also found its own professional direction in the exploration.

When GF Fund was established in 2003, China's public fund industry had already entered its sixth year, and there were already "old ten" pioneers in the market, such as Huaxia Fund and Southern Fund. How could the newly established GF Fund find its own place?

Lin Chuanhui, general manager of GF Fund, objectively analyzed the company's talent characteristics: the core members of the company all came from GF Securities, who were novices in the fund industry but veterans in the securities industry. Chen Shide, then general manager of GF Fund's Investment Management Department, was the fund manager of the former "GF I," while Yi Yangfang, the fund manager, came from GF Securities' Proprietary Department, both of whom had many years of experience in equity investment at that time. The core members had their own unique perspectives on listed companies and stock investment, and the core talent team of GF Fund had obvious professional advantages in stock investment.

After in-depth consideration and analysis, GF Fund's early development strategy was established: to focus on active equity business as the development direction, and to establish professional competence and brand in the niche area within three years. The strategic direction was set, and the choice of the way to achieve it became a difficult problem facing GF Fund.

Yi Yangfang, the current executive vice president of GF Fund and then manager of GF Jufu Fund, recalled that he had engaged in investment banking and was more concerned about the value of companies, so he would consciously replace some popular stocks that were over-speculated at that time with undervalued high-quality company stocks in advance when the market was overheated, but such a practice was not understood by outsiders: "At that time I was very helpless. I often went to the company on weekends to work overtime, trying to figure out the problems that I could not. Moreover, sell-side research was just emerging, and there were only one or two outside institutions that could provide sell-side services. At that time, a researcher from a famous institution came to Guangzhou for a roadshow and did not come to GF Fund. To listen to his roadshow, I was not allowed to choose to go to the nearby E Fund, but had to go to another fund company farther away."

Many of the key members of GF Fund's investment research system were from the GF Securities investment banking team, and the investment banking process for judging the value of the company was quite strict. Investment bankers had to have a good understanding of the industry to which the company belonged, the company's continuous annual financial and business development. They must also conduct a thorough investigation of the company's suppliers and distributors, and even go to visit each production line, inventory, and finished products of the company. This meticulous "investment banking perspective" had gradually become an important feature of GF's investment research team to analyze fundamentals and explore company value.

In 2004, Zhu Ping joined GF Fund as the investment director, and he actively advocated learning Western value investment concepts, formulated a sound system and process in the selection and training of investment research staff, and established a set of strict value investment systems.

At that time, the market did not know much about value investment, so in order to address public doubts, Zhu Ping opened a column in *Shanghai Securities News* to promote the concept of value investment with high frequency and density. He firmly believed that the securities market was mainly for investment, and that it was a way of life, not for speculation. He argued that the principles of investment could actually be very simple. These op-eds became a window to understand value investment and GF, and later Zhu Ping wrote these investment insights into books such as *Investment Is a Way of Life* and *Beating Institutional Investors*, which became essential titles on the desk of many ordinary investors and professionals.

Although value investing was the inevitable choice that must be made to become professional, at that time it was also a thorny and lonely path: "Even if others know about value investing, they don't necessarily do it seriously." He Zhen, the first fund manager of GF Fund, laughs: "We were a group of 'academics.' Although we were all novices, but the good thing was that they had a solid foundation."

Under the influence of the strong atmosphere of value investment, the two fund companies of GF had been working to identify the best companies. Facing market fluctuations, they often became bolder to buy as the market fell further, forming a clear stream that was very different from the popular trend investment at that time.

The A-share market in 2005 was a painful memory for Chinese stockholders, with the Shanghai Stock Exchange Index hitting a low of over 900 points in June, a new low in 8 years. At this time, GF Fund's non-ferrous researcher was somewhat depressed. Contrary to the downturn of the market, he was concerned that the forecast data about the research targets' earnings was too optimistic.

Not long before, based on the future development of the aluminum industry, he and his team went to research Yunnan Aluminum. According to Yunnan Aluminum's information, the company's production had increased tenfold, while aluminum was still in short supply in the market. After coming back, this non-ferrous researcher wrote a report. In light of the alumina price increase, market demand, capacity increment, and other data, he calculated one by one, and finally surprisingly got the conclusion that the expected return would grow ten times in the future. The fund managers and researchers present at the meeting found it incredible to hear, and then researcher Wang Qi laughed: "No one had ever dared to mention such an optimistic expectation, and we all thought at the time that he was writing nonsense."

GF Fund's investment research team did not put the research results on hold just because they were "unbelievable": "Without investigation, there is no right to speak." The investment research team went to the company again with doubts about the conclusion: "It took them several months of field research. They clarified all data from beginning to end several times, but the conclusion was still ten times." Wang Qi remembers very well that without any model to refer to, the great workload was manual calculation. At that time, even the listed company itself did not believe the earnings forecast. The market was still shrouded in the pessimism of the bear market, but GF Fund made an investment judgment based on objective facts and the law of development, and firmly bought Yunnan Aluminum's shares. Eventually, this stock created a tenfold return. Adhering to the spirit of professionalism and firm value investment philosophy, GF Fund's investment research team had successfully discovered the wealth of value in the vast market.

"From the seller of brokerage investment banking to the buyer of fund investment, what remained unchanged was the grasp of the essence of investment, i.e. the ability of reasonable pricing of assets," Lin Chuanhui said to summarize the transformation of the two identities. This professional ability to judge the value of assets had not only laid the foundation for the major strategic choices of the company's development, but also helped GF Fund to rapidly accumulate advantages in the active equity market, and put wings on GF Fund for its rapid development for many years after.

Since its inception, GF had formed an investment research culture focusing on research and learning, which had laid a solid foundation for a robust investment style. Focusing on the business layout of equity funds and implementing the value investment philosophy, GF had shown excellent investment ability in the early stage. In 2004, GF's first fund, GF Jufu, ranked first among its peers with a positive return of 7.55 percent and was named "Golden Bull Fund." In 2005, "GF Stable Growth" ranked first in the market with a return of 16.93 percent, and "GF Jufu" ranked fifth with a return of 13.34 percent. The average performance of GF's equity funds ranked first among all funds.

In the midst of the bear market, GF Fund became the focus of attention of the market and the industry for its outstanding performance in two consecutive years. GF Wenjian and GF Jufu funds were once called "GF Double Top Performers" by fund research institutions, establishing a good reputation in the hearts of channels and investors.

Dr. Ma Qingquan, who was chairman of GF Fund at that time, proposed and advocated that GF Fund should establish the ideal of "managing the country's wealth for all its people." The company not only wanted to enable the holders to keep the value of their wealth appreciating, but also wanted to enable more ordinary people to understand and accept investment, and turn investment into a way of life. This would form a more sound, efficient, and mutually beneficial investment ecology, which would benefit all participants and allow more efficient allocation of capital, thus increasing the total wealth of society.

With such a lofty goal in mind, GF Fund firmly believed that it shouldered the trust of thousands of investors and the historical mission of serving the real economy. It understood that only by adhering to true value investment could it steadily make progress on the road of wealth management and live up to the trust of its clients and the trust of the times.

Therefore, no matter how the external investment environment changed in the short term, GF Fund always firmly took value investment as its investment philosophy. General Manager Lin Chuanhui said at the beginning of the company that, "Value investment is to be adhered to in the long term, in normal times and even more so when the market is volatile." In 2007, GF Fund withstood the test of the value investment philosophy by market fluctuations.

From January to March 2007, value investment stocks rose slowly, while low-priced stocks, junk stocks, and theme stocks rose more. At that time, GF held several meetings to discuss the investment strategy. Through thorough analysis and argumentation, the company believed that there was nothing wrong with value investment at that time, and there was no need to make major portfolio adjustment. After May 30, the market returned to value investment, and all of GF's equity funds achieved excellent investment performance, ranking in the top third of its category for all of 2007, with four equity funds in the top fifth of their category. With the outstanding investment performance, GF funds were favored by investors.

The two young fund companies of GF demonstrated to the market the value of professional investment philosophy with their continuous excellent investment performance, and raised the banner of value investment in the Chinese investment field, making their own contribution to the rational development of the Chinese capital markets.

2. Reflection and transformation

Reflections over development

At the beginning of 2007, the number of new fund accounts even exceeded the number of new A-share accounts in the same period by 50 percent, the scale of new fund issuance reached record highs, and the total asset management scale of funds also expanded rapidly. In the midst of the prosperous scene, there were some concerns within the two funds GF.

In January 2007, the Shanghai and Shenzhen markets added 1.85 million new fund users, a record high. In response to this hot news, a reporter from the *21st Century Business Herald* interviewed Dr. Ma Qingquan, chairman of GF Fund, who was also a vice chairman of the Securities Association of China at that time. It turned out that Dr. Ma was not as relaxed and happy as he thought, but was calm and sensible. Dr. Ma worried: "In the past, funds needed to worry about being 'killed by the stick,' but now they have to be wary of the risk of being 'killed by the hype.'" He even pointed out unapologetically, "The quality of investors cannot fully adapt to the changes in the market.... Now quite a few people do not understand the capital markets and funds. They blindly pursue them. In this case, it is extremely easy to get hurt."

Standing at the height of the industry, he seriously pointed out two contradictions prevailing in the fund industry: one was the contradiction between the expansion of fund scale and the faulty internal control system and governance structure of funds. The second was the contradiction between the development of the fund industry and the lack of effective coordination between the development of various subsystems of the financial industry.

Some of my old colleagues were still impressed by this interview. In early 2007, funds were highly sought after. Dr. Ma Qingquan's public statement was close to "giving a wakeup call" to the fund industry, and it could even be said that he was "taking a risk of going against the will of all."

In the midst of the bull market of 2007, the leadership's sense of concern set a calm tone for both GF funds.

In an interview, the reporter asked, "The boom in the stock market has driven the fund boom, and the size of the funds is also growing rapidly. But as the stock index continues to climb higher, as professional institutions that manage money for the public, what measures do you think funds should take to control the risk?"

Liu Xiaoyan said heartily: "The most important thing is that when the size of the fund is soaring and the performance is skyrocketing, the company should instead keep a cool head. This year the market complains that E Fund is very quiet. In fact, the company's policy at the beginning of the year is to be calm and sensible. We have to adapt the scale of expansion to the level that we can afford, and we should not blindly expand the scale and make money indiscriminately.

When the market is good, we have to think about when the market is bad, and when people line up for subscription of the fund, we have to think that there may also be a line for redemption. With these ideas and concepts, it is natural that we have made systematic arrangements and considerations accordingly."

These remarks show the calm and restrained business thinking of the GF funds. When the market was caught in the feast of the bull market and customers were lining up to buy funds, the funds GF were quietly doing investor education instead.

An interesting figure was that in a market where investors were actively buying funds in 2007, E Fund invested 12.26 million yuan in investor education, a budget level that was at the top of both horizontal and vertical comparisons. In response to the changing structure of investors and the characteristics of trading behavior, E Fund focused its education on small and medium-sized individual investors and client managers of sales channels, and mainly used the forms of on-site and off-site education. The specific work included the opening of the "Investor Education" column and on-site investor education with the four themes of "3+1 Happiness," "Journey of Peace of Mind," "Better Understanding E Fund," and "Rational Life." In order to guide customers to invest for the long term, E Fund also focused on promoting fixed-term business in 2007, guiding customers to diversify the risks hidden in the bull market by investing in groups.

In addition, in order to prevent market risks, E Fund also focused on strengthening the company's internal control. To improve the system and strengthen implementation, the company focused on the management of moral risk, market risk, credit risk, and operational risk. In particular, in response to possible market volatility and redemption risk, the company strengthened liquidity risk management and fully prepared to maximize the protection of the interests of fund holders.

These practices might seem "overly worried" at that time, but today, looking back, we can see that it is because they kept a clear head during this period of "heated market development" that E Fund and GF Fund were able to reflect and transform early during the "dark times" that followed, and were able to march in the forefront of the industry quickly and steadily.

At the beginning of 2008, the Southern region of China was hit by a snowstorm of a kind rarely seen in a century. It was at this coldest moment that the global financial turmoil also quietly spread to China. The A-share market did not usher in the long-awaited "Olympic-based rise," but the Shanghai Composite Index fell from 6,124 points to 1,664 points. Before the Chinese fund industry could look back on the good times of 2007, it was plunged into the pain of the fall brought by the international financial crisis.

Many years later, Yi Yangfang, who had witnessed many rounds of bull and bear changes in China's capital markets, recalled the period of time and still affirmed, "The year 2008 was the hardest year for the whole company, including me personally."

"In fact, the market decline was one aspect, but more than that, our internal ideas were in violent collision." Yi Yangfang recalled that that year was more of an ordeal for GF Fund because of the change in philosophy.

On September 19, 2008, the Chinese stock market, which had been battered by the bear market for 11 months, was stimulated by good news such as the entry of Central Huijin Investment Ltd. into the market, and all stocks reached their upper level of the daily trading limit. This was the first time in the history of A-shares that Central Huijin Investment Ltd. rescued the market.

The whole GF Fund investment research system was boiling. Everyone was discussing now that the index rose to the upper level of the daily trading limit, could they still buy? At that time there were diametrically opposing views. One was that they could still wait, while the other firmly believed that they should increase positions. Some said that "the crisis in the United States has just begun as Lehman Brothers have just collapsed, so we should wait and see." Others said, "The index is still going up. It has been rising for two days, so we cannot wait." In October of that year when investment researchers met, the internal differences were still very large.

"This was the limitations of public funds at the time," reflected Lin Chuanhui, general manager of GF Fund. The institutional characteristics of equity funds determined that it was difficult to avoid systemic risk. In the most difficult "dark times," Lin Chuanhui repeatedly communicated with the investment researchers to cheer them up: "You have experienced ups and downs in two years of a kind rarely seen in a century. We have seen these after we have been in the securities market for more than ten years. You have a long way to go in life. From a different perspective, as professional investors, this experience can later make us more alert and experienced and help us improve our investment."

After this difficult time, GF Fund's investment research team learned a painful lesson and began to make bold reforms.

First, macroeconomic and strategic research was elevated to a more important position. Yi Yangfang explained: "Because in the framework of China's development, you have to study what others do; otherwise you can't beat them. Furthermore, after the scale is large, strategy and asset allocation become very important to fund performance."

Immediately afterwards, GF established an investment strategy group under the Investment Decision Committee, with Yi Yangfang as head. The group included two macro researchers as well as the head of the Research Department. It operated mainly by providing monthly strategy reports to the Investment Decision Committee. The strategy team's investment strategy recommendations were provided to the fund managers for reference after they were approved by the Investment Decision Committee.

In addition, GF Fund also modified many internal self-restraints in response to the prevailing market situation. It increased the fund manager authority threshold, established a special fund manager group, and repeatedly worked on and revised the investment approach, and encouraged the development of a more diversified investment style for fund managers.

At E Fund, the pace of contemplation, review, perseverance, and reform never stopped. "At an extremely unusual time, in the face of a complex, changing and severe market environment, we overcame many difficulties and still held on to our investment research philosophy," a fund manager who experienced the stock market turmoil in 2008 recalls. In addition, E Fund strengthened its macroeconomic research and improved its asset allocation process. It basically solved the problem of alternative investment pool coverage and raised the requirements for in-depth exploration of industries and individual stocks in the bear market. It held individuals responsible for the tracking research of the top 100 stocks with long positions. It conducted field research on 452 companies throughout the year (accounting for one third of the total number of listed companies in China that year), with an average of 1.6 times per company. The company had basically covered the key companies in each industry.

These reforms made the investment research systems of the two funds of GF more stable, more mature, and more diversified, and more able to withstand market risks, laying a solid foundation for moving faster and more steadily in the asset management industry in the future.

A "bridge to the hearts" in the cold winter

For Xiao Wen, then deputy general manager of GF Fund, who was working in the frontline of fund sales, 2008 was also a year engraved in her heart. Xiao Wen, who is familiar to many people in the fund industry, was a passionate and competent person from GF Securities' Brokerage Business Headquarters. She was good at thinking and innovative. She was full of love for the fund industry and was very good at seizing opportunities to promote fund knowledge to others. Some reporters originally came to interview her, but after listening to her sincere narrative, they also unknowingly became fund investors, so the media jokingly called her the "fund preacher."

But during the international financial crisis in 2008, the market was hard hit, and fund investors suffered heavy losses. It is now impossible to imagine how many complaints and how much pressure Xiao Wen had to face from all over the country when she was moving around on the frontline every day. On this point, the optimistic and positive Xiao rarely said anything mentioned. But the most painful thing for her was that in this wave of the market, most investors were investing in funds at a point above 4,800 points for the A-share, and then the index fell all the way to around 1,664. Most of the funds inevitably lost money. Faced with the loss, heartache, and even tears of customers, fund companies and distribution channels could hardly do anything with such systemic risk.

Faced with such a situation, Xiao Wen began to think deeply about the sales model of public funds. At that time, China's public fund industry generally focused on two results, namely size and ranking. But Xiao Wen suggested that while focusing on these two results, she wanted to focus more on the process, because when clients invested in a fund, it included the process and experience in addition to the return. She realized that what clients wanted was not a single product, but a solution.

Xiao Wen said at the time, "The market doesn't give funds much of a chance, so it's more important for our fund to communicate and interact more with our clients, refine our efforts in customer service, and remind them of their investment behavior and approach." She says vividly, "We have to build a 'bridge' to the hearts and minds of our clients."

In order to build a trusting relationship between the fund and its clients, Xiao Wen set out to create a series of brand activities unique to GF Fund: the "Bridge to the Hearts Initiative." Many people may not know that this activity, which had been accompanying GF's clients for more than ten years, but the initiative to build a "heart-to-heart" communication bridge was born in this financial crisis.

"You can't change the market, but you can inform your clients of the reasons for the market decline. You can face and understand the market with your clients, and give investors moral support and comfort. This was also the starting point of GF Fund's 'Bridge to the Hearts' initiative," Xiao Wen explained.

Through the "Bridge to the Hearts" initiative, GF Fund invited a number of customers to come to the fund in person. It visited listed companies and fund managers with its customers and held "wealth salons" with them. Perhaps these activities did not directly increase sales, but they provided a way for clients to understand the investment decision process of the fund, helped them improve their own investment behavior, raised their investment ability, and constructed a sales model with a virtuous cycle in which customers and the fund trusted each other and taught each other.

In 2008, the recession in the securities market caused a downturn in fund sales, and many funds were even faced with the dilemma of borrowing money to ensure "new funds are issued." However, in that year, E Fund sold six new funds against the trend, making the year a record single-year jump in the number of funds sold since its establishment.

The sluggishness and even depression of fund sales in the market forced E Fund's sales department to make its work more practical, detailed, and innovative. By carefully planning each new fund launch and analyzing the selling points of each fund as well as the distribution channels, the sales team of E Fund concentrated on understanding the key sales channels and focused its marketing plan on priorities.

From October 14 to November 7, 2008 was the launch period of the fund Kehui during which it shifted from a closed-end to an open-end fund. During that period, China's stock market was experiencing the greatest decline and investor confidence was at a low point, and all bank channels were unable to sell the fund.

"There was really no willingness to sell at all at the channel end, and our hearts were heavy at that time," said a man who was involved in the sale of the fund Kehui when it shifted from a closed-end to an open-end fund.

But from an investment point of view, this was a good time to build a position. The market had oversold, and it was a good to buy a large number of stocks. So E Fund' sales force shifted its thinking. "We realized that brokerages, especially large brokerages with interest, could be a breakthrough." Immediately, the sales team split up to communicate with large brokerages in depth and detail, implement marketing plans after finalizing sales brokerages, and focus on allocating the sales work to each brokerage's brokerage branches.

In addition to focusing on innovation in the conventional sales methods, the sales model had also changed. Liu Xiaoyan judged that the fixed investment business should be the focus of sales efforts and then planned a theme marketing that had a great impact in the market. The "I Love My Baby" fixed investment marketing campaign was widely praised by the industry and customers:

"The campaign was well received. Through a beautifully crafted 'I Love My Baby' financial commemorative booklet full of cartoon drawings, E Fund strung together the process of parents' annual fixed investment for their children, and also strung together the growth of their children. The letter from the investment director in the souvenir book not only talks about the changes in the economy and stock market in that year, but also gives financial education to the children," a client manager recalls. "This had served us well in developing and maintaining clients."

In an unfavorable market, E Fund achieved better sales performance in the industry over the same period through continuous sales innovation. It issued 106.505 billion shares of its public funds, an increase of 26 percent over the same period in 2007.

In the face of the market winter, the two fund companies of GF did not limit themselves to the momentary gains and losses, but always put the interests of customers first. They boldly changed their sales models, resisted the enormous pressure of the bear market in which it was extremely difficult to complete the sales, stood firmly with investors, and built a "bridge" to the hearts of customers.

The transition from equity to "comprehensive business"

If 2008 was a year of conceptual impact for the investment research team and was a year of radical reform for the sales team, but for the two helmsmen of E Fund and GF, Ye Junying and Lin Chuanhui, they were thinking more about the transformation at the strategic level. Looking back on that time, Lin Chuanhui said, "The market impact in 2008 was a wakeup call for both GF and myself, and made us change, giving us a deeper understanding of the asset management industry."

Lin Chuanhui keenly felt that the economic situation was changing, as were capital markets and people's investment mentality, and that the previous practice of focusing only on developing equity investments could no longer adapt to the new situation. He believed: "The essence of public funds lies in managing money for the public and pursuing sound returns. Our mission is to help investors share the fruits of economic development, rather than just going for high returns in spite of risk."

In its past operations, GF Fund had left investors with the straightforward impression that it was "a fund with strong stock speculation ability." However, in the face of such an evaluation, Lin Chuanhui maintained a high degree of calmness, "This is a kind of affirmation, but from the perspective of varied products, it is also a kind of negation."

After repeatedly reviewing reports, studying foreign development experience, and researching the frontier of domestic and international market development, Lin Chuanhui got the answer he wanted: the era of "with one skill, a fund can make good fortune" in the fund industry had passed, and with the continuous development of China's capital markets, the market environment had become more complex and volatile, and investors' needs were increasingly diversified, and the market's requirements for fund products were becoming more diverse. He realized that this was both a challenge and a historical and strategic opportunity for fund companies.

In 2009, Lin Chuanhui gave his colleagues in charge of planning and development a new project: to study the development of the fund industry in the United States from the 1970s to the early 1980s. The Chinese economy at that time had similarities with the US economy in the 1970s and 1980s, as both were undergoing a transition in their economic growth patterns. Their research concluded that the US fund industry experienced rapid growth in fixed income products during the period of economic stagnation.

This conclusion coincided with the direction that Chuanhui Lin was thinking about. Earlier, he had begun to focus on fixed-income products: "In the past few years we have mainly concentrated on equity funds. In the future, we want to do well in low-risk products." To this end, Lin Chuanhui was eager to recruit more outstanding talents in bond investment for GF.

However, at that time, there were not many mature bond fund practitioners in the market, and where the talents would come from became a problem facing him. In this regard, GF Fund gave a "smart" answer: from the campus. "Almost all the members of our Fixed Income Department at that time were recruited from campuses," Kong Weiying, head of the Human Resources Department, recalls: "There were not so many ready-made people to recruit, so we looked for them from the school and trained them ourselves."

When you're new on the job, you inevitably stumble a bit. "At the beginning, we even used Excel to calculate cash flow, duration and so on," Xie Jun, the fund manager of GF Fund's first bond fund "GF Qiangzhai," still recalls, when remembering the year with a lot of emotions.

In mid-2008, due to the fear of inflationary pressure, the bond market sentiment was generally pessimistic. Xie Jun decided to buy 10-year government bonds through in-depth research and analysis, judging that there was a certain downside risk in the macroeconomy at that time. The trader chose "public inquiry" when trading, and many industry peers called Xie Jun after seeing it: "How come GF Fund is so bullish on the bond market?"

Later on, Xie Jun's operation, which was dubbed as "fierce," proved to be very prescient as he had bought before the inflection point and entered earlier than most people in the market. GF Qiangzhai Fund, established in March 2008, ranked among the top funds of its type with a yield of 11.5 percent by the end of the year.

The success of GF Qiangzhai Fund kicked off a good start for GF Fund's business transformation. Subsequently, GF Fund started to make multi-point efforts to transform into a diversified and comprehensive fund management company, with the establishment of the International Business Department, the Quantitative Investment Department, and the Quantitative Investment Department. Despite its remote location in Guangzhou, GF had always been able to seize opportunities at critical moments, and it only took just over ten years to develop from being a "one-man show" in active equity to "blooming" in fixed income, quantitative investment, overseas investment, alternative investment, and other diversified investment capabilities.

In the nineteenth century, Friedrich Nietzsche once wrote, "That which doesn't kill us makes us stronger." In 2008, in order to actively respond to the rapid changes in the market, E Fund set up a strategic research group to provide a basis for the Investment Decision Committee's asset allocation decisions. The reforms forced by the international financial crisis in 2008 had laid an important foundation for E Fund to manage larger or even trillion yuan assets in the future. In addition, according to the development trend of fixed income business, E Fund made the decision to relocate the whole fixed income management team to Beijing.

More importantly, the market shocks in 2008 made E Fund more determined to pursue "consolidation and improvement, and innovation and overtaking." To become a trustworthy asset management company in a complex and changing market, E Fund needed to continuously consolidate, improve, and upgrade its work and lay an overall solid foundation for the development of E Fund in terms of team building, systems and processes, information systems, management thinking, service awareness, and brand strategy. This consolidation and improvement work was especially important after the industry's great development in 2007 and the problems and reflections in 2008.

In terms of strategy, after years of reflection and the market test in 2008, E Fund clearly set out its strategic goal for the first time, which was "to become a leading comprehensive asset management company in China." The fund also put forward specific connotations such as "remaining as a Top Five in the industry in terms of total asset size, a balanced business structure, and a solid foundation for development." The fund worked to make steady progress for the long run. Under the guidance of such strategic objectives, E Fund successfully launched index funds and became the largest fund company managing index funds in China. It secured large and medium-sized dedicated wealth management and company annuity projects. It rapidly developed its institutional wealth management business. It had actively explored investment management methods adapted to large integrated asset management companies and strengthened its risk management capabilities. It also started to explore the start-up of quantitative investment business.

Based on these business breakthroughs and in light of E Fund's continuous thinking about the development of the fund industry and the upcoming era of large capital management, E Fund established the strategic "pyramid-shaped" business development policy in 2013. Based on the size and sustainability of investors' needs, a hierarchical business structure was formed with clear risk-return characteristics, clear business logic, progressive product technology, and coordinated internal relationships. At the bottom of the pyramid were products with low risk, high liquidity, and stable and competitive return expectations. The higher the tip of the pyramid, the higher the technical content of the products, which was where the fund company formed its characteristics and core competitiveness.

At this point, E Fund had begun to emerge as a "leading large integrated asset management company in China." This also confirms the words written by Ye Junying during the international financial crisis in 2008: "E Fund should keep reflecting, exploring, and brewing. It should embrace changes with an optimistic and positive attitude. It should adjust, learn and grow in difficulties and crises. It should strive to grasp opportunities, make pioneering progress, turn crises into opportunities, and achieve transcendence."

Changing to doing things selectively

In the long journey of fund industry development, how does one distinguish which opportunities are beneficial to holders in the face of opportunities and temptations? Which opportunities can help the company's long-term healthy development? What should be done and what should not? It is these numerous strategic choices that determine the future development of a company. Standing at the crossroads of "fate," GF people always kept in mind that the asset management industry should return to the principle of always putting the interests of holders first.

In August 2006, the CSRC officially launched the pilot QDII products for funds. In June 2007, the CSRC issued the Trial Measures for the Administration of Overseas Securities Investment by Qualified Domestic Institutional Investors, giving the fund industry the go-ahead to carry out QDII business. After the new track was open, although both E Fund and GF were qualified to apply, they were both "late" in the business out of caution in terms of actual product issuance.

From the beginning of the CSRC pilot, E Fund actively prepared for it and set up an offshore investment business group through global recruitment in 2007, and submitted the QDII qualification application in a relatively short period of time. The application was approved by the CSRC at the end of the year, making E Fund one of the earlier funds to carry out QDII investment management.

The bull market boosted investors' fervent pursuit of QDII fund products, and many QDII fund products issued in the second half of 2007 had applications far exceeding the target on the first day and eventually had to be proportionally allocated.

E Fund could have joined this camp and raised a larger fund by issuing QDII fund products at the hottest time of the market. "But we considered that the market was at a relatively high position at the time and it was not the right time to build a position," said a member of E Fund's core investment research team at the time.

E Fund resisted the urge to pursue short-term size growth and turned its head to hard work at QDII products. Its investment Research Department actively researched and prepared for the investment operation of QDII products, and built up an alternative pool of overseas investment products. In addition, in accordance with the CSRC's Regulations on the Establishment of Institutions in Hong Kong by Securities Investment Fund Management Companies, E Fund actively explored the establishment of a wholly-owned subsidiary in Hong Kong, set up a research platform for overseas equity investment, and built its own overseas team.

In 2007, the market considered E Fund "silly and rigid," but it recognized it in 2008. In 2007, when the global market was in a bearish state, the funds that tried out overseas stock markets in the heat of the moment lost at least half of their money and at the most 63 percent. In just one year, the market's most sought-after fund product underwent a dramatic fall to the bottom.

"We must bring investors real investment returns, so that they steadily and consistently earn money," Ye Junying often said. In exercising restraint in launching QDII products, E Fund's "inaction" was precisely the embodiment of this philosophy. In the end, it was not until 2010 that E Fund raised its first QDII product—E Fund Asia Select Securities Investment Fund.

At the same point, the same problem of choice was also placed in front of Lin Chuanhui, general manager of GF Fund.

From the trend of industry development, before 2007, the business of the whole industry was mainly focused on domestic public offerings, with a relatively single type of business. In 2007, with the successful completion of the reform of non-tradable shares, market style change, and policy adjustment of the regulatory authorities, the fund industry began to diversify its investment varieties and investment scope. The regulatory authorities also encouraged funds to "go global" through QDII products. Therefore, GF established an international business department in 2007 and conducted staff reserve and product feasibility study.

At that time, many funds applied to provide QDII products. In such a situation where everyone was competing for first place, GF Fund's delay caused widespread concern in the market, and the media frequently came to ask for the reason. Lin Chuanhui gave a particularly "plain" answer: "I think the market is not ripe yet."

Regardless of whether others criticize GF Fund for this "absence," Lin Chuanhui insisted that the international market situation was uncertain and preparations were not yet in place, so it could be rushed. In an internal meeting of GF Fund, he said earnestly to all present: "The company's business development cannot be separated from the actual situation of the market, but it also must be conducted in light of its own development, which is also the embodiment of responsibility to investors."

Opportunity came with the wait. After the international financial crisis in 2008, overseas markets began to return to rationality and domestic investors began to mature. GF Fund made repeated internal arguments and judged that the market timing and its own conditions were ready to start QDII operation.

In August 2010, GF issued its first QDII fund—GF Asia-Pacific Select Equity Fund, which was "two years late" and achieved positive returns in the same year. Subsequently, the company gradually promoted its overseas business and established a more comprehensive overseas public offering products covering active equity, passive indices, bonds, and REITs. Although it started late, after years of building up, GF Fund is now one of the funds with the largest number of QDII funds and the most comprehensive investment areas in the industry. It is also regarded as the most complete provider of overseas products. In addition, in terms of investment performance, GF Fund won the "Golden Bull Fund Company for Overseas Investment" award four times, and its ability to invest overseas was recognized by the industry.

In the first half of 2015, bull market enthusiasm continued to rise, with "state-owned company reform expectations," "Internet+," "Industry 4.0," and "high-end equipment manufacturing" as the major causes. The Shanghai Index started from the closing point of 3,234.68 on December 31, 2014, and rocketed all the way up to the 5,000-point mark after seven years.

In the frenzied market conditions, the graded funds skyrocketed, with their size expanding from 138.8 billion yuan to 457.9 billion yuan in just six months. Immersed in the bull market, investors finally found the Graded B which could hit the upper level of the daily trading limit, experiencing the thrill of speculating in funds like a stock speculation.

In the face of the "graded fund wave" in full swing, GF Fund, which was considering how to develop passive investment products, was also hesitant about which should come first: issuing graded funds during the ongoing fever, or focusing on the direction of ETF (Exchange Traded Open Index Fund) based on mature market experience? The management of GF Fund considered that graded funds were a kind of products endowed with leverage characteristics, but not every investor could clearly understand the leverage characteristics of the products themselves. As GF Fund believed that this might make conservative and prudent investors buy such products due to the limitation of perception, bringing uncertainty beyond their own ability, it chose ETF in order to protect its investors.

Since June 2014, GF have issued 42 ETFs and feeder funds, covering broad-based, industry, thematic, and overseas investment categories, including Guangdong-Hong Kong-Macao Greater Bay Area ETF, central government company innovation drive ETF, and other innovative products that contribute to the development of the real economy and SOE reform. As of the end of June 2020, the size of ETFs in the market had grown from more than 100 billion yuan in 2015 to 648.7 billion yuan, and the development situation was booming.

Compared with the booming development of ETFs, graded funds were completely reduced to be meaningless. In just a few years, the total size of graded funds shrank significantly from the peak of 457.9 billion yuan in 2015, and the "new regulations on capital management" announced in April 2018 clarified the rule that "public offering products shall not be graded in terms of shares." By the end of June 2019, graded funds with a total share of less than 300 million yuan would need to be cleaned up, while the deadline for clearing up graded funds with a total share of 300 million yuan or more would be by the end of 2020.

At this moment, GF people, who had stood at a crossroads, once again verified and strengthened the development concept that anchors the principle of asset management industry.

After several circuit breakers of A-shares at the beginning of 2016, the shadow of bear market became a haze that could not be lifted from investors' minds. It became the consensus of investors across the market to look for low-risk assets with stable returns. By the end of December 2016, the total scale of public funds reached 9.25 trillion yuan, of which the scale of money funds alone reached 4.4 trillion yuan, accounting for half of the public funds.

When money funds gradually became the "giant" of public funds, many people were also vaguely worried about the risk of the market: the scale was so large, and the concentration of institutions was high, would there be problems?

According to Murphy's Law, if something has the potential to go bad, no matter how unlikely it is, it will always happen. Since late November 2016, market funding had continued to be tight, with the one-month pledged repo rate soaring from 3.0 percent to 6.55 percent, and non-bank institutions such as public funds had faced an unprecedented test: the financial frauds, the rumors of negative equity in the investors' accounts due to leveraged trading on margins, and the high short-term funding rates made money funds the first to be sold by institutions.

The money fund of GF Fund also experienced huge redemption pressure at that time. "Our money fund was one of the most redeemed money funds in the market at the time. We had set aside 60 percent of the fund in anticipation of the tight funding at the end of the year, but eventually the redemption ratio reached 80 percent to almost 100 billion yuan. The shortfall could only be made up while selling assets to fully meet the redemption demand of customers," Wen Xiujuan, manager of GF money fund, said.

This massive currency redemption crisis had added a profound lesson to Wen Xiujuan's cash management career, and also made a big case in the history of GF Fund for successfully dealing with liquidity risk: "The liquidity impact on GF was not significant and my colleagues were calm and collected. First, we had reserved adequate funds. We had discussed what the worst case scenario would be and how to deal with it, but the reality was that it was actually okay and the worst did not appear. Second, we were also very cautious and did not go after high yield in particular. The maximum duration of the money fund was 180 days, and we had already reduced the duration to 90 days before the redemption occurred, so we won't suffer great losses even if interest rates rose."

It's no coincidence that in 2006, 10 years previous, GF also survived such a large redemption crisis in its money fund. In the first half of 2006, the bond market weakened while the A-share market continued to strengthen, resulting in a wave of money fund redemption with an average net redemption rate of 48.31 percent. The average net redemption rate was as high as 48.31 percent. At that time, many funds had money funds of tens of billions of yuan, and the largest money fund was over 40 billion yuan in size, while the largest GF money fund was just over five billion yuan in size. GF Fund General Manager Lin Chuanhui asked the money fund manager about the matter with doubts, but the fund manager said that the operation of a single-minded pursuit of money fund returns was risky. Lin Chuanhui approved the fund managers' idea of prudent operation. "He made the situation clear, and we felt it was right to follow his advice to avoid risks and stop envying the size of others' money funds, which later also proved him right." As the bond market weakened and the A-share market continued to strengthen, the money fund saw a "redemption wave," with the usual net redemption rate of 48.31 percent. Because GF Fund pursued prudent operation and avoided blind pursuit of income and scale, it successfully defused this risk.

Shouldering the heavy responsibility of the Social Security Fund

Leung Ting-bong, former chairman of the Hong Kong Securities and Futures Commission and chief advisor to the CSRC, once recalled a conversation with Premier Zhu Rongji:

> By 2050, you won't be around anymore, neither will I, but the future premier would ask: "What did Zhu Rongji actually do when he had the chance to do something back then?"
>
> If we do nothing now, then by 2050, I'm afraid we won't be able to provide

> for the lives of Chinese people over the age of 60. The state guarantee fund will soon run out. We cannot fully solve the problem of security for the aging population if our fund just sits in the bank.
>
> The best way to solve this problem is to have an annual return on capital of more than four percent, or even eight percent, over the next 30 years. The only way to achieve this goal is to develop broad capital markets. One of the most powerful vehicles for investing retirement savings is the stock investment fund.

These passages illustrate very well the important role of the fund industry for the cause of national basic security.

The Social Security Fund was the largest pioneer of diversified investment operation of the pension fund in China. At the beginning of its establishment, the core concepts of long-term investment, value investment, and responsible investment were set. From the early selection of the entrusted managers, the Social Security Fund acted on high standards and strict requirements. Such an institutional principal, which had a large amount of capital and a clear philosophy, management style, and selection criteria, advocated in the evaluation method that the entrusted managers must have their own clear and explicit investment philosophy, turn the investment philosophy into an institutionalized, procedural and systematic way of operation, and also test the principal through objective data, focusing on the consistency of words and deeds between philosophy and practice.

All this coincided with the original aspiration of E Fund. In 2002, the National Council for Social Security Fund selected six public fund management companies as the first national Social Security Fund investment managers. According to the election rules, only the "old ten" funds were eligible, and newly established funds were not eligible. E Fund, which had been established only one year previously, missed the election, but it paid more attention to the future opportunities of the business and started to prepare for the bidding process.

In 2004, the National Council for Social Security Fund started the second round of investment manager selection. At this time, the Social Security Working Group, headed by General Manager Ye Junying, had been operating in an orderly manner for more than two years. In order to manage the "pension money" of ordinary Chinese people well, during the previous two years, E Fund had continuously improved its investment research, risk control, and operation capabilities, and polished its institutional process and operation system to meet the requirements of social security investment.

Take the fund performance evaluation model as an example. The Social Security Fund pursued continuous and stable investment performance, so the investment managers were required to continuously track the industry allocation and individual stock contribution. However, at that time, China's fund performance was mainly evaluated by simple models such as Sharpe's Mixed Index, and there was no model or system that could be used as reference. The investment research team hired an external expert, State Street Global Advisors (Hong Kong), and introduced the internationally advanced Brinson performance decomposition model as a reference. Based on their actual conditions, the investment research team finally researched and formed an analysis model that exceeded the criteria of Social Security Fund examination, which not only could analyze the attribution of industry and individual stock dimensions, but also additionally considered variables such as interactive returns. The model became a model commonly used in the industry later.

With a sense of responsibility to the people and a sense of sacred mission to the pension fund business, E Fund strived for improvement and made every effort in the process of seeking and participating in the management of the Social Security Fund, exceeding the requirements of the Social Security Fund in terms of system, process, and investment research system. With first place in the overall score, E Fund was selected among 29 participating funds and securities companies to be qualified as a national social security fund investment manager.

The qualification was a historic event for E Fund. Ye Junying called it "a landmark event that reflected the company's comprehensive strength and a milestone for the company to have the opportunity to directly participate in the pension business and make its own contribution to the development of the pension business." The process of preparing for the qualification of Social Security Fund investment manager was also a process of summarizing the company's experience, improving the system and refining the essence of investment, a process of improvement, and a process of overall advancement, with the importance of building on past achievements and opening up the future.

The Social Security Fund investment manager defense was held in a small building in the secluded hills of Huairou, Beijing. An employee who participated in the defense recalled that she still remembered riding in a jeep to the airport after the defense that day: "The view from the front row was wide open, and the view of Beijing in early autumn was beautiful, full of golden scenes, reflecting the stretch and longing in the heart." What was more worthy of longing was the broad future of the development of the pension business.

In order to manage the pension business represented by Social Security Fund, E Fund had formed a professional management model of "centralized leadership, professional division of labor and unified coordination," and set up a leadership and coordination group at the company level to unify the deployment of various resources to support the development of the pension business. It set up a pension business department at the business level, with the investment department responsible for its implementation, so that the pension business was always developed along a systematic path. After years of practice, this investment management model and the performance it brought were recognized by clients. For example, since 2015, when the National Council for Social Security Fund made public the results of its evaluation, E Fund's portfolio has been awarded the highest A grade every year.

It can be said that at the crossroads of fate, E Fund firmly chose the social security business and vice versa, which was the right choice for both of them. Along the way, the social security business had been "a great credit" to the growth of E Fund, and E Fund had also become the best friend of the Social Security Fund for more than ten years.

Whether it was the radical reform of the investment and research systems, the continuous improvement of asset management ability, the bold change of the sales model, or the courage to reject temptation, and the determination of doing things selectively, the road to prosperity was bound to be accompanied by constant trial and error and numerous difficult choices. However, the two funds of GF adhered to the "GF spirit" inherited from GF Securities of being low-key and pragmatic, striving for progress, sticking to the original aspiration and making a contribution to society, and staying at the forefront of the industry with a more stable, inclusive, and diversified posture.

3. Staying at the forefront of changes in capital management

Since its birth in 1998, China's fund industry has developed for more than 20 years. During this tumultuous process, some collapsed, some rode the waves, and some rose to catch up.

In terms of industry ranking changes, it was not easy to maintain the industry leadership in the long term. Only a few funds that ranked in the top 10 of the industry in 2003 remained in the top 10 list in 2020. The fierce competition in the industry and the cruelty of the elimination of losers were shocking. In the competition, a fund is like a boat sailing against the current: it must either forge ahead or fall behind. No matter how successful and experienced a fund has been before, if it does not have the core competitiveness to drive development and the courage to innovate, it is difficult to maintain excellent investment performance and asset management scale.

With the deepening of social development and financial reform, the asset management industry will face more complex challenges and uncertainties: the increasingly diversified needs of investors will put higher demands on the diversified investment capabilities of funds. While funds compete with domestic banks, insurance companies, and independent companies, top international asset management companies have already entered China's fund industry. The ever-changing financial technology has not only overturned the traditional operation mode, but has also created new opportunities for the development of the fund industry.... An era of intertwined hopes and challenges for asset management has arrived.

With the unique GF gene and arduous efforts, E Fund and GF Fund has been running all the way, surpassing and overtaking others all the time. In the face of the rapidly arriving new era, the two companies have started to adjust their postures in running, actively reinventing themselves, breaking the boundaries of their capabilities, glowing with stronger strength in moving forward, and embracing the future with a more positive posture.

Actively embracing the new capital management era under the new normal

Since the eighteenth National Party Congress was held in 2012, the central government has started to adjust its thinking on economic development and promote economic transformation and upgrading. Guided by the objectives of "maintaining stable growth, promoting reform, making structural adjustments, improving people's lives, and guarding against risks," China's economy has entered a new era, shifting from a high-speed growth stage to a high-quality development stage. This has brought changes to the asset management industry: social capital has gradually returned to rationality from the high return expectations of the past, and low-risk and stable-return varieties have gradually become more attractive. In addition, new investment strategies with risk-hedging features have emerged despite the difficulties during the "structural adjustment."

Under the new normal of economic development, the fund industry has also ushered in a new phase of development. The newly revised Securities Investment Fund Law in June 2013 was implemented, which relaxed the investment scope and business scope of the industry and provided huge room for funds to innovate and develop. In addition, this market also ushered in more competitive entities, and the policy restrictions for securities companies, insurance asset management companies, private equity funds, and other institutions to enter the public fund business were broken through. For the first time, the national law encouraged public fund managers to implement professional stock ownership plans and establish long-term effective incentive and restraint mechanisms, showing a blooming situation.

At this time, GF Fund had just reached its tenth year of development. In this decade, from the initial asset size of 3.1 billion yuan to 115 billion yuan, from the thirtieth to the sixth largest fund in the industry, GF Fund established its own circle of competence in the complex and changing market. In an era of change, how could the fund maintain its core competencies while expanding the boundaries of its capabilities to keep pace with the times?

"Change" was the word most mentioned by General Manager Lin Chuanhui at the 2013 year-end work conference, including not only mechanism innovation and management innovation, but also business innovation and product innovation. In the face of the new economic situation, with investors' demand for steady returns, funds needed to continuously broaden the boundaries of their investment capabilities and strengthen their core investment capabilities, including the application of new tools, new strategies, and new markets, in addition to the traditional equity investment management capabilities. Diversification of investment capabilities was the only way to meet the needs of different client groups in different market stages.

Under this strategic thinking, GF started to strengthen the forward-looking research of the product layout, and made efforts to lay out the underlying products, focusing on diversifying a rich variety of products. It not only laid out the most complete industry ETFs in the industry, but also laid out products in multiple regions, becoming the fund with the largest number of QDII products in the industry. It also achieved full coverage of fixed income strategies and clarification of active equity investment style types. These underlying assets with rich categories and clear styles not only provided investors with suitable investment tools in different market environments and economic cycles, but also provided important support for the company to build its asset allocation capabilities.

In addition, General Manager Lin Chuanhui and the management team also actively cultivated and built asset allocation capabilities. As the first company in the industry to prepare for asset allocation team building and talent reserve, GF Fund introduced Wall Street elites and insurance FOF talents to build an investment team with excellent overall strength, rich practical experience, multi-perspectives, and diversified complementarity. Thanks to efforts of the team, GF Fund formed a scientific asset allocation investment and research system, stocked a variety of asset allocation solutions such as allocation, relative return, absolute return, and special targets. It established core competitiveness at three levels: general asset allocation, fund selection, and portfolio management. The expanded asset allocation capabilities under strategic thinking integrated the framework of the company's many years of investment research experience and practical experience in China, as well as absorbed advanced portfolio management experience from overseas.

All preparations were made for a more glorious mission. In September 2016, the CSRC issued the Guidelines for the Operation of Publicly Raised Securities Investment Funds No. 2: Fund-of-Funds Guidelines, and public FOFs (Fund-of-Funds) took the stage in history. FOF products focused on the allocation of general asset classes and risk control, which was more in line with investors' demand for stable returns and also matched the investment direction of pension funds, and the fund industry officially entered the asset allocation era. At this time, GF had been "practicing hard" in asset allocation for more than three years.

The core of competition in the asset management industry was the strength of professional investment research, and the industry also tested the foresight and insight of funds on the development of the industry. Looking back at the previous development history of GF Fund, whenever GF Fund faced a key market opportunity, it had always been able to understand the changing market trend and seize the business high ground. As Jack Welch said, "The world is changing too fast for us to be prepared for every change, but we must be prepared for any change."

Also in 2013, the board of directors of E Fund, just across the Pearl River, formally proposed the company's strategic thinking for three to five years: to adhere to the strategic positioning of "being the leading comprehensive asset management institution in China," to improve the pyramid-shaped business and organizational structure, and to provide investors with investment products with different risk and return characteristics and a fast, easy, and friendly user experience.

At the end of 2015, there were 2,700 public fund products and excellent fund managers emerged in the market in China. The full development of public funds and excellent investment managers provided the basis for FOF and MOM (manager of managers) investment management for fund allocation. From the demand side, the capital managed by banking, insurance, and other institutions increased considerably, while professional investment managers were scarce and needed to manage large-scale funds through a smaller number of products. In addition, bank finance products were facing the demand for transformation to net worth. In the communication with customers and observation of the market, Liu Xiaoyan, general manager of E Fund, keenly felt the new changes in business development. She once wrote when laying out her work in 2015: "In terms of new business, we will strive to develop new business areas and new business models, focusing on the innovative direction of carrying out general asset allocation business, researching FOF, and exploring effective models of providing general asset allocation services for institutional and high net worth clients and internet platform clients. "

FOF and MOM and other similar multi-asset allocation business are a milestone in the development of a country's fund industry to a certain level of maturity, and are an important means for the modernization of the fund industry. The key to investment lies in asset allocation and fund selection, where asset allocation includes both strategic and tactical asset allocation, requiring not only in-depth research on the long-term history of each general asset, but also a clear judgment of the current economic situation and policy direction, and the ability to respond quickly to changes in the market environment. The selection of a good fund is a time-consuming and systematic project, which requires not only a scientific classification of various fund products in the market and a quantitative analysis of their historical performance and positions, but also in-depth due diligence and long-term tracking of fund managers and investment research teams, combining qualitative and quantitative factors. All this places extremely high demands on the ability of the managers.

After active preparation, in 2016, Wang Lanying, who had nearly 20 years of rich experience in general asset allocation, led the establishment of the Multi-Asset Investment Department. Its members had more than 10 years of experience in investment and most of them came from domestic and foreign sovereign funds, pension funds and other investment institutions and had engaged in fund research and investment for many years.

As soon as the department was established, it worked to improve its skills.

Under the guidance of a set of standardized systems and processes and a clear investment research philosophy and values, E Fund formed its own three unique secrets: a complete fund and manager database, a real-time and efficient monitoring and surveillance system, and a strong technical resource and institutional foundation. The three systems supported each other and worked closely together, demonstrating unique efficiency advantages. Those who saw this market-wide, localized fund evaluation system exclaimed, "It's awesome." Some institutional clients also reported that they were willing to pay a high price to use this set of "supreme treasures" for internal fund and fund manager analysis. A mature asset allocation system was set up and operated in E Fund.

"Diversify risk, stabilize growth, and give you steady happiness." This vision of FOF coincided with the needs of pensions. In February 2018, the CSRC officially released the Guidelines for Pension-Oriented Securities Investment Funds (for Trial Implementation), which meant that public funds' deep involvement in the cause of personal pensions would move from theory to practice and funds would be able to give full play to their asset allocation capabilities.

With their asset allocation ability and long-term excellent performance, E Fund and GF funds were approved to be two of the first pension-oriented securities investment funds in China at the same time. The two companies took a more active stance in the road of inclusive finance to take up the heavy responsibility of pensions and root their business development in the soil of enhancing people's wellbeing.

Going global in the new era

With the introduction of a series of financial policies, the capital management industry further deepened its opening to the outside world, and more and more efforts were made to "go global" and "bring in." For the young Chinese fund industry, the road of international development was destined to be arduous and tortuous.

The two-way opening of the capital markets opened up policy space for domestic funds to conduct business and invest globally. E Fund saw a strategic opportunity for international development: with the development of China's economy, global institutional investors have a strong desire to participate in the Chinese market and cooperate with excellent local asset management companies. Global institutional investors managed huge capital and had high professionalism requirements, and leading Chinese asset management companies could provide them with professional and high-quality investment management services. In addition, with the growth of domestic wealth, global allocation had also become a major demand for domestic investors.

Moreover, the entry of foreign institutions into China would bring advanced management concepts and investment methods from mature overseas markets. Exchanges and cooperation with outstanding foreign institutions would help

E Fund reach international excellence in management philosophy, investment research strength, product design, risk control level, and customer service capability, and come in full line with international first-class financial companies.

However, the early start of "going global" encountered difficulties and obstacles. The first group of QDII funds in 2007 was born at a bad time and experienced the whole process of the international financial crisis. Many investors suffered losses, so the asset size of related products had decreased since their establishment. In addition, the diversity and complexity of overseas markets objectively led to the lack of awareness of overseas markets and QDII products among Chinese bank channels and fund clients. This made it more difficult for QDII funds to promote sales and educate investors. The road to "go global" was still long and bumpy.

In contrast, "bringing in" was going smoothly. "We should focus on international business to meet the demand for global asset allocation for individuals and institutions in the process of China's economic downturn, while providing products and services for international investors in the Chinese market. International business requires long-term efforts to cultivate capabilities, build platforms, and establish brands. Although it may not necessarily bring significant scale growth in the short term, it is an indispensable part of the company's long-term development strategy and business layout," said Liu Xiaoyan, president of E Fund, in her 2015 work report.

In October of that year, E Fund officially established a global investment client department to focus on serving international institutional investors. Since the end of 2015, E Fund has signed cooperation agreements with a number of large overseas asset management institutions, including State Street Global Advisors, the third-largest asset management institution in the world, and APG, the largest pension manager in Europe.

The partnership with APG, a pension fund manager headquartered in the Netherlands with a management scale of over 4 trillion yuan, was not easy to come by. As APG was an internationally renowned pension fund manager, it had high and detailed requirements for its partners and investigated E Fund for more than two years for due diligence and in-depth understanding. The due diligence not only involved the investment research E Fund, but also covered the middle and back offices including technical operation, accounting, trading, compliance, risk control, and other aspects of business.

During the due diligence process, in order to avoid the time delay caused by the sentence-by-sentence translation, each business department communicated with their foreign colleagues in English. This was a challenge for most of E Fund employees who were not native English speakers and whose daily working language was not English. One of the department heads who participated in the due diligence once joked that his English skills had improved rapidly since the APG due diligence, and he was even able to "joke" with his clients: when introducing eRisk, an internal risk control platform developed by E Fund, he wisely and humorously told the foreign clients that eRisk means eliminating risks. This impressed the clients.

The consistent conscientiousness and hard work of E Fund employees won the affirmation and appreciation of the foreign party. APG commented that "E Fund's performance in due diligence was the highest level among all institutions that could be on par with BlackRock."

Over the next four years, the two sides made substantial progress in investment management, staff exchange, and knowledge sharing. During the exchange, E Fund also learned, accumulated, and refined the successful experience and methods from the mature European market. Among them, the ESG factor and responsible investment philosophy had the most profound impact on E Fund and the Chinese fund industry as a whole.

In early 2017, E Fund was the first in the Chinese fund industry to join the United Nations Principles for Responsible Investment (PRI) and became a member of the Asian Corporate Governance Association (ACGA). In September of the same year, together with APG, E Fund launched the first pension management product that followed the framework and standards of sustainable and responsible investment in the international market and invested in the Chinese A-share market. In early 2018, E Fund became one of the only two Chinese funds in the China-UK Financial Disclosure Panel. In June of the same year, E Fund and State Street Global Advisors, jointly launched an environmental investment strategy covering Chinese A-share listed companies. In September 2019, E Fund issued the first ESG responsible investment equity public fund in China, followed by China's first responsible investment fixed income strategy jointly launched with APG in November.

Looking back, with professional pursuit and innovative breakthroughs, from simple copying and imitation of overseas experience, to selectively improving and upgrading in light of China's market reality, to now launching system innovation and product service innovation with distinctive local market characteristics and in line with China's national conditions, E Fund has gone further and further on the road of internationalization.

Liu Xiaoyan is an optimist, stating that, "The era, believe it or not, is rolling forward, and what we need is a little more patience, a little more sense of discipline, and a little less complaining."

Evolving in innovation for the future

In August 2018, GF Fund celebrated its fifteenth anniversary, and GF people who had contributed their wisdom and sweat and felt the hardship of starting a business on the stage of fund business over the previous many years, stretched their smiling brows, sang their hearty songs, and shed tears of joy to their heart's content.

At the anniversary party, General Manager Lin Chuanhui, while reviewing the achievements of the company, also put forward a question for consideration: "In the future, can we do better? How can we do better?"

In the face of the unceasing torrent of the times and the roaring changes in the capital markets, Lin Chuanhui realized that the public fund industry would face more complex challenges and greater uncertainties in the future. The increasingly diverse needs of investors had slowly overflowed beyond the familiar asset classes of the existing public fund industry and crossed the boundaries of the fund industry's existing investment capabilities; banks, insurance companies, brokerage firms, independent companies, and other market players were increasing, and top international asset management companies such as Pioneer, Fidelity, and BlackRock had eagerly entered China's public funds. All this would bring more changes to China's fund industry. As part of this industry, GF Fund could become healthier with a long and vigorous vitality and cope with the upcoming unpredictable future only by constantly breaking the old pattern and keeping changing, moving, and surpassing itself.

After the anniversary, GF Fund once again embarked on the road of all-around self-innovation. Lin Chuanhui chose to fire the "first shot" of change in the active equity department and began to clarify the company's active equity investment style and diversify active equity investment management capability, including adjusting the investment department structure, strengthening the process management, and strengthening reform.

In the early stage of consultation, everyone agreed that the direction of reform was right, but when the change entered the deep water zone, it meant changing the status quo, which was a self-revolution. After a long gestation period, GF Fund proposed a restructuring plan for the active equity investment department: by adjusting the structure of the investment department, it would allow each fund manager to focus on his or her own circle of competence according to his or her own knowledge and resources, and clarify the investment style. This was a major change to the operation mode of GF Fund's entire investment research system and meant that everyone had to leave their existing comfort zone to adapt to the new management operation mechanism.

The corporate culture of GF Fund always maintained a spirit of self-innovation and renewed strength, which was also the "gene" of truth-seeking and innovation originated from GF Securities and was deeply integrated into the bloodline of GF people.

GF Fund started to reengineer the investment process as a whole, grouping fund managers according to their styles, dividing the original active equity department into three departments: value, strategy, and growth, and determining the departments' respective positions and development directions. Making fund managers the earliest investors to discover the value of companies was one of the key points of this reform. Grouping fund managers with the same philosophy and similar style into one group would help them communicate and cooperate better and form a synergy. The three divisions were different yet harmonious, maximizing individual capabilities and amplifying the advantages of GF Fund's platform as a large asset management company.

After the reform of the active equity department, the fund managers' attention became more focused, but how could the fund managers achieve maximum alpha within a relatively limited scope to enhance investment returns? The answer given by Zhu Ping, who was specifically responsible for promoting this reform, was to make investment a science. The company profiled the fund managers' investment styles, identifying the areas in which they excelled and strengthening the styles through professional training to improve the winning rate of stock selection.

The method of "special training" for fund managers' investment styles sounded very strange in the fund industry, because this method did not originate from the financial industry, but from the NBA training across the Pacific Ocean. Under the guidance of this method, the Financial Engineering Department of GF Fund built a big data system based on all the fund managers' past stock positions, trading data, profitable and loss-making stocks, analyzed the characteristics of each fund manager's profitable stocks and loss-making stocks, summarized the stocks for which fund managers had a higher winning rate, and discovered each fund manager's ability.

In fact, the fund managers' investment portraits were used not only to improve the winning rate of stock selection, but also to reduce mistakes. There were many temptations and distractions in the market, and when there were rising stocks, many people instinctively rushed in, but such a reaction could easily lead to mistakes in investing, bringing volatility and losses. Let's say, for an oncoming punch, most people's instinctive reaction is to close their eyes and swing their head, but the correct response is to open your eyes to see where the punch is coming from and then decide whether to dodge or block, and the prerequisite for making the correct judgment is countless hours of training.

By establishing a scientific training system, GF Fund strengthened the process management of investment, and through strict process management, it tried to avoid losses of fund managers by investing in companies they were unfamiliar with and not good at, and reduce the probability of making mistakes.

Just like Warren Buffett's baseball investment philosophy, if no efforts are made to catch bad balls, there will be no demerits. The same goes for investing; when a fund manager realizes which ball has a high miss rate and does not catch that ball, there will be no negative contribution to the portfolio. When fund managers focus on their own areas of expertise to find opportunities, the correct rate of stock selection will increase, and the return on investment will naturally increase.

The effect of GF Fund's modernizing its investment research system was immediately visible. Not only did it enable fund managers of different investment styles to pursue better returns while maintaining a stable style, but also more importantly, explored a path to create long-term, stable, and sustainable returns for investors.

With harmony comes prosperity, with culture comes a firm foundation

Some people say that the funds in GF were very fortunate: they were not the first funds to be established, but their management scale has been among the top ten in the industry for a long time; they have avoided the impact on the first funds, but actually shared the scale-large growth brought by the bull market in 2006–2007; they have not fallen into the stagnation on the management scale of 100 billion yuan, and instead embarked on the road of diversification.

These two funds, which came out of GF Securities, have been in the forefront of competition and have continuously transformed, forming a unique "GF phenomenon" in the fund industry. What was the core competitiveness behind their rapid development?

Perhaps we can get a glimpse of it from the cultural genes of GF Securities. All along, GF Securities has been adhering to the "people-oriented" concept of talent. Dr. Chen Yunxian advocated that GF people "should be not only explorers of theories but also practitioners of the capital markets; not only be the owners of material wealth under the protection of the system, but also be the adherents of noble virtues." This philosophy of employment makes the funds of "GF" emphasize the universal development and sustainable growth of talents, especially the harmonious coexistence between people and themselves, the market and the whole of society. This healthy and positive view of talent allows like-minded people with diverse styles to work together harmoniously so that the best talents can realize their self-worth and create maximum social value.

Looking back on the road of development in the past, Lin Chuanhui, head of GF Fund, explained this. The biggest advantage of GF Fund is the simple relationship between shareholders and the company management, the good relationship between the chairman and general managers, and the harmonious relationship between colleagues, and all this forms a synergy.

Wang Qi, investment manager of GF Fund's Research Department, was deeply convinced of this corporate culture inherited from GF Securities. In her opinion, harmony but not uniformity, simplicity and unsophisticatedness were one of the core competitive advantages of GF's investment research team: "The feedback between researchers and investment managers was very direct and efficient, and in the interaction, the original thinking could be revised and updated, and information could be fully flowed within the investment research system, forming a virtuous cycle."

A fund manager of GF Fund lamented, "Because of this, we were very simple and transparent in investment research communication. Investment researchers were only responsible for investment results, and did not have too many other interfering factors. All of them had a standard that put the market before superiors and authorities."

In fact, heated arguments in business seminars were very common within

GF Fund. General Manager Lin Chuanhui strongly encouraged such business debates: "GF Fund advocated a culture of active participation in decision-making, encouraging employees to put forward opinions that differed from those of the principal leader, but once a decision was made, it must be implemented. No one could be authoritative even if he or she was wrong in GF Fund, and we supported whoever was right." Differences of opinion at work did not affect the relationship between employees, but rather stimulated the potential of each of them.

It was this united and harmonious corporate culture, which had a strong attraction to talents, that GF Fund's management always remained stable, with few changes in core personnel, and talents and successful experiences could be passed on from one generation to the next. In the fund industry, E Fund's talent stability was always praised. In the first year of E Fund's establishment, there were only 41 employees, 27 of whom are still working there today. What's even more surprising was that the investment research team was always the hardest hit by the talent drain in the fund industry. But at E Fund, there was a record of three consecutive years of no public fund manager departures.

What was the reason why E Fund was able to retain so many industry elites? This was due to the inclusive working environment and the attentive service to employees. A reporter had an exchange with a young fund manager of E Fund: "What do you think of E Fund?" "I think that E Fund is like a school."

This attitude of education and cultivation ran through the entire talent system of E Fund. Because it did not want fund managers to focus too much on short-term ranking and cause short-sightedness in investment, E Fund introduced a long-term assessment mechanism in the performance evaluation of its investment staff. Such a system gave fund managers a good space to make long-term investment layouts.

Fu Hao, a fund manager who has been with E Fund for more than 15 years, said in an interview: "The company's assessment is long-term. It will not deny you because of bad performance in the short term before the day when you do well." He used to be in charge of E Fund's Kerui Fund and did not top the list of performance in any year. However, his good cumulative ranking over the years won him the "2010 Morningstar Closed-End Fund Award."

In the industry, the culture of E Fund's investment research team was praised. Open, honest, and relaxed, the investment research team respected individual research and did not believe in authority. Sometimes, because of a stock, young researchers without seniority dared to challenge the "old guards" and often the latter were convinced. This was because Jiang Zuoliang and Xiao Jian, the two "teachers," believed that only if the investment philosophy was not rigid, it could be constantly upgraded to adapt to the changes of the times, so that, as described in the brand motto of E Fund, "we are obsessed with winning in the long run."

In addition to providing a good and inclusive environment for employees at work, E Fund was also known in the industry for its care for employees in their daily lives. In 2006, E Fund set up the first cafeteria in the fund industry, making it as safe, hygienic and healthy as possible for employees to eat. This kind of care and love for employees enabled E Fund employees to work without distractions in the sense of belonging to a "home."

In January 2011, Dr. Ma Qingquan, the then chairman of GF Securities, made his last speech at the company's year-end meeting before his retirement at Crowne Plaza Guangzhou Science City.

> I has always emphasized that with harmony comes prosperity, because the problem of unity of leaders can lead to worrisome development prospects for the company. Fortunately, GF Fund's management team has a positive style, a record of good performance and a grasp of the company's future development. I hope the company will continue to maintain this style in the future, with one external voice and one banner that cannot be shaken. It is with harmony that prosperity comes.

Dr. Ma Qingquan, who experienced the changes in the capital markets for many years, knew that the prosperity of a company first came from the prosperity of its corporate culture, while the decay of a company also came from the disintegration and deterioration of its corporate culture. The corporate culture was transformed into the genes of the company's operation, shifting complexity into simplicity, and became an inexhaustible source of strength. The root of this culture was the "GF Spirit," which was the core of GF Securities' corporate culture and shaped the harmonious atmosphere of the company's management.

If a person's fate is determined by his or her character, the "GF Spirit" inherited from GF Securities was the gear that determined the fate of the two funds. This "GF Spirit," as Dr. Chen Yunxian said, "is to truly inspire the team to have a sense of historical responsibility and mission for the country and the nation, and knowledge should be used to serve the country and the people."

With the simple ideal of "making money for ordinary people" and the mission of "serving the country with finance," the young intellectuals from GF Securities pioneered the fund industry and paved their way through trial and error. Whether it was the establishment of rules and regulations and the value-based approach in the early stage of establishment, doing things selectively at the crossroads, or the self-revolution in the new pattern of the industry, the idealistic spirit of "serving the country and the people" was like a fertile ground that nourished the organizational cells, allowing internal harmony and coexistence with vigorous vitality. This spiritual heritage has permeated the thoughts and actions of every generation of GF people since the company was founded, and has become the principle that GF people adhere to.

Chapter XI: GF People in the Futures Industry

The worst enemy is the absence of a strong conviction.

—Romain Rolland

On November 30, 2019, at the fifteenth China (Shenzhen) International Futures Conference, Fang Xinghai, vice chairman of the CSRC, stated in his speech that, "The pace of international development of futures companies has accelerated. Twenty-one futures companies have set up branches overseas, and some futures companies have become members of overseas exchanges such as the CME and LME. Among them, GF Futures' UK subsidiary has become a member of the LME circle and has achieved better profits."

Also during this weekend, Zhao Guiping, chairwoman of GF Futures, who was attending a meeting at GF Securities Tower, kept receiving messages that fellow futures companies were congratulating GF Futures. She could not suppress her excitement and shared the messages with every GF Futures employee. Vice Chairman Fang Xinghai's praise at the conference represented a high recognition of GF Futures' internationalization work by the regulatory leaders. The international expansion was a beautiful business card of GF Futures, a well-established Chinese futures company.

Founded in 1993 as a subsidiary of GF Securities, GF Futures witnessed the early ups and downs of China's futures industry. After the clean-up of the futures market in 2001, GF Securities wholly owned GF Futures and provided strong support, which led to the rapid development of GF Futures for nearly two decades.

The lyrics of a Cantonese song are: "As the road beside you, though far away,

I'm not tired, accompanying you on a long journey, one section after another. Crossing over the peak, another peak appears again. Though the goal is far, the ideal should always come first." This is a true reflection of the industry status of GF Futures against its parent company GF Securities. Inheriting the genes of GF Securities, GF Futures has been forging ahead and has been rated AA by the CSRC for many years in a row, ranking among the top ten domestic futures companies in various indicators. At present, GF Futures' business offices are found in 26 cities and regions in China, with GF Trading Co., Ltd., GF Futures (Hong Kong) Co., Ltd. and GF Financial Trading (UK) Co., Ltd., forming a business network "based in the Pearl River Delta, covering all major cities in China, and radiating the global derivatives market through Hong Kong and London." It is the goal of all GF Futures people to develop into a comprehensive futures and derivatives provider offering domestic and overseas, multi-market and multi-species risk management solutions and wealth management services to clients.

1. The fire of futures in winter

Origin of GF futures

At the beginning of Guangdong Development Bank, in addition to traditional banking, it set up the Trust And Investment Department, Securities Department, Fund Department and Futures Department before 1993. In order to develop foreign exchange and enter the international market, Guangdong Development Bank actively planned international futures. At that time, the Futures Department was mainly engaged in domestic commodity futures trading, and Hu Yousheng, a graduate of Beijing Institute of Economics, was its head.

On January 20, 1993, with the approval by the Guangdong Provincial People's Government's Y.B.H. [1993] No. 27 document, GF Industrial Investment Company, a subsidiary of Guangdong Development Bank, invested 88.61 percent, Guangdong Yueneng Energy Co., Ltd. invested 5.93 percent and Guangdong Huizhou Lingnan Biochemical Group Company invested 5.46 percent to jointly establish Guangdong Huayin International Commodity Futures Company, which became the predecessor of GF Futures. The company had a registered capital of 10 million yuan and was mainly engaged in international commodity futures trading and information consulting services. The legal representative was Wang Zhiwei and the general manager was Hu Yousheng. The company was located on the thirteenth floor of the South Tower of Guangzhou World Trade Center on Huanshi East Road. On December 19, 1994, the company was granted a futures license by the CSRC.

On May 28, 1993, GF Securities became a member of the South China Commodity Futures Exchange. On the same day, Guangdong GF Futures Clearing Company, a joint venture of GF Securities, Guangzhou Rubber Futures Exchange, and Guangdong Overseas Chinese Investment Company, was established with the three companies serving as its controlling stakeholder, becoming the first company in China to start futures and futures clearing business, with Zeng Qingmin as the general manager.

On September 29, 1993, the Securities Department of Guangdong Development Bank held a securities working meeting, which was attended by Ding Lisong, vice chairman of Guangdong Development Bank, and presided over by Dr. Chen Yunxian. This was a significant meeting, which clarified that the Futures Department of Guangdong Development Bank was subsumed under the direct management of the Securities Department, and its head, computer manager, and manager of the Planning and Finance Department would be all appointed by the Securities Department.

On December 20, 1993, the Futures Department of Guangdong Development Bank merged with Guangdong Huayin International Commodity Futures Company to form Guangdong Huayin International Futures Brokerage Co., Ltd., and the office was moved from the World Trade Center to the ninth floor of Huashan Hotel. On March 28, 1995, the company formally changed its name to Guangdong GF Futures Brokerage Co., Ltd., with a registered capital of 10 million yuan and the legal representative changed to Chen Yunxian.

At this point, GF Securities' futures companies included a wholly-owned Guangdong Guangfa Futures Brokerage Co., Ltd. and a participating GF Futures Clearing Co., Ltd. In addition to his positions in Guangdong Development Bank and GF Securities, Dr. Chen Yunxian was also chairman of Guangdong United Futures Exchange, chairman of GF Futures Clearing Company, and chairman of Guangdong GF Futures Brokerage Co., Ltd.

On January 31, 1994, at the first working meeting of Guangdong GF Securities Company, Dr. Chen Yunxian shared his thoughts on investment banking with all executives. When talking about the specialization of investment banking, he listed the financial business innovations of various international securities companies and investment banks. Among them, serving major clients in the secondary market could provide value-added services through interest rate swaps, futures and spot hedging, foreign exchange, gold, and other new financial instruments derivatives. On March 27, 1994, in front of the representatives of securities brokerage branches of all branches of Guangdong Development Bank, Dr. Chen Yunxian stressed again that the business of investment banking needed to include futures business, and pointed out that "the business of GF Securities is a business in line with the trend of global development." In Dr. Chen's mind, futures derivatives services were an integral part of international investment banking.

In his 1995 monograph *On Investment Banking*, Dr. Chen pointed out that, "One of the keys to competitive investment banking is the rapid creation of financial 'new products.' Innovation in financial instruments provides investment banking with the greatest flexibility in terms of business development. Whether it is options trading, futures trading, forward trading or swaps, they can all help investors to hedge risk and increase returns. In addition, investment banking gains from the establishment and trading of financial innovation instruments." As can be seen, Dr. Chen always believed that providing derivatives services was an important part of investment banking and that a wealth of financial instruments could help clients hedge their risks.

The start and consolidation of the futures market

In the 1980s, in the process of changing from a planned economy to a socialist market economy, price breakthroughs became an important goal of reform. On February 10, 1988, Li Peng instructed the Development Research Center of the State Council to "consider the possibility of organizing a few people to study foreign futures and apply futures to the purchase and sale of urban foodstuffs, especially vegetables and pork. This should be done to protect the interests both producers and consumers and keep market prices basically stable." On March 25, 1988, Li Peng pointed out in his government work report at the First Session of the Seventh National People's Congress that, "We will speed up the reform of the commercial system, actively develop various types of wholesale markets." On May 26, 1988, Li Peng approved the Report of the Working Group on the Study of Futures Market on the Trial Operation of the Futures Market in the Light of the National Conditions, clearly stating that, "I agree to pilot the market, but we should work out a plan in the light of China's actual situation." Finally, on October 12, 1990, the Zhengzhou Grain Wholesale Market, the first pilot futures market approved by the State Council, was officially opened.

The establishment of the Zhengzhou Grain Wholesale Market marked the beginning of futures trading in China, and the market established the first standardized futures trading system in China. After that, futures exchanges were established in many regions, including Suzhou, Shenzhen, and Shanghai. Among them, the Shenzhen Nonferrous Metals Exchange was the first futures market for production materials in China and the first futures exchange named after "exchange" in China. In October 1992, the Shenzhen Nonferrous Metals Exchange launched the special grade aluminum futures contract, which was the first standardized futures contract in China.

After the fourteenth National Party Congress, the futures market developed rapidly, with futures brokerage firms springing up and futures exchanges being established in an extensive manner everywhere. By the end of 1993, there were more than 50 futures exchanges, 300 futures brokerage firms, and 2,000 futures institutions (banks, securities companies, and trust companies) in China. 1993 to 1995 were undoubtedly good years for the rapid development of the futures market, with the turnover of the national futures market increasing from 552.2 billion yuan to 10 trillion yuan. The growth rate was phenomenal.

In order to seize the opportunity of the rapid development of China's futures market and benchmark the business layout of international investment bankers, Dr. Chen Yunxian decided to strengthen the futures company. In 1993, At this time, Zhao Guiping, general manager of GF Securities' Third Brokerage Branch, came into Dr. Chen's view. Dr. Chen interviewed Zhao Guiping personally and assigned her to set up the Tianhe Road Brokerage Branch and serve as the first general manager. As a master of automation from South China University of Technology, Zhao Guiping was not only logical, but also undaunted and determined in customer service and frontline operation.

On October 23, 1994, Zhao Guiping suddenly received an arrangement from Dr. Chen Yunxian to draft a report on the future development vision of the futures company, including the current situation of the futures company and analysis of futures business and varieties. Through this report, Zhao Guiping got to know more about GF Futures.

Two months later, Dr. Chen contacted Zhao Guiping by phone and expressed the idea of developing the futures business and assigning her to GF Futures as the general manager. Dr. Chen further pointed out that the futures company should be "internationalized, standardized, and modernized." With a vision of the futures industry, Zhao Guiping came to GF Futures, ready to start a career.

On December 27, 1994, GF Securities held a special meeting in Huatai Hotel to strengthen the management of its subsidiaries. Dr. Chen made the following points clear at the meeting:

> The management of personnel, property and materials of the subsidiaries would be further decentralized. While general managers, deputy general managers and planning and finance managers would be appointed by the Head Office, all other personnel (including the veteran employees) would be appointed, recruited, or dismissed by the subsidiaries.
>
> The management of capital utilization, investment, and finance of the subsidiaries would be strengthened.
>
> The business of the subsidiaries would be guided by the Head Office.
>
> Party organizations' affairs of the subsidiaries would be handled by the Head Office.
>
> In general, the Head Office would manage its subsidiaries mainly by appointing core management personnel and assessing annual profits.

On January 12, 1995, in the new board of directors of GF Futures, Dr. Chen Yunxian was chairman, Wu Chuanbin and Dou Xinyuan were vice chairmen, Director Zhao Guiping was general manager, and Lü Ping was the shareholder director. Liu Jie and Hu Yousheng no longer served as directors of GF Futures.

During this period, GF Futures' domestic business was mainly commodity futures and government bond futures, and its international business was foreign exchange and HSI futures. In 1994, GF Futures had total revenue of 1,655,800 yuan, expenses of 4,075,800, profit of -2,420,000 yuan, and accounts receivable of over 5,000,000 yuan. With regard to the business direction, the board of directors required GF Futures to give play to the advantage of doing both futures and spot goods, and go into a virtuous cycle through cross-market treasury bond arbitrage and stock futures and spot arbitrage. The board of directors focused on the assessment of profit targets for GF Futures, requiring a minimum profit contribution of five percent.

With the support of GF Securities, GF Futures started to lay out its business. It increased its external promotion efforts, and created links with the stock market. It sent market representatives to the Beijing Commodity Futures Exchange (government bonds and mung beans), the Suzhou Commodity Futures Exchange (plywood and red beans), and the Guangdong United Futures Exchange (soybean meal and indica rice). It started a direct point-to-point connection with the Hainan China Commodity Futures Exchange (palm oil, natural rubber, and coffee), the Zhengzhou Commodity Exchange (mung beans and plywood), and the Shanghai Metal Exchange (copper and aluminum). GF Futures started the secondary agency of government bond futures, and carried out Hang Seng Index futures trading simultaneously with the second and third brokerage branches, the Shekou, Zhongshan, Zhuhai, and Hainan brokerage branches, and the secondary agency in Yichang outside GF Securities. The number of employees of GF Futures grew to 24 and its own R&D department was established with reference to GF Securities. At that time, GF Futures advertised its strengths to the public as the first trading venue in Guangzhou that integrated stock trading and government bond futures. However, due to the application of multiple exchange seats, the advance of basic margin also consumed a lot of cash of GF Futures.

In the second half of 1994, the government bond futures market began to explode, and the market scale expanded quickly. The daily turnover of government bond futures on the Shanghai Stock Exchange reached a maximum of more than 80 billion yuan, and the total turnover in 1994 reached 2.35 trillion yuan, accounting for 96.7 percent of the total turnover of the entire government bond market, while the turnover of stocks on the Shanghai Stock Exchange during the same period was only 573.507 billion yuan, which was less than one quarter of the total turnover of government bond futures.

While the trading volume increased rapidly, different varieties of government bond futures were also listed on several domestic stock or futures exchanges one after another. On December 15, 1993, the Beijing Commodity Exchange launched four varieties of government bond futures, and the commodity exchanges in Wuhan, Guangzhou, Dalian, and Zhengzhou also launched government bond futures. The Shenzhen Stock Exchange also launched government bond futures in September 1994 and developed it rapidly. At its peak, there were once as many as 18 exchanges that launched government bond futures across the country. The trading of government bond futures was in full swing, and the trading volume of government bonds of GF Futures also increased rapidly, and securities business offices also carried out secondary agency. Road shows and reports of GF Futures were held intensively. In the midst of the prosperous scene, the staff of GF Futures was once close to 50 people. Few people realized that a crisis was imminent.

In 1995, one of the most significant events in the history of China's futures market, the 327 Bond Futures Incident, broke out. On February 23, due to the irregular trading of Wanguo Securities, the Securities Regulatory Commission and the Shanghai Stock Exchange announced that all transactions of the "327" government bond in the last eight minutes of that afternoon were invalid, and Wanguo Securities, as a short-seller, suffered huge losses. In order to strengthen the management of government bond futures trading and regulate the market operation, the Securities Regulatory Commission and the Ministry of Finance issued the Interim Measures for the Administration of Government Bond Futures Trading. Three months later, on May 17, 1995, the CSRC issued the Emergency Circular on the Suspension of Pilot Trading of Government Bond Futures, which suspended the pilot trading of government bond futures nationwide. As China's first financial derivative, government bond futures were aborted.

The State Council began to consolidate the futures market by abolishing and merging the exchanges, reducing their number from more than 50 to 15, and by consolidating and reducing the number of futures brokers and practitioners. In November 1994, the Securities Commission of the State Council issued the Interim Measures for the Management of Practitioners of Futures Institutions, and promulgated a series of management measures for brokerage firms. In addition, the futures varieties were cleaned up and reorganized, overseas futures trading was strictly prohibited, and futures varieties that were not qualified for listing, such as steel, sugar, coal, japonica rice, oil, and red wheat, were stopped, and disguised futures trading was prohibited. As a result of this consolidation, the futures market turnover fell rapidly from a peak of nearly 10 trillion yuan in 1995 to 8.4 trillion yuan in 1996, a decline of 16 percent, and 6.1 trillion yuan in 1997, a decline of 28 percent.

Due to the shrinking trading volume, GF Futures lost its main source of business, and the company's cash flow was immediately strained. At this time, GF Futures had to both standardize its business and reduce costs by reducing staff and relocating to a smaller site. The company moved from Huashan Hotel to Tianhe Building with seven offices at low rent. On April 23, 1995, Zhao Guiping held a general meeting with all the employees to inform them of the current situation of the company and to express the confidence in "strengthening unity and solidarity to tide over the difficulties."

In February 1996, the Circular on Further Strengthening the Supervision of the Futures Market was issued, prohibiting financial institutions from participating in futures trading. In order to implement the spirit of strict consolidation, the CSRC issued the Circular on Certain Issues concerning the Regulation of Futures Brokers' Acceptance of Capital Contribution on December 23, 1996, which made restrictive regulations on the acceptance of equity investment by futures brokers and stipulated that futures brokers were not allowed to accept investment from financial institutions. In the background of the separation of futures and securities operations, GF Securities could no longer participate in futures brokerage companies. In December 1996, GF Securities decided to transfer its shares in GF Futures.

Dr. Chen Yunxian had a blueprint for the development of GF Securities in his mind. He believed that GF Securities should actively participate in the futures market according to the trend of the world capital markets, but with the rapid expansion of the futures market, the abnormal development of the system lagging behind the market also worried him deeply. Against the backdrop of the withdrawal of securities companies from the futures market, Dr. Chen saw that the development of the real economy could not be separated from the hedging of the futures market and that to develop its economy, China needed to grasp the pricing power of commodities, and that the investment banking could not be separated from the innovation of financial instruments.

Through the fog of market adjustment, Dr. Chen Yunxian continued to be confident in long-term development of China's futures industry and requested GF Securities to retain part of the equity of GF Futures and asked Zhao Guiping to continue to serve as chairwoman of the board. After negotiations, it was finally decided that GF Securities would transfer 58.61 percent of its equity interest in GF Futures to Henan Zhongyuan Venture Industry and Trade Company, while retaining 30 percent of its equity interest and putting it in the custody of Shenzhen Heng'anxin Enterprise Trust Company, a subsidiary of GF Securities. This move allowed GF Securities to wait for the time to rise again.

At this time, Zhao Guiping was in a very complicated and uncomfortable mood, as her enthusiasm for the futures industry was extinguished by the 327 Government Bond Futures Incident. Under Dr. Chen's supervision, Zhao Guiping replaced Chen Wenzhan to take charge of the Institutional Management Department of GF Securities.

After that, the equity of GF Futures changed in the course of operation, and the major shareholder, Henan Zhongyuan Venture Industry and Trade Company, failed in futures trading and subsequently transferred its equity to its old shareholder, GF Securities, by mortgage. By 1999, Shenzhen Heng'anxin Enterprise Trust Company held 58% of the equity of GF Futures. For the three years from 1997 to 1999, GF Futures went into "hibernation" with operating income of 9.52 million yuan and profit of 645,000 yuan, struggling to survive.

The Chinese futures market as a whole also entered a cold winter. After 1996, consolidation documents were issued one after another. In December 1997, the Circular on Deepening Financial Reform, Rectifying Financial Order, and Preventing Financial Risks clearly stated that China would continue to rectify and merge existing futures exchanges and futures brokerage institutions. In August 1998, the Notice on Further Rectification and Regulation of the Futures Market started the second round of review and rectification of the futures market. In June 1999, the Interim Regulations on the Administration of Futures Trading were issued, clarifying that the futures market would be supervised by the CSRC in a unified way. Of the more than 50 futures exchanges around the country, only three remained by 1999: the Shanghai Futures Exchange, the Zhengzhou Commodity Exchange, and the Dalian Commodity Exchange; futures brokerage firms were reduced from more than 300 to more than 200; and more than 2,000 futures institutions were banned. A large number of futures varieties were also banned, and the margin ratios for the retained varieties were increased. In the end, only four futures varieties were retained: copper and aluminum on the Shanghai Futures Exchange, wheat on the Zhengzhou Commodity Exchange, and soybeans on the Dalian Commodity Exchange. With the sudden tightening of the regulatory environment, trading in the futures market became depressed. In 1996, the turnover of the national futures market was still 8.4 trillion yuan, and it declined year by year thereafter, to a turnover of only 1.6 trillion yuan in 2000, a contraction of more than 80 percent over four years.

Recovery in spring after winter

The futures industry finally ushered in spring in the twenty-first century.

In June 1999, the Interim Regulations on Futures Trading were promulgated, and the leaders of the CSRC gave a positive assessment: the futures market had moved from the non-regulated stage to the regulated stage. After two rounds of consolidation in the futures market, the futures market environment was purified and the market entered a more standardized development stage from 2000 onwards. The whole futures industry felt the breath of recovery, but the road to the "unfreezing" of GF Futures was difficult.

At the end of 1999, in a special report of the *China Securities Journal* on the new board of directors of the Securities Association of China, the messages of a number of leading figures from securities firms were published, in which Dr. Chen Yunxian uniquely proposed that "the future of the securities industry is to have both spot goods and futures."

Just as Dr. Chen had been "one step ahead" many times before, he keenly captured the footsteps of spring in the futures market. Based on the "four-pronged" approach (shareholding, conglomeration, internationalization, and standardization) of GF Securities, Zhao Guiping submitted a report "suggesting to take back the equity of GF Futures," which was greatly supported by Lü Ping. Dr. Chen asked all departments to study it seriously. Subsequently, the issue of whether to "take back" GF Futures was put on the agenda within GF Securities.

At this time, GF Securities was moving forward with its listing plan, and the standardization of its equity holding subsidiaries became a very important step. Based on the principle of prudence, GF Securities held five meetings in less than six months to focus on the issue of the retention of GF Futures.

On April 3, 2001, at a working meeting of GF Securities, Zhao Guiping, chairwoman of GF Futures, reported again to the company's leaders on the futures market and the situation of GF Futures, hoping that the company would take back 100 percent of the shares of GF Futures. Lü Ping was in favor of the suggestion. Other participants of the meeting, considering the change of equity and customer disputes in GF Futures, thought that it might affect the company's listing, and they took the position that GF Futures must be liquidated. After the meeting, Zhao Guiping approached Lü Ping and made a suggestion: Dr. Chen wanted to keep the fire, and should we write a letter to him to report the situation? At this time, Dr. Chen Yunxian was studying at Harvard University in the United States.

On April 24, 2001, GF Futures held a shareholders' meeting and a board of directors' meeting, which made it clear that the main work of the company for the year was to complete the asset restructuring. After the meeting, Zhao Guiping, chairman of the Board of Directors, Wu Chuanbin, the supervisor, and Wei Qingsong, general manager of GF Futures, were immediately engaged in the search for a restructuring party. Initially, the focus of the restructuring work was on the proposal of repossession of GF Futures by GF Securities, but the road did not go smoothly.

On October 10, 2001, considering the listing process, GF Securities decided to liquidate its equity interest in GF Futures, using the shareholders' meeting resolution to dissolve the company. By November, the liquidation of GF Futures entered a substantial stage and GF Futures was on the "verge of death."

In October 2001, just one month after GF Securities decided to liquidate GF Futures, strong takeover intentions were expressed by Hantang Securities, Shenzhen Jinfengxin Investment Co., Ltd., Shanghai Jinbang Investment Company, Shenzhen Jingbao Investment Development Company, and Guangdong Qiaoxin Group. In addition, the futures industry was picking up and financial futures was gaining momentum, so brokerage firms accelerated the pace of acquiring futures companies, with Everbright Securities holding Everbright Futures, Dapeng Securities holding Pengxin Futures, Guotai Securities holding Baoyuan Futures, and Ping An Securities holding Ping An Futures. At the time, a license for the futures company in Guangzhou rose to six to eight million yuan.

In the Measures for the Administration of Securities Companies (Draft for Public Comments) issued in June 2001, there was a clear clause that securities companies could participate in investment in futures companies. In addition, GF Securities also learned from the Futures Department of the China Securities Regulatory Commission that securities firms would soon not have to take a detour to participate in the futures market. This news was like a thunderbolt in spring, adding impetus for GF Securities to take back GF Futures. At this point, Dr. Chen Yunxian decided to re-evaluate the work related to GF Futures.

On December 17, 2001, an emergency meeting was held in the conference room of the president's office on the forty-second floor of Metropolis Plaza to decide the fate of GF Futures. The discussion among Chen Yunxian, Fang Jiachun, Dong Zhengqing, Li Jianyong, Li Suina, Li Shuiquan, Shen Hao, Song Yuxi, Zhong Yunbo, Lü Ping, and Zhao Guiping would determine "whether GF Futures should be retained or liquidated."

After some discussion, the voice of support for liquidation prevailed. After listening to the views of all parties, Dr. Fang Jiachun concluded, "As I have heard, except for Lü Ping and Zhao Guiping, who thought they wanted to keep it, all parties, including capital and accounting departments, wanted to write off GF Futures." Hearing this, Zhao Guiping choked back tears. In the previous five years, GF Futures had survived the long winter of the futures industry, gradually depleting its capital and resolving one after another the disputes over additional margins, and ensuring the company's difficult survival in the harsh winter of the futures industry. In the absence of a major shareholder, Zhao Guiping had been representing the non-controlling shareholder as instructed by Dr. Chen Yunxian. She had been able to keep GF Futures in the right direction during the market review and consolidation phase, and the company did not fall, but now it was about to face liquidation. She had overwhelming grievances no one could help relieve; she could not but shed tears.

"How big is the risk to the company if it is not liquidated?" Dr. Chen Yunxian asked, "The general environment of the futures market will probably pick up next year, so please think carefully whether the company still wants to wind up GF Futures or not." These words of Dr. Chen gave GF Futures a ray of hope. On the night the meeting ended, Dr. Chen Yunxian called to comfort Zhao Guiping and expressed his support for keeping GF Futures. "It was really dangerous at that time. GF Futures was almost gone"; recalling the past, Zhao Guiping's heart still flutters with fear.

In the end, with the direct support and request of Dr. Chen Yunxian, the restructuring work started quickly after the meeting. Just after New Year's Day 2001, GF Securities set up a working group to restructure GF Futures, with Executive Vice President Dong Zhengqing in charge of the work and Xie Min, then general manager of Northwest China's Investment Banking Department, as the leader. The shareholders' meeting held on February 3, 2002 passed the resolution to restructure GF Futures.

On February 7, 2002, the shareholders' meeting of GF Futures passed a resolution to transfer 47 percent of the shares held by Huizhou Lingnan Biochemical Group in GF Futures Brokerage Company to GF Securities. As a result, GF Securities owned 98 percent of the shares of GF Futures. Through the equity transformation, GF Futures became a subsidiary of GF Securities again, and also became one of the first batch of broker-held futures companies. In May 2002, the board of directors of GF Futures was adjusted, with Lü Ping replacing Zhao Guiping as chairman of GF Futures and Xiao Cheng as general manager of GF Futures.

In fact, the importance attached to futures companies was evident in many of Dr. Chen Yunxian's books.

In his 1995 book *On Investment Banking*, Dr. Chen suggested that financial instruments such as futures and options could provide investment banking with flexibility in business development and could help investors hedge risks.

In his 1998 book *Risk-Return Correspondence*, Dr. Chen further analyzed that the theory of risk-return correspondence led investment banking to implement "the principle of portfolio investment and risk diversification." Derivatives could serve to fully diversify investment risks and increase the stability of returns.

Based on these studies, in 2002, after years of the Chinese futures market review, Dr. Chen believed that the Chinese financial derivatives market would definitely launch derivatives instruments such as stock index futures, interest rate futures, and foreign exchange futures in the near future.

In addition, the recovery of GF Futures was also an important choice for GF Securities' four-pronged approach. From the perspective of conglomeration, GF Securities had to build up the whole conglomeration structure in addition to its main business of securities. GF Securities was already a leading brokerage firm in the industry, and it should have its own futures platform, and recovering GF Futures was the most convenient and lowest-cost way to have one. Dr. Chen Yunxian judged that the futures industry had just restarted and the process of licensing could be lengthy, all of which were uncertainties in re-establishing a futures company. Future regulatory policies also confirmed that repossession was a better option than establishing a new one, and a number of brokerages ended up having to enter the futures market by acquiring futures companies.

Six years had passed from the time when the fire of futures was retained upon the transfer of equity in 1996 to the full recovery of equity in GF Futures in 2002. This six-year journey was so arduous. GF Securities once again succeeded in its planning strategy for moving later.

2. The new futures army in the conglomeration blueprint of GF Securities

In 2002, GF Futures had a registered capital of only 30 million yuan and only one business office in Beijing in addition to the head office's business office in Guangzhou. Among more than 120 futures companies in China, GF Futures ranked ninety-seventh in terms of the overall performance index, which was in the middle and lower level of the industry. At that time, GF Futures was tantamount to starting from scratch. After years of consolidation in the futures market, the company had very little capital left, its business space was small and was maintained by only a few large investors.

In May 2002, Dr. Xiao Cheng left securities brokerage and funds and started to be responsible for the management of GF Futures. When he first became the general manager of GF Futures, Xiao Cheng's biggest worry was to go to the meetings of GF Securities. At 2003 mid-year working meeting, when the company leaders read out the performance of each department and subsidiary, some people in the audience couldn't help laughing when it was mentioned that GF Futures had made a profit of 6,000 yuan in six months. But by the end of that year, GF Futures had already made a profit of a million yuan, announcing a fundamental change since the establishment of GF Futures.

In 2004, GF Futures ranked among the top ten in the futures industry nationwide, and the following year, it was awarded the "Top Ten Most Influential Brands" in China's futures industry, and became the "top futures company" in a short span of two years. In the following decade, GF Futures had been at the forefront of comprehensive futures service providers in China.

The core values of "knowledge-based development and pragmatism-based dedication" that GF Futures had been practicing for a long time were also matching with GF Securities.

Looking back on his career at GF Securities, Dr. Xiao Cheng said, "If I was first 'exposed' to the corporate culture of GF Securities when I first joined GF Securities, and then I worked for a period of time when I was 'integrated' into the corporate culture of GF Securities, and then, in the operation and management of GF Futures, I really 'practiced and 'spread' the corporate culture of GF Securities."

GF Securities supports the strategic layout

In 2002, shareholders were still divided over the development orientation of GF Futures. Some shareholders believed that GF Futures could simply maintain its current size and that it would not be too late to develop after the launch of stock index futures.

Xiao Cheng insisted that there was no clear-cut boundary between financial futures and commodity futures, and that using the existing commodity futures development to train the team and increase the company's market influence before the launch of financial futures would increase the benefits for the GF Securities group internally and enhance its influence in China's futures market externally. This idea was supported by Dr. Chen Yunxian. Dr. Chen encouraged Xiao Cheng to make GF Futures bigger and stronger while ensuring no systemic risk to the company.

At the beginning of the new century, the futures industry had many problems, the scope of business of futures companies was narrow, the reliance on brokerage business was strong, and the number of business offices had a great impact on performance. In 2002, GF Futures had only two business offices.

Facing this situation, GF Futures put forward the strategic layout of "being based in south China, developing nationwide and connecting with Hong Kong" for its brokerage branches from 2003. At that time, most of the futures companies had fewer business offices and this strategy of GF Futures was advanced.

The layout of GF futures outlets first spread in Guangdong Province, with Zhuhai and Meizhou business offices established first in 2003. In 2007, Nanning and Fuzhou business officers established, and the flag of GF Futures was hoisted in Guangxi and Fujian, meaning the company had taken the first step to shift from "being based in Guangdong" to "being based in south China."

In 2007, Zhao Guiping succeeded Lü Ping as the chairwoman of GF Futures. When Dong Zhengqing approached Zhao Guiping, he said, "Stock index futures are in the pipeline, and you are the only one among our executives who have done futures, who will go if you don't?" These words poked Zhao Guiping's lingering attachment to futures. After thinking about it for a while, she reassumed the chairwomanship of GF Futures, determined to leverage the strong outlet advantages of the shareholder to connect with securities and wealth management institutions and achieve resource sharing in the era of great wealth management and capital management.

The period from the end of 2007 to 2008 witnessed the most rapid expansion of GF Futures' business network. Especially in Guangdong Province, in less than a year, business offices were established in Foshan, Jiangmen, Zhaoqing, Dongguan, Zhongshan, and Shenzhen, and the Shantou business office was also established in 2010. GF Futures started the road of expansion along the footsteps of GF Securities.

The construction of nationwide outlets was also in full swing. By 2008, GF Futures had set up 16 business offices one after another, spreading its territory to the north and south of China.

In order to support business expansion, GF Securities continued to increase capital for GF Futures. After GF Securities bought back GF Futures, it completed nine capital increase plans. The registered capital of GF Futures increased from the initial 10 million yuan to 55.218 million yuan. On October 31, 2007, GF Futures officially became a wholly-owned subsidiary of GF Securities, and its registered capital was changed from 55.218 million yuan to 120 million yuan. On August 5, 2009, the registered capital was increased to 200 million yuan. On May 18, 2010, the registered capital was increased to 400 million yuan, and on May 5, 2011, it was increased to 600 million yuan. In September of the same year, GF Securities increased its capital to GF Futures by 500 million yuan. Thus, the registered capital of GF Futures increased to 1.1 billion yuan, surpassing Haitong Futures with a capital of 1 billion yuan to become the largest futures company in China.

With the development of the futures market, the regulatory authorities increased their demand for the net capital strength of futures companies. After the launch of stock index futures in 2010, in order to prevent risks, the regulatory policy stipulated that the registered capital of futures companies participating in stock index futures brokerage business should not be less than six percent of the client's margin. With the entry of large capital into the futures market, the margin size of futures companies rose significantly, and the net capital of futures companies had to increase simultaneously. The increase in the registered capital of GF Futures to 1.1 billion yuan had strongly supported the development of business and risk resistance.

In 2015, GF Futures rode on the back of the H-share listing of GF Securities and received capital increases of 100 million yuan from GF Securities in July and December, respectively, and provided capital support of US$70 million to its UK subsidiary. On November 30, 2017, GF Securities increased its capital to GF Futures by another 100 million yuan. As of 2019, the registered capital of GF Futures was 1.4 billion yuan.

Making services more professional

Dr. Chen Yunxian once proposed three orientations for the GF Securities Development Research Center: creating a brand, serving business, and reserving talents. Dr. Xiao Cheng, who had worked in the Development Research Center, brought this concept of Dr. Chen Yunxian to GF Futures.

Comparing the development strategies of domestic and international futures companies, GF Futures saw R&D as a powerful tool to "achieve curve overtaking." In order to realize its three abovementioned goals, the GF Futures Development Research Center integrated principle with practice, which organically unified the creation of a research brand and the enhancement of research practicality. The Development Research Center actively undertook research projects of the China Futures Association and the China Futures Exchange. It undertook research and writing work on many projects of the China Futures Association and participated in many projects of the China Futures Exchange. For example, during the preparation for the listing of fuel oil and carbon emissions rights, the Development Research Center set up research groups to cooperate with the exchange in pre-listing research.

After the review and consolidation, there was a shortage of talents in the futures market. Dr. Xiao Cheng introduced the successful experience of GF Securities' "PhD Legion" and quickly gathered a group of highly educated people who were willing to join the futures market to join GF Futures. The year 2004 saw the appearance of articles analyzing GF Futures' industry in many media, which raised the company's visibility in a short period of time. The Development and Research Center became an ace card of GF Futures, winning such honors as "Best Futures Research Institution" for more than ten consecutive years.

With the support of its shareholders, GF Futures took advantage of the momentum of commodity futures and industry recovery to increase its business scale, with operating income steadily rising year by year and customer equity exceeding 10 billion yuan in 2015 from less than 100 million yuan in 2003. With the development of the futures industry, GF Futures carried forward GF Securities' philosophy of sound operation and gained opportunities in the orientation of the futures industry to support the best and suppress the worst, and was among the first in the industry to obtain licenses for the investment consulting business, capital management business, and risk management business.

Leveraging the advantages of the shareholder to lead the futures index

While everyone was still talking about the restorative growth of futures in 2003 and 2004, the futures industry had a shock in 2005. The futures market shrank significantly throughout the year with few new listings, increased regulation, and the delisting of futures companies.

The market expectation for stock index futures was growing day by day. In July 2006, the rules and regulations of stock index futures trading and the draft stock index futures contract proposal were released for public comment. In September, the China Financial Futures Exchange (CFFE) was established in Shanghai, and in October, the CFFE launched simulation trading of CSI 300 stock index futures. After years of brewing, the stock index futures were finally listed on April 16, 2010.

Taking advantage of the listing of stock index futures, GF Securities mobilized the advantages of brokerage business and IB business to fully support the development of GF Futures. After six years of perseverance, GF Futures finally saw the light of the moon and seized the opportunity to develop stock index futures business and increase its market share. In the year of opening stock index futures, GF Futures ranked among the top in trading volume on the China Financial Futures Exchange and successfully entered this "blue ocean."

Prior to that, GF Futures' monthly turnover remained around 400 billion yuan, which quickly doubled after the launch of stock index futures. With the continuous development of business, GF Futures continued to set new records in total turnover, reaching 1.6 trillion yuan in November 2010. In 2010, GF Futures' turnover of stock index futures was 43.07 percent, much higher than the market average of 26.57 percent. In 2010, GF Futures' market share in the China Financial Futures Exchange reached 4.95 percent, comfortably ranking fourth in the market.

In the development of stock index futures business, GF Futures assisted GF Securities throughout the process of opening its own hedging account for stock index futures. Without any experience in the industry, GF Futures repeatedly communicated with the China Financial Futures Exchange and the China Futures Margin Monitoring Center to develop the details of the system, becoming the first institution in China to open a special institutional legal person account, and played a role in promoting the development of the relevant system in the industry.

At that time, the gate for QFII participation in stock index futures had not yet been liberalized, but as one of the worthiest positions for future business, GF Futures did not relax its preparations and kept in touch with the original QFII institutions, informing them of the latest progress in business as soon as it was available. GF Futures also participated in Barclays Bank's global cooperation tender for the China stock index futures business, as well as GF Securities' outreach to Hong Kong institutional clients.

With the business development of stock index futures, GF Futures gained a high reputation among its peers and investor groups. In the first year of stock index futures listing, GF Futures was awarded the annual Gold Award for Outstanding Member, Investor Education Award, and Customer Management Award by the China Financial Futures Exchange.

3. An internationalization futures leader

As for the development direction of GF Futures, Dr. Chen Yunxian explicitly requested that the development of futures should be benchmarked against international investment banking, and expressed his strong support for the development of GF Futures' internationalization. He wrote, "Due to the pressure of competition and the drive of interests, the limited diversification of business development prompts the internationalization of business development, and the internationalization of business competition accelerates the specialization of business.... Merrill Lynch provides not only commodity services, but also economic consulting and research services to major companies around the world."

In May 2001, the CSRC issued the Measures for the Administration of Overseas Futures Hedging Business of SOEs. Since then, 31 SOEs had been approved to engage in offshore futures hedging business, and the curtain had been raised on the internationalization of the futures market.

As we all know, commodities have natural international attributes. In the context of China's rapid economic development, companies had a huge demand for raw materials such as iron ore, copper, and crude oil, and a significant portion of them came from imports. Risk management was very important in the face of international exchange rate fluctuations and shipping effects. Companies were in urgent need of commodity research reports, trading and settlement services when they engaged in transactions abroad.

Chinese futures companies started to explore the path of "going global," and there were only two options: one was to go overseas directly to set up institutions, obtain financial licenses, obtain membership in major global exchanges one by one, and establish business networks; and the other was to acquire and merge, taking over the financial licenses and memberships of the target companies, and quickly building business networks. Due to the different regulatory policies in each country, the former would take a long time to complete, while the latter could start quickly on the strength of acquired companies.

Going overseas and cooperating with Hong Kong

In 2006, under the guidance of the CEPA agreement signed between the mainland and Hong Kong, the CSRC approved a number of securities and futures companies to set up branches in Hong Kong. Six mainland futures companies, including GF Futures, set up subsidiaries in Hong Kong. This was seen as the first step for the Chinese futures industry to try to "go global" and build a platform for China's futures companies to go international.

Compared to other "going global" financial institutions such as banks and brokerages, the overall strength and resources of futures companies were relatively weak. In the fierce competition in overseas markets, it was very challenging for new branches to survive on their own, let alone to accomplish the strategic international tasks. In order to solve the above problems, GF Securities supported GF Futures to develop overseas through capital increase, and the internationalization of GF Futures set sail from then on.

In May 2006, GF Futures (Hong Kong) Co., Ltd. (hereinafter referred to as the Hong Kong subsidiary) was officially established with a registered capital of HK$10 million. The Hong Kong subsidiary obtained a futures contract trading license from the Hong Kong Securities and Futures Commission and obtained the Hong Kong Futures Exchange Participant status and Clearing House General Clearing status. On March 3, 2010, the Hong Kong subsidiary became the first trading member company of EUREX with Chinese background, and later became the first trading member company of LIFFE and SGX with Chinese background. The Hong Kong subsidiary became the first EUREX member firm with a Chinese background on March 3, 2010, and later became the first LIFFE and SGX member firm with a Chinese background.

Hong Kong and Guangzhou had deep ties on many levels. In the beginning, the Hong Kong subsidiary focused on HKEx futures indices and derivatives, with a single type of business and a small number of Chinese institutions and natural persons as clients. As the starting point of GF Futures' international business, the Hong Kong subsidiary made a profit in its first year of operation, which gave everyone strong confidence and strengthened GF Futures' determination to promote its internationalization strategy. Through Hong Kong as a "bridgehead" for international business development, GF Futures could deeply explore the needs of existing clients for overseas business, understand the rules of international market operation and regulatory policies, and cultivate a team of talents who were familiar with international markets. The Hong Kong subsidiary was the internationalization testing ground, which could provide good opportunities and experience to GF Futures.

The Hong Kong subsidiary also carried out some business in European and American markets, such as participating in the business of overseas exchanges such as LME, CBOT, CME, NYMEX, and TOCOM, but the business of trading and settlement still required the agency of the primary member and this secondary agency model was the main method of foreign agency for Chinese futures companies at that time.

The secondary agency model was the main way for futures companies to develop their international trading business. This indicated that the trading channel connecting Chinese and overseas futures markets was still fragmented to a certain extent, which not only reduced the efficiency of risk management for industrial clients in China, but also might leak the overall trading positions of futures companies' clients and the commercial secrets contained in the positions. In addition, this made it difficult for Chinese futures companies to access the operation modes of advanced foreign companies for a long time and improve their own operation level. This also put Chinese futures companies at a disadvantage in the competition with foreign futures companies, which was not conducive to their long-term development.

Moreover, under this model, it was difficult for futures companies to control their agencies' own risks, and careless selection of an agency or even the collapse of an agency could have a huge impact on Chinese futures companies. For example, the collapse of the global futures giant Man Financial in 2011 implicated many Chinese futures companies, and before that, Refco, Lehman Brothers, and Bear Stearns all posed risks to the safety of capital for secondary sponsors. In addition, the secondary agency model had problems such as increased cost of futures companies (which needed to pay agency transaction and settlement fees), information asymmetry or information lag.

If a futures company in China or its Hong Kong subsidiary could apply directly for clearing membership in the major global exchanges, it could seize a favorable position in the upstream of the brokerage business. Directly engaging in brokerage business as a clearing member could reduce the additional costs incurred by agencies and also make it possible for them to provide agency services to Chinese non-member financial institutions. However, it would take a long time to apply for clearing memberships of major global exchanges. To apply for CME clearing membership, for example, applicants needed to apply to the US NFA and CFTC, in addition to the CME clearing house, to become a registered FCM, which would take about a year and a half at the earliest. Moreover, to become a clearing member, you needed to establish a local presence.

Considering all factors, becoming a clearing member of an overseas exchange directly became an important choice for internationalization.

The Hong Kong financial market was a mixed industry with a licensing system. Whether it was a securities company, futures company or fund company which wanted to set up branches in Hong Kong, it could apply for multiple licenses by virtue of their status as financial holding companies. With more and more institutions coming to Hong Kong, there was a situation of "too many monks and not enough porridge." At this point, individual investors, who were sensitive to commission prices in the market, became the target of competition from various institutions. In addition, the Hong Kong subsidiary had never established a special variety in commodities, which made it difficult to attract large institutional funds. With a retail client structure and single means of service, the revenue and profit of the Hong Kong subsidiary hit a bottleneck and once declined.

Would GF Futures continue to consolidate the Hong Kong market or move on to the major global commodity trading locations? How exactly should GF Futures develop its international business? The business of a futures company boiled down to seller services. GF Futures could and should have a try in the international arena to provide cross-market and cross-species services to its clients.

At the end of August 2011, the CSRC officially approved three domestic futures companies to participate in the preparation of the pilot offshore futures brokerage business. After the reopening of the offshore futures business, Chinese companies would be able to directly interface with major global commodity futures trading markets such as the US and the UK through pilot qualified futures companies, establishing a channel between Chinese futures and world futures. Chinese futures companies could seize the opportunity to select suitable target companies to implement takeovers and develop overseas markets.

In the distribution picture of overseas commodity markets, there were agricultural products, crude oil, foreign exchange, and various types of option derivatives markets such as Chicago and New York in the United States, foreign exchange and nonferrous metals markets in London, the UK, and Asia-Pacific markets such as Singapore and Hong Kong, China. By analyzing the distribution and pattern of commodity markets, GF Futures set its targets as Europe and America.

Dr. Xiao Cheng approached Zhao Guiping to discuss his ideas, and the two sides coincided. The layout of the internationalization of futures was gradually clarified during their excited conversation, and the idea of internationalization was then reported to GF Securities. GF Securities supported the internationalization from commodities, but required that the acquiring company must be controlling or wholly owned. Zhao Guiping arranged for Xiao Cheng to actively search for a suitable "shell" and set up the GF Futures International Department as the executive arm of the work.

GF Futures found two projects, namely Sucden and Metdist. Sucden is a well-established company specializing in futures brokerage and ranking among the top three in the London Metal Exchange in terms of trading volume. The buyout team negotiated with the shareholders of Sucden, but no agreement was reached. The approach with Metdist was also abandoned as it was not possible to take a controlling interest. GF Futures had been waiting for the opportunity to complete its takeover plan.

Takeover of NCM in the UK

After the international financial crisis in 2008, the US introduced the Dodd-Frank Act, which increased net capital requirements for derivatives management. Realizing that regulatory costs would rise and profit margins would fall, international investment banks had cut their commodity divisions, and many overseas financial institutions were considering what to do after the crisis. In 2012, the French Bank for Foreign Trade decided to sell its commodity trading company Natixis Commodity Markets Limited (NCM) after a comprehensive consideration.

One day in September 2012, Dr. Xiao Cheng, who was attending an executive training course in the United States organized by the China Futures Association in Chicago, learned of an announcement from the London Metal Exchange (LME) that its clearing member, NCM, was going out of business and asked its customers to stop opening new positions and close them gradually. Xiao Cheng first made a phone call to Zhao Guiping who was in China across the Pacific Ocean. Zhao Guiping also considered this a rare opportunity and immediately asked Xiao Cheng to fly directly to the UK to understand clearly.

Xiao Cheng learned that the French Bank for Foreign Trade had submitted a report to the LME that NCM Futures would be closed and liquidated on April 30, 2013, and that the front office was being cleaned up. NCM Futures was a registered member of the UK Financial Services Authority (FSA), one of the LME Circle members, and a member of the ICE Europe, London Clearing House (LCH), Euronext, London International Financial Futures Exchange (LIFFE), London Platinum and Palladium Market Association (LPPM), Dubai Gold Commodity Exchange (DGCX), London Bullion Market Association (LBMA), and was a well-known futures broker on the London Metal Exchange.

The LME trades mainly in copper, zinc, nickel, aluminum, and tin. As a centennial exchange, the LME was also an OTC market, offering customers convenience in the form of flexible floor quotations, electronic trading, telephone orders, and settlement methods. Moreover, the London market was the only global derivatives market where credit trading was available. China had the second highest demand for copper in the world and preferred the LME for hedging and arbitrage transactions in the global market, and Chinese clients contributed 20 percent of the LME's 2014 transactions.

On December 18, 2012, the working meeting of GF Securities tentatively agreed to the takeover intention, and the takeover work was kicked off. Considering the obligation of information confidentiality of listed companies, the takeover project was called the "Rose Project Team" and it was decided that the takeover team would be composed of Luo Binhua and Zhao Guiping, vice presidents of GF Securities, Cai Tiezheng, Deng Hui, Yi Xinyu, and Xian Yaoting, and GF Futures' Xiao Cheng, Luo Mansheng, Wang Weiqiu, Qiu Jingjing, Shi

Shaohui, Ye Mei, Feng Liang, Tian Jun, and Lu Renqing, with Luo Binhua as the leader and general coordinator and Zhao Guiping as the deputy leader. Four groups were established for finance, legality, IT, and business. On December 28, GF Futures formally engaged PricewaterhouseCoopers, UK, as the auditor to carry out financial analysis and due diligence on the target company, and the project was scheduled to be completed for delivery on April 30, 2013. This was the first overseas M&A in the history of GF Securities, involving regulatory policies of two countries, the most important of which was the policy of the CSRC on overseas takeover of securities companies, foreign regulatory policy. The working team also needed to translate a large number of written documents in both Chinese and English. (See Figure 10)

On January 11, 2013, with the consent of GF Securities, GF Futures signed a memorandum of understanding with the French Bank for Foreign Trade on the purchase of its NCM.

During the 2013 Spring Festival holiday, members of the takeover team—Luo Binhua, Zhao Guiping, Xiao Cheng, and Cai Tiezheng—assembled in London to conduct due diligence and takeover negotiations. The Guangzhou team back in China moved to understand the regulatory policies and reporting and approval procedures of international takeovers by the regulatory authorities.

During the negotiations, GF Futures found that the price and asset quality of the subject were ideal. The net assets of NCM was US$36.14 million, and the final consideration paid was that much, equivalent to no premium transaction. And, according to UK regulatory laws, a minimum net capital of £5 million was required to become a clearing member of a major UK exchange, and a minimum purchase of B-shares in the LME (about £2.5 million at the then quoted price) was required to become a clearing member of the London Metal Exchange, which together would require a minimum of £7.5 million, or about HK$94 million. Taking into account possible initial losses, it would be appropriate to set aside at least HK$120 million. Obviously, it would had been too difficult and time-consuming to set up a new branch in the UK to meet these requirements.

Due to the constraints of China's regulatory environment at the time, the final decision was to have the Hong Kong subsidiary implement the takeover. The registered capital and capital of the Hong Kong subsidiary was limited, and the prerequisite for completing the takeover was that the Hong Kong subsidiary achieve capital increase. There were two ways to increase the capital. One was to directly inject capital into the Hong Kong subsidiary through GF Futures, and the other was for the Hong Kong subsidiary to raise its own capital through overseas financing. Both of these methods required the approval of the CSRC. Considering that the borrowing rate in Hong Kong at that time was generally three percent to four percent, and the overseas financing would increase the operating cost of the Hong Kong subsidiary by as much as £600,000 to £800,000 per year, the takeover team finally chose to increase the capital of the Hong Kong subsidiary by direct capital injection.

The takeover of the overseas futures company also received the attention of the CSRC, the People's Bank of China, the State Administration of Foreign Exchange, and the Guangdong Securities Regulatory Bureau. The timely resolution of the capital increase became a key prerequisite for the realization of the takeover.

From the initial contact between the two parties to the completion of the agreement, after nearly 10 months of an arduous journey, the GF Securities takeover team cooperated fully with the external intermediaries, overcoming time difference, and language, cultural, legal, and regulatory barriers, and battled around the clock. In the final negotiation session, the French Bank for Foreign Trade hired Clifford Chance, the largest law firm in the UK, and GF hired the PwC legal team. The two teams engaged in a heated exchange, gesturing at every disagreement. While adjourning the meeting midway, each discussed with their lawyers for ten minutes, and then continued to focus on the discussion. This went on for more than ten hours. After several rounds, the parties gradually reached a consensus on the takeover agreement.

On July 23, 2013, the Hong Kong subsidiary formally completed the takeover of 100 percent of the shares of NCM, a subsidiary of the French Bank for Foreign Trade, and renamed it GF Financial Marketing (UK) Co., Ltd. (GFFM). This equity takeover was the "first" overseas M&A of a futures company with a Chinese background, which was a landmark in the development history of China's futures industry and a significant step forward for GF Securities on the road to internationalization. After becoming the first trading member of SGX with a Chinese background and the first trading member of EUREX from China, GF Futures became the first mainland futures company to acquire an overseas futures company and the first mainland futures company to have overseas futures clearing qualification.

According to the resolution of the first board meeting of GFFM, the company retained the first level trading membership in the London Metal Exchange, applied for a seat in the London Stock Exchange, applied for an asset management license, and elected Xiao Cheng chairman and Andy Gooch general manager.

On September 10, 2013, GFFM held a meeting regarding GFFM. The meeting considered that the takeover of overseas futures companies was a very important step in the internationalization of GF Securities. Regarding the management of GFFM, GF Securities would keep an eye on the status of the company and support its long-term development.

Overcoming difficult cultural differences

In an M&A, it is often 30 percent takeover, 70 percent integration: the success of an M&A lies in integration, and the hallmark of success is whether the takeover is profitable and sustainable. GF Futures had successfully acquired NCM through its Hong Kong subsidiary, but this was only the completion of the takeover and overseas deployment. In terms of revenue and profit share of overseas business, it was still far from internationalization.

With the increase of Chinese mainland companies in the Hong Kong market, the competition intensified, and the gradual decrease of retail investors, the revenue and profit of the Hong Kong subsidiary showed a downward trend. From a historical best of HK$47,288,400 in revenue and HK$23,349,400 in profit, it went to HK$19,044,200 in revenue and only HK$502,700 in profit in 2015.

In 2016, Zhao Guiping invoked Bonnie Liu, who had previously served as the head of the Commodities Department of the Hong Kong Stock Exchange, to serve as the general manager of the Hong Kong subsidiary and a director of GFFM in the United Kingdom. During the previous work contact, Bonnie Liu was clear-minded, progressive, and diligent, which impressed Zhao Guiping.

GF Securities gave strong support to the development of GFFM. In June 2015, GF Futures invested an additional 100 million yuan (US$15.77 million) through its Hong Kong subsidiary; in January 2018, an additional US$5 million was added; and in September 2018, an additional 200 million yuan (approximately US$28.9 million) was added. Considering that GFFM's core business was credit business, GF Futures also guaranteed guaranteed US$70 million of the line of offshore debt under onshore guarantee.

However, GFFM remained in loss for a long period of time. Although the amount of loss was decreasing year by year, the overseas business did not generate income for several years, and GF Futures encountered a cold current on the road to internationalization.

In 2016, Zhao Guiping, chairwoman of GF Futures, became chairwoman of GFFM. Zhao Guiping was very worried about the continuous loss of GFFM. As a 24-year veteran of GF Securities and a long-time veteran in charge of brokerage business, Zhao Guiping had participated in and presided over more than ten external M&As of GF Securities, and chose to show courage under the pressure. In the face of difficulties, GF people's answer was that there was no such thing as a mountain that they could not surmount. She was determined to carry out a complete overhaul of GFFM.

The differences between Chinese and Western cultures had a very important impact on the fact that GFFM had not been profitable for four years. Zhao Guiping observed that Chinese employees were more proactive in their work and brave to seek breakthroughs, while British employees were relatively conservative and their concepts were not easy to change. There were also differences in efficiency. For the same license application, Chinese employees often worked overtime to compile the documents and quickly report to their superiors, while British employees usually took three to six months to complete the reporting process. In addition, the former NCM company mainly served the major shareholder banks' commodity clients, and had a weak concept of active marketing. It was not highly receptive to the marketing suggestions made by the GF Futures headquarters, and was not willing to learn new business. British employees were generally older and used to rely on their own experience in the workplace, often ignoring the advice of their Chinese colleagues. In terms of business variety, although the crude oil team was established at the end of 2015, there was a delay in launching business.

In April 2017, Zhao Guiping provided an analysis report to GF Securities, hoping to improve the management structure of GFFM, streamline the process, and improve efficiency. She also hoped that the headquarters would support GF Futures to strengthen the management of GFFM, and expressed GF Futures' confidence to turn it into a profit.

This report soon gained the support of GF Securities, which authorized GF Futures to manage GFFM under the premise of vertical management of risk control, compliance, and finance. GF Futures began a second restructuring of GFFM, and Zhao Guiping made up her mind to adjust the principals if necessary.

In mid-2016, Bonnie Liu, general manager of the Hong Kong subsidiary, proposed to cooperate with GFFM for iron ore business. However, after several months, due to the lack of agreement on internal profit-sharing, coupled with the fact that GFFM had been doing business in the London market for a long time, it did not understand the iron ore varieties in Singapore and was intimidated. Moreover, Zhao Guiping communicated with the general manager of GFFM many times, hoping that he would jointly develop the iron ore customers of the Singapore Exchange to broaden the revenue channel of GFFM, but GFFM was slow to respond.

Second integration for the fast track

In May 2017, the Singapore Exchange held an "Iron Ore Week." During a visit to the Singapore Exchange, the staff gave Zhao Guiping a detailed account of the explosive growth of iron ore on the Singapore Exchange in recent years. Zhao Guiping realized that this was a rare opportunity, and recalling Bonnie Liu's previous advice to promote the iron ore variety, she felt that the business was worth doing.

However, Zhao Guiping was still a bit apprehensive about whether the risk of OTC varieties was manageable and whether the Head Office would agree. She called Li Jianhua, chief risk officer of GF Futures in Guangzhou, and asked him to quickly organize the development of a risk management plan for the iron ore business of the Singapore Exchange OTC variety and report to GF Securities' Risk Control Department as a new variety.

"Change your thinking or get dismissed." On June 5, 2017, Zhao Guiping took the project team to London, UK, and officially embarked on the road to secondary integration.

The handling of employees by overseas organizations of Chinese companies was often in the news. The UK was one of the countries where labor laws were well enforced, which makes companies very cautious about the appointment and removal of executives. If labor disputes arose, there was the concern of "losing money and affecting reputation."

On June 7, the project team asked Wang Qian, a Chinese lawyer from Zhong Lun Law Firm in the UK, to discuss the dismissal of Gooch and the management restructuring plan of GFFM. Based on Ms. Wang's advice, the project team studied the specific operation plan, the details of the settlement agreement, the legal details involved, the possible results and difficulties, and the response strategy, and it decided to first communicate with Gooch about the shareholders' decision and the content of the separation settlement agreement before deciding on the next step. If Gooch would not accept the voluntary severance, a mandatory restructuring would be initiated.

On June 8, Zhao Guiping formally proposed to Gooch that the shareholder had decided not to have a CEO and asked him to resign voluntarily and reach a settlement agreement with the company. Gooch promised to consider it, but said he needed some time. During the days of waiting, the project team was a bit anxious.

Finally, on June 12, Gooch replied that he agreed to leave, and a few days later he formally submitted his resignation and signed a settlement agreement. In order to minimize the impact, at the GFFM all-staff meeting on June 19, Chairwoman Zhao Guiping delivered a speech to encourage the GFFM staff, announced a bonus allowance program, and clarified various work arrangements for the transition period after Andy's resignation. In order to stabilize the business, without violating the local regulatory requirements, the board of shareholders began to perform their duties in advance, with Chairwoman Zhao Guiping in charge of decision-making and Director Bonnie Liu in charge of the front office business.

GFFM also adjusted its management structure. The Hong Kong subsidiary undertook customer development and maintenance of GFFM, while GFFM focused on credit, settlement, and risk control, with an additional front office in Hong Kong. The two operated together, developed and expanded commodity varieties, and added iron ore business in Singapore. The Hong Kong subsidiary assists GFFM in activating customers and developing lost customers, targeting the leading Chinese steel and nonferrous companies and making them clients of GFFM. GFFM further improved its team.

After a year of unremitting efforts, GFFM finally turned around. In 2018, GFFM's revenue was 92,214,500 yuan and net profit turned positive to 27,782,800 yuan. After another year of struggle in 2019, revenue increased to 115,453,200 yuan and net profit reached 48,312,700 yuan. Meanwhile, the performance of the Hong Kong subsidiary also improved significantly.

The two international business subsidiaries helped each other to make a qualitative change in the proportion of revenue and profit related to the international business of GF Futures. In 2018 and 2019, the proportion of revenue from overseas business in the total revenue of GF Futures was maintained at around 25 percent, and the proportion of net profit was maintained at around 30 percent.

Looking back on this journey, Zhao Guiping was deeply touched by the great market fluctuations experienced by GFFM, and her cell phone was on 24 hours a day to keep an eye on the ever-changing international futures market and communicate in a timely manner despite the time difference. In April 2018, the US announced sanctions against Rusal, followed by the LME's announcement of a ban on metals from sanctioned companies entering LME warehouses. The extreme market conditions thereafter exposed many Chinese companies to one-sided market risk. In particular, industrial customers who were mainly engaged in hedging demanded additional margin. Zhao Guiping had a sleepless night and was in close contact with GFFM to follow up on customer positions and additional margin in real time to control the liquidity problem.

In the process of participating in the international market, GF Futures always took the liquidity of GFFM as the most important indicator. The biggest difference between GFFM's business and Chinese futures brokerage business was the credit business. Through the ups and downs of the market, GFFM had developed certain experience in risk control and was able to help clients manage risks better.

After going through the initial integration of the takeover, GF Futures' GFFM and Hong Kong subsidiaries were fully connected in 2018, relying on each other and leveraging their respective strengths to develop business synergies.

The full cooperation of the two overseas subsidiaries achieved multiple effects. First, a 24-hour trading platform covering all major global commodity exchanges was created, with GFFM covering the European time zone and the Hong Kong subsidiary covering the Asian time zone. GFFM was responsible for European, Middle Eastern, North and South American clients, while the Hong Kong subsidiary was responsible for Asia-Pacific clients, mainly Chinese clients. Secondly, GFFM's credit business served all overseas clients as a unique highlight. Thirdly, risk control was integrated. GFFM and the Hong Kong subsidiary cooperated to share information according to different trading market control risks, covering all processes of clients from account opening review to transaction management. Meanwhile, the risk control management was verticalized from GF Securities to GFFM.

GF Futures provided overseas futures products and hedging services to many Chinese companies going abroad, and listed companies engaged in Belt and Road-related projects and overseas subsidiaries of SOEs. As of 2018, GF Futures' international business platform had hedged about 1.5 million tons of copper, 200,000 tons of aluminum, 20 million tons of crude oil, 10 million tons of iron ore, 35 tons of zinc, and 100,000 tons of lead for its industrial clients. In the second half of 2017, the two overseas subsidiaries of GF Futures launched the iron ore swap business on the Singapore Exchange, which was welcomed by many Chinese ferrous industry clients due to the advantages of flexible hedging time, fast transaction speed and large market depth.

At the beginning of 2018, iron ore futures prices were at a stage high and the hedging demand of many large Chinese steel mills was very strong. At that time, GFFM had just contacted a large Chinese steel mill. The client suddenly asked the company to open an account for it immediately as it had just purchased two shipments of about 200,000 tons of iron ore abroad and needed to hedge them urgently. According to the normal company process, it would take about one month for the client to open an account with GFFM. In order to respond to the customer's request in a timely manner, GF Futures' management called its overseas subsidiary to conduct due diligence on the customer at the first time, and completed the entire account opening process within one week with full cooperation from both inside and outside China. The customer hedged 200,000 tons of iron ore the day after the account was successfully opened, basically hedging the price risk of the whole production process. The client was very impressed with the efficient service provided by GF Futures. As of September 2018, the client had hedged nearly 1 million tons of iron ore on GF Futures' offshore platform.

On November 29, 2019, the Singapore Exchange awarded GF Futures (Hong Kong) Co., Ltd. the title of "Best Chinese Futures Broker of the Year (Iron Ore Species)" at the Derivatives Awards Ceremony due to the high turnover of GF Futures' Singapore Exchange iron ore species. Standing on the award platform, Zhao Guiping was very excited to see that most of the award-winning representatives around her were from international investment bankers such as Goldman Sachs and Morgan Stanley. In her opinion, GF Futures stood on the same stage with the world's top brokers at least in the commodities sector. In 2019, GF Futures' foreign exchange business occupied a considerable share in the Hong Kong Exchange and Singapore Exchange, and ranked first among Chinese institutions in the iron ore variety of the Singapore Exchange.

On September 25, 2019, the FOW Awards ceremony, an international futures and options event, was held in Singapore. The conference awarded GF Futures the "Best Chinese Futures Company of the Year Award" and Zhao Guiping received the award on stage with great emotion. She said, "I was also here in 2014 to receive the FOW 'China Futures Company of the Year' award for the takeover of NCM in the UK in 2013. But at the time, our international commodities business was nil and we only had the A50 variant on the Singapore Exchange. At that time, I set the ambition that GF Futures should be the most international futures company in China and the most Chinese futures company in the international arena. Receiving this award today shows that GF Futures' commodity trading services have been recognized by its international peers, and GF Futures' international business has mapped out a path and entered the fast lane of development."

In the fast-changing futures industry, GF Futures was ranked seventy-eighth in 2002, rose to seventeenth in 2003, and was ranked among the top 10 in 2004, and since then had been achieving healthy development and had steadily ranked among the top futures companies. The internationalization of its business around

2013 was a landmark in the history of China's futures industry.

The history of the development of GF Futures over 20 years was also the history of the growth of the excellent genes of GF Securities in the futures sub-sector. GF Securities had provided capital export and business export for GF Futures, but more importantly, it had provided personnel export and culture export. It was the continuity of cultural bloodline that allowed these "GF people" to grow together at a high speed in different market segments.

Adhering to the principle of "sound operation" of the parent company, GF Futures always worked to control risks while rapidly expanding its businesses. Under the code of conduct of compliance and risk control, GF Futures did not experience any major risk events or capital problems for a long time, which made GF Futures one of the few steady movers in the industry. Since 2009, when the CSRC opened the classification and evaluation of the futures industry, GF Futures has maintained the status of Class A futures dealer, and after 2014, GF Futures received the highest rating of AA for six consecutive years.

As one of the models of innovative futures brokers, GF Futures has engraved the mark of "GF People" on the historical coordinates of the development of China's futures market. It will contribute to the development of GF Securities into a leading international financial institution through its competitive advantages of specialization, diversification, and innovation.

Chapter XII: Contemplation for the Future

The best that history gives us is the enthusiasm it arouses.

—Johann Wolfgang von Goethe

The year 2020 was the prelude to the third decade of the twenty-first century, and not a tranquil year for the world. Along with the Chinese securities industry's 30-year journey, GF Securities will also be celebrating its thirtieth anniversary. History serves the reality and the future. Standing on the ladder of 30 years, GF people have a relatively mature understanding of these questions: "Who am I? Where do I come from? Where do I want to go?"

In the name of history

The contemporary Western masterpiece *Guns, Germs, and Steel: The Fates of Human Societies* is a far-reaching book. The author, Jared Diamond, is a renowned American scholar with many titles. He blends history, geography, biology, sociology, and other disciplines in this book. "Why did the Inca emperor not capture the Spanish king?" "Why is it not the natives of the Americas and Africa, but the people of Eurasia, who eventually crossed the ocean to kill, conquer, and exterminate?" Looking at the long process of human civilization over 10,000 years, Diamond presents groundbreaking perspectives, first by focusing the study on the early stages of the creation of human tribes, and second by focusing on the introduction of physical geography and human social factors.

At the beginning of civilization, the domestication advantages of different human tribes to the surrounding plants and animals, and even the horizontal and vertical axis configuration of the continental plates they were located in, all caused the disparate differences in the radial evolution of different groups. On this basis, different groups evolved different economic models and social structures, and eventually formed the distribution pattern of wealth and power in modern civilization.

These straightforward and insightful perspectives on "geographical advantage" and "the power of the incipient structure" are a powerful reversal of the previously circulated "theory of human racial superiority and inferiority."

We are interested in the broader question of whether the elements of "geography" and "incipient structures," which determine the dominance of populations, are still true in the broader context. Or, which of these two elements is more decisive?

The 30-year history of China's securities industry seems to be characterized by a strong "geographic determinism" if brokerages were viewed as different groups in the financial ecology. From 1990, when the main business was government bonds, to 2020, when the financial industry opened up to the outside world at an accelerated pace, Beijing, Shanghai, and Shenzhen have always been the first-tier cities in the capital markets. Excellent securities firms have kept emerging in the three regions with deep barriers and form a majority of China's top brokerage firms. In May 2020, a financial media in Shenzhen launched a series of heavyweight reports with wording such as "lost," "sigh" and "anxiety." Based on a large number of surveys and statistics, the articles reported the trend of further concentration of high-quality resources in the securities industry to Beijing and Shanghai, and expressed the eager expectation for the revival of Shenzhen brokerage firms. With sharp words and distinctive style, the articles instantly attracted the attention of the industry.

In fact, compared with its Shenzhen counterparts, GF Securities has a less obvious advantage in terms of "geographical environment." In terms of the ecological distribution of the financial and securities industries, at the early stage of reform and opening up, the geographical location of GF Securities was indeed a relative disadvantage compared with its securities counterparts in Beijing, Shanghai and Shenzhen. Guangzhou is the location where GF Securities started its business and grew up, but compared with Beijing, Shanghai and Shenzhen, which has financial decision-making authorities and stock exchanges, Guangzhou, which has a strong business tradition, has not been among the "first-tier financial cities" for a long time. Although Guangdong Province has a high-quality customer base, GF Securities does not have the innate ability to acquire customers in front of local securities firms established earlier and with state-owned background. Although Guangdong Development Bank is the parent of GF Securities, the securities business is not the main business of the bank, and the two were decoupled earlier in the financial industry, and GF Securities ha not had the background of a mixed financial group for a long time.

In a flash of 30 years, the top-ranking camp of the brokerage industry has changed several times. The overall advantages of Beijing and Shanghai brokerage firms have become increasingly obvious, Shenzhen brokerage firms have seen their popularity diminish, while Guangzhou brokerage firms had mostly ended up in regret.

However, the accident of history has gradually sprouted on the fertile ground of reform and opening up in Guangdong.

Perhaps what puzzles experts in Chinese securities history is that GF Securities, which does not have the "geographical advantage," has been among the top ten brokerage firms in China since 1994. Among the earliest brokerage firms in the industry, GF Securities is one of the very few that have not been restructured by M&As and have not received policy capital injection. Compared with the industry leaders, GF Securities today has much to learn and catch up with. However, history also proves that, as one of the few non-Beijing, Shanghai, and Shenzhen brokerage firms at the forefront of the industry, GF Securities has the ability to stand proudly among the Chinese brokerage firms in the midst of fierce competition.

With its longstanding roots in Guangzhou, GF Securities has been able to transcend "geographic determinism" thanks to what Diamond calls another advantage: "the power of the incipient structure."

According to historical materialism, "The ultimate cause and driving force of all important historical events is the economic development of society. Development and is the change in the mode of production and exchange." In the history of GF Securities, there is no doubt that the changes in production relations and economic operation mechanisms brought about by the reform and opening up of contemporary China are the fundamental reasons for its brilliant achievements. Against this historical background, the unique entrepreneurial practice of GF Securities and the simultaneous existence of the two elements of the "incipient structure," i.e. "balanced equity structure" and "sound internal operation mechanism," are the decisive factors for GF Securities' "historical accident" and the fundamental guarantee for its steady progress.

The balanced equity structure is not unique to GF Securities. According to a study conducted by the Securities Association of China in 2000, there were quite a few securities companies with evenly distributed or laddered shareholdings during this period, such as Nanfang Securities, Huaxia Securities, Guoxin Securities, and Xiangcai Securities.[1] But unlike the superficially similar equity structure and management model among peers, GF Securities has a robust internal operating mechanism based on its unique culture. In other words, GF Securities' robust operating mechanism under a balanced equity structure has enabled it to stand out from the fierce competition in the industry, but it has been able to do so because of the unique corporate culture it possesses.

1 Securities Association of China. *Research on the Frontier Issues of China's Securities Market Development* [M]. Beijing: China Financial Publishing House, 2000.

The power of culture

The core issue of what kind of corporate culture to cultivate was a matter of great importance to the leadership of GF Securities when it was first established. Dr. Yunxian Chen began to think deeply about this early in his career. In 1993, he proposed the GF Securities Spirit of "unity, pioneering, pragmatism, and efficiency." In 1997, GF Securities organized a special discussion on the humanistic spirit at the doctoral and master's symposiums in that year. After years of brewing, the concept of "corporate culture" matured. Beyond the equity structure and internal operation mechanism, GF Securities constantly examined the cultural soul that fit with it.

In June 1999, Dr. Chen Yunxian formally put forward the core concept of "knowledge-based development and pragmatism-based dedication," and the company issued the first version of the GF Securities Corporate Culture Program accordingly.

This Program discusses and makes requirements concerning the core concept, development strategy, enterprise spirit, code of conduct, talent concept, realization mechanism, and evaluation criteria. Requirements such as "a sense of mission, career-mindedness, and professional pursuit," and "scale motivation, interest motivation and mechanism motivation" and statements that GF Securities should "be both a theoretical explorer and capital market practitioner; and be the owner of material wealth under the protection of the system and, more importantly, be the upholder of noble character" are marked with the distinctive brand of intellectual entrepreneurship. They are Dr. Chen Yunxian's generalization of and foresight into the cultural character of GF Securities following his three theoretical book and four-pronged approach. After GF Securities achieved initiative success at the turn of the century, this program gained a high degree of internal recognition. At one time, "knowledge-based development and pragmatism-based dedication" became the brand phrase of GF Securities and appeared on large billboards beside the overpasses in Beijing and the airport expressway in Shanghai, reflecting the image of the "PhD Legion."

The official release of why GF Securities Corporate Culture Program is not a "cultural project" in the general sense. As Dr. Chen Yunxian said, "Principles must be established on a down-to-earth manner and implemented from a high perspective." In the context of the official implementation of the Securities Law in 1999 and the active promotion of placement of GF Securities, the corporate culture program was born at the right time and had a strong practical significance. Corporate culture is the gene of the company's development, and only when it is fully integrated into all the living entities of the company can it truly release its energy and play its role.

If we say that the "balanced equity structure" is the conscious design of the founding team of GF Securities under the background of the separation of banking and securities in the mid-1990s, and the "sound internal operation mechanism" is the neural network system of the company gradually established and improved by the "PhD Legion" of GF Securities with their high-level financial professional background in the development of the company's business, then the secret to make these two elements play the most effective role is embedded in the corporate culture of GF Securities.

The operating mechanism and cultural elements of the company are ultimately reflected and implemented in the pyramidal structure of specific executives, organizations, and employees. The values, business ability, dedication and stability of the management team and thousands of key employees of GF Securities was a beautiful sight for the whole Chinese financial industry for a long time after the establishment of GF Securities.

Pragmatically speaking, the exemplary role of the person at the helm of any company, his or her prestige, contribution and self-restraint, are an important part and even a core constituent of its corporate culture. Formed in the 1990s, the corporate culture of GF Securities, with "knowledge-based development and pragmatism-based dedication" as its core, was proposed in a top-down manner, and then was enriched and developed from the bottom up. As an important assistant of Dr. Chen Yunxian during the founding period, Dr. Ma Qingquan once summarized the connotation of GF Securities' corporate culture as follows: the unity and hard work of Hakka culture, the passion of educated youth's culture, and the cultural bloodline of traditional Chinese intellectuals—a sense of history, sense of mission, and sense of self-discipline. These cultural elements or traits were clearly reflected by Dr. Chen Yunxian and other early leaders of the company.

We review the history of the emergence and cultivation of GF Securities' culture, not to sing the praises of historical figures who played an important role in the company's development history. The purpose of reviewing the history is to remind the future GF people to consciously maintain, enrich, and develop the excellent corporate culture of GF Securities. People are social animals. It should be soberly recognized that with the development of the company, the view of wealth, desire for power, sense of solidarity, spirit of innovation, and pursuit of life of the management and even all other employees of the company will be tested as society and the company develop. The history of GF Securities between its founding in 1991 and its IPO in 2010 is a true testament to this, with both positive and, unfortunately, negative testimonies. The question of whether GF culture may change for the worse in the future is one that should always be watched.

GF Securities' corporate anthem "Future Glory" has been sung for many years. The repeated concluding line of the song, written by Dr. Chen Yunxian, should always accompany the growth of the company:

A strong eagle, with knowledge and unity as its wings;
Soaring to realize dreams and create future glory.

"Knowledge" and "unity" are the two wings of the company's development. With the two wings working together, the eagle can cross the streams and mountains to pursue future glory, which is the image of the rapid rise of GF Securities in the early days. Times and people change. Even an eagle that has been flying high will face the risk of failure if it fails to hone its beak and change its feathers, and if either of the wings of "knowledge" and "unity" is injured. "If the wind and waves come up, everything may soon be doomed." This should be a warning for any future company leader.

Market opportunities and risks coexist, management power and responsibility coexist, and the sword of Damocles is always hanging above the company. "Microsoft is always only 18 months away from bankruptcy" and "We have to think about about winter in spring and summer; Huawei's winter may come colder and much colder." These words of Bill Gates and Ren Zhengfei reflect their deep-rooted sense of crisis and have made Microsoft and Huawei achieve excellence and move toward the path of a century-old company.

It is also the dream of GF Securities to be a "100-year enterprise." The corporate culture program of 1999 described the "external motivation" and "internal motivation" for the development of GF Securities, emphasizing that the "internal motivation" is infinite and is the real power of the company's existence and development and that "knowledge," "synergy," and "a sense of mission" will be the internal and fundamental motivation for the continuous development of GF Securities. In 2015, the new version of GF Securities Corporate Culture Program further carries on and develops this concept, gives it a new connotation, and strengthens the sense of mission. It proposes to "build GF Securities into a modern investment bank with international competitiveness, brand influence, and systemic importance and achieve the dream of strengthening China's finance through value creation."

There are many landmark buildings on Wall Street in the United States, and most of the companies that own these buildings have survived difficulties, and their profound system and cultural accumulation are as solid and lofty as the landmark buildings. China's modern corporate system is in many cases borrowed from the West, having a "latecomer advantage," but the accumulation of culture is impossible to achieve quickly. For example, the culture of professional managers has been relatively mature in developed market economies, which has provided succession support for the inheritance and prosperity of centuries-old companies such as IBM and Ford, while there are few successful cases of professional managerial culture in the Chinese corporate world. The absence of good professional managers often leads to entanglement of equity structure and internal management, which becomes the cause of the decline of many Chinese companies.

The growth of a southern banyan tree into a century-old tree in the jungle requires the convergence of many factors. Looking back on the past brilliant achievements, it is necessary to reflect on the tendency of alienation and decline at the cultural level, and seriously write down a warning to oneself about the dangers of the times.

The cases of the securities industry are still fresh in our minds: an upward culture can make a brokerage firm rise in three to five years whereas a downward culture can bring about a disaster in a matter of seconds. GF Securities needs to improve itself and work continuously and stay vigilant all the time. It must be alert to the bad tendencies in the corporate culture, continue to ensure that "knowledge and unity are the wings," uphold the core values, and achieve the intergenerational inheritance on the way to a century-old company.

Future glory

The light of history shines into reality, and then is cast into the future.

In Greek mythology, Prometheus, in order to benefit humankind, broke through the taboo despite danger and stole fire for humankind. This is the divinized version of the history of social development. It is due to the unremitting efforts of generations that humanity is less dark and flooded in the future for which countless Prometheuses have given their lives. French futurist Jacques Attali once wrote a masterpiece *A Brief History of the Future: A Brave and Controversial Look at the Twenty-First Century*. The GF Securities version of *A Brief History of the Future* will continue to be written by generations of GF people.

Today, doctoral degree is no longer the rarest resource in society, but the "PhD Legion" is still the irreplaceable logo of GF Securities, and the pursuit of the "PhD Legion" will continue in the future of GF Securities.

In the future, the corporate governance structure and management model will have new connotations, but the principle of being responsible for all shareholders, employees, and stakeholders will continue in the future of GF Securities.

In the future, with the ever-changing trends, the word "entrepreneurship" will take on a new meaning, and the profit-seeking orientation of quick materialization in society may be stronger, but the faith and perseverance derived from the entrepreneurial journey will continue in the future of GF Securities.

This is because the "GF dream" of several generations has not changed. GF Securities has been promoting entrepreneurship for the past 30 years, and will continue to do so for the next 30 and 100 years.

Standing at the crossroads for the future, we will stay alert to danger and create greater glory in finance as our contribution to the rejuvenation of the Chinese nation.

Have faith in the new glory in the future.

Afterword

After one year and five drafts, *The Entrepreneurship of GF Securities in the Capital Markets* is now available to readers.

First of all, I would like to thank Dr. Chen Yunxian, the founder of GF Securities. Dr. Chen gave important guidance on the policy by which this book should be written; on how to understand the policy concerning the important events in the development history of GF Securities, stay accurate and objective on them and explore them in depth; and how to arrange chapters in the book.

I thank my colleagues, Zhao Guiping and Wang Liangzhong. They led the team to organize the complicated archival materials, interviewed many enthusiastic key employees of the entrepreneurship period, and wrote about several major events of GF Securities as personal witnesses.

My thanks also go to Li Zhongwen, Zhou Wei, Yu Huiping, Wang Mingchi, Wang Qing, Zhang Mingxing, Zhou Zhengyi, Wu Sifan, and Ma Donglei of GF Securities, Li Min, Bai Mei, Wang Yan, Zheng Xu, Hu An, Liu Qingli, and Wu Jingwen of GF Futures, Zhang Wancheng, Rao Li'an, and Lu Menghan of GF Fund, Qu Fei, Xie Cong, Wang Xi, and Yang Yueying of E Fund and other young colleagues. Their dedication made relevant chapters much better. Wang Mingchi did much proofreading.

I also thank Mr. Wu Chixin, former chairman of Guangdong Development Bank, former leaders of GF Securities, and my former colleagues from the business and administrative teams. They were interviewed by the book writing team many times in their busy schedules and provided extremely valuable historical information and memories of the history of GF's entrepreneurship.

Mr. Sun Shuming, chairman of GF Securities, Mr. Lin Chuanhui, general manager of GF Securities, and other leaders of the company gave strong support to the creation of this book. Mr. Liu Zhao of China Financial Publishing House did a lot of meticulous work for the editing and publication of this book. I thank them all.

Ma Qingquan
December 2020